VANGUARD TO TRIDENT

VANGUARD
to
TRIDENT

•

British Naval Policy
since World War II

by
Eric J. Grove

NAVAL INSTITUTE PRESS   Annapolis, Maryland

Library of Congress Cataloging-in-Publication Data
Grove, Eric.
    Vanguard to Trident.
    Bibliography: p.
    Includes index.
    1. Great Britain. Royal Navy—History—20th
century. 2. Great Britain—Military policy. I. Title.
VA454.G76 1987   359'.03'0941   86-33143
ISBN 0-87021-552-3

All photos not otherwise credited are from the Ministry of
Defence (Navy).

Printed in the United States of America

To my Mother and Father.

CONTENTS

PREFACE

Four decades after the end of the Second World War seems a good moment to pause and survey the evolution of postwar British naval policy. Not only do the mid-1980s witness the more complete institutional integration of the Royal Navy with the other two services, but they also see Britain's naval forces at a major crossroads. The point may finally have been reached where the United Kingdom is going to have to choose what kind of navy she wants, a strategic nuclear deterrent and little else (i.e., procurement of the new Trident missile system), or a sea control and power projection force of the traditional type. Even if Trident does not finally appear, its dominance of current naval policy merits its inclusion in the title.

The four decades since VJ-Day have seen Britain's political and naval decision makers grappling with the intractable problems of too many commitments chasing too few resources. Not that governments have been too niggardly in their budgetary allocations or Naval Staffs too unsuccessful in extorting funds from their paymasters. In 1984 the United Kingdom was spending more on her peacetime navy than ever before. Moreover, that money was buying an active fleet that in tonnage terms was little short of the operational fleet of thirty years before. Yet there could be no doubt that Britain *relatively* was not the naval power she had been. In 1955 she was still number two in the world in naval capabilities if not in sheer size of fleet. By 1985 she had fallen way behind the Soviet Union into third place, and Frenchmen might question even her status there. In 1982 Britain was clearly fully extended defeating the naval and air forces of Argentina, a Latin American rival who would not even have dared give battle half a century or so previously.

Yet this unwelcome situation was much more due to the gains in power of other states than Britain's absolute decline. To have remained the power she was, Britain would have had to undergo a political and economic transformation of truly revolutionary proportions. Her success even in that endeavor would even then have been dubious; the U.S. defense budget is approximately the same as the entire British gross national product! When one British postwar government did try massive rearmament, the country soon showed that it could not provide the required resources and maintain its desired way of life. Moreover, that government did not last long in office.

British governments, therefore, have had to manage their decline as a major naval power as best they could, sometimes attempting radical solutions, more often, as today, trying to keep up appearances maintaining the maximum apparent capability by skimping here and there on less obvious necessities. The following will attempt to chart this process, relating Britain's naval policy and the performance of her navy to the decisions taken in the highest levels of government. It is hoped that the account will do something to explain to those interested why the Royal Navy is the size and shape it is today, and how it is that it has got to the point from which it must address itself to perhaps its biggest postwar challenges yet.

Any exercise in contemporary history must face fundamental methodological problems. For the period back beyond the British "Thirty Year Rule," the historian can rest his account on a relatively firm foundation. Many (though far from all) the relevant documents are available in the Public Record Office. The final year for which documents were available to the author was 1954, which conveniently coincides with a significant break in the story, at the end of the final phase of Churchill's "Radical Reviews" of defense and the beginning of the "Mountbatten era" of naval policy. Moreover, having seen the system working in the period 1945– 54, it is the easier to "read between the lines" of official statements and put together the historical jigsaw from the available public documentation, press reports, and other literature that exists for the later period. The excellent academic work on general postwar British defense policy has been of great value, and special mention must be made of Admiral Crowe's fascinating and pioneering doctoral dissertation on British Naval Policy 1945–63, which the author has generously allowed me to use freely. I must also express particular thanks to those participants in the events described who granted interviews, notably Sir Ian Jacob, Commander J.C. Jacob, Rear Admiral J.H. Adams, Admiral Sir Frank Hopkins, Lord Mayhew, and Dr. David Owen.

Many others must be thanked for the help they have been in the production of this book. Nicholas Rodger and his colleagues at the Public Record Office, at all levels, have done their sometimes difficult and often thankless job with great good humor. Material from Crown-copyright records in the P.R.O. appears by kind permission of the Controller of H.M. Stationery Office. David Lyon and his erstwhile assistants in the Chart Room at the National Maritime Museum were unfailingly hospitable and helpful, and made working there a rare pleasure. David Brown and his staff in the Naval Library and Naval Historical Branch have also been of considerable assistance, as has Professor Peter Nailor of the Royal Naval College, Greenwich, and Dr. John Simpson of the University of Southampton. Lieutenant James Goldrick, RAN, read the typescript in its various forms and generously offered very sound and useful advice. Lieutenant Peter Jones, RAN, has contributed the excellent drawings of "ships that never were." The Fleet Photographic Unit at HMS *Excellent* in Portsmouth, and the Imperial War Museum were most helpful in the provision of photographs, and Michael Chapman of the MOD (Central) Library was his usual efficient self in getting hold of some of the more obscure secondary sources.

I must also pay tribute to my ex-colleagues at the Britannia Royal Naval College, in particular to my successive departmental heads, Louis Wreford Brown and

Richard Alexander for their encouragement in my research. My colleague Evan Davies also deserves a special mention for his intellectual stimulation in this field over a long period. The college librarian, Richard Kennell, always proved unfailingly helpful. More recently Anne Jappie, one-time research officer at the Council for Arms Control, was of considerable help in putting the finishing touches to the original version of the typescript. Norman Friedman was kind enough to carry that bulky document over the Atlantic. More recently, Babs Murray gave essential help with last-minute typing.

A very special mention must be made of two friends and colleagues. First is Norman Polmar, who first suggested this book be written, and whose backing and encouragement have been of great and much appreciated value. Second is Ned Willmott, who finally persuaded me to go ahead with the project and who has selflessly given enormous time to reading and improving the various drafts.

Thanks must be expressed to Deborah Guberti Estes and Carol Swartz of the U.S. Naval Institute, the first for her patience with the unavoidable delays in the production of this volume, and the second for her indefatigable efforts editing and improving it. Finally I must thank my wife, Elizabeth, for her encouragement and help, and her endurance of her husband's preoccupation with little else over the last three years, and, above all, my long-suffering mother, Mrs. Irene Grove, the only typist who has a chance of coping with my manuscripts and who can read my illegible handwriting even better than I can! With enormous patience she coped with a multitude of drafts and, without doubt, is the heroine of this particular volume.

While many have helped and shared responsibility for the merits, if any, of what follows, responsibility for the defects is mine alone. In no sense is this book an official statement of the Ministry of Defence.

VANGUARD TO TRIDENT

CHAPTER · ONE

POSTWAR PROBLEMS

The Royal Navy entered the twentieth century supreme upon the world's oceans. Britain deployed the world's most powerful and ubiquitous navy with squadrons, scattered around the world, sufficiently strong to be the major naval forces in their respective areas of interest. European waters were dominated by increasingly powerful British battlefleets. Never had the Pax Britannica appeared to be more serene or secure. Yet the seeds of decline were already planted. It was not only that the economic expansion of Britain and her empire was faltering. More importantly, growing naval rivals required impossibly great efforts from Britain if she was to retain maritime dominion.

British naval supremacy in the nineteenth century resulted as much from the weakness and preoccupations of others as from her own intrinsic strength. As long as the sea remained the dominant means of world communication, Britain's seaborne empire, the last and greatest such imperium, gave her the firmest possible economic foundation. By the second half of the nineteenth century, however, the development of the railway was unlocking the industrial power of large land masses. When this revolution was combined with the growth of new large political units of continental or semicontinental scale, it was only a matter of time before Britain found her naval supremacy slipping away. By the opening of the new century the United States was fast becoming the dominant naval power in the Western Hemisphere. Moreover, Germany was beginning to demonstrate the naval potential of continental resources closer to home, adding her weight to the already worrying rise in the naval strength of Britain's traditional French and Russian rivals. Even in Asia, Japan was beginning to carve out an empire both maritime and continental in scope, backed up by an increasingly powerful fleet.[1]

Britain's reaction to this new situation was as rapid as it was radical. The attempt simply to outbuild every rival was abandoned. Rivals were neutralized by political detente or entente; the Western Hemisphere was conceded to the U.S.A. and Eastern Asian waters to Japan (although small British squdrons remained in both areas). The main strength of the fleet was concentrated in home waters. France and Russia became allies. Even the Mediterranean, the maritime keystone of the empire, was stripped of British ships. The aim was to concentrate in home waters the new dreadnought battleships and battlecruisers, whose development Britain had pioneered in order to maintain sufficient superiority over Germany, her most dangerous opponent. When war came in 1914, the Royal Navy was able to contain the German battlefleet, but this success was almost neutralized by the direct menace of the U-boat to Britain's merchant shipping. All the navy could achieve by its extended, and increasingly expensive, efforts was to keep Britain in the war and thereby enable her biggest army ever on the Continent to play the dominant role in grinding down Germany's military strength. Only thus could the latter be defeated. No strictly naval action could assure Germany's defeat; and if that were not enough, the new phenomenon of air power promised to add a direct threat to Britain's security, a threat at least as dangerous as naval blockade and all the more worrying given its novelty and unknown potential.

Great Britain, bankrupted and enervated by war, was forced to manage the two interwar decades as best she could. Victory over Germany and naval arms agreements with Japan and the U.S.A. provided some relief from an unwinnable naval building race. For two more decades Britain kept her position as the leading naval power, although her lead was now officially shared with the U.S.A. One price paid for this was the enmity of Japan. Britain could not afford a permanent Far Eastern Fleet, neither its ships nor its bases. All that could be afforded, and that only just barely, was an operating base at Singapore on which the Home and Mediterranean fleets could concentrate if required. This presupposed no threats elsewhere. The 1930s saw British diplomacy attempt, unsuccessfully, to cope with the Royal Navy's request to reduce the number of Britain's enemies. A settlement with Germany proved impossible, despite the Admiralty doing all it could to create a positive diplomatic climate, even to the extent of approving limited German naval rearmament. Italy was, in the Navy's eyes, gratuitously alienated because of Ethiopia. As rearmament began in the middle of the decade, British defense planners had to measure the conflicting priorities of a naval buildup (one that itself required choices between various types of naval forces) with the needs of air defense and deterrence and the possibility of being forced to send an army to the Continent. Behind it all was the overriding need to maintain economic health, "the fourth arm of defense."[2]

There was no way that Britain could solve this conundrum. She was unable to prevent a war that put at risk Britain's entire world position. Whatever her misgivings at entering such a conflict, once committed Britain put more resources into fighting a war than she had ever done before. At sea she deployed fewer spectacular battleships or cruisers, but amassed flotillas of new escort vessels, both old types and new, to deal with the evergrowing submarine menace. Maritime air forces, which Britain could ill afford given the conflicting priorities of home defense and strategic offense, were an expensive new addition to Britain's naval requirements. Britain could simply not afford both a powerful general-purpose air force and the carrier air groups that would be required in a new-style battlefleet. When Japan finally went on the offensive in 1941–42, there was no fleet to send to the Far East capable of standing up to Japanese maritime air power. When the defeat of the European Axis powers finally allowed carriers to be sent East, they went with air groups largely made up of American lend-lease equipment. Weaknesses in the air, moreover, were but one aspect of a set of logistical and infrastructural problems that severely limited Britain from extending her sea power across Pacific distances.[3]

In the Pacific the British encountered a level of naval capability far beyond their own means. Britain had been left far behind, even with her inflated wartime fleet of almost 900 major warships and 866,000 men and women. This is not to denigrate the skill, courage, and determination of Britain's naval officers and men who distinguished themselves against the odds in a more impressive way than had their First World War predecessors. It was a mark of the greater intensity both of the fighting and of the threats that Britain suffered such grievous naval losses between 1939 and 1945, some 224 major surface ships of corvette size and above. More destroyers were lost (139) than were in service in May 1945 (108). In all, some 1,525 British warships of all types were lost, totaling almost a million tons. Over 50,000 British naval personnel lost their lives, 20,000 more than in 1914–18.[4]

The war provided salutary lessons for Britain's postwar naval planners. There were serious questions over the continued utility of large, gun-armed warships, especially battleships such as the new HMS *Vanguard*, begun during the war and approaching completion on the Clyde. An expensive carrier-based air force, with all of its overheads of shore bases and supply backup, was a "battlefleet" of greater usefulness and importance, if also of greater expense. Escort vessels and techniques could not be ignored as they had been in the 1920s and 1930s. Not only was naval power more expensive than ever before, it had to be deployed more extensively than previously. Britain ended the war with her forces spread around the world in an unprecedented way, from Berlin and Trieste to Saigon and Djakarta. Some of the commitments could be quickly liquidated, albeit not without some trouble, as colonies were handed back to their previous owners. Yet Britain's own colonies remained as much responsibilities as assets, at least until alternative arrangements could be made to shed the most onerous burdens.

That such alternatives, however unwelcome, would have to be faced was dictated by Britain's parlous economic state. With every resource put into the war effort Britain was effectively bankrupt. She had become totally dependent on American aid to sustain her, and when that aid was cut off only an American loan, negotiated on far from favorable terms, allowed Britain a short breathing space. This meant that any British government's vital and overriding priority was domestic reconstruction. The fact that the government was a Labour administration rather than a Conservative one, following the former's landslide victory in the 1945 election, only altered the emphasis a little more towards social reconstruction as well as economic.[5]

If all this was not enough, the whole postwar strategic environment had been changed by the manner in which the war had come to an end—by the use of nuclear weapons. Within a week of Hiroshima the Naval Staff, that body of officers within the British Admiralty tasked with formulating higher policy, was grappling with the implications of "the Atomic Bomb." It was clear that nuclear weapons might make the prospect of a long, drawnout total war in the future less likely. The principles of deterrence were quickly grasped by some:

> Probably the most effective countermeasure is the threat of retaliation which may well help deter any nation from using the Atomic Bomb. For such a threat to be effective it is necessary that no one should be able to destroy another country's store of atomic bombs or its apparatus for launching them in a sudden attack. . . . The traditional functions of defending our lines of communication may be pointless if these lines are better attacked at their end points. Even

more broadly, it is possible that the whole war might be decided by an attack
on civilian morale or industry before the Navy had time to mobilize. . . . The
net effect of the Atomic Bomb is that the price worth paying for peace is now
very much higher and that the main function of our armed forces should be the
prevention of a major war, rather than the ability to fight it on purely military
grounds after the war has already been decided either by the collapse of civilian
morale, or the destruction of ports and civilian installations.[6]

The Staff argued that the navy might well have a part to play in strategic nuclear
bombardment with carrier- or submarine- or ship-launched weapons, including
rockets. But there were doubts whether a strategic nuclear attack could achieve
decisive results, especially against dispersed targets, and given the suggestion that
Britain's war industry be spread throughout the empire, it was felt that there would
still be a need to protect shipping from submarine and rocket attack in the event
of general war. Moreover, there would remain "conflicts between small nations in
which we may be involved and threats to our own territory which may be settled
without any use of atomic weapons, and in which a more or less normal navy would
play its usual part." There was a consensus that both in the short term (until the
full implications of nuclear warfare became clear) and in the long term a navy of
some kind was still needed. The various enthusiasts for each naval platform tended
to argue the case of their own "union" and the Gunnery Division even looked
forward to a future battleship defended by nuclear-tipped surface-to-air missiles.
Nevertheless, this initial reponse to the nuclear challenge demonstrated that the
Admiralty would not be defenseless in its struggle to maintain the Royal Navy in
arguably the least favorable economic, political, strategic, and financial environment that it had ever faced.

Before going any further it will be of use to readers to sketch the basic framework
of the naval policy decision-making process.[7] Ultimate authority, of course, rested
with the Cabinet, the supreme collective executive body chaired by the head of
the government, the prime minister. By September 1945 the latter was Clement
Attlee. Attlee was very fond of delegating detailed matters of policy to the cabinet
committees,[8] and defense policy was discussed in the Defence Committee (Operations) left over from World War II, which was taking on the attributes of the
later Cabinet Defence Committee in its roles of reviewer of strategy and force
levels. Attlee, for the time being, retained the title of minister of defense, with
the services being represented in full Cabinet by three separate ministers.

The navy minister, or first lord of the Admiralty, to give him his official title,
was chairman of the Board of Admiralty, the time-honored body of "lords com-
missioners for executing the office of Lord High Admiral."[9] The government department directed by this body, the Admiralty, had the job of "building, maintaining and administering" the Royal Navy. The Admiralty was made up of three
main parts other than the Board itself. First came the Naval Staff, which advised
the Board "in strategical and operational planning, in disposing of the Fleet and
in the formulation of broad naval policy, on the requirements of material, and of
tactical doctrine." Its "responsibilities" were defined as:

> . . . the study of the whole field of naval strategy and tactics, the collection of
> intelligence, the framing of long term plans for the build up and disposition of
> the Fleet as well as its bases, the development of the principles of weapon
> training, the study and development of the basic methods of the various forms

of naval warfare, the specification of the broad aims to be pursued in the development of weapons and equipment and advice on the priorities to govern the effort devoted thereto.[10]

Chief of the Naval Staff was always the first sea lord, the professional head of the service, in 1945 still the distinguished wartime leader, Admiral of the Fleet Sir Andrew Cunningham. The first sea lord's wartime work load necessitated a deputy (DCNS) during the war, but the post was abolished shortly afterwards. The postwar arrangement was to have three officers immediately subordinate to the first sea lord, all with seats on the Board of Admiralty. The senior was vice chief of Naval Staff (VCNS) who was in charge of operational policy. Under him, therefore, came the following divisions, Naval Intelligence, Plans, Plans (Q) (an administrative and logistical planning division), Signals, Operations, and Trade. The second subordinate officer was the fifth sea lord, the Royal Navy's head of aviation, who held the staff post of deputy chief of Naval Staff (Air) with supervision of two divisions, the Directorate of Air Warfare, and the Directorate of Air Organisation and Training. The most junior of CNS's immediate subordinates was the assistant chief of Naval Staff (ACNS), who was in direct charge of the formulation of staff requirements, the evolution of tactics, and the direction of weapons-training policy. ACNS had supervision of four divisions: Tactical and Staff Duties; Gunnery and Anti-Air Warfare; Torpedo, Anti-Submarine and Mine Warfare; and Navigation and Direction. He also supervised a directorate outside the Naval Staff proper, that of Operational Research. In early 1951 ACNS was redesignated deputy chief of Naval Staff and a "new" ACNS, without a seat on the Board, was created to act as assistant to VCNS. In 1953 DCNS also acquired an assistant in the shape of ACNS (Warfare). Director of Plans (Q) became director of Administrative Planning in 1952, the Gunnery Division lost its supplementary AA Warfare suffix in 1953, and DTASW became the Underwater and Warfare Division (DUSW) in 1954. The same year the DTSD was renamed Tactical, Ship Requirements and Staff Duties Division. This brings the evolution of the Staff to the mid-1950s. We shall return to its evolving structure in chapter 5.[11]

The other naval members of the Board of Admiralty were the second sea lord and chief of naval personnel responsible for all personnel questions (recruiting, training and education, administration, discipline, and welfare), the third sea lord and controller responsible for material questions (ships, aircraft procurement, weapons, and dockyards) and the fourth sea lord and chief of supplies and transport responsible for stores, victualling, and logistics in general. These officers headed substantial departments divided, like the Naval Staff, into various directorates.

In addition to the above seven officers, there were three civilian members of the Board of Admiralty. Two were junior ministers, the parliamentary and financial secretary, a sort of assistant first lord, and the civil lord with direct responsibility for certain material matters. Last, but by no means least, was the permanent secretary, the Admiralty's senior civil servant, who headed the large and powerful Secretariat. The power of the Secretariat was clear in its official role, ". . . the interior economy of the Admiralty office, the procedure for the conduct of Admiralty business, all the communications in the name of the Board and the provision and administration of the Civil Staff."[12] The Secretariat had primary responsibility for finance, accounting, and liaison with the Treasury, the all powerful department

TABLE 1-1.

THE NAVAL STAFF BY 1947.

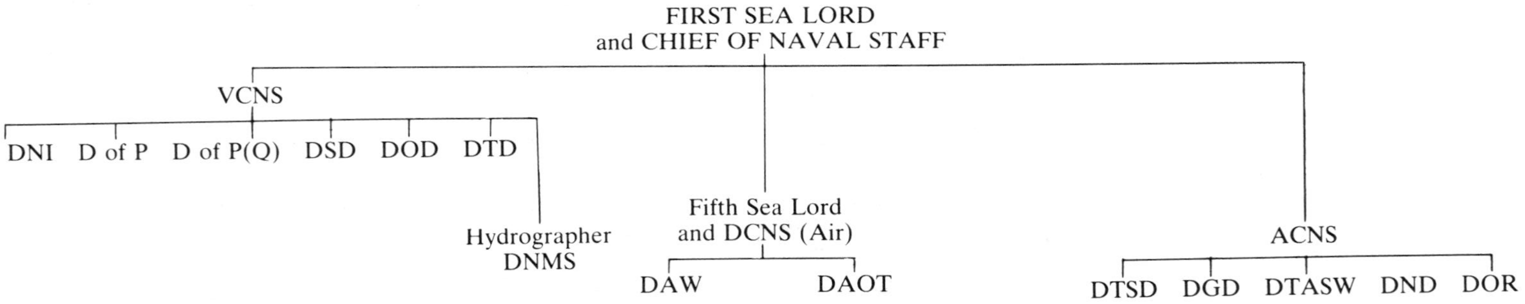

FIRST SEA LORD
and CHIEF OF NAVAL STAFF

VCNS

DNI D of P D of P(Q) DSD DOD DTD

Hydrographer
DNMS

Fifth Sea Lord
and DCNS (Air)

DAW DAOT

ACNS

DTSD DGD DTASW DND DOR

of state responsible for financing government policy. Inevitably, the Treasury's political chief, the chancellor of the exchequer, with his responsibility for matching national resources to policies, was the greatest opponent that successive Boards of Admiralty had to face.

The struggle for resources was to be the central problem of postwar British naval policy. Perhaps inevitably, the Plans Division of the Naval Staff, which with commendable foresight had been working on the size and shape of Britain's postwar fleet since 1943, set its sights far too high. In any future general war, it concluded, Britain would need a fleet comparable to the one she had mustered in the last, with heavy forces of carriers and battleships in home and eastern waters and lighter forces spread more widely, notably in the Atlantic where ten operational escort groups would be required to keep the convoys moving.[13] Between 400,000 and 600,000 personnel would be required to man this armada.

No one suggested that Britain should maintain such a huge navy in peacetime. Nevertheless, Plans Division called for a very substantial peacetime fleet trained for war to safeguard British lives and property and to further British interests abroad. Training was a two-fold task: the training of conscripts and other new entries, and the development of up-to-date means and methods of naval warfare. It was felt desirable to maintain two "main fleets" in order to stimulate competitive interaction. Both these fleets were to contain battleships, as only these ships could deliver the heaviest blows and "keep on striking them under any conditions of geographical position, weather or light. . . ." Battleships were, therefore, to be retained, albeit in small numbers, "until they had outlived their usefulness." As for the safeguarding of British lives and property overseas, it was still held desirable to have squadrons in various parts of the world in order to nip trouble in the bud and demonstrate British resolve. Finally, the desirability of putting on a good show of naval strength was stressed, "showing the flag" being seen as a major means of fostering British trade, and as the foundation of both Britain's standard of living and her armed strength. The requirements of such a policy were a peacetime strength of no less than four battleships, four fleet carriers, ten light fleet carriers, thirty-two cruisers, sixty-four destroyers, sixty escorts, and forty-five submarines. These would be disposed between the two main fleets, one at home and one in the Mediterranean, and four other foreign "stations" that would each have a force of cruisers and escort vessels and sometimes even a light carrier. Half the submarine force would be in the Pacific. Australia, New Zealand, and Canada would contribute two light carriers, five cruisers, sixteen destroyers, and sixteen escorts as part of the above total.

The traditional assumptions behind this overambitious thinking had already been spelled out before V.E. Day by the deputy director of Plans, Captain Godfrey French. He took his stand on the vital importance of sea communications to the survival of the empire. French argued that sea power was still an essential component of the armed strength that would sustain the British Empire's status as a first-class power. It seemed that little had changed since 1939, or even 1897.[14]

Yet there had been changes, fundamental ones. When the Cabinet received the armed forces' postwar requirements, the immediate, and higher, priority was obvious, to get Britain back on its economic feet. Foreign trade and civil manufacture had been neglected when the country mobilized for war to an extent only matched, perhaps, by Soviet Russia. The urgent requirement was to get British industry back into production to recover its overseas markets and earn the vital foreign currency required to pay for Britain's food and raw materials. In this struggle manpower locked up in unproductive warships, airfields, and army camps was no asset. Indeed, as consumers of material and, even more important, as spenders of scarce foreign exchange, the armed forces seemed to the Treasury to be a positive menace to Britain's economic recovery. The latter factor was only mitigated by much of the expenditure being in the sterling area, the closed currency area using pounds for its trade, which allowed such money spent within it to come back to Britain in payments for export of goods and services. Moreover, parts of the empire, e.g., Malaya, did contribute favorably to the earning of all-too-scarce dollars. Nevertheless, the chancellor, Hugh Dalton, was stressing the balance of payments problems incurred by overseas deployments in the Cabinet's Defence Committee (Operations) less than two weeks after V.J. Day in terms that many of his successors would have found very familiar.[15]

The context of these discussions was a chiefs of staff paper that described the expected deployment of Britain's armed forces on 30 June 1946.[16] This outlined a still-massive British naval force disposed in three full-scale fleets, "Home," "Mediterranean," and "British Pacific" with two small squadrons, "South American and West Indies" and "South Atlantic." Ominously for the naval planners, however, it was a fleet both smaller than they considered desirable and larger than the government thought possible. Attlee was especially critical of the Mediterranean deployment, small though it was in comparison with the intended long-term postwar plan: two light fleet carriers, five cruisers, sixteen destroyers, eight escorts, and eight submarines. The government was far from certain as to the precise role of such a substantial navy and enquired whom these forces were to be used against. Albert V. Alexander, first lord of the Admiralty in the wartime coalition and now back in office under Attlee, put up a typically dogged defense of the Admiralty position. He said the ships were for worldwide security and pointed to the reduced number of battleships (one at home and three in the Pacific) compared to prewar times. Attlee was unconvinced and said that Britain ought to recognize that the United States of America was now the dominant naval power and that it was prepared to take over the responsibility for the Pacific and part of the Atlantic. Even Ernest Bevin, the foreign secretary and a strong supporter of Britain's maintaining her world responsibilities, believed that annual defense estimates of £500 million, considered by the wartime government as an appropriate level of peacetime expenditure, ought to be the starting point for postwar planning. He believed that in Britain's straitened circumstances the coat would have to be cut from the available cloth. Alexander, who put the opposite case, that the armed services should decide the forces required to support the government's foreign policy without regard to cost, got short shrift from his colleagues on the Defence Committee.[17]

Within the Admiralty organization, the realities of financial life were in fact already being taken into account. The war had ended with a substantial building program of ships still incomplete. Under construction, on order, or projected in October 1945 were three battleships, seven fleet carriers, eleven cruisers, ninety destroyers, thirty-four submarines, thirty-four escort vessels, and a minesweeper.[18] The carriers were an impressive bunch; three 36,800-ton ships, *Audacious, Ark Royal*, and *Eagle*, and four splendid 46,900-ton vessels, *Malta, New Zealand, Gibraltar*, and *Africa* (the last-named originally intended to be an *Ark Royal*). It had

For the postwar decade the light fleet carriers of the *Colossus* class were the Royal
Navy's main operational units. Economical in manpower they were able to operate
with little modification, the early piston-engined generations of postwar aircraft. This
view of Malta shows two of the ships, relatively late in their operational careers, in
1953 with the *Ocean* returning from active service in Korea. Sea Furies and Fireflies
can be clearly seen on her deck. In the background is her sister, the Mediterranean
Fleet's recently deployed carrier *Glory*. On the latter's deck are some just-delivered
Avenger ASW aircraft. (Imperial War Museum)

been decided in May 1944, at the request of the naval aviators, to build these big
carriers to American design principles, with unarmored decks and hangars in order
to facilitate the launching of large aircraft strikes. This had seriously delayed the
design, and none had reached the laying down stage by the end of the war; two
were already suspended. The incomplete light fleets came in three basic categories:
three of the original 13,000-ton *Colossus* type, six of a slightly modified *Majestic*
class with different messing facilities, and eight of the 22,000-ton *Hermes* class
enlarged to operate the latest projected aircraft. The cruisers were of two types:
five were of the *Tiger* class, 8,885-ton improvements of the prewar "Colony" design.
One, the *Superb*, was about to be commissioned, but the others were far from
completion. Not yet even laid down were six, big 15,000-ton *Neptune*s to be armed
with twelve rapid-firing 6-inch guns in four triple turrets. The destroyers included
vessels of the large "Battle" and medium *C* classes that were already entering
service along with three new types. These comprised two flotillas (eight ships each)
of big 2,600-ton *Daring*s, twenty 1,965-ton "Weapons" designed specifically for
antisubmarine and antiair duties, and a flotilla of eight *Gallant*s, improved and
slightly enlarged "Weapons" with heavier armament. The escort vessels and minesweepers were of the existing improved *Black Swan*, "Bay," and *Algerine* classes,
although the four escorts of the 1945 program were to be of a new design. The
submarines were mostly of the long-range *A* type designed for Pacific service, but
none were completed in time to see action in their intended theater. There were

The only "Tiger"-class cruiser to be completed to the original design was HMS *Superb*, seen here at Malta in the late 1940s. She led an active life as a flagship in the 1950s, and modernization to a similar standard to her sisters was considered. These plans were reduced to a new secondary armament only and were then abandoned altogether. The *Superb* was placed in reserve in 1958 and scrapped two years later.

a few older *T*s still on the stocks and one new experimental boat projected "to be built in slow time," in which it was hoped to develop revolutionary improvements in underwater performance.

In addition to the *Vanguard* there were two battleships on order, the *Lion* and *Temeraire*. The need for any new ships of this type had been questioned in Cabinet in December 1944 by Lord Cherwell, paymaster general and scientific adviser to the prime minister.[19] He quoted the development of guided bombs and argued the case for the battleship's replacement by the aircraft carrier and land-based strike aircraft. This was not too attractive an argument for the sea lords, who had a few months before, in May 1944, decided that "the basis of the strength of the fleet is the battleship. Besides providing support for all classes of ship, the battleship is the most powerful unit for destroying the enemy's surface forces once they are brought into action. A heavier broadside than the enemy is still a very telling weapon in a naval action."[20] The Admiralty's replies to Cherwell, drafted in February 1945, were conciliatory in tone, but took their stand on the need for balanced battle groups, with the battleship protecting the carrier with its guns in bad weather conditions that made flying impossible. One argued an interesting case for the concept of a "heavy support ship," which at present might take the form of a battleship but which could in the future use antiair and antiship guided missiles instead of guns, thus diminishing its size over the next decade and a half. Wartime experience, such as the sinking of the carrier *Glorious* by German heavy surface units, was quoted as evidence of the need for balanced battle groups. The conclusions of the 1936 "Committee on the Vulnerability of Capital Ships" were even quoted: "The advocates of the extreme air view wish this Country to build no capital ships (other powers still continuing to build them). If their theories turn out to be well founded we will have wasted money, if ill founded we would in putting them to the test have lost the Empire."[21] Again, it was almost as if nothing had changed.

These arguments won the day, and the restarting of two *Lion*s found its way

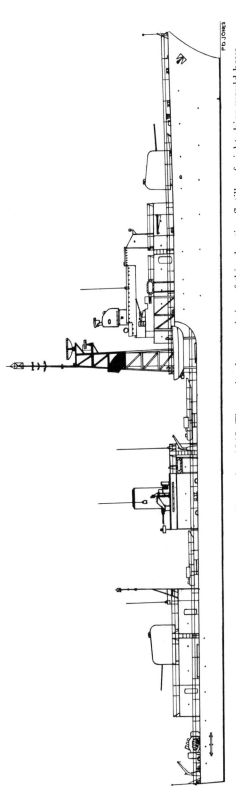

The "G"- or "Gallant"-class destroyers, cancelled in December 1945. The main characteristics of this abortive flotilla of eight ships would have been:

Dimensions: 365' o.a. × 39'6" beam × 14'2" draft
Displacement: 1,995 tons standard; 2,740 tons full load
Armament: Two twin 4.5" Mark 6
Two twin 40/60 STAAG (amidships)
Two single 40/60 Mark 7 (bridge wings)
Two quintuple 21" torpedo tubes
One triple Squid antisubmarine launcher
Electronics: One Type 293 surveillance radar
One Type 978 navigation radar
One Type 37 fire-control director (U.S. design)
Names: *Gallant, Gael, Gauntlet, Gift, Glowworm, Grafton, Greyhound, Guernsey*

into the 1945 building program.[22] The ships were duly reordered to be completed in 1952, but their shape was the subject of almost as much controversy as the need to build them.[23] The design, based on the Staff requirement, was a huge monster of almost 60,000 tons armed with nine 16-inch guns and fitted with 14-inch armor. The director of Naval Construction, C.S. Lillicrap, denounced the design as wrong-headed; even protection on the massive scale suggested would not guarantee invulnerability. A committee met in April 1945 under the chairmanship of Rear Admiral R.M. Servaes, and despite the doubts of some witnesses, it recommended a smaller ship of 45,000 tons armed with six 16-inch guns in two triple turrets forward, up to twenty-four 4.5-inch dual-purpose guns, sixty 40-mm Bofors AA guns and 12½-inch armor. The committee felt that these ships would be needed to counter postwar Soviet and, to a lesser extent, French battleship construction.

The ambitious new program from battleships and carriers to frigates and submarines amounted to over a third of the proposed postwar fleet and, as C.E.B. Simeon, the deputy controller, pointed out, it implied naval estimates of half the total £500 million likely to be allocated to defense.[24] Postwar naval estimates of £150 million were much closer to expected realities, and of that about £25 million would be available for new construction. This implied some substantial cuts, and the cancellation of ships whose construction was already suspended, including the *Africa*, *Gibraltar*, and four of the *Hermes*-class carriers, twenty-one destroyers, twelve submarines, and ten escorts. A few more "Weapon"-class destroyers were to go, along with the *Tiger*-class cruiser *Hawke*. The laying down of the second flotilla of *Daring*s and the two remaining large carriers, *Malta* and *New Zealand*, should, Simeon argued, be deferred for a year along with the ordering of the six *Neptune*-class cruisers. Having thus reduced expenditure, Simeon hoped that a new replacement program could be begun with roughly one battleship or large carrier every two years, beginning in 1949, two cruisers or light fleet carriers per year from 1950, one destroyer flotilla of eight ships per year from 1949, and a series of prototype escort vessels and submarines from 1947.

The first lord held a meeting to discuss the matter on 15 October, with all present aware of the new postwar financial climate. In these circumstances, and with the chances of getting new battleships through the Cabinet in its present mood slim indeed, the *Lion* and *Temeraire* were finally cancelled, "nor is it likely that such ships will be included in any new program during the next few years." The meeting accepted Simeon's suggestions, but it was specifically stated that there was still a desire to proceed with the *Neptune*s at a slow rate, with two to be laid down as soon as the design was finally settled. So ended the era of new battleship construction in Britain but not the new era of cuts and cancellations. This new age, time was to show, was only just beginning.[25]

In November in front of the Cabinet's Defence Committee (Operations), the Royal Navy defended its remaining program on the grounds that it would be uneconomical to scrap vessels in an advanced stage of construction.[26] The Admiralty argued that some new units, built with the benefit of war experience, would be needed for the postwar fleet, but it accepted that, given the over-riding priority of rebuilding and repairing the merchant marine, new construction could not proceed quickly. Work on warships was only being done to prevent the dislocation of labor as the yards changed over to merchant shipbuilding. It was estimated, in fact, that only twenty-thousand men would be employed on warship construction by the year's end, a fall of over half since 1 October 1945. Ten times that number would be employed on mercantile work.

This did not satisfy the chancellor or other ministers. It was vital to release labor, they argued, especially the scarce electricians and wood workers who were required in the housing program to rebuild battered Britain. They needed to leave shipbuilding altogether. Both Alexander and Cunningham argued that there should be a proper plan for a postwar navy before further cuts were made, and that equipment had to be kept up-to-date, but even Bevin said that there had to be further cuts in the short term, i.e., 1946–47. He was worried about accumulations of obsolete equipment and felt that it would be better to wait until 1948 or so before putting into effect the lessons of the war. For his part, Dalton hinted that money and other resources might be more available then.

The chancellor strengthened his pressure on Alexander for further reductions with a personal letter on 13 November 1945, less than a week after the previous discussion. Reluctantly the first lord accepted the need for still further cuts, and his deliberations were assisted by the information being quietly passed on to him by the secretariat about the sea lords' discussion on the subject. The latter seemed willing to accept the end of the *Gibraltar* and *Malta*, the second *Daring* flotilla, the *Gallant* flotilla, and two more of the "Weapons." They wanted to retain the cruisers and all the incomplete light fleet carriers as well as the six remaining "Weapons," arguing the case largely on the grounds of shipyard dislocation if the ships were cancelled. The first lord's civil advisers were dubious about the strength of this argument.

Thus armed, the first lord met his naval advisers on 13 December. Agreement was soon reached on the two big carriers and the *Daring* and *Gallant* flotillas, but there was a division of opinion on the two least-complete "Weapons," the controller standing out against the Naval Staff in favor of keeping them to avoid dislocation at Yarrow and Thornycroft. As a compromise it was agreed to cancel only if half the cost of them had not been spent. The desire not to waste money already spent also helped save the four least-complete *Majestic*-class light fleet carriers. Their utility as anything other than escort carriers was dubious, but that, the Naval Staff argued, was an important requirement. The naval representatives also made the point of their possible sales potential, or their being used to replace older light fleets sold or loaned to foreign or Commonwealth navies. Alexander, who had been inclined to cut losses and scrap the incomplete hulks of these ships, was convinced and decided they should be kept, subject to other carriers being sold.[27]

Matters did not quite end there. F.W. Mottershead, Alexander's principal private secretary, informed the first lord of the director of Plans' suggestions to cancel also the quarter-complete carrier *Eagle* and the four *Neptune*-class large cruisers that were projected but were not proposed to be started in the near future. The Treasury was wanting still more cuts, and these seemed suitable sacrifices, along with the two controversial "Weapons." These ships had indeed already used up more than 50 percent of their proposed cost, but the Treasury now laid it down that reducing future expenditure was more important; good money should not be thrown after bad. A private office memorandum by Mottershead on 23 December confirmed the cancellation of the unfortunate destroyers, leaving only four of the class to be completed as an experimental ASW flotilla. The four *Neptunes*, unwittingly placed on the chopping block by director of Plans were not quite cancelled, but Dalton had forced Alexander to concede that specific Treasury authorization would be required to lay them down. The *Eagle* was, however, to go despite the opposition of the naval airmen, the *Audacious* duly being renamed *Eagle* to keep the old carrier name alive. As for all six *Majestics*, they, like the three still uncompleted *Tiger*-class cruisers, were to continue, albeit at a slow pace. The first lord agreed with the chancellor that he would try to find buyers for two or three older *Colossus*-class carriers to make places for the *Majestics* in the active fleet.[28]

It is easy to criticize the Admiralty in general, and Alexander in particular, for these reductions, but it is hard to see what else could have been done. Caught between Dalton and the admirals, Alexander had little choice but to release as many resources as possible for use in more important areas. With large amounts of money locked up in terminal charges left over from the war effort (such things as release leave pay and war gratuities), a massive training effort to sustain, an expensive naval air arm to support, and a large fleet still scattered around the world clearing up after the war and transporting thousands of men home, there was little left over for new construction. In 1945 Britain had far more warships than she could operate or even maintain in reserve. To spend scarce financial and labor resources on new construction seemed unwise.

The revised 1945 "peacetime" building program retained only the experimental submarine and two escort vessels—a cut of three submarines, two escorts, and two battleships over the earlier 1945 wartime plans.[29] Scrapping of the oldest and least battle-worthy ships in the fleet also began, including the *R*-class battleships, the badly war-damaged battleship *Warspite*, and the two obsolete and worn out carriers, *Furious* and *Argus*.[30]

In 1945 an official Admiralty committee judged that naval aviation had "developed in a comparatively few years from what may be described as an adjunct to naval power to a vital and integral part of it."[31] To signify this the name Fleet Air Arm was abolished and in an order dated 6 September 1946 replaced by "Naval Aviation."[32] In mid-1945 the Royal Navy had a first-line establishment of some 1,600 aircraft, with almost seven hundred embarked in carriers. Actual strength in August 1945 was slightly less with 1,118 aircraft operational, but 2,564 training and second-line machines were also on hand.[33] Initial postwar plans were to reduce the establishment by half to eight hundred—five hundred of which would be in first-line squadrons. The reduction would be obtained by getting rid of all the American aircraft, which had allowed the wartime F.A.A. rapidly to improve its capabilities. Indeed, of the aircraft embarked in British carriers at the end of the war, only just over a third were British. Despite their excellent quality, these U.S. aircraft—Corsairs, Avengers, and Hellcats—were somewhat condescendingly regarded by the Admiralty in London as stopgaps. Although the Americans did not want combat Lend-Lease types returned, scarce dollars were required to keep these machines in the air, and it was decided that they should be disposed of as rapidly as possible, by July 1946 at the latest. Transport and communications aircraft had to be returned to the United States, or paid for, and this was done by sending them back in the escort carriers that also had to be returned, for possible mercantile reconversion. (The British only retained a single escort carrier, HMS *Campania*, in their postwar fleet.) As for the stockpiles of surplus U.S. combat types (and old British aircraft), hundreds were put over the sides of ships in mass ditchings. It was far too expensive to maintain personnel to look after these machines for which no further use was considered possible. For example, on 1 January 1946 orders were issued to ditch some 1,262 Avengers, Corsairs, Hellcats, and Wildcats. By July 1946 only the two Corsair squadrons embarked in the East Indies light fleet carriers, *Colossus* and *Vengeance*, remained in first-line service, and these ships were on passage to the United Kingdom.[34] U.S. aircraft had duly disappeared from Royal Naval operational service by August 1946, although a few second-line Harvards, Baltimores, Expeditors, Vengeances, and even Corsairs left behind at Trincomalee, Hong Kong, and Singapore remained for a time to remind people of the wartime American contribution to British naval aviation.[35]

The intended shape of Naval Aviation in the late 1940s was given in an Admiralty paper of August 1944 that speculated that in four years' time the Royal Navy would have eight hundred first-line combat aircraft. Of these 385 would be fighters. These would be of five types: the Seafire, a modification of the land-based Spitfire and never a satisfactory carrier aircraft (although with good speed and climb characteristics for a piston-engined machine); the Firefly, a slow two-seater more useful for reconnaissance, strike, and antisubmarine duties than engaging enemy aircraft; the Sea Hornet, a new high-performance twin-engined aircraft but large and heavy; the Sea Fury, a promising new conversion of a land-based single-seater but with a high landing speed; and the Wyvern, a large, high-performance, heavy single-seater in an early stage of development. In addition to these there would be between eighty and one hundred Firebrand single-seat torpedo strike aircraft, a similar number of larger, single-engined Fairey Spearfish bombers, and one hundred Sea Mosquito and Short Sturgeon twin-engined bomber reconnaissance aircraft.[36] Even before the end of the war, delays had occurred in this program, especially to the Wyvern project, which was given a low priority.[37] In May 1945, 150 Supermarine Seafang fighters were ordered as a stopgap.[38] Nevertheless, great hopes were placed

One of the large and heavy aircraft planned for Naval Aviation in 1946 but cancelled with the end of the war: the 22,000-lb. Fairey Spearfish torpedo/dive bomber-reconnaissance aircraft. (Imperial War Museum)

in the new types when and if they did arrive, especially the Wyvern, Spearfish, and Sturgeon. They were massive and expensive aircraft, with an emphasis on range rather than speed. The main problem was, however, that, due to weight and size limitations, no existing carriers could operate them.

The *Ark Royal*-type fleet carriers and *Hermes*-class light fleet carriers were the only ships able to operate such big aircraft, but these were still far from completion. Moves were made to accelerate the *Hermes*-class ship, HMS *Albion*, at Swan Hunter on the Tyne in early 1946, but merchant shipbuilding prevented this.[39] The Royal Navy would be forced to make do, in the short term at least, with its existing carrier fleet.

This was numerically quite impressive, but relatively large numbers belied significant qualitative problems. Britain's six armored-hangar fleet carriers had been conceived in the 1930s on the basis of some very restrictive assumptions about the role of the carrier and the number, size, and performance of the aircraft she carried. Even during the war severe problems had been faced in operating high-performance aircraft in sufficient quantities from British ships. Attempts were made to improve the problem of limited hangar space. Only three, the *Illustrious*, *Formidable*, and *Victorious*, were completed to the original design. *Indomitable* was given an extra half hangar while under construction, and *Implacable* and *Indefatigable* were heavily modified with two full-length hangars of reduced height. These expedients created problems of their own—*Implacable* and *Indefatigable* could not operate any American fighters as all types, when their wings were folded, were too high for their hangars. The new generation of aircraft promised still greater problems (see table 1–2).[40]

When the fleet carriers finally came home after duty as transports repatriating prisoners and demobilized personnel, they were either put into a well-earned reserve or demoted to second-line duties. The *Illustrious*, with her limited modifications, continued in service as a deck-landing trials ships, while the *Implacable* became the training carrier for advanced flying. The latter was given modified barriers and arrester gear in 1947, and the same year the *Victorious*, unmodified and without aircraft, joined the battleships *Anson* and *Howe* in the training squadron. There was little point in running such large carriers operationally, as the size of a contemporary air group, around twenty-four aircraft, was well within the capacity of an unarmored light fleet carrier of the *Colossus* class. These little 13,000-ton vessels, built during the war to boost the Royal Navy's quantity of flight decks as rapidly as possible, had a ship's company of 850 men, half a fleet carrier's complement. Hardly surprisingly, therefore, it was these ships that provided the backbone of the Royal Navy's carrier force in the immediate postwar years. With two on loan (see below) and two, the *Perseus* and *Pioneer*, completed as aircraft maintenance support ships (a lesson of the Pacific War), the Royal Navy was left with six of these useful and economical aircraft carriers: the *Glory*, *Ocean*, *Theseus*, *Triumph*, *Venerable*, and *Vengeance*. No more than three or four were usually in commission at any one time. With their relatively large lifts and hangars they could stow any of the new aircraft, although their arrester gear, crash barriers, and lifts required modifications to operate all the new generation. The *Majestic*s were to be completed with a full set of modifications to operate 20,000-lb. aircraft, but work was proceeding on these ships only at a snail's pace.[41]

The short-term solution to the carrier aircraft problem was dictated by the

TABLE 1–2.

THE POSTWAR CARRIER PROBLEM

	SHIP			
	*Illustrious**	*Formidable and Victorious*	*Indomitable*	*Implacable and Indefatigable*
New Aircraft				
Sea Mosquito	Folded width too wide for lifts	Folded width too wide for lifts	Too heavy for lifts and too high for lower hangar	Folded width too wide for lift to lower hangar
Seafang	"	"	Folded width too wide for lifts to lower hangar	"
Sea Hornet	"	"	"	"
Spearfish	Height too great for hangars	Too heavy for lifts and too high for hangars	Too heavy for lifts and too high for hangars	Too high for hangars
Sturgeon	"	"	Too high for hangars	"
Wyvern	Could operate	"	Too heavy for lifts	"
Sea Fury	"	Could operate	Too high for upper hangar	"

*(Modified 1945–46 with 20,000-lb. lifts, barriers, and arrester gear for deck landing trials.)

financial climate as much as by any other single factor. The Royal Navy's aircraft orders were repeatedly slashed. As soon as the war ended, the Sturgeon and Spearfish orders were reduced to a few development aircraft (the Sturgeon later saw limited use as a target tug; it was considered for ASW duties but never developed as such). Nevertheless, there were still over 1,500 naval aircraft on order in November 1945 for delivery before December 1946.[42] The chancellor specifically singled out these for attention in his correspondence with the Admiralty. The numbers were duly cut once more, and still further reductions occurred later in 1946. The Seafang, for example, was cancelled as an operational type, perhaps no bad thing given its poor handling qualities. When not cancelled, aircraft were delayed, and those machines that did arrive had problems that prevented them getting to carriers. The Firebrand TF 4 had to be grounded for an extended period as a result of aileron and elevator oscillation, and eventually the one squadron of these aircraft, 813, was temporarily disbanded. In August 1946 naval air strength was down to a minimum of some 122 operational aircraft, little more than a tenth the level of a year before. Even of this handful, the only available single-seat fighters, the Seafire 15 and 18 models, were temporarily banned from carriers because of supercharger problems.

This was perhaps the all-time low point of Naval Aviation. No squadrons were deployed in carriers in August, although the *Glory*, *Ocean*, and *Theseus* were back

The Royal Navy's main strike aircraft of the postwar decade, the troublesome Blackburn Firebrand. The first operational squadron, 813, formed in 1945, but development problems caused temporary disbandment and the squadron only became fully operational in 1949. A second Firebrand squadron, 827, was formed in 1950. The latter disbanded in 1952 to re-form with Wyverns two years later. 813 Squadron re-equipped with Wyverns in 1953. (Imperial War Museum)

at sea—with all Firefly air groups—by September 1946. Slowly the aircraft situation improved in the following months. Seafires were reembarked and a semi-usable Firebrand finally appeared with 813 Squadron in April 1947. It was still not an entirely satisfactory aircraft, but at least it could be operated from carriers. Perhaps the most unfortunate squadron of this period was 811, equipped with the special naval variant of the Mosquito, the TR 33, in April 1946 (having operated an RAF version, the FB 6, since September 1945). With no carriers capable of taking its aircraft, the squadron disbanded on 1 July 1947, having served only at shore stations. The Sea Mosquito had been intended to carry the large "Uncle Tom" rocket, an air-launched underwater attack weapon, ten inches in diameter and weighing 1,000 lbs. This was designed to be launched in level flight at a range of 2,000 yards, but was cancelled about the time the Sea Mosquitoes were taken out of service. Also abortive were rather odd air-to-surface projects like the "Zoster" winged torpedo, a "jet-propelled torpedo" called Bootleg and a "supersonic weapon with underwater run" code-named "Nozzle." Naval strike aircraft had to make do with bombs, 3-inch rockets, and the 18-inch torpedo.[43]

It is a serious error to gauge British naval air strength in the immediate postwar period from a mere perusal of the pages about carriers that appeared in naval reference books. Carrier air power has always meant much more than mere numbers of flight decks, and in no period was that more true than in the years immediately after the war. It was unsurprising that this most expensive and taxing dimension of naval power should have continued to demonstrate the Royal Navy's serious shortfalls in resources. One way out of the problem was to attempt to spread the load more widely. The Royal Navy helped foster the aviation components of friendly navies within and without the Commonwealth. Arrangements were made shortly after the war to dispose of two redundant escort carriers to the Dutch and the French respectively. The former was a pressing requirement, as the British wished the Dutch to acquire as soon as possible the wherewithal to control the Indonesian

Nationalists, with whom fighting had broken out. The carrier *Nairana* was duly lent to the Dutch in 1946 as the *Karel Doorman*, with the agreement that a *Colossus* class would be sold "at full depreciated price" in 1948. This deal was duly consummated and *Venerable* was sold, taking *Nairana*'s Dutch name. (The escort carrier became a merchantman.) France wished to purchase the *Pretoria Castle*, but the chancellor and Ministry of War Transport insisted that she be immediately converted back to a merchantman. The French Navy could not afford to purchase a *Colossus*, and partly to put into effect Alexander's agreement with the chancellor to dispose of two of these ships and partly to recover lost wartime goodwill, the Admiralty offered the *Colossus* herself in early 1946, on a loan of five years with the option to buy at the end of that time "at . . . depreciated value." She duly became the *Arromanches* in August (and was purchased in 1951). Negotiations were also in progress with the Canadians and Australians. The former received the *Warrior* of the *Colossus* class on loan in 1946, pending completion of a *Majestic* for the RCN. The Australians opened negotiations for two *Majestics*, and in September 1946 the British, anxious to find the incomplete ships a suitable and economical home, offered to meet half the cost, £2.75 million.[44]

Britain's inability to run more carriers herself reflected perhaps the greatest, and certainly the most chronic, postwar naval problem—shortage of manpower. In the immediate postwar period the problems were especially acute. A massive turnover of personnel had to be arranged. The planned run-down was 665,000 (excluding trainees) at the end of 1945, 540,000 on 31 March 1946, and 415,000 by 30 June 1946 (brought forward to mid-May).[45] Reconciling this exodus with the maintenance of both morale and combat effectiveness was not easy. It had been recognized well before the end of the war that: "The fundamental problem which will be presented when hostilities against Germany cease will be how to balance the necessities of material and operational efficiency against the peace of mind and contentment of personnel, large numbers of whom will be concentrating their thoughts more and more on getting back to civil life . . . without contentment we cannot expect efficiency."[46] The lessons of unrest of 1918–19 had been learned, and perhaps some of those of the Invergordon Mutiny of 1931.[47] The situation was indeed a sensitive one requiring a soft touch. Ships were being noted as having "strangely apathetic" crews, and cases of "wilful disobedience" were becoming more common.[48]

Such dissatisfied men had to be returned to civilian life as quickly as possible, but this was not easy given the chronic shortage of regular personnel. Few had taken up long service engagements since 1939, especially in certain specializations such as stokers and writers. What regulars there were tended to be in senior noncommissioned ranks, although this at least helped mitigate some of the problems caused by the return of senior "Hostilities Only" ("HO") men to civilian life. Both rank and specialization structures were unbalanced, and this had an impact on the rate of release of "HOs." It also necessitated a considerable training load for new regulars and new postwar conscripts, not to mention those men in specializations where there was a surplus, who had to be retrained in functions for which there was a shortfall. The loss of regulars as they came to the end of their engagement was a problem, too, as neither they, nor "HO" men, were keen to reengage. It was hoped that a new pay code would solve this particular problem, but it was not introduced until 31 July 1946, and it was not universally welcomed even then.[49]

The first step, at least, was to get some agreement on the number of personnel, traditionally called "Vote A," to be authorized by Parliament. The existing authorized strength of the Royal Navy's regular personnel was that of 1939, 135,000. Although this was larger than the actual number of regulars on strength in 1945, about 133,500, it would still not be enough to meet increasing personnel requirements of the postwar fleet. This increase was caused by the growing complexity of existing ships (e.g., the requirement for radar specialists), the plans to retain vessels and forces not provided for in the prewar navy (e.g., a significant flotilla of fast patrol boats) and the requirements of Naval Aviation. The number of regulars required to man this inflated service was estimated to be 170,000. Conscription did not help this particular problem, as some 10,000 more regulars over and above this total would be required to train the conscripts. The Admiralty understandably, therefore, tended to view conscription as something of a burden. The Royal Navy did not regard short-term peacetime conscripts as especially useful for complement billets. Their only usefulness was to form a wartime reserve. Initially, therefore, it estimated its requirements for new conscripts as 35,000 men out of a total Vote A of 215,000. This would make the Royal Navy the smallest of the three services, a change from the prewar situation. The Royal Air Force numbered only 116,000 men in 1939; estimates of its postwar strength were four or five times as large.

Inevitably, perhaps, Dalton insisted on a reduction in these notional figures before accepting them, in December 1945, and he asked for a reduction of regular Vote A to 136,000. The second sea lord was unhappy about this, as it limited his extra recruiting capacity to 22,500, which would not cover the new branches created during the war. It was also insufficient to cover the shortages in other branches that had not been recruited during the war, such as stokers and writers. Dalton relented and at the beginning of 1946 allowed the Royal Navy a planning total or "bid on account" of 144,000 regulars. In fact, the numbers of regulars went down; by late 1946 only 105,000 were serving.[50]

No sooner had this minor success with the Treasury been gained than the real manning situation was thrown into confusion once more by economic pressures. Dalton was becoming increasingly gloomy in the cabinet about Britain's economic difficulties. If overseas military expenditure was not cut quickly and massively, he arged, then cuts would have to be made on the importation of machinery vital to the export drive. By January 1946 he was prophesying to the Defence Committee (Operations) "economic disaster" if defense expenditure was not cut and manpower redeployed to civil industry.[51] Attlee agreed; the nation, he felt, simply could not afford the armed forces requested by the Chiefs of Staff for the end of the financial year 1946–47 (almost 1,400,000 men; 225,000 in the Royal Navy). Total strength would have to come down from the present 1.9 million to 1.1 million, naval total Vote A (excluding new conscripts) from 330,000 to almost half, 175,000. Alexander complained that this would wreck his release scheme and that of his colleagues and stressed the continuing postwar commitments. Attlee was unimpressed. "It was not necessary in present circumstances to have a large fleet ready for instant action as there was no one to fight. We had to face realities in the present situation and a certain amount of inefficiency might have to be expected."[52]

The chiefs of staff spelled out precisely what the inefficiencies would be in a joint paper signed for the navy by Vice Admiral Sir Rhoderick McGrigor, vice chief of Naval Staff.[53] The ships of the navy, the service chiefs argued, would have to be reduced to such a low level of effectiveness that they would not be able to meet a major threat until after the situation had stabilized. It would have to be assumed, therefore, that there would be no great crisis for the next two or three years.

The navy's total 1947 complement of 194,000 would be made up of 98,000 regulars, 77,000 experienced "H.O." men entered since 1943, plus a new conscript intake of 24,000. A staggering half million men would have left the service by the end of 1946. The planned effect on the fleet would be to run down the forces based east of Suez and at home, concentrating strength once more in the Mediterranean. (See table 1–3.)

The reduced levels were considered to be the lowest possible to meet commitments in the Mediterranean, East Indies, and Pacific. The other smaller stations would not be at the level perceived necessary by the Admiralty to maintain British prestige, and McGrigor had dire warnings about the negative effects of this on British trade. The planned postwar naval air arm would be postponed. Most important of all, VCNS warned, the disruption of technical training, the reduction of complements in all ships, the "drastic dilution" of complements in home waters with semitrained conscripts, and the prevention of continuity would mean a new low in fighting efficiency.[54]

Despite this strongly worded argument, when the Defence Committee (Operations) met once more on 16 February, Attlee was adamant. The risk of war in the next two or three years would have to be accepted. No hostile fleets were in being "or in sight within the next few years." Alexander disagreed. He pointed to the interest Russia seemed to be showing in setting up a powerful fleet and taking over German vessels. She might well be a menace in the future. He disagreed with Attlee's continued doubts about the need to maintain communications in the Mediterranean. The VCNS supported his political chief, and McGrigor stressed that the Royal Navy at the end of 1946 would be little more than a police force. Even its speed would be limited by fuel shortages. Nevertheless, the meeting concluded with the laying down of three important defense planning assumptions: first, there would be no major war in the next two to three years; second, America would be "probably on our side and not against us" in any future crisis; third (and most importantly for the navy), "no fleet capable of being a menace to us will exist in the next few years."[55] These assumptions proved not to be ill founded. Moreover, given the large pool of naval manpower trained in modern methods and experienced in warfare who were recently discharged and still on call for mobilization, and the serviceability of much of the existing Reserve Fleet, it was not too unstatesmanlike to take some risks. These were, however, assets that would rapidly waste away.

Economy thus became even more the order of the day. The Naval Staff's minimum fleet was still further reduced. No naval building program was drawn up for 1946, and the 1946–47 naval estimates were reduced from a departmental requirement of over £351 million to £255,075,000. The savings were concentrated on Votes 8 and 9, shipbuilding and naval armaments, and the victims were those ships not yet cancelled but still lying incomplete in the yards. In May 1946 three of the *Majestic*s were laid up and put in a state of preservation with their contracts cancelled. This saved about £2 million. As for the rest of the class, the building of the

TABLE 1–3.

PROPOSED REDISPOSITION AND REDUCTION OF THE FLEET IN 1946*

BRITISH PACIFIC FLEET	FEBRUARY	DECEMBER
Battleships	2	none
Fleet Carrier	1	none
Light Fleet Carriers	2	2[a]
Cruisers	7	4[a]
Destroyers	16	8
Escorts	16	12
Submarines	10	10
Fleet Minesweepers	8	none
EAST INDIES FLEET		
Light Fleet Carriers	2	2[b]
Cruisers	4	4
Destroyers	8	none
Escorts	20	4
Fleet Minesweepers	24	8
MEDITERRANEAN FLEET	JUNE	DECEMBER
Light Fleet Carriers	1	1
Cruisers	5	5
Destroyers	16	24
Escorts	11	10[c]
Submarines	10	10
Fleet Minesweepers	24	16
AMERICA AND WEST INDIES STATION		
Cruisers	2	1
Escorts	4	4
SOUTH ATLANTIC (AFRICA) STATION		
Cruisers	2	1
Escorts	4	2
HOME FLEET		
Battleships	2	3[d]
Fleet Carriers	2	2[e]
Other Carriers	2[e]	2[e]
Cruisers	7	5
Destroyers	16	16
Escorts	30[f]	16[g]
Submarines	25	25
Fleet Minesweepers	32	16
RESERVE FLEET (by 31 December 1946; including stationary training ships)		
Battleships	6	
Fleet Carriers	4	
Other Carriers	5	
Cruisers	15	
Destroyers	49	
Escorts	126	
Submarines	40	

*Source: DO(46)20 of 14 February 1946—CAB 131/2.
[a]Assuming one Commonwealth
[b]For consideration in March depending on Indian political situation. In the event, the two carriers were withdrawn, and the BPF's two carriers deployed in the Indian Ocean as required.
[c]Including Red Sea
[d]2 with reduced complements
[e]Trials and training duties—reduced complements
[f]For ASW training and air/sea rescue
[g]For ASW training

Majestic herself was temporarily suspended while Vickers concentrated on merchant ships. Work continued slowly on Canada's *Magnificent* and Australia's *Terrible*. To get them completed at all meant abandoning the full *Majestic* specification.[56]

Money was not the only problem. Delays in construction reflected a sheer inability to design and build the ships. Not only was the labor force building warships in the Royal Dockyards reduced to a mere 10,000 by early 1947 (a reduction of 90 percent from the wartime peak), but the numbers working in the shipyards were down to 195,000 (a reduction of 25 percent). The main preoccupation of this reduced work force was rebuilding the merchant fleet. An additional problem that affected warship programs was a chronic shortage of technical design staff, especially for electrical equipment. The *Hermes* class was in a sorry state; *Albion*, the furthest advanced was launched in 1947 but immediately laid up due to a shortage of electrical designers. Work on the *Hermes* herself was stopped and not likely to start again for some time because of Vickers' merchant ship commitments. A Board decision in mid-1946 to alter the catapults to accommodate the latest aircraft promised to delay all four ships of the class. The design of the two fleet carriers, *Ark Royal* and *Audacious* (soon to be renamed *Eagle*), was modified, also putting back their completion dates. It was hoped to get the *Eagle* out before the end of 1948 (if extra design staff were provided), but it proved impossible to man her, and her eventual completion date was 1950. As for the *Ark Royal*, she was not to see service (in a further modified form) until 1955, five years after the late 1950 date anticipated in 1946–47.[57]

Cruisers suffered the same fate as carriers. The 1946 cutbacks led to the complete suspension of the *Tiger*-class cruiser, *Defence*. She suffered the ignominy of having her incomplete hull towed away from Scotts yard at Greenock, as there was no room for her there. It had been hoped to complete her in Portsmouth Dockyard after the carrier *Terrible*, but her incomplete hulk was to remain in the Gareloch for many years. The *Tiger* and *Blake* were delayed by both the reductions in expenditure and the shortage of design staff. The latter meant that the intended "Flyplane" fire control could not be fitted, and first the *Blake* was laid up, and then the *Tiger*, which was to have been completed in 1949, suffered the same fate. By 1948 all three were laid up indefinitely, their contracts cancelled. By the time they were re-started, they would be able to carry a totally new armament being developed for the projected large cruiser class.[58]

In August 1946 the design of the *Neptune*s was revised to include a twin dual-purpose automatic 6-inch mounting instead of the previously intended triple (savings in the latter contributed to the cuts in the 1946–47 estimates). Various designs were produced with five and four turrets, and at a sea lords' meeting in June 1946 the consensus was in favor of a five-turret design with a secondary armament of sixteen automatic 3-inch weapons in twin turrets. These 15,000-ton "Minotaurs," as they were now called, would have been fine-looking ships, but doubts were already being expressed about whether such large and expensive vessels should be built until the trends in ship design became clearer. The *Neptune* class was officially abandoned in favor of the *Minotaur* by Board decision on 28 August and the latter design "kept in the cupboard" for better days that, in fact, never came.[59]

The first sea lord who set his name to this recommendation was Admiral Sir John Cunningham, who replaced Lord Cunningham of Hyndhope (as he had now become) on 10 June 1946. As one contemporary put it: "It would be difficult to

Admiral of the Fleet Sir John Cunningham. (Imperial War Museum)

find two men less alike than 'ABC' and John D. Cunningham. The former fiery, aggressive, active and intolerant; the latter quiet, thoughtful, rather lethargic, very kind but possessed of an acid tongue. ABC scintillating, successful and inclined to be schoolboyishly boastful. John D., with an unlucky series of operations—Norway, Dakar and the Dodecanese—behind him, very cautious, cynical and suspicious of adventure.'' The late Stephen Roskill, who knew them both, considered Sir John to have ''far the better brain,'' and this, plus his general style, perhaps suited the times of even greater adversity into which his service was about to pass.[60]

Sir John Cunningham inherited a major new row with the government over naval manning levels. In early 1946, the government "Manpower Committee" produced proposals on the allocation of personnel to the armed forces that the chiefs of staff found completely unacceptable.[61] In the Admiralty's eyes the proposed Royal Navy of only 173,000 by the end of 1951, when combined with a proposed postwar conscription period of only a year, implied both too low a level of efficiency and an inadequate basis for wartime expansion. By May the Admiralty was willing to concede a navy of 182,000 personnel, compared to the contemporary total of 194,000. It continued, however, to demand a longer period of service for conscripts.[62]

Attlee went on the offensive. In July he sent a memorandum to Alexander asking why so many men were required when 119,000 had been deemed sufficient to cope with the German, Italian, and Japanese navies in 1938. The U.S.A. was now the only major naval power in the world, and the Defence Committee had specifically ruled out war with her. Yet manpower requirements were much higher than before the war. Rather peremptorily he asked for a full report on the state of the fleet.[63]

Alexander's reply, dated 24 July 1946, gives a fascinating insight into the prewar and postwar navies.[64] The tables, which compared *expected* strength in December 1947 with strength in 1938, are reproduced here:

TABLE 1–4A.

COMPARISON OF THE PLANNED POSTWAR (1947) WITH THE PREWAR (1938) ROYAL NAVY*

Ships	Full Commission		Training and Instructional		Reserve	
	1938	*1947*	*1938*	*1947*	*1938*	*1947*
Battleships	11	3	1	2	4	4
Cruisers	31	20	3	2	25	14
Destroyers	69	40	40	38	66	50
Escorts	20	28	10	25	none	145
Submarines	27	25	20	20	12	28
Fleet Minesweepers	none	16	13	8	20	32
Other Minesweepers	none	4	6	2	none	62
Gunboats	18	none	none	none	none	5
Survey Ships	8	7	none	none	none	none
Coastal Forces	18	12	6	10	none	32
Depot Ships	4	6	2	none	1	1
Repair Ships	1	1	none	none	none	4
Maintenance Ships	none	1	none	none	none	4
Wreck Dispersal Ships	none	20	none	none	none	none
Miscellaneous Auxiliary Craft	2	8	28	52	none	17
Fleet Carriers	none	3	none	2	none	1
Other Carriers	5	5	2	1	1	6
Naval Air Tenders	none	54	none	none	none	none

Aircraft	1938	1947
Naval Air Arm Aircraft	none (due to Fleet Air Arm being RAF)	204 first-line, 750 second-line, 100 reserve, 1,530 in storage.
Naval Air Stations and Establishments	none (due to Fleet Air Arm being RAF)	30

Other Commitments	1938	1947
Combined Operations Craft and Depots	none	Battalion lift with training and development together with reserve craft for Brigade lift.
Dockyards and Bases	13	14 + 4 in care and maintenance.
New Entry Training Establishments	4	11
Instructional Schools and Technical Training Establishments	15	31
Wireless Stations	16	21
Royal Naval Volunteer Reserve Divisions	11	12
Hospitals	10 + 1 ship	13 + 1 ship
Boom Defence Organisation	4 vessels	20 vessels
Royal Marines	As required for shore depots	As required for shore depots plus commandos.

TABLE 1–4B.

PLANNED DISPOSITION OF THE ACTIVE FLEET (12/47) COMPARED WITH ACTUAL DISPOSITION IN 1938*

	PACIFIC		EAST INDIES		SOUTH ATLANTIC		AMERICA & WEST INDIES		MEDI-TERRANEAN		HOME	
	1938	1947	1938	1947	1938	1947	1938	1947	1938	1947	1938	1947
Battleships	—	—	—	—	—	—	—	—	5	1	6	2
Cruisers	7	4	3	3	2	1	5	2	7	5	7	5
Destroyers	9	8	—	—	—	—	—	—	35	16	25	16
Escorts	7	10	6	4	4	2	2	4	1	8	—	—
Submarines	15	9	—	—	—	—	—	—	7	8	5	8
Fleet Minesweepers	—	—	—	—	—	—	—	—	—	8	—	8
Other Minesweepers	—	—	—	—	—	—	—	—	—	2	—	2
Gunboats	18	—	—	—	—	—	—	—	—	—	—	—
Survey Ships	1	1	—	1	—	—	—	—	—	1	7	4
Depot Ships	1	1	—	—	—	—	—	—	2	2	1	3
Repair Ships	—	1	—	—	—	—	—	—	1	—	—	—
Maintenance Ships	—	—	—	—	—	—	—	—	—	—	—	1
Miscellaneous Ancillary Craft	—	5	—	1	—	—	—	—	2	2	—	—
Wreck Dispersal Ships	—	—	—	—	—	—	—	—	—	—	—	20
Coastal Forces	12	—	—	—	—	—	—	—	6	—	—	12
Fleet Carriers	—	—	—	—	—	—	—	—	—	—	—	3
Other Carriers	2	2	—	—	—	—	—	—	1	2	2	1

Manpower	*1938*	*1947*
Effective		
Ships in Full Commission	61,300	55,500
Ships for Training, etc.	7,200	10,000
Reserve Fleet	5,600	9,000
Naval Aviation (ashore)	none	24,000
Combined Operations	none	5,500
Dockyards, Shore Training, etc.	12,200	22,000
Royal Marines	2,500	6,500
	88,800	132,500
Non-Effective		
New Entry and Initial Training	13,150	23,000
Officers on Courses/Men Training for Rates	5,500	9,500
Drafting Margin/Sickness/Leave/Conscript Releases	11,550	17,000
	30,200	49,500

*Source for tables 1–4A and 1–4B: "Size of the Navy," DO(46)97 in CAB131/3.

It must be remembered that the figures, like the previous ones for demobilization, are plans rather than actual strengths; for example, there was no battleship in the Mediterranean when December 1947 came round. Nevertheless, they do show the real differences between the prewar and postwar navies. In the accompanying paper, the first sea lord strongly defended the state of his service and its role. Britain, Alexander argued, was more, rather than less, vulnerable than it had been before the war. He warned that if a British naval presence was withdrawn, the situation in many parts of the world would deteriorate and British prestige would suffer. In perhaps surprising words for a member of the Labour Party,

Alexander expressed the role of the Royal Navy in deliciously Victorian form: "A visit by a cruiser has often been cited as a deterrent, and the presence of H.M. ships has always been welcomed as a steadying influence by H.M. representatives in different parts of the world and by governors of our Colonial possessions." The fleet as it stood, he insisted, was inadequate for a country of Britain's position. A capacity to fight a war to defend "ocean routes," especially against submarine attack, was essential for British security. Alexander did not forget the surface threat. Enemy raiders would have to be neutralized by being sunk at sea or possibly by attacking or even capturing their bases. Because of the difficulty of striking potential enemies (at this time RAF bombers could not reach into the U.S.S.R.), Alexander pointed to the carriers as a forward deployed base for air strikes against an opponent.

The first lord pointed out that the prewar navy had not had enough ships to fight both Germany and Italy and that there had been no fleet for the Far East when the time to send it out had come. If Axis naval forces had been handled more efficiently, the situation could have been disastrous. Given the enemy's initiative, a superiority of force to defend sea communications was essential. Even if there was no obvious naval enemy, the Admiralty view was "that if we are to hold our world position we must maintain our sea power and the security of our communications on which the life of the United Kingdom and the British Commonwealth depends." The penalty for challenging Britain at sea had to be "severe, obvious and certain." In fact, one great power—the U.S.S.R., although this was not mentioned because of Attlee's reluctance to adopt too overt an anti-Soviet policy too soon—was building up a powerful fleet, and other powers were reorganizing also. Continued superiority would deter a naval building race, and Britain should concentrate on those areas where she had an advantage.

As for the high manpower figures in relation to active ships, he justified them by citing the large reserve fleet to be maintained compared to prewar times. It was essential that the reserve of ASW vessels and minesweepers be kept up to prevent a repetition of the events of 1939–42. The naval air arm employed 24,000 men in shore establishments alone; the combined operations organization for amphibious warfare took up another ten thousand. To meet wireless and radar requirements, another four thousand were needed. He repeated that conscription *raised* the numbers of trained men locked up in instructional duties and that the shorter the period of National Service eventually decided upon the greater this load would be for a proportional reduction in the usefulness of the conscripts. Research locked up more resources on the shore. He summed up his case as follows:

> The introduction of the large carrier, the heavy increase in anti-aircraft guns, the immense growth in technical equipment, the development of radar and W/T, the speed of the modern commerce destroying submarine, the advent of combined operations and the introduction of short term conscription have substantially changed the situation and their cumulative effect has been largely to increase the number of men required to maintain a given number of naval ships, units and training depots and schools.

It was a powerful, if slightly prolix and repetitive, argument showing Alexander's qualities of devotion to his department to good effect. Attlee, however, had a new post in mind for "A.V.," as a result of the government's plans to reform the central organization of Britain's defenses.[65] A single Cabinet Defence Committee of concerned ministers and the chiefs of staff was to be set up to act as the main strategic review and service coordination body. Although the prime minister would still retain "supreme responsibility" for defense, a new separate "minister of defense" was to be created to chair normal meetings of the Defence Committee for the prime minister and to head a small government department to assist him in the limited task of coordinating the three service ministries and supervising those bodies already set up for joint service planning, intelligence, and staff training. The Admiralty, along with the War Office and Air Ministry, were to remain as separate and powerful government departments with their own ministers. The latter were no longer to be ex-officio Cabinet members, but they were members of the Defence Committee along with their professional advisers, the chiefs of staff, and they were usually called in to full Cabinet when defense matters were under discussion. The task of the minister of defense was a thankless and unenviable one. Not only did he have to referee the struggle of the three services for slices of a defense "cake," but he also had to defend the total size of the "cake" from the chancellor's depredations. The chancellor felt that the minister of defense gave in weakly to service interests; the services felt that the minister of defense did not defend them from Treasury pressure.

Attlee chose Alexander as the first of the new-style ministers of defense. Criticisms of the latter as a "passenger"[66] or "uninterested"[67] are wide of the mark and do not tally with the strong and conscientious man revealed in recently released documents. His outwardly unimpressive and pompous manner covered a strength of mind that could emerge if provoked. He placed a high priority on Britain's defenses, her navy in particular, with some of whose officers at least he had forged a remarkably close relationship of mutual respect.[68] Nevertheless, Alexander, with his background in the cooperative retailing movement, recognized that defense was but one priority among the many pressing preoccupations of postwar British austerity. Alexander's successor at the Admiralty was George, Lord Hall, an ex-miner who had been civil lord in the Labour Government in 1929–31 and who had been at the Admiralty once more as financial secretary in 1942–43. Hall was a gentle and warm-hearted man, highly respected for his integrity and sincerity. He developed a "deep personal interest in the affairs of the Royal Navy" and its personnel,[69] but he was a much less weighty figure than Alexander, as was only fitting given his office's reduced status. Hall took over in October when the new defense proposals were enacted. Alexander became "minister without portfolio" in the Cabinet pending the creation of his new ministry on the first day of 1947. No longer was Britain's navy minister a member of the Cabinet.

The most pressing question facing the new regime of Cunningham and Hall was still the National Service conscription system. The Board of Admiralty was divided, the Second Sea Lord and Chief of Naval Personnel Vice Admiral Sir Arthur Power having become convinced that the system's advantages were outweighed by its disadvantages. The peacetime fleet, he argued, could be manned without conscripts, and some 300,000 men might be obtained for war by voluntary reserves alone, without the burden of the enlarged training establishment and numbers of partly trained and unusable men inherent in conscription. This line received support from John Dugdale, the parliamentary and financial secretary, who said it would be difficult to convince the Cabinet that the service required the stabilized peacetime

Lord Hall (right), First Lord of the Admiralty for most of the Attlee Government.
He is visiting Malta as guest of Admiral Algernon Willis, CinC, Mediterranean Fleet.
(Imperial War Museum)

numbers now being put forward—170,000 regulars, plus about 10,000 to train the
conscripts and the slightly reduced total of 27,000 conscripts themselves. This might
raise 350,000 in war, but, echoing the prime minister's line, he wondered where
the enemy was who would require such a massive mobilization. He even went so
far as to doubt the relevance of a mobilizable reserve in the nuclear age.[70]

The majority Board view was that nuclear weapons had, if anything, emphasized
the need for quick mobilization of the Reserve Fleet and the Naval Air Arm. The
threat of the modern submarine and attack from the air meant that the maximum
number of men would have to be mobilized in the minimum possible time. Conscription was therefore vital to maintain a trained ready reserve, and the navy, it
was decided, should insist upon at least an eighteen-month period of service so
that conscripts could gain some sea time and some might be trained as aircrew.[71]
This was the thrust of an eloquent speech before the Defence Committee (Operations) by Sir Rhoderick McGrigor, VCNS, on 16 October.[72] With the support of
the first lord, he reported in detail the Soviets' naval strength, both surface and
subsurface. They already had 3 battleships, 10 cruisers, 58 destroyers, and 216
submarines, with more vessels under construction. It was vital to meet this threat
to sea communications as quickly as possible. American help could not be relied
on at war's outset. The following day the committee duly approved the adoption
of a conscription plan with a period of eighteen months. This was a compromise
between the services, who generally wanted a two-year period in order to get the
most out of the conscripts, and others of the cabinet who feared both the political
unpopularity of too long a period of service and the economic impact of diverting
too many young hands from productive work.[73] The Treasury and the Board of
Trade were particularly unhappy with these conscription plans, given the demands

of such large armed forces on resources, money, and manpower. It would be impossible, their ministers argued, if defense expenditure remained uncurbed, to meet in full the planned targets in industrial investment, housing, and education or to maintain prewar levels of employment in industries for domestic consumption. The consequences of such a large conscription would be continued austerity or a mortgaged future.

The battle over service manpower went on into 1947, with the Royal Navy suffering a steady series of reverses, leading by the end of the year to some of the most serious and sudden cuts in its capability it had ever known. This was not because of any want of advocacy by the new defense minister. At the beginning of the year he had proposed to the Cabinet's Defence Committee a naval manpower total of 189,000 to 1948, of which 164,000 would be trained and usable.[74] These numbers almost met the undiluted Admiralty demands, and Dalton, the chancellor, came out strongly against them. He had been hoping to get defense expenditure down to £750 million, but the minister of defense wanted £963 million, the equivalent of an extra two shillings (ten pence) in the pound on income tax. Moreover, the country was still 650,000 workers short. The chancellor argued for earlier releases of men from all the armed services, but he was especially critical of naval manpower demands, which seemed the least urgent. He repeated the prime minister's arguments about the lack of an enemy. The Soviet Navy was weaker than any of the German, Italian, or Japanese navies before the war. Yet in 1933 the Royal Navy's strength had only been 94,000 and in 1938 only 119,000. The immediate threat was economic and financial overstrain and collapse rather than a military or strategic one.[75]

Both Alexander and Cunningham joined to beat off this attack when the committee met on 14 January.[76] An increased estimate of Soviet naval strength (230 submarines, 17 cruisers, 69 destroyers) was produced to make the point of the Royal Navy's slim margin of superiority. Despite hints in the following days of resignation by the chancellor and a "first-class row" between Dalton and Alexander, the defense cuts were only minor, the reduced naval manpower total (182,000) having, indeed, been deemed acceptable by the navy six months before. As 1947 wore on, however, two factors beyond the control of either the Admiralty or the Ministry of Defence intervened to upset these plans.

The first was the economy. Within six months, in July, the chancellor was circulating a paper among his Cabinet colleagues that spelled out the "simple and very unpleasant" facts of Britain's economic life.[77] The gist of Dalton's paper was that the American loan was running out. It would be gone by the end of the year. Exports had to be increased and imports reduced, but all overseas commitments "which are the equivalent of imports" would have to be examined. Alexander protected the navy from the worst of the emergency cuts he was forced to draw up immediately, as the balance of payments impact of army and RAF deployments was greater. Nevertheless, the proposed March 1948 figure of naval strength was edged downwards once more to 178,000.[78] Predictably the Admiralty protested, although its cuts were only 5 percent of the total package. Reductions would have to be made in the active fleet, and anything more would lead to the "relative immobilization of the Navy." Perhaps Cunningham and his staff did not think that was a likely possibility. Their worst nightmares, however, were soon to come to pass.

The second blow came from the government's back benches. A Labour Party revolt had forced a reversion of the conscription period from eighteen months to only one year before the National Service Act finally received the Royal Assent in July 1947. Initial forecasts were that this would reduce "Vote A" to 166,250 by the beginning of the financial year 1948–49. Coupled with the less useful nature of the one-year conscript and and the still considerable training load, this gave the navy the worst of both worlds, and Admiralty papers growled once more about the "grossly inadequate sea going fleet" that this reduced "Vote A" could mean.[79]

Given this economic and political background, it is a little disappointing that the Admiralty's policy makers could not be more realistic in their future fleet planning. In the summer of 1947, the economic storm clouds grew bleaker still. In negotiating the vital American loan, the British had been forced to concede that from July 15, 1947, sterling would be freely convertible to other currencies. This led to a fierce run on the pound, which meant that within a month or two Britain's reserves of convertible currency were almost exhausted. Despite this growing crisis the Admiralty was producing plans for a future fleet with which even the government of an economically healthy Britain would probably have demurred. These plans had their origins in the first serious moves taken a year before by the chiefs of staff to draw up a long-term British defense policy once the dislocation of demobilization ended.

In mid-1946 the chiefs of staff had begun a series of important studies of strategy and future defense problems, and the new minister of defense soon made it clear that he felt that the armed forces must know "where they are going and how they are to get there."[80] In January 1947 at an important chiefs of staff meeting chaired by Attlee himself, the United Kingdom's "Principles of Defence" were defined as (a) the defense of the Commonwealth's resources with which to fight a major war until an offensive with allies could be developed and (b) the holding of bases for this offensive. In order to do this basic defense missions were laid down as the "three pillars" of British defense strategy: first, the defense of the United Kingdom; second, the maintenance of sea communications; and third, "a firm hold" in the Middle East. The Royal Navy had a fundamental role to play in this emerging strategy both in maintaining control of the seas around the United Kingdom and elsewhere. "The most important sea communications are those in the Atlantic and approaches to the United Kingdom, hardly less important are the sea communications throughout the Mediterranean to the Middle East and with the Dominions and with sources of raw materials throughout the world. This will necessitate Naval and Air Forces mutually organised to meet any threat to these communications." The main threat came, it was argued, from the airplane and the submarine in both the Atlantic and Mediterranean, "although the surface threat must also be guarded against." Cunningham was obviously pleased at this naval emphasis in Britain's declared priorities and the level of agreement among the chiefs of staff, the continentalist ideas of the Chief of the Imperial General Staff, General Lord Montgomery, having for the time being been suppressed.[81]

The following month Alexander tried to edge the long-term planning process a stage further and provide it with a context in which to work. He reminded the service chiefs, Cunningham, Tedder, and Montgomery, of the need for a strong national economy, using Montgomery's own ideas to make his point. He stressed the importance of scientific development and the need, therefore, not to rush into decisions. Ominously, he doubted whether large naval or other forces could be sustained. Risks would have to be taken but, significantly, he specifically ruled out any return to the prewar "Ten Year No War Rule." This was "a mistake which we must not make again." As general assumptions, however, he did suggest a ten-year planning framework and a total defense budget of no more than £600 million — a sum which would, nevertheless, be "a heavy strain on the national resources." Alexander recommended that the navy concentrate on antisubmarine forces, albeit with the backing of some surface and carrier capability. The extent of the latter, however, was a matter of some debate, especially the future of the battleship and the large carrier. He hinted that some relatively early decisions would be helpful before the 1948–49 estimates were framed, as that year would be the first of the long-term planning period.[82]

The chiefs of staff received some basis on which to make their plans when they were given the long-awaited "Review of Defence Problems," prepared over the winter by a special "Future Planning Section" of their joint planning staff. This review confirmed the emphasis on the Soviet air and submarine threat, and also the menace of the mine, but it cast doubts that the next war would be a long-drawn-out affair in which traditional sea power would be effective. The initial Soviet attack would quickly overrun Western Europe, close the Mediterranean within two months, and capture the oilfields. With Soviet forces on Britain's door-step it would be a relatively easy matter for them to neutralize the United Kingdom in perhaps six weeks using conventional weapons alone. The war would certainly be past its crisis within nine months at the most, six if the Soviets had nuclear weapons. The planners stressed the need for American help and an immediate nuclear air offensive if Britain were to survive.[83]

Not surprisingly, the chiefs of staff disagreed with some of these opinions. Cunningham, in particular, especially questioned the implications of a short war/strategic bombing strategy, and the unanimous COS position was that one could not be specific about the length of a future conflict, but that there would be much less time than previously before the full weight of an enemy attack was felt. The chiefs were unwilling to commit themselves to the immediate use of nuclear weapons and felt it was possible that both sides would be mutually deterred from nuclear use as they had been with gas in the Second World War. Britain had to be prepared to use nuclear weapons, however, because such was the best deterrent to war. (Indeed only three months before Britain had made the decision to build nuclear bombs.) The review also made one more vital point: it was unlikely that the Soviet Union would begin premeditated war until the second half of the 1950s, by which time she would have completed her economic recovery from the war and built up her own stockpile of nuclear bombs.[84]

The agreed positions on the review were confirmed at a meeting between Alexander and the chiefs of staff on 17 April 1947.[85] Together with the January decisions, they were to be written into a paper on "Future Defence Policy" that would govern the buildup of Britain's armed forces in the period from financial year 1948–49, "the first year of a long term development and re-organisation plan for the armed forces." Basic to the strategy and the force goals based on them would be a ten-year planning assumption based on the future policy section's findings: "Planning should proceed on the assumption that the likelihood of war in the next five years will be small. The risk will then increase gradually in the following five years and increase more steeply after ten years. The risk of war at any time will be comparably decreased to the extent that we and our potential allies show strength." The last sentence in particular, and the lack of a "rolling" planning date, differentiates this planning assumption fundamentally from the prewar version.[86]

The "Future Defence Policy" paper that was completed by the end of May reiterated the probable inability of the main potential enemy, the Soviet Union, to support her armed forces in a major war until the late 1950s. The paper stressed the overriding importance of strategic air forces and the Middle East priority. A major military threat to Commonwealth interests in the Far East was considered to be "remote." In any case Britain would be unable to sustain major forces there, and the area would be left to the Americans. Britain should concentrate on research and development and bomber and fighter forces, but "sea communications" with the U.S.A., the Commonwealth, and other parts of the world should be defended against air and submarine threats. That would be the major naval priority, and other naval tasks, such as amphibious operations, could be downgraded since they would not be required in the early stages of a war.[87]

The emphasis on the primacy of strategic air warfare was perhaps a little worrying for the Admiralty, but the requirement to fight a traditional sea war in defense of merchant shipping and troopships was enough to sustain naval force goals that were grand indeed. Alexander had warned the services not to be too ambitious. In a paper of 30 May he reiterated the £600 million limit for peacetime forces and significantly strengthened the "5+5 Rule." The chance of war in the next five years, he asserted, was "negligible," and given the dynamic nature of defense technology, numbers of wartime forces could only be tentative.[88]

In their figures for the shape of the future peacetime and wartime navy that appeared in the summer, the Naval Staff effectively ignored these strictures. The war paper came first, and its strategic framework was very traditional.[89] It called for two "battle forces," one for home waters, the other for the Mediterranean, both to outmatch any naval forces a potential enemy might deploy. These forces had to be able to find, fix, and destroy the enemy in all conditions, and, on Pacific war experience, this was deemed to require four carriers and two "capital" ships (i.e., battleships) with each group, which, with spares, meant a requirement for ten and six of each type respectively. This was based on the assumption that the potential enemy had no more than four capital ships. It was thus held desirable to keep the five modern battleships that Britain still deployed, plus at least three of the older vessels that would still be useful for convoy escort against surface forces and for shore bombardment if nothing else.

The requirement for convoy escorts against enemy surface forces and antiair defense of battle lines necessitated a considerable cruiser fleet—six with each battle force, plus sixteen for escort duty. Given a margin for refits, etc., this required some thirty-five vessels. The reduced numbers of cruisers as compared with prewar assessments was due to the increasing reliance on light fleet carriers and shore-based aircraft as escorts.

The number of light fleet carriers required for "direct control of sea communications, whether in hunting groups or as close escort to convoys," was twelve; with four others being used as replenishment carriers for the battle forces, four to maintain essential training, and five spares, this meant twenty-five ships. Only the twelve operational light fleet carriers would require aircraft—some 432—while battle-force carriers would have 528, bringing the total front-line aircraft requirement (with 240 spares) to 1,200. Of these, some 900 would be required at the outbreak of war, 100 being the Commonwealth contribution.

Some 120 destroyers would be required, 48 (with 12 spares) for battle-group operations and a similar number for operations with the cruisers and light fleet carriers. A new type of ship was envisaged in the fleet air defense picket, six of which would be deployed with each battle force, with three spares. Initial plans for these vessels called for a "large destroyer"-type ship slightly bigger than the existing *Daring* class. As for other types of escort vessels, the requirement was enormous, even with the Pacific responsibility going to the Americans. Twelve ships were required per escort group, ten of which were needed as close escorts for Atlantic convoys, six for Mediterranean convoys, and thirty for escorting logistical support ships. This came to 552 escorts.

To combat the mining threat, some 200 minesweepers (48 large "fleet" vessels and 152 smaller craft) were deemed necessary. As for submarines, the requirement for offensive operations against enemy seaborne movements, reconnaissance, and clandestine operations was some eighty boats—forty for "Northern Waters," twenty for the Mediterranean, and twenty for training. The coastal force requirement was fifty motor torpedo boats and motor gunboats and a hundred motor launches. Seven small minelayers were necessary to lay defensive ASW minefields, and five depot ships were needed, two for destroyers and three for submarines.

It is true that this was still conceived as an "Imperial" fleet, but of the above totals the dominions would be expected to supply only four light carriers, five cruisers, twenty destroyers, and thirty-two escorts. The British contribution was still enormous and a good illustration of the unrealistic near "super power" terms in which the Naval Staff were still thinking. Preparing such a force to the latest standards would cost an astronomical amount of money.

The burden that this wartime fighting fleet would actually put on the peacetime defense estimates was spelled out in the second Admiralty paper.[90] All the ships in the wartime fleet, it was argued, had to exist in peacetime. At least half the 382,000 men required to man the wartime forces had to be peacetime regulars, and the balance had to be capable of recall in the first four months of hostilities. The peacetime manpower requirement was set, therefore, at 191,000 regular men and women. It was assumed that 20,500 National Servicemen (i.e., conscripts) would be serving and that the National Service Reserve would provide 80,500 men to man the reserve fleet on mobilization, along with 90,000 non–National Service reservists.

The desired peacetime fleet was based on two "Tactical Training Forces," the nascent "Battle Forces." These would normally have a peacetime strength of a battleship apiece, two fleet carriers, one light carrier, three cruisers, sixteen destroyers, and four aircraft direction pickets. A training force for convoy escorts would deploy two light carriers, a cruiser, and sixteen frigates. Extra ships were required for policing duties (including four light fleet carriers and a battleship), bringing the total peacetime fleet (excluding "experimental and school" ships) to three battleships, four fleet carriers, eight light carriers, seven cruisers, forty-eight destroyers, eight A/D pickets, fifty other escort vessels, twenty-nine submarines, and four fleet minesweepers. Five hundred front-line combat aircraft would be maintained.

The need to keep the fleet, active and reserve, up-to-date was stressed. Convoy escorts posed special problems. The existing force of relatively slow frigates and corvettes was of only dubious use, given the threat of modern high-speed submarines. Four-fifths of the existing inventory would have to be replaced by modern frigates. Even new battleships might be needed, although, prudently, there was no allowance in the building plan for this due to the surplus of holdings over requirements in this category. The program required for the proposed fleet of 1956–57 comprised 2 new fleet carriers and 6 modernizations (the old armored hangar ships), 6 new light fleet carriers and 11 modernizations, the 6 new *Minotaur*-class cruisers, 8 new destroyers, 14 new A/D pickets, 263 new frigates and 31 frigate modernizations, and 80 new submarines, not to mention almost 150 coastal craft. It was proposed to begin the construction of the new light carriers in 1949, the new frigates in 1950, the six cruisers along with the A/D pickets in 1951, and the two new fleet carriers in 1952.

This program, including the manpower required to achieve it, would cost, assuming labor and shipyards were available, some £236 million in 1948–49, rising to a peak of £465 million in 1954–55. The whole program was priced at £3.32 billion over the period 1948–57. It was admitted that Alexander had told the Admiralty that the *total* figure made available for defense in general should be limited to £600 million, and various options were discussed as to how to keep expenditures down to meet this limit, such as extending the preparedness deadline to 1960, reducing the number of ships in commission, or cancelling or slowing down new construction. The last "would amount to acceptance of the fact that we could never produce a fleet which it has been calculated is necessary to our security." Unfortunately, this would indeed prove to be true, at least in the terms proposed by the Naval Staff.

The ambitious programs set out in these documents were considered "unrealistic" even inside the Admiralty.[91] When discussed at Board level, it was clearly realized that they were out of the question if only because of limited dockyard and works capacity. The Board had no hope of the government authorizing the plan, and it was forwarded to Alexander only as an "ideal" to be compared with the plans of the other services.[92] All three service plans were, of course, equally overambitious, and Alexander was clearly unhappy, if perhaps not too surprised. His reaction was no doubt sharpened by the denouement of the Convertibility Crisis on 20 August, when an increasingly desperate Cabinet had been forced to protect the pound once more. Only three days later the defense minister sent a sharply worded memo to the service departments taking them to task for their somewhat silly proposals. Their estimates, Alexander maintained, were "far beyond anything which the country would be able to afford either in 1948–49 or in later years." These were not £600 million programs but a £900 million program for 1948–49 and £1,250 million programs for "normal years." The services, Alexander went on, would have to accept realities, and reexamination was to start at once based on three assumptions.

Britain, the somewhat pained minister of defense pointed out, needed economic and industrial health as its first priority for war preparedness as well as peacetime prosperity. Alexander insisted that total defense expenditure stay within an annual ceiling of £600 million. Second, war was ruled out in the next five years, and the risk would increase only gradually in the next five: "If attacked we must fight with what we have." Third, it had to be accepted that risks would have to be taken and that it was not possible to build up to the levels previously felt necessary upon the outbreak of war. Priority should be given to those forces that offered the best chance of survival. Further principles were laid down for the composition of the forces, notably that the most visible forces should be given priority—i.e., those with the greatest deterrent power—and that long-term research and development should be emphasized.[93]

The Admiralty now turned to organizing on paper a fleet that could be fitted into a ceiling of £190 million in 1948–49 and £180 million thereafter. This was a far cry from the heady optimism of a month or two before. With war ruled out for the next five years, the immediate tasks were to maintain essential foreign-service commitments and a proper training system. Existing ships would be maintained by refit with as much modernization, especially of carriers, as could be afforded. New construction would be limited to experimental and prototype ships. As for the Naval Air Arm, a strength of 190 first-line aircraft was required. Training had to be kept up in order to replace aircrews still serving on wartime engagements. Wartime aircraft, like the Barracuda, were to be used up. Only aircraft that were completely worn out were to be replaced. The recruiting figure for male regulars should be left at 144,000, and conscripts would be reduced to a token two thousand. They were a luxury the service would have to do without.

New construction and the many ships in a state of partial completion were to be further slowed down. No vessel bigger than a frigate was to be built in the next five years and then only in prototype form. Carrier modernization would be carried out (it was, after all, essential), but it might be limited to two fleets and two light fleets. The costly Reserve Fleet could be reduced by scrapping.[94]

A minimum fleet was worked out that would require a total manning strength of 167,800 at the end of the financial year 1947–48 and 142,000 or so in 1949–50. Numbers would rise, it was hoped, to 157,000 by the end of 1952. Much equipment would have to be forfeited if the estimates were reduced to £180 million, and carrier modernization would have to be traded off against Reserve Fleet refits. If the estimates were reduced to £160 million, the closure of establishments and even dockyards might be necessary, along with the cancellation of ships like the *Daring*s and the *Majestic*s.

Alexander, perhaps shocked by the events of August and the proximity of financial disaster, now had the bit between his teeth. He felt that the services were not moving fast enough to give him coordinated plans for cutbacks. He would, therefore, have to take the initiative himself. On 5 September he contacted the Admiralty informally to ask them what would happen if their estimates were reduced to £150 million. The defense minister had decided that if risks and political consequences were accepted, such reductions were possible. The Admiralty reply, given four days later, was that manpower would have to be reduced to 147,000 in the next six months. It would also involve, among other things, scrapping a substantial number of warships, including five battleships, eleven cruisers, fifty-five to sixty destroyers and frigates; limiting the American and West Indies Squadron to one cruiser and one frigate; reducing the Pacific Fleet to two cruisers and four frigates; and reducing the operational Home Fleet to one battleship, one fleet carrier, three cruisers, and eight destroyers and at the same time immobilizing much of this strength so that men due for release could go without replacement.

Virtually all work on new construction would indeed be stopped, the naval aircraft program cut, and all modernization of carriers deferred. Five air stations would have to be shut down, and one dockyard, Chatham perhaps, might have to be put on a care and maintenance basis.[95]

At the meeting of the Defence Committee where these proposals were presented, Attlee was decidedly unsympathetic to the navy's case and that of the other services. He could not see why expenditure that still totaled over £700 million should virtually immobilize the armed forces. Alexander stressed that he had gone as far as he could.[96] Asked to carry out an investigation into further cuts, he did so, but came back to the Defence Committee to say they were impractical. "I do not see how the Navy could do more."[97]

So in the aftermath of one of the most serious economic crises of the postwar period, the Royal Navy suffered some of its most savage cuts. Although no formal building program was drawn up for 1948, attempts were made to mitigate some of the impact on future capabilities, and the worst cuts fell on the active fleet. In December the active Home Fleet was down to one small 5.25-inch-gun cruiser, a couple of "Battle" class destroyers, half a dozen frigates, and twenty submarines. The South Atlantic Station was made up of a 6-inch-gun cruiser and two frigates, as was the American and West Indies Station. The East Indies Station could boast an extra cruiser, an 8-inch-gun vessel. In the Persian Gulf was a single frigate. The British Pacific Fleet deployed two heavy cruisers, one light cruiser, four C-class destroyers, four frigates, and three operational submarines. Only in the Mediterranean was there a fleet worthy of the name, with Britain's sole operational carrier, HMS *Triumph* (twelve Seafires and sixteen Fireflies), four 6-inch-gun cruisers, eleven destroyers, nine frigates, and two submarines. Plenty of other ships adorned the pages of *Jane's Fighting Ships* and many otherwise usable vessels were in the dockyards "temporarily immobilised" or preparing to become so, but in terms of immediate operational capability this was probably the Royal Navy's postwar nadir.[98]

Although the full scrapping program was whittled down, none of the old battleships, the *Nelson, Rodney, Queen Elizabeth*, and *Valiant* nor the battlecruiser *Renown* escaped being scrapped. So symbolic were the doomed great ships that Hall did not make a decision until it had been discussed at the Defence Committee meeting at No. 10 Downing Street.[99] This discussion reflected many strategic concerns that had a decidedly conservative flavor. Britain, it was argued, might have to guard against all the available European battleships being taken over by the Russians if they overran Western Europe; the Oran syndrome ran deep. It was considered, however, that the four *King George V*s and the new *Vanguard* gave sufficient insurance against any possible threat. The *Nelson* and *Rodney* would cost £2 million to refit, the *Renown* £1 million, the *Queen Elizabeth* the same, and the *Valiant* three quarters of a million. Full scale modernization would cost £4–5 million and take four years and a lot of dockyard resources that were better allocated to other ships. Even reserve refits would cost £7 million for them all and necessitate a reserve crew of fifteen officers and 380 men each at a total annual cost of £100,000. And these were the men that would have to be cut to get the manning ceiling down to 147,000. Any spare money, if available, was needed for carrier modernization. The case was unanswerable.[100]

It was indeed symbolic that the death warrant of these old warriors should be signed at this particular moment, when Britain's naval power was perhaps at its lowest point in centuries. But Britain herself had never been in such dire economic straits. The government and the Admiralty still fondly hoped that these problems were but a passing phase. The dockyards and harbors were still full of ships, a considerable latent force that could be flashed back into life as soon as money allowed. In the yards were considerable numbers of incomplete vessels that would provide a stock of new ships to keep the navy going for another decade. Two keys were needed to unlock this latent power; greater financial health and a greater sense of perceived threat. The first was still elusive, but the second now appeared. Relations with the Soviet Union were getting more icy by the month. The term *Cold War* was just beginning to enter the official vocabulary. In early 1948 the Communist takeover of Czechoslovakia created a sense of imminent crisis. The times were a little more propitious for some, albeit limited, naval recovery.

CHAPTER · TWO

THE REVISED RESTRICTED FLEET

At the beginning of 1948 the Defence Committee of the Cabinet held a series of important meetings that they hoped would decide the shape and size of Britain's armed forces for the next few years. They had under consideration two papers, one by the chiefs of staff and the other by the minister of defense. The former reluctantly accepted that the economic reconstruction of the country came first and that Britain could not expect to be fully prepared for war before 1957. In the meantime the emphasis in Britain's military preparations would be on air and sea forces sufficiently strong to act as a deterrent to a hot war and as a foundation for "Britain's fighting the 'Cold War' " at a political level. Top priority was the creation of a nuclear bomber force as rapidly as possible, but a navy based on air and ASW forces was also vital. Both the Royal Navy and the Royal Air Force were planning a buildup of forces intended to provide a basis for expansion in war. The army, under Montgomery, felt it could not follow this policy. Its only practical option was the maintenance of a force solely to meet peacetime policing commitments. Even so, the combined chiefs of staff submission implied an annual defense expenditure of £662 million (£180 million would go to the Royal Navy). The considerable peacetime navy would require about 150,000 men out of a total armed force of 685,000.[1]

Alexander was still unhappy with this and put forward his own reduced proposals for a £600 million defense policy, a £150 million naval estimate, and 145,000 RN personnel out of a total armed forces strength of 650,000. Naval plans would have to be scaled down, the minister argued, especially those concerning the maintenance of "large capital ships." Presumably the Admiralty would have to think again about its plans to maintain three battleships in commission. The service would have to concentrate on carriers, cruisers, and smaller craft. The minister of defense's proposals were duly accepted, including the reassertion of the assumption that the danger of war in the next five years was small, but that it would grow and might become grave by 1957. "If by a miscalculation or by design war is forced upon us in the next few years, we should have to fight with such forces and weapons as we possess."[2]

The Defence Committee accepted this, Dalton reluctantly signing the £600 million check; he would have preferred £500 million.[3] Within a month or so the possibility of "fighting with what we have" suddenly became a real one as the Cold War took a turn for the worse. In January 1948 the chiefs of staff considered an intelligence document examining the prospect of war before 1956. It concurred in the view that the chance was slim, but argued that Soviet expansion would take place in forms short of war.[4] Within weeks these conclusions seemed to be borne out when the Communist coup occurred in Prague in February 1948. Soon, the British Cabinet was perusing documents with titles like "The Threat to Western Civilisation."[5] The atmosphere of crisis was real, and war, although still considered unlikely if the Western powers held together and made clear what were the limits of acceptable Soviet conduct, became a significantly greater possibility. The cabinet ordered the services to begin a process of "stocktaking," to see what forces would be available should Britain indeed have to fight with what she had in the next eighteen months.[6]

The Naval Staff's "stocktaking" paper was presented to the chiefs of staff in April. It first surveyed Soviet naval strength and concluded that Russia could "mount a considerable maritime force against us" in 1949. Given American and Dominion support, the smallest naval force that it was deemed Britain could get away with in the Atlantic was composed of a battleship, four carriers (with 120 aircraft), nine cruisers, thirty-eight destroyers, a dozen groups of eight frigates each, forty-eight minesweepers, and twenty-seven submarines. The Mediterranean and Middle East would require another battleship, three carriers (with ninety-six aircraft), seven cruisers, twenty-four destroyers, five frigate groups, seventeen minesweepers, and ten submarines. Unfortunately, it did not look as if the Royal Navy would be able to meet even these reduced force goals. If scarce dockyard resources were concentrated on preparing reserve ships for service, the battleship, cruiser, and destroyer numbers could be met. The problems would concern carriers, frigates, and minesweepers. With the carriers there would only be enough aircraft and personnel to mobilize a single fleet carrier, the training ship, *Implacable* (with an expanded air group of forty-nine aircraft), and four light fleet carriers (twenty-five aircraft each), with another light fleet carrier being manned three months after mobilization. As for frigates and minesweepers, there would only be enough to meet half the requirement. There are also great deficiencies in stores, oil, etc., for fitting out an emergency fleet. Mobilization of reservists would be necessary to man the extra ships, the actve-list personnel being enough for only two-thirds of the planned vessels.

Although certain constraints, notably dockyard capacity, were fixed, the Admiralty argued that measures could be taken to improve the situation. By working more overtime and by putting refits out to commercial yards, all but thirty-six of the frigates and a few more minesweepers could be obtained. There would still be a shortage of navy logistical support vessels, however. Ammunition production could be stepped up. Extra oil could be obtained, although supplies would still be short. Other stores would be available in sufficient quantities. Extra personnel were needed to facilitate mobilization. The cost would be of the order of £100 million, and the Admiralty admitted that national economic recovery would be affected.[7]

The nature of the problem was demonstrated by the state of the Home Fleet at the beginning of March. Only the "Operational Force," the cruiser *Superb* and five "Battle"-class destroyers, was ready for action (although even these ships

Retained in the postwar fleet were two active fast minelayers that proved to be useful as flagships as well as in their designed role. Remarkable and unusual vessels of very high speed (40 knots), the *Manxman* was converted into a minesweeper depot ship in 1962. The *Apollo*, seen here, was scrapped in 1962.

needed extra men, torpedoes, and ASW equipment).[8] The absence of proper maintenance personnel meant that the rest of the fleet's destroyers' guns were at a week's notice. The 5.25-inch guns of the two small cruisers, *Sirius* and *Diadem*, were at two week's notice. Even most of the armament of the fleet's centerpiece, the *Duke of York*—both quadruple 14-inch turrets, four 5.25-inch turrets, and most of the close-range armament—was at a month's notice. Ammunition was in short supply, a week being required to re-supply the *Duke of York*. Electrical equipment was in poor condition, the loss of skilled "Hostilities Only" men being felt particularly in this area. The fleet.commander was ignorant as to what air support he would have, no operational carriers being available for him (the only fully operational carriers, both *Colossus*-class ships, *Ocean* and *Triumph*, were in the Mediterranean).

The deteriorating international situation soon forced the government into improving the fleet's short-term operational readiness. In July 1948 the Russians began their blockade of Berlin, and at the end of the month Alexander presented the Defence Committee with tri-service proposals containing the navy's revised shopping list of measures required to be ready to fight should war break out in the short term. If these measures were not taken to improve the situation, Alexander warned, shipping losses would be heavy. A £50 million naval program was proposed to accelerate refits, ready the Reserve Fleet, buy stores and fuel, and build up manpower strength by keeping personnel about to be released from service. It was felt that, despite everything, the navy, at least, was in a better condition to fight than it had been in 1940. The Soviet mine and submarine threat meant that top priority should go to preparing the smaller ships in reserve for ASW and mine-sweeping duties.[9]

Attlee, a little reluctant to go so far so fast, limited the proposed measures to those that could be made without publicity. The chiefs of staff were soon voicing their alarm in a strongly worded July 29 memorandum that included dire predictions of disaster if immediate steps were not taken to improve readiness.[10] This did the trick, and in mid-August decisions were taken to take public-readiness measures, notably the suspension for three months of releases from the armed forces. The prime minister was unwilling to go as far as the recall of regular reservists, which the navy felt it needed, but the proposals to defer releases were accepted by the Cabinet on 26 August, along with the refit and restocking programs.[11] The period of national service was also increased to eighteen months. All this helped solve the navy's problems, to some extent at least, and helped to put the fleet back into a semioperational state. By the end of the year two light fleet carriers, the *Theseus* and *Vengeance*, were back with the Home Fleet, which also now deployed its full cruiser strength, the *Superb, Cleopatra, Diadem,* and *Sirius*.[12]

Alongside this work of improving immediate operational readiness, planning for the 1957 target date went on. In July 1948 the Board of Admiralty considered a long-term production plan. This plan stressed the need to begin the process of bringing the fleet to full war readiness as soon as possible, as the amount of work was such that it would be impossible to carry out if left too long. The dockyards would have to concentrate on working on the fleet rather than the commercial work that had been taking priority since the end of the war. Private facilities would also have to be used. The nine-year program was scaled down in comparison with some of the Royal Navy's postwar ambitions, but it was still a considerable one requiring the expenditure of £1,235 million, 1.5 million tons of steel, and almost 1.7 million man years of labor (between 11 and 14 percent of Britain's shipbuilding work force).

The program planned to complete the carrier *Eagle* in 1949–50; the *Ark Royal* was deferred to 1952–53. As for the priority *Hermes*-class ships, they were expected in 1951–52. Further modifications to the design had been approved in October 1947, which added an extra catapult, a modified island superstructure, centralized messing facilities, and better habitability and increased the cost of each ship from £2.8 million to over £4.5 million. It was not considered worth completing the four remaining *Majestics* until new 20,000-pound lifts became available, which it was estimated would delay matters until 1954 at the earliest.

As for the necessary modernization of existing carriers, the Admiralty knew what it wanted but didn't dare tell the government. At the end of 1946 an internal committee was set up under Rear Admiral G.N. Oliver, ACNS, to investigate the carrier problem. It reported in mid-1947 and called for an ambitious plan not only of completing the *Ark Royal, Hermes,* and *Majestic* classes but also modernizing the other carriers so that they could operate the aircraft expected in the mid-1950s. The civilians on the Board, led by Hall and Lang, the head of the Secretariat, were worried by the expense, and given the serious financial crisis, it was decided to delay presenting the plan to the Defence Committee. Indeed, not until June 1948 was the draft even presented to the board. Its modernization provision covered all six armored hangar ships, six *Colossus*-class light fleets, and the two Commonwealth *Majestics*. Canadian and Australian contributions would help cover the £23 million cost of the program. By 1956 five fleet carriers and four light fleets would be able to operate all available aircraft, while seven light fleets would be capable of carrying modern aircraft sufficient for convoy escort duties. Even in the slightly more favorable atmosphere of 1948 this was too much for any government to stomach, and the first sea lord and controller decided to defer matters once more, although the *Formidable* was tentatively earmarked for full modernization starting in 1949. In the meantime, the *Implacable* was given a limited refit in 1948–49 to make her fully operational as Home Fleet flagship. The *Illustrious*, given a rather more extensive refit in 1948, would now have to double as trials and training carrier, a role she fulfilled for the next six years. She emerged from the yard with a reshaped bow and stern that gave more flight-deck space. The *Indomitable* was taken out of reserve and received similar modifications shortly afterwards to come back into service to relieve the *Implacable* as the operational fleet carrier and Home Fleet flagship in September 1950. The *Indomitable*'s large hangar space made her perhaps the most useful of the war veterans in an unmodernized state. The *Implacable* would, it was hoped, then be taken in hand for the next full modernization. The full process called for by the Oliver Committee promised to be an expensive one indeed, effectively a complete rebuild from hangar floor up, putting an enormous strain on limited dockyard capacity as well as the Admiralty's budget.[13]

Not just carriers suffered from the shortage of money and other resources, but frigates too. The beginning of the two prototype frigates of the 1945 program was

A Sea Hornet NP21 of 809 Squadron takes off from HMS *Indomitable*. (Imperial War Museum)

now postponed until 1951. One was to be an antiaircraft ship, the other to be used for control and direction of aircraft in convoy defense. A new antisubmarine frigate would be begun at the same time. Further construction of the new ships would be on a limited scale up to 1955. The main improvement in the frigate force would come from conversions of existing World War II fleet destroyers, some fifty-nine being earmarked for conversion between 1948 and 1957 into fast antisubmarine frigates. Another scheme to fill a gap was the conversion of a fast minelayer of the *Ariadne* class into a fleet air direction escort, but this proposal was later changed to convert the small cruiser *Scylla* instead.[14]

As for aircraft, it was hoped that production might be more than doubled from just over 350 per year in 1949–50 to some 750 by 1956–57. Jet fighters were already coming into service in the shape of thirty 500 mph Supermarine Attackers due in 1949–50 and thirty more in 1950–51. These planes were intended to provide not only experience with jets but also insurance against delays in the Admiralty's preferred aircraft, the slightly faster and substantially longer-ranged N7/46 being developed by Hawker (the Sea Hawk). A more advanced twin-jet day interceptor was in the early development stage with Supermarine to specification N9/47 (this eventually evolved into the Scimitar). A new all-weather fighter project, the N40/46 was being developed by both Blackburn and Fairey, and it was thought that a strike version of this aircraft might be procured also. These two traditional manufacturers of naval aircraft were also competing for the new ASW machine, the GR17/45, but it appeared that technical problems would delay it beyond its expected 1952–53 in-service date. Not the least of these problems was finding a suitable power plant: both turboprops and piston engines were under consideration. The development of the aircraft was not helped either by the novel weapons it was intended to carry. The Zeta-winged torpedo caused considerable difficulties and was cancelled, and the large Pentane homing torpedo required a large and heavy plane, with obvious implications for carrier modernization.[15]

The GR17/45 was an important contract; a third of all naval aircraft to be produced in 1956–57 would be of this type. The Fairey Company was especially anxious to secure the contract as it had suffered a serious cancellation in 1947—a large turboprop-driven two-seat naval strike fighter to specification N16/45. The ASW/fighter priority advised against putting too many scarce resources into strike aircraft but, nevertheless, in mid-1948 studies began of a new heavy attack aircraft with a range of perhaps two to three thousand miles. Such a machine would give the Royal Navy the same kind of nuclear attack capabilities as were being so assiduously pursued by the United States Navy.[16]

Although the Naval Staff had been none too impressed by the Sikorsky helicopters it had received from the U.S.A. under lend-lease, it claimed to be "fully aware of the need for helicopters in naval aviation" and by 1948 was preparing specifications for both light and heavy helicopters. The main role of the former would be search and rescue, sharing it for the time being with amphibious aircraft. The previous year the Royal Navy had formed its first all-helicopter squadron, 705, with R-4B and R-6 machines left over from the war, with which it worked on the techniques of helicopter search and rescue. A British-built license version of the improved Sikorsky S-51 was intended to replace the older aircraft, but at this stage helicopter deliveries were only intended to be about half a dozen or so a year. A heavy ASW and mine-spotting machine was also projected, and Bristol began work on a large twin-rotor aircraft the following year. It was not expected to enter service for about a decade, and indeed doubts were soon being expressed about whether it should be continued or replaced by a compact general-purpose machine.[17]

However moderate the Admiralty's helicopter plans were at this time, its overall program was still overambitious. When the naval estimates for 1949–50 came up for discussion, it was clear that the original "Nine Year Plan" based on the 1957 planning date could not go forward. The sketch estimates that included provision for the plan came to over £237 million. This, taken with the other service requirements, totaled some £833 million. A new chancellor had now taken over following Dalton's resignation over a budget indiscretion. He was Sir Stafford Cripps, one of the most intellectual members of a talented administration. He insisted that £700 million was the limit beyond which he could not go, and of this, £177 million would be the navy estimates. Such were the ground rules for a "bitter fight" between Alexander and Cripps, with the navy's allocation coming in for special attention. The navy argued that such a figure would necessitate the abandonment of the recently agreed measures to improve readiness. In effect the service would be reduced to its winter 1947–48 state, with a return to the immobilization of ships. The new and able first sea lord, Lord Fraser of the North Cape,[18] backed these points up strongly before the Defence Committee in December 1948. Not only would the Home Fleet be immobilized, but the refitting program of the Reserve Fleet would be practically stopped and refits of the seagoing fleet slowed down. The entry of conscripts into the navy would have to stop, recruitment of regulars would have to be slowed down, and the naval air strength stabilized at the "deplorably low" figure of 170 first-line aircraft. In the end a compromise was reached, with Cripps eventually being forced up to £760 million, of which £190 million was to go to the Admiralty.[19]

It was not just the shortage of funds that constrained naval recovery but the shortage of manpower too. Raising pay for regulars at the end of 1948 did not solve the serious problems caused by the unwillingness of ratings to reenlist or accept higher ranks and a long-term career in the service. In the middle of 1949 the second sea lord, Admiral Sir Cecil Harcourt, was warning of a "first class breakdown" in two years. The situation was indeed serious. Instead of 61 percent of seamen reengaging as they had done in 1938, only 22 percent were doing so in 1948. The reengagement rate for petty officer and chief petty officer had slumped from 93 percent to 26 percent, for lower ranks of seamen from 45 percent to 10 percent, stoker and mechanician POs and CPOs from 76 percent to 21 percent, and lower ranks of stoker and mechanician from 46 percent to a mere 4 percent! The admirals felt that the postwar Welfare State, together with full employment, had diminished the advantages of service in the Royal Navy. As Rear Admiral Sir William Agnew, deputy chief of Naval Personnel, picturesquely put it, civilian life seemed to have become "a free and easy Tom Tiddler's ground on which he (i.e., the sailor) would be advised to stake a claim at the earliest possible moment." The Admiralty attitude at this time was that improved conditions of service, married quarters, etc. should only be used in moderation, "over indulgence leads to a craving for further alleviation, to a loss of independence, decreasing efficiency and mobility and to rising costs." Some might argue that it was the prevalence of such attitudes in the higher echelons of the service that was helping cause the problem in the first place. The only long-term solution would be massive improvement in conditions of service afloat and ashore as well as pay. The Admiralty preferred to put their trust in the latter, however, especially for senior rates.[20]

The wastage situation, combined with pressure from the government to take more rather than less young conscripts, made the Admiralty take a new look at the usefulness of the National Serviceman. The problem was the need to prevent too great a fluctuation in numbers of National Servicemen, given cutbacks in the armed forces and diminished service requirements. The Admiralty, which had announced plans to take only a token 2,000 conscripts in the 1947–48 Estimates Statement, came under pressure in early 1948 from Alexander to recruit more. It still felt, however, that this would tie up too many people merely being trained as a future reserve, not to mention the regulars tied up in training itself. There would be insufficient men to man the seagoing fleet, and using conscripts at home would displace regulars into unpopular foreign service and premature resignation. In May 1948, however, the second sea lord had reversed his position and was looking at extra conscripts as a way of solving his manpower shortage, and the Admiralty was soon requesting the allocation of ten thousand conscripts a year from 1 October 1948. It was better to man ships with National Servicemen than to leave them unmanned. That number could be absorbed, the Admiralty now calculated, without opening additional training establishments.[21]

Nevertheless, this did not solve the problem of the loss of experienced ratings. Ships needing large amounts of manpower, like battleships, were a particular problem. It was reluctantly decided in October 1948 to decommission HMS *Duke of York* in 1949, and by the summer of that year the first sea lord was going even further. Fraser was a gunnery officer and the *Duke of York* had been his flagship in December 1943 when she had fought and won the last battleship action in the Royal Navy's history: the sinking of the *Scharnhorst*. Nevertheless, he had considerable carrier experience and had also fathered the crash program of escort construction at the beginning of World War II. His enthusiasm for the traditional capital ship was always tempered by his recognition of these other naval priorities. Thus he did not shy away from the question of what to do with the battleships. In June 1949 he spelled out the situation to the Defence Committee. The first priority was the maintenance of a full complement of destroyers, frigates, and minesweepers "on which the heaviest immediate call would be made if an emergency came upon us in the near future."

The Royal Navy's Training Squadron at that time was composed of the battleships *King George V* and *Anson*, together with the empty fleet carrier *Victorious*. The *Vanguard*, which was acting effectively as an impressive royal yacht, had been diverted to active duty due to the King's ill health and was in the Mediterranean (see chapter 4). She was now to go to Portland to replace the two *King George V*s as a higher-capacity training ship. Both existing training battleships were to be banished, without refits, to the Gareloch in Category "C" reserve, where they would await possible use in the second stage of wartime fleet expansion. The *Duke of York*, recently decommissioned for refit, would remain after that in Category "C" at Portsmouth as flagship of the Reserve Fleet. The *Howe*, the final *K.G.V.*, was to be kept in Category "A" reserve (at one to two month's notice) as an immediate replacement for the *Vanguard* should she be called away on royal tour. It was, in effect, the end of the careers of these warships, after less than a decade

Britain's last battleship, HMS *Vanguard*, at Malta in 1949. Clearly visible is the royal sun lounge fitted for her duty as Royal Yacht.

of service. None was commissioned again. The Royal Navy was now down to one operational battleship, and even she was not fully combatant.[22]

The future of the battleship was one of the questions posed by a radical secret report on Britain's future defense policy that now, in the summer of 1949, became the focus of discussion on the subject. Despite the report's radical suggestions for huge cuts and withdrawals, it is doubtful that the service chiefs were too shocked. They themselves had decided to set up the Harwood Committee in November 1948 when the Treasury was making its stand on the £700 million expenditure ceiling for Britain's armed forces. Cripps had asked that an inquiry be made into the prospect of reducing expenses to that figure. The chiefs of staff jumped at the chance; they wanted to demonstrate dramatically what the strategic price of such a budgetary ceiling might be. The "Inter Service Working Party on the Shape and Size of the Armed Forces" was chaired by Edmund Harwood, a civil servant who had been with the Ministry of Food since 1939 except for a brief spell as civilian director at the Imperial Defence College in 1947. His Working Party was made up of three senior officers, one from each service, the naval representative being Rear Admiral Charles Lambe, a torpedo specialist but since 1944 closely involved with naval aviation. The Harwood Committee had begun its deliberations in December 1948 and produced its report in February 1949.

The report covered the three years 1950–53 and was based on the latest variant of the chiefs of staffs' requirements for British defense policy: that Britain should meet her existing commitments and "wage the Cold War effectively," that some provision should be made for being involved in unpremeditated war in the near future, and that a start should be made in preparing for Soviet premeditated aggression in 1957. The Working Party took as its starting point the £700 million limit and what could be purchased for it. The three priorities they decided were first meeting Cold War demands, second a "limited insurance against the less likely threat of accidental war in the short term," and, third, "maximum" insurance against the more likely threat of war in 1957 or after.

The Working Party, therefore, echoed the existing official priority on research and development and reequipment for the future. Readiness in 1957, it argued, should not be sacrificed to maintain overlarge forces in being. The Royal Navy's requirements to defend sea communications in the approaches to the United Kingdom were given priority by Harwood, although in actual figures the Royal Navy's was the smallest individual share of the money his Working Party allocated. The cash available for the peacetime forces was just under £1.4 million over the three years, which would support 600,000 service personnel (against the 750,000 planned for 1 April 1950). The Working Party postulated annual naval estimates of just over £166 million per annum. This would mean a drastic reshaping of the navy. The stress would be on a carrier and small-ship force whose main wartime role would be the protection of Britain and its direct sea communications against attack. The assumption would be made of American support in general war right from the start. There was, therefore, little point in duplicating American capabilities in larger ships, given the massive United States naval superiority.

Apart from some commitment to escorting early troop convoys in the Mediterranean before the Americans took over the theater, the British effort would be very largely confined to the Eastern Atlantic, English Channel, and North Sea. In addition to the Mediterranean, the Americans were to look after the Far East and partially to look after the Persian Gulf. The latter area in part and the Indian Ocean in total would be a Dominion, not British, responsibility.

Battleships would leave the fleet entirely, and the number of carriers in the wartime target fleet was to come down from fourteen to twelve, nine modernized fleets and three modernized light fleets. The cruiser force would be heavily reduced from twenty-three to twelve. The planned escort fleet was, however, to go up from 230 to 249 and the minesweeper force from 237 to 330. Coastal forces (fast patrol boats) would also be increased. As for the peacetime fleet, manning levels would come down to 90,000 by 1952–53, with an average strength over the entire three-year period of just over 100,000. This would mean substantial withdrawals, abandonment indeed, of all the worldwide stations except for a small Hong Kong squadron. An Australian naval command would be substituted for the British in Singapore, whose dockyard, together with that of Trincomalee, would be abandoned. Bermuda and Simonstown would be placed on a care-and-maintenance basis, and the naval air stations at Malta would be closed. At home, Sheerness, Portland, and possibly Chatham dockyards would go also.

After cutting back massively on shore infrastructure, it was hoped to be able to deploy in peacetime a main carrier task force of three carriers, one cruiser, one fast minelayer, sixteen destroyers, eight frigates, and four minesweepers to provide the British naval presence in the Atlantic and Mediterranean. An ASW training squadron with a carrier and sixteen escorts would also be maintained, plus eighteen submarines and miscellaneous warships totaling one carrier (trials and deck-landing training), one cadet-training cruiser, sixteen destroyers, twenty-four frigates, and twenty-four minesweepers. In the Mediterranean a small permanent squadron of three cruisers, a destroyer flotilla, eight minesweepers, and twelve submarines would look after British interests both there and in the Persian Gulf, while two cruisers and four minesweepers would suffice for Hong Kong. The numbers of front-line aircraft would be increased to 200 by 1952 and thereafter to 300. It was hoped to maintain the Reserve Fleet, despite its increased size, with only ten thousand men by increased use of dehumidification and other non-manpower-intensive methods. Some 47.5 percent of uniformed manpower would be in the operational peacetime fleet as opposed to 44 percent in 1948. There would be no National Servicemen in this slimmed-down Navy. The Women's Royal Naval Service would be abolished, while the army would be asked to take over the Royal Marines.

There was a great deal in these proposals that was as much a deliberate re-orientation of the navy in a modern direction as a mere exercise in the saving of money. The Working Party argued that the existing Navy was far too big to sustain a proper program of capital reequipment. There were many shore establishments set up by the war that needed closure. What the Harwood Committee was aiming at, except in its stress on mobilization for war, was in most ways the definitive shape of the postwar navy: carriers and escorts, a peacetime strength of less than 100,000, deployment in the Eastern Atlantic, and withdrawal from overseas bases. It was a vision of the future, one that horrified contemporaries unready to come to terms with postwar power realities and, perhaps more important, unable to extricate themselves from commitments that seemed at the time unescapable and perhaps even were.[23]

At the chiefs of staff meeting with the committee in March 1949 and at their own meeting in April, Fraser and the Board of Admiralty made their disagreement with the Harwood findings obvious. Although Fraser had his doubts about over-reliance on the Americans, the Board agreed with Hall that it should be accepted that British naval forces were complementary rather than competitive with American forces. Nevertheless, it found serious fault with the balance of the Harwood fleet and its adequacy to meet peacetime commitments. The ratio of carriers to cruisers was questioned, and the lack of battleships was also found to be "not acceptable." The Admiralty agreed that a reduction to 90,000 men would cause severe manpower difficulties and would not provide an adequate wartime reserve once the existing large reserve of wartime conscripts dried up. It felt that the abolition of the W.R.N.S. just after their future had been announced as being secure would be especially embarrassing. As for the Royal Marines, they ought to be retained "in view of the great traditions of the Corps and their important contribution to the discipline and morale of the Naval Service and their value as a striking force."[24]

One gets the impression, however, that the three service chiefs were secretly delighted with the "courageous" and "workmanlike" job the Working Party had done. The Harwood Committee had done the task expected of it. The chiefs had never regarded the exercise as a serious policy proposal at all. Fraser said that all that was needed was "to submit it to ministers as proof that present Government policy could not be executed on £700 million annually for defence." The first sea lord wanted to pass on the report as it stood, expecting instant rejection by the Cabinet, but his fellow service chiefs felt it safer to produce an "authoritative document" for the government, spelling out the report's lack of acceptability.[25] The COS paper was duly completed by mid-June, the Admiralty playing a large part in its drafting. It doubted whether even the reduced Harwood forces would cost less than £700 million. In any case the forces were seriously inadequate either for war or to carry out British peacetime foreign and colonial policy.

As for the specifically naval proposals, the chiefs of staff considered that the main "Peripatetic Task Force" would soon lose its coherence, and would be split into small units that would be unable to carry out fleet training for war. Reducing strength in the Mediterranean, they felt, would discourage, rather than encourage, American aid in the defense of the area. The chiefs of staff pointed to the strategic vacuum that would be created in Southeast Asia and the Indian Ocean. The proposed Far East Squadron would be inadequate for normal tasks, even without "the Chinese Communist threat." They doubted whether the Dominions would take up the slack and worried about the relationship of an Australian naval commander with the two British commanders in Singapore. Withdrawal from Simonstown would alienate an already wobbly South Africa, and it would probably be impossible to keep any title to the base. It would also be impossible to deal with emergencies in the West African colonies. Withdrawal from the American and West Indies Station would mean no forces to deal with emergencies in the area, "particularly in the event of trouble in British Honduras and the Falkland Isles Dependencies."

As for the wartime fleet, it was doubted that there would be enough shipbuilding capacity to build it by 1957. Even if it were achieved, there would be a shortage of carriers for escort duties, mine countermeasures vessels, and cruisers. The chiefs even criticized the destroyer and frigate provision, especially the lack of "offensive anti-submarine hunter/killer groups." The chiefs also were critical of the cuts in administrative infrastructure, as they would create mobilization problems.[26]

When these comments and those on Harwood's proposals for the other services were taken by the committee in which the three service ministers regularly met, the first lord denounced the report as unacceptable, and the defense minister agreed that it was "folly to withdraw forces from the food and dollar producing colonial territories of Southeast Asia."[27] These views were developed at more length in a paper by Alexander, produced on 27 June 1949 for a meeting of a ministerial committee specially convened to discuss Harwood in early July. Alexander summed up the problem. It was a question of "whether, after the economic exhaustion of the war years we have the power and the resources to maintain the armed forces equipped to modern standards to permit us to play the role of a great power." Moreover, it was "folly" to sacrifice the prospects of "victory" in the Cold War, or at least finding a long-term modus vivendi with the Russians, to free resources for preparations for a war that might never happen. Wholesale abandonment of commitments was "unthinkable," not least because it would undermine Britain's new alliances. The previous year, 1948, Britain had sponsored the Western Union Alliance with France, Belgium, the Netherlands, and Luxembourg, and in April 1949 it was expanded into the "Atlantic Pact" with the U.S.A. The latter implied a major British defense contribution to maintain American interest and add weight to areas the U.S.A. might feel were less important but which were crucial to Britain—e.g., the Middle East. As for the Cold War, the chiefs of staff argued that withdrawal of forces from the colonies would merely invite in hostile influences at great economic, as well as political, cost. Alexander also made a powerful plea for more defense expenditure, casting doubts on the view that it was a direct drain on the economy. He recommended that the chiefs of staff draw up a new plan reflecting the need to maintain forces for the next three years primarily for Cold

War tasks and the requirement to spend more on reequipment, albeit spread over a longer time period. It was decided in July, therefore, to set up yet another working party, this time chaired by Sir Harold Parker, permanent secretary at the Ministry of Defence. This would evolve into an "intermediate" coordinated defense scheme less risky than Harwood's.[28]

Harwood had, nevertheless, demonstrated to the Admiralty that the economic situation required a major scaling down of their proposals for the rejuvenation of the fleet. The director of Plans had duly been asked to prepare a paper showing the shape and size of the navy that could be afforded on £200 million per annum. This "Restricted Fleet" was considered at the beginning of May, but it was still thought to be too ambitious.[29]

The requirement that the fleet should be able to move immediately on to a wartime footing was, therefore, dropped. The criteria laid down now, therefore, were (a) that the fleet should be capable of carrying out the foreign and colonial policy of the government in peacetime, and (b) that it should be able to meet the *immediate* requirements of war in 1957, serving as a *nucleus* for expansion after the outbreak.

So was born the "Revised Restricted Fleet," presented to the Board at the end of May 1949.[30] With a few amendments it was issued within the Admiralty as an internal "Shape and Size" memorandum in June. Fraser considered it "very near practical politics." It later went to the COS and to the Parker Committee in July.[31] The new document set out figures for both peacetime and wartime fleets. It also showed the Reserve Fleet at the various stages of readiness (see table). The wartime fleet was somewhat reduced over 1948 estimates, with fewer carriers, cruisers, frigates, and submarines. The fleet A/D escort program disappeared and battleship modernization was delayed until the advent of guided weapons. Reliance would have to be placed on the U.S. Navy for half the forces controlling sea communications in the Atlantic and Mediterranean. The South Atlantic and Pacific would be given over entirely in war to the U.S. Navy, and the Indian Ocean to the Royal Australian and Royal New Zealand Navies.

Given the emerging priority for Cold War tasks, the peacetime fleet was a little larger than the one presently deployed, although a series of cuts in training and administration, as suggested by Harwood, would provide substantial economies. These included reductions in the strength of the Royal Marines and W.R.N.S. and the closure of Sheerness, Bermuda, and Trincomalee dockyards. These economies would save some twenty thousand men, and conscripts for the navy would have to be abandoned except for a small number, two thousand per annum or less, entered via the Royal Naval Volunteer Reserve to keep up the latter's strength. A number of cruisers, frigates, and submarines were to be scrapped, and other ships would follow when new vessels came into service.

The new construction program itself was drastically reduced, the new proposals being detailed in a document entitled by the controller's department, perhaps a little cynically, "The Phantom Fleet." The two *Ark Royal*s and four *Hermes*-class ships remained (all expected to be completed by 1952), but the *Majestic*s disappeared from the program. It was hoped to finish the three *Tiger*s by 1954 and start new cruiser construction again in 1957. The *Daring*s were also retained and four new destroyers were to start by 1957. Only twenty-one new frigates would be built from 1950–57—four A/D, five AA, and twelve ASW. Six new submarines and 176 new mine countermeasures vessels of various sizes would also be built. Four

TABLE 2–1.

REVISED RESTRICTED FLEET*

	WAR FLEET†	PEACETIME FLEET		RESERVE FLEET‡		
		Full Commission	*Training*	*A*	*B*	*C*
Battleships	1 + 4	—	1	—	—	4
Fleet Carriers	5 + 1 (deck landing and trials ship)	2	1	1	2	—
Light Fleet Carriers	4	3	1	—	—	2
Cruisers	18	13	—	2	2	1
Disarmed Cruisers	—	—	2	—	—	—
Fast Minelayers	3	2	—	1	—	—
Destroyers	62	38	2	6	8	—
Frigates	182	32	33	23	40	54
A/S Experimental Ships	1	—	1	—	—	—
Submarines	53	20	20	13	—	—
Ocean Minesweepers	61	16	7	16	16	6
Coastal/Inshore Minesweepers	250	20	—	230	—	—
Coastal Forces	50	—	12	38	—	—
Midget Submarines	2	—	2	—	—	—
Combined Operations	Brigade lift	⅓ Brigade lift for training	—	⅔ Brigade lift	—	—
Aircraft	250	250	—	60 in RNVR squadrons.		

*Source: B590 in ADM167/133 and DEFE7/609.
†In 1957.
‡A = less than 3 months notice.
 B = 3 months notice.
 C = after Category B.

fleet carriers would be modernized between 1950 and 1957, one for deck landing trials only. Modernization would be carried out to five cruisers: two *Dido*s were to get new radar and fire control, and three prewar "Town"-class 6-inch-gun cruisers were to receive modernized electronics and radar. There was some dispute within the Naval Staff over the question of their rearmament to projected *Tiger* standards with the new 6-inch and 3-inch guns. The old heavy cruiser *Cumberland* was to become an armament trials ship to test these weapons. Some fifty-four existing destroyers were to have new ASW equipment and sensors, better fire control systems, propeller silencing, and improved electronics. Twenty-seven slightly older vessels were now to be converted to fast ASW frigates, and limited improvements were to be carried out to older frigate classes also. The fast battery-drive submarine conversion would be applied to only six "T"-class boats. The naval estimates to sustain this program would be £203 million in 1951–52 rising to £241 million in 1957–58, 25 percent of each year's estimate going for new construction, conversion, and new equipment and 5 percent for research and development.

In comparison with the Harwood proposals the major differences were that the battleships were retained "as essential insurance" against the Soviets building heavy ships, the cruiser force was increased to eighteen to carry out peacetime commitments and meet wartime requirements, and the numbers of small craft were drastically reduced because of the lack of money and manpower to build and maintain them. Front-line aircraft strength would be 250, a *reduction* of 50 on the "pro-air" Harwood proposal, but the average strength of the Royal Navy would come down to 124,000, 25 percent more than the Harwood average.

The Parker Committee's terms of reference were that the total defense burden should not exceed £810 million (£10 million to cover contingencies) and that manpower should come down to 650,000 by 1952–53. The service departments submitted figures that exceeded these to some extent; the total for 1 April 1953 (including a naval total of 124,000) was almost 700,000, and the forces also cost well over the planned figure. Somewhat doubtfully the committee began to prune the service figures and presented the Admiralty with the prospect of estimates of £197 million, i.e., within the £800 million ceiling. The result, the Admiralty argued, would be reductions in the aircraft and submarine programs, and other cuts, including the closure of Simonstown. In the end the Admiralty was able to return to above £200 million. This would sustain the fleet at "Revised Restricted" level, although some of the "Phantom Fleet" would be deferred and reduced. Only one fleet carrier would be taken in hand for modernization in the next three financial years, along with one cruiser, twelve destroyers, nine frigates, ten destroyer-to-frigate conversions, and two submarines. In short, bringing the fleet up-to-date was being sacrificed to the maintenance of a barely adequate operational fleet.[32]

The need for economy was becoming more urgent as 1949 went on. The month Parker began his deliberations the cabinet began to worry about the drain on the gold and dollar reserves. British exports were suffering due to the American recession, as were those of the entire sterling area. By 29 August 1949 the Cabinet had been forced to agree in principle on the devaluation of the pound in order to try to improve the position of the British economy and restore American confidence in it.[33] Devaluation was announced by Cripps in mid-September, and the following month saw the drawing up of a set of public expenditure cuts in order to concentrate maximum resources on the export drive, to limit inflation, and to keep down the prices of British goods. Defense came out well from this exercise, only £35 million of the total £256.5 million coming from reductions in that budget, less than the cuts made in the housing program. It did, however, become even more important to the chancellor that he hold to his £700 million defense expenditure ceiling.[34]

The argument went on in the Defence Committee into November, with the minister of defense and the chiefs of staff stressing Britain's Cold War role and making out a powerful case that Britain was the only country that could discharge the required defense responsibilities in the various parts of the world. Even Philip Noel Baker, colonial secretary and no supporter of inflated armaments, stressed the vital need for Britain to maintain its commitments. He pointed to the destabilization caused by Britain's withdrawals of 1947. As the discussions went on, some criticism was expressed of the cruiser priority in the Admiralty's plans. It was argued, however, that eighteen cruisers only meant thirteen in commission, and all these were required for potential Cold War duties. In wartime, British cruisers would be needed to match Soviet ones. The possible substitution of naval air power for cruisers was suggested. The counterargument perhaps sounded a little odd in 1949. "It was pointed out in reply that the provision of aircraft carriers was very costly, and that it was better to make a severe cut here than to reduce still further the cruiser strength." The doubts about over-providing naval forces came out again, with Attlee expressing his old opinions of three years before. The first lord took his stand on the navy's concentration on underwater threats and the wastefulness of scrapping the nearly completed carriers and destroyers. In the end Attlee decided that the 1950–51 estimates would total £780 million, with the possibility of supplementary estimates to cover any further increases. The question of defense expenditure for later years was left open, but the "Revised Restricted Fleet" had indeed become "practical politics."[35]

In 1949, therefore, the Royal Navy admitted, a little reluctantly, that its affordable wartime force posture only made sense as part of a joint Anglo-American naval capability. In fact, ever since the spring of 1948 American and British planners had been working on emergency war plans in case of conflict with the Soviet Union.[36] These discussions raised the problem of who was to control the maritime war. In the Mediterranean the Americans would be the dominant naval partners with a huge force of eight fleet carriers, two battleships, twelve cruisers and fifty-two destroyers planned for D + 3 months. This rather overshadowed the British contribution of one fleet carrier, two light fleets, eight cruisers, two fast minelayers, and forty-eight destroyers and frigates. The functions of these two forces were different. The British fleet's main task was the defense of sea communications (with the help of a growing number of extra United States ships). The American task was to use air power in support of the land battle.[37] Initial arrangements reflected this, the American Commander-in-Chief U.S. Forces, North Eastern Atlantic and Mediterranean (CINCNELM) Admiral Richard L. Conolly being earmarked in overall command of the theater, with a separate British naval commander and American task force commander.[38]

Contacts were made on the spot between Admiral Conolly and Admiral Sir Arthur Power, now the British Mediterranean Fleet commander. Despite the latter's reservations about not controlling all allied assets in the Mediterranean, plans were agreed upon and drawn up. Exercises involving combined carrier air strikes began to be carried out.[39] As the planning process went on, however, difficulties began to arise. The Atlantic Command question became a bone of contention. Agreement could be obtained at first on dividing the ocean on the 42nd parallel. The British commander-in-chief Home Fleet would control the North Atlantic sector and an American the Central and South Atlantic. However, the Americans insisted that their commander-in-chief Atlantic Fleet should be placed over both these commands, whereas the British wished to maintain the North Atlantic as a British responsibility, with the American chief of naval operations and the combined Anglo-American staff in Washington being the coordinating authority.[40] In mid-1949 the British conceded the important principle of American command for the Atlantic as a whole, but this did not solve the problem, as the Americans now moved to the idea of a north-south division with eastern and western Atlantic areas. The eastern commander would be British, the western, American. The British would not have complete command of the North Atlantic under these arrangements, as they would have done if the ocean had been split at 42°N.[41]

The signature of the North Atlantic Treaty in April 1949 meant that the Anglo-American bilateral discussions had merged into the process of setting up a NATO maritime command structure. The British still held out for the longitudinal Atlantic split. They also set their sights higher in the Mediterranean, arguing for one (British) naval CinC to whom the U.S. carrier task force would be subordinate. There had been some reduction in American forces earmarked for the Mediterranean, which gave some strategic logic to this British assertiveness, but there was also a considerable amount of pride on both sides. The North Atlantic and Mediterranean were both traditional areas of British naval concern. The Royal Navy found it unacceptable that the United States Navy should control both theaters, an opinion that was widely shared in government and among the public at large. The dispute grumbled on into the early 1950s.[42]

Although the British refused to accept the unfortunate command implications of their reduced relative naval circumstances, reluctantly they did begin to dismantle their scattered worldwide base structure, starting with the dockyard closest to the U.S.A., Bermuda. In future the West Indies Station would be maintained in home dockyards. Plans to transfer the administration of the station to Jamaica were, however, abandoned. It was soon seen that the other closures were easier decided upon than executed. Trincomalee raised touchy questions of Commonwealth relations, and Simonstown was even more sensitive—abandonment perhaps leading to a completely neutralist stance by the Nationalist South African Government; closure plans were, therefore, abandoned, although it was decided to run the installations down to the lowest level possible. The potential closure of Sheerness, at home, raised serious employment questions. In fact, it was soon clear that the expected savings from closing shore establishments, in both money and manpower, had been overestimated.[43]

The financial problems of the period also forced the Admiralty to concentrate resources on the most important naval threats. The battleships continued to fade away. Not long after the decision to put them all into reserve, the *King George V*s were all placed in Category *C*, with armament maintenance completely abandoned on two of them.[44] Yet the Naval Staff was reluctant to go the whole way and scrap them. As late as 1948 Staff documents put forward a case for the battleship as the type most able to withstand the impact of modern weapons. They argued that if bomber development was outstripping that of fighters, then gun or missile defense,

Sir Bruce Fraser at Exercise Trident. (Imperial War Museum)

based on large and relatively invulnerable platforms, might be the only answer to air attack. Battleships were also seen as perhaps making up for the lack of powerful cruisers, especially given the demise of the last of the older, fully combatant 8-inch-gun ships in the 1948–49 cuts. At the Royal Naval College, Greenwich, in April 1949 a major combined exercise, known as "Trident," was held. The aim was to investigate the role of all types of naval forces in the defense of sea communications. At the accompanying press conference Lord Fraser put the case for the battleship thus: "We think in the Navy that we must have battleships and we must continue to have battleships, whether we keep them all in commission or not, or whether we keep any in commission at the moment; we must keep one or two. There has always been a demand for the strongest and heaviest and most powerful things that we have. . . . In addition to that, of course, in the future it is possible that the battleship will be the only platform on which you can mount the weapons of the future, like guided missiles. When every armed landing has taken place there has always been the cry for battleships, so we intend to keep the battleship because we think it will be of the greatest value."[45]

The only battleship remaining in commission was the *Vanguard* in her training role. Prestige and the desire to secure a return on a recent expensive investment were finely balanced against financial and manpower costs in the decision whether or not to retain her. The pro-battleship arguments were, however, not strong enough to recommission HMS *Howe* of the *King George V* class when the *Vanguard* went in for refit. This would mean decommissioning a cruiser and three destroyers or frigates to provide sufficient engine-room ratings. The smaller ships were much more useful, in peace or war.[46]

The carrier was clearly the major surface ship. There was some debate over the primary duty of these ships, whether they were mainly for offensive purposes in attacking enemy naval bases or for defensive use dealing with air and submarine threats to high-value convoys. The Americans had both the ships and the aircraft to bear the brunt of the offensive against land targets, and this they duly agreed to do. Development of the heavy attack aircraft was deliberately stopped, although another factor in this decision was the fact that a propeller-driven machine would be out-of-date before it was deployed. The emphasis was on high-performance fighters for fleet carriers and ASW aircraft, supported by low-performance fighters in the light fleets. The former would operate against the threat of land-based aircraft (in the Mediterranean in particular), the latter would primarily serve in the Atlantic. The emphasis on convoy escort was clear. As Fraser put it to the fifth sea lord in 1948: "Planning can only proceed on something we know we must do; escort safely our convoys." This view did not find complete acceptance among Fraser's colleagues, especially the airmen, who instinctively demanded a more theoretically "offensive" role.[47]

The Americans, however, insisted that carrier strikes, the preferred "offensive" strategy, had to be made en masse with two hundred aircraft as a minimum. Not only was this way beyond Naval Aviation's strength in strike aircraft, it was more than its entire strength! In theory the Royal Navy had thirty-six strike aircraft (three squadrons) in its front line. In reality it only had twelve (not until the end of 1950 did a second squadron form). Firefly two-seat fighters had to act as light strike aircraft in addition to their other duties. Once the three hoped-for squadrons were formed, however, they were not to be thrown at the Soviets in the early stages of a conflict. The Royal Navy saw them as a cadre for an eventual force of two hundred aircraft in four carriers that could act as a sufficiently strong offensive force during some future war. By that time the Firebrand's replacement, the Wyvern, might have solved its development problems. The immediate priority for Naval Aviation, however, was implied by the first sea lord's dictum—direct defense of shipping against air and submarine attack. This required a front line of seventy-five day fighters, twenty night fighters, and seventy-five ASW aircraft.[48]

For the ASW task two approaches were taken. Firstly, and rather desperately, in accordance with the Defence Ministry's wishes the old Barracuda was resuscitated as an operational type. On 1 December 1947 815 Squadron was formed from 744 ASW Training Squadron and regularly operated from fleet carriers on exercises over the next few years. The Firefly carried out ASW tasks for the light fleet carriers. The standard "fighter reconnaissance" variant had a limited ASW capability, but specialized ASW Fireflies, equipped with sonobuoys, were also procured. The great advantage of these aircraft was that they did not require expensive carrier modifications. As for day fighters, the Seafire soldiered on, its final Mark 47 version entering service from 1948. It began to be replaced, however, by the Sea Fury before the end of the year. This more flexible aircraft had not been without developmental problems of its own, and because of its high landing speed it also required modifications to the arrester gear and barriers of *Colossus*-class carriers. Finally in the autumn of 1948 the Home Fleet's light fleet carriers, *Vengeance* and *Theseus*, took Sea Furies to sea. The squadron of twelve twin-engined Sea Hornets, 801, finally began regular deployment in *Implacable* in 1949. Fireflies at first provided night-fighter capability, but one squadron, 809, which went to sea in HMS *Vengeance* in 1950, was equipped with an NF21 Sea Hornet variant.[49]

As for the carriers, synergistic shipbuilding and financial difficulties pushed completion dates for building and modernization ever further into the future. By early 1950 the planned completion date for the *Eagle* was March 1951, with the four *Hermes* light fleet carriers due between the end of that year and 1953, and the *Ark Royal* coming out at the end of 1952.[50] Modifications were agreed upon in mid-1950 to make the *Ark Royal* better able to operate the larger jet fighters planned for the mid-fifties. This would delay the carrier for another five months.[51] But at least the long-discussed policy of full modernization for fleet carriers was getting under way. There had been a false start in 1949 when the *Formidable* was surveyed and was found to be in too bad a condition to begin modernization. The *Victorious* was picked instead, and her modifications were approved in the summer of 1950. She would be able to operate much larger and heavier aircraft than previously and would be given a shorter but higher hangar. This would necessitate effectively cutting the ship down to hangar deck level and building anew. The new hangar, unlike the old one, would have a deck thicker than its side protection. The ship's displacement would increase to 33,000 tons from just over 29,000. It was hoped that the *Victorious* would operate up to fifty-six modern aircraft.[52] As for the poor *Majestics*, work began again on the name ship of the class for the Australians. Unlike the two already completed ships of the class, HMCS *Magnificent* and HMAS *Sydney* (ex-*Terrible*), both commissioned in 1948, the *Majestic* herself would be completed to the modernized design, capable of operating the GR17/45 and a jet fighter of limited performance (precisely how limited became a matter of some dispute). Alas, there was still no money to do the same to the three remaining *Majestic*s that had not yet found a buyer, and they remained in their state of suspended animation. With their clear inability, even when modernized, to operate the second generation of planned jets it seemed inadvisable to spend scarce resources on them; much better to continue to concentrate on bringing the four larger, more flexible *Hermes*-class ships to completion.[53]

The reaction of the Admiralty to the Harwood Exercise had shown that there were those who considered the cruiser as important as the carrier, at least for Cold War tasks. There was much debate over cruiser policy in 1949, but in the spring of 1950 an agreed policy was presented to the Board. The *Minotaur* program was tacitly abandoned, and resources were to be concentrated on existing light cruiser hulls. The last operational 8-inch-gun armed heavy cruisers of the "County" class had just gone for scrap. Both the modernized *London* and two more original surviving ships, *Sussex* and *Norfolk*, had served on in the late 1940s in the Far East and East Indies. But they would require a virtual rebuilding to give them new equipment, as their gun mountings, etc., were worn out. Plans to use the hulls as the basis for escort carriers foundered on shortages of draftsmen if nothing else. There was little alternative but to dispose of these imposing veterans, although the *Cumberland* was kept running in her trials role for almost another decade and the *Devonshire*, which was disarmed, became Cadet Training Ship in 1947. She survived until 1954.[54]

Other famous war veterans among the light cruisers had also just been scrapped, notably the *Leander* and *Ajax*, both of which had served in the Mediterranean after the war. Of the twenty-four more modern 6-inch and 5.25-inch armed cruisers still either in commission or reserve, fifteen were to be modified to provide, when the *Tiger*s were completed, a total force of eighteen combat-worthy ships available for service in the first six months of war. Modernization was constrained by a shortage of funds, as the Admiralty could not maintain an adequate fleet for its normal peacetime functions and prepare fully for war. In any case the new automatic 6-inch and 3-inch guns and the new MRS3 fire-control system now planned for the three *Tiger*s would not be available until the mid-1950s. So it was decided to leave the main armaments of the older retained cruisers unchanged, to improve their fire-control radar, and to fit entirely new secondary armament fire control when it was available and could be afforded. Given their more robust prewar construction and their greater size, which allowed for greater habitability and more space for new equipment, the five "Town"-class cruisers were preferred over the later "Colonies." Three were scheduled for "large repairs" and two for more extensive modernization. Their larger half-sister *Belfast* was to receive full modernization also. Only one "Colony," the *Newfoundland*, was slated for repair as were the two related but more modern ships *Swiftsure* and *Superb* (the latter the only *Tiger* built to the original design). Despite their small size, the *Dido*s of just under 6,000 tons were valued as being capable of conversion into "satisfactory dual-purpose cruisers for relatively little cost." Four were to be modernized and two given "large repairs." The rest of the existing cruiser fleet, seven "Colonies" and *Dido* classes, would be scrapped or sold when no longer necessary as reserves.[55]

As for completed new ships, 1948–49 had also seen a certain amount of effort spent on the best design to fulfill the roles of the cruiser in the future. These functions were defined by the Naval Staff as:

(a) Protection of seaborne trade against surface attack by cruiser, large destroyer, or armed merchant ship of speeds up to 25 knots.

(b) Ability to assist in the protection of other ships in company, self-protection against air attack.

(c) To be logistically independent of bases or Fleet Train for long periods.

At the end of 1948 the naval constructors, bearing in mind the latest Staff thinking on having a minimum of funnels and upperworks in order to allow radars and other electronic sensors maximum unrestricted areas of operation, drew up four completely new "1960 cruiser" designs. These designs varied in size from 10,500 tons to 14,500 tons. Proposed main armament was either the new 6-inch automatic twin mount or a completely new 5-inch gun that was in an early stage of development. One design substituted a surface-to-air missile launcher for some guns. A compromise 12,250-ton ship with three 6-inch turrets and eight 3-inch guns was chosen to be the basis of the next large cruiser, a decision that seems to have marked the effective end of the *Minotaur* project with its more traditional layout. Rather ambitiously, it was hoped that the new cruiser might be able to carry two of the large 984 radars so that it could carry out the fleet air warning and control functions of the abandoned pickets.[56]

It was recognized, however, that there could not be enough big cruisers to fulfil requirements. As Rear Admiral Ralph Edwards, ACNS, argued in an important paper on future fleet requirements, the functions for which these large ships were traditionally needed were simply less important given the needs of more urgent priorities. The best way around this problem, the Staff thought, was to enhance the antisurface capabilities of the new destroyers, which would have to be large vessels anyway in order to make them effective antiair and antisubmarine screens for carrier groups. The Staff saw the new destroyer planned for the mid-1950s as a 5,000-ton "cruiser/destroyer" that would carry large 5-inch dual-purpose guns (able to deliver in a given time a weight of shell equivalent to that of a *Tiger*-class cruiser), light AA guns, good ASW sensors, and both "Limbo" antisubmarine mortars and antisurface/ASW torpedo armament. As well as being able to "handle" a Soviet *Kirov*-class cruiser (two would be able to deal with such a ship), they would make good flag-showing vessels, and would be more economical to operate than the existing cruiser force. The cost was £3 million each compared to £1.75 million for a contemporary destroyer of the *Daring* class and the estimated £5.2 million cost of a *Tiger*. (A new 12,000-ton cruiser was estimated to cost £6 million.) The complement would be 350–400, less than half that of a *Tiger* and about 50 percent more than a *Daring*. Fifty of these ships might do the wartime task of twenty-three cruisers and fifty-eight destroyers, with thirty kept in commission in peacetime. The new cruiser plan called for commencing the first of these ships in 1953, with one laid down every year to 1956, by which time the first would be completed. Money would come in part from scrapping the two *Dido*-class cruisers scheduled for large repairs. Design studies were carried out on the cruiser/destroyers in late 1949; they proposed vessels in the 4,700-ton to 4,800-ton category with various arrangements of three single 5-inch mounts. Various radar fits were suggested, including the 984 in one, again with the fleet aircraft direction/warning role in mind.[57]

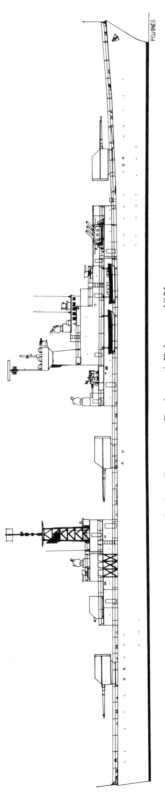

Cruiser-Destroyer Design—1 February 1951

Length: 463'

Armament: Three single 5" Mark 1 DP automatic guns (270 rounds each)
Two single 3"/50 DP guns
Two rocket/flare launchers
One triple-barrel Limbo antisubmarine mortar
One RULER anti-torpedo weapon system

Electronics: One Type 992 surveillance radar
One Type 960 air-search radar
One Type 978 navigation radar
One Type 277Q height-finding radar
Three Type MRS 3 fire-control radars (5")
Two 3"/50 fire-control radars

As for the frigates, the first priority was to provide a new convoy escort force with some capability against the new menace of the fast submarine. The existing ASW frigate force, although capable of some modification, was only able to deal with World War II type boats that had a submerged speed of 7 knots. A new design had been prepared to deal with the 17–18 knot high-performance, conventionally powered submarine. A 35-knot surface escort to cope with 25-knot boats was considered impractical for the time being, and even meeting the 17–18 knot threat was considered a difficult problem, given the requirements for endurance and minimum displacement. The new ASW frigate had to be able to escort a 10-knot convoy across the Atlantic. The endurance required was 4,500 miles at 12 knots. These design parameters were agreed upon in 1948 and one prototype was included in the 1949 Building Programme. Its main armament was to be a double set of the new "Limbo" long-range depth-charge mortars with a range of 1,000 yards and enough ammunition for twenty salvos; "Bidder" ASW torpedoes would also be carried. These weapons would be directed by an advanced Type 170 sonar and fully automated fire-control system with analog computer. To allow the ship to take part in the AA defense of convoys, a new automatic twin 3-inch mount was specified, along with a twin 40-mm Bofors mount. Since the new guns would not be available for some time, twin 4.5-inch guns would be mounted as an interim measure.[58] And since these new ships would not be available in sufficient quantities soon enough, the main thrust of the frigate program was the conversion of the large numbers of wartime destroyers, which had considerable life in them if refitted, but which were of only limited use with their existing antisurface ship weapon suites.

Two designs were placed before the Board of Admiralty in March 1949, one a prototype full conversion, the other a simplified variant. In the full conversion, which was to be applied first to HMS *Rocket* and *Relentless*, the hull was to be stiffened to allow the ship to maintain 25 knots in the roughest North Atlantic gales. Range was set at 3,350 miles at 15 knots. The 170 sonar and fire-control suite would be fitted, and the main armament would again be the double "Limbo" and ASW homing torpedoes. As a contribution to convoy air defense, a twin 4-inch mounting was placed amidships, as the forecastle would be too wet to operate the guns when the ship was being driven into a heavy Atlantic swell. A twin Bofors mount would cover the forward arcs.[59]

The limited conversion was originally envisaged as a more rapid way of improving the fast convoy escort position while tests with the full conversions were completed, and the intention in early 1949 was that ten ships were to receive less extensive modifications once the two full conversions had been done. The less capable "Squid" ASW system would be fitted, and the destroyers' forward torpedo tubes would be retained to fire ASW homing torpedoes when available. In general the appearance of the old destroyer was kept, although an AA armament would be substituted for the original.[60] In June 1949 the cuts in the 1949–50 estimates and the new "Revised Restricted Fleet" plans almost meant the end of the "Limited Conversion" program because of the decision to spend available resources on full-scale conversions. The still further financial cutbacks of late 1949 demonstrated, however, that there was little likelihood of getting enough fast frigates on the full conversion/new construction basis. It was decided, therefore, to convert the *Tenacious* on the more austere basis as a prototype for a modification that could be quickly applied to other ships when the financial situation improved or the political situation deteriorated. The

Board accepted this *volte face* in February 1950, and Hall even suggested that the expensive full conversion scheme might be abandoned, or dramatically reduced, in order to get more conversions or more new ships.[61]

In this confused climate the Naval Staff now compromised. It was decided that mixed flotillas of "First Rate" and "Second Rate" ships were the most cost-effective answer to the frigate problem, and a new-construction "Second Rate" design was developed. It was to have the same range, ASW armament, and sonar capability as the new "First Rate" antisubmarine design, but was much smaller (1,290 tons) and carried very limited communications equipment. It carried only a minimum AA armament of three 40-mm guns. Speed was marginally reduced to 25 knots, but this was probably sufficient to deal with a 17-knot submarine. The complement was only 143, compared to 240 in the "First Rate" ship. The Ship Design Policy Committee was much enamored of the design and regarded it as "being of great importance," recommending its inclusion in the 1951/52 program. This ship was also "the nearest approach available to an up-to-date ocean going anti-submarine vessel that could be produced rapidly in a future war, as with the corvette in the late war."[62]

The Board approved the sketch design in May 1950, recommending a new name for this type of ship to differentiate it from the more capable "First Rate" vessels.[63] It was, however, decided not to depart from the generic name "frigate," which had only been adopted in 1948. Instead, the always fertile mind of Edwards, ACNS,

In the late 1940s it became clear that Britain would not be able to afford sufficient fully capable ASW frigates to meet her numerical requirements in a third battle of the Atlantic. Hence, a new class was designed, meeting the latest ASW capabilities with a cheap, prefabricated hull. After some debate, the classification "Second-Rate" frigate was given to these ships, named after Nelson's captains as the "Blackwood" class. A large program was intended, 23 units, but only 12 were delivered. This view shows the ships' main armament of two Mark 10 ASW mortars directed by a 170 sonar. The lightweight hulls proved weak and had to be strengthened for the fishery protection duties often allocated to them.

suggested that frigates should be given the prefix "antisubmarine," "antiaircraft," and "aircraft direction," with a type number to indicate specific characteristics like size and armament. This was eventually approved, and the new "First Rate" ASW frigates became Type 12, the new "Second Rates," Type 14, the full conversion, Type 15, and the limited conversion, Type 16. At the same time as this was approved, July 1950, the Type 16 conversion secured Board approval. The ship's gun armament, designed to engage a surfaced submarine as well as deal with the self-defense problem, was two 4-inch and seven Bofors guns. The lack of proper fire control prevented the ship being able to make much of a contribution to the air defense of convoys. It was hoped that the somewhat inadequate double "Squid" arrangement might be replaced by a single "Limbo" later.[64]

As for the protection of convoys from air attack, two completely new types of ship were planned. As stated above, it had been decided that the 1945 program's two frigates were to be completed as prototypes, one an antiaircraft weapons platform and the other as a radar and fighter-control station for the direction of shore- or carrier-based aircraft. Lack of funds delayed these ships, and sketch proposals were not laid before the Board until April 1948. The maximum degree of standardization between the two ships was desired in order to facilitate mass production. Displacement was 1,665 tons for the A/D ship and 1,770 tons for the AA. Diesel engines were to be fitted to allow rapid production in large numbers, and the whole design of the ship was drawn up with mass production with minimum labor in wartime in mind. The diesel engines gave a maximum speed of only 23 knots, but this was deemed to be enough for the intended work. The armament was to be four 4.5-inch guns and four Bofors for the AA ship, with half that armament for the A/D vessel. Three-inch automatics were to be fitted when ready instead of the 4.5s.

Full drawings did not appear until September 1950. By then the AA ship had grown to 1,855 tons, and its additional roles were described as carrying out "minor offensive operations for which fleet destroyers are unsuitable" and assisting in ASW operations. For the latter a "Squid" ASW system was to be carried. The A/D ship was still at 1,665 tons, with additional roles as a coastal force directing ship, assisting in ASW defense of convoys, and contributing to the AA defense of convoys and anchorages. A comprehensive radar fit was the main feature of the design, with Type 293Q target-designation radar, Type 960 long-range air-warning radar, Type 982 aircraft-direction radar, and Type 277Q combined air/surface warning radar. No ship demonstrated better the growing electronic sophistication (and expense) of the hitherto cheap escort vessel. Under the new system the AA frigates were Type 41 and the A/D ships Type 61.[65]

As for the older AA frigates, a major argument broke out about their future. A number of old surplus frigates, thirty-nine, were to be scrapped under the latest plans. "Hunt"-class ships in reserve seemed especially good targets for disposal. The range of the erstwhile "escort destroyers," now "AA frigates," was limited and their development potential small due to inadequate reserves of stability. It was proposed in April 1950 to scrap some twenty-nine "Hunts" and nine old "River"-class ASW ships (one "Hunt" had already gone). This was strongly opposed by the newly appointed parliamentary secretary, James Callaghan, son of a chief petty officer and a wartime acting lieutenant in the Royal Naval Volunteer Reserve, who was taking a much more forward part in board discussions than any of his recent predecessors. The Naval Staff stressed the poor condition of the ships due to a lack of proper preservation and care. It would cost £3,250,000 to put the ships in a state of preservation and £300,000–£400,000 a year to look after them properly. It was doubtful whether these vessels would ever be mobilized in war. Callaghan stressed the threat posed by Soviet submarines and the need for every possible escort vessel. He reminded the Board of the part played by the fifty old American destroyers in World War II. The "Hunts," he argued, were fast and of use for both antiaircraft and ASW purposes. Even the "Rivers" might still be of use, and the Canadians planned to modernize them and keep them until the late 1950s. Retaining both classes, Callaghan pointed out, would provide the vital numbers of escorts required; on this occasion, quantity was more important than quality. Callaghan angered the Naval Staff by going down to Plymouth to inspect the ships himself and enlist the support of Admiral Sir Rhoderick McGrigor, the local commander-in-chief. Their condition did not seem to be as bad as the admirals in London thought. The argument prevailed into the Korean War period and the ships were saved. Indeed, once the Korean War broke out, investigations into their possible modernization were carried out.[66]

The Admiralty might have felt that some of its less-capable frigates were expendable, but it was in no doubt about the importance of the convoy escort. These were the top-priority surface vessels, and it seems that the lessons of the World War II had been very clearly learned. There was no question but that convoy would be reintroduced at the outbreak of any future war in the North Atlantic and Mediterranean. A draft convoy system, very reminiscent of that of 1939–45, was ready. Although plans also included offensive antisubmarine forces and hunter-killer groups, there was no doubt that giving shipping in these theaters proper escort was the first priority in both deployment and procurement.[67]

Yet there was another threat exceeding that of the submarine. By 1949–50 Alliance planners were putting the mine at the top of the list of threats to be countered.[68] The Russians were known to have a predilection for this kind of warfare and, given their lack of experience in oceanic submarine warfare, it provided perhaps the easiest and most convenient means of challenging shipping coming and going from British ports. The requirement for mine-countermeasure vessels was, therefore, pressing, and the Admiralty set up a special Mine Counter-measures Equipment Working Party to study the situation.[69]

It was clear that much of the Royal Navy's existing mine-countermeasures equipment was dangerously out-of-date. Influence mines, the new pressure type as well as the established magnetic and acoustic types, were now the main threat. Locating such devices and disposing of them by diving was becoming more significant than old-fashioned sweeping. There were fears about the sensitivity of the new Soviet mines, designed with all the benefits of a war experience on both sides. Big ships like the existing ocean minesweepers, of which over sixty had been retained in service or reserve, were probably going to be vulnerable and useless against much of this new threat. In any case, the mines would be laid largely in coastal and inshore waters for maximum effectiveness; the outstanding need, therefore, was to replace the existing fleet of smaller vessels. There remained about seventy World War II-type coastal minesweepers and a similar number of inshore minesweeping motor launches (about 75 percent of all MCM craft were in reserve). In wartime almost one hundred trawlers would also be recommended for mobilization. In order to make a start on a modern MCM force, it was planned to replace the coastals and inshores by new, improved vessels. A new coastal vessel was put into the 1949 program, and the Board considered drawings in September 1949. Made of aluminum and wood, the new ship could sweep mines faster and could deal with magnetic mines in shallower water (4 fathoms) than previous ships. At the same time a new inshore sweeper design was presented, along with a mine-locating version. A mine-locating design of the coastal minesweeper (CMS) appeared in October. An advanced new sonar, the 178, was under development for the mine-location vessels. Three more CMS, five inshore minesweepers (IMS) and three each of the mine locaters were duly put into the 1950–51 program. Thus was born the prolific "Ton," "Ham", and "Ley" classes that were to be the backbone of the Royal Navy's force of smaller warships in the second half of the twentieth century.[70]

In February 1950 Mr. Attlee called a general election, which resulted in a narrow Labour victory. The Cabinet was reshuffled and Alexander replaced as minister of defense by the erstwhile army minister, Emanuel Shinwell.[71] Both Shinwell's capacity and inclination for anti-navy mischief were rather greater than Alexander's, and he was soon leading an attack by his ministry on the Royal Navy's carrier program. Not only were the ships themselves vulnerable due to their expense, but also the Admiralty was insisting on the development of its own expensive, high-performance carrier jets that could contest control of the Mediterranean with shore-based Soviet aircraft.

The government was anxious to limit expenditure by reducing the number of different airframes under development, and the Admiralty was willing to accept a navalized version of the RAF's Venom, which could fulfil its need for all-weather fighters to shoot down low-performance reconnaissance aircraft in the Atlantic. The scales were finally tipped by the RAN's request for a jet fighter suitable for operations from the modified *Melbourne* (ex-*Majestic*). This meant that the total size of the buy would be big enough to justify the Venom, the only aircraft that could fit the modified *Majestic* design. The Naval Staff felt, however, that the Sea Venom could not deal with massed bomber attacks in the Mediterranean and insisted that the development of its own advanced single-seat fighter, the N9/47, be continued. Only this aircraft had the very high rate of climb required for naval operations with expected radar and fighter-control facilities. In 1949 the N40/46 two-seat all-weather fighter specification was also rewritten in a much more advanced form as N14/49. Both Fairey and De Havilland offered designs. The RAF had superficially similar projects for both a single-engined day fighter and a twin-engined all-weather fighter, but the Admiralty considered both specifications unsuitable for carrier conversion. Indeed, De Havilland, whose DH 110 offered one potential common solution to both services' all-weather fighter plans, suffered the double setback of being rejected by both the Admiralty and the Air Ministry. To officials in the Ministry of Defence and Supply this all looked like unnecessary duplication. Moreover, the Admiralty's airmen were treading increasingly on the RAF's toes by strengthening their case that offensive air strikes would be the key to securing command of the sea in the intensive opening phase of a future war. They repeated their requirements for a specialized strike version of N14/49 (or

N9/47) to replace the troublesome turboprop Wyverns, which would, in any case, be obsolete by 1957. The RAF had serious reservations about too much penetration by Naval Aviation into the strike role.[72]

The feeling that Britain needed to rationalize its maritime air effort prompted Chief of the Air Staff (CAS) Sir John Slessor to write to the first sea lord in April 1950 with a radical proposal. He suggested the merging of RAF Coastal Command with Naval Aviation in order to form a joint Maritime Air Force. This, he argued, would allow the most rational use of the limited resources available. Slessor felt that the existing plans invested too heavily in aircraft as ASW weapons, as it was currently assessed that they had only limited ability against modern submarines. The emphasis on carrier-based rather than shore-based aircraft seemed to him to be too great, and given the planned strength of both RAF Coastal Command and Naval Aviation, the air war at sea in general was taking up a disproportionate share of Britain's limited stock of military aircraft. Indeed, according to Slessor's calculations, this share represented more aircraft than were used for land warfare or even the air defense of the United Kingdom itself. In his reply, Fraser stood firm on the question of Naval Aviation, deprecating any reversion to the dual-control system of 1924–39 that had led to so much interservice wrangling and had contributed to the limited development of British naval air power.[73]

That month the anticarrier feeling within Shinwell's ministry gathered strength. A director of the Fairey company wrote with regard to the largest carriers: "Ministry of Defence recommend them out; Admiralty want them retained. General opinion: we cannot afford them." Fairey was interested, as the cancellation of the carrier building and modernization program might well mean the end of not just their N14/49 but also the GR17/45 (Gannet) ASW aircraft. It could also mean the substitution of a much more austere aircraft that would be operated from the unmodified light fleet carriers with which the Navy might well be left. The Gannet by now was clearly going to be too large and heavy for operation from such ships.[74] Shinwell, however, clearly thought that large carriers did not fit in an era in which, more than ever before, we had "to cut our coat according to our cloth." At a conference with the chiefs of staff on 11 May, he openly questioned the need for fleet carriers, given the priorities of ASW and mine countermeasures. VCNS Vice Admiral Sir George Creasey defended the Admiralty, saying that due weight was being given to the minister's points. Nevertheless, he insisted, fleet carriers were of great value. Significantly, Slessor steadfastly refused to be drawn by the minister. He insisted that Fraser himself be present to defend the Admiralty position before the question was pursued.[75]

In private, Slessor was keeping up the pressure on Fraser for a joint Maritime Air Force. In a second letter to the first sea lord he addressed the issue of the Admiralty's plans for fighter and strike aircraft in light of the agreed chiefs of staff policy on the Navy's role in defense of sea communications. The CAS cited disapprovingly the "Trident Exercise," in which attacks on Soviet bases were made from carriers deployed to the North Cape. It was clear, he felt, that the Admiralty should be concentrating on more direct ASW measures. Slessor also argued that the context was different from before the war. Then, he argued, interservice relations had been poisoned by the question of aircraft vs. battlefleet. Now everyone accepted that aircraft were major weapons; the open question was who should control them and train their crews. It made sense, he reiterated, to get the maximum unification of air effort. He warned that another Harwood affair was in the air, implying that under Shinwell its proposals this time might be accepted. Under the circumstances Britain had to produce the most cost-effective defense policy possible. Surface ASW forces, and the optimum combination of carrier-based ASW aircraft and land-based ASW machines, would provide such a posture, leaving the RAF to look after the fighter/strike functions.[76]

The 11 May meeting had considered an important policy paper on "Defence Policy and Global Strategy." This document confirmed a significant realignment from the strategic decisions of 1947. It reinforced the increasing stress on the defense of Europe begun in 1948, when the decision was taken to fight on the Continent rather than withdraw the troops there to the Middle East. This had already been significantly supplemented in March 1950 by the decision to send reinforcements to Europe rather than to the Middle East. Not only was this deemed essential to maintain French morale, but the occupation of the Channel coast by Soviet forces would make British survival very dubious. Much had changed since 1940 to make more formidable the threat of strategic air attack on the United Kingdom. The Soviet Union had both rockets and nuclear weapons. Moreover, as Fraser and the other chiefs of staff had argued, "even if it were possible to hold the UK, many years would elapse before we would be in a position to mount an operation on the scale of Overlord to liberate Europe. By that time the Russian occupation would have put an end to Western Civilisation."[77]

This 1950 "Global Strategy" paper boded ill for the Admiralty, especially for its carrier program. It emphasized the alternative demands on the aircraft industry—air forces on the Continent to support the enhanced commitment of ground troops there, and enlarged air defenses of the United Kingdom. The chiefs of staff decided on a committee to study the question of maritime aviation, but before it could meet the political and strategic context had been fundamentally altered by the outbreak of the Korean War in June. Not only did this give the Royal Navy a chance to show off the combat capabilities of its carriers in the limited war role, but it also seemed to bring the prospect of general war nearer. This was reflected in the terms of reference of the Maritime Air Defence Committee "to examine the whole problem of air defence of sea communications and to make recommendations to the Chiefs of Staff for the most efficient maritime air defence system for war against Russia starting in 1954."[78]

The chairman of the committee was Lieutenant General Sir Gerald Templer, a distinguished soldier soon to go on to still greater success in Malaya against the Communist insurgents. He acted as neutral arbiter between four Admiralty representatives and four officers from the Air Ministry. After considering much evidence (which gives a fascinating insight into the anticipated shape of naval war in 1950), the committee's report, completed in October, was a triumphant vindication for the Admiralty. Templer and his assistants argued a case for the complementary use of land- and sea-based air power, the former being judged more cost-effective for ASW out to 550 miles, the latter being best for the areas beyond. The Mediterranean scenario for the fleet carriers was reaffirmed, and the committee also came out in favor of a limited number of carrier-based antishipping strike aircraft to deal with the surface threat in the Atlantic. The committee set the requirement for defense of sea communications at 7 carriers, 306 carrier-borne aircraft, 50 very long range maritime patrol aircraft, and 300 or more shorter range maritime patrol aircraft.[79]

By the time the report came out, there was some chance that such goals might be met. Rearmament had become the order of the day on a shorter timetable than the 1957 target date of previous plans. Increasingly, as with the Templer Committee, 1954 began to be used as the planning target for the rest of 1950; this was the date by which NATO wished to get its forces into order. At the end of the year, target dates were abandoned and Britain began to rearm as quickly as she could.[80] The rationale for rearmament was set out by Shinwell when the first installment was discussed in the Defence Committee on 24 July:

> The general situation was difficult. There might be other surprise attacks, as in Korea or there might be no trouble for several years. The potential enemy was formidable especially on land but his forces were powerful also in the air and at sea. It was necessary to build up some adequate defence against him.[81]

Shinwell felt that one might expect less support from the Americans than previously, given their commitment to Korea, and that this made it even more important to improve the readiness of the armed forces. In relation to the Navy he specifically mentioned its need for new submarines, minesweepers, and frigates. He wanted £200 million more for defense, £30 million to be added immediately to the 1950–51 defense estimates (a third for the Admiralty) in order to lay the groundwork for much larger increases after April 1951. Attlee supported his defense minister, stressing the importance of Britain showing a good example both to her European allies and to the United States, who "might be prepared to increase their assistance to Western Union countries if they were satisfied that Western Union countries were doing all they could to help themselves." The chancellor supported higher spending, although he cut the higher figure by half, and in the Cabinet discussions the following day it was suggested that rearmament might actually have positive economic effects in deferring the unemployment that was beginning to develop in the shipbuilding and ship-repairing industries. The Cabinet duly authorized the increase of £100 million (£22 million to go to the Admiralty) and kept the possibility open of still greater increases.[82]

An immediate problem being faced by the Admiralty was a shortage of manpower in the Far East Fleet, which had to be rectified if it was to fight the war effectively. At the 24 July Defence Committee meeting the first lord obtained authorization for suspension of releases and a call-up of naval aircrew from the Royal Fleet Reserve.[83] The immediate needs of the war were held to require the manpower measures but, as the second sea lord admitted a few months later, more basic structural problems were the real culprits, especially the shortage of petty officers. The wartime shortage of regulars meant that no one was available to replace the twelve-year men leaving the service from the last prewar entries. The cuts in shore establishments of 1949–50 had indeed not been enough.[84] Limited manpower continued to be a significant constraint on rearmament because of Korea, and delays in ships' completion (such as the relatively manpower-intensive *Daring*-class ships) were more welcome than they might otherwise have been. In 1951 the need to decommission ships in service to man new construction had to

A fine view of the "C"-class destroyer HMS *Charity*, which led an active life in the Far East in the early 1950s. After a period in reserve, she was sold to Pakistan in 1958.

be accepted. This was despite the increases in pay announced at the end of August 1950 and the extension of National Service to two years.[85]

The decision to increase the National Service period was taken while the Cabinet was considering the desired financial level of rearmament. One or two Cabinet members, notably Aneurin Bevan, expressed doubts about the effect of too large a program on the government's domestic priorities, but Gaitskell, the chancellor, was sanguine about the affordability of the economic costs. The increase in defense expenditure would be substantial, to over £1,000 million per year from 1951–52 onwards, but some members of the government doubted if even that would satisfy the Americans or public opinion at home. The three-year program, approved in principle by the Cabinet on 1 August 1950, totaled £3.4 billion over three years, and this went up to £3.6 billion with the decision to lengthen conscription and give pay increases to the armed forces. Substantial United States aid was expected, over half a billion pounds worth, and the services began to draw up shopping lists. The Admiralty wanted Sikorsky S-55 ASW helicopters and Skyraider aircraft for airborne early warning, both forms of naval airpower unavailable as yet from home industry. The Admiralty, in drawing up its increased production plans, was warned of the constraints on rearmament. The economy was to stay a "peacetime" one; there would be no direction of labor or sequestration of factories. It was assumed that as well as supplying military aid the Americans would underwrite any export losses.[86]

The Naval Staff set about drawing up a blueprint for expansion, and this duly appeared as the "Fraser Plan" in October. The plan was modest in extent, being insufficient to build up a fleet that the Admiralty felt was fully sufficient for war or a fleet big enough to meet the force goals being worked out for the NATO Medium Term Plan. Instead, it proposed a "minimum balanced fleet, having regard to what the country can reasonably afford." Its size was generally as planned in 1949, although money would be spent more quickly to meet the revised readiness date of 1954. The fleet available after six months of mobilization that year would be modestly increased by six destroyers, sixty-one coastal and inshore minesweepers, and sixty-three aircraft over the war fleet planned previously. Mine countermeasures were still a major preoccupation, with fifty-six coastal and forty-five inshore craft planned in the four yearly construction programs from 1950 to 1954. This would help meet the shortfall of 152 vessels of these types. Twenty-seven frigates and eight submarines were now to be laid down, while coastal forces would get a more substantial number of new vessels: thirty-three fast attack craft and eighteen "seaward defence boats," a new type designed to replace the old harbor defense motor launches in guarding anchorages against submarine attack. (In the end some twenty of these "Ford"-class vessels were built over the next seven years.) The stabilized personnel strength of the fleet would be 132,000 rather than the 124,000 planned for 1952. This fleet would be more capable of "fighting with what it had" than the fleet of 1950.[87]

The pace of rearmament was soon stepped up even further. Attlee had rushed to Washington at the beginning of December, fearing escalation of the war. Truman had requested Britain to increase its defense expenditure still more. Attlee, troubled at American fears of general war in the next year or two, felt that the maximum defense effort was required to avert it. The Americans were about to ask publicly for yet more expenditure on defense from the Europeans, and Attlee felt the British had to show a good example: "One could not ignore the risk, however remote it might seem, that the United States might lose interest in the defence of Europe, if her allies in the North Atlantic Treaty Organisation failed to play their proper part."[88]

The Admiralty immediately set about producing an "Accelerated Fraser Plan." There were severe constraints, as problems concerning provision of propelling machinery and other equipment meant that building a new major combatant took at least two years. Only small craft could be built, notably MCM vessels. The number of mine countermeasures vessels was increased still further to sixty new coastals by the end of 1953 and sixty two new inshore vessels by the same date. The completion of fast ASW frigate conversions would also be sped up to have twenty-five by early 1953 and forty-five by 1955 (twenty-seven full and eighteen limited). Frontline aircraft strength could be increased to almost 230 aircraft in 1952 by ordering more of the types in, or about to go into, production than by waiting for more advanced later types. More Attacker jet fighters were ordered, along with a much modified Mark 7 version of the Firefly for ASW. Only a year or two's service was expected of these interim machines but semicapable aircraft were needed in the shortest possible term. The increased production in all areas would mean the displacement of civilian work, particularly in the electrical and electronic industries. A number of extra ships were to be added to the fleet in commission, and it was hoped to restore the Home and Mediterranean Fleets to a healthier manning level. The increased cost would be £26.5 million in 1951–52 and £64 million in 1952–53. Over twelve thousand extra men would be required, to be met by deferred releases and call-up of men mainly from the regular Royal Fleet Reserve but a few ex-"Hostilities Only" World War II veterans in "Class Z" reserve. This "£1,610 Million Plan" was presented to another working party, again chaired by Sir Harold Parker. This party endorsed the proposals and pointed out that all the services' demands would mean that the total labor force engaged in defense production in 1954 would be over a million, compared to less than half a million at present. The cost of the defense plan as a whole was over £4.5 billion.[89]

When the Cabinet's Defence Committee considered the expanded program, Attlee agreed that strong naval forces were necessary to deter Soviet initiatives, although the prime minister asked that care be taken not to dissipate efforts on measures not likely to have a deterrent effect. He had been impressed, however, by the size of the Soviet submarine force, which he now called the largest in the world. The chancellor, perhaps a little more complacently, argued that the economic strain could be taken up by limiting the current consumption of consumer goods, radios, television sets, and "frigidaires." The supply of consumer goods would fall by 2 percent per annum, and the standard of living, the rate of industrial reequipment, and the amount of building would fall. A 4 percent rate of increase in manufacturing output, it was hoped, would mitigate the worst economic impact of the program.[90]

In reality the chancellor seems to have recognized the economic dangers of the program, which he summarized in his written memorandum to the cabinet. The total program, including civil defense, was costed at £4,760 million. Although it would be impossible to maintain a favorable balance of payments, Gaitskell insisted that overseas earnings be maintained to keep "a net surplus" of £200 million when stockpiling had been taken out of the calculations. He pointed out the unfavorable movements in terms of trade against Britain and the shortages of raw materials that were already becoming apparent. Rearmament would increase demand in a comparatively small range of industries, especially those metal-using industries that supplied half of Britain's exports and the investment goods upon which the future health of the economy depended. It was hoped to switch labor and other resources into those industries, but it was also clear that exports and investment might well suffer. A series of measures, including direction of labor, prohibition of the production of some articles, and increases in purchase tax were considered, although it was admitted that the time was not yet ripe for them. Gaitskell called for agreement on the necessary measures to control the economy so that the burden fell where it was intended. On 27 January 1951 the Cabinet accepted the program and its "general economic implications," although it was agreed that it might be delayed by raw-material shortages and that no definite public commitment should be made. Indeed, when it was announced in Parliament two days later, Attlee limited himself to saying that expenditure *might* total £4.7 billion rather than saying it *would*.[91]

The program indeed soon ran into economic and political difficulties. The Cabinet crisis caused by the introduction of charges for spectacles and dentures into the National Health Service rocked the government and contributed to its defeat in the election in October 1951.[92] As far as the Admiralty was concerned, however, the new bonanza conditions were to be exploited. The existing rearmament program, expensive as it was, did not provide Britain with a fleet that met her full NATO force goals. At a meeting of the Alliance's Defence Committee in Washington in October 1950 a "Medium Term Plan" (DC28) had been worked out for completion by 1954. This set Britain the task of deploying in the NATO area one fleet carrier and four light carriers (with 271 aircraft), 5 cruisers, 262 destroyers and frigates, 44 smaller escorts (under 300 tons), 15 submarines, 8 minelayers, and no less than 791 minesweepers. For outside the NATO area the British planners felt the Royal Navy required one more fleet carrier and two light carriers (with 175 aircraft), nine cruisers, 39 destroyers and frigates, 12 submarines, one minelayer, and 109 minesweepers. Within six months of mobilization an extra carrier and cruiser, twenty-two destroyer/frigates, 74 carrier-borne aircraft, and three submarines would be required.[93] The perceived shortfalls between these goals and contemporary plans impelled the Naval Staff to try its luck with a third "Exercise C" expansion plan that was presented to the Board of Admiralty in July 1951. More ASW and mine countermeasures vessels were proposed, but the most notable inclusion was a brand new fleet carrier! The Naval Staff thought that this could all be afforded more or less within the government's £4,700 million defense plan, although they did make the somewhat optimistic assumptions that the naval share would be slightly increased and that the same level of expenditure would be kept up even after the plan was completed. Callaghan was unimpressed. He would rather see what money there was used to bring to completion the three remaining *Majestics* as ASW carriers rather than to build a completely new larger ship. The Naval Staff argued in return that a new carrier was vital for an "up to date and balanced" naval task force. "Exercise C" received the Board's approval as a statement of intention, nothing more.[94]

In retrospect, such hopes look especially unrealistic, as it must have been clear that rearmament was running into serious trouble. Aircraft carriers provide a good case study of the fundamental problems that both government and Admiralty faced. It was not so much a question of spending money on new ships; it was finding the material wherewithal to design and construct them. At the very beginning of the design process the naval constructors had insufficient staff to work on all the projects the Naval Staff required. This factor was often decisive in delaying designs to the point where changing conditions advised cancellation. Draftsmen were also short in the shipyards, causing enormous difficulties, especially given the various modifications to the new carriers to allow them to operate the most modern aircraft possible. The design of three of the *Hermes*-class ships was deliberately frozen due to the drafting office bottleneck and the need to get modern ships into service as soon as possible. There was also a shortage of workers in the yards, especially electricians, plumbers, and fitters, and the procurement authorities were soon bemoaning the poor distribution of labor. So many shipwrights were taken up by the conversion of *Victorious* at Portsmouth that construction of a proposed A/D frigate was moved to a private shipyard. Other problems, however, were almost as serious: such as late delivery of pipes, valves, and electrical fittings and labor disputes.[95]

The result of this tale of woe was that the proposed completion dates for new carriers slipped steadily. Also, such new improvements as the steam catapult could not be fitted if any new carriers were to be in service by the newly advanced date of intended readiness, 1954. In February 1951 the carrier program was still an optimistic one.[96]

(a) World War II armored-hangar fleet carriers

    Implacable—to be modernized 1953–55; to relieve the *Eagle* on refit 1956.

    Indefatigable—to be modernized 1954–57.

    Indomitable—harbor training 1953–57; modernization as training carrier 1957.

    Victorious—modernization complete 1954*; then trials carrier replacing the *Illustrious*.

(b) *Colossus*-class light fleet carriers

    Vengeance—limited modernization to begin 1953 then to Category "C" reserve.

    Warrior—limited modernization 1952–53 then to Home Fleet.

(c) *Hermes*-class light fleet carriers

    Hermes—to complete 1955 to modernized design; then to relieve HMS *Glory*.

    Albion—to complete end 1952; then to relieve HMS *Theseus*.

    Centaur—to complete early 1953; then to relieve HMS *Triumph* (as training carrier).

    Bulwark—to complete 1954; then to relieve HMS *Ocean*.

(d) *Ark Royal*-class fleet carriers

    Eagle—to complete August 1951; to refit with steam catapult 1956.

    Ark Royal—to complete 1954.

This was basically the "Revised Restricted Fleet" program, with two *Colossus* modernizations added after the decision to keep an extra light fleet carrier at sea. The *Colossus* modernizations were of a somewhat austere type, producing ships that could just operate the Gannet/Sea Venom combination but nothing more.[97] It was not planned to give them such an extensive conversion as the Australians' HMS *Majestic*, which was allocated both a valuable steam catapult and priority over the *Hermes* at Vickers' Barrow yard. This was perhaps only politic, given the uneasiness of the Australians over the bargain they were getting with their light fleet carrier purchases from the British.[98]

To fly from these ships when they eventually appeared, some 300 front-line aircraft were planned for 1955, an increase of fifty over the original "Fraser Plan." By 1954–55 almost all first-line aircraft were to have gas-turbine engines, the actual planned number being 88 Sea Hawks, 48 Sea Venoms, 24 Wyverns, 112 Gannets (this Fairey type having finally defeated the Blackburn offering for the GR17/45 specification at the beginning of 1951), and 28 Skyraider AEW aircraft (the only piston-engined type). The continued emphasis on fighters and ASW aircraft is noteworthy.[99] This was an increase of over 50 percent compared to 1951, but it was still only the complement of three to four U.S. carriers. Nevertheless, the projected improvement in quality would greatly enhance Naval Aviation's capabilities, especially against Soviet submarines and jet bombers, the two major perceived threats in the Atlantic and Mediterranean respectively. As for second-

*Projected loading for a modernized carrier: 20 Seahawk, 10 Sea Venom, 10 Wyvern, 10 Gannet, 4 Skyraider.

generation jet aircraft, the N9/47 single-seat fighter had become the N113, with even higher performance expectations and an equally extended time scale for development. As so often occurs in the history of British naval aircraft, the Naval Staff felt forced reluctantly to consider navalized versions of RAF land-based types. The Swift single-engined day fighter was considered as an interim swept-wing aircraft but rejected, a happy outcome considering its later RAF history. As for the next all-weather fighter, the navy became increasingly dissatisfied with Fairey's work on the N19/49 and brought De Havilland back into the program. After considering a swept-wing Sea Venom, the DH116, the Admiralty returned to the twin-engined DH110, two prototypes of which, to RAF specification, had survived cancellation in favor of the delta-winged Gloster Javelin. The decision was eventually taken to "navalize" the DH110, a process that involved 80 percent re-design. At the other end of the scale, in 1951 the Admiralty issued requirement NA32 for a modern light ASW aircraft to operate from unconverted light fleet carriers that could not take the Gannet.[100]

The "£1,610 Million Plan" allowed for a new destroyer modernization program. First, the eight Ca-class ships of 1944–45 were to be turned into A/S escort group leaders. The Staff Requirement of 1 November 1951, however, stressed the fleet role of these ships. Their main role was to screen heavy ships against attacks by submarine, aircraft, and light surface forces, with an offensive role against enemy light forces and merchant ships. Their secondary functions were to supplement cruisers in independent operations, to support amphibious operations, and to torpedo heavy ships. An enlarged bridge and an operations room were to be fitted, and the new balance of armament was reflected in that there were only three dual-purpose 4.5-inch mounts (directed by modern fire control); one gun and one set of 21-inch torpedo tubes were sacrificed for Squid ASW mortars and an improved Bofors close-range AA armament. It was also the intention to give five other Cs the same treatment and thirteen others an interim modification with less advanced sonar and radar.[101]

As for the earlier destroyers, the Naval Staff had tentative plans for all fifty-seven survivors of the M to Z classes. Twenty-seven were to be Type 15 conversions (four for R, five for V, four for W, seven for U, and seven for Z) and eighteen Type 16 limited conversions (seven for T, five for N, two for P, and four for O). As for the rest (five for M, four flotilla leaders, one for S, and two for W), a new role had appeared in the Fraser Plan, the Aircraft Direction conversion. This "Type 62" had first been suggested in 1949, and only the five large prewar Ms were ever seriously considered for it. The conversion involved fitting them with radar similar to that carried by new-construction Type 61 frigates. An armament of two 4-inch guns, one twin Bofors 40-mm AA mount, and a single Squid ASW mortar allowed the ships some three-dimensional capability: they could defend themselves, and they could also defend the convoys and amphibious groups they were intended to support. With the limited availability of new A/D frigates and the importance of RAF and naval aircraft in shipping defense, these A/D conversions were felt, for a time, to be especially important.[102]

The Type 62 conversion plans began to come under increased scrutiny in 1951 with the appearance of a new conversion option, the Type 18 "improved limited" ASW frigate. This frigate was first suggested in July 1950 as an attempt to upgrade the Type 16, about whose ASW potential there were increasing doubts. The Type

A common sight around the coast of Britain in the 1950s were rows of mothballed warships, the massive reserve fleet, relics of World War II waiting for a recall to arms. Keeping these ships fit for mobilization was a significant drain on the Royal Navy's resources. Here at Penarth in Wales (second row from the left) are four destroyers of the "M" class: the *Marne* (D 135), *Matchless*, *Meteor*, and *Milne*. Plans to convert them into aircraft direction frigates never came to fruition, and they were sold to Turkey in 1957. Ahead are four more destroyers and two "River"-class frigates. Astern are three small "Castle"-class frigates.

18 ended up as a considerably improved vessel, with a sensor fit and armament very like the Type 15 although with much less structural modification. The saving was some £150,000 on the £600,000 cost of the Type 15. But instead of the Type 18 being substituted for the Type 15, as was suggested at one time, it was decided instead to upgrade eight of the eighteen planned limited conversions to Type 18s, keeping all twenty-seven Type 15s. The need to save money seemed, for a time, less compelling. The priority was "a conversion of greater military value," always assuming, of course, that resources were available. That they were not is demonstrated by the main reason for not adopting the Type 18 earlier—the lack of draftsmen—which forced the retention of the Type 16 if *any* improved ASW ships were to be in the water soon, and also by the difficulties that were soon apparent in deliveries of the new ASW mortar system.[103]

Nevertheless, it was noted that numbers had to be kept up at some sacrifice in quality. The increasing recognition that even the austere "Second Rate" Type 14 frigate, with its hard-to-produce turbines and sophisticated ASW weapons and sonar suite, was not the ideal approach to a mass-production frigate stimulated work on even "cheaper" designs. By 1951 work had begun on a Type 17 gunboat type, or "Third Rate" frigate, with a single Squid, one 40-mm gun, reduced sonar, and less-powerful engines. It was hoped to build a 900-ton prototype in 1953–54 along with another new vessel, a rather larger Type 42 gun-armed diesel frigate, designed for "anti-E Boat" duties in coastal waters.[104]

It might have been better if the Naval Staff had devoted even more attention to such ships as these, as the rearmament bonanza was looking less and less realistic as the weeks of 1951 went by. The Attlee administration, in increasingly deep

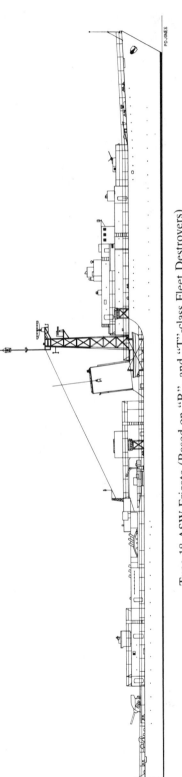

Type 18 ASW Frigate (Based on "R"- and "T"-class Fleet Destroyers)

Armament: One twin 4"/45 Mark 19 DP gun (aft)
             One twin Bofors 40/60 Mark 5 AA gun (fwd)
             One quadruple 21" torpedo tube
             Two Limbo triple-barrel antisubmarine mortars
Electronics: One Type 293 surveillance radar
             One Type 978 navigation radar

political trouble, was intending to devote some 14 percent of national income to defense, a proportion greater than that of 1939. The new Conservative Government of Winston Churchill was elected in October 1951 with a clear commitment to continue rearmament. Whether it would continue to do so was another matter, given its reassessment of Britain's economic difficulties. However, economic factors were not the only issue. Was the very idea of massive conventional rearmament a good one in an age that was already nuclear, with America about to embark on an even greater thermonuclear revolution in the technology of mass-destruction? Up to now the assumption had been that the war would be long. In 1949 American planners had Allied armies, 150 divisions strong, attacking across Europe in the third year of war, with the aim of occupying the Soviet Union. Nuclear weapons would add to the destructiveness of such a World War III, but they would not be themselves decisive. There would be time for mobilization and traditional long-drawn-out naval operations; 150 divisions would require an enormous amount of supply by sea.[105] Would politicians facing economic problems of crisis proportions continue to think in such terms? It would soon be clear that they would not.

CHAPTER · THREE

GLOBAL STRATEGY
AND RADICAL REVIEW

In the new Conservative Government, Winston Churchill restored for a time the wartime link between the premiership and the Ministry of Defence, and James Thomas (later Viscount Cilcennin) became first lord of the Admiralty. They inherited a new rearmament program that was already creaking under the strain. It was true that planned additions of ships to the active fleet, the most notable of which was the belated completion of the new 43,000-ton fleet carrier *Eagle*, were taking place. But the future looked bleaker, due to the probable reduction in the number of ships in commission in order to provide crews for new construction. The larger complement of the Type 15s and 16s meant that only two-thirds the number of frigates would be possible for each flotilla. Shortages of draftsmen as well as materials were delaying work on the new-construction program, less than half of the minesweepers and no new frigates having been laid down. Indeed, the substantial 1951–52 new-construction program (four new "First Rate" ASW frigates, twelve new "Second Rate" ASW frigates, four new AA frigates, three new A/D frigates, and forty each of coastal and inshore minesweepers, plus other vessels) had not yet been officially approved by the Defence Committee.

As for aircraft, first-line strength, 169 machines on 1 November 1951, was still short two squadrons of the authorized end-1951 total. In commission were six day-fighter squadrons, one of night fighters, eight ASW, and two torpedo strike squadrons. The first squadron of Attacker jet fighters had just been formed, but there had been problems and difficulties caused by raw material shortages. "Technical and production difficulties" were continuing to delay the Wyvern strike fighter, while labor shortages at Hawker's works at Kingston were delaying Sea Fury deliveries and the forthcoming entry into service of the Sea Hawk jet.[1]

Given the unwillingness of the Attlee Government to take draconian measures to control the economy, such delays caused by shortages of labor and materials were probably inevitable. But the strain of the rearmament program went much deeper. The new chancellor of the exchequer, R.A. Butler, was clearly horrified by the economic situation he found on taking office. Within a month he had drafted a paper for the cabinet setting out the need for drastic measures to be taken with the defense program. The import bill had risen massively, and exports of consumer goods had been disappointing. The steel shortage had limited engineering exports as well as defense production and industrial investment. A speedy solution to these problems was vital; present policies, Butler argued, were leading to ruin.

The major difficulty was the balance of payments. The government had inherited a prospective 1952 import bill of £540 million. Emergency import controls, it was hoped, would reduce these by some £350 million, but that was not enough. Exports, the chancellor insisted, would have to be increased, and the only scope for such an increase was in the engineering products of the "metal using industries," a phrase that was to dominate discussions for many months. There were such shortages of coal and semifinished products that further exports of these were not possible. Not only did engineering production have to be released for exports, Butler argued, but there also had to be a higher priority for investment in the civilian sector in plant, machinery, and vehicles in order to increase the capacity to export. Defense building would also have to be cut to release scarce building resources for use elsewhere.[2]

Even while the chancellor was making his powerful case, the Ministry of Defence was reworking its programs on the basis of spreading the existing program over four rather than three years. Nevertheless, the Admiralty planners were still aiming at an annual expenditure of over £400 million per annum. It soon seemed that even this was an unreasonable prospect. At a meeting held to discuss the "Progress of the Defence Programme," held under Churchill's chairmanship on 12 December 1951, the conflict with the Treasury became clear. Sir John Lang, the extremely able permanent secretary of the Admiralty, explained to Churchill that the estimates had been raised at the beginning of the year to over £300 million, but it seemed as if only some £279 million would actually be spent—an index of the shortfalls in the program. The estimates for the year 1952–53, it was hoped, would be some £402 million. The controller, Vice Admiral Sir Michael Denny, then explained what new vessels this money would buy, concentrating on smaller vessels and submarines.[3]

The controller made no mention of the Admiralty's more ambitious proposals, such as the new carrier, and Butler complimented the Admiralty on its moderation. Nevertheless, the chancellor insisted on cuts even to the proposals as presented. Churchill agreed, and three days later the Admiralty was faced with a note from the prime minister asking it to reduce its 1952–53 requirements from £402 million to £330 million. This was a very substantial cut that would deeply affect the new construction program and the ship modernization plans. The conversion of the carrier *Implacable* would be delayed, the recommencement of work on the *Tiger*-class cruisers postponed, and the new ships, including two projected 1,500-ton ocean minesweepers (see drawing), would have to be deferred. Stocks of equipment would not be increased after March 1952, and Reserve Fleet refits would be curtailed. Substantial cuts in the works program would also be necessary, despite the effects on morale of a continuance of poor conditions on shore. In total the Admiralty offered to reduce its program by £72 million.[4]

The effect of these cuts would be grave, but pushing them to the total level required by the Treasury or beyond would, the Admiralty argued, be disastrous, making the complete disorganization of the fleet "even more spectacular" than that of 1948. The Admiralty's case was discussed at a meeting with Churchill and Butler on 20 December. The prime minister laid down two principles for any cuts

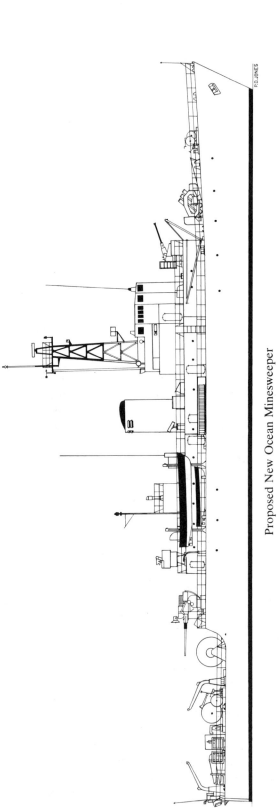

P.D. JONES

Proposed New Ocean Minesweeper

Length: 230 ft.
Armament: One single 3″/50 DP gun
One single Bofors 40/60 Mark 9 AA gun
Two 2″ rocket/flare launchers
One Squid antisubmarine mortar
Electronics: One Type 974 navigation radar
Space for Type 960 radar (AYE, AYD, AYC aerial)
One IFF Mark 10 transponder
One FM 12 MF/DF
One Type 164 sonar
One Type 63 3″ gun director

in the naval program. First, work on ships approaching completion (such as the *Daring*-class destroyers) should have priority. Second, the emphasis should be on the "maximum war power" during the next year, 1952. This principle allowed the Admiralty to save some of its program, especially its small craft, and it was able to extract from Butler estimates of £358 million for 1952. The other two services suffered more serious reductions.[5]

These cuts, agreed upon in full Cabinet on 14 January 1952, were not enough.[6] Only eight days later the Cabinet was hearing that the balance of payments situation was again resembling the disastrous situation that had led to the devaluation crisis of 1949. On the 25th, Butler was insisting that "the total burden of production for defence and exports was greater than the economy could bear." He felt that further defense cuts of £40 million might solve the problem by allowing an immediate increase in engineering exports. It would be better, the chancellor went on, to reduce the program of rearmament rather than just starve it of raw materials. The beleaguered program now acquired a new champion, Viscount Alexander of Tunis, the distinguished World War II commander, who had been picked by Churchill to take over the Defence portfolio. The failing prime minister felt that he could no longer do it full justice; Alexander was a trustworthy and "professional" alternative who, Churchill felt, could be relied upon to take a relatively docile and apolitical line. At his first cabinet meeting of 29 February, Alexander said he would begin discussions on ensuring a positive balance of payments impact for the £40 million of defense cuts, either by selling military equipment abroad, or by setting free the capacity of the "metal using industries."[7]

Finance was not the only pressure for a strategic reassessment at this time. From the prime minister downwards there was a feeling that Britain's defense preparations were somewhat wrong-headed. Britain was about to explode her nuclear bomb, and a naval task group was being formed to carry out the test in the Monte Bello Islands. The Soviet Union already had such weapons, and even more horrendous thermonuclear devices that promised another quantum leap in destructive power were under development in the U.S.A. Was it really prudent to rearm for a long-drawn-out World War II-type war under the new conditions? Would the next war not be sudden, intense, and short, with nuclear air power playing the major role? Such questions had been around since 1945, but by 1952 they had acquired greater force. In November 1951 the chiefs of staff had submitted a report on the likelihood of war with the U.S.S.R. They had concluded that the Soviets did not intend to start a total war, although as long as the West was weak in conventional arms, the Russians would exploit that weakness by "Cold War methods and local aggression." The main deterrent to war was the West's (i.e., the U.S.A.'s) "overwhelming superiority in atomic weapons." The Russians would not risk this awesome power being used against them, given their incapacity to retaliate in kind and their relatively weak (as yet) air defenses. They could not be sure that their economy would stand up to American nuclear bombardment. Intentional war was, therefore, unlikely, and unintentional conflict arising out of some escalation from limited war, or a preventive war designed to preempt the growth of Western strength, could be prevented by a judicious mixture of "resolution and restraint." By 1952 Britain's strategic problem was no longer a "one-off" buildup of forces to fight on some specific date. She was beginning to realize that the essence of her future defense policy was to maintain in the long term peacetime forces strong enough to deter an enemy, but cheap enough not to strain the economy enough to cause internal decay. Such decay was what the Russians primarily relied upon to secure their long-term goals. In effect, the British were the first to realize that the West had to find an affordable deterrent posture for the "long haul."[8]

In January 1952 the chiefs of staff asked the Joint Planning Staff to review the existing formulation of British "Global Strategy." This was enshrined in the paper that had originated in 1950 (see previous chapter) but which had been revised in May 1951. The amended document seems to have been very much a recapitulation of previous strategic thought, spiced by fears of an earlier possible Soviet attack. It still called for ambitious force goals and major rearmament. The joint planners recommended a greater stress on "fighting the Cold War" even at the expense of preparations for a hot war. The chiefs still seem to have been thinking in terms of further amendment, but the minister was wanting more than that. A meeting was arranged between the service chiefs and Alexander in early March and the minister seems to have made clear, either then or shortly afterwards, that a fundamentally new document should be drawn up. On Friday 14 April, at the suggestion of Sir John Slessor, chief of the Air Staff, the chiefs decided on a time and place for their discussion. Admiral Sir Rhoderick McGrigor, first sea lord since the end of 1951, cannily suggested the Royal Naval College, Greenwich, an offer that was duly accepted. Perhaps McGrigor reasoned that it would be difficult against such a naval background to write off the future role of the Royal Navy. The discussions were to last a week from Monday, 28 April, to Friday, 2 May.[9]

Thus took place the "Greenwich Exercise," perhaps one of the most remarkable attempts of its kind to rethink national strategy as far as possible from first principles. The three chiefs of staff made an interesting trio. There was Field Marshal

Admiral of the Fleet Sir Rhoderick McGrigor. (Imperial War Museum)

Slim, conqueror of Burma but no mere combat commander, being perhaps the most intelligent and articulate soldier of his generation. Equally intellectually gifted was Slessor, one of the Royal Air Force's prominent staff officers of the late thirties and early war years before moving on to head up Coastal Command at the time when the Battle of the Atlantic was won. Slessor had succeeded Slim as commandant of the Imperial Defence College in 1948, leaving to become chief of the Air Staff. Against these two big guns the first sea lord, Sir Rhoderick McGrigor, perhaps seemed slightly outranged, although he was no mean intellect himself, having finished top of his term at Dartmouth, despite losing time to illness. A torpedo specialist, McGrigor had a mind that was more technically orientated than those of the other chiefs, and his talents were perhaps more suited to the fighting fleet than Whitehall. A shy man, he was better on paper than in conversation, but when he felt his service, or its interests, threatened he could turn his enormous energy to good effect and put up a strong fight with not a little success.[10]

The other official to have significant impact on the results of this group's deliberations was Sir Ian Jacob. He had been military assistant secretary to the War Cabinet during the Second World War, and Churchill had demanded his appointment as chief staff officer to the Ministry of Defence soon after resuming office. The BBC, of which Jacob was now director general, reluctantly gave a year's leave of absence, and Jacob returned to the center of defense policy making the very week the chiefs of staff went to Greenwich. Jacob felt that the paper that emerged from the chiefs' deliberations was too obviously an uneasy compromise between the services, with the mark of three different authors. Something more unified was required and Jacob prevailed upon the chiefs of staff and their secretary, Brigadier F.W. Ewbank, to produce a more coherent document for presentation to the Cabinet.[11]

The first draft of "Defence Policy and Global Strategy" was ready by the middle of May. An all-day meeting of the COS Committee was held on the 20th to discuss it, and Jacob was invited to supervise the preparation of a second draft by the end of the month. This was duly done, and the new draft was discussed by the chiefs of staff, Jacob, and Sir Frederick Brundrett, a member of the Admiralty's scientific service since 1919 and now the COS's trusted chief scientific advisor. Discussions went on in early June with no less than seven meetings and yet another redrafting by the indefatigable Ewbank. Sir Pierson Dixon of the Foreign Office was invited to one meeting, and the first part was amended on his advice. Finally on the 14th of June the chiefs (and Jacob) decided that the final draft was at last satisfactory and that the paper should be forwarded to Churchill.[12]

The "Global Strategy Paper" of 1952 was one of the most significant documents in the history of postwar British defense policy.[13] It set the strategic context for the Conservative Government's defense reviews of the next five years. Given the existing intelligence assessment of the chiefs of staff, there could be no quarrel over the declared primary object of Britain's future defense program—"to provide the forces required to protect our world wide interests in the Cold War." This implied an emphasis on peace-keeping and limited war forces. The next object was unexceptionable also: "To build up with our allies in the North Atlantic Treaty Organisation forces of a strength and composition likely to provide a reliable deterrent against aggression." The problem came with the third object: "To make reasonable preparations for a hot war should it break out." The definition of "reasonable" was a contentious one, for much of Global Strategy's logic cast real doubts on the relevance of naval forces fighting a war in the new nuclear age.

The chiefs came to the disturbing, but inevitable, conclusion that no complete defense against nuclear attack was possible in the foreseeable future. The RAF fighter and bomber force would limit damage to the best extent possible; indeed, the primary role of Britain's new strategic medium bombers was held to be a counteroffensive against Soviet nuclear forces. It was accepted, however, that the main deterrent to war with the Soviets would come from the nuclear offensive threat posed by the United States Air Force. The main role of the future British nuclear bomber force was to gain influence over the direction of an Allied strategic nuclear offensive towards targets of the greatest importance to the United Kingdom.

The paper predicted that a "future war would begin with a short period of great intensity which would be followed, if a decision had not been reached in the first period, by an indefinite period of 'broken-backed' hostilities during which both sides would seek to recuperate from the wounds they had sustained and to recover strength for a further intensive effort." Little would be done to prepare for broken-backed war; war reserves were to be subordinated to preparations for the first intense period when everything British would be directed against the enemy's forces, not against his logistical or industrial bases. The emphasis in the Allies' war preparations should be "to concentrate on measures which will contribute both to their defence in the opening phase and to the violence of the initial assault on the enemy." The nuclear bombers had top priority. The paper argued for a reduced force but big enough for about a month's operations at significant strength. Then came the army, whose continued ability to make a contribution to European defense was held to be vital. As the chiefs of staff summarized their argument a few months later: "The main conclusion was that provided the deterrents of atomic air power and adequate forces on the ground were properly built up and maintained, the likelihood of war would be much diminished and we could in consequence ease our economic position by accepting a smaller and slower build up of forces, equipment and reserves for war."

There was no mention of the Royal Navy's role here, but when the paper specifically discussed naval forces, it maintained that keeping open the "vital sea lanes" against mine, submarine, surface, and air attacks would still be required. Only the previous February, Sir Henry Tizard, chairman of the Defence Research Policy Committee, had reported to the chiefs that the threat to sea communications was equal in importance to that of nuclear attack on Britain itself.[14] Submarine attacks, it was felt, would be on a larger scale than at the beginning of World War II. It would, therefore, be necessary to fight a relatively conventional naval war from the outset, but it was in the second stage that the navy would really come into its own. The most intensive theater of broken-backed war would be at sea, the chiefs' paper argued: "U-boats will continue to operate and there will still be many mines laid in the first phase still to be swept besides those which may be laid thereafter." Not only was it assumed that there would be enough people left to be worth supplying: destruction at home made foreign supply even more important. As for the problem of bombing major harbors, imports to maintain basic subsistence for the British people and to sustain their recovery could be brought in through smaller ports or even over the beaches. On this slightly tenuous basis, the paper argued that the Royal Navy should not aim to increase the quantity of ships for the ASW, antiair, and antisurface roles, but it should concentrate on improving their quality. The only area where it was recommended that numbers should be increased was in mine countermeasures vessels that would sweep the approaches to the small ports. The planned total of new frigates for 1956 would be cut by some 40 percent from the previous government's figures, the total of modernized frigates by 15 percent, and front-line aircraft by 25 percent.

McGrigor had done an excellent job in "fighting his corner" by insisting not only on the broken-backed concept but, even more importantly, on the Cold War tasks of the services and the particular contribution of the navy in fulfilling them. The first sea lord won considerable support for this latter line of reasoning in a paper presented to the Cabinet at the same time as the Global Strategy Paper.[15] In it, Anthony Eden, the foreign secretary, argued strongly that the U.K. had world responsibilities "inherited from several hundred years as a great power," that the U.K. was not self-sufficient, and that the country faced an "external threat" from the Communist world. He noted, however, that Britain was fully, if not over, committed. There was nothing in reserve and, indeed, the burden of Britain's responsibilities already seemed to be somewhat beyond her resources. Some obligations, Eden felt, might be transferred to others or reduced without seriously affecting Britain's world position, but the point might come where the choice was between a lower standard of living or "second class power status," which would cause the British people "injury to their essential interests and way of life of which they can have little conception." Precipitate withdrawal from major commitments would cause power vacuums that Russia would fill, harming Western security and economic interests. Britain's status and prestige were even more important. "Once the prestige of a country has started to slide," the foreign secretary ominously stated, "there is no knowing where it will stop." Loss of prestige would have tangible effects, such as economic and trading losses, but it is clear from the whole tenor of the paper that it was something that was deeply feared in itself.

Eden ran through the impressive list of commitments to the defense of Western Europe and to the "maintenance of a world system of garrisons and bases, e.g., Gibraltar, Malta, Persian Gulf, Singapore, Falkland Islands." He was unwilling to give up even the smallest of them. "A very minor commitment which we could endeavour to dispose of to the United States is the Falkland Island Dependencies. I do not, however, advise such action, for public admission of inability to maintain these traditional possessions would cause a loss of prestige wholly out of proportion to the saving of money obtained. It might precipitate a scramble by the numerous claimants to various parts of British territory." The study stressed that Britain should continue to carry out as extensive a world role as possible. Only thus could she convince America that the burdens were worth sharing. Eden priced Britain's overseas commitments at about half the prospective deficit on the balance of payments.

Although the Global Strategy paper promised some significant defense savings, Eden's paper showed how politically and emotionally difficult it would be to cut commitments significantly. And only by cutting these commitments could further savings be made. The alternative—forces at smaller than the Global Strategy levels to service existing commitments—was specifically warned against by the chiefs of staff. As it was, they wrote: "The reductions which we recommend in the build up and equipment of our forces can be undertaken only by incurring real and serious risks. These risks are only justifiable in the face of the threat of economic disaster."

Yet the imperatives of the economic position seemed to be that still further risks were, indeed, necessary. In June a special "Defence and Economic Policy Committee," numbered in the Cabinet Series GEN411, began to meet under Churchill's chairmanship. Its aim was to come up with ways of dealing with the balance of payments problems, both short and medium term, and to consider "to what extent, if any, does the Chiefs of Staff report on 'Global Strategy' warrant any net reduction in our defence effort?" One of the papers they had before them was a report of a working party (chaired by Mr. Richard Powell, deputy secretary of the Ministry of Defence) that had met to look at the burden defense production was putting on the "Metal Using Industries." The existing program, as spread over four years instead of three, was going to load the industries to the tune of up to £630 million by 1954, £175 million being the Admiralty demand. The committee had looked at three reduced options: A—£500 million; B—£450 million; and C—£400 million. Even option A would affect the navy by reducing stores, ammunition, aircraft deliveries, and ship modernizations and by cancelling a large number of projected warships. The only ships that would survive in the years 1952–55 would be those already ordered plus 140 new minesweepers, these being the Admiralty's absolute top priority. Among the cancellations were the restarting of the *Tiger*-class cruisers and seven new frigates that were to have been laid down in 1954–55. In option B the stores, ammunition, and aircraft cuts would be even more serious, along with further new-construction cuts, including all the twenty-five new frigates on order and the forty-five inshore minesweepers due in 1953–54. If only 420 aircraft were produced in 1954–55, then Britain would not be able to equip one of its NATO-allocated carriers, while, "most seriously of all," she would only be able to meet her goal in frigates with obsolete and rather useless ships. No new frigates would be available, or even under construction, at a time of revolutionary change in antisubmarine warfare. Option C would be marginally worse still: the fifty-seven inshore minesweepers that had not yet been laid down would be cancelled, as would the six submarines that had been ordered. Even the new royal yacht would have to go. Only the coastal minesweepers would survive. As Thomas said, implementing such cuts as these would destroy naval rearmament altogether.[16]

In early July Churchill conceded that the £500 million limit (option A) should be used to pay for the forces required for Global Strategy. The day after, on the 9th, the paper was officially adopted by the Cabinet's Defence Committee "as a basis for the revision of planned forces and defence production programmes." The Admiralty reluctantly decided that some extra marginal cuts in addition to those included in the chiefs of staff paper would reduce the metal-using load to the requisite ceiling. These included the deferment of construction of three fast tankers and some motor torpedo boats, delaying some ship modernization, and substituting four limited for four full ASW frigate conversions. The proposed Global Strategy defense budgets were duly reduced to £1,759 million for 1953–54, £1,857 million for 1954–55, and £1,867 million for 1955–56.[17]

Butler strongly opposed these figures, which he still described as "frightening." He said a rise in defense expenditure beyond the existing level of £1,462 million was not possible, and accepting the Global Strategy costings would mean that over half of the total government expenditure would be directed to defense-related construction. That would be the equivalent of an extra 2 shillings (10 pence) in the pound on the income tax. Equally the chancellor deprecated the idea that defense expenditure could continue to rise in an "unending vista." He wished to hold defense expenditure at existing levels and reduce the load on the metal-using industries to at least £450 million.[18]

Butler made his case before GEN411 on 21 July.[19] The discussion centered on the industrial question, and Alexander was conciliatory, offering to get as far towards a loading of £450 million as he could. He supported the view, however, first put by Duncan Sandys, minister of supply, that saving in overall demand might not release the specific engineering capacity required for exports. It was duly decided that that would be borne in mind when cuts were made. When the arena moved to the cabinet two days later, Alexander stoutly defended the basic costs of Global Strategy. Butler restated his position, which Alexander said was "tantamount to an abandonment of the rearmament programme." Alexander pointed out that the rearmament program was approaching maturity, with lots of equipment plans about to come to fruition, and that the chancellor's proposed cuts would make sure "that the results will be inefficient and dangerously incomplete." The defense minister offered to go as far as he could to meet the chancellor, but the Cabinet should recognize, he concluded, that it would soon be clear to allies that defense was being sacrificed to housing, consumer goods, and social services. He stated that the only way the forces could be reduced in size was by cutting commitments both in peace and war.

The Cabinet mulled the matter over. The choices seemed to be between keeping the forces at their 1952 size and not reequipping them, or cutting them and providing them with new equipment. In reply to discussion that the government's domestic spending might be cut, Butler said that he was indeed cutting investment, the social services, and consumption. Churchill himself was caught between his instinct for military security and his often-forgotten instinct for peacetime cuts in defense expenditure. He decided to let the situation ride for a while, while further discussions and investigations took place.[20]

These occurred at two levels. The relevant ministers met under Alexander's chairmanship on 31 July to decide on the general approach, their deliberations revealing a significant difference between the services. Thomas wanted each individual service to negotiate independently with the chancellor, with only minor adjustments being made for Global Strategy priorities. Lord De L'Isle, Minister for Air, shared Slessor's doubts about the navy's true commitment to the concepts of the Global Strategy paper and recognized that the RAF stood to gain from a coordinated approach based on the paper's nuclear assumptions. He suggested an agreement with the chancellor on a figure for total defense expenditure, and this was accepted. In correspondence with Butler, Alexander had already suggested a reduced figure of £1,600 million for 1953–54 and £1,700 million thereafter. The metal-using load would rise from £457 million in 1953 to £525 million by 1955. At a face-to-face meeting on 8 August Butler insisted on still lower figures—£1,600 million over three years with a £450 million limit on the use of metal. Moreover, he reiterated his preference for a still lower metal-using load, if possible. Alexander resisted quite violently. Such a program, he insisted, would result "not in a rearmament programme but in a disarmament programme." The reductions would have disastrous results on Cold War commitments, obligations to allies, and in preparations for a possible "hot war."[21]

To examine ways in which "Global Strategy" costs could be pruned, the chiefs of staff appointed a "Committee on the Reconsideration of Defence Programmes," once more under the chairmanship of the redoubtable deputy secretary. This new Powell Committee included the third sea lord and vice chiefs of staff of the other two services. The group reported to the Defence Committee via the chiefs of staff at the end of September. Its report did indeed revise Global Strategy costs down a little, an exercise from which the Admiralty actually benefited—the proposed naval expenditure over the 1953–56 period going up from £1,133 million out of £5,483 million to £1,147 million out of £5,286 million. The three proposed annual defense expenditures under Global Strategy were now held to be:

1953–54	1954–55	1955–56
£1,719m	£1,777m	£1,790m

Against this benchmark the committee looked at two reduced sums resulting from specific agreed reductions to the Global Strategy program. Cuts were made in items whose deletion would have the "least harmful" effects. The actual figures were:

	1953–54	1954–55	1955–56
Exercise I	£1,598m	£1,657m	£1,710m
Exercise II	£1,570m	£1,583m	£1,612m

Exercise I would involve, as far as the Royal Navy was concerned, losing forty minesweepers and deferring some ship modernizations. Exercise II would involve a reduction in ASW escorts "anti U-boat vessels, which the Admiralty have been at pains to safeguard under both 'Global Strategy' and Exercise I."[22] In the covering note the service chiefs made a strong plea for maintaining the Global Strategy forces. "We do not underestimate," they wrote, "the importance of restoring our economic position if we are to hold our full status and influence as a major partner of the United States in world affairs. But this in itself will be insufficient unless we can maintain our position as a strong military power, not only in NATO but in the Middle East and Asia. Our standard of living stems from our status as a great power, and this depends to no small extent on the visible indication of our greatness which our forces, particularly overseas, provide." The chiefs made clear the unacceptability of both reduced programs.[23]

Alexander decided to compromise. When he reported to the Cabinet, he supported the chiefs of staff in general terms, but came up with a slightly cut version of Global Strategy based on the doctrine of "equal misery." The army's Conqueror tank program would be cut, the RAF's (non-nuclear) B29s would be handed back to the U.S.A., and forty new RN minesweepers would be offered to the Americans for allocation to NATO. This would produce figures of:

1953–54	1954–55	1955–56
£1,645m	£1,688m	£1698m

The metal-using load was £485 million, £540 million, and £550 million respectively. Alexander argued strongly that the differences between these figures and the chancellor's were not significant given the total metal-using production of £3,500 to £4,000 million. Alexander wrote to the prime minister in strong terms that he could go no further. The chancellor was still unimpressed. The immediate crisis over the balance of payments was past, but the long-term export position had to be safeguarded. The defense load was a quarter of the metal-using industries' output of goods for export and capital investment at home. There was also the question of an uncontrolled rise in public expenditure that if not cut would be politically embarrassing and economically unhelpful. The extra defense measures in 1953–54 were equivalent to one shilling (5p) in the pound on the income tax. If the defense expenditure was really essential, then "we must partly go over to a war economy" with major changes in social and economic policy. The chancellor grudgingly conceded a future budget level of £1,550 million and a metal-using load of £450 million. That would still imply an extra balance of payments loss of £650 million, 25 percent of total visible exports and 50 percent of food imports.[24]

The dispute went on into October and November. The chancellor went up marginally to £1,570 million, the Ministry of Defence stuck to £1,645 million at July 1952 prices. On 5 November the Defence Committee thrashed the matter out, with Churchill in the chair. There were only faint possibilities of cuts in army deployments, such as on the continent if Germany rearmed. The "metal-using industries" factor now seemed less important, as it was being recognized that high costs and the resulting lack of competitiveness limited any exploitation of a reduced defense load. The prime minister, surprised at the impact on capability of relatively small amounts of money, was assured that all possible costs in support had already been made, hence the impact on combat arms. The chancellor was impressed by the magnitude of the cuts in capability the chiefs of staff had pointed out would be necessary to meet his figures. In a new paper before the committee, the service chiefs stressed this very point. Churchill was still unconvinced that cuts in both active forces and new construction were really necessary, but he decided that the full Cabinet at its next meeting should settle the matter of next year's defense expenditure.[25]

In their position papers for this vital confrontation, the various sides in the dispute set out their respective cases. Butler summed up Britain's postwar economic predicament: the need to boost exports to avoid balance of payments crises and the dependence on American aid, and the need to invest in industry to retain competitiveness. "The claims of defence and industrial investment and of our best exports are directly and inescapably competitive; they all depend on the same sections of the engineering industry." He argued that he was not anti-defense, but Britain was attempting a defense program unprecedentedly high in peacetime. In total, when all things like civil defense and atomic energy were considered, a third of all expenditure was defense related. He did not see how Britain could continue to afford armed forces of 850,000 plus a million civilians employed supporting and equipping them, some 10 percent of the work force in total. He made a plea for an agreed upon, affordable defense program that could be maintained in the long term. For their part the service ministers wrote a joint paper defending themselves from the Churchillian accusation of overspending on support services and maintenance, and arguing that there was little scope for further cuts.[26]

On 8 November, a day later, the full Cabinet debated the issue. It was a classic straight fight between the minister of defense and the chancellor. Butler said he was willing to go to £1,600 million and a £480 million metal-using load, but only "provided that a radical review of the future pattern of our defence effort is undertaken at once with due regard not only to strategic needs and foreign commitments but also to economic and financial factors." He was quite prepared to cut social programs, but his main concern was to increase industry's productivity and competitiveness by investment, which would be impossible if even the Ministry of Defence's reduced figures were accepted. It was a plain choice: defense or investment, and the non-defense cabinet members put their weight behind the view that "to accept a defence budget beyond what was economically wise now would lead to a still lower figure for defence in subsequent years."

Eventually Churchill decided the issue by giving Alexander a slight increase to £1,610 million for 1953–54 with additions allowed in certain circumstances to cover wage rises and increases in costs in Germany. (In the event, the estimates were just over £1,636 million.) Churchill reiterated his desire to see the minimum cuts in combat forces and the Cabinet decided that, as suggested by the chancellor, a "radical review" of defense policy should begin to decide on an affordable defense program. The chiefs of staff had been given their chance, but their goals were still too ambitious. The government was looking for an alternative approach that, when it came, carried the service chiefs' own logic significantly further, in directions diametrically opposed to the interests of the Royal Navy.[27]

The cuts already decided upon had a serious enough effect on naval personnel. Conscription was due to come down quite significantly during 1953–54 as retained and recalled men were allowed to leave once more. Some ten thousand seagoing billets were to be abolished at minimum cost to the active fleet. To sustain the navy's Cold War commitments some drastic manning expedients were resorted to that made many ships at least semioperational. Cruisers, fast minelayers, the "second rate" frigates of the *Black Swan*, "Bay," and "Loch" classes, and ocean minesweepers were singled out for the "temporary peacetime complements." This had the following effect on the ships' operational capabilities:

	Main Armament	Secondary Armament (if fitted)	Close-Range Armament	Sonar
Cruisers	30% manned	50% manned	30% manned	maintained not manned
Fast Minelayers	30% manned	N/A	60% manned	maintained not manned
Frigates (second-rate)	33⅓% manned	N/A	70% manned	manned
Ocean Mine-sweepers	manned	N/A	N/A	maintained not manned

Further manpower cuts, VCNS argued in a paper to the chiefs of staff, would have to mean a cut in commitments if the Royal Navy was to become anything but the "shop window" force that it was rapidly approaching.[28]

Such arguments were placed before the "Radical Review," whose first, not very radical, stage opened in January 1953. Sir Norman Brook, Secretary to the Cabinet, was made chairman of a ministerial committee tasked with studying the implications and effects of various policy changes, e.g., the end of commitments such as Korea. The chiefs of staff kept a firm watch on Brook's deliberations, and despite recommending some reductions in deployment, notably in the Far East, his report did not depart much from the basic tenets of Global Strategy. The first sea lord could take satisfaction from its reaffirmation that a short war was not an absolute certainty and that "the first aim of rearmament programmes should be to ensure national survival in the initial attack and to safeguard sea communications in the succeeding phase." Unfortunately, its repriced defense program totalled £1,830 million for 1955–56.[29]

Churchill did not think this good enough and convened a meeting on 18 June of the chancellor, Lord Cherwell (paymaster general and prime ministerial adviser), the ministers of defense and supply, and three service ministers. Butler once more took up the call for defense cuts to maintain full employment, a healthy balance of payments, and growth in industrial production. Much to the chagrin of the service ministers, Alexander acquiesced in this policy, but it was the contribution of Duncan Sandys, minister of supply and Churchill's son-in-law, that especially infuriated the first lord and his advisers. Sandys put forward an extension of Global Strategy logic that redefined the "short war" strategy in stark terms. Only those forces that contributed in peacetime to Britain's position as a world power and which were relevant to the first six weeks of war should be maintained. The following day Alexander duly dropped something of a bombshell on the service ministers and the chiefs of staff. They had to find savings of some £308 million on the 1955–56 program, and the assumption for these savings would be "that the period of the first six weeks should be considered as the time during which the United Kingdom might rely on the United States Strategic Air Force to break the Russian will to fight; our survival forces would be those to ensure the survival of the United Kingdom during that period." The defense minister defined three "categories" of forces. Most important at Category I were "minimum forces required to carry out essential Commonwealth commitments in peace." Category II comprised forces necessary to "survival" in the opening phase of a war. Lowest in priority at Category III were forces for broken-backed war.[30]

McGrigor, already very unhappy with the Radical Review, now became more belligerent than ever and emerged as its major opponent. In a chiefs of staff meeting on June 22nd he firmly asserted the navy's case to be included in Category II: "During the survival period it is a matter of critical importance that imports into the United Kingdom and lines of communication to our forces in Europe should be protected. Balanced naval forces for the survival phase are, therefore, a prime requirement."[31] He also refused to give up the broken-backed war concept.[32]

He wrote to his colleagues on 10 July reiterating the idea that the Allies could not plan exclusively on a short war and suggesting "that the first six weeks should be considered as the time during which the major atomic attacks on both sides will be delivered." "Our survival forces," McGrigor insisted, "will be those required to ensure the survival of the United Kingdom during that period, in order that she may play her part in the ensuing phase of broken-backed war which will lead to final victory."[33]

The naval tasks required to be carried out in the first six weeks of war were now defined by the Admiralty's Plans Division as:

(i) the rapid deployment of forces and their supplies to the Continent in order to delay enemy advances into Central Europe;

(ii) ensuring the supply and possible reinforcement of the NATO allies in Scandinavia to prevent its use as an enemy base against the U.K.;

(iii) the deployment of minelaying and light surface forces to shut the Baltic for as long as possible;

(iv) air, antisubmarine and mine countermeasures protection to coastal shipping so that supplies might be distributed;

(v) ensuring the "safe and timely arrival" of ocean shipping into British and European ports since it would be impossible to subsist on stockpiled supplies for any length of time.

This was deemed to require cross-Channel, North Sea, coastal, and Atlantic convoys protected against air, submarine, surface, and mining threats, plus the reinforcement of Scandinavian naval forces in both the Baltic and northern waters by surface units backed by aircraft. Given the tasks of direct convoy defense plus providing a carrier striking fleet (which might be entirely British in the first two to three weeks), the total requirement in the North Atlantic and Channel at the outbreak of war would be two fleet carriers, two light fleet carriers, four cruisers, forty-five destroyers and frigates, sixteen ocean minesweepers, twelve coastal minesweepers, eleven inshore minesweepers, one fast minelayer, twenty-one submarines, and eight motor torpedo boats. Within a month these would be reinforced by forty-six destroyers and frigates, nineteen ocean minesweepers, eighty-five coastal minesweepers, fifty-five inshore minesweepers, a fast minelayer, and four motor torpedo boats.

In order to maintain Britain's "world power" position in peacetime, a number of extra ships were required in the active fleet—the battleship *Vanguard*, one light fleet carrier, seven cruisers, thirty-one destroyers and frigates, eleven submarines, four ocean minesweepers, and five coastal minesweepers. The Admiralty also insisted that many of its reserve vessels not available in the first six weeks would be "essential for continuing the war at sea subsequently." It was "imperative" that the following ships be retained for mobilization in the first months of a future war: four cruisers, seventy-five destroyers and frigates, twenty-two ocean minesweepers, thirty-seven coastal minesweepers, and forty-three inshore minesweepers. Even the rest of the Reserve Fleet, not capable of use for six months, "might well play a valuable part in the war at sea." The chiefs of staff decided, however, that *all* the reserve ships were in Category III according to the minister of defense's definitions. It was assessed that a "Category I and II" fleet would require about 130,000 men by 1955, a reduction of some 15,000 men on 1953 strength, and it would cost around £400 million per annum to maintain. Reserve vessels only made a marginal difference to these costs, some £9 million per year.[34]

By July it was clear that perhaps the main anti-Admiralty influence in the government was Duncan Sandys. It was decided, therefore, to send two of the ablest members of the Naval Staff to see him and give him a seminar on naval strategy. On July 10th the vice chief of Naval Staff, Vice Admiral Sir Guy Grantham, and Rear Admiral Sir Anthony Buzzard, the director of Naval Intelligence, tried hard to convince Sandys of the naval case, but despite a three-hour session they had little success. The minister of supply continued to attack the Royal Navy, in particular its carrier and cruiser forces. Sandys felt that the RAF should take priority. Not only did Sandys argue that bombers and maritime patrol aircraft could take over some of the navy's direct roles, but he insisted that strategic bombers and air-defense fighter forces should have first call on the restricted defense budget. Grantham and Buzzard felt they had made some impression on the difficult minister, and in a meeting of the Radical Review Defence Ministers Committee three days later Sandys seemed to get the worst of the argument. He was not, however, to be so easily defeated.[35]

In late June Churchill had been laid low by a stroke. This left Butler, the formidable chancellor, in charge of the government, which augured ill for the Ministry of Defence and the armed forces. Sandys reopened his attack on the Admiralty when Butler reconvened the previously ad hoc Radical Review group of top ministers, now the "Defence Policy Committee," on 17 July. The minister of supply restated the need to abide by the original Alexander directive; he specifically singled out carriers and cruisers for scrutiny, asserted that land-based aircraft were more cost-effective answers to the ASW problem, and opposed cuts in the RAF's proposed force of strategic medium bombers. These ideas offered beguiling possibilities for economies. At the end of July the chancellor wrote to the minister of defense that the maximum figure he could offer him for his 1955–56 budget would be £1,650 million. He also specifically asked for "all the relief" possible in the 1954–55 estimates. Alexander divided Butler's figure up into various headings, the Admiralty receiving some £360 million of the total (only about two thirds the amount specifically allocated to each of the other service ministries). The defense minister asked for statements on the force levels that this budget would produce and the reductions that would be necessary. The £1,650 million figure was to be taken as a ceiling for succeeding years, and the "six week" criterion was always to be borne in mind. The minister allowed the services to say if a marginal increase in expenditure would lead to a major increase in capability.[36]

The Admiralty duly produced a very gloomy answer on 31 August. Thomas, the first lord, wrote plainly that the submissions contained were "not proposals that the Admiralty considered sound either from a strategic or political point of view and they are only put forward as a result of the instructions in your directive." He emphasized that the Admiralty viewed them "with grave concern." The first lord disagreed with Alexander's priorities, which were an "unsuitable basis on which to plan naval expenditure, as they place insufficient emphasis on the Navy's role in support of our foreign or colonial policy in peace, or in Cold War, and give little attention to the difficulties of getting food and raw materials into this island after the first six weeks of an atomic war." As for the services' peacetime roles, the Admiralty took its stand once more on traditional ground, quoting Britain's dependence on the sea and the dependence on the Royal Navy of British communities and trading interests all over the world. The Admiralty argued that further cuts were impossible in an active fleet that was at full stretch, although it was willing to try to run on a reduced manning level of 132,000. This would be done by serious cuts in the Royal Marines (two out of three commando units), scrapping many ships in Class III Reserve (i.e., those at extended notice that required a refit before being ready for service), and by decommissioning the *Vanguard*. The Admiralty was reluctant to lose its last battleship, which it regarded as a valuable status symbol.[37]

Indeed, HMS *Vanguard* was effectively only a status symbol in 1952–53, being officially maintained primarily for peacetime rather than wartime functions. Although allocated to the Mediterranean in Admiralty war plans, she was being used as Home Fleet flagship, having taken up this active duty in 1951. Churchill reportedly took a special interest in the ship and its importance to British prestige. The battleship's complement, however, was still much reduced, which meant that her armament would be available to NATO only at ninety days' notice! Indeed, a pessimistic Gunnery Division of the Naval Staff thought that seven months rather than three was nearer the mark for getting the ship operational. A sun lounge, fitted for the ship's "royal yacht" duties (and used in normal circumstances by the *Vanguard*'s midshipmen), made the closest main gun mount (X turret) unusable. It had long been in a state of preservation, but there were insufficient men on board fully to man the other three turrets or their magazines. Usually no main armament ammunition was carried, and to get that on board and to work up the guns' crews would take the time. The ship did carry out periodical main armament shoots with her forward turrets, both to keep up appearances and maintain morale, but these were special occasions.

As for the eight 5.25-inch turrets, all were on immediate notice materially, but only two were operational to fire starshells for tactical exercises; it would take at least a month to get the rest of the secondary armament equipped and worked up for service. As for the very impressive 40-mm AA armament, only four of the ten sextuple mountings were operational, and even these lacked directors, all of which were stored ashore (as was one mounting). Only 25 percent of the 5.25-inch magazines were filled (with starshells) and 5 percent of the 40-mm spaces, some of which had been taken up by the royal accommodation. Manning the armament, even to only 85 percent, would require over seven hundred extra men. Moreover, providing these men was not the only problem. The battleship was officially overweight thanks to its accommodation for royalty (including as well as the sun lounge and sun deck a special air-conditioning plant), plus many other alterations and additions designed to improve habitability. HMS *Vanguard* was a pleasant and spacious flagship, but a Naval Staff anxious to increase her combat efficiency seemed faced with a choice between filling an overweight ship with ammunition or with fuel should she actually ever be made into a fully combatant unit. Such matters, however, discussed at length in classified documents, did not detract from the ship's impressive appearance. The first lord summed up the situation thus: "*Vanguard* alone may not have a fighting value as decisive as the rest of the active fleet in the opening stages of a war but I have come to the conclusion that, despite the heavy cost of keeping her in commission she has a value for prestige purposes that makes it important to retain her if this can be contrived without the sacrifice of even more important things." The price paid was in fact relatively small. Putting the battleship in reserve would save a million pounds a year, scrapping her £1.6 million.[38]

When the prime minister, restored to health in September, was apprised of the course of the Radical Review, it was clear that his assessment of what were the "important things" did not entirely agree with that of the Naval Staff. He wrote a note criticizing the Admiralty for being "penny wise and pound foolish" in its willingness to scrap old major reserve warships, such as the *King George V*-class battleships, and the old armored-hangar carriers not earmarked for reconstruction. If Britain wanted the prestige of battleships, he argued, she needed a reserve to back up the single ship in commission. Plans Division felt this attitude at best ill-advised. In a paper it produced to rebut Churchill it argued as follows: "In any future war our requirements will more than ever before be for numbers of smaller ships needed to combat the menace of submarine and mine. We should be well advised, therefore, to continue concentrating a liberal measure of our financial resources on providing such vessels even if by doing so we are obliged to allow some older and larger ships to pass out of service." Together, the *King George V*s and the old carriers took 900 men and almost £500,000 annually to maintain them in reserve. The storage of some 13,000 rounds of 14-inch ammunition cost about a million pounds per year in valuable storage space. There were not very large sums, but in the prevailing climate, with the fleet possibly reduced on current plans by 50 percent over the next ten years, every saving was significant.[39]

The matter was discussed, as all battleship disposals were, before the Cabinet's Defence Committee on 10 October. The Admiralty could well turn this situation to advantage. The prime minister was, after all, adding his not inconsiderable weight to the importance of reserve vessels in broken-backed war, one of the main planks of the Admiralty's platform. If the prime minister would endorse the latter concept, a million or two on some useless old warships (probably only the battleships) was a small price to pay. The old prime minister duly said what the navy wanted to hear: "In the 'broken-backed' warfare that is likely to succeed the first atomic phase of a future war, these ships would be able to fulfil a valuable role. The more modern vessels on either side might well be lost and the situation might easily arise in which the older ships might be able to hold their own against anything left in active service on the enemy's side." Churchill went on to quote the lessons of World War II and the usefulness of the old British and U.S.-built destroyers in convoy escort. If a million pounds was at stake, the prime minister suggested, it would be better to reduce personnel. Alexander, perhaps a little angry at the apparent abandonment of his "six week's prescription," stated that no final decision had yet been made.[40]

Having received this powerful endorsement of the broken-backed scenario, the Admiralty moved into a full counteroffensive. Thomas had already put in a bid on 7 October for an allocation of £369 million, and he persisted in his request that this should be taken as the basis for a future naval budget, "which gives a minimum coherent naval strategy." In his letters and at meetings he pushed the broken-backed war scenario as a primary naval function and a reason for a large active fleet, a strong reserve, and a substantial naval manpower total. The Admiralty now argued that the P.M.'s wishes on the all-important battleships could be fulfilled on £369 million but not on sums reduced still further. Other cuts would remain, however—old fleet carriers, the war reserve of aircraft, foreign bases. Personnel strength would come down to 135,000, and there would still be some cuts in the active fleet and in new construction, albeit on a smaller scale. The Admiralty thought that the *Vanguard* and the two threatened commando units might scrape into the £369 million Navy, "a most hurtful cut" though that figure might be.[41]

The naval "£360 million" memorandum of 31 August was now rewritten in a stronger form arguing, with prime ministerial authority, that Alexander's infamous directive had now to be reinterpreted "with a recognition that naval plans must take account of the period after the initial phase." All the battleships ought to be retained, the Admiralty argued, following Churchill's line, with further reductions of the frigate conversion program to pay for them. The Admiralty made it even clearer that they found the £360 million formula a recipe for naval decline: "It must be emphasised that unless the Navy is allocated a higher proportion of the Defence Vote in the years following 1955–56 it will not be possible to make any appreciable progress with the replacement of our ageing ships and the fleet will steadily dwindle away." In monetary terms this meant nine million more than the chancellor's 1955–56 ceiling that year, twelve million more the year after, and twenty million more after that. The Admiralty predicted still larger defense estimates in the 1960s.[42]

As the Naval Staff made their bid for more money, Rhoderick McGrigor made his increasing concern at the dangers of naval cuts felt at the chiefs of staff level. In October 1953 he brought up the constitutional position of the chiefs of staff as the prime movers in the making of strategy. He asserted that their recommendations of Global Strategy were being effectively changed without their approval. It was agreed that, while reductions in the defense budget for 1954–55 might be accepted, further reductions should only be made after due consideration by the proper authorities. McGrigor and Grantham, vice chief of Naval Staff, kept up the pressure for the rest of the year, trying to get the chiefs of staff to assert their collective responsibility and bring the Radical Review under control.[43]

In truth, however, the Admiralty was skating on increasingly thin ice, especially as the other services were becoming reconciled to the chancellor's cuts. Not only was broken-backed war a relatively weak concept in itself, it implied the maintenance of an old reserve fleet rather than the build-up of a powerful, modern active one. Some within the Admiralty were putting forward ideas that might form alternative rationales for the maintenance of large naval forces. A key figure in the Admiralty Secretariat was Philip Newell, a brilliant mathematician and, as head of the military or "M" branch, the main civilian adviser to the first lord on strategy and doctrinal matters. He argued that, given the logic of mutual nuclear deterrence, war between the great powers might be limited to the conventional level. Even more radical was the director of Naval Intelligence, Rear Admiral Sir Anthony Buzzard. In July 1953 he made out a powerful root and branch critique of the "mass destruction policy" based on the immediate use of American strategic air power. He denounced it on grounds of uncertain effectiveness, arguing that the Soviet Union might well sustain grievous blows and continue fighting. He regarded the assumption of quick results as a somewhat dangerous gamble. Not only was Buzzard unhappy with the ethics of immediate attacks on civil targets, but he denounced strategic countercity bombardment as an unstable and escalatory strategy making general war less avoidable. It would bring devastating retaliation and would ultimately, once the Soviets had numerous and efficient delivery systems, be suicidal for the U.K. He also argued that this emphasis on mass destruction diverted attention away from military targets that were significant to the actual conduct of the war. Buzzard was in favor of limiting nuclear weapons to military targets in the first instance, keeping a deterrent force in reserve to prevent attack on Western urban industrial targets. The "survival period," he argued, should be defined as up to a year, and NATO should deploy conventional forces sufficient at least to hold Scandinavia or France.[44]

It seems that such ideas were not shared by many of Buzzard's colleagues, or by Rhoderick McGrigor. The first sea lord, for one, was becoming attracted by the prospect of naval forces adding their weight to a "mass-destruction" nuclear attack. In the future, he argued, naval platforms such as submarines might prove the best launchers for long-range bombardment. For the time being the carrier provided the best solution. There can be little doubt that such analyses enhanced a growing tendency of British naval doctrine to emphasize just the kind of carrier strike fleet operations of which Slessor had been so critical in 1950. At that time Slessor was probably underestimating the Admiralty's commitment to convoy defense, but the appearance of a spectacular new naval surface threat after 1950 did edge the Admiralty firmly away from the direct defense of shipping as the major case for its carrier fleet. The commissioning of the impressive 16,000-ton *Sverdlov*-class cruisers caused an enormous stir, as these seemed to be excellent long-range raiders. The best counter was obviously the Admiralty's carrier force, but, rather to its surprise, the Naval Staff found that it was highly doubtful that any of its existing or near-term aircraft could inflict damage to a *Sverdlov* with bombs or rockets. Naval Aviation's only real strike aircraft, the Firebrand, was considered to have some potential with either a 2,000-lb. armor-piercing bomb or torpedo, but there were doubts over the bomb's ability to kill the ship, or the torpedo's capability of hitting a fast, freely maneuvering target. In any case there were only two squadrons of these aircraft. The Firebrand replacement, the Wyvern, was still suffering technical problems, and some of its weapons, such as an HTP-powered torpedo, were still at an early stage of development (and never in fact appeared). The main operational rationale for recommissioning the *Vanguard* in 1951 was that her guns and the 6-inch main armaments of Britain's own cruisers were considered to be rather more reliable "*Sverdlov* killers" than aircraft. Antisurface-ship warfare was placed as a top priority in the design of the new 5-inch armed cruiser-destroyer. In addition to these developments the proportion of front-line aircraft was signif-

The threat that dominated much Royal Navy thought in the early 1950s, the Soviet *Sverdlov*-class cruiser. The name ship of the class, seen here, made a suitably salutary impression at the Coronation Review of 1953. (Imperial War Museum)

icantly altered. Instead of devoting almost half of the navy's combat air strength to ASW operations, this type of aircraft would now be reduced to just over a quarter. Strike aircraft would rise from a tenth of the inventory to almost a fifth.[45]

There is no doubt that the creation of NATO reinforced the tendency towards forming a British Atlantic strike fleet strategy. By early 1953 the Mediterranean was no longer providing the main war scenario for the British fleet carrier force. That theater would get but one light carrier in the opening stages of a future war. What fleet carriers there were available would make up Carrier Group 2 of the NATO Striking Fleet in the Atlantic. This "battlefleet" had an aura that the traditional Mahanian instincts of the Naval Staff found irresistible.

The offensive striking fleet allowed the Naval Staff to argue for increases in both its fighter force and its bomber force. The main Soviet counter to striking fleet operations would be the Soviet Naval Air Force, which was increasingly becoming equipped with Tupolev Type 35 jet bombers (later NATO code-named Bosun: Soviet designation Tu16). Defense against these aircraft would require both more and better fighters. In August 1952 the ASW proportions in the front line were reduced yet again to boost the fighter strength. Developing the new ultra-high-performance N113 fighter (later named Scimitar) remained just as important in the new context as it had been in its originally intended role of defending sea communications in the Mediterranean (not that that function might not still be necessary). The new high-performance, all-weather fighter, the DH110 also remained an essential complement. Not only did the Admiralty insist on keeping these two sophisticated types, but it was actively pursuing once again the concept of a nuclear-capable heavy attack aircraft. Some kind of navalized variant of the RAF's Canberra bomber was considered, and this led to a requirement, issued in June 1952, for a new jet strike aircraft of much more advanced design and performance, the NA39. It was to have a range of over 400 miles, be capable of Mach 0.85 at 200 feet, and would be very suitable for attacking land targets as well as sweeping *Sverdlov*s from the seas. The Ministry of Aviation issued specification M148T in August, and various designs were offered by, among others, Blackburn and Hawker.[46]

It was perhaps no coincidence that the same month that the NA39 requirement was issued the Admiralty gave provisional approval for its new fleet carrier. This was a slightly ironic result of the first stages of Butler's cuts. The decision to run rearmament over four years, not three, caused the *Implacable*'s scheduled modernization to be delayed. This delay turned out to be fatal. As Butler kept up the pressure for cuts in 1952, the whole modernization scheme for the remaining ships was abandoned. This gave an additional rationale for the Admiralty's planners to push ahead with the completely new 50,000 tonner. In June 1952 the Board decided on this policy and hoped the ship would be completed by 1958. The prime minister was initially enthusiastic. In the prevailing spirit of economy, the old carrier *Formidable* and the old "Hunt"-class escort destroyers would provide the steel for the new ship. It was specifically stated that the new ship was to be capable of operating a large strike aircraft to carry the planned "tactical" nuclear bomb.[47]

This thrust for a strike and high-performance fighter capability inevitably brought upon the Admiralty the ire of the RAF, strongly supported by Mr. Duncan Sandys and his Ministry of Supply, to which Admiralty ambitions seemed something of a duplication of effort in the prevailing atmosphere of financial cuts. Ever since

Global Strategy, the fundamental controversy between Air Ministry and Admiralty over the maritime air question, which had been smothered by the Korean War and the rearmament program, had begun to smolder once more. The Maritime Air Defence Committee had been called back into being in the autumn of 1952, with Sir Frederick Brundrett of the Ministry of Defence in the chair, to enquire into the question of a greater integration of Naval Aviation and the RAF. The committee's deliberations mainly concerned the ASW role, and Brundrett and his assistants came out even more in favor of carriers and their aircraft than Templer had done. Helicopters were specifically endorsed because of their much greater capability against deep, quiet submarines than sonobuoy-fitted aircraft. New operational concepts were explored, such as the use of large passive sonar arrays to vector ASW forces on to submarines, but convoy was still the main scenario. The naval representatives on the committee, however, used the opportunity to assert the role of carriers in striking at precise long-range targets, perhaps even with nuclear weapons.[48] In February 1953 the VCNS and his RAF counterpart produced a mutual statement for the chiefs of staff that seemed to be something in the nature of a truce. Its terms set down that naval aircraft could be "employed in the attack of targets and the support of land forces in areas where shore based aircraft cannot be deployed economically or based within range." Carriers were necessary, the vice chiefs argued, at distances of more than fifty miles from the shore, and their presence with escort groups or fleets conferred great tactical advantages. They were also very useful for carrying troops. Shore-based aircraft were also necessary, however, when bases were favorably placed or when the weather made carrier operations impossible.[49]

This report concluded with the usual desire for more maritime aircraft, but in the context of the Radical Review this was not very likely. Indeed, the Admiralty's carrier plans were pruned significantly to reflect the new financial climate. On 8 July 1953 the new fleet carrier project was abandoned, although preliminary design work continued on a smaller ship to be laid down, it was hoped, in 1957. At first the Naval Staff looked at ships in the 20,000–24,000-ton bracket, which would be useful as convoy escort fighter carriers, with complements of twenty-four to twenty-eight aircraft, and which might in the future operate vertical take off and landing (VTOL) aircraft. Some radical and novel flight-deck layouts were examined. In the medium term the immediate problem was ensuring the procurement of a second generation of conventional jet aircraft, and modernizing existing carriers to operate them. The aircraft production plans were reduced slightly to sustain a slightly smaller front line (230 rather than 260), but this still meant expenditure of about £35–36 million per annum on aircraft in the mid-1950s, rising to around £50 million by 1960. The higher figures were necessitated by the new types coming into service from 1957 onwards, the N113 (Scimitar) day fighter, with nuclear strike capability, and the DH110 (Sea Vixen) all-weather fighter. These would completely replace the Sea Hawk and Sea Venom jets and the Wyvern turboprop strike aircraft in carriers by 1960.[50]

To operate the new fighters and the new NA39 bomber due about 1961, both the *Victorious* and *Hermes* had their modernization specifications expanded to include 984 three-dimensional radar, Mk.13 arrester gear, and those two vital modifications developed by British officers grappling with the problems of operating modern aircraft from inadequate platforms, fully angled flight decks and steam

The only armored hangar carrier to receive a full rebuild to modern standards was the *Victorious*, seen here in the early 1960s with "Buccaneer" and Sea Vixen aircraft. Note the large 984 three-dimensional radar and the American three-inch guns.

catapults. This delayed their completion until 1958 and 1959 respectively. The *Eagle* was slated for full modernization to the same standard by 1961, and the Admiralty also hoped to convert both the *Centaur* and *Bulwark* to fully modified *Hermes* standards by 1962. This would give a carrier fleet of five ships capable of operating every type of modern aircraft and carrying out strike missions with nuclear weapons into the next decade. In the shorter term, by 1956 the Royal Navy hoped to have two fleet carriers, the *Ark Royal* and *Eagle*, and four light fleets, the *Centaur*, *Albion*, *Bulwark*, and *Warrior*, all with partially angled decks and capable of operating the combination of Sea Hawk day fighters, Sea Venom all-weather fighters, and Gannet ASW aircraft. (The *Vengeance* was now deleted from the partial modernization plan, being loaned instead to Australia to cover for delays to the

The arrival in the mid-1950s of the *Hermes*-class light fleet carriers coincided with the appearance in quantity of jet aircraft with the Fleet Air Arm. Here refueling from the tanker *Tidereach* is HMS *Bulwark*, last of the three unmodified ships to be commissioned, at the end of 1954. She is operating Sea Hawk and Sea Venom fighters, and a Skyraider AEW aircraft is clearly visible aft.

820 Squadron received the Gannet AS1 in March 1955 and embarked in *Bulwark*, the Trials and Training carrier for the exercises in September of that year. Here two aircraft are catapulted off. (Imperial War Museum)

Melbourne.) The carrier program was costed at £3.3 million for 1954–55, rising to £9.7 million for 1957–58.[51]

At the end of October the question of the Royal Navy's aviation plans was raised at a defense ministers' meeting. Thomas, the first lord, was asked to define the roles, both wartime and peacetime, of the different types of carrier, the targets against which they should be used, and the proposed strength, both active and reserve. The Admiralty's answer was ready in time for a defense ministers' Radical Review meeting on 10 November. Thomas explained the different roles of the different carrier types. The fleet carriers were for offensive operations and for air defense of naval forces and convoys against heavy air attack outside the range of land-based fighters. Light fleet carriers were (a) for the defense of convoys and shipping in the open ocean against lighter air attacks and (b) the ASW defense with up-to-date ASW aircraft of ocean convoys. They could also carry strike aircraft if required to face a surface threat. The Admiralty also cited the continued usefulness of escort carriers being attached to important convoys to give enhanced ASW protection. Only one wartime CVE, the *Campania*, had been retained (used variously as a Festival of Britain exhibition ship and an HQ vessel for Britain's first nuclear test). She would revert to her designed role in war. The four unmodernized light fleet carriers, *Theseus*, *Ocean*, *Glory*, and *Triumph*, that were being demoted to non-flying training duties as the *Hermes* class appeared, also had a wartime CVE role. These ships would operate the NA32, the Seamew, when it appeared. The paper also made the fact that carriers were essential for many peacetime roles, not the least being their capacity to transport large quantities of troops.[52]

In a strongly worded covering note, Thomas tried to correct any misconceptions that he felt might exist about Admiralty policy. The first lord made it clear that the Admiralty had no intention of building a fleet carrier in the American *Forrestal* category. The British carriers had a vital role to play in the striking fleet, whose function was "analogous to the Grand Fleet of World War I and the British Home Fleet of World War II, namely the offensive force for Atlantic and northern waters, and the essential cover under which defensive forces, protecting our shipping from attack by aircraft, submarine and mine can do their work." Attacks "at source" by the striking fleet on the various threats to sea communications could "materially reduce these threats," but Thomas was careful to argue, quoting General Omar Bradley, chairman of the U.S. Joint Chiefs, that the carriers were an additional, complementary deterrent, not a substitute. The paper rehearsed the arguments about the British carrier striking force being the only one available in northern waters until D + 15, and the voice it gave to Britain in the employment of the whole fleet. Shore-based aircraft could only provide cover in the North Atlantic and Mediterranean; carriers could provide air cover and air strikes in other areas at short notice. The first lord concluded by pointing out ". . . the disastrous results which would follow if, in spite of the strategic need, fleet carriers were abolished from the Royal Navy. In the eyes of the rest of the world we would cease to be a major naval power." Thomas concluded in a serious vein: "I must ask you to bear in mind the effect of this on the morale of the Royal Navy and on its confidence in any Board of Admiralty which agreed to such a measure."[53]

The 10 November meeting first discussed the £1,650 million total, and Thomas and Sandys immediately clashed on the viability of this figure. De L'Isle, the air minister, loyally supported the minister of supply, and the army representatives reluctantly acquiesced in the limit also. Thomas held out for his extra £9 million for 1955–56, but Sandys held out the prospect of extra savings: some of the extra £11 million he would need that year on present plans could be effected by reductions in the Fleet Air Arm. After this sparring, the ministers got down to the naval air question. Thomas insisted that: "However little money was allocated to the Admiralty they [sic] would certainly give naval air a high priority for expenditure within it. The Navy simply could not do its job without it."[54]

Sandys counterattacked strongly. As he understood it naval aircraft were needed for three purposes: (1) the defense of Norway, (2) offensive operations in the Baltic and North Sea and minelaying in enemy waters, and (3) the protection of Atlantic convoys against Russian raiders. The first role, he argued, "bore no relation as a matter of strategic priority to the defence of Western Europe or of the United Kingdom," and the other two functions could be carried out by land-based aircraft and the U.S. fleet. Sandys ended by agreeing that "carriers were desirable and should be provided if money were unlimited," but "he could not argue that, in the situation with which we were faced, we could afford to spend any money on them." De L'Isle chimed in at this point to say that an early decision was required. In his view "the share of the Defence Budget allocated to the Royal Air Force must certainly increase."[55]

It was decided that the various protagonists should produce papers setting out their positions. The Admiralty drafted a memorandum on the role of aircraft carriers that set out its case cogently and powerfully. It argued that aviation was integral to the fleet and that the Fleet Air Arm played a vital role in Cold War

Duncan Sandys (center), Minister of Supply and the Royal Navy's most implacable and indefatigable opponent of the 1950s, especially on the carrier question, after just being flown on board HMS *Eagle*. On his left is his anti-carrier ally, Lord de L'Isle and Dudley, the air minister. (Imperial War Museum)

tasks. All three types of carrier—fleet, light fleet, and escort—were required as part of the deterrent against war and to protect vital sea communications if war came. The point about NATO commands was given its due weight. "To play a part in world affairs, particularly within NATO, worthy of a nation whose greatness is founded upon and whose survival depends upon seaborne trade, and which now holds the major Allied sea commands in the crucial areas, we need a Navy wherein the Fleet Air Arm is an essential component. Otherwise we forfeit our right to be considered as a major naval power and therefore as a world power."[56]

It must be remembered that the NATO command question was an especially sensitive one at this time. In August 1950 Britain had reluctantly accepted the American proposals on the Atlantic command, and two months later they were approved at the October meeting of the North Atlantic Defence Committee.[57] The news leaked out in early 1951 and caused such an outcry that the question was discussed at Cabinet level. Some ministers made their displeasure felt, and their feelings and those of the other critics were reflected in a *Times* editorial: "Nothing for many years has aroused so much deep and heated feeling—and real alarm—as the news that supreme naval command in the North Atlantic Treaty Organisation was to go to an American admiral. This was no mere matter of hurt national pride. It was rather the sense that the safety itself of these Islands was being put at outside disposal, the fear that the responsibility of British admirals for the British lifeline was being put into commission."[58]

It remained still to be decided what SACA's powers should be, however (the acronym SACLANT came later). As VCNS described it to the Cabinet's Defence

Committee in March 1951 ". . . after a considerable amount of argument it was proposed that in peace he should exercise operational planning functions only and should be responsible for the co-ordination and training exercises of Allied Fleets. He should have no right of inspection, no power to recommend the deployment of navies and no power to command except for training exercises during peacetime." The commander of the Eastern Atlantic was the British CinC Home Fleet. A British admiral was also to be deputy supreme commander. The British hoped that the Americans had not gained a great deal by having the supreme command as CINCEASTLANT would be the main operational commander.[59]

Churchill, in opposition, led the attack on these proposals, and his election delayed their introduction. Only after a visit to Washington as new prime minister at the beginning of 1952 was it agreed finally, against Churchill's "better judgement," that the agreement should go through as planned with the chop line between the Eastern and Western Atlantic moved somewhat farther west to the 100-fathom line. It was also agreed that a Channel command should be set up, as suggested in October 1950 by the Dutch, to supervise cross-Channel convoys. The British desire to assert national control over these was resisted by the French and Dutch, and a separate international Channel command structure was set up with the British Commander in Chief Portsmouth as Allied CinC Channel.[60]

Command arrangements in the Mediterranean posed still greater problems. The Americans were determined to keep the carriers and amphibious forces of their Sixth Fleet firmly tied into the land battle on the southern flank of the NATO European command. An American admiral was appointed to the Southern European Command, and the Americans proposed that he control all the Mediterranean except the far eastern end, which would be under a British admiral associated with a British Middle Eastern Command. The British were determined to maintain their Mediterranean Fleet's responsibility for sea communications throughout the Mediterranean, and although they were willing to concede some special provisions for U.S. naval support of the Southern Flank land battle, they held out for a British naval CinC, directly subordinate to Supreme Allied Commander Europe (SACEUR). The Americans conceded the principle of a British commander but insisted on his continued subordination to CINCSOUTH. Personal negotiations were held between Admiral Fechteler, the American chief of naval operations, and the British chiefs of staff, but both sides stuck to their positions. When he was appointed British CinC Mediterranean Fleet in 1952, Vice Admiral Mountbatten (as he then was) was ordered not to do anything that implied subordination to CINCSOUTH. Relations between the British command at Malta and the Americans at Naples steadily deteriorated. The main problem was over the transfer of submarine and convoy planning to Malta, but at last in December 1952 a compromise was made. The British Mediterranean Fleet Commander was to become NATO CinC Allied Forces, Mediterranean (CINCAFMED), responsible to SACEUR for all naval operations *except* those of the Sixth Fleet, which remained directly subordinated to CINCSOUTH. The new NATO Headquarters became operational at Malta in March 1953, but relations remained very uneasy with Naples and its rival naval "Strike Force Headquarters." Only when Admiral Carney was replaced at Naples by Admiral Fechteler did relations improve.[61]

The final source of Anglo-American friction on the question of naval command was the IBERLANT affair. The U.S.A. had wanted to set up a CINCIBERLANT, coequal with CINCEASTLANT under the Atlantic Supreme Commander. This proposed area covered the waters off Spain and Portugal to the west of Gibraltar. The Americans, anxious about reinforcing both their southern armies and the Sixth Fleet, wished to set up a major NATO command under an American officer at Lisbon. The British, claiming dominant interest in the shipping in the area, and a flag officer at Gibraltar, strongly disagreed. A modus vivendi was patched up in which the proposed IBERLANT area was delegated to EASTLANT, with a small integrated staff element at Gibraltar. The British wanted this to become an IB-ERLANT HQ under CINCEASTLANT's overall command. In the end British opposition delayed the creation of an IBERLANT command as desired by the Americans until as late as the mid-1960s![62]

Britain had, in fact, done quite well in the allocation of NATO Commands: Eastern Atlantic, Allied Forces North, Mediterranean, and Channel. The Naval Staff were to reiterate increasingly the possibility of losing these positions if the British withdrew from the striking fleet. This argument, and the related one that the British Carrier Group 2 gave Britain a powerful say in the utilization of the whole Allied carrier force, came to become more important as the attack began to center on the continued British possession of *fleet* carriers. Sandys and his Air Ministry allies emphasized the duplication of effort these ships implied, both with the Americans and with the RAF, in the role of bombing land targets. In return the Admiralty made the point that the main argument in favor of the RAF's planned medium-bomber force was the influence it might give over the general Western bomber offensive. It was as important to have influence over the main NATO Striking Fleet's AJ-1s or A3Ds as it was over the United States Air Force's B47s and B36s.[63]

At the end of November 1953, at a meeting of the full Defence Policy Committee, Churchill ordered an enquiry into the carrier question "before a great deal more money was spent on the production of expensive naval aircraft and the moderni-zation of carriers."[64] At the beginning of December, the faithful Alexander duly asked the Admiralty what would be the effect on both its aircraft production and carrier modernization program if carriers were limited to the "local protection of convoys and fleets operating with them against attack by submarines and aircraft particularly in the North Atlantic."[65] At first the Admiralty "assumed" that the two fleet carriers, if withdrawn, would be replaced by CVLs on convoy duties. It also considered that both of its new fighters were necessary to cope with current Soviet aircraft and their successors. The Ministry of Defence asked for new costs on the basis of not replacing the fleet carriers by CVLs, on the assumption that the two fleet carriers would be mobilized for convoy escort duties in war. It also expressed the opinion that the Sea Hawk and Sea Venom were perfectly adequate to deal with the long-range recce aircraft met in the open oceans for the foreseeable future, and that a much simpler fighter than the DH110 or N113 could be procured to replace them. Much to the annoyance of the admirals, the Treasury was refusing to sanction any orders for the DH110. (The Ministry of Supply was also holding up orders for the NA39.)[66]

The Defence Ministry's compromise proposals were drafted in January 1954. Alexander had found a chink in the Admiralty's armor. Cutting back on fleet carriers would save, on their own admission, some £10 million in 1954–55, £20 million in 1955–56, £23 million in 1956–57, and £12.5 million in 1957–58. This was perhaps the only area where such short-term savings could be made. As Alexander put it: "The problem is . . . not simply one of the intrinsic desirability or otherwise of maintaining fleet carriers but one of priority for the expenditure of scarce resources and of obtaining the best value for money." To do this Alexander suggested a compromise solution: the *Ark Royal* was to be completed (to cancel her at this stage would have been difficult), but she would only be equipped as a *light* fleet carrier. The *Eagle* would be relegated to trials duties and the *Illustrious* maintained for training. Three light fleet carriers would be retained, but not an extra ship for trials and training. The front-line air establishment would be reduced from 250 to 160. Most significant of all, both the *Victorious* and *Hermes* would be cancelled. This would leave sufficient carrier capability to defend fleets and convoys from submarines and aircraft in the open oceans, but the U.S. Navy would be relied upon to deal with raiders and for attacks on shore targets.[67]

Hardly surprisingly the Admiralty rejected these proposals. It counterattacked by casting serious doubt on the viability of the RAF's planned medium bombers against evolving Soviet defenses. There were echoes both of the bomber vs. battleship controversies of the 1930s and of the B36 controversy in the U.S.A. only a few years before in the competitive costings of fleet carriers and strategic bombers; two fleet carriers were deemed to be the equivalent of only twenty-seven medium bombers and their bases. The Admiralty made the case strongly that naval aircraft might well be a more viable means of nuclear delivery than the high-flying Valiants, Vulcans, and Victors (the "V" bombers). Carrier aircraft could carry out surprise raids at low altitudes, possibly at longer ranges than those at which a medium bomber was capable. They were also more effective minelayers. Yet the Admiralty and Naval Staff also recognized that if they made too much of this point, the RAF might well dig in its heels more firmly. More powerful were the arguments that the minister's proposals *still* implied a new generation of combat aircraft and that Alexander's apparent recent softening on the question of the use of aircraft to protect against enemy surface warships meant that the NA39 was required to deal with the *Sverdlov* in the open sea, "all that is saved by omitting from the naval tasks offensive action against enemy targets at source and offensive minelaying are relatively minor adaptations to some of these aircraft." Rather disingenuously the Naval Staff stated that it would "not feel itself justified in setting a requirement for an aircraft solely to attack shore objectives and to lay mines." The NA39, it said, was primarily a *Sverdlov* killer, although it might be an "economical method" of delivering "small atomic bombs" on important targets "within a few hundred miles of the enemy coast."[68]

On 22 February 1954 the first lord wrote to Churchill to reiterate the "very strong" feeling of the Board of Admiralty on the carrier question. The Alexander compromise would, he said, take away the striking power of the navy, and the Admiralty felt that the promise to NATO of the two heavy carriers fully equipped with the latest aircraft was of "supreme importance." He asserted the navy's need for nuclear-capable aircraft and argued that "all naval circles, British and Allied, would be alarmed to see that the finest heavy carriers in the world for North Atlantic conditions are not to be used for the purpose for which they were built and for which they are so well suited." Knowing the prime minister's sensitivity on this point, Thomas raised the NATO Command question once more and went on to assert that the retention of fleet carriers was absolutely vital to the navy's self-respect. He also pointed out the political opportunities that the cancellations would give to the Opposition.[69]

By this time the tide was turning in the Admiralty's favor. One important factor was that Duncan Sandys was hors de combat due to illness. Another was that the RAF had been made to recognize that it was treading on dangerous ground. As the attack on the carrier had risen in strength, so the navy had reopened an offensive for the transfer of RAF Coastal Command. There was a danger of this being considered as a compensation for the loss of the fleet carriers (and it is clear that the first lord and Naval Staff had some reservations about the transfer), but it was a good way of exerting pressure on the RAF and giving them an actual interest in the navy's retention of fleet carriers. Similarly, the growing attack on the V bombers threatened the RAF at its most sensitive point of all.[70]

As early as December 1953 McGrigor and Air Chief Marshal Sir William Dixon, the chief of the Air Staff, seem to have come to an informal agreement that was the basis for a truce. Bomber Command, they agreed, could not substitute for the Striking Fleet without substantial reinforcement. Even the latter might not make possible attacks on northern Soviet air bases. It was even agreed that a carrier strike might be more effective against northern targets and that carrier aircraft might be better suited to mining in northern waters. The two officers agreed that ". . . a contribution of two fleet carriers was a small price to pay for having a say in the employment of the Striking Force." Having got the carriers, it was "wasteful not to use them."[71]

On this basis a settlement seems to have been made at the end of February or shortly afterwards. The Admiralty accepted £360 million (£375 million at 1955 prices), but were allowed to fit a fleet carrier capability into that figure (realistically, the Naval Staff had been planning on this basis since August 1953). Newell felt that the key to victory had been that "if the RAF was to be allowed to keep up with the American Joneses then the principal applied also to the navy, and possibly with greater force since our carriers exist and it would be folly not to spend the few million to use them."[72]

In March 1954 the Naval Staff confirmed its victory with Alexander by impressing him with its ability to think ahead. Thomas had been stung by a *Times* editorial of 31 December 1953 that argued that "the weakness of the admirals' case until now has been their inability to make up their minds about the types and numbers of new ships they want to build for an atomic age." McGrigor claimed in reply that there were such plans, constantly updated as the expected financial provision changed. On 21 January, however, Thomas received a letter from the defense minister that seemed to demonstrate that Alexander and his advisers shared the views of the *Times* leader writer. A draft on long-term plans was quickly cobbled together by Plans Division from two existing long-term planning papers, and in February it was shown to the Admiralty's friend at court in the Defence Ministry, Sir Frederick Brundrett. With his comments on the navy's importance as an "ancillary deterrent" in the future, the paper was duly forwarded to Alexander by Thomas on 2 March.[73]

The paper, entitled "The Navy of the Future," began by asserting that the aim of the Royal Navy would still be a traditional one, "to use the sea to impose our will upon the enemy, while denying him its use and preventing his interference with our essential sea communications." Various long-term technical advances were quoted, plentiful atomic weapons, antiaircraft missiles, long-range detection of enemy submarines, VTOL aircraft, nuclear-propelled ships, 200-mile-range anti-ship missiles and "the possibility of the development of ship-launched ballistic rockets of considerable range which will carry atomic warheads and land accurately." The implications of these developments were held to be (a) the end of the gun-armed ship, with aircraft and missiles taking over the offensive role; (b) the decline in importance of convoy escort after the next decade and its replacement by torpedo countermeasures, interception of submarines in transit, and attacks on bases. Considerable confidence was expressed in the efficacy of these new anti-submarine measures and it was thought that this would increase the importance of air attack. To protect against that, VTOL fighters from the small carriers and AA missiles would provide defense, along with offensive strikes on airfields. Mine warfare would also remain important.

In addition to the "accepted naval tasks," the Naval Staff argued that the declining effectiveness of long-range bombers against missile defenses meant that long-range rockets were going to become much more important. The sea, the Staff argued, provided a useful base for these new weapons, drawing counterfire away from the vulnerable United Kingdom and allowing the deployment of shorter-ranged weapons that might well be available earlier, both ballistic or any other "unmanned vehicle of air attack." In a prescient passage the paper stated, "If the launching ship were submersible, her vulnerability to enemy attack would be reduced."

The future fleet, therefore, would be composed of: (a) ballistic-missile ships, both surface and submarine; (b) various other types of missile ships; (c) aircraft carriers; (d) offensive ASW vessels; (e) vessels for controlling convoys and directing A/S helicopters; (f) submarines, primarily for ASW duties; (g) "mine huntin', fishin' and shootin' forces"(!). By 1965 the Naval Planners estimated that helicopters for ASW and antimine warfare would be in service, guided missiles would have replaced AA guns for high-level defense, nuclear weapons would be available for carrier-based aircraft, and midget submarines and long-range shore sonar stations should be operating. Vertical or short take off and landing aircraft might allow the use of small carriers and one or two "seaborne ballistic rocket launchers," and nuclear-powered submarines might be operational. The rockets they carried might have a range of only some 1,000 miles or less. "The strategic air offensive will thus still primarily be conducted by aircraft," the Naval Staff stated, but "naval forces will form a necessary part of this offensive." Due to the increasing vulnerability of large high-flying bombers and the existence of targets only reachable by carrier-based aircraft, "low flying attacks from fighter supported carrier aircraft will, therefore, need to be fully exploited."

The Admiralty, therefore, looked forward to a fleet as shown in table 3-1. The expected 1965 figures were set alongside the projected figures for end-1954, and they make an interesting comparison. It was a brave vision, and remarkably accurate in some ways. The defense minister was impressed. Alexander congratulated Thomas on the paper's imagination and "careful forward looking thought." But the Royal Navy in 1965 would be somewhat smaller than expected in early 1954. The reason was that further financial pressures could not be so easily staved off. Alexander might be satisfied with the Royal Navy's plans, but Churchill was not.[74]

Only the following month a new second round of the Radical Review opened.

TABLE 3–1.

THE PROPOSED ROYAL NAVY FROM END 1954 TO 1965.

	1965	End 1954
Aircraft Carriers:		
New light fleet carriers for jet reaction aircraft	2*	—
Modernised (able to operate all naval aircraft in service in 1956)	7	—
Interim modernised (able to operate all naval aircraft in service in 1954)	—	5
Partially interim modernised (able to operate certain modern aircraft in 1954)	—	1
Unmodernised (only able to operate obsolete aircraft and helicopters) M.A.C. Ships (merchant ships selected for conversion to aircraft carriers in war—will also be able to operate these aircraft)	5	11
	14*	17
Battleships and Cruisers	7	31
Guided Weapon Ships (including conversion of existing hulls)	4	—
Fleet and Convoy small G.W. Ships and AA Gun Ships	70–80	
Fleet, Convoy and Offensive A/S vessels	75–85	Destroyers 270
Fleet and Convoy Air Control and Air Warning Ships	15–20	Fleet and Convoy Escorts
	160–185	
Ocean Minesweepers	40	64
Coastal and Inshore Anti-Mine Vessels	315	200
Submarines	50	57
X Craft (Midget Submarines)	8	2
and appropriate Fleet Train, small craft for local defence and other purposes and auxiliaries.		

Source: Section 8A, ADM205/102.
*Plus 2 building

The immediate cause was the sudden British recognition of the overwhelming power of the hydrogen bomb. Not only did Churchill want Britain to build this weapon, but the prime minister and chancellor saw its advent as yet another opportunity to reduce the defense budget still further. In April, the very month Churchill's special Cabinet Committee on the H-bomb question (GEN464) first met, a new phase of the Radical Review opened with a new Defence Expenditure Committee being tasked with assessing the scope for yet more reductions in defense expenditure. The options looked at were cuts of £30 million or £60 million. This review was to be simultaneous with another chiefs of staff Global Strategy assessment.[75]

The Admiralty reluctantly listed possible cuts in descending order of acceptability. At the top were: disposing of surplus tank-landing ships to the Ministry of

Transport; scrapping a large number of reserve ships (including the battleships); and reducing the *Vanguard* to reserve. At the bottom were cuts in the hard-fought-for carrier program. The Admiralty was indeed able to retain its two fleet carriers, but had to come down to only two running CVLs, the *Centaur* and *Albion*. The *Bulwark* was to be relegated to trials and training duties, but the *Warrior* was retained to cover the *Centaur*'s planned modernization from 1956. This, plus a front-line establishment of 225 aircraft, contributed to the agreed savings of £25 million on the Naval Estimates. The role of the NATO Striking Fleet in the opening offensive seemed at least to have been fully accepted. What was cut was the conversion of escort vessels and the future building of the mine countermeasures fleet. There could now be no more scruples over the Reserve Fleet, and four old carriers, seven cruisers, and about eighty old destroyers and frigates were consigned to the scrapyard. New building and modernization would in future "be confined to those ships which can play a valuable role in both war and peace." The building program was to be spread over a longer period. The new carrier, which had now grown to some 30,000 tons, remained in the new-construction program but was deferred until 1959–60 at the earliest.[76]

On June 16th, the Cabinet's Defence Committee decided to go ahead with a British thermonuclear weapons program, and by the end of July the full Cabinet had given its approval. At the same time, the results of both the "Second Radical Review" and the chiefs of staff "thermonuclear" appreciation were presented to the Cabinet. The latter is still classified, but a version was presented to the Commonwealth prime ministers at the end of the year, from which its gist can be gleaned. The chiefs considered that the hydrogen bomb or "the revolution in weapons of war over the last two years" had "completely altered the world situation." After putting the "world-wide" threat of "Communist subversion and expansion" in stark terms, the chiefs placed their main emphasis on "subversion backed by the supply of arms and financial aid as opposed to overt attack or invasion." Given American nuclear superiority over the Soviet Union, the chiefs felt that deliberate war was unlikely over the next three or four years, even as the Soviets gained the capability to attack the U.S.A., and that a situation of mutual deterrence was likely if both sides showed restraint. The Cold War was likely to continue for a long time, with more open conflict mainly deterred by the West's accumulation of nuclear weapons. If war did, after all, break out, "an immediate and overwhelming counter offensive with the most powerful nuclear weapons appears the only hope of defeating the enemy's attempt to destroy us and bring[ing] the war to an early halt." Top priority, therefore, was the build-up of nuclear forces, although the chiefs also stressed the importance of "a shield of land and air forces in Western Europe and of naval and air forces for the protection of Allied sea communications" as "an essential complement for the main deterrent."[77]

On the specific question of sea communications, McGrigor managed to obtain the following statement: "Besides deploying a vast army and possessing a very large and modern air force Russia has now emerged as a first class naval power. We can expect that, concurrently with strategic air operations major attacks will be made by Soviet naval, land and amphibious forces, supported by part of the Soviet nuclear potential against Western Europe and our sea communications." The best way of coping with this offensive was a Western attempt "to gain command of the sea at the outset by destroying her [i.e., Russia's] fleet, her mercantile marine, and her bases." With the offensive strategy confirmed in such robust terms, it made sense for the Admiralty to concentrate even more on their proto-nuclear carrier force. The latter, in conventional guise, also had considerable Cold War utility.[78]

The plans to cut the defense program and the strategic appreciation had gone along in parallel. Despite Newell's fears expressed in April about the attempt to "catalogue amputations . . . before you decide whether you wish to play football or fives,"[79] there was much logic in the joint submission. Ominously, however, in the Cabinet Sandys and De L'Isle, the air minister, buoyed up by the overwhelming emphasis on strategic air warfare, "suggested that further study was needed to ensure that the proposed reduction in defence expenditure was correctly apportioned between the various elements in our defence programmes." The chancellor also made it clear that the proposed defense budget was substantially above his revised upper limit of £1,500 million. Churchill agreed and called for yet "further scrutiny" of the defense budget by a small group of ministers.[80]

The complexion of this small ministerial group did not fill the Admiralty with much cheer. In the chair was Lord Swinton, Commonwealth Secretary, who as air minister had asserted the Royal Air Force's priority in the rearmament process of the 1930s. Then came Duncan Sandys, now fully restored both to health and to his anticarrier crusade. Finally there was Nigel Birch, parliamentary secretary at the Ministry of Defence, who had been parliamentary under secretary at the Air Ministry in 1951–52. Only a few months before, the Naval Staff had been expending its efforts refuting Birch's claims that the proposed V bombers could provide the vital offensive air capability for all three services. The chiefs of staff and service ministers were to advise this small Swinton Committee as required.[81]

Despite the best efforts of Thomas and McGrigor and their advisers, the Swinton Committee reopened the arguments the Admiralty thought had been settled in their favor. Indeed, if anything, it went further than before in its attack not only on the carrier but on the whole place of the Royal Navy in Britain's overall defense posture. The crucial paragraph read as follows:

> The three Services are equal in honour and will remain so. But each must vary in size and character as changes take place in the science of war and the course of world events. In the new strategic conditions the relative importance of sea power in our defences is evidently diminishing and there is no sign that this trend will be arrested. There can be no question of having a larger Navy than we need, or can afford; and we must make the best use of existing material. It is natural that the Navy should wish to have their share in air power, which is growing in importance. The cost of the Fleet Air Arm, however—already about £70 million and expected to rise sharply—appears to impose a burden disproportionate to the results. Moreover, the role of the aircraft carrier is already restricted through the ever increasing range of shore based aircraft."[82]

Ironically, the Swinton Committee used one of the navy's own weapons, broken-backed war, against it. This was an argument that still had considerable appeal to the old prime minister, who endorsed the committee's recommendations when he presented them to the Cabinet in November 1954. Swinton and his colleagues considered that "two light carriers would be insufficient for the important task of defending our Atlantic lifelines, upon which in the later stages of a war our life might depend. In this role, moreover, carrier borne aircraft cannot effectively be replaced by shore based aircraft." The two fleet carriers would, therefore, be retained, but "manned and equipped for the escort role only." In peacetime they would only carry a reduced CVL aircraft complement. NATO was to be told of these proposals, "but we should not be deterred by the possibility that this may re-open the question of our share in the Naval command structure of NATO. As we should be retaining four aircraft carriers with the Fleet, but putting them to better use, we have a good answer if any proposal were made to re-open the question of command."[83]

The Admiralty had offered savings in reserve aircraft totals to the tune of some £3½ million, but the reduced carrier complement would increase this to £5.5 million, and possibly more later given the consequential reductions in the reserve. Finally Swinton and his colleagues called for an investigation into "the future strategic role of the Fleet Air Arm and the longer term plans for the development of new types of naval aircraft." Ominously the report added: "This review should cover the possibility of further reducing the number of aircraft required to support the front line strength of the Fleet Air Arm."[84]

As for cruisers, another of Sandys's traditional targets, the committee recommended that the number planned to remain in commission be reduced from ten to eight, the spare crews being used to maintain the *Vanguard* in commission "for prestige purposes and for having a vessel superior to the latest Russian cruiser." This somewhat shameless appeal to the prime minister's prejudices must have jarred the Admiralty somewhat, whose planners must have smiled ironically when they read that the Swinton Committee "accepted the importance of the peacetime role of the cruiser in police duties and showing the flag," but nonetheless recommended that "it should be possible to make more extensive use of our aircraft carriers for these duties."[85]

The Swinton Committee finally turned its attack on the minesweeper program. Two hundred coastal and inshore MCM vessels were under construction, and a new ocean minesweeper was about to be laid down. Ten new coastal minesweepers per year were to be laid down, but the committee argued that, given the diminished emphasis on minesweeping in the new strategic concept, this could be reduced to six a year. It would have preferred to have abandoned new minesweeper construction entirely, but saw some strength in the argument that this would force closure upon the small shipyards that specialized in their construction.[86]

The Admiralty, more than a little aggrieved, now mounted a major counterattack. Circumstances, not as constitutional practice eleven years later, prevented the first lord being present at the Cabinet meeting, but he could produce a paper to be presented by Parliamentary and Financial Secretary Alan Noble (a retired officer), backed by Sir Rhoderick McGrigor. The Naval Staff and "M" Branch produced comprehensive briefings, paying special attention to the carrier question. The NA39 strike aircraft was, the fifth sea lord made clear, a bomber specifically tailor-made to Britain's requirements with an 800-mile high-level range for anti-*Sverdlov* duties in a "hot war" and a 400-mile range for land attacks in "warm (i.e., limited) war." The possession of carriers, he argued, was essential to the navy to carry out its agreed functions, as defined by the Swinton Committee itself. The vice chief of Naval Staff pointed out the trivial nature of the savings being proposed, 0.125 percent of the defense budget; the Fleet Air Arm as a whole was less than 5 percent of the whole defense budget. In return for these savings the

Royal Navy was being deprived of its entire ability to deal with targets at sea as well as on shore. The ever-perceptive Newell, however, made an interesting point in a briefing paper produced on the day of the Cabinet meeting (Guy Fawkes Night, 5 November 1954): "Fireworks from the Prime Minister may be expected but I suggest it may well be that the whole object of plugging the half empty carrier in the Defence Review Report may be to make certain that the Admiralty accept everything else and feel thankful they are to be spared the last straw."[87]

Entitled "Defence Policy: The Fleet Air Arm," the Admiralty's submission to the cabinet was very strongly worded indeed, especially for the "amiable, sensible and complaisant" first lord. It stated that the Swinton Report "contains a number of expressions of opinion and recommendations which are not in accordance with the views of the Board of Admiralty and to which the First Sea Lord and I have taken every opportunity of objecting."[88]

He denounced the report as unrealistic. It failed to take into account the cumulative effect on the navy of the severe cuts already made and of the further reductions envisaged by the Board. The Admiralty, the first lord argued, had gone as far as it could in contributing to defense cuts. Thomas argued that recent discussions had "brought clearly into focus the strategic role of the Fleet Air Arm— a role complementary to, and not in competition with, that of the Royal Air Force. Heavy carriers with their full complement of the right types of aircraft are essential in order that we may be ready to undertake our share of the Allied naval task." Only fleet carriers could embark all types of aircraft, airborne early warning, fighter and ASW, as well as sufficient aircraft for a "worthwhile blow at whatever threatens us by sea." Swinton's recommendations "would deny carriers capable of taking their place in the covering force on which our control of the sea depends." Thomas quoted the united opposition to these proposals of himself, the first sea lord and Lord Alexander (who had resigned as minister of defense the previous month). Ominously, he stated that: "The present Board of Admiralty feels most strongly in this matter." At the very least Thomas asked for a decision to be delayed until he could be present.[89]

As for the less spectacular minesweepers, Noble agreed that the mining threat was reduced. "This view," he wrote, with not a little understatement, "is based both on the assumption that the enemy would put our major ports out of action by thermonuclear attack, which would be more durable than mining their approaches, and on the long term effect of the Allied strategic air offensive on the enemy's logistic support." Nevertheless, Noble (and the Naval Staff) asserted that "supplies will . . . still have to reach this country by sea." Soviet mining capabilities both by sea and air were very great. Reducing the program in the way suggested would further increase the shortfall of minesweepers as the old World War II motor minesweepers finally wore out. Some 600 were required: there would only be 215, compared to 345 in 1956. More importantly, the demise of building capacity would prevent any emergency program. "It is this double effect," Noble argued, "that confirmed the Board in its conclusion that it would be most imprudent to plan on fewer than ten a year."[90]

Sir Rhoderick McGrigor spoke first for the Admiralty at the Cabinet meeting. It was perhaps his finest hour. On the preeminent carrier question the first sea lord defended the Striking Fleet's role protecting shipping from Soviet surface forces. As the Americans wanted three British carriers, he said, the least the British could do was provide two, properly equipped. British carriers were also needed to counter the Soviet fleet alone until the Americans arrived. As an extra role they could also help defend Norway from amphibious attack, but this task was "only incidental to the primary strategic role of defeating the Soviet surface fleet." Noble followed McGrigor, saying the Admiralty was willing to make some reductions in the Fleet Air Arm to make the £3.5 million cut to which the report had referred. This was over and above the £25 million reduction of the Radical Review.[91]

A new minister of supply was now in office, Selwyn Lloyd, and he now came to the Admiralty's defense quoting the dislocation the reduction in the naval air program would cause. Butler was his usual implacable self and stood out for a defense budget no greater than £1,525 million. The new defense minister, Harold Macmillan, suggested that the question of the strategic use of heavy carriers in a future war be examined in greater detail in consultation with the Admiralty. Churchill growled that "he was not convinced that the large and increasing resources which would be absorbed by the Fleet Air Arm were justified by the contribution which it would make to our defences." He would not, however, "press for the immediate adoption of the particular proposals" of the Swinton Report "if the Minister of Defence were ready to explore with the Admiralty alternative means of securing savings in naval expenditure." In the circumstances the Admiralty gave up its minesweepers without more of a fight.[92]

So the Admiralty had saved the day. Newell had been right, and the navy's victory was confirmed before the end of the month when Macmillan rang Thomas, in bed, to say that he need not worry about any review of the Fleet Air Arm's functions. Its future was no longer in doubt, at least as regards 1955–56. In December 1954 Macmillan dictated a draft paper that could have come from the Admiralty itself. It made the point of the importance of the commitment of two fleet carriers to NATO and the importance of fleet carriers with their considerable capacities for self-defense in "cold or warm roles." Light carriers had only sufficed in Korea, the paper argued, because of the lack of risk. The paper endorsed the navy's fears about loss of morale should the fleet carriers disappear. It was at least uncertain that the land-based aircraft could do the job of carriers, and this uncertainty did not justify "a course of action which would be most damaging to the authority of the fleet and the prestige of this country." Such a blow was not worth a saving of about £2.5 million per year.[93]

The Admiralty had played a skillful game, looking for chinks in their opponents' armor and going on the offensive themselves when required, e.g., over Coastal Command and the V bombers. Thus it captured, or at least threatened, bureaucratic "territory" that could be exchanged for concessions on the carrier question. The basic structure of the bureaucratic environment was favorable, with the first lord given full access to the cabinet and most of the top-level Cabinet committees. Thomas was not a strong figure himself, but he was excellently briefed by Newell. McGrigor may not have been the most articulate of first sea lords, but he made up for it in rugged Scottish strength of character and dogged determination to do the best for his service both in the chiefs of staff committee and the Cabinet.

Sandys was the core of the anticarrier group, but his illness and then his transfer to the Housing portfolio when Harold Macmillan went to defense in October took away some of his influence at the center of defense decision making. Butler, the chancellor, was interested in getting savings rather than the specific areas from which they came, but there is little doubt that Churchill had become anticarrier and antinavy by the second half of 1954. His naval horizon always comprehended dreadnoughts rather than carriers. The Admiralty was lucky that the prime minister's powers were distinctly on the wane by the closing months of 1954. He, and everyone else, knew that there was no question of his ramming through an unpopular program of carrier cuts on his own authority.

Alexander, the minister of defense for most of the controversy, was a neutral arbiter rather than a strong personality. He could be swayed by Churchill to come up with rational "compromises," but he was equally willing to be argued out of them on professional, military, and strategic grounds. His successor, Macmillan, was a great contrast. His acute political sense recognized the futility of forcing a major defense crisis to get marginal savings, especially with a change of leadership and an election in prospect. If the Admiralty had something that it felt it could give up, i.e., the minesweeper program, then it made sense to take that and give the Admiralty its precious carriers, at least for the time being.

McGrigor and the Naval Staff saw many of their high hopes of a year or two before dashed. Cancellations of many cherished projects had reluctantly been accepted. Yet these were not aimless cuts; what emerged from the repeated traumas of 1952, 1953, and 1954 was a significantly reorientated Royal Navy. Ships that had made more sense in the long-drawn-out Battle of the Atlantic were sacrificed to ships that were useful in (a) the Royal Navy's peacetime tasks; (b) the opening offensive against the enemy in the survival period. Indeed, even broken-backed war was not yet quite buried. In the 1955 Defence White Paper the following rider to reliance on strategic nuclear air power appeared: "Our policy," the paper said, "must aim at impressing on a potential enemy that a sudden attack even with nuclear weapons would not be conclusive. It must also demonstrate that we have both the will to survive and the power to insure victory. The vast conventional forces controlled by the Communist world include a large and growing navy. On our side, we must have a Navy . . . which, with the Allied Navies, can seek out and destroy the enemy's naval forces and preserve effective command of sea communications." This use of the traditional words "seek out and destroy" meant more than just the attack "at source." The Americans' long-range passive sonar arrays were beginning to come into use. With the nuclear "new look" now being exhibited in the United States, SACLANT was increasingly thinking in terms of hunter-killer groups armed with nuclear depth charges using the information gleaned from these arrays. The days predicted by the March 1954 future policy paper might be coming sooner than the Naval Staff had thought. One might well, therefore, spend less on special forces for convoy escort work and direct the resources toward maintaining and enhancing the forces directed to the Cold War/Strike Fleet strategy, which could fight the future Atlantic battle too. It all began to fit together nicely to produce a more secure naval future.[94]

The 1955 Naval Estimates put the best possible face on the cuts of the previous few years. They included an extended discussion of "The Role of the Royal Navy in an Age of Thermonuclear Weapons." The main thrust of its argument was a defiant assertion that changes in weapons did not lessen the requirement for navies; indeed, the need was all the greater given the relevance of the fleet as a support of the nation's foreign policy and trade in peace and limited war. This did not mean that wartime functions could be forgotten, however; searching out and destroying enemy ships wherever they were, preventing use of the sea by the enemy, protecting sea communications, and providing air support for operations ashore that could not be provided by land-based air power all remained important duties.[95]

The aircraft carriers, "the fists of the fleet," were central to the new posture. Carrier groups, the paper asserted, were "the strength upon which all naval activities depend." Four carriers were operational, with an equal number being used on trials and training duties. The second fleet carrier was the *Ark Royal*, finally commissioned in the same month as the Estimates appeared, February 1955. Given all the problems naval shipbuilding had faced in the early 1950s, even this delayed entry into service was something of an achievement. The *Ark Royal* entered service with a partially angled deck and modifications to allow her to operate modern aircraft. These included another important development, the mirror landing aid. The latter modification and a partially angled deck had also just been installed in the *Eagle*, which reentered service after refit at virtually the same time as the *Ark Royal* began her trials. Steam catapults for the *Eagle* would have to await a full rebuild. This may have been no bad thing in some ways, as the *Ark Royal* was plagued by problems with her catapults during her first few months in service.[96]

The other two fully operational carriers in 1955 were the two *Hermes*-class light fleet carriers, *Centaur* and *Albion*. The *Centaur* had almost made her intended completion date, being only about six months late in September 1953, but the *Albion*'s builders, Swan Hunter, had such problems with her that she was eighteen months late, only completing in May 1954. Both were soon given angled decks on the same 5½° interim pattern as their larger cousins. The *Bulwark*, another *Hermes*-class ship, was completed more or less on schedule in 1954 and became trials and training carrier, to replace the old *Illustrious*. The *Hermes* herself was going to be very late, however, given the considerable modifications to her design that had been approved and which made her, since 1951, a separate *Hermes* (modified) class. There was doubt within the Admiralty over the practicality of giving this standard of capability to other *Hermes*-class carriers or whether to concentrate on new construction.[97]

As for the smaller light fleet carriers, the *Warrior* was receiving her planned flight deck improvements. The *Ocean* was briefly earmarked for similar treatment when the *Vengeance* went to Australia, but ended up serving as a training ship with no aircraft, along with the *Theseus* and *Triumph*. The light fleets had been converted to these duties because of their much greater economy of manpower compared to the old armored-hangar fleet carriers *Implacable* and *Indefatigable* that were previously used. The *Glory* was in reserve after use as a trooping and ferry ship. The *Majestic* was approaching completion for Australia and sailed from Barrow as HMAS *Melbourne* in October 1955. The *Powerful* had been taken over by Canada in 1952 for similar treatment and was commissioned as the *Bonaventure* in 1957. As late as 1953 the Staff expressed hopes that the *Hercules* and *Leviathan* would be completed as repeat *Majestic*s with steam catapult, angled deck, etc. Alas, the Radical Review process finally put paid to such intentions, and the 1955 Estimates listed the two ships as still suspended. As for the old armored-hangar ships, the crippled *Formidable* had gone for scrap as early as 1953. The other four ships, finally doomed by the decisions of mid-1954, were all taken out of service that year. They went for scrap in 1955–56.[98]

The 1955 Naval Estimates proudly spoke of new aircraft types becoming available

Most heavily modernized of the British *Colossus*-class carriers was HMS *Warrior*. In 1952–53 she received a modified island and radar. She then served actively in the Far East with a Sea Fury/Firefly air group as seen here. In her next refit in 1955–56, she received a partially angled deck and modified arrester gear to allow the operation of Sea Venoms and Gannets. Defense reviews and reductions in the number of running carriers meant that her only subsequent service was as control ship during the "Grapple" thermonuclear test of 1957. The following year she was sold to Argentina as the *Independencia*.

that spelled the doom of the old ships. The Sea Hawk fighter was entering into service in large numbers, the first squadron having formed in 1953. Sea Venoms were also reaching the front line. Sixteen American-built Skyraiders provided the airborne early warning for these fighters. The new jets also had a respectable ground attack capability that made up for weaknesses in specialized strike aircraft. The Wyvern was, however, entering service after a decade or so of troubled development. Contingency plans to purchase American Corsairs to provide a usable strike aircraft proved in the end unnecessary. Only two Wyvern squadrons were to be maintained at any one time, one for each operational fleet carrier. American aid was resorted to, however, in the ASW field because of delays to the Gannet and the failure of the Firefly 7. One hundred Avengers were needed to equip four front-line squadrons in 1953–55. The first Gannet squadrons belatedly formed by early 1955, development and labor problems and the late delivery of components having taken their toll. Five squadrons were operational before the end of the year. There was, however, the first operational ASW helicopter squadron of U.S.-built Sikorsky S-55s and another squadron of these aircraft in the counterinsurgency role. (See next chapter.) ASW aircraft were beginning to receive better weapons. Although "Pentane," a large 21-inch active sonar homing torpedo, was cancelled as development became more difficult, an 18-inch lightweight passive homer, "Dealer B," did enter service as the Mark 30 in 1954. This was, for its time and despite its limited speed, an effective torpedo, rather better than the smaller American Mark 43 that was chosen to replace it in 1955–56.[99]

Turning to surface ships, the *Vanguard* was under refit to allow her to return to service at the end of the year. A long active life seems to have been foreseen for her. It was hoped that she would sail for her next commission in a more combatant condition than at any time since 1946, as she would be carrying her full stock of 15-inch shells. Three of her four turrets would be operational along with half of the rest of her armament. The royal apartments were being removed, but the improved habitability modifications still made her somewhat overweight, so her fuel load would have to be restricted. Unlike the doomed old carriers, the four battleships of the *King George V* class were kept in reserve, as requested by Prime Minister Churchill.[100]

Cruisers, the other large, gun-armed ships, were as useful as Cold War weapons as carriers in the eyes of the Admiralty, and almost as high in priority, although the squeeze on funds had caused two "Towns," the *Liverpool* and *Glasgow*, and two *Dido*s, *Sirius* and *Phoebe*, to have their modernizations cancelled in 1952. Only the three ships given "large repairs" in 1950–52, the *Newcastle*, *Birmingham*, and *Newfoundland*, received their modifications on schedule, being given an enclosed bridge, improved radar, a modern action information organization, and improved MRS6 fire control for their 4-inch secondary armament. They were now deemed to be capable of defending themselves from air attack in all conditions, and from other ships in clear weather. The *Sheffield* was given a "large repair" in 1949–51 when policy was still being decided, and although modernized in some ways did not receive all these improvements.

The emphasis on Cold War duties after Global Strategy had a significant effect on the cruiser plans. The *Dido*s seemed less useful, especially since improving their effectiveness cost substantial amounts of money, dockyard time, and resources. What was needed, it was felt, were relatively impressive ships that could bombard the shore effectively with minimal modernization. The "Colonies" seemed excellent ships for this task, and at the beginning of 1953 Plans Division put four of them (in better physical shape than the *Glasgow* and *Liverpool*) back into the planned cruiser fleet to replace the four cancellations. They were earmarked for limited fire-control improvement to allow them to defend themselves from the air, at least in clear conditions. At the end of the year three of the four *Dido*s planned for improvements were taken out of the program (one modernization and the two "large repairs") and only HMS *Royalist* survived to receive a full modernization in 1954–56. This allowed three more "Colony"-class ships to survive in reserve at least, in order to be sure of keeping the notional (D + six months) war fleet at its newly reduced figure of sixteen.

It was still felt, however, that some combat-worthy cruisers were required that could play their full part as fleet vessels protecting other ships from air attack. The only "new" ships were the three modified *Tigers*, work on which eventually began again (after much consideration) in 1954. The first sea lord proudly predicted at the end of the year that, given the vote of confidence in the gun-armed cruiser shown by the Soviet building program, these three much-delayed vessels would be "a very valuable asset." The previous year, 1953, it had also been decided to enhance the plans for the *Swiftsure*, *Superb*, and *Belfast*. The two former vessels were to get the new advanced MRS3 fire-control system and a completely new 3-inch secondary armament, similar to that of the *Tiger* and her sisters. The *Belfast* could not take the new guns due to her magazine arrangements, but she was to get MRS3 for her 4-inch guns (see drawing). Modernization of the "best of those cruisers in commission" was specifically endorsed in the 1955 Estimates, so these

Britain's largest operational cruiser for most of the postwar period was HMS *Belfast*, now preserved in the pool of London. She spent most of her time in the Far East, often serving as a flagship. She is seen here in European waters shortly before starting a four-year "large repair" in 1955 that gave her a new bridge structure. The reconstruction was not as extensive as that originally planned, however (see drawing on the next page). The ship in the background is a newly completed *Hermes*-class light fleet carrier.

plans seemed still alive. A program of four completely new gun-armed cruisers for the late 1950s had fallen by the wayside. Studies on such ships had gone on into 1954, and various ships in the 16,850–18,200-ton class were considered, with six 6-inch and three 3-inch guns, or four 6-inch and four 3-inch.[101]

The 1955 Naval Estimates made clear that the plans for new cruisers had been replaced by, or at least combined with, those for a single new guided-missile ship to carry the Sea Slug surface-to-air missile. This weapon had been under development since 1944 when a Naval Staff target was stated for a long-range "GAP" (guided antiaircraft projectile). It had priority over antisurface weapons in 1945, and it was hoped that a prototype would be available in two years. It was to be capable of shooting down aircraft at heights of up to 50,000 feet and at speeds of up to 700 miles per hour. Weight was to be kept as small as possible.[102]

Given postwar shortages of men and materials, and dislocation caused by administrative reorganization, by 1947 the project was far from the hardware stage. Yet at least it was now given the highest priority: the Defence Research Policy Committee hoped that it would be in service in some numbers within the ten-year defense planning time scale adopted that year. By 1948 certain decisions had been taken on the missile. It was to have wrap-around boosters and fly down a radar beam to the target. The same year, however, it became clear that there were not enough resources for four missile projects, and the following year the DRPC and the Defence Committee decided to concentrate on Sea Slug as a common sea- *and* ground-based weapon with a range of 30,000 yards for air defense not only of sea communications but of the United Kingdom itself. Development began to fall behind, and it did not look as if Sea Slug would meet its 1957 target date. In 1950,

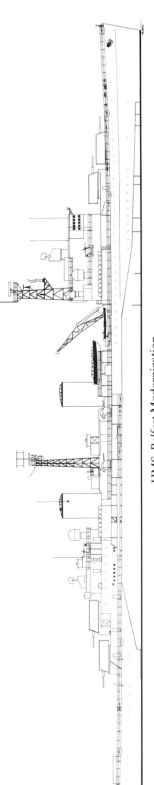

HMS *Belfast* Modernization

Armament:
Four triple 6"/50 guns
Four twin 4" Mark 19 DP guns
Six twin Bofors 40/60 Mark 5 AA guns
Two triple 21" torpedoes

Electronics:
One Type 960 air-search radar (AQQ aerial)
One Type 992 surveillance radar (AKC aerial)
One Type 277Q height-finding radar (ANU aerial)
One Type 974 navigation radar (AKL aerial)
Two 6" gunnery directors with Type 274 radar (AUM aerial)
Two Type MRS 3 fire-control systems
Four CRBFD Bofors directors
IFF Mark 10 associated with Type 960 radar

therefore, with Korean rearmament, missile development was given equivalent priority to the nuclear program, which stepped up its progress. By then Sea Slug size had been more or less settled. It was somewhat bigger than expected at 20 feet long and over 1 foot in diameter with a wing span in the region of five feet. Clearly it was only going to be operated by relatively large ships. The Admiralty did consider trying to argue for the more compact American Terrier missile, to get a SAM into service more quickly, but given the uncertainty as to whether the Americans would supply the system, and the desire not to be dependent on foreign supplies, nothing came of this proposal.[103]

Consideration had been given to various platforms for Sea Slug, from the *Vanguard* downwards, but by the end of 1950 serious thought was being given to two concepts, a fast fleet vessel and a slow coastal convoy escort. When HMS *Girdleness* was first earmarked for conversion to a trials ship, it was hoped that she might double as a Sea Slug escort ship as well, but difficulties in accommodating a full war complement meant that when she began her conversion in 1953 it was as a trials ship only. This decision, taken in July 1952, saw the beginning of work on a new-construction convoy escort missile ship for ocean as well as coastal work. By 1953 designs in the 10,000-ton class were being considered by the Ship Design Policy Committee, which considered them rather large for convoy work. With the new strategic policy emphasizing carrier escort rather than convoy work and with the example of the contemporary missile conversions of U.S. cruisers, minds in the Admiralty turned back to missile conversions of major warships. From these, in 1954, emerged the idea of a purpose-built missile cruiser. This was conceived as a high-speed ship of over 10,000 tons, of mixed armament, with a Sea Slug launcher aft, and medium-caliber guns forward to deal with any *Sverdlov* menace. Once the proposed Blue Slug surface-to-surface missile was ready, the cruiser could be altered to "double-ended" configuration, with a launcher at each end.[104]

In 1953 the 5-inch large destroyer/small cruiser project came to an end. It was clear that its guns were not going to have a sufficient rate of fire to take on *Sverdlov*s with any chance of success. Instead, emphasis shifted to a fast escort based on the existing *Daring*-class large destroyers, which could screen strike carriers. At least one of the options considered for this design was an ASW ship of Type 12 frigate capabilities but with a speed of 40 knots. Two such "Fleet Escort Ships" were duly announced in the 1955 Estimates, although their characteristics were left studiously vague, probably reflecting Naval Staff indecision on their design. Two more were in the building program. In the meantime the main modern fleet escort was the existing *Daring* class, all eight of which were now in commission. These 2,830-ton ships, "the finest escort vessels in existence," were deemed to be too large to be classified destroyers and were referred to in fleet listings as a separate category. They were also run on more formal "big ship" lines. Their roles were described as "attacking heavy ships with torpedoes, destroying light forces, sinking submarines, and contributing to defence against air attack."[105]

The 1955 Naval Estimates statement spoke proudly of the progress that had been made in improving the fleet of smaller destroyers and frigates, of which "bitter experience had shown that it was impossible to have too many." There was indeed much of which the Admiralty could be proud. Twenty-seven Type 15 and 16 ASW frigates were in service with six more conversions in hand. Nevertheless, the frigate conversion program had not escaped unscathed. Equipment shortages had meant

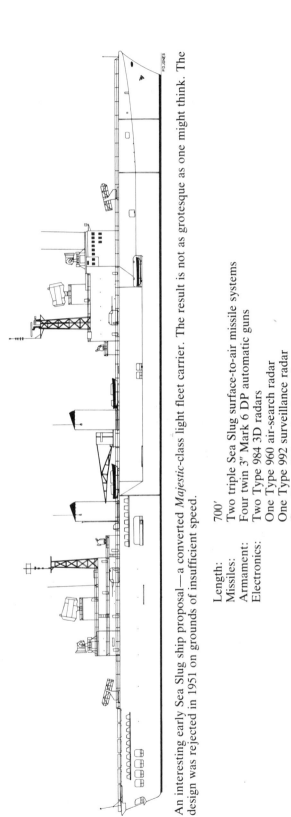

P.D.JONES

An interesting early Sea Slug ship proposal—a converted *Majestic*-class light fleet carrier. The result is not as grotesque as one might think. The design was rejected in 1951 on grounds of insufficient speed.

Length: 700'
Missiles: Two triple Sea Slug surface-to-air missile systems
Armament: Four twin 3" Mark 6 DP automatic guns
Electronics: Two Type 984 3D radars
One Type 960 air-search radar
One Type 992 surveillance radar
One Type 978 navigation radar
Two Type 901 Sea Slug fire-control radars
Four Type MRS 3 gun fire-control radars
IFF Mark 10 associated with Type 984 radars

One of the later Type 15 conversions of a wartime destroyer into a fast ASW frigate was the *Troubridge*, converted in 1955–57 after a period in reserve since 1949. (Imperial War Museum)

that Type 15s had to enter service with older Squid mortars instead of the intended Mark Xs. Moreover, two conversion projects had to be abandoned—the Type 18 intermediate ASW conversions and the Type 62 aircraft direction conversions. The old destroyers specifically earmarked for these conversions, the *N* and *M* classes respectively, remained in reserve. The former were early candidates for scrapping, the latter were eventually sold to Turkey. It seemed to make more sense in the context of 1954–55 to concentrate on maintaining the program of converting the *Ca*-class destroyers, which could combine an enhanced ASW capability with a 4.5-inch main armament, had high speed and, not least, good rakish looks. They were excellent "roving protectors of this country's interests throughout the world"— against limited opposition at least.[106]

As for the new-construction frigates, two more projects had been abandoned completely, the Type 42 "anti-E-boat" coastal escort and the Type 17 Third Rate ASW frigate. One of each had been in the building program, but both ships made more sense in traditional World War II scenarios than in the new world defined strategically by the chiefs of staff 1952 Paper and financially by the Radical Review and its successor. The rest of the frigate program was greatly altered also, with much juggling of hulls between types. As late as the beginning of 1953 the plan was to build only eight Type 12 ASW frigates, but some eleven Type 41 AA frigates and ten Type 61 aircraft-direction ships, the last three of the latter to a new enlarged design "with full equipment." In order to slow the program down within the bounds of affordability, one of the first five Type 41s, HMS *Panther*, was transferred to India, and another two later hulls were also earmarked for the Indians. This left at least five 41s and seven 61s on order or projected for the Royal Navy. The remaining orders were transferred to the Type 12 program, which was also slowed down somewhat by selling two 1955 program ships to India, and two more were projected at the end of the production run to complete in 1963. By 1955 the first six of these fast steam-powered vessels were under construction, two more were being ordered, and ten more were projected to provide the Royal Navy with useful escorts for task forces as well as convoys.[107]

The newly completed Type 61 aircraft direction frigate *Chichester* firing her Squid ASW mortar. The comprehensive radar fit of these convoy escort ships made them useful additions to carrier groups, but their slow speed was a drawback, and with the move to a more carrier-centered "fleet" strategy, the Type 61 program was reduced from ten ships to four. The Sea Hawk fighter ground/attack aircraft are on board HMS *Albion*.

The Type 14 Second Rate frigate program, that had been boosted to no less than twenty-three hulls, was cut back to twelve ships. Three were ordered for India, one was cancelled completely, and seven were reprogrammed to a new design. An alternative Second Rate frigate had already been planned, a "common-hull" design on the pattern of the old "Loch" and "Bay" classes of World War II. Three antisubmarine variants and one antiaircraft ship were in the building program by 1953 for construction in the mid-1950s. In 1954 a new "general-purpose" design concept was adopted for these ships, the term "sloop" being used, as "frigate" implied a specialized role. The ships were intended to replace the *Black Swan*- and "Loch"-class frigates that had been kept operational since 1945, primarily for colonial policing duties. The latter day "sloops" were conceived primarily for the Persian Gulf, and a wooden deck was specified, despite the weight penalty, both for insulation and appearance. Eleven ships seem to have been projected, with eight being ordered initially. In the meantime plans to modernize eleven *Black Swans* with Squid, etc., were quietly dropped, as the ships were perfectly adequate "policing" gunboats as they were. One scheme that did go through, however, was the modernization of seven of the "Loch"-class ASW ships to improve their gun armament. Such conversions improved the effectiveness of the World War II ASW frigates in gunboat and limited-war duties, but even this program was curtailed to only half that originally intended.[108]

Also cancelled were the plans for sixteen new ocean minesweepers, 1,500-ton ships that would have greater mobility and range than the coastals. This decision,

One of the prolific "Ton" class of coastal minesweepers, HMS *Dartington* seen here had a relatively short but active career in commission. Completed in Dartmouth in 1958, she was allocated first to the Mediterranean's 108th Minesweeper Squadron. However, by the end of 1959 she was deployed to Singapore. These small ships proved to be useful patrol vessels in the Indonesian confrontation, being able to penetrate up rivers as well as to cover coastal areas.

and the abandonment of the Third Rate coastal escort, may well have led to a somewhat belated program of modernizing the *Algerines* with a Squid ASW mortar on the forecastle. The "Ton"-class coastal minesweepers would have to bear the brunt of future mine countermeasures tasks, and the first of them were coming into service. At one time it had been intended that the RN would receive over 170 of these craft. The program was cut to 167 and then to 137, but in the end less than 120 were actually delivered. The plan to complete some as mine-location vessels died in 1952 with the failure of the "brilliant and innovative" 178 sonar. The inshore mine-countermeasures vessel program was also seriously curtailed, over 150 having been intended: 123 remained programmed in 1953, and just over 100 were built. Most were of the "Ham" class, but ten were "Leys," mine-location vessels with 179 sonar, a much less sophisticated set than the abortive 178.[109]

Many of the mine countermeasures vessels went straight into the Reserve. The 1955 Estimates announced significant changes in Reserve Fleet policy. The vulnerability to nuclear attack of lines of ships awaiting mobilization was recognized in the 1955 Estimates Statement. It announced that resources were to be concentrated on a reduced number of ships that would form an operational reserve at the highest possible readiness for sea. This implied that other less useful ships would cease to be maintained. Much of the Reserve Fleet was now being looked after in private yards on a contract basis, which also released dockyard facilities for maintenance of the active fleet. This arrangement also helped disperse reserve ships.[110]

Cuts in the number of ships helped save manpower, but the situation still remained serious. It had only proved possible to man the *Ark Royal* by decommissioning the *Implacable* and *Indefatigable*. By April 1955 the Royal Navy's manpower ceiling had been reduced to 133,000, and there was to be a further reduction of 6,000 over the following fiscal year. Recruiting was disappointing in the full-employment economy that Butler's policies had fostered. Despite new amenities, more married quarters, and increased pay and allowances, both recruitment and retention were below expectations. The situation for aircrew was a special problem, with only half the required number of recruits and those of a "deplorably low" standard. It was decided, therefore, in 1953 to restore the more glamorous title "Fleet Air Arm" in order to encourage more, and better quality, entries. Across all the branches voluntary recruitment of lower ranks dropped from 11,100 in 1951–52 to just over 8,000 in 1954–55. Only just over a third of the Royal Navy's personnel was staying on after the initial period of service, which was especially serious given the low recruitment rate of regulars during the war, thus reducing the numbers who could re-engage. The year 1954 saw the end of men retained compulsorily or recalled from the reserves, and an intake of 5,000 National Servicemen a year was still required to keep up numbers. A two-year period of service, a relic of Korea, allowed time for the conscripts to serve at sea. In order to make longer service more attractive and to gain greater flexibility in deployment, a new system of "General Service" ship commissions was introduced in 1954. These were shorter than previous commissions—eighteen months as against thirty—and ships' companies would spend only up to a year abroad. Men on specific "Foreign Service" commissions would now be accompanied by their families.[111]

Despite these difficulties and the significant cuts in capability that had resulted from the traumas of the continued process of review that had marked almost all his career as first sea lord, Rhoderick McGrigor might feel satisfied with the state of affairs described in the Naval Estimates when he retired in April 1955. His leadership had seen the service respond positively and aggressively to the challenge of the Churchill Government's policies. Out of the ruins of the old rearmament policy, the Royal Navy was committing itself to a course that accepted new strategic priorities and realities. Moreover, the emphasis on "fleet forces" rather than duller ASW and minesweeping ships helped maintain prestige and professional self-respect. Yet the outlook was still stormy, despite the departure of Churchill, who had so clearly turned against the Admiralty. In 1955, almost simultaneous with the appearance of the Naval Estimates and McGrigor's departure, the old prime minister resigned to be replaced by Sir Anthony Eden.

The new chancellor was Harold Macmillan, a politican whose commitment to domestic investment and living standards was considerable. He had already ably maintained the priority of his housing program in the early 1950s. Despite his willingness, as defense minister, to compromise over aircraft carriers at the end of 1954, Macmillan felt that defense expenditure in general should be still further controlled. The navy and the other services were about to come under an even more serious attack. They were, however, in a somewhat stronger position tempered by the experience of the Radical Review. Moreover, the Admiralty would have an even more effective first sea lord, an officer of the very greatest political skill and influence, Lord Louis Mountbatten. It would be his task to take up the torch once more, eventually against the old enemy, Duncan Sandys, in the most serious attack yet on the Royal Navy's position. Mountbatten's "Naval Case" would rest even less on war fighting and more on the fleet's role as a sustainer of Britain's peacetime influence and interests. Since 1945 the RN had been playing a remarkably active part in this respect. It is to the record of these events, which were to a large extent the key to the service's survival in a very hostile environment, that we shall now turn.

CHAPTER · FOUR

A FAMILIAR ROUTINE
IN A CHANGING WORLD

When the Plans Division of the Naval Staff surveyed the future in mid-1945 it assumed that the postwar world would differ little from that of pre-1939, or even pre-1905. "British interests are world wide," it wrote, "and will require the stationing of ships in all parts of the world. Besides exerting British influence and rendering assistance to British nationals in case of civil disorder and other calamities the Navy has an important role in 'showing the flag.'" Now came the contemporary twist: "This latter function should result in greatly expanded exports, without which it is certain that the country's finances will be unable to support a large Navy except when at war."[1] So the Royal Navy took up its peacetime stations intending to act as the world's maritime policeman, and indeed, apart from the United States Navy, there was no one else *capable* of acting as such. By 1947, therefore, the distant stations were reestablished and the Royal Navy seemed to have returned to a pattern of deployment that was described as being on "familiar pre-war lines." In many ways this was similar to that of the days of Pax Britannica a century before. In addition to the fleet at home, two others, each based around a pair of light fleet carriers, patrolled the waters of the Mediterranean and the Pacific. (The latter station would lose its carriers the following year, one permanently and the other temporarily. It would also be renamed Far East Fleet rather than Pacific Fleet and move its HQ from Hong Kong to Singapore.) The South Atlantic Station had been restored at Simonstown in South Africa with a cruiser and two frigates. On the American and West Indies Station, based at Bermuda, twice that number of ships kept the White Ensign flying within the Western Hemisphere. Based at Trincomalee, the East Indies Station, a couple of cruisers and two frigates oversaw the traumas of Indian independence, which included a 1946 mutiny of the Indian Navy, which had required the rapid deployment of the cruiser HMS *Glasgow*. The East Indies Station had access to the British Pacific Fleet's carriers if required. It also controlled the British naval presence in the Persian Gulf. Here a frigate or two operated against slavers and other disturbers of law and order.[2]

Yet the clock could not be turned back completely. Plans Division hoped to restore a Yangtse flotilla of shallow draft gunboats, which it considered an adjunct to British commercial and consular activity. It disagreed with the Foreign Office view that the renunciation of extraterritorial privileges in China, made in 1943, made the ostentatious presence of foreign warships in Chinese waters, without local permission, ill advised and illegal. Undeterred, the Admiralty set about collecting five suitable river gunboats. None were operational, but it was hoped that they could be deployed to Singapore relatively quickly to be held in readiness for deployment on the Yangtse. Landing craft would be used to patrol the West River. British ships indeed did reappear on the Yangtse in the wake of the American occupation forces, but these were temporary deployments and the flotilla was not restored, the old river gunboats themselves proving to be too worn out for future service. Armed landing craft could have been used, but the new political situation made traditional gunboat diplomacy in the upper reaches of Chinese rivers unacceptable to the Chinese, whether Communist or Nationalist.[3]

The Civil War between these two factions, however, created a perceived need for some British naval presence on the lower Yangtse to support the British Embassy at Nanking. In the autumn of 1948, with the permission of the Chinese Nationalist Government, a guard ship had been restored there to provide a point of potential refuge and a source of considerable comfort to Commonwealth ambassadors and diplomats. In January 1949, Admiral Sir Patrick Brind, CinC of the Far Eastern Station, signaled his desire that British ships should establish the precedent of movement up and down river. He preferred an incident, should one occur, to happen before an evacuation. He was confident of its outcome, "Unhampered ships should be able to look after themselves."[4]

In early February the chances of such an incident increased as the advance of Communist forces from the north reached the river. On the 9th the Nationalists announced that shipping on the Yangtse moved at its own risk. The possibility of danger to Commonwealth nationals in the capital seemed to make it even more important to maintain a naval presence until the Communists, who seemed to be winning, had taken the city and "restored order." It was, therefore, decided to relieve the destroyer *Consort* by the Australian frigate *Shoalhaven*. The British Pacific Station commanders had been told by the Australian Government only to use the *Shoalhaven* on errands of "mercy," and the enhanced chances of an incident with Communist forces poised to cross the river, coupled with the need to keep the relieving ship at Nanking for some time, led Vice Admiral A.C.G. Madden (flag officer, second in command) to decide to replace her with HMS *Amethyst*. The latter frigate had been the last Nanking guard ship and was presently slated for duty at Shanghai, where a frigate was also kept to safeguard British nationals. The *Consort*'s relief had been delayed for some time by the threat of a Communist river crossing and was becoming urgent as supplies ran low. It seemed possible that if the *Amethyst* was sent up before the 21st, the exchange might go off without incident. As Madden put it, "As both H.M. Ambassador and I understood that a cease fire order was in force . . . until the night of the 20th of April and as both ships should by then be clear of the danger area I decided to allow the movements to continue as I considered the risk justifiable."

The *Amethyst* left Shanghai on the 19th as news reached the British that the Communists were expected to cross two days later. Perhaps a little unwisely, the frigate anchored for the night with some Nationalist warships at Kiang Lin and acceded to the Chinese senior officer's request to darken ship. Early the following day the *Amethyst* set out again, but the morning was misty, and she was forced to stop for an hour until the fog cleared. There was still some mist around when, at 0830, the ship came under rather inaccurate fire from the Communist-held northern bank. Since December RN vessels had been authorized to fire back on batteries if they were endangering the ship, but they first had to be clearly located, and this the *Amethyst*'s gunnery director was unable to do before firing ceased.

So, the frigate, now displaying two large union flags to indicate her nationality, as well as a number of white ensigns, continued upriver. But the Communist gunners probably had never seen these flags before and did not recognize them. As the frigate came into a narrower part of the channel between Rose Island and San-chiang-ying, she came under more accurate fire. (See map.) The effect was devastating. The first hit was on the wheelhouse, and the next two on the bridge, just after the *Amethyst*'s captain, Lieutenant Commander B.M. Skinner, had given the order to open fire. A fourth shell hit the ship's low-power electric generators, effectively putting out of action her centralized fire control. If the *Amethyst*'s nerve center had not been knocked out, she might well have run through the gauntlet of the hostile fire and escaped. It was not to be. Control of the helm was restored but not of the engines and, with the starboard engine telegraph jammed at full ahead, the ship ran aground on to the mudbanks of Rose Island. Only the after twin 4-inch mounting would bear on the Communists, and it was able to fire about thirty rounds before being knocked out. The Communist guns continued to fire, however, even as the ship was being evacuated of a portion of its crew to save lives. Before the firing finally died down, the *Amethyst* had received some fifty-three hits from 105-mm, 75-mm, and 37-mm shells.

At 1230 the *Amethyst* received some welcome, but perhaps slightly embarrassing, support, when a Nationalist air strike was made on the artillery positions. Then, about ninety minutes later, HMS *Consort*, on the way downriver, tried to extricate the *Amethyst* from her predicament. The destroyer had already been in action before sighting the stranded frigate, silencing some small-arms fire with a single 4.5-inch salvo as she rushed downriver at 26 knots, flooding the riverbanks with her wake. Manpower shortages meant that the *Consort* could only man three of her four 4.5-inch guns, but the available armament was used to good effect as the ship now replied to the fire by the batteries that had disabled the *Amethyst*. Three guns were knocked out, but the *Consort* received three hits by 105-mm shells. After sailing by the frigate and trying to communicate, with limited success, the *Consort* returned at 8 knots in a systematic attempt to silence the Communist artillery and tow off the *Amethyst*.

The action was a fierce one. First, a 105-mm Chinese shell hit the *Consort*'s petty officers' mess, then a 75-mm crashed into the wheelhouse killing the coxswain. The *Consort* had to go over to emergency steering from aft. Hits forward by 75-mm and 37-mm rounds put the *A* gun out of action, but the *Consort*'s remaining two guns claimed three Chinese artillery positions in return. Then the bridge was hit, putting out of action the engine telegraphs; shortly thereafter *B* gun was knocked out. The gun director support was next struck, cutting the main firing circuits. The *X* gun went over to quarters firing and silenced a fourth Chinese gun. The hitherto unmanned and unused *Y* gun was brought into action by the survivors of *A* and *B* guns, but it was clear that the Communists were being reinforced by antitank guns brought into action by the troops waiting to cross the river. The risk of being put out of action was too great, and the already seriously damaged *Consort*

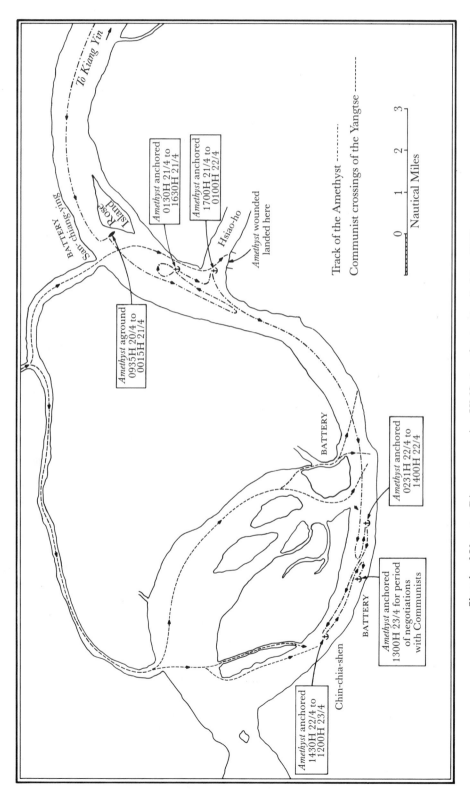

Sketch of Yangtse River concerning HMS *Amethyst*—April–May 1949

Within the figure:

To Kuang Yin

BATTERY San chiang ying

Rose Island

Amethyst anchored 0130H 21/4 to 1630H 21/4

Amethyst anchored 1700H 21/4 to 0100H 22/4

Hsiao-ho

Amethyst wounded landed here

Amethyst aground 0935H 20/4 to 0015H 21/4

BATTERY

Amethyst anchored 0231H 22/4 to 1400H 22/4

Amethyst anchored 1300H 23/4 for period of negotiations with Communists

BATTERY

Chin-chia-shen

Amethyst anchored 1430H 22/4 to 1200H 23/4

Track of the Amethyst ------
Communist crossings of the Yangtse ------

0   1   2   3
Nautical Miles

decided to abandon the rescue mission. The *Amethyst* herself had signaled that the operation was too dangerous under Communist fire. So the destroyer turned back and sped downriver. Within ten minutes she was again being fired at by a 75-mm battery from the north bank, and the two remaining British guns knocked out six of the eight Chinese weapons. The destroyer was badly hit again, however, being struck four times in just over a minute; six of her eight ratings killed in these actions were victims of this final engagement. In all the *Consort* had fired no less than 240 rounds of main armament ammunition and 25 percent of her light AA rounds.

The following day the Royal Navy tried again, and an even bigger battle resulted. Madden had decided to sail upriver to the *Amethyst*'s assistance in his flagship, HMS *London*, with the frigate *Black Swan* in support. The rebuilt heavy cruiser was an impressive ship, but her modern looks belied her age and her main 8-inch gun turrets were "long past their prime." Madden hoped that the mere presence of the cruiser would be enough, but it was soon clear that the Chinese Communists were not to be overawed by a warship, however impressive, sailing towards their vital river crossings. Within ten minutes of beginning her upriver dash, the *London* was under fire from 105-mm and 37-mm guns. She replied with her main armament and secondary 4-inch guns. Then a new, more numerous, battery joined in, and Madden began to consider withdrawal. Again the Communists scored hits on their opponent's bridge, and the cruiser turned back. Still, however, she was fired at, the action being heavier on the return trip than before. The *London* had both her forward turrets put out of action and one of her aft turrets hit also. The 4-inch guns were struck, the crew suffering over a third casualties (one crew was operating both port and starboard batteries). Nevertheless, the ship was still able to reply to her final opponents before the action ended at 1340, just over three hours after it had begun. Against five Chinese batteries, the *London* had expended 132 8-inch,

The heavy cruiser *London*, the last Royal Navy warship to fire eight-inch guns in anger, passing through the Suez Canal after the heavy engagement in the Yangtse incident. (Imperial War Museum)

449 4-inch, and over 2,000 rounds from her light AA guns. Her casualties were thirteen killed and thirty wounded. The *Black Swan* had accompanied the cruiser part of the way, but was held back out of serious danger to give the *London* cover with her 4-inch main armament. She fired some 313 rounds in twenty-five minutes at batteries observed shooting at the cruiser. There was some confusion as to whether all the guns engaged by the *Black Swan* were in fact Communist or Nationalist.

After this not inconsiderable battle, the heaviest engagement of the entire incident, the *Amethyst* had to be left to do the best she could. The ship floated off the sandbank during the night and moved slightly upriver, preparing to sail away with her would-be rescuers. She was fired at again, especially when a Sunderland flying boat appeared and brought in an RAF doctor to replace her own medical officer killed in the initial shelling. The frigate tried to find a safe anchorage in an inlet on the southern bank but, frustrated by shallow water, moved on Madden's orders some eight miles upriver in the early hours of the 22nd to get away from the batteries, only to come under small-arms fire from the southern shore. Moving back a mile out of danger the ship anchored once more. When on the 22nd the Sunderland returned, another bombardment ensued, but the *Amethyst* sailed upriver and the firing stopped. The ship was now at her farthest point up the Yangtse, off Chin-chia-shen, and at this point she received a new captain. Skinner had been mortally wounded by the first hits. Lieutenant Commander John Kerans, the assistant attaché at Nanking, was ordered to attempt to join the ship. Narrowly missing her once, because of one of her moves upriver, he eventually got on board with the help of a Nationalist landing craft.

The apparent setting up of a gun battery on the northern shore made it seem as if a crossing of the river was about to take place in his vicinity, and Kerans decided to move to get out of the crossfire. As he moved upriver, however, he was shot at once more and so he turned back to anchor out of danger. Movement was impossible, and the Communists had succeeded in getting the *Amethyst* out of the immediate area of their river crossings, which began that afternoon on either side of the British ship. Kerans decided not to compromise himself by trying to escape by attaching the *Amethyst* to the Nationalist naval forces that tried that night to oppose the landings. On 26 April negotiations, which dragged on for three months, began with the Communists, who tried to make the British take responsibility not only for the whole incident but also for the 252 Chinese casualties suffered so far in action with the Royal Navy warships. Supplies began to run out, although the Communists did allow 54 tons of RN fuel stockpiled at Nanking to be brought downriver on 10 July.

As the Chinese position appeared to harden after this, Kerans entered into a tortuous telegraphic conversation with Admiral Brind on the subject of a possible breakout. Circuitous language had to be used due to the early destruction of the *Amethyst*'s codes. At first Kerans had problems getting the Admiral's meaning, which in effect authorized a breakout, and Brind had doubts about Kerans's morale. In late July, however, Kerans got the message, and a new cypher, laboriously constructed on board, signalled on the 30th that he intended to break out that evening. Brind, who had already encouraged this, had sent a telegram to London on the 29th warning that unless fuel and stores arrived within ten days it might be necessary to destroy the *Amethyst*. Fraser, the first sea lord, was away from the

HMS *Amethyst* on arrival at Malta on her way home after the Yangtse incident. (Imperial War Museum)

Admiralty staying with friends, and he had to be given the gist of this highly secret message on an open telephone line. The first sea lord's immediate reaction was that the government should be told before anything drastic occurred, and he ordered a signal to be sent telling Brind that the *Amethyst* should not break out without reference to the Admiralty. A slightly embarrassed Brind signaled back, "Too late to stop *Amethyst* now." The *Amethyst* was indeed just about to slip anchor, and Brind did not feel he could stop her, a decision which Fraser later supported.[5]

With her silhouette disguised with canvas, prepared for destruction if something went wrong, and with *B* 4-inch and light weapons manned, the *Amethyst* prepared to leave. She was extraordinarily lucky in that just as the planned moment for escape occurred, a river passenger steamer appeared sailing in the same direction. Kerans decided to follow her, and for half an hour all went well. Then the *Amethyst* was challenged by a Communist landing craft and came under heavy fire once more from the shore. Some of the ship's plates were sprung by a near miss, but she replied with her lighter guns and one 4-inch round. The Communist fire was confused and heavily damaged the steamer and their own landing craft. With the new leak stopped, but old ones causing trouble, the frigate, helped by the current, raced down the river at 22 knots, well over her official maximum speed, coming under fire once more from the Kiang Yin naval base. The boom was safely negotiated, a Chinese patrol boat was smothered with fire at point-blank range, a small junk running without lights was cut in two, and the forts at Woosung at the river mouth were safely passed. Just as dawn broke the *Amethyst* met the destroyer *Concord*, sent up to engage the Woosung forts if they opposed the *Amethyst*. The escape was accomplished, and a relieved Brind, on board his flagship, the cruiser *Belfast*, received Kerans's famous signal: "Have rejoined the Fleet south of Woosung. No damage or casualties. God Save the King."

It had been a daring operation, and the whole Yangtse incident reflected well on the junior officers and ratings involved. Nevertheless, at this range it does seem slightly provocative to have sailed a warship across the front of an army about to engage on a potentially tricky amphibious operation. The battery that first hit the *Amethyst* was guarding a major concentration of Communist assault shipping, and the gunners may well have taken the *Amethyst* for a Chinese Nationalist vessel, despite her flags. The *Amethyst* had sailed from an enemy anchorage from which the Communists expected no movement, as the ships there were known to be wavering in their loyalties. The *Amethyst* might well have been an enemy vessel, as the Nationalists operated ex-British ships. The gunners and their local commanders could take no risks, and it is significant that the *Amethyst* came under greatest pressure when she was close to the actual planned crossing points. Furthermore, the Nationalist air strike might well have confirmed her belligerency in the eyes of the gunners, especially in view of the *Consort*'s systematic bombardment just afterwards. Once the Communists had their mistake confirmed, face had to be saved at all costs. Although the ship escaped, the Communists had made a strong political point. Foreign warships were certainly no longer welcome in Chinese internal waters; they could now be opposed only too effectively. The door that had been opened with the Opium Wars of a hundred years before was now slammed firmly shut.

Ironically it soon seemed quite likely that RN warships would be breaking a blockade by Nationalist forces of Communist-controlled territory. Even before Kerans's escape a Blue Funnel liner, the *Anchises*, was forced ashore by Nationalist Mustang fighter bombers in the Whangpoo River. The *Black Swan* had not been allowed to take action, as to do so would have meant a possible clash with Communist Chinese forces when the *Amethyst* was still imprisoned. The lessons of the Yangtse incident had been learned. In June the Nationalists declared a full-scale blockade of Shanghai, now Communist controlled, and the British government came under pressure from ship owners to assist British-owned merchantmen in the Yangtse Estuary. The owners recognized the dangers of clashes with Communists if warships went too far upriver but wished the Royal Navy to provide "unobtrusive" salvage-and-rescue assistance if British ships encountered difficulties above Woosung or the Taku Bar. Orders to this effect were duly issued on 26 June, with a supplementary order the following day that if there was no Communist opposition, there was no objection to H.M. ships going to the Whangpoo entrance. It was confirmed the following day that ships were not to face either Communist fire or go into waters over which the Nationalists still had de facto jurisdiction.

There was a difference of opinion between Fraser and the Admiralty on the one hand and Brind on the other over the extent of the action to be taken to keep trade flowing to Shanghai, where there were still considerable British commercial interests and four thousand British nationals. Fraser was very anxious that there not be any overt British action on behalf of the Nationalists, support for which he compared (with feeling, given his imprisonment by the Bolsheviks thirty years before) with the fruitless support given by the British to the White Russians and to the Greeks against the Turks in the years after the First World War. He argued that the Nationalists had never been especially friendly to Britain and that it was quite obvious that they were going to be losers with whom the U.K. should not identify. The only way to divorce the Communists from the Soviets was to show the former their dependence on commercial connections with the West. Fraser was in favor of as much assistance as possible being given, if necessary covertly, to the blockade runners. He and the Admiralty also felt strongly about the danger in permitting them precedent of forces that had not been granted belligerent rights in international law (this applied to both sides in the Chinese Civil War) interfering with British vessels on the high seas. Brind disagreed. He tended to take a more

"American" and anti-Communist view of affairs. He wished to keep up all kinds of pressure on the Communists. When a major blockade-busting operation was suggested in August 1949, he signalled to London his unhappiness at the prospect. His men were anti-Communist following the Yangtse incident, he argued, and the operation would divert attention from Hong Kong's security, which was a greater priority than Shanghai. Moreover, it would not make the Communists any more amenable on the subject of Hong Kong. He hinted strongly at the resulting feelings of the Americans and the local anti-Communist establishment with which he, somewhat naturally, identified: "The problem with our men could no doubt be solved, but their outlook is typical of views which will be strongly held elsewhere by people who will not be so ready to understand the real British purpose."[6]

This attitude perhaps goes some way to explain the relatively unaggressive stance adopted by the Royal Navy in the *Anchises* incident and others. Certainly by early September 1949 the ship owners were becoming concerned at the low profile being adopted. British merchantmen were indeed arrested but this was sometimes due to ships missing their escort. British warships were now authorized to use force if the Nationalists did so and to enter Chinese territorial waters. Brind was reinforced with a light fleet carrier from the Mediterranean, HMS *Triumph*, and plans were laid for her to cover a major convoy into Shanghai with a cruiser and up to ten destroyers or frigates giving additional protection. The chiefs of staff were somewhat anxious about the political repercussions of a Nationalist ship being sunk or aircraft shot down, but the plan was being discussed by the Cabinet late in August 1949, with the possibility of air strikes on Nationalist airfields if the convoy was attacked on the high seas. Only the decision of the government's law officers that the Shanghai blockade was legal after all, prevented what might have been another major Chinese incident.[7]

In November there was renewed pressure from the Foreign Office for action. Bevin felt that it was high time that the Royal Navy took action to force the Nationalists to allow British ships into Shanghai. Hall, the first lord, reminded the foreign secretary that it had been decided in August that such action was illegal. The problem persisted into 1950, with Fraser and the Naval Staff getting quite belligerent about the continued blockade and persistent bombings of British ships and their crews. In February Sir George Creasey, VCNS, urged action to be taken as a "matter of urgency," although he recognized the danger to British lives and property from Nationalist air attacks in reprisal. This opened up the possible requirement of bombing the airfields in Formosa, something perhaps slightly beyond the capabilities of the Pacific Station's single light fleet carrier *Triumph* with its twelve Seafires and twelve old Fireflies (the Nationalist Air Force deployed an estimated 260 fighters, 105 light bombers, and 25 long-range Liberator bombers). Even when giving cover to ships approaching Shanghai, the best a light fleet carrier could do was to maintain two to four aircraft for two periods of three days each with an interval of four days between. It could not even do that on a continuous basis for much more than forty days. The carrier would be operating 800 miles from its base, making any damage it might receive even more embarrassing. The Joint Planning Staff made these points in a paper presented to the chiefs of staff in early March, which pointed out the unfortunate broader effects of fighting the Nationalists: weakening them against the Communists, provoking them into action against Hong Kong, and forcing Britain into the appearance of siding with the

The Seafires and Firefly Is of HMS *Triumph*, the first British carrier air group committed to the Korean War in 1950. (Imperial War Museum)

Communist Chinese against the United States. The Foreign Office was particularly anxious about the last of these three, although others pointed out the usefulness of keeping a viable British merchant community in China as a way of weaning the new Communist regime away from the Russians.[8]

The Joint Planners pointed out that if Chinese territorial waters were not to be violated, as the Foreign Office insisted, the only action possible was to take measures against the Nationalist blockading ships themselves. Minesweeping could only be done with the approval of the Communist authorities, and even then it would be difficult to give the operation air cover. The only way the air threat could be seriously diminished was to blockade the supply of aviation fuel to Formosa. It was recognized that any operation rested on the unlikely foundation of U.S. acquiescence and the report did not receive the chiefs of staff's approval.[9] British warships did remain in the Yangtse Estuary until the Korean War forced their withdrawal in June 1950. Some ships were, however, retained on patrol on the Chinese coast, especially in the area of Hong Kong and Formosa as interference with maritime traffic continued.[10]

Although much had obviously changed, British warships in Chinese waters did not entirely abandon their traditional roles or attitudes. For example, in November 1950 the frigate HMS *Cardigan Bay* secured the release of the British steamship *Shun Lee*, detained by the Nationalists in the Pe Chin Islands. The *Cardigan Bay* found the ship anchored under a 75-mm gun battery, "a fact," her captain, W.L.M. Brown, reported, which "fortified my belief that diplomacy not force was the right method of approach." The Nationalist warship, *Lee Chun*, now appeared and invited Brown on board for dinner; Brown refused, and the following day, on board the *Shun Lee*, politely informed the Chinese that there was little point in detaining the ship as she would have to sail eventually, and then the ship "would come under the orders of the ubiquitous British Navy who would remove the guard if necessary." After this point had been made, the RN officers accepted invitations to a banquet that evening. The *Shun Lee* was duly released the following day. The whole incident might have taken place any time in the previous century.[11]

Trouble with the Nationalist blockade of the mainland and vice versa persisted, and from mid-1952 to the beginning of 1954 there were some forty cases of British ships being intercepted off the China coast. British naval patrols were sometimes successful. In 1953 the *St. Bride's Bay* prevented a Nationalist warship from seizing a British merchant ship in the Formosa Straits. There was also trouble with the Communists as the Korean War exacerbated tensions. In 1952 the destroyer *Consort* and frigate *Burghead Bay* were fired on by Communist batteries near Hong Kong. On 9 September 1953 a more serious incident occurred when the small RN harbour defence motor launch (HDML) 1323 was badly shot up in the Pearl River by a Communist landing ship, with the loss of six of her crew and a member of the Hong Kong Defence Force. With the help of the destroyer *Concord*, the HDML was able to return to Hong Kong with all but two of the survivors wounded.[12]

If patrols protecting merchantmen from ill-controlled Chinese soldiers and sailors were part of the Royal Navy's "familiar routine," so, in a sense, was fighting limited wars with Chinese and other Asian forces. There had been a series of such conflicts in the nineteenth century, and another broke out on 25 June 1950. On that day heavy fighting started between North and South Korea. Several Royal Navy warships were in the area. HMS *Triumph* had just left Japan en route to Hong Kong. The cruiser *Jamaica* was also on passage to Hong Kong, while the cruiser *Belfast*, destroyers *Consort* and *Cossack*, and the frigates *Black Swan* and *Alacrity* were in Japanese ports. The frigate HMS *Hart* was on her way to Japan. Rear Admiral W.G. Andrewes, who had taken over from Madden as second in command to Brind, was flying his flag in the *Belfast* and was soon at sea on his way to Yokosuka for consultations with Vice Admiral C. Turner Joy, the American Commander Naval Forces Far East (COMNAVFE). As the *Belfast* butted through the stormy night of the 26th, a signal arrived from Brind warning Andrewes that British ships might be called on for action under the U.N. Charter. The Security Council, with the Soviet representative absent, had already condemned the North Korean invasion and ordered the evacuation of Communist forces from the South. On the 27th the Northern attack was further denounced, and U.N. members were authorized to help South Korea defend herself.[13]

The following day the Cabinet Defence Committee met in the prime minister's room in the House of Commons to consider the chiefs of staff memorandum recommending that British naval forces in Japanese waters should be placed at the disposal of the U.S. naval commander for U.N. operations in aid of South Korea. Fraser put the COS's case. Successful action in Korea would help the situations in Malaya and Hong Kong. The Russians showed no sign of helping the North Koreans, and British forces should not be used in the protection of Formosa or against China. Action by sea and air forces alone would not be enough, but the service chiefs felt that no land forces could be made available, or indeed RAF units. The main aim was to show solidarity with the Americans. Commonwealth governments would be asked to take similar action.[14]

The previous day the *Belfast* had arrived at Yokosuka, and Andrewes went to see Turner Joy in Tokyo. The latter, worried about possible Soviet intervention, advised Andrewes to concentrate his ships at sea south of Japan, and by the afternoon the *Belfast* had sailed, followed next day by the three frigates. On the 29th, as the *Belfast*, *Jamaica*, and *Cossack* rendezvoused, orders arrived from London to place all RN forces at Joy's disposal in support of the resolutions of the Security Council. On the orders of COMNAVFE, the *Jamaica*, *Black Swan*, and *Alacrity* were sent to the east coast of Korea to join Rear Admiral J.M. Higgins, commander of Joy's "Support Force" and flying his flag in the 6,000-ton antiaircraft cruiser *Juneau*, escorted by two U.S. destroyers. The cruisers met just south of the 38th Parallel in the fading light of the 30th, and next day they patrolled around the coast of South Korea. At midnight the three British frigates arrived; HMS *Alacrity* was then sent to the west coast of the peninsula, and the American destroyers also seem to have been detached. So it was that as 2 July 1950 dawned clear and fine, the *Juneau*, *Jamaica*, and *Black Swan* were patrolling together near Chumunjin and about to fight the one real surface action of the war.

The North Korean Navy had been built up by the Soviets over the previous few years as a coastal force of around fifty small vessels. Among these were a number of little 14-ton G-5-class motor torpedo boats, four of which were detected at dawn escorting a convoy of about ten trawlers. The MTBs were fitted to carry torpedoes launched over the stern, but these could be removed to carry troops or supplies. It is quite likely that this was the case on the 2nd, as when the four boats raced in to attack the two cruisers they confined themselves to gunfire. With nothing better than machine guns they stood little chance against the much heavier armament of their adversaries, and a rain of shells blew up one of the attackers immediately. A second was badly hit and stopped ablaze, dead in the water, to sink later. The two remaining G-5s raced off in opposite directions. One was forced ashore and destroyed by gunfire, but the second's maximum speed of 45 knots proved too much for the 19–20 knot *Black Swan* that was in pursuit, and the North Korean boat escaped. The U.S./U.K. force then turned its attention to the remaining North Korean vessels, and three of the trawlers were soon despatched. Light artillery opened up from the shore, and the warships were forced to withdraw. It was thought that the convoy's survivors had taken shelter in Chumunjin, and the *Black Swan* carried out two bombardments of the port later in the day with her six 4-inch guns. Due to lack of proper observation, results were doubtful although next day the Americans claimed the destruction of most, if not all, of the rest of the convoy by a bombardment carried out by the *Juneau*.

As these first shots were being fired, to the south HMS *Triumph*, with the *Belfast*, *Cossack*, and *Consort* as escort, was joining the U.S. Seventh Fleet. As ordered by Turner Joy, Andrewes had set sail for the Seventh Fleet's Okinawa base on 28 June, arriving on 1 July. There he conferred with the fleet commander, Vice Admiral Arthur D. Struble, who wished to use the *Triumph* to supplement his carrier *Valley Forge* in air strikes against North Korea. There was a considerable speed differential (8 knots) between the two carriers, but problems of RN/USN cooperation were remarkably few in the newly constituted Task Force 77. In the spring, joint Anglo-American exercises had been held, and these proved to have been useful in familiarizing the British ships with U.S. signal books and procedures. Many of Andrewes's personnel also had had experience serving with U.S. forces in World War II.

The first attacks were carried out on 3 July, the *Triumph* launching the first carrier strike of the war at 0545. Her air group comprised 800 Squadron with twelve Seafire 47 single-seat fighters and 827 Squadron with a similar number of Firefly I two-seat fighter-reconnaissance aircraft. The Seafire 47 was an excellent interceptor, but its combat radius and weapons load were severely limited. The old Firefly I was even worse as regards range, and strikes could not be planned for more than 120–130 miles away. This meant that whereas the *Valley Forge*'s Skyraiders and Corsairs, covered by Panther jet fighters, were tasked with bombing targets near Pyongyang, the enemy capital, the Fleet Air Arm machines had to make do with Haeju, just north of the 38th Parallel. The British were somewhat jealous of the greater flexibility of the American air group. All twelve Fireflies and nine Seafires were launched to hit the airfield there with rockets. No aircraft were spotted, but damage was inflicted on buildings and hangars; all machines returned safely.

With combat air patrols to fly, the *Triumph* could not muster enough Seafires for another strike that day, and on the 4th the RN flying operations had to be delayed until 1100 as the *Valley Forge*'s high speed had taken the force too far from potential targets. At last, however, 827 Squadron and seven Fireflies were launched to attack the railway between Haeju across the 38th Parallel to Yonan. Two hits were scored on a bridge, and a column of marching troops was strafed. One British aircraft was damaged by ground fire.

On 4 July President Truman announced a blockade of the Korean coast, and two days later Admiral Joy told Andrewes that with the "non-American" U.N. naval contribution he was to take responsibility for the west side of the peninsula. So began the main Royal Navy commitment of the war. The west coast of Korea was the more difficult of the two geographically, with its islands, bays, shoals, mudbanks, and its wide tidal range, over 30 feet in places. But this was only one problem for Andrewes; another was that of building up base facilities in Sasebo. A headquarters ship was an urgent requirement and, as no proper depot ship was

Headquarters ship for the Royal Navy effort in the Korean War was the converted Yangtse steamer, HMS *Ladybird*. (Imperial War Museum)

available, Admiral Brind provided his despatch vessel, HMS *Alert*. She was replaced from September by HMS *Ladybird*, a converted Yangtse steamer. Only in April 1953, shortly before the war's end, did a proper depot ship arrive, HMS *Tyne*.

As for the blockade itself, Andrewes issued his orders on 8 July. His objects were: the blockade of the North Korean coast against supply vessels, transports, and North Korean warships; the prevention of any infiltration into South Korea by sea; the provision of naval support against North Korean targets ashore. Welcome reinforcements had arrived in the shape of another cruiser, HMS *Kenya* and two more destroyers, the *Comus* and *Cockade,* and Andrewes was able to divide his "Task Group" into three "Task Units" each of one cruiser escorted by one or two destroyers or frigates.

HMS *Jamaica* now returned from the east coast where she had just suffered the first British casualties of the war. Following the surface action of 2 July, she had refuelled in Sasebo and then relieved the USS *Juneau* in the Chumunjin area. Bombardments of various coastal targets were carried out in an attempt to slow down the Communist invasion, and on 7 July, together with the frigate HMS *Hart* and the U.S. destroyer *Lyman K. Swenson*, she bombarded Yangyang in North Korea itself. On the 8th the *Jamaica* and *Swenson* moved south to where there were suitable cliff roads for bombardment. Moving at only 6 knots to gain accuracy, the British cruiser was taken under fire by a hidden 76.2-mm gun battery, which scored a hit on the starboard tripod of the mainmast, killing two and wounding others. The Communist guns were soon silenced, and the two ships returned to their original targets.

At 0600 on the 9th Andrewes had set off to inaugurate the blockade with the *Belfast, Cossack,* and *Consort*. Apart from a brief bombardment by the *Cossack*, little of note occurred before the unit was relieved. The *Belfast* and *Cossack* only had 48 hours in Japan, however, before the deteriorating situation caused them to be sent post haste to help relieve pressure on the Pusan perimeter. Unable to give close support due to lack of observers, the two ships blasted more distant targets farther up the east coast. By 19 July, however, proper arrangements had been made for ground spotting, and with the additional help of air observation, greater results were achieved. Rear Admiral Higgins was impressed by the *Belfast*'s bombardment in which 350 rounds of 6-inch were fired. Yondok was almost completely destroyed and was recaptured by South Korean forces on the 21st, supported once more by the *Belfast*'s fire.

Carrier strikes from the *Valley Forge* were making their contribution to stemming the Communist advance. The *Triumph* was having vibration problems with her shafts, but her more important difficulty was the range of her aircraft, which restricted the carrier to the role of flying combat air patrols with her Seafires and ASW patrols with her Fireflies. The only opposition came from a USAF B-29 that shot down a Seafire, no doubt mistaking it for a Soviet-built Yak. Miles of high-power running were exacerbating mechanical problems in the *Triumph*, and her relief at the end of July by the USS *Philippine Sea* allowed ten days of much-needed self-maintenance.

The carrier next began supporting the west coast blockade whose routine was being kept up by the three cruiser-based groups in cooperation with South Korean patrol vessels and minesweepers. Despite some American doubts, little, if anything,

The destroyer HMS *Cossack* in the ice off the island of Cho-do, an active area of British operations in the Korean War. (Imperial War Museum)

was getting through to the Communists by sea. Shore bombardments were also being carried out, a particularly heavy attack on Inchon being made by both the *Belfast* and *Kenya*, supported by the *Cossack* and *Charity*, on 5 August; on this occasion the *Belfast* fired 252 rounds of 6-inch ammunition, the *Kenya* 163. The return of the *Triumph* allowed Andrewes, now flying his flag in her, to tighten up the blockade, and her aircraft flew various patrols and strikes in which a number of North Korean vessels were sunk. Opposition to the blockade was minimal, but on 23 August HMS *Comus* was attacked by two Ilyushin Il-10 bombers 85 miles west of Kunsan. The "Shturmoviks" attacked singly from astern. The first dropped four bombs that holed the ship on the port side, killing one sailor and wounding another. The second dropped its load ahead of the ship and missed completely. The *Comus* immediately made for Kure for repairs, escorted by her sister, HMS *Consort*, and covered by U.S. carrier fighters.

Despite the opposition of the chiefs of staff, Attlee had insisted in late July that ground forces be sent to Korea in order to please the Americans "who had hinted very strongly that even small land forces would be very acceptable."[15] At the end of August the first two British infantry battalions to reach Korea arrived in the cruiser *Ceylon* and the ferry carrier *Unicorn*. The former, on loan from the East Indies Station, was replacing the *Belfast* while the latter was making a second trip to reinforce the *Triumph*'s air group. She was carrying the last fourteen of the twenty-six reserve aircraft (fourteen Seafires, twelve Fireflies) at Singapore, and these were transferred to HMS *Triumph* at Sasebo to replace operational losses and unserviceable machines. Seafires were always difficult to operate, and 800 Squadron by this time was down to two-thirds serviceability. The "new" aircraft, however, being the oldest and in the worst condition, were even more difficult to keep in the air, as the *Triumph*'s hard-pressed crew found in her next operational period. The American fleet carriers had been withdrawn for maintenance, and the British carrier did her best to replace them in their task of interdicting the supply lines of the North Korean forces pressing on the Pusan perimeter. Despite bad weather her planes carried out some effective strikes on rail and road targets. The price was high: rough seas led to hard landings, which worsened the Seafires' weak rear fuselage problem. Although there were no losses to enemy action, accidents and unserviceability reduced the *Triumph*'s stock of useable aircraft to about a dozen.

Planning was now in progress for the landings at Inchon, which were to turn the tide of the war against the North Koreans. This was kept an American affair, but the 6-inch guns of HMS *Kenya* and HMS *Jamaica* were a valuable addition to the gunfire support groups of Task Force 90. Admiral Andrewes's Task Force 91 of Commonwealth and South Korean forces was to maintain the western blockade, provide cover and reconnaissance for the attack force and air spotting for the two British cruisers. Andrewes divided his force into two groups, a northern and southern, and his British units, *Triumph, Ceylon, Charity, Cockade,* and *Cossack,* were concentrated in the former. As the U.S. landing forces sailed round the Korean peninsula on 13 and 14 September, the *Triumph* flew search missions to check on their positions and normal blockade patrols. Two Seafires were kept on deck for immediate launch. With her reduced air group this was all the British light carrier could do. During the night of the 14th/15th, the *Charity* was sent north to form a barrier patrol protecting the landings, and the *Ceylon* joined the main covering group, which took up position to the west of Inchon. If Soviet submarines were found, they were to be attacked—something that rather worried Andrewes.

As the first glimmers of the rising sun appeared on the eastern horizon on the 15th, D-Day, two Fireflies roared down the *Triumph*'s deck, the first spotting missions for the British cruisers' guns. Bombardment of Inchon had begun on the 13th and continued through the next day, the two British cruisers adding their share to the general effort. American aerial spotting of variable but increasing effectiveness had been used, and by the middle of the 14th the peninsula of Walmi-do, the first objective of the landing forces, had been silenced. On D-Day itself the *Kenya* and *Jamaica,* with the two U.S. heavy cruisers *Rochester* and *Toledo,* opened fire on Walmi-do at 0545. Each British cruiser had one spotting Firefly allocated to her, and as the U.S. Marines approached the beaches, the aircraft designated new targets in the town of Inchon itself. The bombardment went on at intervals all day, the *Triumph* providing three pairs of Fireflies in constant rotation. The attempt was made to limit fire to known military targets, and HMS *Jamaica* succeeded in hitting an ammunition dump with spectacular results. The *Kenya* was withdrawn just before the second stage of the landings began, but the *Jamaica* played her part in the final pre-landing bombardment.

The two British cruisers were not required for bombardment work the next day, but there was greater excitement on the 17th. Just before 0600 two aircraft appeared overhead. They were initially mistaken for "friendlies," but as the first approached the USS *Rochester,* it dived and released two bombs, which fell astern. The second also dropped a bomb that landed on the American cruiser's crane but failed to explode. The two North Korean machines, a Yak-9 and Shturmovik, then made for HMS *Jamaica,* which had already opened fire. As it flew over the *Jamaica,* the Il-10 raked her port side with gunfire, and one sailor was killed and two others wounded. One machine gun bullet penetrated the 1-inch armor protecting the rear of the 6-inch gun turret, grazing—and surprising—the one rating inside. The

Shturmovik was badly hit, however, and was brought down; the more nimble Yak got away.

By 19 September it had become difficult for the *Triumph*'s spotters to find worthwhile targets for the two ships and they left Inchon. General MacArthur had already signaled the British admiral in typically expansive terms that his ships had "added another glamorous page to the long and brilliant histories of the Navies of the British Commonwealth." Certainly the cruisers had been worked hard keeping the ships at constant readiness. The *Jamaica*'s crews had fired 1,290 rounds of 6-inch and 393 rounds of 4-inch ammunition, the *Kenya*'s 1,242 rounds of 6-inch and 205 of 4-inch.

Off the coast Admiral Andrewes had spun out his air group's limited strength to continue the duller, but no less arduous, tasks of blockade. Attacks were carried out on any enemy craft seen, and a particularly heavy raid was mounted on the port of Chinnampo on D-Day itself. On the 17th HMS *Charity* treated a small North Korean gun battery near Haeju to a 4.5-inch bombardment, and HMS *Ceylon* engaged another battery near Fankochi Point with her 6-inch guns. By the 20th, with the landings safely accomplished, Andrewes withdrew, leaving HMS *Ceylon*, three British and two Canadian destroyers to continue the routine blockade.

There was, however, a third Royal Navy contribution to the Inchon landings. From the beginning of the war British frigates had escorted the troop and supply ships that ran between Japan and South Korea. For Inchon the "Escort Element," composed of the *Mounts Bay, Whitesand Bay,* two "Loch"-class New Zealand frigates, three American-manned "River"-class ships (ironically recently returned from Soviet service), and an old French sloop, formed Task Force 90.7 under American command. The element's job was forming an "Iron Ring" 40 miles to the southwest of Inchon and 50 miles long to protect the landings against attacks by submarines, aircraft, or small surface forces, to watch for and destroy mines, and to prevent any enemy movement between the offshore islands. The "Iron Ring" was maintained successfully until the middle of October. The only excitement to break the boring routine of patrolling and challenging was when HMS *Mounts Bay* spotted enemy forces building gun emplacements and fired 118 rounds from her 4-inch guns at them.

By late September HMS *Triumph* was at the end of her tether operationally. Only eight Fireflies and three Seafires remained serviceable. HMS *Theseus,* with a higher performance air group, was about to arrive, and on 25 September the *Triumph* sailed for home. The *Theseus* arrived on 5 October with 807 Squadron's Sea Fury FB11 single-seat fighter bombers and 810 Squadron's Firefly 5 two-seater fighter recce ASW aircraft. The Sea Fury was a superior aircraft to the Seafire both in terms of reliability and general combat flexibility, especially at lower altitudes. The Seafire was the better interceptor, but with little or no air threat the Sea Fury's longer range and heavier weapons load were more useful in Korean conditions. The Firefly 5 had a more powerful engine than the 1 and better radius of action and endurance.

Despite a deck landing accident that cut 810's strength by 25 percent, the *Theseus* went into action on 9 October with eighteen Sea Furies and nine Fireflies. The North Koreans were by now in full retreat, and U.N. forces had crossed the 38th Parallel. There was little sign of activity, but attacks were carried out against rail and road targets and the port of Chinnampo. Attacks were eventually suspended due to the difficulty of separating friend from foe in such a fluid situation. White flags were appearing all over the area covered by the *Theseus*'s planes, and aircraft were sent to overfly Pyongyang in order to discourage resistance. The enemy capital fell on 21 October, by which time the *Theseus*'s two squadrons were trying to find targets in the far northwest of Korea. There was little left to bomb by this time, and on the 21st the *Theseus* turned for Japan.

Some of the craft sunk at Chinnampo were small auxiliary minelayers, and the threat from this type of warfare had become serious by the middle of October. The Russians had supplied the North Koreans with mines and advisers on their use. Mines were first sighted by HMS *Kenya* and HMS *Charity* off Chinnampo on 17 September, and three weeks later they scored their first success inflicting heavy damage on an American destroyer off the east coast. With the great tidal range on the west coast, spotting moored minefields from the air was not too difficult, but new fields were being laid by night to catch blockading or bombarding vessels, and mines were floated down rivers out to sea. At the end of September this caused limits to be placed on the operations of the blockading ships.

As the U.N. forces advanced, mined harbors had to be cleared, and there was an acute shortage of mine countermeasure vessels; Japanese vessels used to clear their home waters for the Occupation authorities were pressed into service, some under the command of British frigates. Mines also kept at bay the U.N. attempt to mount a major amphibious operation at Wonsan, the main port on the east coast of North Korea. Admiral Andrewes had requested that British ships take some part in operations at Wonsan and HMS *Ceylon* and *Cockade* were included in the gunfire support group and HMS *Mounts Bay* and *Morecambe Bay* in the screening forces.

Despite these difficulties, however, by late October it seemed that the war was won. Andrewes was already laying plans for the British naval presence after victory. The *Theseus* had worn out its catapult and was limited to operating a reduced number of aircraft (thirteen Sea Furies and eight Fireflies) on combat air patrols for the minesweeping operations. She was eventually sent to Hong Kong. Andrewes himself sailed for Hong Kong in the middle of November in HMS *Kenya,* turning over to Captain Lloyd Davies a reduced western blockade group: the *Ceylon, Cossack, Morecambe Bay, Cardigan Bay,* seven Commonwealth destroyers and frigates, and a Dutch destroyer. On that day General MacArthur stated that the war would be over by Christmas.

It was not to be, for on 27 November the Communist Chinese, anxious to keep a Communist North Korea as a buffer between themselves and the Americans, launched a major offensive that soon had the U.N. forces in full retreat. On the 30th Joy requested the return of all RN ships available. The *Theseus, Kenya, Constance,* and *Concord* were soon on their way back through the winter gales to Korea, the recently promoted Vice Admiral Andrewes flying his flag in the carrier, which was carrying her squadrons' full complement of twenty-one Sea Furies and twelve Fireflies. The British ships were given the task of protecting the evacuation of the American 8th Army from Chinnampo, which was accomplished successfully with no opposition, and then reinstating the blockade and covering Inchon. Things temporarily quietened down ashore, but the *Theseus* kept up the pressure against

Communist communications, as many as 630 sorties being flown between December 5th and 26th. Morale was not high.

On New Year's Eve the Chinese offensive reopened. Seoul fell once more and Inchon had to be evacuated, covered by the gunfire of the cruisers *Kenya, Ceylon,* and the USS *Rochester*. On 7 January Royal Navy aircraft, for the first time, began flying close support missions for the United States Army. After a week's operations the *Theseus*'s catapult again began causing trouble, and rocket assistance had to be used to launch fully armed Fireflies, while the Furies were operated with reduced fuel loads. The regular rotation of an American CVL or CVE with the British carrier on the west coast was now agreed upon with the 7th Fleet commander, and the USS *Bataan* relieved the *Theseus* on 16 January.

As the Chinese advance recovered all of North Korea and some of the South, Andrewes suggested that the islands off the coast should be retained with South Korean garrisons as bases for the inshore blockade and to limit a renewal of the mining threat. Garrisons were, therefore, landed on islands as far north as the Yalu Gulf. Pengyong was the HQ for an American-officered guerrilla organization called Leopard, which began to work in close cooperation with the blockading forces. The same could not be said of the various other C.I.A. and American-armed-forces-controlled clandestine groups that began to infest this west coast area. It was very difficult for Admiral Andrewes, or his successors, to find out about their operations, and considerable confusion resulted—sometimes with tragic results.

In the middle of January 1951 the U.N. forces had once more begun to drive the Communists back up the peninsula. The *Theseus* provided air support, flying up to sixty-six sorties a day, and HMS *Ceylon* helped bombard Inchon, being replaced by the *Belfast* at the end of January on her return from the U.K. Admiral Andrewes wished to create a feint landing threat here, but although the preliminary bombardments were carried out, the port fell before the full-scale operation could be mounted on 10 February. As the U.N. forces advanced, the policy of continued diversionary bombardment pressure was kept up.

Since his promotion, Vice Admiral Andrewes had been serving under American Rear Admiral A.E. Smith, the commander of Task Force 95, the U.N. Blockade and Escort Force. Much to his surprise, the Americans decided to promote Andrewes to command the whole task force, with Smith in control of all operational groups except those on the west coast. With Andrewes in overall command, the policy of sending Commonwealth ships to the east coast was confirmed, and British and other west coast ships were sent to reinforce the siege of Wonsan, where islands off the port were captured and held by South Korean forces, and U.N. warships kept up a constant bombardment of the shore. The *Belfast* began this reinforcement on 19 February, but more usually the British contribution was a destroyer or *Black Swan*-class frigate.

Air and gunfire support to the advance continued as it ground its way north through March and April. AA fire claimed some of the *Theseus*'s planes, and the carrier acquired an American helicopter for rescue duties. Vice Admiral Andrewes came to the end of his distinguished tour of duty at the beginning of April and was relieved by Rear Admiral A. Scott Moncrieff, who arrived in Japan in HMS *Belfast* on 14 April. Task Force 95 now reverted to USN command.

During April 1951 HMS *Theseus* and the USS *Bataan* operated together off the

The vile conditions experienced in winter off Korea are vividly portrayed by this picture of Sea Furies and Fireflies on the deck of the *Theseus* in 1951. (Imperial War Museum)

east coast of Korea during the temporary withdrawal of the Seventh Fleet's ships. Again the comparative slowness of the British ship created problems, but friendly rivalry between the two carriers speeded up air operations to a significant extent. Strikes were made against a variety of targets, and gunnery spotting missions were also flown. Opposition was the worst yet experienced. In 276 sorties three Sea Furies and a Firefly were shot down by AA fire, and another Sea Fury was forced to land at an airfield ashore. A fifth Sea Fury was badly damaged by mistake by USMC Corsairs. The U.S. helicopter again proved of value in the rescue role. After a final spell on the west coast, the *Theseus* sailed for home on 25 April, having flown almost 3,500 operational sorties with no losses, apart from those inflicted by enemy action. The lack of deck landing accidents especially impressed the U.S. Navy.

The replacement British carrier was HMS *Glory* with 804 Squadron (twenty-one Sea Furies) and 812 Squadron (twelve Firefly 5s). She also carried an RN Dragonfly search-and-rescue helicopter. The *Glory* was soon called upon to add her weight to blunting the abortive Chinese spring offensive that opened on 22 April. The pressure of air and gunnery bombardment was also kept up over the succeeding weeks. Again there were joint operations with the USS *Bataan*, but the difference in the endurance of the American Corsairs and the British Fireflies continued to cause problems. The speed differential of the carriers compounded the difficulties once more, especially as the *Glory* was suffering engine problems and was getting even slower. In early May she was reduced to 23 knots, in mid-May to 18.

In May a diversionary landing was organized near the island of Choda. A major demonstration was arranged with carrier air strikes from the *Glory* and a gun bombardment from HMS *Ceylon* and the heterogeneous frigate force (that now included a Colombian vessel). Marines from HMS *Ceylon* carried out the landing, operating from an American LSD. Not many Communist forces seemed to be around to witness this operation, but afterwards, the enemy did seem to put more effort into defending the area.

The blunting of the spring offensive and the successful U.N. counterattack led to the opening of armistice negotiations in July. The war now acquired the static character that it was to retain until its end. Before negotiations began, the *Glory*'s aircraft had intensified their pressure on the Hwanghae/Taedong area. Despite catapult problems, some fifty-one sorties were flown per day in groups or 'events,' one of seven and four of eleven aircraft on combat air patrol, ASW patrol, and armed reconnaissance missions. About 100 tons of explosives were landed on the enemy for the loss of two machines. Once talks were under way, it became important to dispute Communist control in the Han Estuary area, which had been South Korean before the war. The *Glory* flew air strikes, and groups of ships were sent into the estuary to bombard targets and generally exert a positive U.N. presence. Poor charts and badly briefed U.S. aircraft pilots proved something of a danger in these difficult waters, but for the rest of 1951 HMS *Comus, Black Swan, Amethyst, Cardigan Bay, Mounts Bay, Morecambe Bay, Whitesand Bay,* and *St. Bride's Bay* were all used on these duties, firing many thousands of rounds. Small-scale landings and bombardments were carried out elsewhere, unusual participants in these being the despatch vessel *Alert* and even the ferry carrier *Unicorn* (that was armed with eight 4-inch guns), one the of oddest shore-bombardment vessels in naval history.

Towards the end of 1951 the Communists began to go over to the offensive against the offshore islands. On the night of 30 November/1 December a major assault was mounted by one thousand men in junks and rubber boats against Tae Wha Do in the far north. HMS *Cockade* rushed to the rescue and was hit by the shore batteries on one of her after gun mountings; one sailor was killed. She sank two or three of the Communist craft, including a naval motor patrol vessel, but was unable to get in touch with the guerrillas on shore to give direct help. The "Leopard" men swiftly evacuated in their own boats. To protect Sok To and Choda, Captain G.A. Thring of HMS *Ceylon* instituted Operation Smoking Concert, a series of systematic patrols in the swept channels around the islands, which led to a series of sharp little engagements in December. Protection also had to be given to islands in the Han Estuary.

Shore bombardments increased in their intensity in the first part of 1952, and in May almost 15,000 rounds of 4-, 4.5- and 6-inch ammunition were fired by Scott Moncrieff's ships. Orders went out to confine fire to observed targets, and when air spotting was not available, naval and Royal Marine personnel were landed to control the bombardment. Deep behind enemy lines these spotting groups often could not resist the odd ambush against enemy forces. British ships also took part in bombardments on the east coast, to which a frigate or destroyer was regularly rotated. The ships sometimes closed the coast to 40-mm gun range, well within reach of enemy fire. On 7 February HMS *Alacrity* was hit no less than seven times, and in April HMS *Concord* was hit on her *Y* gun by a shell that killed two men and wounded four. Trains were the major target, and in July a "Train Buster's Club" was organized by the Allied ships; HMS *Charity* was able to claim membership with a score of two.

The year 1952 saw several changes in the RN forces off Korea. In September

HMS *Newcastle* pounding Chinnampo with her six-inch guns. (Imperial War Museum)

Scott Moncrieff was replaced by Rear Admiral E.G. Clifford, and the two cruisers *Belfast* and *Ceylon* were replaced by HMS *Newcastle* and *Manchester* in July and September respectively. The *Glory* and *Ocean* successively provided the carrier support in an air campaign that steadily escalated as restrictions on "strategic" targets were lifted. On 24 June six electrical transformers were successfully attacked by the *Ocean*'s aircraft, and in July her Sea Furies and Fireflies (802 and 825 Squadrons) took part in the large-scale attacks on Pyongyang.

Enemy MiG jets now began to be encountered, a potent threat to piston-engined machines such as the *Ocean*'s. On 5 August a flight of four Sea Furies was attacked by eight of the jets. In the low-altitude dogfight the superior slow-speed maneuverability of the piston-engined fighters was exploited by the RN pilots, and one MiG was actually shot down by Lieutenant P. Carmichael; later the same day another MiG was damaged. Over the next few days there were more encounters with the Communist jets, and arrangements were made for American jet fighter cover.

HMS *Glory* with 801 Squadron (Sea Furies) and 821 Squadron (Fireflies) replaced the *Ocean* in November. The winter weather interfered with operations once more, and the Fireflies proved particularly vulnerable to engine problems. Nevertheless, the routine of attacks and patrols was kept up into 1953, and leaflet raids and attacks in support of the guerrillas added to the variety. In January the *Ocean*'s aircraft spotted for shore bombardments carried out by the battleship USS *Missouri*. Although they usually remained silent when big ships were in the vicinity, the Communist guns were now becoming tougher opponents, some being mounted in caves. Even the 16-inch shells of the *Missouri* or her sister ship *New Jersey*, which came to the west coast in May, were unable to silence them permanently. By May the spotters were from HMS *Ocean,* which had just reappeared with 807 Squadron (Sea Furies) and 810 Squadron (Fireflies). Her aircraft were also soon in action giving close air support against the Communist offensives that marked the final stages of the negotiations at Panmunjom. In July the *Ocean* landed three Firefly night fighters to counter the threat of Polikarpov PO-2 light aircraft that had spread their "nuisance" bombing operations to the Seoul area. The raiders had been operational around Choppeki Point since April, and one even attacked HMS *Newcastle,* which could not shoot it down, despite, or perhaps because of, her new AA gunnery system, intended for rather faster targets than a slow biplane.

In June, as the Panmunjom negotiations moved belatedly towards an armistice, the *Birmingham, Newcastle, Modeste,* and *Sparrow* supported American landing craft evacuating thousands of friendly Koreans from islands off the northwest coast. HMS *Tyne* sailed to the area to provide HQ facilities. All the Korean civilians were removed from the islands before the final signing of the armistice on 27 July, and the evacuation of military forces took until 1 August. The Korean War was over.

Over the previous three years thirty-two Royal Navy warships had seen service around Korea. They steamed over two million miles and used up over half a million tons of fuel. Ten of thousands of rounds had been fired by the British cruisers, destroyers, frigates, and HMS *Unicorn,* and over 20,000 carrier sorties flown. It had been a major British naval war, a fact too often forgotten in later years. Some 17,000 Royal Navy, Royal Marines, and Royal Fleet Auxiliary personnel served

HMS *Unicorn,* laid down before World War II as an aircraft maintenance ship to support the armored hangar carriers, saw postwar service in the Far East. She served in the Korean War in ferry, maintenance, and even short-bombardment roles. She went into reserve at the end of 1953 and, although refitted as an aircraft supply and repair ship in 1955, never went to sea again. She was scrapped in 1959. (Imperial War Museum)

in Korea and thirty-three RN officers and thirty-three ratings became casualties, twenty-five and seventeen respectively being killed or missing.

The cost in lives had not been very high because, except for their shore batteries and mines, Communist opposition to the U.N.'s naval offensive had been minimal. In this "limited" or, as the Admiralty put it, "warm" war the sea was the "sanctuary" from which U.N. forces had operated, almost as much as China was the "sanctuary" for the Communists. Nevertheless, the British ships in Korean waters had to stay constantly on the alert in case of enemy escalation, and weather conditions were often foul enough to make up for the lack of any man-made threat. Moreover, the lightness of British casualties does not detract from the positive contribution made by RN warships. Operations on the west coast were organized by British officers during the whole war, and British warships were the core of the multi-national naval force there. RN ships also made their presence felt on the east coast, and for a brief period an RN officer had been in charge of the entire blockading force. The British had in fact made a vital contribution in denying use of the sea to the enemy and rendering his land operations within range of ships' guns extremely dangerous.

British carrier-based planes were able to play an important role in the air offensive, the ship and air crews getting the most out of their dubious equipment by excellent training and skill. British carriers might only carry a few relatively low performance aircraft, but their operational efficiency was now second to none. The sortie rates achieved were much better than those of the British Pacific Fleet in 1945. The general RN effort could not have been greater as the main strength of the fleet had to be kept at home to face the apparent menace of a Soviet attack in Europe presaged by the Korean "diversion." By the beginning of 1953 the Admiralty was feeling the strain of the Korean commitment, especially in terms of manpower. It was also regarded as "providing very little even in the way of sound experience." The sea lords breathed a sigh of relief when operations finally came to an end.[16]

The end of the war in Korea did not mean that the Pacific Station ceased combat against Communist forces. The "emergency" in Malaya had broken out in June 1948, and the Royal Navy was soon making a contribution to operations against it. Flying from the shore bases at Sembawang, aircraft normally deployed in HMS *Triumph* struck against the guerrillas in October 1949. Surface units, such as the frigate *Amethyst,* patrolled off the coast, showing the flag of government authority and preventing any possible guerrilla sea traffic. There was never any evidence of attempts to land supplies or men, but the Royal Navy patrols on the east and west coast of the peninsula, with their constant searches of coastal traffic, may well have played some role in this effective isolation of the insurgents. More directly useful were the naval patrols in and around the Johore Straits between Singapore and Malaya that caused serious problems to small craft used by the Communists for logistical support. Even during the Korean War a number of ships were deployed in the waters around Malaya and Singapore. There were two frigates, a destroyer, and three MLs stationed there in July 1951. Shore bombardments continued, as, for example, in 1952 when the *Amethyst* sailed thirty miles up the Perak River to attack a guerrilla camp. This was but one of some thirty-nine bombardments that year by destroyers, frigates, and minesweepers, supported by five carrier air strikes. As the Communists retreated into the interior, it became more difficult to attack

A cruiser on Cold War duties: HMS *Newfoundland* bombards Communist positions in Malaya. (Imperial War Museum)

them from the sea. Larger guns were required, as when the cruiser *Newfoundland* carried out a 6-inch bombardment in 1954 of Kedah Peak in retaliation for the killing of the area's chief political officer. Carrier air power, now released from Korea, also became even more valuable in these conditions, and in the same year the newly refitted HMS *Warrior* was in action against the guerrillas with her Sea Furies and Fireflies. Both shelling and bombing, however, were only dubiously effective against an elusive foe. One cruiser spent an entire day firing a single shell every few minutes at a guerrilla supply route in the hope of hitting something. In early 1955 in an offensive against fifty to sixty guerrillas hiding in the Selangor swamps, naval gunfire from the destroyer *Comus* and cruiser *Newcastle* was added to army mortar bombs and attacks by RAF Lincoln bombers in an attempt to destroy the enemy by fire. The bombardment was kept up for a week. The year 1955 saw fifteen further bombardments by ten warships.[17]

Perhaps more useful than its gunfire was the Royal Navy's contribution to the transportation of ground forces along the coast and up rivers, the latter in landing craft and other small vessels. Similar craft were used for riverine patrols. Another vital contribution was a squadron of Royal Navy transport helicopters. It is perhaps strange that the Royal Navy's first operational helicopter squadron should go into action in a land-based troop transport role, but Britain was woefully short of helicopters in the early 1950s. In mid-1952 there were only ten helicopters, four Dragonflies and six Sycamores, in the RAF, and the Dragonflies were all in Malaya on casualty evacuation duties. The Royal Navy had nine Dragonflies for rescue, training, and trials. The Royal Air Force was expecting only six more machines in the next few months, but the Royal Navy was expecting to receive no less than forty-six more Dragonflies. As an interim measure, the Admiralty lent six of these to the RAF to bring the Malaya deployment to twelve. The Dragonfly, although a proven rescue machine, was of little use as a transport, but the potential of more powerful machines as anti-guerrilla weapons was obvious, and Sir Gerald Templer, the High Commissioner, was crying out for them. They could concentrate troops before located guerrillas could disperse, they could land troops for ambush and surprise attack, and they could rapidly reinforce the outlying estates. The only suitable helicopters in the pipeline were the American-built Sikorsky S-55s, twenty-five of which were about to be delivered from the U.S.A. for anti-submarine duties with the Royal Navy. (Some forty-five had been bid for under the Mutual Defence Aid Programme, but the Americans had only allowed the reduced figure.) The Americans were asked to accelerate delivery of the first ten, and the Royal Navy was persuaded to release these helicopters for use in Malaya. The latter did so on condition that they were operated by Naval Aviation.[18]

So it was that the Royal Navy's first front-line helicopter squadron, 848, was formed in October 1952 with Sikorsky Whirlwinds that were configured as HAR21 transports and not as ASW aircraft. They travelled to Singapore at the end of the year in the maintenance carrier *Perseus* and were rushed into service since the RAF's Dragonflies were non-operational in the adverse conditions. After starting operations in January with casualty evacuation, the squadron was soon positioning hundreds of soldiers at a time at jungle locations where guerrilla activity was expected. As the RAF official history put it: "The most important development stemming from 848 Squadron's arrival was the ability to handle the tactical movement of troops in respectable numbers which had not previously been practical."[19]

Although limited war activities against the Communists on the Asian mainland took up most of the Pacific/Far East Fleet's attention, there was one other significant

The Royal Navy's first operational helicopter squadron, 848, landing troops in Malaya from an American-built Sikorsky Whirlwind HAR21. (Imperial War Museum)

use of sea power in the area in a slightly less violent form. In the summer of 1947 unrest occurred in the Solomon Islands due to the activities of an organization called "Marching Rule." It was thought prudent to have a warship standing by when the movement's leaders were arrested, and the destroyer *Contest* duly arrived to carry out the mission. The "natives" seemed suitably overawed, and the British made the point of their continued power a little later when the carrier *Theseus* and destroyer *Cockade* called there on passage between Australia and Asian waters. As the naval estimates put it drily: "The visit of these two ships had a calming effect on the population."[20]

Following Indian independence the East Indies Station found most of its activity up in the Arabian Gulf/Horn of Africa area. Some of this was very traditional, as when at the end of 1953 the frigate *Flamingo* recaptured an Indian-owned dhow that had been captured by pirates and towed back to Aden. Warships were also rushed to ports threatened with unrest. Two *C*-class destroyers on passage between Britain and the Far East were able to give aid at Aden in December 1947, their crews joining those from the survey ship HMS *Challenger* to hold off the incensed Arab mobs intent on attacking Jewish houses in Palestine-related riots. A month later when clashes between Italians and Somalis erupted in Mogadishu, Somaliland, the frigate *Loch Quoich* was sent down from the Gulf to give assistance as required.[21]

More serious, and more indicative of the problems caused by the newly released forces of twentieth-century nationalism, was the crisis when the Iranian prime minister, Muhammas Mussadiq, nationalized the Anglo-Iranian Oil Company and its refinery at Abadan in 1951. This was a cheap source of much of the Royal Navy's oil. The Cabinet considered military action to reclaim the oilfields, but a few days' reflection convinced its members that "Operation Buccaneer" would be inexpedient. Action would only be taken, the government decided, if British lives were at risk. Property would only be defended if a "Communist" regime were set up. With the cooperation of Iraq, a cruiser, HMS *Mauritius* of the East Indies Station, was sent into the Shatt-al-Arab to cover the refinery. She arrived at the end of June and the following month was replaced by the smaller cruiser *Euryalus* and four *C*-class destroyers. The latter were later replaced by four larger, more impressive "Battle"-class destroyers. A tank-landing ship was also sent to the Gulf and another was mobilized from the reserve at Malta. The *Mauritius* reappeared to relieve the *Euryalus* after two months, and this larger ship took off the company staff in the early days of October.[22]

The Mediterranean Fleet was by far the largest of the British overseas naval deployments, and it could still put on a fine show of strength, even at the lowest point of the Royal Navy's fortunes in 1947–48. It also led an active operational life maintaining British interests in the traditional manner, although the opposition, as in China, was beginning to get a little more serious. A sign of this came in 1946 with a major incident in the Corfu Channel.[23] In May of that year the two cruisers *Orion* and *Superb* were shot at from the Albanian side as they sailed through the Channel, a strait where right of innocent passage was internationally recognized. Albania, however, now claimed the right to control sailings through the strait. The British stated they would reply to any further fire, and London hinted strongly to Admiral Sir Algernon Willis, fleet commander, that the passage of some ships through the strait to see "whether the Albanians have learned to behave them-

A cruiser on Cold War duties. HMS *Mauritius* maintains an outwardly impressive British presence at Trieste as flagship of the First Cruiser Squadron in 1946–47. (Imperial War Museum)

selves" would be welcome. Willis duly changed the programs of four of his ships, the cruisers *Mauritius* and *Leander,* and the destroyers *Saumarez* and *Volage.* These were now to sail north instead of south out of Corfu on 22 October, deliberately to test Albanian reactions.

It was a classic "freedom of the seas" operation, but it went disastrously wrong. The Albanians seem to have enlisted Yugoslav help in laying mines. The *Saumarez* duly hit one and was seriously damaged with heavy loss of life—thirty-six ratings. The *Volage* took her under tow only to have her own bows blown off by a second mine. HMS *Ocean* was standing by at sea, her Fireflies ready to act as gunnery spotters if a firefight developed. Immediately on *Saumarez*'s mine hit, the *Ocean* headed for Corfu, her plane guard destroyer, HMS *Raider,* going to the assistance of the stricken ships. Despite her damage, however, and the loss of one officer and seven men, the *Volage* was able to tow the *Saumarez* stern first into Corfu. The *Saumarez* was too badly damaged to be worth repairing, but the *Volage* received new bows and went back into service.

In November the Mediterranean Fleet mounted "Operation Retail" to sweep the offending mines in the Corfu Channel. A force of four ocean minesweepers and seven smaller vessels was covered by the *Ocean,* two cruisers, three destroyers, and two frigates, all the ships being ready for action. Some twenty-two mines were

The Corfu Channel incident: HMS *Saumarez* down by the bows after being mined. The *Volage* and the old light cruiser *Leander* are in the background. (Imperial War Museum)

swept without opposition, but the Albanians never accepted responsibility, despite an extended legal argument and adverse judgment in the International Court. Britain was awarded financial damages, which she has never received, although she also received censure for the minesweeping operation in Albanian waters. Further minesweeping of the old wartime channels (part of a massive operation which the RN conducted in the Atlantic, North Sea, English Channel, and Pacific) made passage of the Corfu Strait no longer dependent on Albanian goodwill. In a sense both sides had made their point.

By the time of the Corfu incident another activity was escalating, the prevention of illegal Jewish immigration into Palestine.[24] In July 1946 the British chiefs of staff had strongly recommended that illegal immigrants no longer be kept in camps in Palestine itself because of Arab hostility and the danger of war on two fronts, which the British could not afford; conflict with the Jews alone was proving difficult enough. The decision led to much greater problems with the illegal immigrant ships than before. This factor, coupled with the prospect of having to deal with faster and heavier blockade runners, led the Admiralty to ask for the right to arrest ships of dubious registration on the high seas. This was not granted due to legal objections, and the RN patrols generally waited until the ships entered Palestinian territorial waters before boarding. Nevertheless, exceptions were allowed, and in April 1947 the first sea lord signalled to CinC Med that he could use his discretion about boarding outside the three-mile limit even though the government could not officially countenance it. The Admiralty had very mixed feelings, however, about encroaching too much on the traditional doctrine of the freedom of the seas, and only a few days after the signal mentioned above, had come round to urging against a general policy of high-seas interception.

Most of the immigrant ships used in 1946 were small sailing caiques with the exception of a Panamian ex-corvette, the *Colon*, alias *Josiah Wedgwood*. This ship was intercepted on 25 June by two *Hunt*-class escort destroyers (later frigates), the *Haydon* and *Talybont*, and the fleet destroyer *Venus*. She was shadowed all night and, typically for the pre-Cyprus days, looked as if she was abandoning ship so that the British would pick up "survivors" to take them to Palestine. The British warships withdrew to discourage this, and the ship was eventually boarded by men from HMS *Venus.*

Few ships slipped through but one or two did, as when the ill-fated *Saumarez* allowed the French ship *Ideros* to land immigrants in August. The following month the serious fighting began. HMS *Childers* and *Chivalrous* stopped the Italian motor schooner *Fede,* alias *The Four Freedoms,* and a boarding party from the *Childers* jumped aboard. Fire hoses were used to help support the boarders who were forced, apparently reluctantly, to fight passengers of both sexes to gain control. The lesson was learned, and the future boarders were given extra training. Rifles were also replaced, on the *Childers'* recommendation, by entrenching-tool hafts, pistols, and bayonets as the boarding parties' major weapons. Another fight took place later in the month when the defenders used iron bars, hatchets, and knives, which led to tear gas and at least one shot being fired.

Another serious incident occurred in February 1947 when almost the entire Palestinian patrol—two destroyers, a frigate, and two ocean minesweepers—intercepted the Honduran *Ulua,* alias *Haim Arlossoroff.* The *Algerine*-class minesweepers *Welfare* and *Rowena* tried to board, but only thirteen men got over and they were overwhelmed and then thrown overboard. One of the destroyers picked them up and the *Rowena* tried again. A party got aboard but was forced to fire over the heads of the immigrants with Lanchester submachine guns and pistols to force a way to the bridge. Tear gas was again used.

In March 1947 as three known ships tried to run the blockade, one successfully, the Palestinian patrol was increased to eight ships—four destroyers, two frigates, and two *Algerine* fleet minesweepers. In April a major "battle" occurred on board one of the two ships boarded, the *Guardian,* carrying 2,622 immigrants; two of the latter were killed and others wounded when shooting broke out. In June, as three ships arrived, trailer pumps began to be used to increase the power of the water jets carried by the British ships. Chinese firecrackers were also found to be effective in clearing spaces.

In July a more important change in strategy occurred as the actual patrol was slightly reduced in size to allow more ships to be stationed all the way from the Western Mediterranean. The main target was the largest illegal yet, the 4,273 gross registered ton *President Warfield* alias *Exodus 1947* with no less than 4,500 passengers. After sailing from Sete on 11 July, it was shadowed by the frigate *Mermaid* who handed over to the destroyer *Cheviot* the following day. In order to overawe the potential immigrants a cruiser, the war veteran *Ajax,* was sailed from Malta, and she shadowed the *Warfield* all the way to Palestine. By the time the *Warfield* reached territorial waters she was accompanied by a veritable British squadron of the cruiser, four C-class destroyers, and a frigate.

As the *Warfield* tried to beach herself near Gaza, the four destroyers moved in to board, the Jewish defenders being outmaneuvered by the warships' use of platforms from bridge level on to the *Warfield's* upper deck. Resistance was heavy with steam jets, oil fuel jets, tear gas bombs, smoke bombs, and even lifesaving floats being projected or thrown at the British ships. Despite an early British conquest of the bridge, the Zionists continued to steer their ship from aft, ramming the *Chieftain* and *Cheviot* so badly that they needed extensive repairs. The fighting on board was generally limited to clubs, but the British resorted to shooting when they felt their lives were in danger. The final score was four British sailors injured to three Jews killed and twenty-seven injured. CinC Mediterranean signaled his congratulations to the boarder. Naval escort was provided to the three ships that took the illegals back westwards on a journey that ended, luckily for Zionist propagandists if not for the hapless immigrants themselves, in Germany.

Interception now generally took place as far to the west as possible with frigates and RAF Lancaster recce aircraft deployed at Gibraltar to act as a first line of defense. In August two suspicious ships, the *Northland* and *Paducah*, were followed right through the Mediterranean and into the Dardanelles, through which they passed to pick up their cargoes in Black Sea ports. RN warships were kept in the Aegean to cover them on their way out, and when the two vessels tried to run the blockade in October, interception duly took place, in each case four to five destroyers and frigates being used in the boarding operation. Meanwhile two more even larger suspicious vessels, the *Pan Crescent* and *Pan York*, were followed to the Dardanelles, and the Aegean squadron was reinforced by a cruiser to intercept the ships when they came out. When intelligence came in December that the ships had sailed from Burgas, Bulgaria, another cruiser was sent to reinforce the Aegean squadron still further. The Palestine patrol was also reinforced in December when the announcement was made that the country was to be partitioned, but the trouble was less than expected. The ships deployed in the eastern Mediterranean were kept busy shuttling between these various assignments.

The Partition announcement partially defused the situation as far as Britain was concerned, although for as long as the Mandate remained anti-immigration patrols continued. Both sides were trying to make political and propaganda capital out of the situation. In late December the destroyers *Chequers* and *Volage* (back in action) and the frigate *Bigbury Bay* intercepted and boarded a small two-masted schooner; they found themselves unpaid extras in a film being made on board (complete with actors!). When the two *Pan* ships sortied from the Dardanelles, carrying well over ten thousand immigrants between them, an "imposing force" was deployed against them, the 6-inch-gun cruiser *Mauritius*, the smaller cruiser *Phoebe*, the destroyers *Chequers*, *Chivalrous*, and *Volage*, and the two frigates *Cardigan Bay* and *Whitesand Bay*. It was hoped that the Zionists would recognize force majeure, which in the circumstances they did, and boarding parties were allowed on board voluntarily. On 1 January 1948 the two ships, with their escort, arrived at Famagusta, Cyprus. They remained at the island under the guard of the frigate *Mermaid*.

Immigrant ships continued to be boarded until the Mandate came to an end in the middle of May 1948. Only one or two got through the blockade. The British were trying to show their "even-handedness" to the Arabs, and the maximum political capital was made out of the Royal Navy's role when Admiral Willis visited the Arab capitals in February and March 1948. As the official report put it, "Although the Commander in Chief's visits to the Arab states were not intended to indicate any measure of support for the Arab cause in Palestine, their primary object was to exploit the high regard in which the British Navy is held by the Arab peoples, particularly for its part in preventing illegal Jewish immigration into Palestine. It is felt, therefore," the document went on, "that quite a number of the most important Arab leaders must feel that Great Britain in general and the Royal Navy in particular have contributed towards giving the Arabs in Palestine a fair deal and are continuing to do so." As part of this diplomatic offensive Willis took his flagship, the large light cruiser HMS *Newcastle,* and the destroyer *Chevron* to Jeddah in Saudi Arabia where, the Foreign Office reported, they made an "excellent impression." It was a classic case study of the diplomatic uses of navies. The British Palestine patrols by early 1948 had become of more "demonstrative" than "purposive" significance. They did more to show a pro-Arab policy orientation than achieve anything very effective in limiting Jewish immigration. It made sense, therefore, to use the navy to emphasize the political point to counter the understandably anti-British Arab feelings caused by the Palestinian partition.[25]

The day before the Palestine Mandate came to an end, a new commander in chief, Mediterranean, Sir Arthur Power, took up his duties. He was deeply suspicious of the new Israeli Government and was not unhappy to lay on the planned show of force with the carrier *Ocean,* four destroyers, and two frigates escorting the High Commissioner out of territorial waters in the cruiser *Euryalus.* Power's ships stayed to cover the withdrawal of the British troops into the Haifa enclave and through Gaza. They were ready to intervene if required on shore, being even prepared to give support to Arab refugee columns. The final evacuation of Haifa was completed at the end of June, another major naval demonstration being mounted. The frigate *Veryan Bay* was placed just outside the main breakwater to engage any opposition with her 40-mm guns. The more heavily armed destroyers *Verulam* and *Venus,* with the 5.25-inch cruiser *Phoebe,* were anchored in the bay, while the carrier *Triumph,* escorted by the *Volage,* acted as more distant cover. When the British troops were taken off in four tank-landing ships, a long-standing, difficult, and somewhat embarrassing naval commitment came to an end.[26]

Despite the Palestinian entanglement and the naval cuts, the Mediterranean Fleet was still able to carry out its more routine duties throughout the period. A British naval presence of at least a frigate or destroyer was maintained in Greek waters and in the Adriatic, where the problem of Trieste simmered. In July 1947 the fleet sailed from Malta on its first postwar summer cruise, making a fine sight with its two carriers and three light cruisers being reinforced (very temporarily) by the three-funnelled heavy cruiser *Norfolk* on passage to take up duties as flagship in the East Indies. In support were six fleet destroyers, two "Hunt"-class frigates, a fleet minesweeper, and the fleet's two small target submarines, *Statesman* and *Solent.* Also with the fleet were the destroyer depot ship *Woolwich* and three tankers of the Royal Fleet Auxiliary. The fleet then split up, and after the main body had made a visit to Istanbul (the first RN call since 1939), the *Liverpool, Chequers,* and *Chaplet* went on to Sevastopol. The Home Fleet had visited Kronshtadt the previous year with the carrier *Triumph* and destroyer *Rapid.* Now it was Willis's turn to try to turn the tide of deteriorating Anglo-Soviet relations, and the visit went well. It was, however, the last such courtesy call for some time.[27]

The fleet next concentrated at Nauplia, where it was visited by the King and Queen of Greece and the usual regattas were held. It returned to Malta after five weeks of flag showing and "useful training" on passage between the various ports. A further set of visits planned for the Western Mediterranean the following month had to be considerably reduced due to the financial crisis, but the fleet once more carried out some of its regular routines redolent of the nineteenth century and the interwar period. It anchored at Aranci Bay for a week in mid-October carrying out more regattas, the three prewar cruisers *Liverpool, Ajax,* and *Leander,* two carriers, half a dozen destroyers, a frigate, and pair of minesweepers being a rather less impressive force than the battleships of yesteryear. Nevertheless, for a country on the verge of international bankruptcy it was perhaps not too bad a show. It was understandable, however, that the senior RN officers at Gibraltar should remark rather wistfully on the occasion of the visit of the American 6th Fleet warships at the end of 1947 that the twenty-six American ships reminded them of the "old days when our combined fleets met here in the Spring."

Willis was reduced to one carrier when the *Ocean* was docked at the end of the year, and there were several operational calls on his resources, not just in Palestine but in the Red Sea, where the frigate *Peacock* was sent to show herself at the various ports to counter a reported revival of the slave trade. She was relieved in January by the fleet minesweepers of the 2nd Minesweeping Flotilla, which were able to mount a general naval presence as well as sweep mines off Massawa as part of the general postwar "clear up." The flotilla moved on to Assab and the Straits of Bab el Mandeb, but further disturbances in Aden caused seven of the nine *Algerine*s to be rushed there for a few days in mid-March.

The previous month, with the *Ocean* a "runner" once more, the 2nd Aircraft Carrier Squadron with escorts went on a spring cruise to the Western Mediterranean. The ships mixed exercises with visits to North Africa, Italy, and the south of France. The destroyers *Chieftain* and *Volage*, later joined by the *Chaplet*, had a particularly successful visit to Nice. This was a time of high tension in Europe due to the Communist coup in Prague, and there were real fears of similar events in France and Italy. So the Foreign Office was especially grateful for the activities of these grey ambassadors. As the consul general wrote on 16 March, "The visit was a great success from many points of view; after so much ink spilled over the decadence of the Royal Navy our friends were encouraged by the lovely lines of modern and perfectly handled ships, and, given the opportunity of showing the admiration and affection they undoubtedly feel, possibly enhanced by the critical period in European affairs which coincided with the Fleet visit." At the ports they visited, the carriers, albeit small ships of their type, created a major impression. Much was made of their similarity to the *Arromanches* (ex-HMS *Colossus*, name ship of the class), which had been loaned to the French Navy. The fleet might have been in reduced circumstances, but it could still impress, and after another concentration in Aranci Bay it retired to Malta in mid-March following an especially successful piece of "flag showing."[28]

So the routine went on as the Royal Navy kept up appearances in an area of traditional concern. In 1949 Admiral Power received Britain's ultimate prestige warship, the battleship *Vanguard*. This was somewhat fortuitous. Since completion the 44,500-ton ship's main role had been that of royal yacht. Six months after commissioning she had been taken in hand at Portsmouth to be converted for royal use, the additions including a sun lounge just forward of "X" turret, which eventually prevented the after turrets being used because of blast problems: X turret itself was in a state of preservation by the early 1950s. Some of the royal furnishings were from the old, unsafe royal yacht *Victoria and Albert*. The *Vanguard*'s first duty in this role was to take the Royal Family on a tour of South Africa in 1947. This was followed by another refit, and in the autumn of 1948 the battleship was sent to the Mediterranean on a "shakedown cruise" before another planned Royal Tour, this time to Australia and New Zealand. The tour had to be cancelled due to the King's ill health, and this left the *Vanguard* to a grateful Admiral Power. He had her for six months, engaging in one main armament shoot before she sailed back to Britain for her new noncombatant duty, that of training ship.

The *Vanguard*'s presence made up to some extent for the loss of his carriers, the *Triumph* to the Far East and the *Ocean* back to Britain to be swapped for her sister, HMS *Glory*. Before departing eastwards the *Triumph* carried out joint exercises with the Sixth Fleet. The F8F Bearcats and F4U Corsairs of the *Philippine Sea* joined with the British carrier's Seafires and Fireflies in the joint strike exercises. These rubbed home to Power the weakness of the light fleets with their two dozen or so rather old-fashioned aircraft, and he engaged in an argument with London over their usefulness in their wartime role of maintaining air superiority in the area. He placed greater reliance on shore-based fighters, but London reassured him that the light fleets could cope with the expected immediate threat. Power was not over-sanguine about his chances if war broke out over Berlin and was pleased when tension seemed to lessen in July, the month he lost the *Vanguard* to her training role.[29]

While she was briefly on duty, one mission for the battleship was to overawe the King of Egypt. Relations with Egypt were far from easy, there being problems over the renegotiation of a new Anglo-Egyptian Treaty, which, among other things, allowed the British to occupy the Suez Canal Zone. These problems grumbled on throughout the late 1940s and into the 50s, and the chiefs of staff formulated a plan for major military intervention in Egypt if things got out of hand. Code-named *Rodeo,* the operation was to be in two parts. The first, Rodeo Bernard, involved moving troops from the Canal Zone to Cairo; the second, Rodeo Flail, would bring them in by air and sea to Alexandria. The intention was to safeguard British lives and interests. Following the Egyptian regime's unilateral abrogation of the 1936 Anglo-Egyptian Treaty in October 1951 and the outbreak of an anti-British campaign of violence in the British-occupied Suez Canal Zone, Rodeo seemed a real possibility. Measures were immediately taken to safeguard passage of ships through the canal. The day after abrogation the cruiser HMS *Gambia* arrived at Port Said for her crew to take up harbor duties. Two days later warships were deployed at the other end of the canal. A system of patrols was set up using small landing craft and ships' launches to watch the canal and ensure safe passage of merchant ships. Warships were also used to bring troops to reinforce the area in case Rodeo should be necessary. In June the light fleet carriers *Warrior* and *Triumph* were used as troopships to carry the Parachute Brigade to Cyprus. In November the *Triumph* returned, together with the trials and training fleet carrier *Illustrious,* to bring the 3rd Infantry Division to Cyprus and the Canal Zone itself.[30]

The situation was at its worst in January 1952 when the British moved against the Egyptian police in Ismailia. This led to riots in Cairo, and Rodeo was brought to forty-eight-hour notice. It was now realized, however, that the Egyptians would probably fight if it were put into effect. This altered the situation entirely, as a vital planning assumption had been that the Egyptian armed forces would remain passive. Not only would this mean resistance to British forces and Egyptian troops leaving foreigners to the mercy of the mob as the troops fought the foreign invaders, but the Canal Zone itself might have to be defended from attacks. The chiefs of staff, therefore, decided to reduce the scope of Rodeo Flail to an armed evacuation of British residents. Forces would then be concentrated in the Canal Zone and on the Cairo operation. The government was clearly relieved when the Egyptians, alarmed at the radicalism of the mob, restored order themselves. Navigation of the Suez Canal also began to get back to normal.[31]

In April 1952 the chiefs of staff reexamined the Rodeo Flail plan. As things stood, three battalions of troops were to be flown into Alexandria and then, twenty-four hours later, the Mediterranean Fleet would arrive to land troops—peacefully it was hoped, forcefully if necessary. Possible landings at Aboukir Bay or other suitable sites were considered. The chiefs were worried that valuable cruisers might be hit in the case of an opposed entry to Alexandria, and it was suggested that merchant ships should be chartered instead for the purpose. The solution adopted seems to have been to earmark mercantile ex-corvettes operated by the army with locally enrolled crews. It was also decided to hold an amphibious exercise, Dryfly, in the Mediterranean that would bring into the area the Royal Navy's small Amphibious Warfare Squadron to reinforce the local landing craft.[32]

In July 1952 King Farouk was overthrown by a military coup. It was decided not to interfere with the movements of the Mediterranean Fleet but to take all measures short of leading to publicity to reduce Rodeo Flail's period of notice to below the existing ninety-six hours. Intervention was only to take place if British lives were at stake or if it looked as if a "Communist" regime was to be set up. In both cases it was felt that Britain would receive a favorable international reaction.[33]

The new regime made it very clear that it would strongly oppose military intervention by foreign powers. Rodeo Flail now looked like being a full-scale operation of war requiring at least a battalion ready to carry out a surprise landing over the beaches of Aboukir Bay simultaneously with the arrival of troops by air. If this was impractical, then the risk would have to be taken of using four destroyers to bring the troops straight into the harbor. The landing troops were to be a Royal Marine Commando unit airlifted from Malta to Port Said for embarkation. In order to maintain sufficient amphibious shipping for the Aboukir Bay landing, the Amphibious Warfare Squadron was to be retained in the Mediterranean. Middle East Land Forces Headquarters, which drew up these revised plans in August, was not optimistic about them. It pointed out to London the dangers of ships being sunk, which might jeopardize the whole operation with consequent loss of prestige. Rodeo Flail was only practical, the local command argued, if a full-scale covering bombardment was provided and if force commanders were allowed to take "such action as will best ensure the success of the operation."[34]

Much to everyone's relief the situation calmed down, and by October 1952 the chiefs of staff were considering Rodeo "unlikely." Nevertheless, it was considered important to maintain an operational carrier in the Mediterranean to cover the Flail landings. At the beginning of 1953 the recently refitted fleet carrier *Indomitable* was deployed to Malta with an air group of one Sea Fury squadron (802) and two Firefly squadrons (820 and 826). Unfortunately, no sooner had she arrived, in early February, than she suffered a serious fuel explosion that caused extensive structural damage. After some consideration it was decided to give her temporary repairs to keep her on station and allow her to appear cosmetically sound in the Coronation Review at Spithead in June. Putting on the best possible show of strength on that occasion was a top priority.[35]

The review placed the naval planners in a quandary. How much of the Medi-

Naval theater: the Coronation Review in 1953. The impressive lineup of carriers deliberately gave a most misleading impression of real British naval strength. Few were real operational carriers with allocated air groups. Note one of the two aircraft maintenance ships fitted out as a viewing platform in the foreground. (Imperial War Museum)

terranean Fleet's strength could be brought back to Spithead given the Egyptian situation? In April the chiefs of staff decided to approve the departure of the cruisers *Glasgow* and *Gambia,* the minelayer *Manxman,* two "Battle"-class destroyers, six frigates, four ocean minesweepers, five submarines, a tank-landing ship, and the depot ship *Forth.* This left behind to cover emergencies the cruiser *Bermuda,* the armament trials cruiser *Cumberland* (with plenty of space for troops on board), four *C*-class destroyers, the tank-landing ships *Dieppe* and *Reggio,* two tank-landing craft, the repair ship *Ranpura,* two fleet tugs, and three fleet auxiliaries. This was a sufficient force to transport the Royal Marine Commando Brigade to Port Said (a move under consideration since the previous August) and to make up two task forces, one to operate the canal and one to be a mobile reserve. If necessary the whole fleet could return in just over a week.[36]

In May these contingency plans had to be put into effect when Anglo-Egyptian negotiations broke down. The Commando Brigade was duly brought to the Canal Zone. Its three commando units were scattered across the Mediterranean area, but the Headquarters and 45 Commando at Malta were swiftly loaded into the *Ranpura* and *Dieppe* and carried to Egypt, while 42 Commando, exercising in Libya, was equally quickly embarked in the *Reggio* and three of the remaining destroyers at Tripoli. By the time these two units had reached the Canal Zone, 40

A cruiser on Cold War duties—HMS *Bermuda* being loaded at Malta with helicopters and other reinforcements during the Cyprus emergency: a Greek Cypriot revolt against British rule began in 1955. (Imperial War Museum)

Commando had been flown in from Malta. After the all-important Coronation Review, the Mediterranean Fleet returned in full strength, with the *Theseus* substituting for the *Indomitable,* which was put into the lowest category of reserve as a prelude to scrapping. The eventual conclusion of an agreement in 1954 on the British evacuation of the Canal Zone seemed to make the chances of further operations in Egypt somewhat less likely. Paradoxically, two years after that agreement a full-scale amphibious landing was to take place.[37]

As well as carrying out its operational duties the Mediterranean Fleet continued to execute a full exercise program that increasingly took on a NATO, rather than national, aspect despite the problems over command. In August 1951 a major exercise was held in "defence" of Malta. Admiral Sir John Edelston, the British CinC Mediterranean, commanded the defenders, which included French and Italian forces, while Vice Admiral Gardiner, USN Commander of the Sixth Fleet, controlled the attackers, who used their long-range carrier aircraft to good effect. In 1952, with command still a sensitive issue, a rather similar exercise was held under the direction of Lord Louis Mountbatten, the new British CinC. Admiral Carney, USN Commander Allied Forces South, organized two major exercises at the beginning and end of the year to which British ships contributed. These operations included convoys and amphibious landings and saw the fast minelayer, HMS *Manxman,* playing the part of a surface raider. The emphasis remained on amphibious landings in 1953, this time in defense of Thrace. The carrier *Theseus* carried out ASW patrols with her Fireflies and provided fighter protection with her Sea Furies, but the main air support came from the American Sixth Fleet. By now Mountbatten had become NATO Commander in Chief and he shared control with Admiral Fechteler, the new USN CINCSOUTH. The Greeks and the Turks were fully involved, the exercises starting with the cruiser HMS *Gambia* escorting a convoy of Greek landing ships.

The following year, the combined exercises with the Home Fleet led by HMS *Vanguard* marked a historic occasion, the last time a British battleship would be seen in the Mediterranean. Later in 1954 American, French, Greek, and British forces "attacked" Malta, which was defended by Anglo-Turkish naval forces supported by American aircraft. Nothing could better illustrate the integration of the Mediterranean Fleet with that of its NATO allies, and with typical Mountbatten showmanship, he staged the first NATO Naval Review for Lord Ismay, Secretary General of the organization. The end of one era and the beginning of another was also symbolized by the withdrawal from Trieste of allied forces, covered by a new naval task group consisting of the recently completed carrier *Centaur* with jet aircraft and two full-conversion ASW frigates, HMS *Whirlwind* and HMS *Roebuck*.[38]

During the postwar decade the Home Fleet could not match the Mediterranean Fleet in operational activities, but once it was reconstituted after its near disappearance in early 1948, it carried out a full program of cruises and exercises. The best that could be done in May 1948 was an exercise in the North Sea, code-named Dawn, in which HMS *Superb* and a small operational force, plus the impressive-looking training battleships *Anson* and *Howe* and the carrier *Implacable*, were attacked by aircraft and submarines. Although at this time used for advanced air training, the *Implacable* had an allocated Carrier Air Group, the First, formed in October 1947. The 1st CAG was made up of 801 Squadron with twelve large Sea Hornet fighters and the only strike squadron in Naval Aviation, 813, with a dozen torpedo-dropping Firebrands. The CAG, in whole or part, was only an occasional visitor to its carrier and for Dawn was based at Arbroath, Scotland, adding its weight to attacks on the "enemy" fleet. The Firebrands mounted torpedo "attacks," and other aircraft including RAF Lincoln bombers also provided an air threat. By September 1948 the Home Fleet proper was operational once more, with Sir Rhoderick McGrigor flying his flag in the battleship *Duke of York*. With him were two light fleet carriers, the *Theseus* and *Vengeance,* each with a combination of eight Fireflies and about a dozen of the latest Sea Furies. Also pressed into service was the *Illustrious,* the trials carrier. With the heavy ships were three small cruisers, the *Diadem, Sirius,* and *Cleopatra,* and two destroyer flotillas, each of six large and impressive "Battle"-class vessels. After exercises, the larger surface ships crossed the Atlantic to the West Indies and the U.S.A., while the two light fleet carriers plus escorts went south to South Africa. The Royal Navy was both demonstrating its resuscitation to its most powerful ally and showing off strength to the Commonwealth country about whose loyalty there were serious fears after the fall of Smuts in May.

The West Indies visit had another purpose, too. The low ebb of British naval power had been a factor in encouraging Guatemala to put pressure on British Honduras earlier in the year. At that time cruisers had duly appeared with Royal Marines and troops of the Gloucestershire Regiment to reinforce the garrison. One of the ships was the regular flagship of the station, HMS *Sheffield,* with her Marines, but the other was the old disarmed training cruiser *Devonshire,* in the West Indies on a training cruise and available as an army transport. It was no coincidence that, later in 1948, British Honduras was on the Home Fleet's list of visits.[39]

When the fleet returned home at the end of the year, it formed up in the Azores, together with the *Illustrious,* which came out from Britain with five more destroyers. The *Illustrious,* now both a trials and training ship, was carrying a mixed, ad hoc group of 815 Squadron's thirteen old World War II Barracudas in the ASW role and two Sea Vampires to evaluate jet operations under operational conditions. The Barracudas normally operated from a shore base in cooperation with the Joint Anti-Submarine School at Londonderry, but went to sea for exercises such as this. The carriers were to run the gauntlet of "enemy" submarines and aircraft to attack the naval base at Plymouth and air bases in Devon and Cornwall, an interesting scenario showing that the offensive use of British naval aviation against the Soviet Fleet bases in the Kola Peninsula had not been ruled out completely. The defenders were also to simulate the use of nuclear weapons against the fleet. Two were allowed to the "Blue" air force to be simulated by photo-flashes.[40]

The weather was very poor, which led to fiasco. In the gale force winds the light fleet carriers had great difficulty in operating their aircraft, although the larger *Illustrious,* operating in a submarine hunting role ahead of the main body, was able to fly her Barracudas every day. She was even able to operate her Vampire jets, which were not cleared for catapulting, on the best day, when a few aircraft got off the light fleets also. Antinuclear disposition was taken up by the fleet, with no destroyer closer than three miles and no big ship closer than four and a half miles, but none of the Bomber Command Lincolns and Lancasters could even find the fleet due to the poor conditions and a little simple electronic deception. Eventually a Coastal Command Lancaster dropped one simulated nuclear bomb, which went off 4,500 yards from the nearest ship to dubious effect. The vile conditions caused the exercise to be called off with no simulated strikes being made by the carriers.

The lessons of this event, Exercise Sunrise, were thought over by the Admiralty who were worried about the limitations it showed in the capabilities of contemporary carriers and their equipment. The commander of the 2nd Cruiser Squadron suggested special aircraft ought to be developed that were flyable in winter conditions from the light fleets. The nuclear threat had proved not very serious and the conventional air threat even less, at least in poor conditions, but McGrigor was not ready to write aircraft off too easily. More study was required. Certainly the exercises could be said to vindicate those who argued the case for the continued importance of the battleship as a strike weapon in poor weather conditions; perhaps more pertinently the exercise seemed to argue the case for better carriers and aircraft.

In 1949 the emphasis switched to the main wartime priority—convoys—with the first Western Union exercise, code-named Verity, carried out with French, Belgian, and Dutch Navies. The exercises was under the command of Admiral McGrigor, flying his flag in the carrier *Implacable,* operational since the beginning of the year with 1st CAG. There were 109 participating warships, but seventy were British. After some maneuvering in an attempt to coordinate the multi-national fleet, an attempt that was none too successful, the movement of a convoy through a minefield off Portland was practiced, with the minesweepers of four nations clearing a path. Much was learned about the problems of making ships of different nationalities operate together as a single tactical unit.[41]

Another Western Union exercise, Activity, took place in 1950, and this time units of the Home Fleet were placed under Dutch command. The ships then visited European ports before going around the south of the British Isles for the "Summer War" in the North West Approaches, an annual event since 1946, but now increasing in size and importance. These "wars" were controlled by the Flag Officer (Submarines) and were based around submarine and ASW tactics. They involved attacks on "convoys" and merchantmen and involved the Home Fleet's ASW forces as well as ships of the training squadrons. In the autumn, Sir Philip Vian, now CinC Home Fleet, took his ships down to Gibraltar. Things were really like old times with Vian and his flag in the training ship *Vanguard,* the *Implacable* being in refit. The *Indefatigable,* a training carrier, kept up appearances while the operational light fleet carrier *Vengeance* provided the real air capability.[42]

In 1951 the pattern was more or less the same, although Progress, the Western Union exercise "fought" in the Bay of Biscay under French command, was smaller than usual. The Home Fleet carried out its summer cruise and made an impressive sight, although two of its big ships, the *Vanguard* and *Indefatigable,* were noncombatant. Only the *Indomitable* and *Vengeance* were active warships, the former carrying a rather ad hoc air group of her own Firebrand strike squadron, *Vengeance*'s Sea Furies, and 815 Squadron's Barracudas. The *Vengeance* herself deployed a special air group of Sea Hornet night fighters and new Firefly ASW aircraft. The latter exercised against submarines in the biggest yet "Summer War." Home Fleet ships were also placed, in June, at the disposal of Sir Arthur Power, CinC Portsmouth, for a major convoy defense exercise that involved ships from almost every RN home deployment, including Fishery Protection ships, as well as from the NATO allies. No one as yet could accuse the Royal Navy of forgetting its wartime lessons of what was for Britain the most important dimension of naval warfare—the defense of convoyed merchantmen against submarine and air attacks.[43]

By 1952 the Atlantic command structure had been finally settled, and the Home Fleet's commander, Admiral Sir George Creasey, now wore his NATO hat of CinC Eastern Atlantic under the command of the first Supreme Allied Commander Atlantic, Admiral L.D. McCormick, USN. CinC Portsmouth was also now CinC Channel, and the first exercise came in his area with another major convoy "battle" in the South Western Approaches, Channel and North Sea. Creasey's moment came when exercise Mainbrace was held in September. This simulated a NATO maritime response to an attack on Norway with CINCEASTLANT providing support for the NATO CINCNORTH, Admiral Sir Patrick Brind, back from the Pacific Station. This was the first time the NATO Striking Fleet had come into being with four American carriers and two British fleet carriers. One of the latter was the new *Eagle,* the first postwar fleet carrier with, by British standards, a powerful and balanced group of two squadrons of Attacker jet fighters, two Firefly 6 ASW squadrons, and the second Firebrand strike squadron, 827. Two Skyraider early-warning aircraft were also carried, making a grand total of forty-four aircraft. The other available carrier was the faithful old *Illustrious,* once more having a few days of operating glory. She was carrying eight Firefly 6 ASW aircraft and two Dutch squadrons, one of Sea Furies and the other of Fireflies, twenty-eight machines in all. The third British member of the Strike Fleet was the *Vanguard,* although it is not clear whether the battleship was carrying any ammunition beyond starshells for her secondary armament. All these ships together made up the recently formed Heavy Squadron of the Home Fleet. Its fourth major member, the light carrier *Theseus,* operated her Sea Furies and Fireflies with two other CVLs, one American and the other the Canadian *Magnificent,* in an ASW carrier group. In all the "Blue" forces consisted of over a hundred major surface combatants (frigates and above) of which almost a third were British.

The Strike Fleet, which also contained an American battleship and five cruisers (British, American, and Canadian), fought enemy submarines (mostly British) and in poor weather provided "air support" and shore bombardment for the NATO forces in Norway. An "enemy surface raider," the Canadian cruiser *Quebec,* playing a *Sverdlov*-class cruiser, was duly "sunk." Convoys were run to and from Bergen with carrier and land-based air support. HMS *Apollo,* the fast minelayer (and the final member of the Heavy Squadron), simulated another "raider" that was "slowed down" by land-based aircraft and then "sunk" by surface forces in the classic manner of prewar RN doctrine. The carriers also gave air support to "landings" in Denmark.[44]

The following year the biggest NATO naval exercise yet took place, Mariner, which covered the entire Atlantic and Channel area from Norway to Gibraltar. Convoys were run as well as large, fast merchantmen simulating independently routed vessels. In addition to these the main NATO Striking Fleet (two U.S. *Essex*-class carriers, the battleship *Iowa,* three American cruisers, one Canadian cruiser, and seventeen destroyers) moved northwestwards towards the Denmark Strait between Iceland and Greenland, with the British fleet contribution coming from Invergordon to join up. This was made up of the available major units of the Heavy Squadron, the *Vanguard, Eagle,* and the cruiser *Sheffield,* the carrier *Theseus* being detached to the Mediterranean on Flail duty. The *Eagle* was carrying over fifty aircraft (Attackers, Sea Hornets, Fireflies, and Skyraiders), but the *Vanguard* proved to be the star of the show. In gale-force winds and stormy seas the British battleship was able to demonstrate her superior sea keeping compared to that of the USS *Iowa.* She steamed at 26 knots "with hardly a movement on her and the spray flying out from either bow . . . directly into the gale . . . a magnificent sight," one observer wrote, "that few of us will ever forget." The *Eagle* also proved much more capable than the American ships of keeping heavy seas off her flight deck. Despite some confusion the enemy "raider" (HMS *Swiftsure*), breaking out through the Denmark Strait, was eventually spotted by a Skyraider early-warning aircraft from the *Eagle,* and the *Vanguard* was directed to her. Just at the moment the battleship was due to "engage," she was "attacked" by U.S. Skyraider bombers in error, but she was judged "undamaged" and the "enemy" cruiser was duly "sunk" by *Vanguard*'s guns and destroyers' torpedoes. The *Swiftsure* now joined the Striking Fleet but suffered more genuine damage the following day.

The British contributed six destroyers to the Striking Fleet, three "Weapons" of the 6th Destroyer Squadron and three of the large *Daring*s allocated like cruisers to the Home Fleet Flotillas' Command. The bad weather made things especially difficult for these smaller vessels and one of the *Daring*s, the *Diamond,* ran into the *Swiftsure.* The cruiser caught fire, so seriously damaging her that in the end

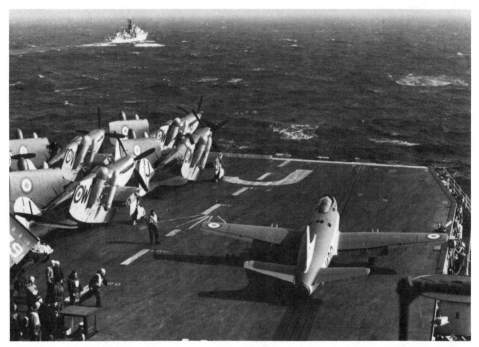

The first jet fighter in front-line service with the Royal Navy was the Supermarine Attacker. This is one of 803 Squadron's aircraft about to be catapulted off the *Eagle* during Exercise Mariner in 1953. On the left are Firefly AS6s of 814 Squadron. (Imperial War Museum)

she never operated again. The two stricken ships were escorted to Iceland by the *Decoy, Battleaxe,* and *Crossbow.* The weather prevented any "air strike" or surface bombardments on Iceland, and as the fleet proceeded south insult was added to injury as RAF Bomber Command aircraft carried out attacks on the Fleet and the weather prevented any fighter defense. After the Striking Fleet split up on 1 October, the American portion suffered a "successful" RAF bomber attack, even though a combat air patrol was airborne. The following morning, 4 October, probably much to the relief of the participants, the exercise ended. Its other aspects had included a mine offensive against ports, coastal convoys, and estuaries.

A convoy was run between Loch Ewe and Bergen, with the old carrier *Illustrious,* about to be withdrawn from service, pressed into operational service once more as escort with a squadron of Firefly 6s, 815 Squadron, now with newly delivered American Avengers, and Dutch squadrons of Sea Furies and Firefly 4s. The ad hoc air group provided useful support against both air and submarine threats. Such was the shape of naval warfare expected in the first half of the 1950s. There were elements of tradition here, such as in the continued use of battleships. Indeed, the supporters of their retention could argue that the point of the continued usefulness of the battleship in weather that made carrier flying impossible had received powerful reinforcement. The airmen countered this by blaming the unreal exercise conditions for preventing these carriers finding more suitable weather. Perhaps the most significant feature was the style of command. CINCEASTLANT, Admiral Creasey, did not exercise his authority from the bridge of the *Vanguard,* or even from the *Eagle,* but from the new shore-based headquarters at Northwood in North

One of the few saving graces of the 1953 Mariner exercise, ruined by weather and collision, was the fine seakeeping of the *Vanguard*, seen here butting through the heavy seas.

Although her normal duty was as a trials and then a trials and training carrier, the *Illustrious* was usually pressed into service during autumn exercises as an operational carrier. She did this in the Mariner exercises in 1953. Seen on deck are 826 Squadron's Firefly AS6s, 815 Squadron's recently delivered Avenger TBM-3Es, and 3rd Royal Netherlands Navy Squadron's Sea Furies.

London. The previous year he had been in a temporary base at Pitreavie in Scotland. The era of the ship-based Home Fleet Commander was coming to an end.[45]

The Royal Navy did see a little operational duty in the Atlantic in the late 1940s and early 1950, in its most southern extremities. It began its postwar conflict with Argentina over the Falkland Islands and their Dependencies in 1948. The American and West Indies Station sent down the frigate *Snipe* to the Falklands in the early part of the year, officially to take the governor on a tour of the "Southern Dependencies," i.e., the South Orkneys and South Shetlands and the Western Antarctic Peninsula. Over the previous five years the conflict over the rights in the area between Britain on the one hand and Chile and Argentina on the other had steadily deteriorated. Hoping to take advantage of British economic and naval weakness, Argentinian and Chilean warships landed parties in the Dependencies in the summer of 1947–48 and asserted rights over the "South American Antarctic." The old Argentine claim to the Falklands themselves and all the Dependencies (including South Georgia and the South Sandwich Islands) was also resuscitated. To back up the *Snipe*, the 6-inch-gun cruiser *Nigeria* was duly despatched south. There was a minor confrontation in Melchior Harbour, off the Antarctic Peninsula where the Argentines had recently built a settlement. The cruiser and two Argentine tugs politely presented notes to each other protesting the other's presence. A warship was maintained in the Falklands into 1949, the *Snipe*'s sister, *Sparrow*, and it was considered prudent to take the governor to South Georgia in February of that year in the company of the CinC of the station, Admiral Sir William Tennant, on board an even larger cruiser, the *Glasgow*. The three contending parties had by then agreed not to send warships south of 60°South on other than routine calls.[46]

In February 1951 the Argentine president, Juan Perón, threatened to reopen the Antarctic offensive with talk of scientific expeditions taking possession of islands claimed by Britain. In December of that year, the Argentines duly occupied the abandoned British base at Hope Bay, first founded in 1944 on the island at the tip of the Antarctic Peninsula. Shortly afterwards, in February 1952, the Argentines shot over the heads of a party from the Antarctic survey vessel *John Biscoe*, landing to reassert a British presence. The party returned to its ship; a strong protest was sent to Buenos Aires, and HMS *Burghead Bay*, already at Port Stanley "to assist in the maintenance of the bases" in the Dependencies, was sent down with the governor, Sir Miles Clifford, to assert British rights. The Argentines now allowed a British scientific party to come ashore, and the Foreign Office felt that the Argentines would now behave. Churchill, however, wanted further action and insisted on the despatch of another frigate to the Falklands from Britain, HMS *Veryan Bay*, with a small detachment of thirty Royal Marines. These forces were duly sent. In the spring of 1952 the Argentines went further, announcing publicly the establishment of a new base at Hope Bay and the forthcoming "progressive occupation" of Antarctic territory.[47]

By early 1953 the British had decided positive action was required to assert their rights. The naval force in the Falklands was reinforced by the flagship of the CinC, Vice Admiral Powlett, flying his flag in the cruiser HMS *Superb*. On 11 February the local frigate, again HMS *Snipe*, embarked the "Falkland Force" of thirty-three Marines to be taken to Deception Island in the South Shetlands to the west of Hope Bay. Once there it was intended to remove the huts the Chileans and Argentinians had recently built close to the British hut on the airstrip. Both foreign huts were duly surrounded on 15 February, two Argentine seamen being arrested before the buildings were demolished. The weather now forced the *Snipe*'s withdrawal, but thirteen Royal Marines were left behind on guard. A very angry Argentine officer, the commander of the demolished hut, who arrived by air the following day, was politely but firmly told to leave. Argentine ships duly appeared shortly after, one to deliver a protest, but the Marines made it clear they were not to be intimidated.

The *Snipe* was now sent back, slipping from alongside the *Superb* at Port William in the Falklands in the early evening of the 21st. Four days later she paid a brief visit to Deception Island but, as the weather deteriorated, decided to move on to Hope Bay. Signs now developed of possible action being taken by the Argentines, three of whose aircraft appeared, one transport and two Lincoln bombers, and the *Snipe* passed a helicopter-equipped transport, the *Bahia Aguirre*, sailing towards Deception. Around midday on the 25th, intelligence was received of a possible attack, and the Marines went on the alert. The *Snipe* was duly ordered to return, and the alerted ship was back at Deception before midnight and landed more Royal Marines. Despite dirty weather, the *Snipe* stayed in the area guarding the troops ashore as the Foreign Office considered the danger of attack to remain real. At the beginning of March Commander Hall Wright checked with the CinC and was left in no doubt about his authorization to use force should it be required. There was no question, however, of going on the offensive against other more important settlements in the area, an agreement having been made that no further attacks would be made on anyone's bases. The *Snipe* duly left on 11 March.[48]

With reports of continued Argentine activity, the Falkland Islands remained "jittery," as noted by the new guardship *Bigbury Bay* in April/May. It was not until the end of 1953, however, that the next serious problem appeared, at Dundee Island just south of Hope Bay, which was threatened by the Argentines. The Chiefs of Staff Committee were by then worried about the capabilities of the Falkland Force, now supported by the frigate HMS *Nereide*. There was no cruiser deployed in the Falklands any more, and it would take two weeks to get the station flagship down there. A second frigate would take even longer. The danger of a highly embarrassing military debacle seemed real and, although it was decided to order the *Nereide* to support a reconnaissance of the threatened spot, the chiefs were loath to risk the troops ashore unnecessarily. "Under current policy," it seemed to them, "the United Kingdom was endeavouring to maintain an interest in the Falkland Islands Dependencies without the proper forces to support them." Alas, the same would be true almost thirty years later.[49]

Britain could not be strong everywhere, for 1953 had seen other calls on British forces in South American and Caribbean waters. British Guiana was the trouble spot with the accession of a new radical government leading to civil disturbances. There were some problems in deploying forces into the area to restore the situation, but in due course the cruiser *Superb* and two frigates, *Burghead Bay* and *Bigbury Bay*, landed both their own Royal Marines and a force of army troops brought from Jamaica. Reinforcement was required, but moving them by air would have required stopping the whole British long-haul civilian airline. The training carrier *Implacable* was duly pressed into service as a troop transport to carry a battalion of the Argyll and Sutherland Highlanders from Plymouth.[50] These American events, among others, were on the mind of Admiral the Earl Mountbatten, CinC Mediterranean as he spoke on the "Role of the Royal Navy" in January 1954. He stressed the peaceful tasks of the service, the Hydrographic Service that had now been rebuilt after the war, and the navy's rescue roles that his own fleet had carried out after the earthquake of the previous year in Cyprus and Greece. He also quoted the policing role, mentioning among other occasions an affair of over a year before when HMS *Alacrity* had put down a mutiny in the British merchantman *Atheldale* near Gibraltar. The role of the cruiser was stressed as being "particularly suitable to afford protection to British lives in any part of the world at very short notice." There was little about war and its preparation and much about policing the seas. Lord Charles Beresford was quoted as arguing that the Royal Navy existed not only for battle but to carry the "British flag and British ideas of justice and good government to every corner of the globe. . . ."[51]

Mountbatten, that dismantler of the British Empire, would probably have been the first to admit that times had changed and that the long-term British problem was the stabilization of a policy of eventual decolonization rather than one of maintaining imperial commitments. Nevertheless, in this talk he was mapping out the line he would take in the great struggle over the service's future that he would inherit in 1955 on taking up office as first sea lord. For the last decade or so the Royal Navy had been acting, or had been prepared to act, as one of the most flexible of the military instruments sustaining Britain's world role. No British political leader of substance was willing as yet to declare that role finished. If decision makers wanted a force that could be deployed in a wide range of peacetime functions, Mountbatten could sell one to them, and he had a wealth of good examples from which to quote: the carrier as both a mobile airfield in limited war and insurgency or as a useful troop transport; the surface combatant as an immediate queller of unrest and symbol of interest.

Moreover he would *have* to take his stand on peacekeeping, limited war, and traditional naval diplomacy, as traditional naval war seemed increasingly unreal and irrelevant. The reason was the dawn of the nuclear era and its threat of a short, all-too-decisive conflict. Ironically, the Royal Navy had played an intimate role in the first British nuclear test in October 1952. The continued British concern with sea communications was shown in the test scenario, nuclear attack on a harbor with the device mounted in a ship, the frigate HMS *Plym*. There seems to have been genuine fear at this time that the Russians, given their weaknesses in long-range air power, might adopt some kind of covert nuclear mining or torpedo threat to ports. The location chosen for the test was the Monte Bello Islands off northwestern Australia, and planning began at the Admiralty in spring 1951. The escort carrier *Campania* (just having completed its job as exhibition ship for the "Festival of Britain") and the tank-landing ships, *Zeebrugge, Narvik,* and *Tracker,* were allocated to the operation, and considerable refit and conversion work was done on the ships to make them suitable for their special task. Loaded with smaller landing craft, the *Zeebrugge* and *Narvik* sailed in February 1952 to begin preparations, while work continued on the *Plym, Tracker* (the radiological safety ship), and *Campania* (the "base ship"). In June 1952 these ships set sail for Australia, where they had all arrived by the end of July. August saw the squadron concentrated on the test site, one Australian frigate acting as guardship and another as a weather observation vessel. Further preparations took almost two months, but the *Plym* was duly vaporized on 5 October. The dirty mushroom cloud that resulted was to cast a long shadow, one that promised dead populations and devastated ports and that made precious little point in trying to defend any shipping in the area. A disconcerting uncertainty hung over the roles of navies in general war. A new rationale based even more firmly on "cold" and "limited" war tasks was an urgent requirement; the time for its refinement and articulation was at hand.[52]

CHAPTER · FIVE

SUEZ AND SANDYS

The Royal Navy might have been forgiven for thinking that the 1955 Defence White Paper would mark at least a breathing space in the process of cuts and review that had been going on constantly since the election of the Conservative Government in 1951. There was, however, to be no respite from financial pressure. In May 1955 Sir Anthony Eden, who had replaced Churchill as prime minister in April, went to the country and received a decisive mandate to continue the policies of the previous four years. By July Chancellor of the Exchequer Selwyn Lloyd was reporting to the prime minister that the defense program as planned, even after all Butler's hard work, would be costing almost £2,000 million by 1959. Eden found this unacceptable. With considerable popular backing, he wished to relieve still further the burden defense put on the economy in the hope that the manpower so released could contribute to solving a still chronic balance of payments problem. So yet another defense review began. It would cover programs up to seven years ahead and put emphasis on further cuts in forces for general war. The thermonuclear weapon seemed to make large conventional forces obsolete: armies and navies were, in the view of the prime minister and others, primarily for the maintenance of still vital overseas commitments. Moreover, of the three services, Eden felt the navy was now the least important. Its current primary strategic rationale, with the Royal Navy fighting on to salvage some "victory" out of the Armageddon of an "initial nuclear blitz," held little appeal to any politician.[1]

Lord Mountbatten, the Admiralty's new professional head, was determined that the active fleet and the new building program should be the last to suffer in the new exercise. He was less convinced than McGrigor had been that the limits of administrative economy had been reached. Indeed, as he later put it, he considered the Royal Navy to be in a "dangerously bloated condition" with its massive infrastructures of shore establishments, not all of which were absolutely necessary to its combat efficiency. In a letter to his American counterpart, Arleigh Burke, Mountbatten explained that "the effort and expense ashore has not in my opinion been reduced to the same extent as the cutting of the active fleet; nor have the resources we have been left with after the reduction been reorganised to meet either present conditions or further developments." Mountbatten wanted a more logical reorganization, and set up the "Way Ahead Committee" to carry out an "Enquiry into the Structure and Supporting Organisation of the Naval Service." The committee first met in June 1955 with the first lord and other political members of the Board deliberately excluded. Under the main committee that defined objectives and gave policy guidance was a "Sub-Board Executive Working Party" chaired by the assistant chief of Naval Staff. This main working party could form smaller subcommittees as required. The "Way Ahead" Board Committee became a kind of streamlined Board of Admiralty whose "wide-ranging and deep investigation began with the requirements of the running of the Fleet over the decade up to 1965, and went through the necessary pattern of command, every aspect of shore support and administration at all levels, the naval air organization and the manpower needed to sustain the Navy of the future." "Way Ahead" proposals were rubber-stamped by the full Board, the first sea lord being determined to ram through reform with as little interference as possible. Mountbatten's biographer argues that Sir John Lang, the permanent secretary of the Admiralty, was opposed to the "Way Ahead" process. This seems, at best, overstated, although Lang may have at times had doubts about the "Way Ahead's" constitutionality. He was a full member of the main Board Committee and had struck up a close relationship with Mountbatten during the latter's time as fourth sea lord. Lang, indeed, urged "unreserved cooperation and exchange of ideas" with the "Way Ahead."[2]

The Reserve Fleet was one of the "Way Ahead's" first targets. Immobilized reserves were not going to be available after a Soviet H-bomb attack on the United Kingdom. This spelled the doom of many members of the Class III reserve of ships at extended notice. The 1956 Naval Estimates duly set out the fate of these ships. They were to be sold to friendly navies or scrapped when they reached the end of their useful lives. The 1956 Estimates also announced the review, not yet complete, of the "whole supporting organisation" and a significant switch to afloat support with the conversion of the carrier *Triumph* into a repair ship, the conversion of the support carrier *Perseus* into a submarine depot ship, and the purchase of a cargo ship for conversion into a stores vessel. Both the vulnerability of fixed bases in the thermonuclear age and the requirements of a mobile peacetime fleet seemed to suggest these developments. The general emphasis was on maintaining the front-line fleet as cheaply and efficiently as possible, at the price of mobilization potential.[3]

This was a significant shift from the priorities of the previous decade. In the late forties reserve ships had been refitted and maintained at the price of a nonexistent Home Fleet. A mobilization infrastructure had been kept at the cost of a reduced front line. Even during the Radical Review the Admiralty had been loath to give up its ideal of mobilizing for a long-drawn-out maritime war. Indeed, it was still unwilling to abandon the concept entirely. Nevertheless, there was no alternative but to adopt the prevailing line of overriding priority for Cold War peacetime commitments. Many in the Admiralty, from the first sea lord downwards, were increasingly happy to develop further the logic begun by McGrigor and his colleagues in 1953–54. Such provided the only sure foundation for the survival of a significant fleet of any kind. As had been clear ever since 1945, Britain had far too many warships, not too few. Bringing them up to modern standards, or even maintaining them, was beyond her financial and manpower means if she wished to keep a modern fleet running in commission. The navy had cause to be grateful for the political pressure to get rid of a reserve that was increasingly becoming a useless encumbrance.

The Defence White Paper and the Naval Estimates for 1956 both stressed the Royal Navy's peacetime role more strongly than their predecessors had done. The former summed up the navy's role as the maintenance of an "effective fleet capable of supporting the country's influence and interests as a world wide power and a member of the Commonwealth and NATO. The further development of new weapons and techniques should enable us to strike whatever may threaten us by sea in the future whether in limited or global war." A little later the emphasis was even more obvious. "By its presence in foreign stations; by its close ties with the navies of other nations and by the goodwill that it engenders in foreign countries; the Navy is a valuable weapon in the Cold War against Communism." There was a significant and new emphasis on "limited war," for which the White Paper specifically argued the case for the carrier task force as a major weapon. It even made the case for cruisers "which, because they are capable of sustained operations far from base," were "the most economical units of sea power." Only then came mention of the British contribution to NATO and the importance of ASW. The ordering of priorities was the same in the Naval Estimates.[4]

The decision had already been taken to maintain the total defense estimate at around £1,500 million, and indeed the net 1956 figures turned out slightly less than that figure. Cuts of £11 million in the previously intended Naval Estimates brought them down to £346 million. As announced by the prime minister at an early stage of his review, total service manpower was to come down to around 700,000 by the end of the financial year 1957–58, as compared with just over 772,000 in the spring of 1956 and over 825,000 the previous year. Vote A plans for the Royal Navy were a strength of 116,500 by 1 April 1957 as opposed to 122,500 at the same date in 1956 and 128,400 in 1955.[5]

Mountbatten was unable to fully protect the active fleet or the future building program (frigate building was slowed down), but the preferred option of cuts in shore support bore its first fruits in the summer of 1956. It was announced that the training system was to be greatly rationalized; for example, all gunnery training was being concentrated at two establishments and all signal training at one. These and other cuts amounted to some six shore establishments and two naval air stations. It was proudly announced that these reductions would release some 5,000 officers and men for use elsewhere. The cuts also marked the formal closures of Scapa Flow and Invergordon. They were perhaps considered to be too exposed to Soviet air attack. Future main fleets, if required at all, would be forced to adopt a more mobile posture than before. The pressure for further cuts in shore bases did not let up. In July 1956 Harold Macmillan, Eden's chancellor since the end of 1955, forced extra reductions of £8 million in defense expenditure.[6]

Eden wished to avoid a constant process of such piecemeal cuts. From the start the emphasis had been on long-term policy, and by the summer of 1956 he had decided to set up a Cabinet Committee of senior ministers to look at the problem. A new Foreign Office paper was prepared for the committee to look at Britain's future world role in the thermonuclear age. It concluded that the United Kingdom had overspent on defense since 1945 and that this was a major contributor to her persistent economic ill health.[7]

Eden stressed to his colleagues the "assumptions" they should bear in mind in the new phase of the review: (1) that the main threat to the U.K.'s security was political and economic rather than military; (2) that as aid from abroad was ending, some £400 million had to be saved on the balance of payments; and (3) that priorities should be shifted from forces concerned with least likely risks, i.e., those concerned with general war, to those of greater importance. A rapid and wide-ranging investigation went on throughout July into every defense issue from National Service and Antarctica to medium-range ballistic missiles. One of the most significant stages in the review was when, in the week beginning on 16 July, there was discussion of a COS Appreciation on a "New Strategy for NATO." This seems to have spelled out a still greater nuclear emphasis in British strategy. Forces in Europe were no longer to be expected to fight too large a land battle; all that would be expected would be to "impose some delay on the progress of a Soviet land invasion until the full impact is felt of the thermonuclear retaliation which would be launched against the Soviet Union."[8]

With the prospect that a future war would be shorter than ever, it was even more important for the Royal Navy to espouse the "policing and limited war scenario." Mountbatten did his best personally to sell to the prime minister the importance of the navy in these duties—with some success. In the week beginning 23 July 1956, the future of the navy was discussed, along with other "forces for limited war and internal security." Eden and his colleagues decided to aim to reduce strength by 1960 to a navy of 90,000 men as part of largely regular forces of about 445,000. Conscription would be abolished as soon as voluntary recruitment could maintain these strengths. Throughout the armed forces the emphasis would be on full-time professionals ready to move worldwide at the shortest possible notice. The events of the following months would do much to confirm the strength of this argument, as well as point to the need for a significant reorientation of Admiralty views on the balance of their forces. The very week that the future of the Royal Navy was being discussed in Eden's Cabinet Committee President Nasser nationalized the Suez Canal in retaliation for the withdrawal of promised Western aid to build the Aswan High Dam.[9]

This is not the place for a detailed discussion of the political background to the Anglo-French-Israeli joint attack on Egypt that ensued in November 1956. Rather this account will concentrate on the navy's role in "Operation Musketeer" and the preparations for it. First, however, it is necessary to discuss the background to the weaknesses in amphibious capability that the operation revealed.

The new emphasis on limited war and Cold War functions had not yet had an effect on the amphibious capabilities of the Royal Navy. In the decade since the Second World War the "Combined Operations" organization had been allowed to wither away almost completely. As far as the Admiralty was concerned, preparations for the major war at sea, be it convoy protection, mine countermeasures work, or the provision of a carrier strike fleet, took priority in the struggle for resources. Cold War functions were not deemed to require more than the forces that could be landed by a "gunboat," be it a cruiser or a frigate. Understandably, given Britain's *possession* of the territories she was policing, the assumption often tended to be that the landing of forces would be unopposed and, if it were not, the ships required might be taken up from the merchant service or out of reserve to deal with the problem.

The war had ended with the Royal Navy well equipped with many amphibious

TABLE 5–1.

AMPHIBIOUS FORCES AS PROPOSED IN FEBRUARY 1947*

TYPE	NUCLEUS TRAINING FLOTILLA	MOBILE FLOTILLA	ASSAULT TRAINING FORCE
Landing Ship Headquarters	—	—	1
Landing Ship Tank (3)	—	—	6
Landing Ship Tank (Assault)	—	4	15
Landing Ship Dock	—	—	1
Landing Craft Headquarters	—	1	3
Landing Craft Tank (Experimental)	—	1	—
Landing Craft Tank (8)	1	3	12
Landing Ship Rocket	—	—	2*
Landing Craft Assault	6	24	108
Landing Craft Navigation	—	—	2
Landing Craft Personnel (Large)	—	8	48
Landing Craft Mechanized (7)	2	2	12
Motor Transport Ship	—	—	1
Coasters	—	—	2
Picket Boat Units	—	—	8

Source COS(47)129, P.R.O. DEFE5/4 Chiefs of Staff Committee Memoranda.
*When built

ships. Many, however, were American serving under lend-lease, among them four very useful dock landing ships (LSD). By 1947, with most amphibious ships either returned to the U.S.A. or reduced to the Reserve, the only operational landing vessels were three of the 4,980-ton British-built tank landing ships of the LST(3) type, a small landing craft headquarters, LCH 243, and four of the 640-ton tank landing craft of the LCT(8) type built for Pacific operations. Six more LCT(8)s were being used for training. In 1946 ambitious plans had been laid for expanding this into a "Post War Assault Training Force" containing two small training flotillas plus a substantial "Assault Training Force," but the simultaneous cuts in manpower and material prevented any moves to set up such an organization. In October of that year the Admiralty claimed that the shortage of manpower would mean that only one training flotilla could be manned before 1949. The other two formations would not be ready before 1952. The following month investigations began into the possibility of doing without the Assault Training Force. While these enquiries were going on, the continued cuts in expenditure led the Admiralty to present the other services with the unpleasant choice of either the "Assault Training Force" idea or reducing the amphibious lift kept in reserve. Field Marshal Montgomery, chief of the Imperial General Staff, fought hard for a minimum lift for a full brigade group (6,000 men and 750 vehicles). This target (agreed upon by the chiefs of staff) received A.V. Alexander's endorsement, but there remained disagreement between the War Office and the Admiralty over whether it meant maintaining in peace the capacity to lift a brigade group immediately in emergency or whether it was just an "ultimate target" that would require four months' mobilization.[10]

The main opponent of the Admiralty in this struggle for an amphibious force was Major General Sir Robert Laycock, an army commando officer with a distinguished war record and still chief of Combined Operations. The army commandos had been disbanded in 1946, and the Royal Marines now monopolized the com-

Two strong supporters of the Royal Navy's amphibious capabilities, Major General Sir Robert Laycock (left), who tried unsuccessfully to increase their priority in the 1940s, and Admiral Lord Louis Mountbatten, who succeeded in the late 1950s. (Imperial War Museum)

mando infantry role; their 3rd Commando Brigade was now Britain's spearhead amphibious force composed of three battalion size Commandos, numbered 40, 42, and 45. The army was still very interested in "Combined Ops," however, and it was recognized that for an operation of any size army forces such as armor and artillery would be necessary, hence the requirement for a Brigade Group lift. It also might prove necessary, Laycock argued, to land army infantry in certain circumstances. Laycock was head of a joint service Combined Operations Headquarters that controlled the School of Combined Operations (later the Joint Service Amphibious Warfare School) at Fremington, near Barnstaple in Devon. This had been set up at Laycock's suggestion close to the existing Combined Operations Experimental Establishment in 1946. Combined Ops HQ and Fremington kept British expertise in amphibious warfare alive, despite attempts by the Admiralty to abolish them, moves that had been stoutly opposed by the army and RAF.[11]

In the summer of 1947 Laycock presented the chiefs of staff with ambitious plans for Britain's peacetime amphibious capability. This comprised a small nucleus training flotilla to see to Fremington's requirements, a larger Mobile Flotilla to serve a new combined training establishment to be set up in the Middle East, plus the controversial Assault Training Force. The total shipping requirements for this proposal are set out in the accompanying table.

These vessels would, if required, become the operational force to lift the required brigade group. A "very formidable" major building and conversion program was required, the surviving large infantry landing ship *Keren* being converted into an HQ ship (LSH) and fifteen LST(3)s into landing ships tank (assault) to handle nine assault landing craft from davits. The latter would do the job of the wartime infantry landing ships (LSI). Two new HQ landing craft (LCH) were to be built along with two new rocket-equipped landing ships (LSR) for close support. Most important of all, a new LSD was to be built, a major item of construction. Not only would all this new building take up scarce dockyard resources, but the proposed force would require 6,300 even more scarce Royal Navy personnel. Laycock suspected what kind of reception his ambitious ideas would get from the Admiralty. He ended, therefore, by saying that an interim solution might be to use the training flotillas, if necessary, to carry a battalion if required operationally, with the rest of the brigade group being delivered in whatever merchantmen were available.[12]

When the chiefs of staff got around to discussing Combined Operations policy in June, the Admiralty reacted to these proposals as expected. Rhoderick McGrigor, then vice chief of Naval Staff, made it clear that "the developments of other weapons and methods of warfare should have priority" over Combined Operations. Montgomery supported Laycock, but the Admiralty remained adamant. The sailors were obviously offended by Laycock's assertion that the neglect of his organization was due to "the natural reluctance on the part of any particular Service Ministry to spend a substantial portion of its vote on projects not directly to its own immediate advantage." His paper's recommendation that one policy option was that the COS might "accept the risk of a reduction in the Royal Navy's ability to retain command of the seas in order that a more substantial effort can be made to meet the future needs of Combined Operations" led the Admiralty to retaliate with a short lesson on the theory of sea power.[13]

In a sharply worded paper, dated 6 August, First Sea Lord Sir John Cunningham wrote acidly that Laycock's paper ignored "the fundamental issue that there can be no strategic mobility unless control of sea communications has been assured by the exercise of sea power. . . ." Laycock's suggested policy option was "basically unsound and utterly inadmissable. . . . Nothing could be more unsound than to risk our ability to gain and maintain control of sea communications, by which alone can the movement of our fighting forces to the points where they can be most effectively used be ensured, in order to provide the actual means, i.e., the ships and craft, of carrying out those movements." Combined Operations forces had not been neglected, Cunningham insisted, they received "the same consideration in the Naval Estimates as all other naval forces," but they were "subject to the same restrictions of manpower and money as other branches."[14]

The Admiralty also poured cold water on a suggestion that there might be a simple reallocation of manpower and resources from army to navy for Combined Operations. The complexities of the navy's manning problems as perceived in 1947 and the vital problem of attracting long-service personnel meant that, come what may, no more than 4,600 trained men could be allocated to amphibious forces. Other constraints like dockyard capacity and the army's own priorities made merely throwing "Army money" at the problem useless.[15]

The Admiralty reminded Laycock and the other chiefs that design work was in progress on a new LST(4) and LCT(9) as requested by Combined Operations, but that the need for these ships to carry the new heavy tanks led to serious design difficulties. Work on a prototype LST(A) conversion was about to begin, and no staff requirement had yet been received for an LSR. The first sea lord might also have made the point in his defense that the New Construction Programme for 1947–48, the first such postwar program after 1945, included a large landing craft personnel, an LCH (to be purchased from the U.S.A. for 95,000 dollars), and even the 4,500-ton LSD. Also included were three amphibious vehicles, one 20-tonner for assault and two 35-tonners for amphibious "build-up."[16]

The increasing pressure for cuts in the aftermath of the financial crisis saw pressure on Combined Operations increase. The new chief, a distinguished Royal Marine, Major General Wildman Lushington, scaled down the figures for proposed Combined Operations forces on the basis of a single battalion group lift with a supporting training establishment. The Assault Training Force was abandoned. Instead there would be but a single seagoing Training Squadron of five LSTs, four LCTs, and sixteen smaller landing craft. Two additional LSTs would be based in the Mediterranean. Twenty-five small landing craft, over half without allocated crews, would be kept for training, while for experimental and demonstration work at Fremington would be the LCH, two LCTs, and seven smaller landing craft. Kept in short-notice reserve for the battalion group lift would be eight LSTs, six LCTs, and thirty-seven smaller landing craft. Wildman Lushington recommended that the *Keren* be sold and the existing *River*-class frigates, *Waveney* and *Meon*, which had been converted during the war into LSH(S) (Landing Ships Headquarters (Small)) be retained instead as more economical substitutes. A third frigate, the *Exe*, was to be converted also, and it was hoped that new HQ ships might be available by the mid-1950s. In the event, the *Exe* was never converted and the *Waveney* spent the next decade in reserve, for even these scaled-down requirements had remained aims rather than become realities.[17]

The LSD was duly cancelled, along with the assault amphibian, and little work had been done on the LCP or the "Build-Up Amphibians" by the time of the appearance of the next building program in 1949. Later in the year it was decided

An important member of the postwar Amphibious Warfare Squadron was HMS *Meon*, and ex-*River*-class frigate converted in 1945 into a Landing Ship Headquarters (Small) or LSH(S). During the late 1940s she was in reserve at Sheerness as an accommodation, but from 1951 to 1965 she acted as Headquarters Ship for the Royal Navy's main amphibious force.

to suspend work on the amphibians. The Revised Restricted Fleet Plan confirmed the concept of battalion lift in peace and brigade lift in war and a small conversion program to improve the existing fleet. It was still hoped to build a small number of all-new LST(4) tank landing ships in the 1950s, and work slowly progressed on a little new Landing Craft Personnel (LCP501). It was not a great deal, but at least the Harwood Committee's recommendations to abolish the Royal Marines and to maintain only raiding forces had been pigeonholed.[18]

Korean rearmament seems to have done little to improve the situation. Various shortcomings were identified, but the Admiralty assured the chiefs of staff that its existing reserve amphibious ships could lift a brigade (albeit one redefined at 4,000 men and 500 vehicles) or indeed supply four divisions over beaches. The latter reflected the "hot war" thinking that still dominated amphibious requirements. The most that was expected offensively was the seizure of small strategic objectives, or operations on the seaward flank of an enemy army. Various deficiencies were identified, twelve landing ships of various kinds and three large LCH, but little was done to remedy them. Worries that the LST(3) and LCT(8) could not carry the new Conqueror heavy tanks were allayed by the knowledge that at least the LCT(8) could carry the new, slightly smaller Centurions "over short distances." The new LCT(9) prototype was still projected, but was not due until 1953–54.[19]

By 1952 the number of available amphibious ships was very small indeed. Only three LST(3)s were operational, one of them the first LST(A), HMS *Reggio*. The remaining thirty-six were either in reserve (nine at fourteen days' notice), on special service, or on loan or charter (at six months' notice). One of the two LST(C)s (an LST(3) modified to carry seven medium-sized landing craft) was in service, the other in reserve. Only two of the LCT(8)s were running, eight were in Category I (fourteen days' notice) Reserve, twenty in Category III (i.e., post-mobilization) Reserve. One battalion could be lifted at relatively short notice, and the Admiralty felt it could do no more in circumstances where there were not enough men to man even cruisers properly. It was admitted that Cold War requirements might require a brigade at short notice, but it was just impossible to meet that request. Rearmament had had some effect on the plans for new amphibious warfare vessels, notably a new LSD in the 10,000-ton class, of which preliminary studies were made (all the wartime LSDs had been returned to the U.S.A.). Some six landing craft projects were under consideration by 1953, but only the smallest raiding craft reached the point of being ordered. The cuts of 1953–55 put paid to anything larger being built—especially the big £4–5 million LSD—but the program on converting LST(3)s to LST(A)s slowly went ahead. Two more had been converted by 1956.[20]

As for vehicles, the British "build-up" amphibian was never put into production. Indeed by the early 1950s the amphibious vehicle situation was parlous in the extreme. Eighty-seven LVTs (Landing Vehicles Tracked) and 222 DUKWs were on hand, but only 37 and 12 respectively were usable. There were plans to try to get new vehicles from the U.S.A., but these never came to fruition. Proposals to improve the operational amphibious capability to give full battalion group lift also fell on stony ground, with the Admiralty opposing even minor increases in the active strength of LSTs and LCTs by one and two respectively. The Admiralty also went on the offensive once more suggesting abolition of the renamed Amphibious Warfare Organisation early in 1953. Its chief, Major General V.D. Thomas, com-

Another portion of the Reserve Fleet at Portsmouth in the mid-1950s. This is part of the more ready reserve of modern ships, some vessels being placed here straight out of conversion, like the two Type 15 ASW frigates visible, *Rapid* (F 138) and *Verulam* (F 29). The former recommissioned ten years later as a training vessel, and the latter became a trials ship in 1958. In the foreground is the impressive "Battle"-class destroyer *St. James* in reserve since 1953; she went for scrap in 1961. Tucked between the *Verulam* and the two cruisers is a new *Daring* class, HMS *Dainty*, completed in 1953, but which spent a year in reserve in 1955–56, there not being enough men to man her.

plained about the constant pressure on his organization. There had been no less than seven investigations into its status and existence in the previous ten years.[21]

By 1953 the amphibious vessels available for training in Britain had been reduced still further by the decision to deploy Britain's sole effective Amphibious Squadron, HMS *Reggio* and two LCT(8)s, to the Mediterranean to support the existing Middle Eastern deployment of two LSTs and two LCTs. Effectively all Britain's amphibious capability was now in this area to help prepare for operations against Egypt (see chapter 4). The initial exercises of this newly augmented amphibious squadron did little to inspire confidence, and they were brought under the direct supervision of the CinC to improve their performance. The Amphibious Warfare Squadron's main "armament," 3rd Commando Brigade, deployed in Egypt, also suffered from the low priority given to amphibious warfare at this time. When the brigade finally withdrew from the Canal Zone in 1954, 42 Commando was reduced to a training cadre and "nucleus" for mobilization.

Thus, the 1956 demand for an amphibious landing in Egypt found Britain woefully ill-prepared. Mountbatten, the old wartime chief of Combined Operations, had since his appointment shown increasing concern with amphibious weaknesses.

The first sea lord encouraged studies of the latest U.S. Marine Corps techniques, notably those of helicopter landing or "vertical envelopment." Mountbatten was outnumbered on the Board of Admiralty by officers who considered cruisers the main ships for Cold War duties and who still did not put a very high priority on amphibious operations. Plans for a carrier to be converted to land Marines by helicopter were made, but given a low priority. Indeed it was announced in 1956 that Fremington would finally succumb to the constant pressure and be closed down to save money. It was to be combined with the Royal Marines' training school at Poole.[22]

The 1956 Naval Estimates listed only one of the small LSH, HMS *Meon*, in commission plus two LST(A)s, four LCT(8)s, and another LST engaged in trials and training. The two operational LST(A)s, HMS *Striker* and HMS *Reggio*, and two of the LCTs, *Bastion* and *Redoubt*, were with the Amphibious Warfare Squadron at Malta. These vessels could only lift a single Commando (about 600 men), and an invasion of Egypt would require a force several times as big. It should have been possible to have moved 3rd Commando Brigade at least (42 Commando was reactivated on 1 August) with the landing ships and craft in commission on fourteen days' notice, but on inspection many of these reserve ships seem to have proved unusable. Recourse had to be made, therefore, to vessels on longer standby, and these needed considerable work to make them seaworthy. In any event the Royal Navy was incapable of manning sufficient amphibious lift to land and sustain all the troops involved. The army had its own fleet of landing ships, a dozen or so LST(3)s, operated by civilian crews for the Royal Army Service Corps or as "Empire" troopships. In September 1956 the chiefs of staff took the decision that the army should henceforth look after its own maritime logistics, and its fleet of landing craft was to be greatly increased. One LCT(8), together with a smaller LCT(4), was quickly sent to Cyprus. In addition another dozen reserve LST(3)s were transferred to the Ministry of Transport for use as civilian-manned troopships. These were still in Britain in November, but a total of eighteen British LSTs were eventually sent to the Mediterranean to be used in the Suez Operation and its immediate support; eight were RN operated and ten civilian. Five more RN LCT(8)s were mobilized to reinforce the Amphibious Warfare Squadron.[23]

Extreme measures had to be taken to mobilize enough amphibious vehicles. One reservist officer arrived at Amphibious Warfare HQ at Fremington in August to find gaily painted DUKWs requisitioned from being used as pleasure boats at seaside resorts! He summed up the consequences of a decade of neglect, "Only a dozen years ago we mounted the major portion of the greatest amphibious operation the world has ever known; now . . . we've got to conscript 'Saucy Sue,' for heaven's sake!" Ordinary merchant ships were also requisitioned to carry troops, among them a liner about to take emigrants to Australia.[24]

The very evening that Nasser had announced nationalization of the Suez Canal, 26 July, Eden met the chiefs of staff and ordered them to prepare contingency plans for military intervention. The Cabinet officially authorized the preparation of plans for military operations against Egypt the following day. The three relevant British commanders in chief, including the naval CinC, Mountbatten's successor Admiral Sir Guy Grantham, were alerted. By the beginning of August a joint Anglo-French team based on the British Joint Planning Staff was drawing up a command organization and going through the options for "Operation Hamilcar," soon changed to "Operation Musketeer." On 11 August command was placed in the hands of General Sir Charles Keightley, CinC Middle East Land Forces, with a French Vice Admiral, P. Barjot, as his deputy. Under him were three "Task Forces," Naval, Land, and Air Force. The naval force was to be commanded by Vice Admiral M. Richmond, who was later succeeded by D.D. Durnford-Slater. His deputy was Rear Admiral Lancelot of the French Navy. Mountbatten later claimed that he argued on 26 July in favor of a *coup de main* by the navy and the commando brigade to seize Port Said. The evidence, however, is that the suggestion was made only to be immediately dismissed by Mountbatten himself. The first sea lord did *not* at the time support such unilateral action by the Royal Navy and Royal Marines, and Sir Gerald Templer, the army chief of staff, was even more strongly opposed to putting lightly armed troops against possible armored counterattacks. At the vital Cabinet meeting on July 27th that formally decided on the use of force if necessary, the chiefs of staff argued that Egyptian strength required the use of the equivalent of three entire divisions. Much more than a "brigade group lift" would be required for this imposing force, and "preparations for mounting the operation would take several weeks."[25]

The chiefs of staff submitted their first ideas for "action against Egypt" on August 1st. Forces were to be built up within striking range and then an ultimatum issued. If this was refused, naval and air action would be begun, and "if this is still necessary" an attack would be made on both the northern end of the canal and a "threat posed" to Alexandria. Heavy air support would be required for the "slender" assault forces, and the maximum possible parachute drop was to be arranged. The Canal Zone would have to be occupied and "law and order" restored in Egypt. A permanent re-occupation of Egypt was not, however, envisaged. The chiefs discussed the first specific plans a week later. The designated land force commanders, General Sir Hugh Stockwell and his French assistant, General André Beaufre, were concerned about Port Said's distance from the amphibious base at Malta. Landing conditions were also poor there. Hence, the first plan was to concentrate on Alexandria. Some 80,000 men would be used and, after a major battle with the Egyptians, the canal would be occupied eight days later. This was soon amended to include a two-day air offensive to destroy the Egyptian Air Force, then an amphibious and airborne assault landing followed by a week's concentration of forces. The denouement would be an advance towards the canal "through the Cairo area." It was assumed that a victorious battle with the Egyptian Army would occur within fourteen days of landing, which would cause Nasser's fall. The assault on Alexandria Harbor itself would be carried out by the British 3rd Commando Brigade. The long concentration period was due to shortages of shipping and the need to bring up sufficient strength. No risks were to be taken with the well-equipped Egyptian forces, although opposition was not expected to be serious.

The plan was adopted by the Special Egypt Committee of the Cabinet on 10 August, with the landing originally planned to take place on 15 September, two days after the bombing of Egypt began. This schedule disappointed Eden, but when one considers pre-crisis British doubts about whether they could move a single brigade within three months of taking the decision to do so, it was far from unambitious. Not only Marines and ordinary infantry would be landed. Shortages of transport aircraft meant that two-thirds of the Parachute Brigade would have to be deployed by sea. Gathering suitable shipping was not the only problem. A goodly proportion of the British specialist forces, both Royal Marines and the soldiers of the Parachute Regiment, had been engaged in counterinsurgency operations in Cyprus. They needed retraining in their original roles before they could be used.

Throughout August the strength of the Mediterranean Fleet was built up. At the end of July Grantham only had a single carrier, albeit the largest one in service, HMS *Eagle* carrying over fifty aircraft, two squadrons of Sea Hawk fighter/ground attack aircraft, a Wyvern strike squadron, a squadron of Sea Venom all-weather fighters, a squadron of Gannet ASW machines, and a flight of Skyraider AEW aircraft. The *Eagle*'s sister *Ark Royal* was unavailable as she was undergoing her first major refit, but reinforcement soon appeared in the shape of the *Hermes*-class light fleet carrier *Bulwark*, which had been mobilized from her trials and training duties and equipped with an ad hoc air group of thirty Sea Hawks (three squadrons). She left Portsmouth for the Mediterranean on August 6th, and after two days in dry dock at Gibraltar, had arrived at Malta by August 25th. The landing ships began to gather in Malta in August too, along with the destroyer depot ship HMS *Tyne* that had just been serving as Home Fleet headquarters vessel and which would be a joint Anglo-French command ship. Her level of facilities soon caused problems, and after an amphibious exercise at Malta in early September, General Beaufre decided to transfer to one of his own navy's vessels. Another significant arrival was the Minesweeping Flotilla's Headquarters ship, *Mull of Galloway*. Extra paratroops and supporting personnel, including the Headquarters of 16th Parachute

When it eventually came into service, the Wyvern equipped two strike squadrons, one intended for each fleet carrier. Here the *Eagle* catapults off one of 827 Squadron's aircraft in 1955. (Imperial War Museum)

Brigade, were brought out to Cyprus in the Training Squadron light fleet carriers *Ocean* and *Theseus* and the armament trials cruiser *Cumberland*.[26]

One major operational difficulty was that Cyprus, Britain's main Middle East base since her withdrawal from the Canal Zone, had very poor harbors and lacked most other facilities: workshops, supply dumps, and even, as yet, airfields. The wharves at Famagusta could only take five ships up to LST size but no larger, and at Limassol all loading had to be carried out by lighter. Malta had a much better harbor and also airfields, but it was over 900 miles away from Egypt, almost a week's sailing for a slow amphibious convoy. Libyan opposition eventually prevented British armor there from being used for the operation. British tank support had to come from Britain where two tank regiments, the 1st and 6th Royal Tank Regiments, were initially allocated to the operation. Gathering the scattered units of these regiments was not easy, and the difficulties were compounded by the belated decision towards the end of August to send the 6th Royal Tanks, the unit designated as the second wave, as the assault regiment. The unit sailed in four mobilized LST(3)s between 23 August and 2 September.[27]

It was hoped that the somewhat public flurry of military activity in August would have the effect of forcing Egypt to back down, but this did not occur. Nevertheless, the British and French still vacillated, and there was progressive postponement of the Alexandria landings to 26 September. In order to give the invasion a legal pretext, the British and French withdrew their canal pilots, which they assumed would effectively close the canal by late September; military intervention would then be "necessary" to reopen the international waterway. On the new schedule a decision in principle was required by 9 September, and the shipping was to set sail on the 15th. By early September, however, various factors were counseling caution. First, the Egyptians were demonstrating an annoying facility to operate the canal with their own pilots. Second, the forces would not all be at Malta by the 9th. Most importantly, opposition to the whole idea of an invasion of Egypt was growing. The U.S.A. had voiced its serious reservations, and even some members of the Cabinet were unhappy. The Admiralty in general seems to have been skeptical about the whole operation; the First Lord, Viscount Cilcennin was opposed and even his successor, Lord Hailsham, while more supportive of the prime minister's line, voiced opposition to the Alexandria plan and the need to bombard the city. Although he was careful not to make his position widely known, Mountbatten made his opposition to the whole operation clear behind the closed doors of the Chiefs of Staff Committee. He felt that a military solution was impossible. Even the prospect of a successful invasion begged the question of what was to happen afterwards. Could a pro-British regime be set up? How long an occupation was being considered? The chiefs were not united. Templer was hawkish, Chief of the Air Staff Sir Dermot Boyle, indecisive, and the chairman and fellow airman, Sir William Dickson, often absent due to illness. Mountbatten contemplated resignation, but was persuaded to stay at his post.

What grew from these divided counsels was a new military consensus that the original Musketeer plan of an invasion through Alexandria and an advance into Egypt was impractical. On 7 September, with the first sea lord playing a leading role, a united front of the minister of defense (Sir Walter Monckton), the chiefs of staff, and General Keightley presented Eden with the prospect of the political embarrassment of heavy loss of Egyptian life in the landings and a long campaign of two to three months. The meeting was acrimonious, but the dubious and angry prime minister was won over and in the afternoon, at full Cabinet, he got agreement on a decision to order the chiefs of staff to draw up a revised plan. The French had begun preparing contingency plans for Port Said since late August, and joint planning on this had been agreed on the 24th of that month. This now provided the basis for "Musketeer Revise," which was drawn up by October 10th. The Anglo-French Force would now take Port Said and reoccupy the Canal Zone. Land operations would be limited to the seizure of the canal, and there was a much greater emphasis than before on preliminary aerial bombardment to break Egyptian morale.

The first date proposed for Musketeer Revise was 1 October, and the force commanders and their staffs set to work to recast their plans as quickly as possible. As the name suggested, the new plan was the old one with its objectives changed. Again the British were to take the harbor. This, at least in part, reflected weaknesses in British amphibious capability, notably the difficulty of landing large numbers of tanks over the flat Egyptian beaches. The French, with an LSD and its embarked Landing Craft Mechanized, were better off in this respect and were allocated a beach assault around Port Fuad. Four British LCT carrying tanks would bring in a squadron of tanks to the beaches to the west of Port Said, but the bigger LST(3)s would have to disembark the rest of the 6th Royal Tanks in the harbor itself.

By the end of September it was clear that any invasion of Egypt would be strongly opposed by both the Labour Opposition and the United States. All this counseled further delay. Referring the issue to the United Nations Security Council put the operation back a week to 8 October. The internal debate continued also. Mountbatten kept up his pressure to consider Britain's capacity to maintain an Egyptian occupation force on Britain's already overextended commitments. Another opponent, Monckton, who voiced open opposition to "premature recourse to force" in Cabinet on September 11, was eventually moved to a ministry that was less closely involved with the proposed operation. This was not a good atmosphere for decisive action, and no decision was taken to put Musketeer Revise into effect by 29 September, the day shipping movements were due to begin. The French were increasingly frustrated at what seemed to them to be British indecision and were already coordinating plans for an Israeli attack on Egypt either as an alternative to, or as a trigger for, British action. In the first part of October, as new plans were being prepared to hold forces over the winter at ten days' notice, the French acted as go-betweens between the British and the Israelis. These negotiations culminated in the secret meetings in a villa at Sèvres on 22 October and 24 October between British, French, and Israeli ministers and officials. At the latter meeting an agreed "record of the discussions" was signed by Sir Patrick Dean, a senior Foreign Office official. This paper set out the plan: Israel would attack on 29 October; the following day Britain and France would appeal for a cease-fire and withdrawal of forces from ten miles each side of the canal to allow Anglo-French occupation of key positions; if Egypt did not agree, an Anglo-French attack would be mounted.

The extra weeks granted by this activity presented both problems and opportunities. The problems were those of boredom amongst the recalled reservists, leading in some cases to mutiny and disorder. The Royal Navy, which had merely cancelled men leaving rather than actually recalling reservists, was less prone to this kind of trouble. Maintenance of equipment loaded into ships many weeks previously was also causing problems. Loads had to be adjusted and plans changed, and this exacerbated problems of harbor pilfering. Nevertheless, the extra time also allowed the forces earmarked for the landings to be steadily improved. The *Eagle*'s air group was amended, the Gannet ASW squadron being replaced by 893 Squadron of Sea Venom all-weather fighters, part of the air group intended for the *Ark Royal*. This meant that the fleet carrier would have fifty machines available for attack missions, twenty-four Sea Hawks, seventeen Sea Venoms, and nine Wyverns. The Mediterranean Fleet's carrier strength was brought up to three ships when the *Albion*, having been rushed through her refit, sailed from Britain on 15 September. The light fleet carrier was operating nineteen Sea Hawks and eight Sea Venoms. Under the command of Vice Admiral M.L. Power, flag officer aircraft carriers and designated Allied carrier force commander, the three British carriers operated together on intensive exercises, practice strikes being flown against the French carriers *Arromanches* and *Lafayette* in the Western Mediterranean. In early October the *Bulwark* lost a Sea Hawk in an accident and also suffered catapult defects that forced her to be docked in Gibraltar. After intensive work she was operational once more by October 23rd, when she sailed for Malta. In all, the carriers deployed seventy-two Sea Hawks, twenty-five Sea Venoms, and nine Wyverns. Both the *Eagle* and *Albion* had flights of four Skyraider AEW aircraft, while the *Bulwark* still had her flight of two Avenger AS5s. Rescue helicopters brought the total of British aircraft in the carrier striking force to 120.

The Port Said Plan also included the novel idea of a helicopter assault on the bridges to the south of the town to ensure a line of advance. To do this it was decided to convert HMS *Ocean* and *Theseus* into extempore helicopter assault ships. The supporters of vertical envelopment were clearly grasping the opportunity to test and prove the concept. The two training carriers had been used as troop transports since late July, having been fitted with thousands of folding camp beds. On their return to the United Kingdom in early September, they were taken in hand to have proper bunks fitted in the hangars: the *Ocean* was also being equipped as a hospital ship. On September 26th these plans were suddenly changed. Fresh work was torn out as the two vessels were swiftly refitted to carry helicopter groups. Two helicopter squadrons were available, one the "Joint Experimental Helicopter Unit" (JEHU), a mixed Army/Royal Air Force organization normally based at Middle Wallop in Hampshire with its six Sycamore 14s and six Whirlwind HAR2s. Although the British-built Westland Whirlwind was not such a good load carrier as the Sikorsky original, it was an adequate helicopter by contemporary standards. The Sycamore, however, could only carry three men and was hardly the best machine for the job. At Royal Naval Air Station Eglinton carrying out antisubmarine exercises were the eight Sikorsky Whirlwind HAS22s and three Westland Whirlwind HAR3s of 845 Squadron, the Royal Navy's first operational ASW helicopter squadron, commissioned in March 1954. Like its sister squadron, 848, it was destined to see its first combat service in the transport role with its American AN/AQS4 "dunking" sonar stripped out. By the end of September JEHU was embarked in the *Theseus* and 845 in the *Ocean* on exercises in the Channel. The exercises were completed on October 10 and it seemed as if the two helicopter squadrons were to revert to normal duties. At this stage it looked as though

"Musketeer Revise" would be indefinitely delayed; the *Ocean* was even returned to her training role! Then 845 was suddenly ordered to embark in the *Theseus*, which sailed for Malta on October 19th. She arrived on the 26th, followed on the 31st by the *Ocean*, retrieved once more from her normal duties and carrying JEHU to war. The change of plan caused by French diplomacy and the Sèvres meeting had obviously been sudden.

Other aids to landings also appeared. Sixteen old Buffalo landing vehicles tracked (LVTs), manned by the hastily mobilized crews of the 1st LVT Troop Royal Armoured Corps, arrived in Malta. They were to operate from LSTs to carry in the first Marine wave, but the mobilized landing ships were too old and decrepit to be safely flooded so that the vehicles would have some buoyancy before driving out of the ship into the sea. Instead, the more risky procedure of driving straight out into the sea "dry" was adopted. A far from united Cabinet approved the invasion plan on 25 October. The chiefs of staff were also expressing doubts about the full implications of moving on to Cairo and Alexandria after a successful occupation of the Canal Zone. Nevertheless, Israel was now forcing the pace, and orders for the landings were issued on Saturday, 27 October. With the cover story that a four day "Exercise Boathook" was about to begin, loading of the reinforced 3rd Commando Brigade (2,150 officers and men and 550 vehicles) began on Tuesday the 30th, the day after the Israelis began their attack into Sinai. Loading had been delayed by the need to make it appear that the operation was a response to the Israeli attack. By the 31st the embarkation was complete and the force was at sea. The reinforced Commando Brigade was being carried in the RN Amphibious Squadron now up to a strength of three LST(A)s, five LST(3)s, and eight LCT(8)s led by the converted frigate *Meon*. The extra LCT(8) had been converted into an LCH, and Motor Launch 2583 was navigational leader. Because of its slow 6–7-knot cruising speed and the slow speed of the minesweeping screen, the squadron was not due to arrive off Port Said for six days. At 1615 on the 30th, President Nasser having refused the ultimatum to withdraw from the canal, the first RAF air attacks on Egypt began.

Even as the British bombers appeared over the Egyptian airfields and the invasion forces began to close in on their target, last minute changes of plan took place amid considerable inter-allied wrangling. The helicopter landings by one of the British commandos were replaced by a French parachute drop. The risks to machines unproven against hostile fire seemed too great, and it was not possible, given the limited capability of the helicopters, to land sufficient men at one time with sufficient security. Instead the *Ocean* and *Theseus*, with their embarked commandos, would act as a general reserve. The decision was also taken to advance the airborne landings by twenty-four hours to 5 November.

One reason for these changes in plan was the increasing certainty that the Egyptians would not be cowed into premature surrender by the bombing and British propaganda. Mountbatten was moved to write to the prime minister on 2 November appealing to him to accept a resolution passed by the United Nations for hostilities to cease and to turn back the assault convoy. Eden replied by telephone refusing to do so, and the final "go" decision was transmitted on the evening of the following day, 3 November. That evening the new British minister of defense, Anthony Head, accompanied by Sir Gerald Templer, chief of the Imperial General Staff, arrived at Cyprus to confer with General Keightley and Admiral Barjot. Templer

The pioneering British experiment with the Commando Carrier concept at Suez was when the *Ocean* and *Theseus* flew 45 Commando ashore. This is the *Theseus* in Port Said after the invasion, with the Whirlwinds and Sycamores of 845 Squadron and the Joint Experimental Helicopter Unit (JEHU) on deck. (Imperial War Museum)

and Head seem to have brought with them the fears of the British chiefs of staff on the subject of civilian casualties and the extent of operations. They made clear that operations were to be limited to the Canal Zone and that the supporting warships were not to use any guns bigger than the 4.5 inch. This affected the French more, perhaps, than the British, as the former had deployed the 15-inch-gun battleship *Jean Bart* with at least one of its quadruple turrets operational. The decision to limit fire to smaller calibers emphasized the role of the large British *Daring*-class destroyers with their heavy armaments of six 4.5-inch weapons. Six of these ships were available with the force. Detailed fire plans had been worked out as the Amphibious Squadron sailed across the Mediterranean, although much of this work proved futile as plans were changed again and again. The news of the gunfire limitations was relayed to the unimpressed amphibious ships. Bombardment plans for the two 6-inch-gun cruisers *Jamaica* and *Ceylon* quickly became the responsibility of the *Daring*s and other destroyers. Even more consternation was caused by last-minute news that the *entire* bombardment was to be scrapped. The commanders on the spot, on their own initiative, made the distinction between "Naval Gunfire Support" and "Bombardment." Effectively they decided to ignore this last order, as they felt that to do otherwise would be suicidal for their troops.

The desire to avoid civilian casualties also limited the air offensive both in targets attacked and bombs dropped. On 1 November the three British carriers, which had been operating together once more since the 29th of October, joined in the air offensive. In addition to the British air groups Vice Admiral Power, flying his flag in the *Eagle*, commanded forty-five more aircraft, thirty-six Corsairs, five Avengers, and four rescue helicopters in the French light carriers *Arromanches* (ex-HMS *Colossus*) and *Lafayette*. Just before dawn Sea Venoms and Sea Hawks attacked the airfields around Cairo with rockets and cannon fire. Later that day the Wyverns, which had been held back in case they ran into higher-performance jet opposition, went into action also. The Egyptian Air Force, untrained in the intricacies of their new Soviet jets and incapable of serious opposition, were evacuating what aircraft they had southwards and were not opposing the Anglo-French air offensive. Attacks went on throughout the day with Sea Hawks flying top cover just in case of opposition. By 2 November the Egyptian Air Force had ceased to exist as a fighting force. The Admiralty claimed some seventy-one aircraft destroyed and fifty more damaged by 355 sorties by British naval aircraft. The Egyptian losses included some modern MiG-15s and Ilyushin Il-28s as well as two old ex-British Lancaster bombers. The British carriers now turned their attention to Egyptian troop and supply concentrations, the *Eagle*'s Wyverns being unleashed on the massed vehicle dump at Huckstep Camp with bombs, rockets, and cannon fire. The only British casualty was one of the *Eagle*'s Sea Venoms, which just made it back to the ship where it crash landed. On the 3rd, limited attacks on identifiable military road traffic were carried out, together with attacks on strategic targets around Port Said. The *Eagle*'s aircraft attacked the bridge to the west of the town over which reinforcements might come. Both Sea Hawks and Wyverns were used to bomb this tough target, and one of the latter was shot down by AA fire, the pilot being rescued by helicopter.

Not only naval aircraft had gone into action on 1 November. On the night of 31 October/1 November just as the RAF began their attacks, the cruiser *Newfoundland*, accompanied by smaller British and French warships, entered the Gulf of Suez. The object of this activity is not clear. Certainly it acted as a useful blockade helping the Israeli attack on Sharm al-Sheikh. The Egyptian frigate *Domiat*, an ex-British "River"-class ship, had been ordered south both to escort a convoy to relieve Sharm al-Sheikh and possibly to mine the Straits of Tiran. The *Domiat* was sailing south with lights on shortly after midnight when she ran into three darkened warships, one of which was the British 6-inch-gun cruiser, *Newfoundland*, which ordered the Egyptian ship to halt. When the cruiser shone a searchlight on the *Domiat*, the latter opened fire. She missed, but the *Newfoundland*'s replying salvo hit the frigate forward. The *Domiat* fired two more 4-inch shots before a second salvo knocked out her main gun. An attempt to ram the cruiser failed when 6-inch shells knocked out the Egyptian's engines and steering. The *Domiat* could only reply with 40-mm fire until her crew were forced to abandon the sinking ship. The *Newfoundland* suffered six casualties; sixty-eight Egyptian survivors were picked up, about half the frigate's crew. Not only the Egyptians suffered from this southern British presence. When four Israeli aircraft attacked the British frigate *Crane*, presumably in error (the Egyptians operated a sister ship), the British ship shot one down.

Another target attacked by naval aircraft on 1 November was the Egyptian LST *Akka*, which had been prepared for sinking as a blockship in Lake Timsah on the canal. Two attacks were made, with only limited success, and the ship was towed into her blocking position before she sank. Thus, somewhat ironically, did the British themselves begin the blocking of the canal, a process the Egyptians hastened to complete in a "subsequent orgy of sinking" that began on 2 November. On 4 November the carrier and shore-based aircraft kept up their pressure around Port Said, preparing the way for the amphibious landings on the 5th. The rules of engagement often limited the activity of the British naval aircraft, but some clear-cut targets appeared when three Soviet built P6-class motor torpedo boats were spotted between Alexandria and Port Said. The *Bulwark*'s Sea Hawks had soon accounted for two and damaged the other. In all the day's attacks the *Bulwark* lost one Sea Hawk, which crashed on landing, and the *Eagle* another that was shot down over land, the pilot being rescued by helicopter.

With the navy for which he was responsible now at war with Egypt, the first sea lord made one final protest. On 4 November, the day before the planned landings, he protested at the fleet being called upon to inflict civilian casualties in the opposed landing. Mountbatten felt that resignation was inappropriate: naval officers had to obey orders, however repugnant, and the officers and men already committed to combat were doing so, no matter what their private feelings. However, he did ask the first lord whether in the circumstances he wished to get a new professional head of the service. Hailsham ordered the first sea lord to remain at his post. Philip Ziegler has summed up Mountbatten's predicament as follows:

> To have resigned . . . would have been contrary to every tradition of the public service; the professional head of the Navy might properly throw up his office if in his view the efficiency and well being of his Service was threatened, but not because the Government decided to wage a war of which he disapproved. Mountbatten could have resigned, but it is unlikely that he would have achieved anything if he had and he would have earned the justified criticism of the Navy by so doing. He could not realistically have been expected to take his opposition further.[28]

As Robert Rhodes James has argued, however, the influential first sea lord was no ordinary officer. If he had made his doubts clearer and earlier, he might have had some significant effect in steering the government away from military action. By early November it was too late. The combination of an aggressive prime minister and a divided and vacillating military leadership in the months leading up to Suez was an almost inevitable recipe for disaster.

On 5 November the airborne troops landed with naval aircraft providing close air support. Some 373 sorties were flown against various targets. A "cab rank" system was operated with up to sixteen RN and French aircraft available to be called down on targets only a hundred yards from the paratroops. Wyverns with 1,000-lb. bombs were called in to deal effectively with the tough coast guard barracks near Gamil Airfield. One was shot down, the pilot being rescued. Helicopters were also used to ferry out wounded to, and fly in supplies from, the amphibious force closing Port Said. Vice Admiral Power reportedly suggested an immediate helicopter landing with 45 Commando in support of the airborne forces but was overruled. This was a pity as the airborne assault alone had caused the local Egyptian commander to consider surrender. Cairo ordered the continuation of resistance, and the seaborne assault went ahead as planned.

On 5 November the invasion force finally coalesced, the convoy from Cyprus joining the Malta amphibious force and the French convoy from Algiers. The Cyprus convoy consisted of commandeered merchantmen, civilian-manned LSTs, and the troopship *Empire Parkstone* (a cross-Channel ferry). Also coming from Cyprus was the flagship, HMS *Tyne*, in which all the task force commanders were concentrated. Under the command of Rear Admiral G.B. Sayer, the two British helicopter assault ships of the "Helicopter Force" had left Malta on the 3rd, with the 600 men of 45 Commando. The two carriers were somewhat faster than the rest of the amphibious forces. The whole Anglo-French force attacking Egypt at this time totaled more than one hundred major British warships and thirty-four French ships, not counting small landing craft, storeships, and supply vessels. The Royal Navy contingent included, in addition to the five carriers, three cruisers, a fast minelayer, six *Daring*s, seven destroyers, six frigates, five submarines, five headquarters and maintenance ships, a survey vessel, and fifteen minesweepers.

A major problem for this huge armada was the activity of the U.S. Sixth Fleet, which was demonstrating American opposition to the operation by "leaning" on the Anglo-French squadrons. On the night of the 4th/5th searchlights were shone on the blacked-out ships, and shortly afterwards U.S. aircraft made dummy attacks on French ships; two closely shadowing American submarines were ordered to the surface. Some very strong signals passed between the Americans and their NATO allies before the U.S. ships finally withdrew.

Despite these activities and despite the orders concerning the shore bombardment, the British landings took place under cover of a preliminary ten-minute air strike and a very heavy forty-five-minute session of "gunfire support on known enemy defences" on the morning of the 6th. A hail of 4.5-inch shells struck the beaches at Port Said. Guided by ML 2583's radar, the LVTs and LCAs from the tank landing ships ran in towards the shore in the first and second waves, five

After all the confusion of their initial deployment, one of the 6th Royal Tanks' Centurions comes ashore at Port Said from HMS *Puncher*. (Imperial War Museum)

minutes apart. Shortly before the landings the naval guns ceased fire and the work of cover was taken over by carrier-based aircraft once more, which raked the shore with rocket and cannon fire. The landings took place at 0650 local time. Shortly after the initial waves touched down, four LCT(8)s landed waterproofed Centurion tanks of the 6th Royal Tank Regiment in four and a half feet of water on the beach on the extreme left of the landing beaches. The Egyptians had some SU100 armor dug in in defense, and one of these dueled with a British destroyer whose 4.5-inch shells set fire to the surrounding buildings; 40 Commando was on the left of the landings with 42 Commando on the right. With armored support, 40 Commando advanced into the town against fierce resistance at first. The object was to clear the harbor to allow more armor to be landed from the LSTs. Under cover of another heavy air strike, 42 Commando, tasked with capturing the outskirts of the town, chose a more mechanized approach using LVTs to get to their objective. To help clear the town, which was still full of snipers, 45 Commando was brought in by helicopter. This unit was first called at 0740, but the landing was delayed when it was found that the initial prepared landing ground, the Sports Stadium, was heavily occupied by Egyptian forces. Instead, the Commando was brought ashore near the De Lesseps statue to the southwest of the landing beaches and next to the canal. Some 415 men and 23 tons of stores were landed between 0815 to 0937. Conditions were not easy. There were no seats or doors, and few handholds for the seven to nine men in each 845 Squadron Sikorsky Whirlwind. The Westland Whirlwinds could only carry five men each and the Sycamores three. In the latter aircraft the three Royal Marines sat on the floor, two with their legs dangling over the side, each carrying a recoilless rifle round, with the center soldier holding on to his companions with the help of the weight of six mortar bombs! Once landed, the men of 45 moved westwards, despite an air strike of British Wyverns called by a mistaken map reference. An LST was able to land the Commando's transport in the afternoon.

As the three RM Commandos tried to control the town, the rest of the British force were having problems. Block ships prevented the rest of the armored force, and the paratroops who were coming in by sea, from getting to their designated off-loading points. HMS *Chevron*, carrying the Queen's Harbourmaster and naval officer in charge, organized two minesweepers to sweep a passage to the fishing port closest to the sea. Soon LSTs were unloading the remaining two squadrons of 6th Royal Tanks at these jetties, but not until early afternoon did British ships enter the main harbor. The carrier *Theseus*, carrying the army's dock-operating company, was the first large warship to enter Port Said. The *Empire Parkstone* and her accompanying tank landing ships began landing the 2nd Battalion Parachute Regiment. As the British ships arrived, Wyverns and Sea Hawks were systematically reducing a major center of resistance, ironically the strongly built edifice of "Navy House," the old Royal Navy Headquarters. The troops went down scrambling nets into lighters to be brought ashore. The tank landing ships went straight for the wharves. The 1st British Parachute Regiment was still waiting offshore by the evening when news came that a cease-fire had been ordered from London to take effect from midnight. The advance down the canal had just begun, albeit in a somewhat desultory fashion, but by the time the cease-fire came into effect, the British forces of 2nd Para were at El Cap, 23 miles south of Port Said.

Britain's superiority over the Egyptians was not matched by her economic strength vis-à-vis her major ally. The United States now demonstrated ruthlessly and decisively her veto over independent British action. With a run on the pound orchestrated by the U.S. Government and threatening Britain's currency reserves, there was no alternative to giving in, as Chancellor of the Exchequer Macmillan reported to the Cabinet on the morning of the landings. A cease-fire by midnight meant an International Monetary Fund loan of £500 million and other means to prop up the tottering pound. There were other factors in the British decision— the fact that the Egyptians and Israelis had indeed ceased fire, the prospect of further defections from the Cabinet and civil service, and Eden's failing health and exhaustion. Nevertheless, the financial motive and, therefore, U.S. pressure seems to have been predominant. The U.S.A. had, perhaps, taken the Soviet threats of intervention a little more seriously than the British, although it was made clear that U.S. support would be given to Britain and France if Russia did intervene. Primarily, however, the Americans were concerned about the effect of the invasion on Western interests in the Middle East. Once Britain decided to withdraw, the French were forced to conform—with considerable resentment.

On 7 November a clearance team moved into Port Said Harbor to begin the work of clearing the twenty-one ships sunk there. It had been assumed that the Egyptians would have made some attempt to block the harbor and HMS *Dalrymple*, a wreck disposal and survey vessel, led a team of two salvage ships and five tugs that had been included in the assault force. More such vessels arrived later. By 9 November a channel had been made and by the 12th LSTs were moving into the inner harbor. On that day Keightley was ordered to remain until the arrival of the U.N. Emergency Force that had been arranged to cover the Anglo-French-Israeli withdrawals. On 11 November two brigades of 3rd Infantry Division arrived by sea to relieve the Marines and paratroops. These brigades had sailed from the United Kingdom at the beginning of the month. Ten days later, on 21 November, the first UNEF battalion arrived, and withdrawal of the 23,000 Anglo-French troops ashore began. This was completed on 22 December, although a small number of British salvage ships remained to help clear the Suez Canal, which had been blocked by over forty obstructions.

The closure of the canal and the economic costs that that imposed on the United Kingdom, which was forced to introduce petrol rationing, was only one negative effect of the Suez Crisis. Indeed, it is hard to find any positive gain from an operation that had a disastrous impact on Anglo-Arab, Anglo-Commonwealth, Anglo-American, and Anglo-French relations. The direction of the military operation had some question marks over it also, particularly as regards the failure to exploit the opportunities offered by the events on the 5th and the effective neutralization of the higher command by the ill-advised attempt to come ashore on the 6th. Nevertheless, as a service the Royal Navy emerged from the operation remarkably well. Although the Admiralty's neglect of, and low priority for, amphibious capability was a direct cause of the extraordinary weaknesses in sea lift that made some contribution to delaying the operation, it is arguable whether that delay was fatal or not. Although an immediate attack was out of the question, a limited invasion with supporting tanks could probably have been landed from mid-September onwards in support of an airborne battalion. To be in a position to do that was no mean achievement given the readiness schedules of many of the ships involved. The delay beyond mid-September was caused fundamentally by political factors and divided opinions at the highest military level, not directly by military and naval weaknesses. Nevertheless the lesson of the need for immediate readiness for intervention forces had been well and truly learned.

The operations had also vindicated the effectiveness of navies in projecting military power ashore. Naval gunfire support, even given the restrictions under which it labored, had proved effective, as had carrier air power. The delays, allowing the carrier force to be strengthened and the "vertical envelopment" by helicopter to be mounted, had helped the navy to make a more effective demonstration of the carrier's continued utility than might otherwise have been the case. Given the mounting criticism of the carrier in general and the fleet carrier in particular, it was useful for the Naval Staff to be able to point out that the low-level type of air strike, as practiced by carrier aircraft, had proved much more effective than the RAF's high-level offensive. The RAF had deployed some fighter bombers of its own, but, from airfields in Cyprus, they only had ten to fifteen minutes on task. The naval aircraft, being closer, were much more flexible in their use. Not all had gone well for the FAA; inexperienced pilots, working with insufficient intelligence briefing, had some problems. Two historians of the operation have compared unfavorably, and a little unfairly, the time taken to destroy the Egyptian Air Force—two whole days—with the results achieved by the Israeli Air Force in 1967. Nevertheless, the basic point of the vital importance of carrier air support in limited war had been reemphasized.

Moreover, it was the big fleet carrier that had proved most efficient. Despite catapult defects, which forced flag officer aircraft carriers temporarily to transfer his flag to the *Bulwark* on November 7th, the *Eagle* had launched some 621 sorties during the six days of the campaign, more than the *Albion* and *Bulwark* combined. However, a new possible use for light carriers had also been opened up by the experiment in helicopter landings. The *Ocean* and *Theseus* and their helicopter groups had, despite everything, landed a Commando significantly faster than would have been possible using landing craft. It is true that opposition was limited, but it had now become an open question whether Britain could carry out any opposed landings on a considerable scale without the support of the U.S.A. More limited interventions might well be the rule in the future, and these helicopters, covered by efficient fleet carrier air groups, would provide a rapid and effective response.

On 9 January 1957, as a direct result of the Suez debacle, Eden informed the Cabinet that he was resigning. He was replaced by the erstwhile chancellor, Harold Macmillan, who immediately set about strengthening his predecessor's Long Term Defence Review. This new exercise was the culmination of the series of reviews begun by the Churchill administration over five years previously, on the Conservatives' assumption of office. Its immediate cause was the financial crisis caused by the Suez debacle. Its main protagonist was Mr. Duncan Sandys's that old enemy of the navy, who Macmillan appointed as his minister of defense. Sandys's predecessor, Anthony Head, who had replaced Monckton because of Suez, had balked at resting Britain's defense posture purely on economic and political logic rather than strategic.[29]

From Macmillan's point of view Duncan Sandys was a good choice. The latter was a minister of considerable experience, much of it in the defense field. He had no obvious single service allegiance. He also had another vital asset, an abrasive force of character that would brook no opposition from entrenched hierarchies and bureaucracies. Macmillan had been minister of defense himself, albeit only briefly, in the final days of Churchill's administration. He had seen the power of the services to blunt the cutting edge of the contemporary Defence Review. As chancellor in Eden's government he had provided the Treasury pressure behind the next Defence Review. Few understood Britain's economic problems and domestic preoccupations better. To the avuncular Macmillan increasing defense budgets that prevented expansion of exports and improvements in domestic standards of living were out of the question. The government had been lucky to survive Suez. If it was going to win the next election, maintenance of living standards and economic health were two overwhelming priorities. Both short-term and long-term factors seemed to call for financial cuts in the defense budget. A complete review of Britain's defense policy was now essential, or so the prime minister thought.

Macmillan began the new review almost immediately on taking up office. Speed was of the essence, as the new annual Defence White Paper, normally due in February, could not be delayed too long. The first priority was to enhance Sandys's institutional authority. Already in October 1955 Eden had expanded the role of the minister of defense ensuring that "the composition and balance" of each service conformed to overall Cabinet policy. A separate chairman of the Chiefs of Staff Committee was also appointed to provide at least some professional military official without total single-service loyalty. Macmillan now strengthened Eden's measures by issuing a new directive of January 1957. He had already told the service ministers that he "proposed to bring some reality" to the Ministry of Defence's task to produce a unified defense policy. His immediate job was to "work out a new defence policy in the light of present strategic needs which would secure a sub-stantial reduction in expenditure and manpower" and "at the same time prepare a plan for reshaping and reorganising the armed forces." Defence Minister Sandys would decide questions of "size, shape, organisation and disposition of the forces, as well as their equipment, supply, their pay and conditions of service." All pro-posals from the service ministries or the Ministry of Supply to the Cabinet Defence Committee had to go through the minister of defense; there could be no more Admiralty maneuvers like that concerning the battleships during the Radical Re-view. The chairman of the Chiefs of Staff Committee became chief of staff to the minister of defense, emphasizing his independent "tri-Service" position. When these measures were published a year later in a White Paper on the Central Or-ganisation of Defence, he officially became "Chief of the Defence Staff." Sandys was also given access to any officers and officials of the service ministries, bypassing where necessary the established single-service institutional hierarchies. The direc-tive was drawn up in consultation with Sandys and the agreement of the new service ministers (including that of the new First Lord, George Douglas Hamilton, Earl of Selkirk) was obtained before they were confirmed in their posts!

The new measures fell short of complete integration of the Central Organisation of Defence and, with weaker ministers and less direct prime ministerial backing, soon had to be strengthened, but as long as Macmillan continued to back him to the hilt they made Sandys the most formidable coordinator of defense policies to date. Mountbatten and the Naval Staff were worried by such developments. They knew Sandys to be an enemy of the carrier program that had become the centerpiece of planning for the future of the surface fleet. He had proved impervious to naval arguments in the Radical Review; it did not seem that he would be any more agreeable now. Sandys by this time had even abandoned his previous support for land-based aircraft. The future, he felt, lay with nuclear-tipped rockets. Manned bombers would fast become an anachronism; carriers, he felt, doubly so. Even before taking office he made it clear that the Royal Navy was a major target for cuts, and the carrier force in particular. Once in office he told the Admiralty that he required convincing of the carrier's continued value. If the Admiralty could not do this, the ships would be phased out.

As in 1953–54 the Admiralty was determined to make out a strong case for the ships. Without these new "capital ships," it still felt, the Royal Navy would suffer a decisive decline in status and prestige. So a justification for the ships was quickly worked out. One area it was decided not to emphasize was the carrier's role as a nuclear strike platform. This caused some controversy within the Admiralty, as the naval aviation lobby was arguing that British carriers, soon to be nuclear capable, had a part to play as part of the NATO Strike Fleet. The new fighters under development, the Scimitar and Sea Vixen, were both capable of carrying the light "Red Beard" fission weapons that were under development in Britain, and the NA39 program was well under way. Nevertheless, the Board of Admiralty as a whole now seems to have felt that on this issue the Minister of Defence might actually have a potential case. British carriers, smaller and less numerous than in the U.S. Navy, were of limited strike potential and also might be too valuable to risk against the increasingly capable Soviet air and submarine forces in waters close to the U.S.S.R. The striking power of Bomber Command with its new higher-yield bombs and modern jet medium bombers, not to mention its future long-range missiles, would always have considerably greater potential as a striking force. It was also recognized that Sandys was probably unshakeable on the issue of the carrier in a nuclear war. He told the American SACLANT, Admiral Wright, on a visit to the United States that he did not believe in the whole strike fleet concept. An assault by the Royal Navy on this entrenched position would only increase Sandys's antipathy to the service as a whole. Although the idea of carriers for a nuclear offensive against the Soviets was not entirely abandoned, "after intense deliberation and discussion" the Admiralty decided not to base their carrier case upon it.[30]

As the Admiralty saw matters, there were three other basic arguments in favor of keeping the Royal Navy's carrier force in being. The first, and essentially least satisfying, was that there had been a substantial investment in these ships over the previous decade; two fleet carriers (the *Ark Royal* and *Eagle*) and three light fleet carriers (the *Albion*, *Bulwark*, and *Centaur*) built; another light fleet carrier (the *Hermes*) approaching completion; a major fleet carrier modernization under way (the *Victorious*), and a limited light fleet carrier modernization (the *Warrior*) completed. It would hardly be prudent, politically or economically, to throw all this away. The one weakness in this case was that only the *Hermes* and *Victorious* would be able to operate the aircraft of the 1960s without expensive modernization.

The next argument was a strategic justification. It was essentially a refinement of the "broken-backed" war argument that McGrigor had succeeded in keeping on the policy agenda. It was not mere familiarity that tempted the Admiralty to keep sailing on this tack. Sandys himself had doubts about the totality of destruction after the first intensive nuclear phase of war. According to one well-informed account, "The Admiralty and Mr. Sandys agreed that it was impossible at that stage to predict with any accuracy what would happen at sea. It was conceivable that a period of conventional war would precede the nuclear strikes or that the nuclear exchange might not prove immediately decisive."[31]

Such wars would require a substantial conventional and/or tactical nuclear naval capability in the Atlantic. The Naval Staff, as we have seen, through their swing towards an offensive strike fleet strategy as the most economical way of fighting this war, had already begun to deemphasize the convoy escort task. Now they felt they could go further. Again, following the Americans, they argued that the ASW war of the future against the submarines that entered the Atlantic was better fought by a relatively small number of "offensive" ASW task forces working on information from static hydrophone systems rather than a large number of convoy escorts. The Americans, never too enamored of British stress on convoys, still wanted this kind of ASW support (and the continued presence of British Carrier Group 2 in the Strike Fleet). Pulling out of the Atlantic battle on top of the troop cuts envisaged on the Continent might have disastrous effects on the cohesion of NATO and the Alliance. Macmillan's Government was out to repair, not rupture, relations with the U.S.A. An overt commitment to the maintenance of the Atlantic "bridge" was a necessity. The beauty of the new strategy for the Admiralty was that it could make that commitment at limited cost with the kind of ships it really wanted. The reserve of convoy escorts could be scrapped, the program for light ASW aircraft for unmodernized ships cancelled.

There was, however, still a danger in an emphasis on ASW, as ASW meant low-performance aircraft such as the Gannet or even just helicopters which now seemed to be the best ASW aircraft. The small *Hermes*-type light fleet carriers were adequate for this role without modernization. If a case was to be made that the Royal Navy stay in the business of flying high-performance jets from larger fleet carriers like the *Ark Royal* and *Eagle*, something more was necessary. The third and key argument in the navy's case for carriers was provided by their utility as a source of mobile air power in limited wars and on "peacekeeping" missions, when using nuclear weapons was neither credible nor relevant. Suez taught new lessons in the need for readiness and speed of response in future operations of this type. The inability to use certain foreign bases, and the limitations of the bases Britain did possess emphasized the importance of the mobile self-contained air base that a modern, properly supported carrier task force provided. The future use of foreign bases did not look promising; already Ceylon had ordered the East Indies Station out of its principal base as a direct result of Suez.

Suez, however, had only heralded the end of Empire for Britain; it did not lead to a policy of immediate withdrawal. British West Africa was approaching independence, but in East Africa there was as yet no decision to decolonize. Even where independence was being granted, notably in Malaya, Britain felt that she still had a duty to make sure that the right kind of successor took over, as pro-Western and as economically and politically stable and acceptable as possible. Such governments might well require the protection of a limited military force while they established themselves. Indeed, a defense agreement was planned for Malaya after independence. The Admiralty insisted that a British carrier task group presence was thus a continuing necessity "East of Suez." Sandys seemed to agree.

The commitment of Macmillan and Sandys to abolish conscription also helped the Admiralty's case. The increasing political unpopularity of National Service, the need to return scarce manpower to civilian industry, and the expense of a large training establishment all seemed to advise abolition. If there was to be an emphasis on smaller, ready, highly mobile forces, then it could be argued that amphibious forces offered even greater potential than air-portable infantry based at home, given the increasing difficulty of gaining over-flying rights. Suez, indeed, led directly to the creation of a Middle East "air barrier" against British flights. The Admiralty itself now had to eat some of its previous words and emphasize the vital importance of, and priority for, amphibious operations, but such forces did provide something to escort that made sense to the new minister. Landing operations also provided an economical role for smaller, unmodernized carriers converted to carry helicopters. Even more crucially, amphibious forces required the support of large strike carriers.

It was this limited/brushfire war role for the carrier force in particular, and the navy in general, that was the key to the strong and remarkably successful case that Mountbatten's Admiralty and Naval Staff produced in the frenzied weeks of January, February, and March 1957. Sandys worked fast and personally wrote up his plan, with the help of senior officials of his own Defence Ministry. An especially important influence was the Chief Scientific Adviser to the Ministry, Sir Frederick Brundrett, who could perhaps provide a little pro-navy pressure that was all the more palatable to Sandys given Brundrett's close involvement and identification with the minister's beloved rocket programs. According to one source, "two senior civil servants both in key positions in the Ministry of Defence were mobilised in the Admiralty's cause"; Brundrett may have been one of these.[32] Relations between Sandys and the service chiefs were not good, and there were some "highly acrimonious" meetings with the minister.[33] Sandys was not to be overwhelmed or outargued. Mountbatten, who developed a "grudging admiration and even affection for Sandys," found him "obstinate and truculent in the defence of his views, but ready to listen to arguments and, once convinced, stalwart in his support."[34] The onus was on the Admiralty's and Naval Staff's talents of argument, which were stretched to the limit. One whose job it was to give the naval case at this time described it thus a few years afterwards: "The walls [of Sandys's office] were lined with charts. The Minister levelled a continuous chain of questions at the Navy's advocates. Evidently nothing was taken for granted, and every statement had to be defended with facts. It was clear that the traditional and trite generalities concerning the merits of sea power did not impress him [i.e., Sandys] in the least. Many of the questions were extremely basic, but nevertheless had not been asked before, and the Navy was often caught unprepared."[35]

The Earl of Selkirk, the first lord, was a "generous and honourable man" who had deliberately been chosen as a relatively self-effacing figure so as not to stand in Sandys's way. Mountbatten, however, almost reveled in the "pretty good tussle" he had with the minister. The most articulate and self-confident first sea lord ever, his abilities to argue a case in committee and back it up by intrigue and influence were exactly what the service needed in its hour of need. He was ably served by his subordinates whom he took great pains to weld into a coherent team. Notable among these, Admiral Sir Charles Lambe, second sea lord, whom Mountbatten

The Board of Admiralty, 1958. The Earl of Selkirk is in the chair, with Sir John Lang, the Permanent Secretary, to his left. Lord Mountbatten, the first sea lord, smiles confidently at the cameras with Sir Caspar John on his right. (Imperial War Museum)

treated as a personal confidant and advisor, was an exceptionally gifted and broad-minded officer, renowned for his sound judgment.[36] It was he who had argued a strong pro-carrier case in the Harwood Exercise of 1948–49. These officers set the tone for the more junior members of the Board and Naval Staff, and the whole service benefited from the new emphasis on argument rather than on tradition and reputation. The naval campaign successfully headed off proposals to cut the service by half over the next year. Mountbatten's greatest victory, however, was perhaps using the "East of Suez" scenario to obtain unanimous endorsement by the Chiefs of Staff Committee, on 19 February 1957, of the Royal Navy's continued possession of carriers. Sandys had no option but to concur.[37]

The minister's proposals were approved in basic form at a weekend meeting of ministers at Chequers on 23 February. Another month was spent drawing up the "final" drafts of the actual statement, settling details and selling the contents of the documents to Britain's allies. The twelfth "final" draft was presented by the full Cabinet on 28 March and, with a few last-minute alterations, was presented to parliament on 4 April. The document, "Defence: Outline of Future Policy," more commonly known as the "Sandys White Paper," self-consciously stressed its radical nature. Previous reviews had merely "pruned" the rearmament program; it was now necessary to "make a fresh appreciation and to adopt a new approach towards it." The changes announced were "the biggest change in military policy ever made in normal times." Strategy, Sandys argued, had been revolutionized by the hydrogen bomb and the rocket. The strategic revolution thus wrought, he went on, would reduce a defense burden that was described in stark and direct terms. "Over the last five years, defence has on average absorbed ten per cent of Britain's gross national product. Some seven per cent of the working population are either in the Services or supporting them. One eighth of the output of the metal using industries, upon which the export trade so largely depends, is devoted to defence. An undue proportion of qualified scientists and engineers are engaged on military work. In addition the retention of such large forces abroad gives rise to heavy charges which put a severe strain upon the balance of payments."[38]

Britain's two defense priorities were set out as (1) contributing to Allied deterrence and resistance to aggression and (2) colonial defense and limited operations overseas. For the first priority, almost complete reliance was placed on nuclear and thermonuclear weapons. Against these it was admitted that there was "no means of providing adequate protection for the people of this country." The RAF's V bombers, increasingly supplemented by ballistic missiles and defended by a reduced fighter force, would provide a significant part of the West's deterrent to such attack. Britain's army on the Continent was to be reduced and the forces equipped with nuclear battlefield missiles. Britain's tactical bomber force would also be reduced and equipped with nuclear bombs. Effectively, Britain's "Continental commitment" would become just a nuclear tripwire to massive thermonuclear retaliation.[39]

As for the Royal Navy's "role . . . in total war," this was described—ominously, perhaps, and much against the Admiralty's will—as "somewhat uncertain." "It may be," the paper went on, "that the initial nuclear bombardment and counter bombardment by aircraft and rockets would be so crippling as to bring the war to an end within a few weeks or even days, in which case naval operations would not play any significant part. On the other hand there is the possibility that the nuclear battle might not prove immediately decisive; and in that event it would be of great importance to defend Atlantic communications against submarine attack." Britain would, therefore, continue to contribute, albeit with fewer ships, to NATO ASW forces in the Atlantic.[40]

However equivocal this statement was, the paper's following paragraphs made it clear that the Admiralty had successfully sold its case on limited war and peacekeeping. Under the heading "Sea Power" the paper asserted that "on account of its mobility, the Royal Navy, together with the Royal Marines, provides another effective means of bringing power rapidly to bear in peacetime emergencies or limited hostilities." The carrier's continued relevance was specifically spelled out: "In modern conditions the role of the aircraft carrier, which is in effect a mobile air station, becomes increasingly significant." It was announced, indeed, that the "carrier group" would be the main deployment pattern for the future Royal Navy. Each group would be composed of a carrier and a relatively small number of escorts. Large vessels, other than carriers, would be "restricted to the minimum." Future surface ships would be in smaller categories where reduced numbers of better-equipped ships would provide escorts for the carriers. Also, the Royal Navy had finally had to choose between forces in being and forces in reserve. The Reserve Fleet, already reformed and reduced by the first set of "Way Ahead" cuts, would become even more a slimmed-down operational reserve for the active fleet rather than a large war reserve. The *King George V*-class battleships were for early disposal. The *Vanguard*, whose recommissioning had fallen victim to the defense reviews of 1955 and which was now Reserve Fleet flagship, was to stay for the time being. The reprieve was short. Britain's last battleship went to the scrapyard in 1960.[41]

The center of gravity of future naval deployments would move significantly eastwards. Forces "East of Suez," as the paper put it, were to remain as at present. Reductions would only occur in forces in European waters. A carrier group would normally be in the Indian Ocean, and although this was not spelled out, the group in the Mediterranean would be available for deployment eastwards if necessary. In the accompanying statement on the Naval Estimates, the "East of Suez" role was reemphasized, the Royal Navy being compared to a "fire brigade" quickly on the spot in case of trouble to stop the "local fire from spreading." It was specifically stated also that the kinds of ships demanded for this role were the same as those required for the murky and "speculative" conditions of total war. Only the most modern ships and weapons would do. The logic of this was not entirely spelled out, but the Soviet Union had begun to equip states friendly to them with modern equipment. If Egypt had been able to operate her MiGs effectively, the FAA strikes would have suffered serious difficulties. The sophisticated missile-equipped units that were already in the pipeline were necessary, therefore, even East of Suez, and they were also suitable for use by forces that might prove useful in the various stages of some future general war. The mobility of such fleets would, the Admiralty argued, give them freedom from nuclear annihilation.[42]

It was yet another victory for the Admiralty. Perhaps the most notable casualty was the projected large missile-equipped cruiser that had increased in size to around 18,000 tons. In part compensation it was announced that the new "Fleet Escorts" would be equipped with Sea Slug. These had increased their size to almost 6,000 tons, making them light cruisers in all but name. The name "destroyer" was too good to lose, however, as it made the ships more acceptable to the politicians and the Treasury. The Admiralty was quite open about it at the time but, nevertheless, this slight of hand does seem to have been a significant factor in lubricating the program through the bureaucratic machine. Work on adding the missile to the previously projected fleet escort had been going on since 1955, and in 1958 the Cabinet Defence Committee approved that the ships be ordered. The first of the new "County"-class ships was laid down in March 1959. Another factor helping these vessels was the previous involvement of Sandys, Brundrett, and others in the earlier parts of the somewhat expensive and protracted Sea Slug program. Some return was expected for the massive investment in the system, development of which had taken over a decade.[43]

The "Counties" would, it seemed, be the largest units of the future surface fleet. The existing gun-armed cruiser force seemed doomed. The three *Tiger*-class ships, *Tiger*, *Lion* (ex-*Defence*), and *Blake*, were eventually approaching completion, and it seemed as if it would not be too long before they were the only cruisers in service. Even before the Sandys Exercise the pressure of the Eden cuts had caused a reduction in the modernization program. The *Belfast* received merely a "large repair" when she went into the yards in 1955, not the extensive modernization intended that would have altered her appearance much more extensively. A similar "repair" was probably intended for the *Swiftsure* and *Superb*, but in the end only the former was taken in hand, the latter being a Sandys casualty. The logic was the same as before. Cold War duties did not demand extensive modernization that diverted resources away from higher-priority projects. Moreover, there were other ships as good as a repaired *Superb* without spending any extra money on them. In the next few years a steady stream of British cruisers went to the scrapyard. By

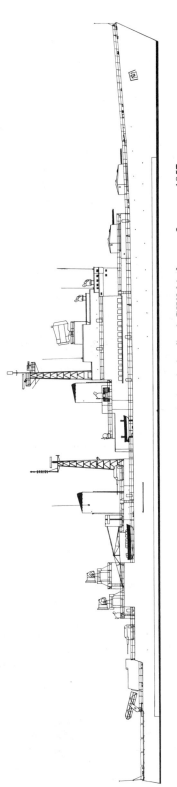

The impressive, large guided-missile cruiser design in its final GW96A form—January 1957.

Dimensions: 687' o.a. (675' w.l.) × 80' beam × 22' draft
Displacement: 18,450 tons
Machinery: 110,000 SHP = 32 knots; 4,500 n. miles @ 20 knots
Armor: 1½" sides, 1" deck (machinery)
1" sides, 1" deck (A10)
1½" sides, 1½" deck (missile and gun magazines)
Armament: One twin Sea Slug surface-to-air missile system
Two twin 6" Mark 26 DP automatic guns
Four Twin 3" Mark 6 DP automatic guns
One helicopter deck

Radar: One Type 984 3D radar
One Type 992 surveillance radar
One Type 978 navigation radar
Two Type 901 Sea Slug fire-control radars
Four Type MRS 3 gunnery fire-control radars
One telemetry aerial
TACAN

Complement: 95 officers, 1,020 ratings

First of the light cruiser-sized "County"-class guided-missile "destroyers" was HMS *Devonshire*, commissioned at the end of 1962. Her three main weapons systems are displayed in this view, in descending order of importance from stern to bow: Sea Slug SAM launcher to deal with aircraft, Wessex search/strike helicopter to deal with submarines, and four 4.5-inch guns for shore bombardment. Great attention was paid to appearance in this design to obtain maximum dramatic effect.

1960 HMS *Sheffield*, her large repairs just completed in 1956–57, was the sole survivor of the old "Towns" in reserve. The *Dido*s were also extinct, the modernized *Royalist* having gone to New Zealand. A couple of "Colony"-class ships remained in service with two more in reserve.

The older destroyers and frigates also began their sad progress to the scrapyards although more modern versions of both types, it was felt, still had a major role to play as a task group escort. The Naval Staff now rather regretted not having

Finally fully operational in 1959 eighteen years after being laid down, HMS *Tiger* returns to Britain after work-up in the Mediterranean. Note the Mark 26 6-inch turrets and the Mark 6 3-inch guns. These rapid-fire weapons could shoot off the entire contents of the ship's magazines in minutes. (Imperial War Museum)

Last survivor of the standard prewar "Town"-class cruisers was HMS *Sheffield*, given a "large repair" in 1949–51 and modernized secondary armament fire control in 1956–57. She served in the Atlantic until 1959 and after refit was in reserve until 1967.

proceeded with any fast aircraft direction ships, and the decision was taken to convert the four "Weapon"-class destroyers into fleet radar pickets with the 965 long-range air-warning radar. Unfortunately, most of the eleven postwar frigates that the Naval Estimates proclaimed to be in service were not unduly suitable for the new strategy, being over-specialized Type 14 Second Rates or relatively slow Type 41s. The fifth Type 41 was cancelled along with two of the Type 61s that had not yet been laid down. A Type 12 ordered the previous year was disposed of to New Zealand, but another ship was added to take her place in the program. Over half the twenty-one frigates on order were the fast ASW type. The new Second Rate general-purpose frigate order was reduced to eight ships.[44]

The coastal and inshore minesweeper program was almost completed, and it was stressed that these vessels had an important peacetime role as patrol vessels. Some sixteen coastals were in full commission with thirteen more on trials and training duties along with seven inshores; thirty-one coastals and eighteen inshores were still under construction, with fifty-two coastals and fifty-nine inshores in reserve. In reality the Admiralty was rather embarrassed by the numbers of these vessels, whose mobilization would be doubtful with the announced reduction in reserve forces. The "Way Ahead" Working Group had, in fact, already recommended a reduction to twenty-one minesweepers in home and Mediterranean waters in its first major report in November 1956.[45]

Another area in which the Way Ahead had preempted Sandys was that of Coastal Forces. The November 1956 report called for the reduction of Britain's fast patrol

With the change in policy in the mid-1950s towards general-purpose ship designs, all of which could act as peacetime gunboats, the *Tribal* class became the standard "Second Rate" frigate of the early 1960s. Designed under the classification "sloop," they were intended primarily for duty in the Gulf. This is HMS *Mohawk*, completed in 1963. In reserve from 1979 to 1981, she fell victim to the Nott defense review and was scrapped in 1982.

boats to a small development cadre. The prevailing "nuclear" and East of Suez logic had little place for such craft. Their main rationale was seen as operations against Soviet forces in the Baltic or even perhaps in the Channel if the Soviet offensive European thrust into Central Europe was successful. The Korean rearmament scheme had, indeed, emphasized these vessels at a time when a swift Soviet move to the sea seemed a real possibility. Motor torpedo boats and motor gunboats had been merged as a single, integrated "Fast Patrol Boat" type in 1950. At that time this force consisted of a number of boats left over from World War II. A few ex-German boats were also operated, two on intelligence gathering in the Baltic. A very limited amount of experimental construction took place under the postwar programs, but serious production of two models, an intermediate petrol-engined *Gay* class and a "Deltic" diesel-engined *Dark* class, began from 1951 under the rearmament program. Some twelve and eighteen boats respectively of each class were built before the program was curtailed. Four gas-turbine-powered boats were also built, two experimental *Bold*-class vessels in 1950–53 and two *Brave*s that were only just begun when the Sandys White Paper appeared. At that time the operational flotilla comprised nine FPBs, two more were occupied on trials and training, with twenty-four in reserve. HMS *Hornet*, the Coastal Forces HQ at Gulfport was closed before the end of 1957, and most of the boats were laid up for disposal. These were sold in the 1960s, but a couple of boats, notably the two *Brave*s, continued to serve in training and fishery protection duties.[46]

The announced abolition of conscription marked a significant strategic shift away from the concept of a mobilized reserve. The Royal Navy, beset by manpower shortages, had been forced to rely on conscripts to an increasing extent. In 1956 almost ten percent of total strength was made up of National Servicemen (11,600 out of 122,100), a higher proportion than at any time since 1949. Cutting these personnel had the double benefit of reducing the training establishment. Massive reductions were also announced in the ready reserve of ex-regular short-service ratings, the so-called Royal Fleet Reserve. This was to come down from 33,000 to 5,000. It was also announced that the Royal Naval Reserve (largely merchant seamen) and the Royal Naval Volunteer Reserve would be significantly cut, particular casualties being the RNVR air squadrons intended to equip the older reserve carriers for convoy protection and support duties. Effectively, the concept of mobilization for old-style wars was being abandoned.[47]

The main victory for which the Admiralty could congratulate itself was the retention of the carrier force. Hopes for a new ship had never been abandoned, but such ambitions were played down in public as the Admiralty settled for two ships that were in the offing—the very much rebuilt fleet carrier *Victorious*, finally recommissioned in 1958, and the much modified *Hermes*, whose belated completion took place at the end of 1959, over fifteen years after the ship was laid down. Sandys's announced abandonment of new manned aircraft projects in favor of missiles affected the navy only to a limited extent. The Scimitar, Sea Vixen, and even the NA39 were safe. The last named, for which the Blackburn design had been chosen in 1955, seemed to have export potential and had been built and was about to be tested with the help of U.S. funds, which it would be embarrassing to seem to have been squandered. Cuts were made in the Gannet ASW aircraft numbers, but an AEW version of the Gannet went ahead, along with a substantial program of British-built Whirlwind ASW helicopters.[48]

The specially austere antisubmarine aircraft, the Short Seamew (whose program had already been cut), was finally abandoned after the twenty-four aircraft delivered had been put into storage. The Seamew had not turned out to be a very good aircraft, and helicopters seemed the better bet for the kind of operations for which it was being purchased. In any case, all the carriers now intended to be kept could operate the Gannet, and the RNVR squadrons for which the aircraft had been intended were being abolished. Another ASW aircraft casualty was the large twin-rotor Bristol 191 helicopter. Sixty-eight had been ordered for the purpose of fulfilling half the RN's requirement for antisubmarine aircraft. The 191 was now to be replaced by a new ASW helicopter based on the American Sikorsky S-58 design that would not take up as much physical space in the strike carriers of the future. The S-58 could also be operated from the new fleet escorts, further economizing on space in the carriers. Although many sophisticated jet projects were now cancelled, the only one that seriously affected the navy was the Saunders Roe P177, an interesting jet- plus rocket-powered interceptor. Sandys felt that the Vixen/ Scimitar combination seemed more than sufficient to deal with the threat in the carriers' prospective sphere of operation. Moreover, he felt that the long-term future of carriers was not so secure as to allow money to be spent on a project that would take some considerable time to come to fruition.[49]

The Royal Navy's campaign against Sandys did not end in April 1957; indeed the pressure, if anything, increased. Sandys was considering cutting the Royal Navy's budget to less than £300 million in 1958, and Mountbatten feared consequent "chaos followed by loss of morale." In June 1957 he prepared a letter to be circulated among his fellow senior admirals justifying his intended resignation and hinting strongly that he wished for assurances that none of them would be prepared to serve as a replacement.[50] In the event it did not have to be sent. Instead, the Naval Staff rose to the occasion and produced arguments to convince a skeptical minister that the navy was still a good investment. In September it drew up a paper, "The Autumn Naval Rethink." The document (1) asserted the importance of the limited war role, (2) made the point of the central role of the aircraft carrier in fulfilling it, and (3) asserted the synergistic relationship of strike aircraft, transport helicopters, and modern amphibious warfare vessels. The chiefs of staff endorsed this doctrine, and it was duly presented to the minister who "was well pleased and considered the paper a major advance in Admiralty thinking."[51]

While the Admiralty put its own doctrinal house in order, it exerted pressure upon the Ministry of Defence, sometimes subtly, sometimes less so. Mountbatten extended his lobbying activities with officials both within the Ministry of Defence and outside, especially in the Foreign Office and Colonial Office. The latter two departments were soon emphasizing to Sandys the critical need for forces East of Suez. Dire warnings of reductions in the naval presence in Singapore to two frigates, and the commercial leasing of the dockyard were given to Robert Scott, Commissioner General in South East Asia, together with requests for him to lobby hard with both the foreign secretary and the minister of defense.[52] Commonwealth politicians and officials were briefed to press the need for a strong British naval presence to the defense minister during his tour of the Far East and to Prime Minister Macmillan when the Commonwealth Prime Ministers' Conference was held. The Americans were also mobilized, with Admiral Denny, senior British representative in Washington, being given broad hints to approach the president via Chairman of the Joint Chiefs of Staff Admiral Radford. Mountbatten used family connections also. Royal patronage was arranged for a conference called "Fairlead" at the Royal Naval College, Greenwich, to make the case for the maintenance of a powerful fleet. Some of the audience of influential gentlemen were soon writing to the *Times* to stress how impressed they had been by the "sound and imaginative" thinking shown by the Admiralty. Serving senior officers were encouraged, in a way that was almost unprecedented, to speak both on and off the record to members of the press to make the naval case, and letters to the quality newspapers were encouraged from retired admirals. This was part of a more general service appeal against Sandys, but the navy probably made the strongest anti-Sandys case. Subtly and effectively, further "anti-Navy" cuts were made impossible.[53]

In November 1957 Mountbatten had the opportunity to entertain Sandys at his house at Broadlands: "no other First Sea Lord would have had the style, the status, or for that matter, the country house to entertain the Minister of Defence on equal terms." Mountbatten exploited the situation to the utmost. One outstanding matter was Sandys's absolute determination to equip the carriers in European waters "predominantly" with ASW aircraft, both fixed and rotary winged. This would allow cuts in aircraft orders as well as allowing administrative rationalization. The Admiralty (with the strong support of SACLANT) was committed to the idea of mixed, general-purpose carrier air groups. Moreover, it was reluctant to lose any more aircraft orders and have an over-specialized, inflexible aircraft support structure. Nevertheless, Mountbatten conceded the point at Broadlands in return for a navy of 88,000 men. The first sea lord must have realized, however, that his concession was just a paper one. The decision was taken about this time to abandon the Gannet and fixed-wing ASW carrier aircraft in general in order to concentrate on dipping-sonar helicopters for antisubmarine duties. Moreover, as described above, the planned British ASW helicopter had just been cancelled in favor of a British-built variant of the Sikorsky S-58. The implementation of Sandys's proposals would thus be delayed until about 1960, by which time a new minister might well be in office. In the event, the Admiralty's stratagem was successful, and after Sandys's departure no more was heard of the idea. How far this "carrier politics" played a part in the original aircraft decisions is uncertain.[54]

At Broadlands Mountbatten also traded some shore air stations for an extra carrier with the fleet and obtained Sandys's acceptance of the conversion of the light fleet carrier *Bulwark* into a "Commando Carrier." The Suez experiment had vindicated the concept of vertical envelopment, and after consideration in the spring of 1957, the Admiralty decision was made in July to try to get ministerial acceptance of the conversion. Both air and amphibious interests combined to back this ship, and the Admiralty carefully built up a strong outside constituency for it too. The support of the War Office was enlisted by taking up the suggestion from Amphibious Warfare Headquarters, which claimed that the ship could carry army troops as well as Royal Marines. The RAF were happy not to have to spend more of their scarce

First of the economical "Commando Carrier" conversions of the *Hermes*-class light fleet carriers was HMS *Bulwark*, commissioned in her new role in 1960. This was an economical way both of maximizing the potential of existing hulls and considerably enhancing amphibious capability.

resources on helicopters and transport aircraft. Even the Treasury was not displeased, as the bill for the conversion of an existing ship was less than £10 million. The converted ship could also contribute to the more general war capability as well as to limited war, as her Whirlwinds could be fitted quite easily from the ship's own resources for ASW duties. In effect, the Royal Navy was maintaining another useful aircraft carrier at minimal expense in addition to the agreed carrier force.[55]

The Royal Marines were now finding themselves in the novel position of being central to the Admiralty's concerns. The Marines' gratification increased still further when in 1958 the dock landing ship reappeared once more in the naval program. Two of these vessels were intended to replace the old ships of the existing Amphibious Warfare Squadron. Again army support was enlisted, and the price for each ship of £7 million was not excessive. The first ship was duly ordered in 1959 and a second was planned. The year 1959 also saw the permanent reactivation of 42 Commando in order to "arm" the *Bulwark*. Yet another Commando, 41, was reestablished in 1960. Many Royal Marines had traditionally embarked as detachments in big ships, manning guns and carrying out other naval duties. Now they were being reorganized for a more overtly amphibious role, both as larger units and as small landing parties of twenty men embarked in frigates, first in the Gulf and later in the West Indies.[56]

Before its permanent reactivation, 42 Commando had been briefly mobilized in order to reinforce Jordan as part of the coordinated Western moves to back up pro-Western states during the Lebanon crisis of that year. In May 1958 a group based around the carrier *Ark Royal* deployed from Malta to cover possible withdrawal of British subjects from Lebanon. The *Ark Royal* was later replaced by the *Eagle*, which provided fighter cover for the parachute brigade being flown into Jordan. The *Albion*, working up for her last commission as a fixed-wing carrier, was diverted to Portsmouth to load 42 Commando and its vehicles for possible use as reinforcements if required. The *Bulwark* was used during her last commission as a fixed-wing carrier to bring in army troops to Aqaba. Both future commando carriers therefore found themselves impelled by force of events into their future role, a vindication of the relevance of the new Admiralty doctrine.[57]

Although the Royal Navy now orientated itself decisively towards limited war and peacekeeping tasks, the nuclear weapon was not entirely forgotten. Although the NATO Strike Fleet role was played down a little, there was still, the Naval Staff argued, a case for nuclear capabilities in the carriers to deter Communist use of such weapons in local wars in the Far East. Sandys was committed to the idea of using nuclear weapons as a matter of course if the situation got out of hand, even in limited war, and found the argument convincing. A special variant of the "Red Beard" kiloton-range "tactical" bomb was developed for naval use. It had a "demanding" specification, being of variable yield (5–20 kt) and capable of use against ships, submarines, protected submarine pens, or harbor installations. Despite RAF opposition, the Defence Ministry gave the go-ahead to provide facilities to carry the modified bombs in the carriers, and the new Scimitars were configured to carry the weapon, which went into production in 1959. Once Sandys had gone, of course, the aircraft could be deployed against Soviet bases and forces as easily as they could be deployed against the Chinese, North Vietnamese, North Koreans, or Indonesians. The nuclear capability would certainly make destroying *Sverdlov*s a good deal easier! Sandys wished the RAF and Royal Navy to cooperate on a single, future nuclear strike aircraft, but the former found the NA39 insufficient for their purposes. Reluctantly, in September 1958 the minister of defense authorized development of both the NA39 and the TSR2 for the RAF. Despite this delay, NA39 prototypes were conducting carrier trials by 1960, and later that year were given the service name of Buccaneer.[58]

At the end of 1957 Mountbatten wrote to the greatest of the prewar first sea lords, Lord Chatfield, with the happy news that "It looks as though Duncan Sandys means to give us a reasonable deal — better than the Army and RAF."[59] The 1958 Defense White Paper listed the newly defined and articulated naval roles that were the key to that happy outcome. The peacekeeping/limited war emphasis was even clearer than before. The roles defined for naval forces were:

> *In peacetime* to help carry out Britain's responsibilities in colonies and protected territories, to defend British shipping and generally to contribute by their presence to the maintenance of peace and security;
> *in limited war* to protect sea communications, to escort troops and supplies to the theatre of operations and give them support in action;
> *in global war* to make an effective contribution to the combined naval forces of the Western Alliance.[60]

The eastern deployment was also emphasized, with the forces East of Suez described as an "Eastern Fleet," a "balanced" force of a strike carrier and a commando carrier screened by a cruiser, destroyers, and frigates, all based at Singapore. Frigates would be based in the Persian Gulf, at Hong Kong, and on the rearranged "West Indies" and "South Atlantic" Stations (as they were now called). The two (ASW) carriers, two cruisers, and other surface forces in European waters would be considered as a contribution to Alliance forces and not as a "fully balanced, all purpose British fleet." The latter was apparently a sop to SACLANT, increasingly disturbed at the prospective loss of his British strike carriers.[61]

The "Way Ahead" process continued its work, and a wide-ranging set of cuts was announced in the 1958 Statement: the abolition of the East Indies Command abroad and the Nore Command at home; closure of the dockyards and major base facilities at Sheerness, Portland, and Hong Kong; and the civilianization of Malta, the abandonment of several facilities at Chatham and a number of Fleet Air Arm establishments. The squadrons of small craft maintained since the end of World War II on the Rhine and Elbe rivers to support the army were also to be wound up. The total of the cuts, it was hoped, would save some 23,000 civilian posts, 7,000 naval personnel ashore, and £15.5 million per annum.[62]

These cuts helped cushion the fall in Naval Estimates that Sandys succeeded in achieving. The 1957–58 estimates totaled only £316 million. The chancellor was still not satisfied, and the Naval Estimates for 1958–59, £339,400,000, were actually a reduction in spending power over the previous year due to higher prices, increases in pay, and the expense of premature retirement necessitated by the manpower cuts. In the end a supplementary estimate of £41.5 million was required. In 1959–60 it was hoped to limit money expenditure to the previous year's amount, £377 million being budgeted.

Cuts in manpower reflected the cuts in finance. The total authorized permanent strength of the Royal Navy and associated services steadily came down from 121,500 in 1957–58 to 112,000 in 1958–59 and 106,000 in 1959–60. Regular recruitment was looking up; by 1959 enough new men were coming into the service to meet the projected strength of ninety to a hundred thousand by the early 1960s (out of a total projected armed forces strength of 375,000). The reduction in the reserves continued, and in 1958 the merging of the Royal Naval Reserve and the Royal Naval Volunteer Reserve was announced. By 1959 the strength of the reserve forces had been reduced by some 26,000 to almost 14,000. Total planned defense expenditure was now around some £1,500 million per annum. This was some 7 percent of GNP, a reduction of almost a third over the proportion for 1956–57, and in 1959 it was agreed that this should become the permanent proportion of national resources to be spent on defense.[63]

Sandys and Macmillan had achieved their aim, but so had Mountbatten and his colleagues. When the first sea lord went on in July 1959 to become the second chief of Defence Staff he could indeed bequeath a firm and clear "Way Ahead" to his chosen successor and closest service friend, Sir Charles Lambe. Lambe's appointment, obtained over the objections of Selkirk the First Lord, reflected a concern on the part of both Duncan Sandys and Macmillan to maintain the Mountbatten approach. No better indication could be obtained of the extent to which he had won the argument. The navy's share of the defense budget seems to have been settled at some 25 percent. Building on the work of his predecessor, Mountbatten had encouraged a more complete reorientation to the concepts of limited war and peacetime policing duties in the attractive and gentler waters of the eastern seas. His own "Way Ahead" process had concentrated cuts in areas of the Admiralty's own preference and helped convince Sandys that the Royal Navy was putting its

Two generations of Royal Navy "cruisers" are shown in this 1950s picture of a jackstay transfer between a larger conventional World War II-type gun-armed light cruiser and one of the new Type 12 ASW frigates, HMS *Scarborough*. The latter is in her original condition, and both aspects of her designed main armament can be clearly seen, the Mark 10 mortars and the ASW torpedo tubes (covered in canvas). The latter were soon removed with the failure of the slow Mark 20 as a surface-launched weapon. During the 1960s the smaller but more flexible frigate would take over larger cruisers' "cold war" functions. Note the *Scarborough*'s original gaunt functional appearance with no concessions to good looks. This was typical of the first postwar generation of World War II warships built as war-fighting vessels in an age of austerity.

The last two classes of British destroyers compared—two *Daring*s and two "Weapons," the *Duchess*, *Crossbow*, *Diamond*, and *Battleaxe*. The larger size of the *Daring*s is noteworthy. The picture was taken in 1961–62 when the ships were operating together as the 5th Destroyer Squadron. Both the "Weapons" are now radar picket aircraft direction escorts with torpedoes removed. The *Daring*s have also lost half their torpedo armament to improve their somewhat cramped accommodation. The alterations made to these ships of wartime conception reflect the changing priorities of the postwar fleet.

own house in order. Yet if the navy owed a lot to Mountbatten, it owed as much to his old enemy, Duncan Sandys, for "he made it think about the Navy's role harder than it ever had before, and face up to the unpleasant realities of post-war British life."[64]

The extent of Mountbatten's winning over of Duncan Sandys was demonstrated in late 1958, when Sandys backed Mountbatten's long-standing wish to see the RAF Coastal Command reintegrated into the Royal Navy. He ordered an enquiry that led to acrimonious meetings of the Chiefs of Staff Committee. The air minister threatened resignation, and Mountbatten, a little embarrassed by breaking his promise of 1957 to the chief of the Air Staff not to raise the issue, did not engage in his usual supportive political activities. The issue was dropped, but this was a relatively minor failure. Between 1955 and 1959 within the Royal Navy itself Mountbatten had carried out much-needed root and branch reform. As he put it to the fleet, in characteristic style, "This may be the end of one era but it was an era of over insurance. Let us think of it rather as the beginning of a new era, as a 'shot in the arm' for those willing to respond. Let us make sure that we use this volcanic moment to boost our morale and put the Senior Service back into its proper position."[65] The volcano sent its earthquakes into the structure of the Naval Staff itself, which reflected Mountbatten's new look in the way it developed from 1957 into the 1960s. In 1957 the posts of fifth sea lord and deputy chief of Naval Staff were combined, a sign of the even greater integration of naval aviation with the rest of the service. The Divisions of Naval Air Warfare (DAW) and Naval Air Organisation and Training (DAOT) were duly added to DCNS's other responsibilities, which also now included the Historical Section. Two years later the Tactical

TABLE 5–2.

THE NAVAL STAFF IN 1960.*

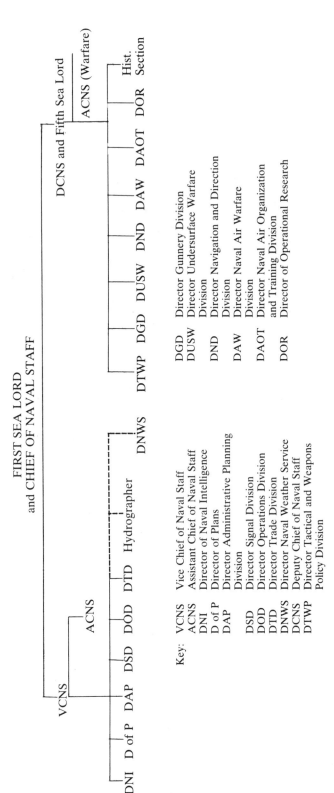

FIRST SEA LORD
and CHIEF OF NAVAL STAFF

Key:
VCNS	Vice Chief of Naval Staff
ACNS	Assistant Chief of Naval Staff
DNI	Director of Naval Intelligence
D of P	Director of Plans
DAP	Director Administrative Planning Division
DSD	Director Signal Division
DOD	Director Operations Division
DTD	Director Trade Division
DNWS	Director Naval Weather Service
DCNS	Deputy Chief of Naval Staff
DTWP	Director Tactical and Weapons Policy Division
DGD	Director Gunnery Division
DUSW	Director Undersurface Warfare Division
DND	Director Navigation and Direction Division
DAW	Director Naval Air Warfare Division
DAOT	Director Naval Air Organization and Training Division
DOR	Director of Operational Research

*Dotted lines represent lines of responsibility to VCNS and DCNS of organizations not officially part of the Naval Staff proper.

Ship Requirements and Staff Duties directorate was further renamed Naval Tactics and Weapons Policy (DTWP). (See table 5-2.) In 1962 there was some rationalization, the Trade and Operations Divisions being combined into one Directorate of Naval Operations and Trade (DNOT) and DAW and DAOT becoming a single Naval Air Division (DNAD). In 1964 the Gunnery Division (DGD) became the Surface Warfare Division and the Navigation and Direction Division (DND) became the Division of Navigation and Tactical Control. The commandant general Royal Marines was also fully integrated into the Staff under VCNS.[66]

Another major reform of the Mountbatten era that must be mentioned is that concerning officer structure. In 1954 the Committee on Officer Structure and Training (COST) had been set up and was chaired by Vice Admiral Sir Aubrey Mansergh. The Mansergh Committee's report, announced as Admiralty Fleet Order 1/56 in January 1956, created a "General List" of officers combining the old Executive, Engineering, Electrical, Supply, and Secretariat Branches. The non-Executive officers had previously been marked by colored "distinction lace," which emphasized their somewhat inferior status. This was now to cease as an outward mark of a process that was meant to integrate more fully, including into the higher echelons of the service, officers with the technical skills demanded by the increasing complexity of naval affairs. The old branches continued as "specializations," but an extra distinction was added to the newly designated "seaman" specialization by creating a special "Post List" for the ranks of commander and beyond. The Post List (or, as they became known, "Wet List") officers were those who would hold command at sea. In some ways this recreated the old Executive/non-Executive split in a new form as officers who remained on the General List with the Engineers and other non-seamen were added to the group of "second-class citizens" doomed to administrative appointments for the rest of their careers. This "damaging and divisive" system of stigmatizing seaman commanders publicly was abolished in 1969, but the distinctions between seamen and non-seamen have persisted, given the requirements for specialists in certain posts and a natural tendency to appoint seamen to the key operational commands.[67] Slowly, however, after January 1957, when AFO1/56 came into force, some non-seamen were able to infiltrate the higher echelons of the service, as Mansergh intended. In addition to the "General List" for full-career officers, a "Supplementary List" of short-service officers was created, first for aircrew only, but later expanded to cover seamen and supply officers also when full-career recruiting began to lag. The old "Branch List" of officers promoted from experienced ratings became the "Special Duties" list. In its essentials, this structure has remained unchanged to the present day.[68]

When Sandys himself left office in September 1959, to be replaced by Harold Watkinson, he seemed to have set both the Royal Navy and Britain's defense forces in general on a secure strategic, administrative, and financial base. It would continue to consume a relatively generous proportion of a rising GNP. The fleet as planned seemed affordable. Unfortunately, given the sluggish performance of the economy and the increasing cost of defense, it eventually proved not to be. Nevertheless, the Sandys Exercise did achieve its fundamental aim. On the slogan, "You've never had it so good," Macmillan's Government scored a smashing victory in the 1959 General Election.

CHAPTER · SIX

PEROXIDE TO POLARIS

One of the most significant developments in the post-1945 Royal Navy was the changing balance between surface forces and submarines. Although subsurface craft were never neglected by the Royal Navy, as long as the latter was mainly concerned with sea control, submarines were viewed as opponents rather than assets. During the postwar decades, however, this situation has changed, for four main reasons. Firstly, the development of nuclear propulsion had given the submarine the size and general characteristics of a capital ship that no navy with any pretension to greatness could be without. Secondly, the combination of this propulsion technology with long-range ballistic missiles had provided the Royal Navy with the means to become the nation's primary nuclear deterrent. Thirdly, the submarine has become increasingly significant as an *anti*-submarine weapon. And finally, as opponents grew in power and three-dimensional threats restricted the utility of the Royal Navy's surface ships as offensive weapons, Britain increasingly had to adopt a sea-denial strategy also, as she had done in the Mediterranean during the Second World War.

A major problem arose, however, as a result of this new emphasis on undersea warfare. The technical complexity of the equipment necessary to prepare for it, and engage in it, put far too great a strain on British resources than they could bear alone. Repeatedly, U.S. technology had to be considered or actually resorted to for almost every aspect of submarine warfare: sensors, propulsion systems, weapons. Although this point should not be overstated, and in one or two areas the exchange was two-way, there can be little doubt that without American aid the capabilities of the British submarine force would have been greatly reduced and the pace of its evolution much slower. Indeed, without an American missile British submarines would never have become the instruments that allowed the Royal Navy to elbow aside the Royal Air Force from its key position in Britain's defense posture for the thermonuclear age.

Another problem that adversely affected the submarine service, especially in the first postwar decade, was its weak bureaucratic position in the Royal Navy itself. Submariners traditionally regarded themselves as members of a specialized arm at one remove from the rest of the service. This was true of naval airmen also, but the latter had separate representation on the Board of Admiralty in the shape of the 5th sea lord. There were also two staff divisions solely concerned with air matters. There was no separate submarine staff division, the Directorate of Torpedo, Anti-Submarine and Mine Warfare being the most concerned, although its perspective was obviously more general and sometimes not a little hostile! In 1954 DTASW became the Directorate of Undersurface Warfare (DUSW), reflecting a change of emphasis in its work with more attention given to pro-submarine operations.[1] There often seems to have been a significant split between the submariners themselves (represented by Flag Officer Submarines and the Flotilla/Squadron Commanders) and the surface-oriented sailors of the Staff. Ideas often changed and projects were pursued briefly, to be delayed or cancelled as enthusiasm waned and Staff doctrines changed. This weakness had unfortunate results, both as regards the lack of clout behind submarine-related developments and also the policy vacillations that had an adverse effect on equipment developments and deliveries.

From 1945 onwards submarines were seen as the only means of carrying on offensive operations close to the increasingly well defended shores of the Soviet Union. As the planners put it: "It must now be accepted that unrestricted attack against merchant ships carrying essential supplies and war materials would always be a necessary form of total warfare." Submarines were, therefore, "needed to enforce blockade in waters close to the enemy's shore where surface vessels are unable to operate and for special reconnaissance operations."[2]

A main target for British submarines on these duties would be Soviet undersea craft. From the beginning of 1948 "the interception and destruction of enemy submarines" was designated the "primary operational function" of the British submarine fleet. In his important paper of 20 April 1949 ACNS emphasized that even a strategy of convoy defense included "offensive submarine patrols off enemy bases" using torpedoes and mines to help in the neutralization of the enemy's submarine offensive at its source. Submarines would also take the offensive against the enemy's surface forces and merchant fleet. They were, as restated a year later, "one of the few opportunities" the contemporary Royal Navy had of "getting to the enemy on his home ground."[3]

The war ended with thirty-one British submarines in service, nineteen in refit, and seventy-four in reserve. The intention was to maintain, indeed slightly increase, the size of the operational force to some forty-five in service or in refit, of which twenty-five would be in home waters, ten in the Mediterranean, and ten in the Pacific. Some forty boats were to be maintained in reserve to provide a full war force of eighty-five submarines. There were some doubts, however, about Britain's capacity to keep such a fleet refitted and up to the required standards of maintenance. *All* submarines, it was deemed, had to be fully refitted in short-term reserve, and there were only fourteen submarine refit facilities available. Further consideration of refit cycles revealed that some seventy existing boats might be maintained, which, with twelve new units, would almost meet the near-term requirement.[4]

In 1947 the submarine fleet in service or refit was still forty-five strong, of which over half were on trials and training duties. The reserve force was, however, down to twenty-eight, although it was still hoped that it would be possible to build up to a total force of eighty boats. But by the end of the year, the Admiralty had reduced this target to sixty-five. Nevertheless, this was still above the total force

strength—some fifty-three boats in 1949, twenty active, a similar number for training, and thirteen in immediate reserve. Korean rearmament plans set a realistic
British submarine force target of sixty-one boats, the most the supporting infrastructure could now manage. Of these, it was hoped around thirty-eight would be
running, and this aim was achieved by 1952–53. The actual figure for the years
1953–55 was, in fact, thirty-seven, twenty-six at home (with three boats in refit),
and six in the Mediterranean (with two in refit). Two more were in Australia,
along with a third there in refit, making up a small 4th Flotilla sent there in 1950
to assist the local navy in ASW training. The 1955 Estimates marked a further
increase, listing an active force of no less than forty-three boats (almost a quarter
more than in 1945), with another fourteen in reserve or under refit. Unlike other
naval units, submarines being used for trials and training were always listed as fully
active in public statements. One reason for the extra boats in 1955 was the basing
of the 6th Squadron of three submarines in Canada for duties similar to those of
the 4th Submarine Squadron in Australia. (Flotillas had become squadrons in 1952
with the adoption of U.S.-style NATO nomenclature.)[5]

In the immediate postwar years British submarines were organized into four
flotillas/squadrons with three in home waters—the 2nd at Portland, the 3rd at
Rothesay, and the 5th at Portsmouth; the 1st was in the Mediterranean. It was
planned to concentrate all Home Fleet submarines at Rothesay in the west of
Scotland in time of war. The 1953 "Submarine War Plan" mentioned the eventual
concentration of three depot ships in that area in dispersed anchorages at least two
miles apart. All the active U.S. submarines in the Atlantic would be operating
farther up the Clyde from the base at Rosneath (on the opposite side of the Gareloch
from the present British submarine base at Faslane). The risk of nuclear attack
advised dispersion from the one crowded base area. NATO submarines would sail
on war patrol between D+2 and D+7. The existing 3rd Submarine Squadron,
based in the old depot ship HMS *Montclare*, would be joined by HMS *Maidstone*
and her 2nd Squadron between D+10 and D+21. The 5th Squadron boats would
split between the two depot ships. Within three months HMS *Adamant* would also
arrive and become the HQ of a new 6th Submarine Squadron, whose role would
be training. The maintenance aircraft carrier *Perseus* was intended to be a replacement for the *Montclare*, but the Sandys period cuts led to the abandonment of that
project. Possibly because the area had become a little less crowded after the American move towards longer-range nuclear submarines and operations from American
waters in defense of the U.S. seaboard, the 3rd Submarine Squadron's depot ship
was eventually moved from Rothesay back to the Gareloch.[6]

The British submarine force of the first postwar decade was mainly composed
of boats of three classes—the 1,090-ton *T* class, the 1,120-ton *A* class, and the
little 715-ton *S* class. The *T*- and *S*-class boats were essentially of prewar design,
and both had proved themselves on active service. Later boats of both classes had
various detailed improvements, notably welded hulls, allowing greater diving depth
(350 feet against 300).

Beginning in 1944 eight *S*-class submarines were given radical modifications to
give them the high underwater speed reported as being characteristic of the German
Type XXI submarines. Higher-capacity batteries and upgraded motors, together
with hull and conning tower streamlining, gave an underwater speed of just over
12.5 knots compared to 8.8 knots for a standard boat. The role of these boats was

Important members of the Royal Navy's postwar submarine fleet were the small 715-ton "S"-class boats. Last in service was HMS *Sea Devil* seen here, which operated until 1962. The snort mast can be clearly seen off of the conning tower. Note also the twin sonar domes widely separated on the forward casing (one is partially obscured by a crew member). By about 1960 many British submarines were so equipped, presumably to obtain maximum bearing accuracy with available hydrophones and to give some passive ranging capacity by triangulation.

to act as high-speed targets to train ASW forces, and the torpedo tube ports were blanked off. The *Seraph* was the pioneer conversion; the other boats were the *Satyr, Sceptre, Selene, Sleuth, Statesman, Solent,* and *Scotsman.* The *Scotsman*'s conversion was the most radical as she was fitted with completely new electric motors like those in the larger *A*-class submarines. She underwent a number of further extensive alterations in the postwar period as a trials boat.

The *A* class had been designed for operations in the Pacific, and along with longer range and better habitability they could dive deeper still, to some 500 feet. The *A*s were also quieter and could dive faster than the old boats. No *A* boat was completed in time to serve in the war, but some sixteen of these valuable submarines were completed between 1945 and 1948. No less than forty-seven of the class were cancelled, however, along with four uncompleted *T*s at the close of hostilities. This left three modified *A*-class submarines of the 1944 program and a new experimental boat of completely new design in the 1945 program. It was hoped to spread construction of these boats around the four submarine building yards to maintain as wide a submarine production base as possible. The four yards were Vickers Armstrong at Barrow, Cammell Laird at Birkenhead, Scotts at Greenock, and Chatham Dockyard. In the end these yards were kept going by work on existing *A*s, as the decision was taken in July 1946 to build only two completely new boats. It was confirmed that the experimental 1945 boat would be powered by hydrogen peroxide (HTP) Walter turbines as developed by the Germans during World War II. (A

Type XVIIB Walter boat, U1407, had been captured and commissioned in the Royal Navy as *N25*, later HMS *Meteorite*.) It seems to have been intended to combine the diesels with HTP motors in the improved *A* boats, but these boats were cancelled and replaced by a second wholly HTP craft, similar to the 1945 boat. This was put into the 1947 building program.[7]

Other German submarines had been acquired, and these were operated in the immediate postwar years. They included two boats of the Type XXI type, U3017 and U2518, and one Type XXIII, U2348, all with high-capacity batteries that gave them high underwater speed. The British decided not to spend money on refitting these German craft, given their dubious safety standards and non-standard equipment. Various alternative options were considered, including the conversion of existing larger boats to the advanced U-boats' standards or building a similar fast battery drive (FBD) boat from scratch. Flag Officer Submarines (FOS/M) in mid-1947 regarded it as urgent to get experience with the latter as quickly as possible, given the "grim" HTP development time scale (see below). He felt that the FBD boats were needed not only to develop ASW tactics against them, but that an operational fleet of such vessels would provide a fleet of the highest possible performance in case of war in the early to mid fifties. He wished both an *A* and a *T* to be converted as quickly as possible and design to start on a completely new boat based on the XXI. Copying the American *Tang*-class "super battery attack submarine" design was considered. In the meantime one crucial German modification, the "Snort," which allowed submarines to cruise underwater on diesels, was being added to existing boats.[8]

An FBD program received strong support from the ship designers, who felt it was a more practical approach to a useful operational boat (current planning envisaged forty new boats, half HTP, half FBD). Preliminary enquiries revealed that the best option was to convert the Ts, whose construction lent itself to the operation. The *T*-class batteries were in three small sections to which a fourth could be relatively easily added abaft the control room. It was hoped to increase the submarine's power by two and a half times to give an underwater speed of 14–15 knots. By mid-1948 it was decided to plan on the conversion of up to twelve *T* boats and the construction of two new FBDs and two operational HTPs in 1949–50, and have six of each new type complete by 1956. Alas, financial realities caused cuts to this program, and the same year the Revised Restricted Fleet proposed just six new FBDs and six converted Ts in addition to the two original experimental HTP submarines.[9]

Not just financial difficulties militated against the ordering of more HTP boats, for despite continued enthusiasm from the submariners, it was becoming clear that the propulsion system was one fraught with many problems. Not only was the machinery difficult to develop in itself, but there were delays in getting existing systems out of Germany and in building the experimental establishment in Britain, due to shortages of cement and steel. The hydrogen peroxide fuel was scarce, tricky to handle, and expensive (some £350–£400 per ton when storage requirements were taken into account). Even the two planned experimental boats, now known as E14 and E15, were going to cost an estimated £4.3 million over the next four years. This was the equivalent of a large cruiser, or refitting a third of the Reserve Fleet. Alternatives were being considered, such as a closed-cycle system using oxygen, but this was not as compact as an HTP system nor did the fuel have such promising energy release characteristics. HTP seemed to be the only way of creating a true submarine within the next decade. The Admiralty feared that the Soviet Union might well have HTP boats in service by 1957, and so E14 and E15 were held to be essential for developing countermeasures. The prospect of operational HTP boats for the British was, however, dropped, at least until the threat of war was "urgent and unquestioned." Even E14 and E15 were suspended until 1950–51 by the general financial squeeze of 1949.[10]

Early 1950 saw the decision to run the two boats with one crew to save manpower, but this was a little premature as neither was yet laid down. Indeed, by June 1950 it was clear that E14 would not be started for at least another year, by which time trials with her engines would be completed. In fact the first of the two 760-ton unarmed boats, named HMS *Explorer*, was only laid down in July 1951 and her sister, *Excalibur*, just over six months later. They were completed by the end of 1956 and at the beginning of 1958 respectively, somewhat later than originally intended. Nevertheless, they did eventually provide the Royal Navy with two useful fast underwater targets, and they also proved the impracticability of the HTP propulsion system. The boats' nicknames, "Exploder" and "Excruciator," were testimony to the difficulties of their operation.[11]

Just as the two experimental HTP boats were being belatedly laid down, the Royal Navy was discovering the difficulties of using existing submarines as ASW platforms. Despite ASW's high priority for a future war, antisubmarine exercises were only number eleven on Flag Officer Submarines' (FOS/M's) list of peacetime activities instructed by the Admiralty. Nevertheless, in June and July 1950 the 3rd Submarine Flotilla carried out some significant trials off the west coast of Scotland simulating offensive British submarine ASW patrols off Soviet bases. The waters between Skye and the small isles of Canna, Rum, and Eigg played the part of the Kola Inlet. The two boats used were the *Truncheon* and *Alcide*, both nonstandard examples of their classes. The *Alcide* had been built with an experimental 152X sonar, a double transducer variant of the standard wartime 129 submarine sonar. The *Truncheon* had a normal 129, but she was also fitted experimentally with an American JT precision tracking hydrophone. This was combined with considerable efforts on the part of HMS *Montclare* to streamline the *Truncheon*'s hull, removing her gun, external torpedo tubes, and other noise-making fittings. The quieter hull and the JT sonar made the *Truncheon* the superior "hunter-killer" submarine. Her

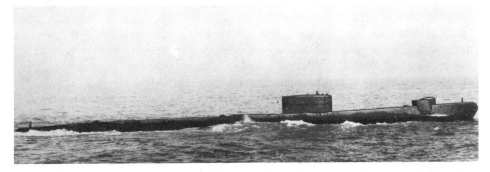

HMS *Explorer*—known less kindly to her crew as HMS "Exploder." One of the pair of unarmed experimental HTP-powered high-speed trials and target boats. (Imperial War Museum)

quieter hull form made her the better silent sonar platform and also enhanced her chances of maneuvering quietly into a good firing position. Nevertheless, neither boat could maneuver silently at more than three knots, which made getting into a good attacking position somewhat difficult.[12]

The two submarines had insufficient sonar capabilities for effective torpedo fire control, but the *Truncheon*'s JT did give significantly superior bearing accuracy (and marginally better detection ranges). Despite her better capacity to estimate a target's course and speed, the *Truncheon* was only able to claim a marginally better success rate: 34 percent from thirty-two sonar-controlled underwater "attacks" against the *Alcide*'s 29 percent from seventeen. When the *Truncheon* was noisily snorting the *Alcide* got six "kills" from seven "attacks"! When the Naval Staff got round to examining these results (not until early 1951!), the conclusions were not optimistic. "It is clear from the report that submarines with the present standard equipment can only be expected to have limited success when employed in their AS role."[13]

More trials were carried out with the *Truncheon* in 1951 before she lost her JT hydrophone to the submarine shore establishment, HMS *Dolphin*, at Gosport. She was set against her standard sister, the *Tireless*, and a boat given partial streamlining, the *Tally Ho*. These two tested new approach-and-attack procedures, and combined with encouraging results from the 1951 "Summer War," both the commander of the 3rd Submarine Flotilla and FOS(M) were moved to state that British submarines stood a "fair" chance of destroying enemy submarines at a worthwhile rate even with current equipment. ASW operations were raised to number seven on FOS(M)'s list of activities in July 1951, and by the autumn of that year it was clear that specialized and intensive training in ASW tactics was required, especially to exploit fully the new boats of enhanced capability that were beginning to come into service.[14]

In January 1950, even before the outbreak of the Korean War, the *T*-class conversion program had been accelerated. Chatham Dockyard was chosen to expedite the work, and the *Taciturn* and *Turpin* were soon in hand there. The staff requirement for these conversions specified the ability "to perform the functions of a fully operational submarine capable of carrying out a war patrol continuously submerged" combined with "the highest possible submerged speed." Surface performance was sacrificed to performance underwater. This involved full streamlining with the loss of guns and external torpedo tubes. Not only did this enhance top speed underwater (to the intended 15 knots), but it improved the speed at which the boat could maintain silence, both to hide herself and to operate her sonar at maximum efficiency. To increase underwater power an extra battery section and a second pair of electric motors were added. This involved cutting the boat in half and adding an extra center section. There were slight differences between the two initial conversions, the *Taciturn* being given a slightly longer section than her sister—14 feet as opposed to 12. The shorter section was the standard for the next two boats to be chosen, the *Thermopylae* and *Totem*. In May 1950 the last of the six boats originally planned were earmarked for conversion, the *Tiptoe* and *Truncheon* (the latter due for a refit in October after her pioneering trials). The choice was constrained by the requirement for welded construction and Lawrence Scott main motors. The first conversion, the *Taciturn*, was running by 1951. The rearmament program put two more boats back into the conversion program, to make

After problems with the earlier boats' fins in rough seas, the last two "T"-class conversions were given the large streamlined structures as designed for the new *Porpoise* class. This is HMS *Tabard*. The boat has not yet been fitted with a 187 sonar and instead seems to be carrying an interim arrangement of a pair of 168 "searchlights" to give a similar "split-beam" effect for improved bearing accuracy.

a total of eight. The *Trump* and *Tabard* were chosen as the extra pair, the former having been planned as one of the original conversions.[15]

The last four converted boats were given longer extra sections, enlarged to 20 feet. The *Trump* and *Tabard* were also given modified fins, as planned for the new-construction FBDs. The original navigational position on the "stepped" fin had proved too wet. Indeed, her poor seakeeping qualities on the surface caused the *Turpin* serious difficulties in the Mainbrace exercises of 1952. Water flooding down the conning tower played havoc with her electrical equipment. Despite these problems, however, the modernized Ts were much improved ASW platforms, and attempts were made to give similar, but less extensive, improvements to some of the riveted members of the class unsuitable for the full modernization. Streamlining and higher-capacity batteries for silent underwater running gave them many of the advantages of the full conversions, notably higher silent speed for sonar purposes, without the time and expense of the full modernization. The *Tradewind* seems to have been given an experimental streamlining around 1950, but the first boat chosen for the official "streamlining" program (complete with new sonar) was the *Tireless*, which had been engaged in trials as the standard "target" in April 1951. She was running trials in her new configuration by 1952. Four more boats were given the same treatment: the *Talent, Token, Tapir,* and *Taredo.*[16]

Obtaining improved submarines was only part of the problem, however. Of at least equal importance were the difficulties faced in acquiring improved sensors and weapons. In antisubmarine operations passive sonar capability was at a premium. Wartime British boats had carried a 138 passive hydrophone on their after casing to supplement their main 129 active/passive set mounted in a keel dome forward. After the war 138 began to be mounted in a streamlined dome on the forward casing for aggressive use rather than mere passive warning. Modifications were carried out to the 129/138 combination to produce an improved 169 active/passive set and 168 hydrophone, and these were tested in HMS *Anchorite* in 1950. Attempts were also made to acquire American AN/BQR3 low-frequency "split-beam" sonars for precision tracking, and forty-five of these sets were ordered, delivery to begin in the spring of 1951 just as the modified *T*s were coming into service. The fate of these sets is unclear. The *Turpin* was completed with a larger than normal sonar dome, but most of the fully modified *T*-class boats seem to have had the smaller dome associated with 169/168 as did the first *T*-class "streamlines."[17]

This was, however, only considered an interim solution to the problem. A totally new submarine sonar set, the 171, based on the "four-square" instrument being designed for the latest ASW surface ships was under development. Great things were expected from this set; it was hoped that it would be both an active attack sonar, as well as have an accurate passive listening capability. Considerable effort went into its development. It was to be combined with a British trainable "split-beam" low-frequency precision tracking hydrophone, the 718. It was intended to fit the later modified *T*s with this suite, and in 1953 the *Thermopylae* was so equipped for trials. It was soon clear, however, that the 171's depth-determination characteristics were inadequate and that it would require computer support, which would be impossible to fit into a contemporary submarine. Since it was determined that it would take at least another six years for the equipment to be fully operational, the 171 was cancelled.

As an interim measure, experiments were carried out with double transducers to improve bearing accuracy. Photographs of 1955 show the *Scotsman* carrying twin domes forward while the relatively unmodified *T*, HMS *Thule*, was fitted with twin domes of rather large size. Experiments also took place with more widely spaced domes, and by 1956 *T*-class streamlines were carrying sonar domes both fore and aft in order to give some passive ranging capacity. These twin sonar domes were fitted to several boats of various classes in the late 1950s, but a more definitive solution appeared in 1958 in the shape of the 187 submarine sonar, effectively a 718 with a limited active capability. It gave greatly improved bearing accuracy and was retrofitted into the fully modernized *T*s. The large inverted dome on the bow attested to the presence of this equipment. Another improvement reportedly fitted to the modernized *T*s was the 186 low-frequency hydrophone array for long-range detection, a development of the German wartime GHG equipment belatedly introduced into British service in 1956. Shortages of resources were partly responsible for these delays, but the official historian of Britain's sonar program argues that the "false starts" of the postwar period were "because the Naval Staff found it difficult to formulate their requirements."[18]

An even more intractable problem, however, was finding a modern submarine weapon. The only system available for one submarine to attack another in 1950–51 was the latest "double star Mod 2" version of the Mark 8 torpedo in service since 1927. This was the most efficient 21-inch torpedo of its generation, but even when fired in salvoes was not an absolute killer of a submerged submarine, given all the uncertainties of bearing and range. Some capability to home on a submarine acoustically would solve many of these difficulties. The Germans had developed acoustic torpedoes for anti-escort work during the war, but because of insufficient staff interest and shortages of resources the British decided largely to rely on the Americans for similar devices. Nevertheless, an active homing variant of the Mark 8 "Trumper" was undergoing trials in mid-1945. The end of the war and the need for short-term savings caused this project to be postponed and finally cancelled in favor of an electrically powered passive homing torpedo code-named "Bidder." This weapon fitted in better with the existing salvo-firing techniques, and it was also suitable as an ASW weapon for surface escorts. During the 1950–51 trials, techniques were worked out as to how Bidders might be fired in groups without mutual interference. It was estimated that Bidder would have doubled the *Truncheon*'s success rate in her "attacks" on *Alcide*.[19]

The torpedo eventually became available in the 1950s as the Mark 20, but only apparently in limited quantities as its low speed and relatively insensitive homer made it a secondary weapon for use against attacking escorts. The trials with improved submarines seem to have demonstrated the need for a fundamentally new approach to attacking enemy submarines, by quietly stalking them with passive sonar and using wire-guided torpedoes. Priority, therefore, switched to "Mackle," a torpedo developed by Vickers based on a German wartime wire-guidance system. Unfortunately, Mackle, tested as a prototype in 1955, proved over-complex and was abandoned in 1956 to be replaced by a simplified "Grog" based on the Mark 20. The trials batch was not ordered until 1959, and it did not enter service, as the Mark 23, until 1966. Reportedly the weapon was not fully operational until 1971![20]

So submarine commanders of the 1950s were forced to rely on salvoes of unguided torpedoes. A good way of increasing the chances of a hit with such weapons was by increasing their speed. Once more following German wartime ideas, an HTP-propelled variant of the Mark 8 was developed under the code names "Ferry" and "Fancy." It was ready in prototype form in 1953 and was adopted as the Mark 12. Unfortunately, on 16 June 1955 a Mark 12 just loaded into HMS *Sidon*, which was alongside the depot ship *Maidstone*, blew up, sinking the submarine. Another Mark 12 exploded shortly afterwards at the Arrochar torpedo range in Scotland. It was found that HTP was incompatible with the materials of the Mark 12 body, and the dangerous devices were withdrawn from service. The Mark 8 remained the British submarine's primary weapon.[21]

With such manifold sensor and weapon difficulties and with the converted *T*s being used to improve techniques, perhaps it made some sense to delay laying down the first new "FBDs" until June 1954, almost four years after the basic design had been completed and just over three years after the first order had been given. It had originally been intended to lay down the first four submarines in fiscal year 1953–54 and the second four in 1954–55. As it was the *Porpoise* was not laid down at Vickers Armstrong, Barrow, until 15 June 1954, followed by her sister, *Rorqual*, in January 1955. Cammell Laird of Birkenhead laid down their first boat, the *Grampus*, in April 1955 and Scotts of Greenock, *Cachalot* in August. Vickers and Cammell Laird both laid down a new submarine each in 1956, and the two final members of the class of eight were begun at Cammell Laird and Scotts in 1958 just as the *Porpoise* entered service. The final boat, the *Sealion*, was delivered in July 1961.

The "Intermediate B" or *Porpoise* class, as they became generally known, were intended primarily for ASW duties and were similar in size to the German Type XXIs that had been their inspiration. They were some 241 feet long overall, 44 feet shorter than a *T*-class conversion, and displaced just over 1,500 tons standard. The boats were built with American-style high-capacity batteries, which gave them twice the storage capacity of any previous new British submarine. The staff requirement was for the boat to maintain 17 knots submerged for twenty minutes. Also, unlike previous British submarines, the *Porpoise* class always worked in diesel-electric or straight electric drive, thus dispensing with noisy direct-diesel propulsion. This helped give excellent silent running characteristics. The high cost of the boat reflected the most up-to-date sonar suite possible: 186, 187, and 719. The torpedoes carried were Marks 8s for the six forward tubes and Marks 20s for the pair of torpedo tubes placed facing aft. (The *T*s had been forced to dispense with this capability on conversion as their aft torpedo tubes were external.) The Admiralty officially noted that the *Porpoise*-class design was "one of the most elaborate and comprehensive the Admiralty has ever produced and containing more novel and untried features." They proved to be excellent units and some of the finest conventional submarines of their time.[22]

While the *Porpoise* class was being constructed, the *A*-class submarines were modernized with new streamlined bows and sterns and large streamlined fins. Battery capacity was increased, although unlike the *T*-class full conversions, the motors were not enlarged as they were more powerful anyway. The *Artful* underwent the first transformation in 1955–56 and by 1960 fourteen boats, all but one of the class (one having been accidently lost in 1951), had been converted. The

Britain's East of Suez presence in the 1960s was maintained by submersible gunboats as well as by surface vessels. Here in the mid-1960s HMS *Andrew*, a modernized "A" boat fully equipped with 187 sonar as well as a 4-inch gun, passes the Type 61 frigate HMS *Lincoln*.

early *A* conversions carried the widely separated twin sonar dome arrangement, but 187 sonar was fitted as it became available.[23]

As larger boats were taken into the yards for modernization, the task of keeping up numbers of running submarines devolved on the little *S* class. Measures were taken to quieten the combatant boats of the class, notably by removing their deck guns. They also seem to have been fitted with improved sonar. The number of *S*-class submarines in the active fleet rapidly rose from three in 1949 to thirteen in 1953 and fifteen in 1955. The mid-1950s also saw the brief return to service of the even smaller *U* class of 545 tons, two of which, the *Upstart* and *Untiring*, were returned from Greece in 1952 and were both active by 1955 with modernized sonar. Both these submarines were taken out of service the following year and were expended as ASW targets in 1957. By this time the *S* class was being rapidly reduced. In 1960 only three of these submarines remained active, and in 1962 the *Sea Devil*, the last one at sea, paid off for disposal. The only *T*s in service were now modernized or streamlined, the last original member of the class, the *Tudor*, having been taken out of service.[24]

The early 1960s also saw the end of the Royal Navy's small force of midget submarines. Two had been included in the Revised Restricted Fleet, and four World War II *XE* craft were kept (two running at any one time) pending new construction. Four new 32-ton midgets were ordered in 1951; a fifth boat was also planned but she was cancelled. Originally just numbered X51 to X54, they received names before they commissioned—the *Stickleback*, *Shrimp*, *Sprat*, and *Minnow*. Only two were normally kept running at any one time. Nuclear weapons gave the midget submarine a new lease on life, and in 1954, the year the *Stickleback* and *Shrimp* were launched, the Naval Staff had foreseen these craft as carrying "an adaption of the atomic bomb" for attacks on harbors. Indeed, this form of delivery was seen at this time as the navy's primary medium-term means of nuclear delivery together with carrier-based aircraft. A nuclear "side charge" never appeared, however, and the *Stickleback* was sold to Sweden in 1958. That same year the *Sprat* was lent to the U.S.A. for three months to test harbor defenses. The three remaining British midgets were all placed on the disposal list in 1961.[25]

By 1962, therefore, the British submarine force of some thirty boats had become entirely "postwar" in capability. The final departure of the wartime submarines was made possible by the rapid delivery of a second class of new "fast battery" boats. These were very much based on the *Porpoise* class, but with a set of incremental improvements to improve quietness and general performance. Reportedly, maximum diving depth was now doubled to over 1,000 feet. The name boat of the class, the *Oberon*, was laid down at Chatham Naval Dockyard even before the private shipyards began the last two *Porpoise*s, and by the end of October 1962 five more were completed and another six were under construction.[26] In more general terms, however, a much greater step forward was the beginning of the trials of a boat that promised a quantum leap in the capabilities not only of the submarine service but of the Royal Navy as a whole: Britain's first nuclear submarine, HMS *Dreadnought*. This, and the decision to make a submarine-launched ballistic missile Britain's primary nuclear delivery system, made 1962 a real watershed in the history of the postwar British submarine.

The Admiralty had first shown interest in nuclear propulsion as early as 1945–46, and one of its scientists was sent to the nuclear research laboratory being set up at Harwell. He was joined in 1948 by two engineering officers. Within two more years sketch designs for nuclear ship-propulsion plants had been drawn up, and a subcommittee of the Ship Design and Policy Committee was formed to put the work on a more systematic basis. Although officially an "important" project, nuclear propulsion research did not receive a high priority, and it does not seem to have been very well funded. Nevertheless, design studies did begin in the 1950s on various types of reactors, including a submarine propulsion plant using enriched uranium. This type of plant presented severe problems, however, as Britain would not possess high enrichment facilities until the end of the decade, and all the enriched uranium available was earmarked for the weapons program. Graphite-moderated low-enrichment gas-cooled uranium reactors, similar in principle to the reactors already producing plutonium for Britain's nuclear weapons program, seemed the only practical way to produce a power source. Design studies soon revealed, however, that such reactors were both too heavy and too vulnerable for use at sea. There would also be a problem in the supply of necessary materials such as helium coolant. Eventually, in October 1952, development work on submarine propulsion reactors was effectively suspended when the chiefs of staff decided it did not have a high enough priority to interfere with plutonium production.[27] In 1952 nuclear power received only a Class II priority in the Ship Design Policy Committee, which in effect meant no priority at all. The Royal Navy's planners in early 1954 considered that production of nuclear submarines would be possible in the 1960s "but only at great cost." Nevertheless, a "few" such boats might be building.[28]

The U.S. Navy commissioned the *Nautilus*, the world's first nuclear-powered submarine, in 1954. This gave the British the impetus to set up, in June of that year, a committee to organize research and development. Admiralty representation at Harwell was also increased. The submarine service was beginning to show greater interest, but it was the advent of Lord Mountbatten as first sea lord in April 1955 that gave the project decisive new impetus. Nuclear propulsion appealed to his enthusiasm for technical novelty and innovation. With Mountbatten's strong support the Admiralty approved the development of both a submarine and its propulsion plant in June. In October, Mountbatten visited the U.S.A., and thanks to his close relationship with the American chief of naval operations, Arleigh Burke, enlisted American naval support for the project. This was important, given the opposition of the American Congress's Joint Committee on Atomic Energy to sharing information with anyone on nuclear propulsion. The legal position was unclear as to whether such knowledge could be transferred to allied states. Negotiations soon began between the American Atomic Energy Commission, the United States Department of Defense, and the United Kingdom to clarify the situation. Things were not helped when the chief of the U.S. nuclear submarine project, the notorious Rear Admiral H.G. Rickover, opposed any sharing of information and refused even to allow Mountbatten on board the *Nautilus*. The U.S. Defense Department supported the British request, however, and, in June 1956, over the objections of Rickover and his friends on Capitol Hill in the JCAE, an agreement was signed to give the U.K. information on ship propulsion reactors and nuclear submarines. In August 1956 Rickover visited London and "fell under the spell and aura of Queen Victoria's great-grandson." According to a member of Mountbatten's staff, "Rickover didn't give a damn whether we as a country got the submarine or not, but he did care whether Lord Mountbatten got one or not!"

This was a decisive factor in causing Rickover to inform Duncan Sandys in early 1957 that he was prepared to withdraw his objections to implementing the agreement. There were also good strategic reasons for the admiral to change his mind. Like his USN colleagues he saw the advantages of improving their ally's capabilities to destroy in transit the Soviet missile and nuclear torpedo-carrying submarines that were beginning to be deployed off the eastern seaboard of the United States.[29]

By this time, early 1957, Mountbatten felt that American aid was less important than it might have been earlier. British ideas were now quite fully developed. The fully fledged "Naval Section" at Harwell independently decided on an American-style pressurized water-cooled reactor (PWR) using the enriched uranium that would soon be available given the H-Bomb-related expansion of Britain's gaseous diffusion facilities at Capenhurst. Treasury approval was obtained early in 1956 to build a land-based experimental plant at Dounreay in Scotland, to be completed and working by mid-1961. The date was later brought forward to January 1960. It was hoped that the first submarine would be commissioned eighteen months later. An agreement was made with Vickers, and work began at Harwell on a small "Neptune" research reactor to investigate highly enriched uranium cores. But as one commentator on the program has stated, "Progress was not rapid, with too few people serving too many masters." A first leaf was taken out of the Americans' book by the appointment of an engineer, Rear Admiral Guy Wilson, as "Rear Admiral Nuclear Propulsion" in order to act as an established project chief. The name *Dreadnought* was chosen for the first Royal Navy nuclear submarine, a self-conscious attempt to compare her with the revolutionary battleship of a half a century before. A design team was formed of three naval constructors, who had been working on the recently cancelled missile cruiser project. The staff requirement for a nuclear submarine (usually known by the American abbreviation SSN) was approved in February 1957, and in May the hull and machinery contracts had been signed. The hull shape would be novel in the Royal Navy, being similar to that developed in the United States for their latest *Skipjack* class of nuclear submarines.[30]

By this time the program had already come under severe financial pressure from the Treasury, which saw an American connection as a good way of cutting research costs. The Admiralty argued the contrary, that U.S. cooperation implied a two-way flow of knowledge and that the British had to have their own independent program in order to have something to give in return for American help. Nevertheless, the financial logic of increasing dependence on the U.S.A. proved too strong, especially as Rickover on a visit to the U.K. in May 1957 expressed his concern at the dilatory rate of progress. The following month a group of twenty-five British nuclear scientists and engineers was sent over to the United States to confer with their American opposite numbers. The British were impressed by the Americans, but there were still suspicions among the latter of attempts to steal commercial secrets. Despite his regard for Mountbatten, Rickover's own desire to put rapid American development above any assistance to allied projects led him to argue that giving detailed technical information to the British "would be tying up our people and we would not be able to do our work."[31]

Perhaps it was this experience with the more unified American organization that helped lead to British attempts to copy transatlantic example more directly. Mountbatten had set up a Nuclear Submarine Advisory Committee that contained all interested parties—naval, nuclear energy, and industrial. It was also decided to set up a special division under the director of naval construction. The Admiralty duly approved the Dreadnought Project Team (DPT) in October 1957. The previous month Admiral Wilson had submitted his requirements for reactor fuel, and this raised the opposition of the Royal Air Force, which still demanded top priority for fissile material for bombs for the growing force of V bombers. The Treasury was also getting restive at a project costing some £31 million. In order to impress Sandys with the potential of nuclear propulsion, a ride was arranged for him in the USS *Nautilus*, which was in European waters for NATO exercises. Details of the remarkable performance of this boat were given wide circulation in the Ministry of Defence. The Defence Research Policy Committee was also lobbied.[32]

These tactics seemed not to be working when Rickover, of all people, came to the rescue. When Lord Selkirk, the First Lord, visited Washington in October 1957 it was hinted by Rickover that a sale of propulsion technology might be possible. Rickover reportedly "informed the Admiralty that he could arrange U.S. agreement if it could manage British approval." There were doubts in the development team about too great a reliance on U.S. help, and Rickover had by now prompted an all too typical adverse response from some British officers. Nevertheless, the advantages of cost, speed of delivery, and of the very survival of the project outweighed all doubts. In December 1957 when Rickover visited London, the completion date of the British SSN was further away than it had been in May. Rickover asked Mountbatten "whether the British Admiralty wanted to satisfy its pride or whether it desired to build a nuclear submarine as quickly as possible." Mountbatten said it was the latter and, despite an initially rather hostile reception by the Advisory Committee, the first sea lord got his way. The plan was confirmed by the British in February/March of 1958 and the U.S. Atomic Energy Act was duly amended that summer. The deal was in the interests of both sides; the British acquired a submarine quickly and at a price the Treasury felt it could afford. The vexed question of fuel was also solved as it too would come from the United States. The Americans gained much from the deal too. They secured the least possible interference with their own program, delayed the arrival of a rival power reactor design, and influenced British ideas in their direction, thus heading off an original competitive propulsion concept.[33]

It took another year before the contract was finalized. Rickover's influence on the project remained strong, and his personality continued to create difficulties. He insisted on choosing the commercial partner who would make the deal with Westinghouse, the American producer. He wished to use Rolls Royce, which created some inconvenience with Vickers, the existing prime contractor. Moreover, the Atomic Energy Authority in the U.K. had monopoly rights on nuclear fuel manufacturing in Britain, and it took a little time before Rolls Royce was allowed to produce nuclear fuel rods. The British, however, resisted American pressure to abandon their own reactor project. For their part the Americans made it clear that if the British continued with their own work there was no commitment to a continuing exchange of information with them.[34]

More helpfully, Rickover had also insisted that the Admiralty still further strengthen its program's centralized direction and control. The choice of chief of DPT helped this enormously. It was assistant director of Naval Construction Rowland Baker who insisted that a complete power plant, including steam turbines, be purchased from the U.S. and also that the complete British research and production program be continued, albeit at a reduced priority. An entirely British submarine front end was designed at Bath, where work had been concentrated. The plans included the latest sonars, developed by the Admiralty's Underwater Weapons Establishment at Portland. A large 2001 active/passive sonar array was to be fitted at the bow along with a 2007 long-range passive array on each side. There were many other novel features in design as well as in the hull shape, including new water-ram torpedo tubes usable at great depth. Baker worked his team hard, bypassing official channels and exerting strong personal authority. Baker's direct access to the third sea lord and Mountbatten also helped lubricate the wheels of bureaucracy where necessary.[35]

An Admiralty team was sent to the U.S.A. to supervise the purchase of the power system. Rickover wished to sell the British the S3W reactor system as used in the USS *Skate*. British representatives were denied access to the Electric Boat submarine construction facilities in Groton, Connecticut, where later-type boats of the *Skipjack* class were under construction. In October 1958 Mountbatten used his personal influence with Rickover to see the *Skipjack*. Both the yards and the new type of submarine were then opened to the British who were able to gain much general information about the most modern nuclear submarine design practice. Rickover also allowed Britain to purchase the *Skipjack*'s S5W reactor system. In 1959 British officers and sailors, including the *Dreadnought*'s designated commander, were given training courses in both the *Nautilus* and *Skipjack*. (Rickover had tried to insist that he personally control the appointment of British officers to nuclear power posts, but Mountbatten had refused!) In June 1959 the *Dreadnought* was actually laid down at the Vickers yard in Barrow, and she was launched just over ten months later. Despite all Baker's efforts she did not commission until 1963, but she was at sea on trials before the end of 1962, the deadline the project managers had given themselves when it became clear that they could not meet the original 1961 timescale.[36]

As the Americans had intended, the national British nuclear program suffered from this U.S. purchase. Hardly surprisingly, the Treasury used it as a strong reason to limit expenditure on British research: the activities of the Naval Section at Harwell were almost stopped. There were constructional problems at Dounreay, and the program was also delayed by the need to recast the British design to incorporate many of the lessons of the S5W propulsion system. Not until 1965 did the Dounreay Submarine Prototype establishment (DS/MP) HMS *Vulcan*, as it was called, become operational. The second British SSN, HMS *Valiant*, was laid down in January 1962 and launched a year after the *Dreadnought* began her trials. She did not commission, however, until July 1966, admittedly only a year later than it had been estimated in 1958 that a wholly British boat would be ready. Delays were partly caused by reactor difficulties and partly by the diversion of materials into a new nuclear submarine program of even greater significance, the Polaris ballistic-missile force.[37]

The Admiralty's attitude toward Polaris paralleled that towards nuclear propulsion, a distinctly limited enthusiasm. In 1954 McGrigor and the naval planners had looked forward to the mid-1960s by which time sea-based rockets launched from both surface ships and submarines would begin to replace the RAF's manned bombers. Such rockets would draw enemy fire away from the U.K., be less vulnerable to counterattack and, being of shorter range, might be in service sooner than weapons capable of being fired from Britain itself. The emphasis on this role faltered a little with the Admiralty's emphasis on a conventional, or, at most, limited nuclear role for the carrier-centered fleet that was at the heart of the mid-1950s "naval case." Other factors confirmed this agnostic, at best, attitude. The opponents of the naval missile program in the U.S.A., notably the U.S. Air Force, reportedly fed their opposite numbers in the Air Ministry and Ministry of Defence with assessments that doubted the practicality of the Polaris project. Morever, even Admiral Rickover advised the British to avoid Polaris until its development problems had been solved. Perhaps, once more, he wished to prevent the British interfering with the most rapid development of the American program.[38]

Nevertheless, the Royal Navy did have a link with the Polaris program from an early stage. The initiative had come, again, from Mountbatten, as a product of his close relationship with Arleigh Burke. As Mountbatten later remarked:

> On 4 November 1955 I was flown to Key West from Washington in order to go to sea in the first submarine designed hydrodynamically for high speed when fully submerged, USS Albacore (owing to nuclear security restrictions still in force I could not then be embarked in the nuclear powered USS Nautilus). On return to harbour Admiral Burke telephoned his office in Washington. He then drove me to the airfield for my return flight and during the journey expressed great indignation. He said that he wished to be friends with the U.S. Air Force and had offered to go shares in their new IRBM, Thor, if they would change the fuel from liquid to solid so that it could be fired from submerged submarines. They had categorically refused. He had then and there given the order to start work at once on a solid fuel IRBM to be mounted in a new class of large nuclear submarine. I said, 'Since the U.S.A.F. does not support you would you accept support from the RN?' I then offered to send a handpicked RN officer, with missile experience, to join his special team. He accepted and thereafter the First Sea Lord had his own representative on the Polaris project.[39]

Burke also "hoped that it might be possible" for the Royal Navy to deploy Polaris missiles. Mountbatten extolled the virtues of the missiles in his First Sea Lord's Quarterly Newsletter in October 1957. Sea-based missiles, he argued, echoing McGrigor, his predecessor three years before, would not invite Soviet preemptive strikes on Britain. Mountbatten, however, foresaw budgetary problems if Polaris was procured and argued for its funding coming from the "overall Defence Vote." In 1958 the first sea lord kept up the pressure, inspiring articles in the press arguing the obsolescence of land-based missiles and calling on senior naval officers to make this point as often and as widely as possible. The same year a British officer was officially appointed as liaison with the Special Projects Office set up to organize the fastest possible development of the Polaris missile in the United States. Personal liaison between Mountbatten and Burke remained close, to an extent that would have caused considerable embarrassment had it become public.[40]

What made these contacts so embarrassing was that the official consensus in Britain was that the best follow-on to the existing V bombers around 1965 should be a 2,000-mile-range, land-based, liquid-fueled intermediate range ballistic missile (IRBM). A project to build such a system, called Blue Streak, was officially announced in 1956, development work having begun in 1953. Following an agreement negotiated in 1954 by Duncan Sandys, as minister of supply, the rocket's designers received substantial U.S. help. The Blue Streak became even more important in 1957 when the complementary supersonic bomber, the Avro 730, was cancelled in the Sandys Defence Review. One of the most controversial features of the 1957 White Paper was its contention that the manned aircraft was obsolete. At the same time agreement was reached to deploy American Thor IRBM manned by British crews in order to give Britain some missile capability until her own longer-ranged, silo-based rocket appeared to replace the V bombers. Blue Streak, it was thought, might have a relatively short service life, and it was openly admitted that Polaris would be the logical system for the 1970s. Cancelling Blue Streak would, however, leave a perceived deterrent "gap" as Britain would not be able to deploy a Polaris force until some time after the V bombers had ceased to be effective. In retrospect, considering that the Avro Vulcan remained in service, albeit in a theater rather than strategic strike role, until the early 1980s and that the V bombers, some equipped with Blue Steel stand-off missiles, remained the primary deterrent until 1969, some of the doubts about the ability of the bomber force seem misplaced. Nevertheless, there were real fears about the technical credibility of the British contribution to the Western deterrent if rockets were not deployed as soon as possible.[41]

Indeed by the end of the 1950s the British strategic nuclear force was being seen by many not so much as a contribution to a general Western capability but as an independent force in its own right. Anglo-American disagreements over Suez, the advent of higher-yield bombs, both fission and fusion, and the increased vulnerability of the United States to rocket attack (as dramatized by Sputnik I and other early Soviet space achievements) all fueled British ambitions for strategic nuclear independence. Sandys was an enthusiastic supporter of this shift, as was the RAF, but the Admiralty and War Office had their doubts, partly because they worried that such a policy might give the Air Force overriding budgetary priority for improved capabilities. Moreover, both Mountbatten and Templer, the retiring chief of the Imperial General Staff, seem to have found strategically incredible the concept of Britain unleashing her nuclear weapons on her own against the Soviet Union. A joint navy/army paper along these lines was discussed at the end of October 1958 at a meeting of the chiefs of staff, chaired by the minister of defense. Mountbatten was a little isolated, as the brand new CIGS, Sir Francis Festing, felt in no position to give a great deal of verbal support to the document he had inherited and signed. The meeting seems to have reached a majority conclusion backing the official emphasis on increased independence, but Mountbatten was careful to record his continued dissent from it. He clearly regarded his proposed future British Polaris force as a limited, cost-effective British contribution to a general Western nuclear force, not as "an independent nuclear deterrent" in its own right.[42]

The top-level professional doubts about the credibility of the British national nuclear force were soon reinforced by serious questions about the viability of its forthcoming technical expression, the Blue Streak IRBM. Although less vulnerable than Thor, Blue Streak soon appeared to be vulnerable to preemptive attack by the improving Soviet missile force. Further attempts to harden Blue Streak would increase its already massive cost, which by 1960 was being estimated at some £600 million. By then Duncan Sandys, Blue Streak's major supporter, had departed. So had another major advocate, Sir Frederick Brundrett, the Ministry of Defence chief scientific adviser. With the operating service, the RAF, less than keen about Sandys's missile policies, there was an insufficient constituency within the defense establishment to sustain Blue Streak, despite the political embarrassment of cancelling a system whose vital importance had been repeatedly stressed. Sandys, now minister of aviation, pushed the missile's case in cabinet, but the chiefs of staff were united in their opposition, founding their case on the vulnerability of the fixed-base system. Mountbatten, now chief of the Defence Staff, no doubt relished the opportunity to put over his long-standing view as the new military consensus.[43]

So, on 24 February 1960, the Cabinet's Defence Committee took the decision, in principle, to cancel Britain's IRBM. Macmillan was to visit Washington at the end of March, and the nature of Blue Streak's replacement was put on the agenda for discussion. Macmillan was able to secure an exchange of notes in which President Eisenhower promised to supply Britain with mobile delivery systems for British-built thermonuclear reentry vehicles. Polaris was one of the systems considered, and Mountbatten and the chiefs of staff now openly supported this as the best *long-term* prospect. Nevertheless, the Americans were unwilling to sign an immediate agreement on Polaris until exploration had taken place for the possibility of a wider NATO Polaris deployment to replace America's vulnerable European-based IRBM.[44]

Polaris had been the subject of an Admiralty study in 1959 that had vindicated both the SLBM's practicality and its desirability as the least-vulnerable nuclear deterrent system. Nevertheless, Polaris remained the most expensive option in the short term and, despite the fact that Mountbatten's advocacy gained it increased support within the Royal Navy, other officers felt that it would divert attention and resources away from the struggle to rebuild the carrier fleet. Even if, as Mountbatten hoped, the extra money could be found to fund the Polaris force in addition to the Admiralty's existing long-term projects, there would be a considerable demand for highly skilled and specially trained officers and men who could not be used elsewhere in the service. If the money was to come out of the Admiralty's budget, the diversion of funds might be considerable indeed. Moreover, the continued RAF involvement in its traditional role of strategic deterrence would weaken its opposition to the Royal Navy providing a substantial part of Britain's air forces for limited war. Once the new British carrier that was planned had been approved, a more progressive and active pro-Polaris policy might be possible and practical.

Even the submariners, still relatively weak as a lobby, were divided in their approach to Polaris. Diverting scarce reactors and building facilities to designated SSBNs would mean a building hiatus in an SSN program that was only just under way. The professional attractions of "hunter-killer" weapons of naval warfare seemed to outweigh those of cruising around keeping out of trouble. The contemporary Polaris missile was a 1,200–1,500-mile-range rocket, somewhat inferior to Skybolt. It seemed to make sense to wait for a longer-range version. Finally, the persistent doubts within the Admiralty about the very "independent deterrent" force itself perhaps did something to weaken the navy's approach to the acquisition of it.[45]

So the chiefs of staff accepted the alternative American offer of the Skybolt air-launched medium-range ballistic missile as the immediate Blue Streak follow on. Skybolt, which had been extensively lobbied for by the RAF, would, it was hoped, come into service about 1964 and take the British deterrent into the early 1970s when Polaris would, in all likelihood, finally be procured (if a general disarmament treaty had not yet been concluded). Although the government was at pains to dissociate the two deals, it had also been agreed by Macmillan and Eisenhower at their Camp David discussions, "more or less in return for Skybolt," to base the new American Polaris submarines with a submarine tender in Holy Loch on the Firth of Clyde. The Cabinet agreed upon the submarine base scheme in September 1960 on the basis of Eisenhower's "broad assurances" of American help with nuclear delivery systems, including Polaris, should this become necessary.[46]

In October 1960 the British Government received the first news that the Skybolt project was in doubt. Its costs were higher than anticipated, over £100 million, and when informed of this by the prime minister, Mountbatten, now CDS, "strongly advised him to use the same money to buy a couple of American-built Polaris submarines." If Skybolt was delayed, as now seemed likely, the RAF offered a ram-jet-powered cruise missile called Pandora, fired from its TSR2 tactical bomber, as an interim strategic system of limited cost, but the chief of Defence Staff expressed skepticism both on the cost and the development time scale. Using the information he was getting from Burke, Mountbatten said at a meeting in November that "Polaris would remain valid as a deterrent for twenty or thirty years as he saw no prospect of anti-submarine measures having the breakthrough of a magnitude needed to attack Polaris submarines over the millions of square miles of ocean or under the North Polar Ice Cap."[47] Harold Watkinson, the minister of defense, was convinced and agreed in principle that if Skybolt was cancelled, then Polaris would be procured in its stead. It was announced in Parliament that it was the official intention of "put in hand an urgent study of the requirement for British built submarines capable of carrying the Polaris type missile."[48]

In fact, the Admiralty had just prepared contingency plans to procure Polaris. In June 1960 an extensive paper written by the director general Weapons, Rear Admiral Michael Le Fanu, a brilliant and unconventional officer with considerable experience of the U.S. Navy in World War II, was accepted by the Board of Admiralty. It recommended that a central executive be set up to organize the project along the lines of the four-and-a-half-year-old American Special Projects Office. This would "cut across the functional department structure of the Admiralty,"[49] but in order not to raise too many bureaucratic hackles, it should work within the Admiralty and not as an autonomous semi-elite organization. Measures were also taken to familiarize British naval designers with Polaris submarines, and an assistant director of Naval Construction, S.J. Palmer, led a team to the United States to inspect progress.[50]

The Royal Air Force, however, was far from defeated and began an aggressive anti-Polaris lobby. A Tri-Service Scientific Committee was set up in 1961 to look at the options for a nuclear deterrent in the 1970s. Before this body the Air Force pushed hard for an improved Skybolt system for the future rather than a Polaris purchase. With their plans for an eventual purchase of Polaris now being undermined, the Admiralty representatives countered by suggesting the immediate replacement of Skybolt by Polaris. The Naval Staff could see that the government was totally committed to an independent deterrent. In these circumstances the Royal Navy might as well be the operating service, especially as it could offer a system it genuinely felt was better and more cost effective. If obtaining Polaris meant accepting it now rather than later, then the nettle would have to be grasped, with all of its potential problems. The aggressive attitude of the RAF also stimulated deeply felt prejudices among the senior sailors. "Even though they had not pressed for Polaris, they disliked seeing the capabilities of sea power undersold."[51] The committee was unable to agree on a successor to Skybolt, but it was agreed that any 1970s nuclear deterrent had to be mobile and constantly ready for action.

The controversy went on into 1962. A new Admiralty–Air Ministry study group of civilian officials was approved to look at the alternatives—Polaris or an improved, airborne-alert Skybolt. The Royal Air Force was able to claim a lower capital expenditure but higher running costs for a ten-thousand-man force. The Royal Navy stressed Polaris's low running costs with a 2,500-man force, despite much higher capital expenditure. Again no agreed upon conclusion was possible, and the two services were still at loggerheads on the 1970s deterrent when it suddenly began to seem that the prospect of a British Polaris force was much closer than previously expected.[52]

Skybolt's severe developmental and financial problems eventually proved to be terminal. As this became all too clear, the Ministry of Defence asked the Admiralty for options if cancellation occurred. The Admiralty suggested three: (1) abolition of the deterrent; (2) building a force of mixed hunter-killer/ballistic-missile submarines with six to eight Polaris tubes each; and (3) a specially assigned SSBN program of boats similar to the American model with sixteen tubes per submarine. The first lord, Lord Carrington, told his superiors, the minister of defense and the prime minister, that the Royal Navy was willing and able to construct a Polaris submarine force, although the actual configuration of the boat was kept open. The favorable report of the Palmer mission to the United States was also transmitted to Prime Minister Macmillan. Thus the Royal Navy came, perhaps still a little reluctantly, to embrace an SSBN force.[53]

In early December Defence Minister Thorneycroft had a "disconcertingly cool" and "wholly unsatisfactory" meeting with American Secretary of Defense Robert McNamara. There were few points of agreement between the American and British defense chiefs, the former trying to assert radically new strategies of "flexible response" and centralized crisis management that had little room for an independent British nuclear force. Moreover, the Kennedy Administration's Defense Department's fixation with "cost effectiveness" had no time for a dubiously effective, rather expensive airborne missile system that was inferior in almost every way both to Polaris and the new solid-fueled, land-based Minuteman ICBM. Skybolt was clearly about to be cancelled, and Prime Minister Macmillan made this the central issue of an already arranged personal meeting with the new president, due to take place a few days later at Nassau in the Bahamas.[54]

At the first meeting on the 19th, the prime minister stressed the previous co-operation between Britain and America in the nuclear field, the 1960 Camp David agreement on Holy Loch, and Eisenhower's assurances that, if necessary, Polaris would be granted to Britain. Despite initial British hopes that Skybolt could be saved, it was soon clear to the prime minister that Skybolt was a "lame horse" and Polaris a "new favourite." Macmillan also moved to head off American fears that further special favor to Britain would alienate their other major European allies, France and Germany, especially the former. The prime minister concluded by hinting darkly at the effect on Anglo-American relations of coercing the U.K. out of the nuclear weapons business.[55]

Kennedy in return offered to go halves with the British on the cost of Skybolt or, alternatively, allow the RAF the jet-powered cruise missile, Hound Dog. He protested that the Americans only wished to cancel Skybolt on technical grounds, but argued that in no way were they committed to supply Britain with Polaris. The Americans were worried (in the event correctly) about the effect of a British Polaris deal on Franco-American relations. Their own Polaris program was ambitious enough without adding any additional burdens. Foreign cooperation would bring extra security risks and a bilateral British program would undermine the current idea of a NATO multilateral force (MLF) of Polaris-equipped surface ships manned by crews of mixed nationality. At Nassau the Americans once more pressed the MLF notion on the British, who felt the idea to be impractical. In the end a compromise formula was worked out: assignment of any British Polaris force to NATO command "but available for national use in time of emergency." The U.S.A. would match the British Polaris NATO assignment with at least equal numbers of SSBNs. It took two more days of often heated argument before an agreement was eventually reached on 21 December. The British were to abandon the now-doomed Skybolt and instead purchase Polaris missiles from the United States; the warheads were to be made in Britain.[56]

The Nassau Agreement was officially approved by the British Cabinet on 3 January 1963[57], but earlier, on Christmas Eve 1962, only three days after its signature, the Board of Admiralty had met and agreed to adopt the general shape of Le Fanu's proposal of two and a half years before. The author of these plans was now third sea lord, responsible for procurement and hence for implementation of the program. A "Polaris Executive" organization was duly set up with Flag Officer Submarines, Rear Admiral H.S. Mackenzie, an officer with a notable war record, as its chief. The organization "was a structure which could place executive responsibility for progressing the project in as few hands as possible, while at the same time enabling the executive cadre thus created to work with and through the existing organisation in order to integrate the project into existing procurement plans rather than to compete with them."[58] Mackenzie did not have his own budget or a place on the Board of Admiralty, being responsible to Le Fanu, but he did have access to the Board if he encountered opposition in other parts of the Admiralty organization. An integral part of the arrangement was a Polaris project officer in the Ministry of Aviation (later the Ministry of Technology), responsible for missile procurement and warhead development. The naval side of the design and construction of the submarines and weapon systems, including the means for firing the Polaris missiles themselves, was headed by the redoubtable Rowland Baker, fresh from his success in the *Dreadnought* project team that the new "Polaris Executive" absorbed (the initials DPT now stood for Director Polaris Technical). The number of staff actually allocated to the Polaris organization was never more than five hundred, although personnel from other departments were designated to work on the project as required. Relatively senior officers were also appointed as "Polaris Liaison Officers" "in order to ensure the support needed for the Polaris programme." A committee was also set up at assistant chief of Naval Staff level to deal with any serious disagreement betwen Mackenzie and the heads of other departments.[59]

While these steps were made to set up what turned out to be a highly successful organization, the first decisions were being taken at Board level on the technical parameters of the British SSBN force. It was felt that the hybrid SSN/SSBN should be abandoned, if for no other reason than that the NATO assignment of the force would prevent their use on anything other than deterrent patrol.[60] On 8 February an office memorandum was signed by Sir Clifford Jarrett, the Admiralty's recently appointed permanent secretary, confirming that the Board had approved four submarines, each equipped with sixteen missiles. This was a fortunate decision on other grounds also. Submarines carrying Polaris would have been much less flexible weapons for any kind of limited war scenario. The deployment of strategic nuclear weapons into any crisis situation would have seemed like an enormous escalation. There was some discussion about the size of the eventual SSBN force, notably over whether a fifth boat would be procured. It was asserted that the V bombers "would cease to provide an effective deterrent" by 1967, and hence acceptance into service of the first SSBN was set for January 1968 with sea trials the previous year. The Board had not given "indiscriminate over-riding priority" to the program, but the intention of keeping to the set timetable was firmly stated. The office memorandum formally approved the organization under the Chief Polaris Executive, or CPE, as the organization came to be known.[61]

In January 1963 transatlantic negotiations began to put some flesh on the bare bones of the Nassau agreement. A high-level U.S. group visited London, and shortly thereafter a British team of senior civil servants and naval officers crossed the Atlantic in the opposite direction. Among the latter group were Admiral Sir Varyl Begg, second sea lord, and Sir Solly Zuckerman, chief scientist at the Defence Ministry, as well as Rear Admiral Mackenzie. Their task was to gather data on which the British could base their ideas for the Polaris program and begin negotiating a sales agreement with the U.S.A. McNamara, a little unhappy still about confirming British nuclear ambitions when the opportunity was there to limit them, was insisting on a British contribution to Polaris development costs, something the U.S. had not sought with Skybolt. Although Macmillan seems to have conceded the principle of such a contribution in December, the British were out for the best possible deal, and at the suggestion of the liaison officer, already in Special Projects, it was agreed that the contribution should only be on costs incurred after 1 January 1963. The British at all levels were determined not to be drawn into an open-ended financial commitment; the missile recommended to them and which they themselves wished to procure, the improved 2,500-mile A3, was far from developed and its costs were unknown. There was, in addition, still considerable scope for interpretation as to the nature and size of the costs to be met by the British. In the end it took a series of personal telephone calls between Macmillan and Kennedy before the Americans reluctantly accepted the British proposals, a fixed additional contribution of 5 percent to the "retail cost" of the missiles. There can be no doubt that the close personal relationship of these two leaders and the mutual desire for a constructive Anglo-American relationship were vital factors behind the whole Polaris agreement.[62]

Formal negotiations began in February with sixteen sessions in the Special Projects Office in Washington, and the Polaris Sales Agreement was finally signed by Secretary of State Rusk and the British ambassador on 6 April 1963. The U.S.A. agreed to supply the British with the missiles themselves and their support equipment and instructions on how to use them. Other than this, no other information on the design of the missiles was to be included. The American Special Projects Office was in charge of procuring the equipment in the U.S.A., and the Americans would also provide training and testing facilities. The British liaison team in the Special Projects Office was greatly expanded following the agreement and placed under a naval captain. In June an American Special Projects Office was opened in London. A Joint Steering Task Group was then formed to oversee the Anglo-American interface, meeting every three months, alternately on each side of the Atlantic. A special subcommittee, the "Joint Re-entry System Working Group," was formed to fit the British-made warheads to the American two-stage solid-fueled rocket and inertial guidance system. In the agreement, despite recurring doubts "about getting too involved with the British," the Americans committed themselves to share information on any improvements in any element of the weapon system and its platform except reentry vehicles. Any improvements suggested by the British would be made available in return. The Americans, however, resisted perceived British attempts to share information on the nuclear submarines themselves, especially the propulsion plants.[63]

The British had indeed secured a bargain that was important both to the prime minister, who did not want an open-ended commitment to meet spiraling development costs, and to the Admiralty, which wanted to limit damage to the rest of the navy. The Admiralty's campaign to contain the financial impact of the program, however, went much further. The Board reportedly toyed with the idea of requesting the transfer of funds from the Air Ministry to set up a special "deterrent" budget, but the idea was dropped as too provocative. Instead, the help of the Defence Ministry was obtained to try to get more funds from the Treasury to cover the extra costs of Polaris. The chancellor's department, hardly surprisingly, proved reluctant to do so and suggested instead to the defense minister that he reallocate funds within his existing budget. Thorneycroft thereupon decided to share the costs of Polaris equally between the three services. There would indeed be a "deterrent" budget after all, one whose impact was shared evenly. This, plus the availability of funds already earmarked for Skybolt, the savings made by the inevitable delays in the SSN program, and, finally, the financially attractive nature of the Polaris Sales Agreement as a whole, generally limited the impact of the SSBN program on the navy's budgetary plans. What it could not do was reduce the impact of the skilled personnel requirements (one obvious and immediate example of this was the fact that a new flag officer submarines was not appointed for some months after Admiral Mackenzie had become CPE). Neither did it do much to placate the Royal Air Force, which now looked like losing the very role that had led to the setting up of an independent air service in 1918, that of strategic bombing. It was now even more necessary for the Air Ministry to assert its claim for a monopoly on the air power Britain deployed for limited war purposes. Moreover, the airmen felt "outmanoeuvred and robbed of their rightful heritage" by Mountbatten and the Admiralty.[64] The Air Ministry was in no mood to compromise as the question of aircraft carriers now moved to the center of the bureaucratic stage.

While that struggle was played out to its denouement in 1966, work on Polaris went forward in a remarkably effective manner. A Programme Evolution Group within the Executive organization created an overall plan for the project, which was modified as required. Modern techniques of "critical path network analysis" were used to create the most effective project management possible. The Executive organization also insisted that these techniques be used by private contractors also, especially the shipbuilders, whose work was considered to be an especially "critical path" in itself. This introduced modern management science to areas both of the Civil Service and to private industry where it had been previously unknown. As with the American Special Projects Group, "management by exception" was the rule with responsibility generally concentrated at the lowest levels possible—i.e., with the contractors and the representatives of the Executive working together. Regular meetings and program management planning by CPE ensured that progress was maintained and bottlenecks avoided. The whole project was also rather self-consciously imbued with a considerable amount of the dynamism that had affected and stimulated the American project.[65]

At the same time as the Zuckerman mission had gone to Washington, R.J. Daniel, the naval constructor responsible for the design of the boats (and later director general ships) had led a separate technical mission to the U.S.A. to update the Admiralty's knowledge on ballistic-missile submarines and "to identify the plans that would be necessary to begin the submarine design work."[66] Vickers of Barrow hoped to be the sole British contractor, but in order to limit the impact on SSN construction and to prevent overinvestment in construction facilities at one yard, it was decided instead to appoint a second builder. The choice fell on Cammell Laird of Birkenhead on the Mersey, and the signing of contracts was duly announced in May 1963. It was initially suggested that American designs be copied, but this was ruled out as it would have involved retooling British industry to produce copies of U.S. patterns or direct dollar purchases of American equipment. An alternative suggestion, to take HMS *Valiant*, the first all-British nuclear submarine, slowly completing at Barrow, and cut her in half to take the Polaris section, was also mooted. Bisecting and lengthening existing SSNs had been the American solution to getting the SSBNs in the water as quickly as possible; Daniel strongly opposed this. His objections were twofold, that the SSN program should not be completely jeopardized and that there were enough new features in the *Valiant* as it was without adding the first British Polaris installation.[67]

The final SSBN design followed the proposals of S.J. Palmer, Daniel's immediate superior, for four boats built new from the keel up. A reactor section similar to that of HMS *Valiant* was grafted via a short extra machinery space on to the American-designed, but largely British-built, missile compartment. A new forward end containing torpedoes and sonar for self-defense completed the vessel. At 425 feet long and displacing 7,500 tons it was the largest British submarine design, over double the displacement even of HMS *Dreadnought*. Vickers produced all the drawings. Two submarines were laid down, one at each yard in 1964 and two more in 1965. Vickers launched the first, HMS *Resolution*, on 15 September 1966; she was commissioned on 2 October 1967 and on her trials by the end of the year. By June 1968 the *Resolution* was on operational patrol. Cammell Laird could not maintain this pace and, despite labor problems, the second Vickers boat, HMS *Repulse*, was commissioned in October 1968, two months before the first Merseyside built SSBN, HMS *Renown*. The fourth submarine, the *Revenge*, was completed a year later in December 1969, six months after the Polaris force had officially taken over the nuclear deterrent role from the V bombers. By the time the two 1965 boats had been laid down, the decision was taken by the new Wilson administration not to build the fifth SSBN. The new government had carried out an enquiry into the Polaris program and considered what reductions were appropriate, both as part of its general defense review and to placate antinuclear opinion within the Labour Party. One interpretation of the Labour election manifesto had been the cancellation of the entire program, but honor seemed to be satisfied by the

The impressive bulk of one of the four British "Polaris" submarines, HMS *Renown*.

cancellation of a single boat. The loss of the fifth boat did diminish the operational flexibility of the force a little, but, nevertheless, at least one SSBN has been on patrol at all times since June 1969.[68]

When the program was first drawn up, it was decided that the first test-firing of a missile would take place on the American range at 1115 on 15 February 1968. The *Resolution* duly fired her first Polaris A3 at the required time and place, a remarkable achievement of planning and management and one perhaps unknown in the postwar history of the Royal Navy. By October 1968 the program had cost some £350 million, only 5 percent greater than the estimated sum.[69] Polaris was undoubtedly the most successful British weapon procurement project of the whole postwar period. The chairman of Vickers, admittedly not the most unbiased of sources, was probably right when he said that: "Polaris was the best defense bargain the British taxpayer ever had."[70] The advent of Polaris also stimulated the construction of a special nuclear submarine base on the Clyde, HMS *Neptune*, at Faslane, which opened in August 1968. The base also provided facilities for the Third Submarine Squadron. In addition a Weapons Store to house the British missile stockpile was constructed a few miles away at Coulport. Running costs of the Polaris were also very reasonable. In the mid-1960s the V bomber strategic force had been taking up to 6 percent of the total defense budget. Ten years later running the Polaris force was consuming less than 1.5 percent.[71]

Nevertheless, a price had to be paid for the program. Only two more SSNs appeared in the sixties, the *Valiant* in 1966 and the *Warspite* in 1967. Indeed the appearance of the latter boat was a considerable achievement given the rush to complete the SSBN *Resolution* on schedule. The next three SSNs, the *Churchill*, *Conqueror*, and *Courageous*, were not in service until 1970–71 (their appearance coinciding with the belated full operational capability of the Mark 23 torpedo).[72] It might be argued that the nuclear-powered submarine had little place in the East of Suez scenario that dominated naval planning and deployments in the 1960s, but Mountbatten had not thought so when he pushed for the SSN force at the end of

HMS *Conqueror*, Britain's sixth nuclear-powered attack submarine, and the first nuclear submarine to sink an enemy warship.

the 1950s. SSNs were seen as especially mobile ASW units, capable of rapid deployment on a worldwide basis, covertly if necessary, and contributing to the defense of a carrier task group. In any case, only three SSNs had appeared before the end of 1967 when the center of gravity of British naval strategy swung once more back to the Atlantic, the theater in which their highly sophisticated capabilities made most sense.

Not that submarines were entirely absent from the Royal Navy's East of Suez operations. In 1959 a new submarine squadron, the 10th, was established at Singapore. By 1961, along with the other smaller British submarine units, it had become a Division, the 7th. By the early 1960s its strength settled down at four modernized *A*-class boats, which often carried 4-inch guns on their casings, a sign of their limited war role. Other divisions deployed away from home at this time were the 5th (the old 1st Submarine Squadron) with perhaps three modernized *T*s at Malta, the 4th (the old 4th Submarine Squadron) at Sydney of similar strength, and the 6th (the old 6th Submarine Squadron) with a couple of modernized *A*s in Nova Scotia. The rest of the submarine force was at home, divided into three new squadrons, the 1st (the old 5th) at HMS *Dolphin*, the 2nd at Plymouth, and the 3rd at Faslane. The total number of boats in the operational fleet increased in the 1960s from thirty to a new peak of thirty-seven in 1965. In some ways these submarines formed the backbone of the operational West of Suez navy while the surface ships worked up and trained for their role of projecting power ashore in the Royal Navy's main operational theater East of Suez. This East of Suez role, much more than the tasks represented by the sleek futuristic monsters taking shape in northern England, was what the Royal Navy of the 1960s seemed to be all about and to it we must now return.[73]

CHAPTER · SEVEN

EAST OF SUEZ

We have already seen how, under the pressure of the series of defense reviews that marked the period 1951–57, the Admiralty successfully formulated and "sold" a case for the Royal Navy based on its role in limited war and peacekeeping tasks in relatively distant areas of the globe. With the Soviet Union increasing its backing of new nationalist regimes in the growing, ex-colonial "Third World," considerations of both world strategy and economic interest seemed to make it advisable for Britain to continue to play the role of a military world power in the Middle East (especially Arabia), the Indian Ocean, and South East Asia—that is, "East of Suez." The Sandys White Paper had made this clear, and the Macmillan Government's commitment to this policy increased, if anything, as the years went by.[1]

In 1958 Macmillan set up a Future Policy Committee to study Britain's possible world role in the late 1960s and 1970s. The main working group was chaired by Sir Patrick Dean of the Foreign Office and contained representatives from all other concerned departments—the Treasury, Colonial Office, Commonwealth Office, Board of Trade, Admiralty, Air Ministry, War Office, and Ministry of Defence. The group apparently had its fears that Britain might become overcommitted East of Suez, but its criticisms were muted by the Committee's steering committee, composed of the chiefs of staff and top civil servants. This less-radical body emphasized Britain's traditional overseas obligations and "greatly watered down" the recommendations of the working group. The final report, which appeared in 1960, duly stressed the unlikelihood of war in Europe and the potential for limited war in Asia, the Middle East, and Africa. Britain's interests were worldwide, the paper argued, and she had a particular responsibility for the Indian Ocean area. Strategically mobile forces would provide a means by which these crucial responsibilities could be maintained for an investment of 7 percent to 8 percent of the GNP on defense. It is arguable how important this report was as a factor in policy making, but it did reflect both the power and the nature of the East of Suez policy, which commanded consensus support among Britain's top policy makers.[2]

As Britain withdrew from direct colonial occupation, she made defense agreements with her former dependencies. In January 1957 the Anglo-Malayan Defence

Agreement was signed, which committed Britain to the external defense of the ex-colony. Forces based in Malaya could be used to protect Singapore (which Britain retained as a self-governing colony), Borneo, and Hong Kong. Malaya's "neutralist" sensibilities were reflected in her desire that British forces there could not be used in support of the American-sponsored anti-Chinese alliance, SEATO. This organization and the British-sponsored anti-Soviet CENTO Middle East alliance provided other treaty commitments that were used in justification of a British world military role. A treaty was signed with Nigeria on independence in 1960, and two agreements were made with small states that were to be of special significance. One was a treaty signed with the Sultan of Brunei in 1958 when autonomous self-government was given to his enclave on the coast of Sarawak, and the other was the 1961 agreement with the Arab Kingdom of Kuwait, which became independent that year.[3]

Kuwait was of special importance to the United Kingdom thanks to the 50 percent share in the Kuwait Oil Company held by B.P., the great oil company controlled by the British Government. By 1960, Kuwait was providing some 50 percent of Britain's oil supplies.[4] Her defense was thus a matter of some significance, and following the Iraqi Revolution of 1958, there was a real threat to Kuwait security. Contingency plans were prepared by the British for Kuwait's defense and in 1960 Plan "Vantage" was produced by the recently set up unified British Arabian Peninsula Command at Aden (Middle East Command from March 1961). The grant of independence headed off any nationalist internal subversion, but by mid-1961, neighboring Iraq had greatly strengthened her military power as a result of substantial Soviet aid, which had doubled her armored strength and greatly increased her air force.[5] Britain also moved to strengthen her own capabilities in the area. In 1960 the Amphibious Squadron, still a small force of two LST(A)s and two LCT(8)s, together with Landing Ship Headquarters HMS *Meon,* was moved from Malta to Arabian waters after being refitted and air-conditioned. This was directly related to Kuwait, as the squadron was intended to move a small force of Centurion tanks from Aden into the kingdom if required. Once more the speed of the force was a matter of concern; the tank base at Aden was some nine days steaming away from Kuwait in a 9-knot LST. It was decided, therefore, to keep an LST with half of the tanks forward deployed on patrol between Sharjah and Bahrein to be within a day or two of the potential trouble spot. HMS *Striker,* with her tanks, was duly in position at Bahrein when the crisis broke, about to be relieved by her War Office-operated sister *Empire Gull,* already in the Gulf with the other half of the tank squadron. At this time the rest of the Royal Navy's Amphibious Warfare Squadron was made up of three LCT(8)s, the *Redoubt, Bastion,* and *Parapet,* and the LSH *Meon,* all at Bahrein where Flag Officer Middle East, Rear Admiral Fitzroy-Talbot, had his headquarters in the shore establishment HMS *Jufair.*[6]

Within a week of the Sheikh of Kuwait's becoming a fully sovereign ruler on 19 June 1961, Iraq was making claims that he was a mere provincial governor. Somewhat fortuitously the British had an asset in the area that was additional to the Vantage plans. In late June HMS *Bulwark,* Britain's first commando carrier, was at Karachi carrying 42 Commando of Royal Marines and 848 Squadron's sixteen Whirlwind HAS 7 helicopters. The *Bulwark* was officially on the Far East Station, but her captain, R.D. Franks had been warned that it might be a "hot summer" in the Gulf and had arranged his program accordingly. He was indeed due to sail

The *Bulwark* in action at Kuwait with the Westland Whirlwind HAS 7s of 848 Squadron. (Imperial War Museum)

in that direction for "hot weather trials," but the accelerated date of Kuwait's independence seems to have upset the program somewhat. On receipt of warnings from the British Embassy in Baghdad, the decision to send the *Bulwark* to the Gulf was made on the 28th, and she sailed forthwith. On 29 June the *Meon* and *Striker* were ordered to sail from Bahrein to stand off the Kuwait coast, out of sight. They were accompanied by the *Loch Alvie*, whose sister ship *Loch Ruthven* was ordered to sail from Mombasa the same day. On 30 June, with two RAF Hunter squadrons in Bahrein and troops on alert, the CinC Middle East, Air Marshal S.C. Elworthy, was able to report that Vantage could be implemented immediately the Kuwait ruler requested assistance. That evening the request duly arrived, and Elworthy ordered the plan put into effect.

Considerable problems were now created when Turkey and Sudan suddenly denied Britain overflying rights, which delayed getting troops to the area. The only immediately available troops were the commandos in the *Bulwark*, by then off Kuwait, together with the *Loch Alvie, Striker,* and *Meon.* The LSH's equipment was vital for communications within the local area and with London. Despite difficult conditions caused by the hot *Shamal* wind, at 0900 a Kuwaiti helicopter led the *Bulwark*'s Whirlwinds into the still incomplete "new" airfield close to the town. The commandos immediately moved twenty-five miles north to dig in on a strategic ridge line. To give armored support, HMS *Striker* also landed its half-squadron of Centurions, although not without some difficulty as the specially prepared concrete ramp had been removed. Air cover was provided by RAF Hunters of 8 Squadron flown in from Bahrein.[7]

Further reinforcements arrived as soon as possible. On 1 July the *Loch Fyne,* the third Persian Gulf frigate, sailed from Karachi after early completion of a self-maintenance period. The available landing ships and craft brought ashore the second half of the tank squadron and an armored car squadron. As new plans were hastily improvised by the RAF, the air-lift of troops went ahead, assisted by the partial relaxation of the overflying bans. By 7 July no less than five more Army infantry battalions had been flown to the area, some units from as far afield as Ceylon. In Kuwait itself by 9 July there were almost 5,700 British service personnel, among them 45 Commando flown in by the RAF from Aden. The Second RAF Hunter Squadron at Bahrein, 208, was also sent to Kuwait, and a force of Canberra bombers was formed at Sharjah. Radar cover from the *Bulwark* proved remarkably effective (out to 80 miles), but the fighter control situation was greatly improved by the arrival on 9 July of HMS *Victorious,* which had been on her way to Hong Kong in company with the destroyer *Cassandra* and the modern frigate *Lincoln.* The force was ordered to turn back and proceed with all despatch to Kuwait. The frigate's relatively low speed (she had been designed as a convoy, not a fleet, escort), plus the need for fuel economy due to a shortage of tankers, meant that the force could only cruise at 22 knots. The carriers' arrival in the Gulf area, however, transformed the air situation for the British, not only because of the *Victorious*'s Sea Vixen and Scimitar fighters, but also due to her advanced 984 radar and aircraft control facilities. Ground-based RAF radar was not available until 18 July.

If the forces in Kuwait were dependent on maritime forces for their communications and air cover, especially in the early stages, they also relied on the sea for logistic support. Britain's available airlift was incapable of bringing in supplies as well as troops, and the *Bulwark*'s helicopters were useful ferrying supplies to the forces in the forward positions. Stockpiles in Kuwait were used, as were those in Bahrein, with both the Amphibious Warfare Squadron and the *Empire Gull* bringing up the supplies. Royal Fleet Auxiliary tankers and stores ships also proved their value in sustaining the force at sea and ashore.

Further naval reinforcements were sent. Egypt supported Britain's action, and permitted the light fleet carrier *Centaur* to pass through the Suez Canal on 5 July, along with the "Battle"-class destroyers *Camperdown, Finisterre,* and *Saintes,* and the LST *Messina.* Another "Loch"-class frigate, *Loch Insch,* was also brought down from the Mediterranean, and the two more modern frigates, *Llandaff* and *Yarmouth,* arrived from the Indian Ocean. "Ton"-class minesweepers were also deployed. The *Centaur,* together with other units, was held back at Aden until she was needed to relieve the *Victorious* and her escorts at the end of the month. The whole operation was controlled by the CinC at a joint headquarters set up at HMS *Jufair* in Bahrein.

This rapid reinforcement operation achieved its objective. Iraq did not attack Kuwait, which was soon accepted as a full member of the Arab League. One cannot say how far the British action did deter Iraq, but it was a significant factor to add to all the other disincentives to aggressive action. Although everything did not go smoothly, and it was perhaps lucky that no fighting ensued, the operation was a very useful demonstration. The Admiralty could point to the vital part played by naval forces from carriers to logistic vessels. It could also make capital of the problems of acclimatization faced by the troops flown in from the U.K., since the

Bulwark had been much in demand as an air-conditioned haven from the Arabian heat! The chiefs of staff in general saw Kuwait as a vindication of their concepts of strategic mobility, and Harold Watkinson, the new minister of defense, told the House of Commons the following spring that the operation was used as the foundation for "much of our future planning." The Americans were also making much of the Kuwait experience. The McNamara Pentagon was pushing hard the idea of limited war and its view that Britain should maintain Western conventional capabilities in "her" Indian Ocean area. British withdrawal would create, it was felt, a power vacuum vulnerable to Soviet exploitation, as the U.S. navy was unwilling to extend its strategic obligations to these waters.

The planning to which Watkinson had referred began in secret at the end of 1961 in a Chiefs of Staff Committee study of Britain's defense commitments and capabilities over the next ten years. The study, which appeared in 1962, emphasized "East of Suez." War in Europe was very unlikely, the paper argued, given the nuclear balance and the growing confrontation between the U.S.S.R. and China. The growing process of decolonization meant an increased likelihood of trouble in Africa and Asia, problems that would be exploited by both Russia and China. Britain, therefore, ought to be increasingly prepared to intervene in these areas, and "this would be her major military role over the next decade."[8]

To sustain this role Britain would continue to spend some 7 percent of GNP per annum on defense, a steadily increasing sum in real terms assuming an economic growth rate of 4 percent per year. This would sustain some re-equipment, although the U.K. would only have a front-line strength that was able to carry out one large operation at a time and no more than one a year. Her reserve capability, or lack of it, meant that there were also limits to the number of minor peacekeeping operations she could carry out. This meant that some care would have to be exercised to make sure that commitments did not outrun capabilities.[9]

Many of the arguments and principles of the chiefs of staff study were reflected in the 1962 Defence White Paper that set out the government's "Five Year Plan" for defense. The paper defined Britain's defense policy as having three objectives:

"(a) to maintain the security of this country,
(b) to carry out our obligations for the protection of British territories overseas and those to whom we owe a special duty by treaty or otherwise,
(c) to make our contribution to the defence of the free world and the prevention of war in accordance with the arrangements we have with individual countries and under collective security treaties."[10]

To ensure the fulfilment of these objectives the White Paper reemphasized the importance of air and sea mobility at a time when the usefulness of fixed bases would become increasingly dubious. Britain's forces had to be "carefully balanced . . . to deter every form of aggression and military threat," although a major war would inevitably escalate to the nuclear level.

The White Paper did not place much importance on Europe or even the Mediterranean as the area where Britain's conventional forces might find their main employment. The paper emphasized the increasing importance of Aden as a British base and of amphibious forces in military operations in the Gulf area. As for the Far East, the paper welcomed the setting up of the wider federation of Malaysia. This combined Malaya, independent since 1957, with the self-governing British colony of Singapore and Britain's colonies in North Borneo and Sarawak. The whole area would be an independent sovereign state, but would receive British protection under an Anglo-Malaysian defense agreement.

It was again no coincidence that the specific discussion of the Royal Navy began with the statement ". . . the sea may in certain circumstances be the one open highway for strategic movements free of international political hindrance." It was seen, therefore, more as a medium for deploying military power than as a highway upon control of which Britain's survival depended. "Balanced" task forces with undersea, surface, air, and amphibious capabilities could exert "seaborne military and air power . . . wherever our interests require it, to preserve or, if necessary, restore the peace."[11] The oft-quoted mobility and flexibility of sea power were asserted once more to make the point that a navy could cope with the rapid changes of the contemporary world. Ships could be "redeployed and concentrated wherever our policies require." Almost as an afterthought was the statement: "A continuing need will be for effective and up-to-date antisubmarine forces and equipment." The emphasis was entirely on projecting power ashore, rather than engaging in traditional naval operations, and a new amphibious warfare organization was announced, a new Joint Service Staff being set up under the chairmanship of a deputy chief of Defence Staff. Amphibious Warfare Headquarters was subsumed in the new framework.[12]

The paper expected Britain's naval posture over the next ten years to be in general an incremental evolution of the fleet as it existed in 1962. The associated "Statement on the Naval Estimates" spelled out its shape. The operational fleet was essentially the Sandys/Mountbatten mix—four strike carriers, two commando ships, four cruisers, two new guided-missile destroyers, twenty conventional destroyers, thirty-two frigates, thirty submarines (including the first SSN), thirty-seven coastal and inshore minesweepers, and seven amphibious warfare vessels. The last named were to be replaced by the new assault ships, the second of which was to be ordered in the coming financial year. The commandos were also to be further reinforced and strengthened by increasing unit size from 600 to 750 to improve combat sustainability and autonomy (a special Army commando artillery unit had been formed in 1961). Four more guided-missile destroyers were now on order, and four older "Battle"-class destroyers were in the process of conversion to fleet aircraft direction ships (a program whose usefulness had been confirmed by the lesson of the *Lincoln* struggling to keep up with the *Victorious*). One C-class destroyer was also being modernized (she was the eighth, and last, of these ships to receive the modernizations planned a decade before).

Since 1957 frigates had outnumbered destroyers in the escort force, and separate "frigate" and "destroyer" squadrons were replaced by mixed "escort squadrons" as new frigates came into service to replace old destroyers. The first "Tribal" second-rate general-purpose frigate was commissioned in 1962 and sent to the Gulf. That year's White Paper also mentioned the ten ships of the *Leander* class that had been ordered. These fast twin-screw vessels were based on the older Type 12s, combining the speed and sea keeping of this design with a Type 965 long-range radar and weapons-delivery helicopter as mounted on the "Tribal." Stabilizers were fitted to allow helicopter operations in as wide a range of weather conditions as possible, the bridge layout was improved, and accommodations enhanced. The *Leander* seems to have originated as a modification of the Type 12 design originally

The *Danae* was the last of the sixteen original *Leander*-class frigates, being laid down in 1965 and completed in 1967. She shows off most of her general-purpose capabilities in this photograph: twin 4.5-inch guns, 20-mm guns in the bridge wings, Sea Cat point-defense antiair missiles, 965 air-warning radar, and Mark 10 ASW mortar. Hidden from view is the main armament, the Wasp helicopter. Instead, the flight deck is filled by the *Danae*'s ship's company smartly attired in tropical rig and perhaps as important to her "peacetime" role as any weapons system. A handsome and well-turned-out ship, the *Danae* demonstrates the way the British naval presence was maintained in the Far East in the closing days of "East of Suez."

undertaken for the Royal New Zealand Navy. To provide for the extra top weight and space requirements the internal arrangement of the ship was almost completely altered. The forecastle deck was extended through to the after end of the ship, and heavy items of equipment, such as the diesel generators, were mounted much lower in the hull. The greatest benefit was, however, obtained from combining the water ballast and fuel tanks, water being let in as fuel was consumed in order to maintain the stability of the ship. (This system was also adopted in the large guided-missile "destroyers.") The Admiralty was offered the new design and took it, the three Type 12s laid down in 1959 being converted to the new configuration while under construction. The fifth Type 61, HMS *Coventry*, ordered but never laid down, was also changed to a Leander, HMS *Penelope*. The *Leander* herself was commissioned in 1963 and soon proved herself an excellent task-force escort. Her charges would now be carriers, amphibious ships, or at least RFAs; the original concept of the Type 12 as a convoy escort had now receded. Design work was also being carried out on an ultra high speed (42-knot) frigate, the Type 19, but this was eventually abandoned. The *Leander* was a much more practical and cost-effective warship, and no less than twenty-six were eventually built.[13]

It will be noted from the above that the active cruiser force was now down almost to the level envisaged in the 1957 White Paper. All three of the *Tiger*-class ships were now in service, their belated completion (eighteen to nineteen years between laying down and commissioning) having become an item of some public and parliamentary concern.[14] The fourth cruiser was a World War II "Colony"-class vessel, HMS *Bermuda,* a ship that had received some modifications for peace-time duties but not a complete modernization. Of the remaining old cruisers, the *Belfast, Sheffield, Gambia,* and *Mauritius* were in reserve or under refit. The *Swiftsure* was in the middle of her large repair, when the decision was made to recommission instead a second commando carrier, HMS *Albion*; the choice of which ship had the higher priority for scarce resources was a clear one. In 1958 Mountbatten had been replaced by Admiral Sir Charles Lambe, a very pro-aviation officer. His Naval Staff would see the *Albion* as a much more flexible instrument than a rather obsolete cruiser, even for flag-showing duties. Moreover, a "large repair" cruiser was almost useless for hot war functions; a commando carrier was at least useful for ASW. The repair was duly abandoned in 1960, and the *Swiftsure* was towed away from Chatham Dockyard for scrap amid rumors of structural problems. As the "Counties" came into service, the need for conventional cruisers diminished anyway, but the *Tiger*s could not just be thrown away. This would not only have been politically inexpedient, but they did have some use as command ships and as troop transports, a traditional Cold War cruiser role that the Admiralty had made much of in the days before commando carriers. A cruiser's guns meant that useful support could be given if required, and to combine this with a capability to transport and land about 450 troops in a more modern manner, it was suggested that some ships—the three *Tiger*s at least—might be rebuilt with a new after section consisting of a helicopter hangar and flight deck.[15]

The official statements on naval policy kept returning to the central importance of amphibious warfare in the new naval strategy. The aim was to have the capability to put two battalions ashore at short notice, with the capacity to expand the force to a full brigade size if a little warning was given. Not only were the two LPDs on the way, but also their associated landing craft (LCM), the first serious small landing craft program since 1945. The civilian-manned LSTs used as army logistic transports also needed replacement, and in August 1960 the chiefs of staff authorized the construction of the prototype of a replacement 3,720-ton Landing Ship Logistic (LSL). Called *Sir Lancelot,* she was launched in June 1963. On the recommendation of the again renamed Joint Warfare Headquarters, these ships were designed to be able to land equipment over beaches as well as to operate as more normal transports. The intention was to land up to 350 troops and their equipment. The ships were to be twice as fast as previous LSTs, with a maximum speed of 17 knots. At a speed of 15 knots they were to have a cruising range of 8,000 miles. The *Sir Lancelot* was a success, and six production sister ships were launched in 1966–67. The original intention was that, like their predecessors, these ships would be operated by a shipping company on behalf of the Ministry of Transport.[16]

The 1962 Naval Estimates spelled out the scenario for the operation of this new fleet in some detail. The paragraph that summed up "the role of the Royal Navy" is worth quoting in full:

> In peace-time the ships of the Royal Navy are stationed all over the world. But when danger threatens they can be quickly assembled to take their place with the Army and Royal Air Force in combined operations to meet the threat. Every ship has her part to play. The commando ships and assault ships put ashore the spearhead of the landing forces with their guns, tanks and vehicles.

The aircraft carriers provide reconnaissance and tactical strike ahead of the landing; air defence for the seaborne force; and close support for the troops ashore—especially when this cannot be done, either adequately or at all, by land based aircraft. Cruisers and escorts reinforce the air and anti-submarine cover, direct our aircraft and give warning of the enemy's and use their guns for bombardment if required. Submarines provide additional protection against hostile submarines and carry out reconnaissance and minelaying. The mine-sweepers clear a way to the land.[17]

In the center of the document was a sketch of such an Amphibious Task Force to make the point still further.[18] It was a far cry from Cunningham's diatribe of fifteen years before: amphibious warfare was now the acknowledged role of the Royal Navy. There was *no* mention of other kinds of operations.

In order to sustain this kind of capability, afloat support became ever more crucial. This emphasized the role of the Royal Fleet Auxiliary, the state-owned and run, but civilian-manned, organization that maintains the Royal Navy's fleet train. The Admiralty intended to replace all the ships designed to replenish ships at sea with oil, fuel, ammunition, and other supplies and stores. By 1962 the program was well in hand. The Naval Estimates Statement listed four new replen-ishment tankers of the "Tide" class. The *Tidespring*, the latest ship that was about to be launched, was the first of a pair fitted with a helicopter hangar following the lessons of Kuwait.[19] Other RN-manned support ships were being modernized or converted also, notably the light fleet carrier HMS *Triumph*, which became a mobile heavy repair ship for Far East service.

To help sustain the escorts deployed "East of Suez," the light fleet carrier *Triumph* was converted into a heavy repair ship between 1958 and 1965. Here she is at Singapore with two Type 12s to port and a Type 15 to starboard. The *Triumph* returned to the United Kingdom in 1972 with the withdrawal from "East of Suez" and was scrapped in 1981, just before she might have been of considerable use in the Falklands War.

As for the other light fleet carriers of the *Colossus* and *Majestic* classes, their fate was sealed by the decisions on the Reserve Fleet and the diminished perceived need for escort carriers for a future general war. After periods in reserve, the *Glory* was broken up in 1961 and the *Ocean* and *Theseus* in 1962. The year 1961 also saw the completion of the *Hercules* for India as the *Vikrant*. Completed to full modified *Majestic* standard with steam catapult and partially angled deck, she could operate Sea Hawk fighters and French Alizé ASW aircraft (similar to the Gannet), but these limited capabilities were not deemed to be worth the cost and effort to give similar treatment to the *Magnificent* and *Leviathan* for the Royal Navy. The two ships lingered on for a little longer, but the *Magnificent* eventually went for scrap in 1965, and the poor, incomplete *Leviathan* was finally towed away from Portsmouth in 1968. She had already been heavily cannibalized for spares for her sisters, notably in 1965–66 when her boilers were used to refit the Dutch *Karel Doorman*. On scrapping, her turbines were removed to refit the latter ship as the Argentinian *Veinticinco de Mayo*.[20]

Modern aircraft were even stretching the larger 22,000-ton light fleet carriers of the *Hermes* class to their limits. The *Albion* and *Bulwark* were converted to helicopter carriers, which solved the problem in one way. HMS *Centaur*, with her interim modernization, could operate Sea Vixens and Scimitars. She would not,

The East of Suez presence of the 1960s is typified by the carrier *Hermes* in full strike carrier form complete with 984 radar, fully angled deck, and an air group of Sea Vixen fighters, Buccaneer bombers, and Gannet airborne early-warning aircraft. Maintaining even a small carrier like the *Hermes* at sea demanded heavy investment in afloat support, like the tanker *Olwen* on the left of the picture and the air stores vessel *Reliant* on the right.

however, be a very suitable platform for the new Buccaneer, which was first deployed in the *Ark Royal* in 1963. The *Hermes,* equipped with more powerful steam catapults, improved arrester gear, and a fully angled deck, could operate Buccaneers satisfactorily, but was only big enough for half a dozen or so in addition to her fighters and ASW aircraft. Even the modernized fleet carrier *Victorious,* which took over the first Buccaneer squadron later in 1963, had difficulties with aircraft of the latest standards of performance, and FAA attrition rates were high. Neither the *Hermes* nor the *Victorious* met the full requirements of modern strike carriers. The margins for error were very narrow, and it is a tribute to the high quality of the British carrier and air crews that operations were carried out as successfully as they were.

A light fleet carrier in the 30,000-ton *Hermes* category had remained in the building program after the proposed 50,000-ton ship was abandoned in 1953. Vertical take off and landing aircraft were considered for the smaller carrier, but despite work in Britain on such aircraft, the Naval Staff view in the late 1950s seems to have been that viable operational types were still a long way off. Although a "modified *Hermes*" would have had several advantages (lower capital and operating costs and, perhaps even more important, economy in drawing office resources), she would have only a minimum capability to operate the "conventional" high-performance aircraft expected to be in service in the 1970s and 1980s. So the Royal Navy's carrier ambitions grew once more. In early 1959 an Admiralty Committee was set up to look at the carrier replacement problem. It called for all five strike carriers (the *Ark Royal, Eagle, Victorious, Centaur,* and *Hermes*—the last named just approaching completion) to be replaced by five new large fleet carriers. The first named would replace the *Victorious* in about 1970–72. The whole class would be complete by about 1980.[21]

The Air Ministry was firmly against such a scheme. The Sandys White Paper's more extreme pro-missile proposals had been quietly reversed, and there were still some manned aircraft planned, notably the TSR2 long-range tactical bomber, a design to replace the existing Canberra. Mountbatten, as chief of Defence Staff, strongly opposed this aircraft as being too expensive. He doubted if it would ever be procured and tried to force the Royal Air Force to buy the Navy's Buccaneer instead. This the Air Force firmly resisted. Indeed the RAF's view was increasingly that the East of Suez scenario should sustain TSR2 and other land-based types as the primary providers of air power for limited war. The Air Ministry had been prepared, always a little reluctantly, to tolerate carriers as long as they were used for "naval" purposes, i.e., attacks on ships or submarines, at sea, if not in harbor. Indeed, carrier-based aircraft could allow economies in land-based RAF maritime reconnaissance and strike aircraft. Now, however, the two services were in direct competition for the same roles, and the Air Ministry, increasingly annoyed at the CDS's tactics, forged an alliance with the Treasury, which was fed with counter-carrier arguments. The chancellor was understandably concerned about the carrier's apparently enormous cost. A large fleet carrier with a £50 million price tag seemed to be an expensive single investment, one that might conceivably disappear in some future wartime attack by increasingly sophisticated weapons or one that might even prove vulnerable to a peacetime accident.[22]

The Board recognized the sensitivity of the situation and trod carefully. Instead of the five fleet carriers recommended by its own enquiry, the Admiralty proposed four, a compromise figure large enough to be cut but small enough to stand a slight chance of acceptance, at least as a future planning target. In early 1960 the plans were presented to the chiefs of staff, where RAF opposition became manifest. The Admiralty had a useful ally in the minister of defense, Mr. Harold Watkinson, a former naval officer and a great improvement, from the Admiralty's point of view, over Duncan Sandys, for whose departure the Admiralty had waited before unveiling its plans. Watkinson was "a businessman who believed in letting the professionals run things while he played an unobtrusive role."[23] He was much under the influence of the chief of Defence Staff, Mountbatten, and was in general in favor of the navy's carrier ambitions. He did make one condition, however, for his support. He wished the Admiralty to join with the RAF in the development of common supersonic fighter aircraft to replace both the former's Sea Vixen and the latter's Hunter. Somewhat reluctantly the Admiralty went along with these ideas, and preliminary studies began, at first to an extremely ambitious requirement for a Mach 2.5+ "fighter/strike" aircraft, OR346, for which "swing-wing" designs were considered.[24]

Unfortunately for the Admiralty, the two services were soon looking for two different kinds of aircraft. The navy was after an advanced interceptor/strike aircraft of more or less conventional layout for operation with catapult and arrester gear from existing and proposed carriers. The Air Staff soon began to take a more optimistic view of vertical/short take off and landing (V/STOL). This was part of a more general emphasis on the limited war role of the RAF, something that predated Skybolt cancellation but was further strengthened by it. Apparently doomed, first of all to be an organization devoted to maintaining missile silos and flying transports and then to acting as a provider of mobile launching platforms for ballistic missiles, the Royal Air Force had felt the need to concentrate on a role that was at once more rewarding professionally and lucrative in budgetary terms. The result was an "island base scheme" by which RAF combat aircraft and transports, it was argued, could match the capability of aircraft and commando carriers. The Air Ministry argued that, based on such places as Ascension, Tristan da Cunha, Prince Edward, Aldebra, Diego Garcia, and Socotra, its land-based combat aircraft could provide air cover for troops landed by air transports. The latter could be moved by an all-British air route to the point where they were required. Moreover, a new fighter/ground-attack aircraft and a tactical transport, both with V/STOL capability, could provide support without the necessity for airfields.

It seems that the island base concept was first proposed in 1960 as a means of circumventing the Middle East air barrier, but it soon acquired wider overtones in self-conscious opposition to the navy's carrier plans. The Air Staff felt that Britain, in the long term, could not afford two limited-war air forces and that it was their business to provide the one that *could* be afforded. The island scheme was submitted to the Chiefs of Staff Committee in "broad outline" in 1961, only to receive a cool reception from Watkinson, Mountbatten, and Sir Caspar John, the first naval aviator to be first sea lord and a strong fleet carrier supporter. Studies went on and by March of 1962 the minister of defense announced publicly that they were in progress. If the COS Committee refused to sanction island bases, it would not sanction the carrier either. Apparently the chief of the Air Staff consistently vetoed a consensus position in favor of the ships. It is possible that if John and the Naval Staff had been willing at this stage to accept a smaller ship, it might have separated the Air Ministry from their Treasury allies sufficiently to tilt the balance in favor of a pro-carrier decision.[25]

The Admiralty, however, was set on a full fleet carrier and, moreover, seemed to be getting its foot in the door. The 1962 Statement on the Navy Estimates stated that although there was "no need to order a new carrier yet . . . the necessary design work . . . had been put in hand."[26] The lines of a major inter-service controversy, perhaps the greatest such controversy of the entire postwar era, were being drawn. Intense activity went on behind the scenes as both sides tried to make their respective cases. The Admiralty at first seemed to have the upper hand. Watkinson was a ready listener to arguments about the high cost of inflexible, immovable fixed bases, even island bases, in both financial and political terms. Eventually the minister decided to make improvements to a "few selected airfields . . . but nothing more."[27]

The minister was, however, holding out for his common fighter ideal that was now beginning to take shape in a form that was both new and unwelcome from the navy's point of view. The 1962 White Paper had spoken, rather darkly and a little ominously, of a new RAF V/STOL type being "capable of operating from the carriers of the day."[28] Two months later a new joint staff requirement (OR356/AW406) was drafted and issued by the Naval and Air Staffs. By August 1962 Hawker was offering two versions of an advanced Mach 2 V/STOL aircraft, the P1154. The naval version was a twin-engined, two-seat carrier-based interceptor, the air force machine a single-seat fighter/ground attack aircraft. Six months later it was announced that two hundred of the former aircraft were planned, and four hundred of the latter. The Naval Staff had little faith in this new aircraft. The fleet carrier supporters were also anxious about the renewed implication that a smaller carrier might serve as a V/STOL ship.[29]

"Political" considerations, however, advised naval support for the P1154. The joint project was firmly endorsed by the new minister of defense, Peter Thorneycroft, who was appointed in mid-1962. The change of minister had little to do with defense. It was part of Prime Minister Macmillan's remarkable major cabinet reconstruction of July that year. Watkinson did not intend to continue in office after the next election and resigned at the prime minister's request. Thorneycroft had been minister of aviation, and initially he shared Duncan Sandys's doubts about the carrier program; indeed, he made his disbelief in the continued usefulness of carriers only too obvious. In order to get an independent view, the new minister appointed a committee of scientists and other experts, but with no naval representation, to look at the problem. It was chaired by J.C. Kendrew, a part-time scientific adviser to the Ministry of Defence.[30]

Perhaps a little to the minister's surprise, the Kendrew Committee came down firmly in favor of the new carrier program. With the Chiefs of Staff Committee (to which the issue now went) still deadlocked, Mountbatten, chief of Defence Staff, was able to present to Thorneycroft his own pro-carrier views, together with a set of Admiralty papers setting out the case for a continued strike-carrier capability. This new study emphasized the sophisticated equipment that was being supplied to potential enemies in South East Asia, such as Indonesia. Small, missile-armed fast patrol boats were coming into service. If the fleet was to be operated against such forces it would need protection, and carrier-based aircraft seemed to be the best way of doing so. The alternative, it was argued, was developing guided-missile ships that might be equally costly but which would be much less tactically flexible. Thorneycroft seemed genuinely convinced and said he was willing to approach the Cabinet Defence Committee with a proposal for new carriers. In return, the Admiralty, which really wished to ditch the P1154, did not press for its cancellation in favor of the option it now preferred, the American Phantom.[31]

So in the spring of 1963 the Admiralty received the welcome news that Thorneycroft approved of new carriers and that he was willing to back it in Cabinet Committee. There would be opposition, however—from Sandys, who was now commonwealth and colonial secretary, and from the air minister. The Defence Ministry felt that to ask for four new carriers was to ask for trouble; two seemed the safer bet. Lord Carrington, the young and able first lord, and Sir Caspar John reluctantly accepted. Indeed, their realism was soon to be subjected to further strain. Carrington discovered, when he carried out informal meetings with the Treasury, that there was deep-seated opposition to two ships. Treasury's view was that a modern aircraft carrier with aircraft and other equipment was going to cost about £100 million a unit, £40 million more than the Admiralty's estimate. Given the implications of sanctioning a program of multiples of these expensive ships, all that the Treasury and the new chancellor, Mr. Maudling, would approve was one new ship and two modernizations to existing ships, HMS *Eagle* (already undergoing a massive five-year rebuild) and HMS *Hermes*. This would keep a force of three carriers going throughout the 1970s with at least one deployed on station East of Suez. In effect the new ship would substitute for both the *Ark Royal* (which would not be modernized) and the *Victorious*, both of which were to be scrapped by the early 1970s.[32]

This new plan was not a popular one with the Board of Admiralty, but it reluctantly conceded, knowing that one new carrier would, in effect, commit the government to continue with the carrier task force strategy East of Suez. It was likely that replacement of the other two ships would take place as a matter of course. To create difficulties by continuing to hold out for two new carriers seemed ill-advised. The Admiralty, therefore, strongly backed the new plan when Thorneycroft presented it to the Defence Committee. As predicted, argument was fierce, but with the strong support of the chief of the Defence Staff, the chancellor and the prime minister, the Air Ministry and its allies were worsted. On 30 July 1963 Thorneycroft informed Parliament of the Cabinet's decision to go ahead and build a new carrier. The ship would, the minister stated, operate the same fighter as the RAF.[33]

This policy fell apart within months, although at first in a way that did not entirely displease the Naval Staff. The requirements for the two versions of the P1154 were almost entirely incompatible, despite the best efforts of the Naval and Air Staffs to reach agreement. The officers of the former were not interested in V/STOL, however, because they were, in effect, building these characteristics into the ship rather than into the aircraft. V/STOL added extra weight to the aircraft design, especially as the Admiralty insisted their P1154 be fitted to operate from carriers in the normal way with catapults and arrester gear to optimize its performance. By October 1963 the Admiralty was willing to concede a single-engine, single-seat plane with reduced electronics. A dual-service P1154, with only limited equipment differences, was duly put forward at a top-level meeting on the project. The meeting decided instead to push the simpler RAF P1154 and delay a decision on the naval aircraft for six months. In the following months rumors of the cancellation of the P1154RN became public. After a final attempt to produce an acceptable twin-engined version of the design, using two Rolls Royce Spey jet engines, the decision was taken to select the Spey-engined Phantom as the future naval fighter. The Royal Navy, which had been cross-decking Phantoms in joint exercises for some time as part of a quiet investigation into the American aircraft's capabilities, heaved a metaphorical sigh of relief. The deal was a good one, the aircraft being offered by the USN "at practically cost and including no development charges." The price was increased by the decision to mount British engines, but the latter made governmental approval a good deal easier and gave the promise of higher power at takeoff making the aircraft more compatible with the smaller British ships. The decision was announced at the end of February 1964 and was another vote of confidence in the fleet carrier program.[34]

Moves were afoot, however, which were to make the confidence of 1963–64 turn to ashes two years later. The interservice battle over the carrier emphasized the need for a more centralized control of defense policy, especially as it was becoming clear that even an increasing defense budget could not easily sustain existing commitments with proposed levels of capability. A passionate supporter of further unification was Mountbatten, who, after having his term of office as chief of the Defence Staff extended for another three years in 1961, was offered the Ministry of Defence itself in 1963 as a "non party" post. As in 1949 when Attlee had offered him the same position, he turned it down, being unwilling to be a member of a cabinet to which he might not be able to be fully loyal. Instead, Mountbatten got a further extension in office of a year until mid-1965. His major preoccupation at that time was unification and integration.[35]

The CDS had already taken the lead in setting up unified commands in the Near East (1960), Middle East (1961), and Far East (1962), which also stimulated further measures of unification at the center.[36] In August and September 1962, in secret consultation with his staff as well as with Macmillan, Thorneycroft, and Sir Robert Scott, permanent under secretary at the Ministry of Defence, Mountbatten wrote a powerfully argued memorandum, "The Reorganisation of Defence." On 9 October, the final draft was completed for presentation to the defense minister the following day. Mountbatten called for nothing less than the abolition of the separate service departments and the creation of a truly unified Ministry of Defence under one secretary of state to implement a long-range plan decided on by the Cabinet and Defence Committee. There would be no separate service staffs that could be subsumed into a single organization under the chief of Defence Staff. Thorneycroft passed the paper to the prime minister who, during a week-end's shooting visit to Mountbatten's home at Broadlands at the beginning of November, was soon convinced of the merits of the plan. On 11 November the prime minister, defense minister, and CDS, together with Scott, Zuckerman (chief scientific officer to the MOD), and the cabinet secretary, Burke Trend, met at Macmillan's temporary residence at Admiralty House. Agreement was reached on the basic plan and on holding a series of further meetings to draw up a plan for presentation to the cabinet.[37]

In early December the service ministers were first apprised of their impending doom, the chiefs of staff having been circulated informally with "Reorganisation of Defence." Hardly surprisingly, the three services now united against this threat to their independence. Sir Caspar John was concerned about the timing of the changes, but his two colleagues, the chief of the Air Staff, Sir Thomas Pike, and chief of the Imperial General Staff, Sir Richard Hull, were strongly opposed, the former vehemently so. The three chiefs prepared a paper whose wording Caspar John toned down, saying it was too personal an attack on the CDS. Daunted by the strength of feeling but sensing the possibility of some reform, the prime minister suggested tasking Lord Ismay and Sir Ian Jacob, both ex-army officers with considerable wartime experience at the center of British defense decision making, to take soundings and draw up authoritative proposals for improvements on the general lines suggested by the CDS. Jacob had co-drafted the 1946 reforms that set up the postwar Ministry of Defence in the first place. Now they sketched out schemes that went a great deal further. Jacob did most of the work, interviewing over two dozen ministers and officials. The report, "Principles for Defence Reorganisation," was completed in six weeks, being available by 20 February 1963. It diagnosed "discord, uncertainty and malaise" in top British defense decision making and recommended making a significant, but not complete, move to an integrated Defence Ministry under a single powerful secretary of state. Macmillan accepted these recommendations and Mountbatten, a little reluctantly, accepted them as an interim solution. A special Defence Organisation Steering Committee was set up to draft detailed proposals and plan their execution.[38]

It was duly announced in July 1963 that a unified Ministry of Defence would indeed be created, although, in accordance with the Ismay-Jacob recommendations, the separate armed services would retain their identity as departments right up to chief of staff level. Nevertheless, they would now be in a single building, responsible to a single Defence Council chaired by the secretary of state for defense. The Defence Council would delegate its authority to individual service boards. This meant the abolition of the historic Board of Admiralty. It now became the "Admiralty Board of the Defence Council." Its senior naval member became the chief of Naval Staff and first sea lord, an interesting reversal of titles, and the name second sea lord was retained for the chief of naval personnel. The controller and the chief of naval supply and transport lost their traditional titles of third and fourth sea lords, respectively. The Royal Air Force refused to allow the deputy chief of Naval Staff and fifth sea lord to be given any special title which reflected a special position as head of the Naval Air Service; he became merely DCNS. Mountbatten had been forced to fight hard even for the retention of the title second sea lord, but there was general service consensus about keeping the first sea lord title for the professional head of the Royal Navy. Indeed, Sir Richard Hull, the CIGS, made the suggestion to keep it. As for "Admiralty Board," it might be argued that a reversion to the title "Navy Board" would have revived an even more historic title and been a reflection of the administrative functions proposed for the single service bodies. "Navy Board" had been the actual intention until opposition in the House of Lords influenced the government to revert to "Admiralty."[39]

Nevertheless, the first lord of the Admiralty was to disappear to be replaced by a minister of state. This confirmed what had been the case in reality for some time. As one well-informed historian has argued in relation to the separate service ministers, "Their titles had caught up with their duties as mere middle level administrators, expediters of logistics and super paymasters, and all these duties were now merely delegated to them from the Secretary of State." Mountbatten had persuaded the queen to take back to herself the office of Lord High Admiral. The Board of Admiralty met for the last time in the historic setting of the Board Room on Thursday, 26 March 1964. In future the new Admiralty Board, a mere subcommittee of the Defence Council, would meet across the road in the new "Main Building."[40]

Given the "root and branch" nature of these reforms, it would be easy to overstate their importance. They were not the complete integration that Mountbatten desired, and, indeed, further moves in this direction were delayed until the 1980s. The extent of centralized control would still in large part depend, as it had always done since 1947, on the personality and attitudes of the minister of defense and the backing he was receiving from the prime minister. Moreover, it was specifically recommended by Ismay and Jacob, against Mountbatten's wishes, that the chiefs of staff should continue to express their views collectively to the Cabinet. Only if there was disagreement could the CDS state his own views and, in such a case, he also had to transmit all the views set out by the three separate chiefs of staff. Although the CDS now had a strengthened staff of his own, he had not received official sanction for the independent line he had been taking on some issues, based on the advice of his own personal staff. This had caused much friction with the three services. The situation was compounded also by the decision not even to follow the Ismay-Jacob recommendations that all senior officers should be carried on a single list responsible to the CDS alone. This made it certain that any senior officer who did find himself on the Defence Staff would have, at best, divided loyalties. His commitment to the center might well be in conflict with the loyalties demanded by his own service hierarchy.[41]

There were important changes that decisively weakened the navy's bureaucratic position. No longer did single service ministers have the right to state their views in Cabinet, either in full session or even in the new Defence and Oversea Policy Committee (DOPC) that had been set up in 1962 in an attempt to secure greater coordination of foreign and defense policy. The old combination of a first lord and first sea lord, fully and skillfully briefed by the Admiralty Secretariat, arguing a specifically naval case at the highest level could no longer be the cutting edge of the Admiralty's argument. The reorganization of the Admiralty's civil servants into a unified Defence Secretariat under the central permanent under secretary also weakened their ability to help in the construction of a specifically naval case. Overdeveloped single service loyalties might well be at a discount for ambitious civil servants in the new context.

This put even more emphasis on the debating skills of the first sea lord in the Chiefs of Staff Committee and on the officers of the Naval Staff itself, a load that they were sadly not as well prepared to bear as, perhaps, they should have been. It was not that naval officers were less intellectually gifted than their fellows in the other two services, but that the Royal Navy, in its inculcation of career skills, had never stressed systematic staff training and education in the higher aspects of the profession. Unlike the other two services, such a background was not compulsory for promotion to senior rank. Because of the more practical nature of the seagoing profession, experience and command at sea were rated far more highly in the Royal Navy's culture. When the perspectives gained there had been complemented by the disciplined minds of the Admiralty Secretariat, and presented with their bureaucratic skills, the Admiralty did extremely well. But from 1 April 1964, after a touching ceremony on Horseguards when the Admiralty flag was hauled down from the Old Admiralty Building, the naval officers had a much greater burden to bear. How would they perform against their better-trained and educated opponents, particularly as the minister of defense now had the independent advice of a greatly strengthened Central Staff?

The answer to that question was not long in coming, as this new and unfamiliar bureaucratic framework became the battlefield for an even more hard-fought round of continuing carrier controversy. Before going on to this battle, however, we need to return East of Suez. The navy's role in this area was no mere exercise in showing the flag. Kuwait had proved the Royal Navy's potential in making real displays of force, and even more active operations had occurred in 1962 when an uprising occurred in Brunei, the British protected sultanate in Borneo.

That year saw a significant increase in the normal piracy around Brunei, and the frigate *Loch Killisport*, together with the minesweepers *Maryton* and *Chawton*, showed themselves off the coast "which brought an immediate renewal of confidence and improvement in morale among the local population." The minesweepers had some success in capturing pirate boats, and in August the *Bulwark* and 42 Commando extended the navy's reach inland in the antipiracy campaign. The destroyer HMS *Caesar* arrived to replace the *Loch Killisport* and had further success in apprehending pirates.[42] In December, however, the trouble acquired a more overtly political hue as a "North Borneo National Army," which opposed the incorporation of Brunei into the proposed Federation of Malaysia, came out in armed revolt. The rebellion also involved parts of Sarawak and North Borneo. The revolt came as no surprise to Admiral Luce, who immediately flew in a force of Gurkhas, followed by the Queen's Own Highlanders. One company of the latter was taken from Singapore to the trouble spot on board the destroyer *Cavalier*. The *Chawton*, now accompanied by the *Fiskerton*, asserted control of all boat traffic in the sultanate's waters. The two minesweepers' crews manned a number of commandeered small craft, including two "Ramp Cargo Lighters" that were used to carry a company of 42 Commando, flown in by the RAF, to rescue the captured British Resident and other hostages at Limbang. The commander of this operation was a Captain Jeremy Moore, who was to achieve even greater fame as a senior operational commander almost two decades later.

The convictions of the 1950s Admiralty as to the Cold War utility of cruisers found belated support when HMS *Tiger* carried an infantry battalion to Miri in Sarawak and to the island of Labuan. The problem of landing at Miri was solved by the local British Resident commandeering more local small craft and an old LCT belonging to an oil company. The *Tiger* had left most of her boats back in Singapore in order to accommodate the battalion's vehicles. On 14 December more specialized amphibious shipping arrived at Kuching, Sarawak, in the shape of HMS *Albion*, the second commando carrier, carrying her invaluable Wessex helicopters and assault landing craft and the seven hundred or so men of 40 Commando. HMS *Blackpool*, a Type 12 frigate, also arrived carrying the commander of 3rd Commando Brigade. The *Albion* proved the more recent policies correct as her helicopters provided mobility for the troops ashore. She also acted as a base for a "trouble shooting" reserve and gave vital logistical support. Two more minesweepers, the *Wilkieston* and *Woolaston*, plus the depot ship *Woodbridge Haven* and an RFA tanker, were in the area before the revolt was crushed by the end of the month. The minesweepers carried out coastal patrols while the depot ship joined the *Albion* in providing a vital communications link. It was another display of the usefulness of sea power in a brushfire situation, but the RAF could also take credit for the prompt airlift and for providing support from the airfield at Labuan, just off the coast. In the event, the successful operations against the Brunei rebels were a good example of the benefits of interservice cooperation.[43]

The *Albion* had sailed posthaste from Mombasa, and it was East Africa that provided the next major operation for Britain's East of Suez mobile forces. In January 1964, just as Britain's former colonies achieved their independence, their armies mutinied. The newly emancipated leaders immediately had to appeal to their former masters for aid. Troops, including Royal Marine commandos, were flown to Kenya and Uganda, but the mutiny in Tanganyika saw a more naval response as the rebels held the airfields. The carrier *Centaur,* the last of the original *Hermes* class not to be converted to the commando role, was at Aden on her way east. Her sister, the *Albion,* was at the other side of the Indian Ocean off Borneo. The *Centaur,* therefore, quickly embarked 45 Commando, part of the Aden garrison, and its transport. She also took on board some scout cars and two large RAF Belvedere helicopters, sister aircraft of the Bristol ASW helicopters cancelled the previous decade. The Belvedere's rotors were nonfolding, and these machines took up a large part of the flight deck. This, plus the storage of equipment on deck, closed the flight deck to the operations of all but the Wessex helicopters of the *Centaur*'s ASW squadron. Most of the Wessexes were stripped of their sonars so as to take up the assault role on arrival. With the *Centaur* steaming close inshore to reduce turnaround time, the commandos were flown ashore at Dar-es-Salaam on 25 January, with the destroyer *Cambrian* providing covering fire in the shape of high 4.5-inch air bursts. The mutineers quickly surrendered to this show of force, and the commandos were flown inland to Tabora in three commandeered civilian transport aircraft escorted by the *Centaur*'s Sea Vixens. The latter also covered another peaceful pacification operation at Natchingwea, south of Dar. In all it had been an even more classic peacekeeping operation, one that demonstrated both the flexibility of the carrier and the importance of interservice cooperation. How the ad hoc force would have performed against real opposition, however, was a matter for speculation.[44]

Operations such as this, and the deployments that made them possible, were expensive in terms of money, ships, and manpower. British defense expenditure, after dropping in real terms in the late 1950s, began to edge upwards in the early 1960s. Then in 1964 the defense spending jumped upwards by some 5 percent. In 1982–83 prices the figures look like this[45]:

Financial Year	Defense Estimate
1961–62	14.3 billion
1962–63	14.6 billion
1963–64	14.9 billion
1964–65	15.7 billion

The rise in Gross Domestic Product prevented this increase from creating a still greater burden on Britain's resources. Indeed the proportion of GDP being spent on defense actually fell to about 6 percent, but there was a growing consensus that this was still too much. Even before the election the Treasury prepared a paper for the winner that argued strongly for a significant reduction in defense spending. Moreover, even if more money were spent, it would not buy enough equipment to meet commitments adequately or pay for the increasingly expensive personnel to man it. To maintain only one carrier and amphibious task force East of Suez required up to half of the personnel of the active fleet. Informed commentators assessed that it required two such forces, with a further 50 percent reserve, to provide an adequate Indian Ocean presence. This was beyond the capabilities of even the sizable navy that the Admiralty had saved from the threats of the 1950s. Moreover, the Royal Navy itself was costing in real terms almost as much as the war-inflated navy of 1946–47 and almost 20 percent more than the fleet of a decade before (see Appendix 6).

Warships and aircraft were becoming more expensive at a rate that far outstripped any possible rate of increase of the defense budget. This was mainly the result of the electronic revolution. A *Leander*-class general-purpose frigate had fifty times the value of electronic equipment in her than a prewar destroyer. The same held true for contemporary carriers even before modernization; once, like the *Eagle*, they had received full modernization, the multiplication factor was no less than 250. The prewar *Ark Royal* had cost £3.2 million, her postwar successor had cost £21.5 million to build, and in 1964 her new sister, the *Eagle*, cost £30 million to refit. The new fleet carrier would cost at least twice that sum. The contemporary Sea Vixen naval all-weather fighter was coming off the production line at seven times the cost of its predecessor, the Sea Venom.[46]

It was not just a question of sustaining the active fleet in terms of hardware. Manpower was, if anything, an even more serious problem by the early 1960s. Reenlistment at first seemed relatively healthy, some 62 percent of personnel staying on in 1961 as opposed to 45 percent in 1957, 34 percent in 1953, and only 26 percent in 1950.[47] By 1962, however, undermanning was beginning to lead to strains, as demonstrated by the outbreak of a minor rash of disciplinary problems.[48] Early in 1963 the announcement was made that HMS *Blake*, so recently completed after a very extended building period, was to go in reserve after refit; her seven hundred officers and men were required elsewhere. This event attracted considerable adverse publicity as one of a spate of apparently bad defense decisions. Nevertheless, it was difficult to see what else the Admiralty could have done given the priority of keeping carriers and their modern escorts in commission. Even encouraging retention rates did not mean that there were enough *skilled* ratings to maintain the manpower-intensive cruiser in service. Modern electronics, as well as more expensive hardware, placed very great demands on the navy's manpower. The advent of the Polaris program, which increased authorized strength by 3,000 to 103,000 for 1964–65, made this worse. By 1964 overall retention had slipped back to 55 percent, a reflection of the strain being put on ships' companies. Moreover, recruiting trends, especially among officers, were not very encouraging either. In 1964 the actual, rather than authorized, strength was expected to be at least 2,200 below the new total by the beginning of the 1965–66 fiscal year.[49]

With all these problems it was even more difficult to maintain ships East of Suez in the required numbers. It was something of an achievement to keep two out of the three available strike carriers, plus a commando ship, in the Indian Ocean in the period 1963–64. The new Labour Government, elected in October 1964 with Harold Wilson as prime minister, inherited the problem, which it soon characterized as "overstretch." As the first Labour navy minister, Christopher Mayhew, later wrote, "Desperate devices were resorted to to overcome the Navy's manpower shortage. It became quite common for ships to embark on overseas commissions without their full complement, and with some of their essential equipment unmanned."[50] The 1966 Defence White Paper made the general point of naval "overstretch" with the following table on the average employment of destroyers/frigates:

	Annual Mileage	Annual Hours Underway	Complete Days Underway	Ratio Sea–Harbor
1956–57	27,600	1,950	81	1:4
1963–64	33,450	2,430	142	1:1.5

As the document went on to say: "In these conditions, both recruiting and re-engagement have fallen short of the target set; this in turn has increased the strain on our already over-stretched Services."[51]

One important reason for these problems was the outbreak of the largest single operational commitment of the entire East of Suez period after 1957. This was the "confrontation" with Indonesia when Britain backed the new Federation of Malaysia against a campaign of subversion and infiltration that President Sukarno's Indonesia had opened in 1963. At first, action was confined to Sarawak and No. Borneo (Sabah). Naval helicopters provided vital mobility for British and Gurkha troops ashore, 845 Squadron's Wessexes being detached from HMS *Albion* for use from shore bases, the two most important of which were at Sibu and Nanga Gaat. When the *Albion* sailed for home in February 1964, some aircraft were left behind, the rest of the squadron transferring to the *Bulwark* at Aden. Shortly after arriving, the *Bulwark* made several operational cruises off the Sarawak coast where Naval Party Kilo had been set up to operate small riverine craft fitted with machine guns.

845 Squadron re-formed with Wessex HAS 1 helicopters for service in the Commando carrier *Albion* in 1962. The squadron distinguished itself in operations in Brunei and Malaysia over the next two and a half years. (Imperial War Museum)

A picture that demonstrates the changes that came over the emphases of British naval policy in the 1950s is this study of the frigate HMS *Londonderry*, designed to escort wartime convoys in the North Atlantic, but completed in 1961 to sustain British peacetime interests in tropical waters. The 1960s saw her being deployed both to the West Indies and the Far East.

Off Sabah's coast guardships of various shapes and sizes were stationed, including the old, fast minelayer *Manxman,* recently converted into a somewhat slower minesweeper support ship. The "Ton"-class minesweepers themselves carried out patrols off the coast and up rivers.[52]

In August 1964 infiltration began across the Straits of Malacca into Malaya itself and tension increased. Britain felt that Indonesian claims over archepelagic waters needed a direct challenge, and a powerful task force was formed south of Java with the carrier *Victorious,* on her way back to Singapore, escorted by the destroyers *Caesar* and *Cavendish.* They were joined by the new guided-missile destroyer *Hampshire* and the fast frigates *Berwick* and *Dido.* The intention had been for these vessels to transit the Sunda Strait between Java and Sumatra but, in the event, this was considered to be too provocative. In the context of the Gulf of Tonkin incident, Indonesia felt it had reason to fear a Western carrier air strike. However, no Buccaneers or Sea Vixens appeared over Djakarta, and the task force took the Lombok Strait, seven hundred less-provocative miles farther from the Indonesian capital.

The British were by then demonstrating their commitment to Malaysia's security with a Far East Fleet that was of a size unheard of since 1953. It comprised over a third of the entire British surface fleet and half the carrier force. Two strike carriers were on station, the *Victorious* and *Centaur* (the latter having been sent east at the end of 1963 in great haste), one commando carrier, the *Bulwark,* the large guided-missile destroyers *Kent* and *Hampshire,* seventeen destroyers and frigates (after reinforcement from the Mediterranean), almost a dozen minesweepers, and five submarines. The total number of warships in Malaysian waters (when auxiliaries were included) was about fifty. Two Australian escorts and a New Zealand frigate were also based at Singapore. New Zealand crews manned

two British minesweepers taken from the Singapore reserve, and Australian minesweepers were also used for patrol work.

With a threat of air attack on Singapore and gaps in the radar, HMS *Kent* was
pressed into service as a radar and missile picket in the Malacca Strait. Gannets
landed from the *Victorious* were also used to provide early warning of possible
attack. To combat infiltration into Malaya, the *Bulwark*'s helicopters quickly deployed troops to round up Indonesian parachutists, and HMS *Ajax* foiled an attempted landing north of Kuala Lumpur. Off the Sabah coast the Indonesians fired
at HMS *Maryton,* and another coastal minesweeper, HMS *Fiskerton,* suffered
minor damage off Singapore in an exchange of fire with a sampan that killed all
three Indonesians on board. The mobilization of more reserve minesweepers and
seaward defense boats in Singapore at the beginning of 1965 caused the decommissioning of similar vessels in home waters. By mid-1966 16,000 personnel and
over seventy vessels of various shapes and sizes were tied up in the Far East. Two
major depot ships were also moved to the area, the ex-carrier *Triumph* and HMS
Forth, the old submarine depot ship refurbished to maintain nuclear-powered submarines.

It was against this background of a Royal Navy committed somewhat beyond
its true level of capability that the new government took office. Following Macmillan's resignation in 1963, there had followed the brief Douglas-Home Government under whom the Conservative's electoral fortunes seemed to be reviving.
When the election was held in October 1964, it almost held on to power, but Harold
Wilson's Labour Party won by a very narrow majority. The party had reunited
under Wilson with a new technocratic image, stressing a scientific, progressive, but
pragmatic, approach to solving Britain's domestic problems. No one better typified
the new approach than Denis Healey, the leading Labour defense expert who
became secretary of state for defense when the government took office in October
1964. A leading "defence intellectual" and member of the limited coterie of British
strategists who had begun the Institute for Strategic Studies a few years before, he
had been impressed by the attempts by American Secretary of Defense Robert
McNamara to produce a cost-effective defense posture across the Atlantic. Just as
Wilson tended to regard himself as a British version of the late President Kennedy,
so Healey felt himself to be the British McNamara, using rigorous intellectual
analysis to squeeze the maximum possible defense from the most cost-effective
armed forces. Thus, he hoped, Britain could maintain her commitments at an
affordable price and concentrate on finally solving her long-standing economic
problems, which were only too clear to a government that inherited a balance of
payments problem of crisis proportions.

It must be stressed that at this stage the Wilson Government had absolutely no
intention of pulling out of the East of Suez role; indeed, its commitment could
hardly have been more explicit. As the prime minister announced to the House of
Commons in December 1964: "I want to make it quite clear that whatever we may
do in the field of cost effectiveness, value for money and a stringent review of
expenditure, we cannot afford to relinquish our world role—our role which for
shorthand purposes is sometimes called our 'East of Suez' role."[53]

In his early days as prime minister, Wilson expressed in extravagant terms his
conviction that Britain still had a major role to play as a world power. Britain's
frontiers lay on the Himalayas, he announced, and the United Kingdom would

guarantee Indian security against China. Playing to anti-American sentiment in his own party, Wilson argued for Britain thus preventing an "eyeball-to-eyeball" U.S.-Chinese confrontation in the area, but the prime minister's real aim was to assert a new special relationship with the Americans based on Britain's looking after general Western security interests in the whole Indian Ocean area. The U.S.A. was already beginning to become fully committed in South East Asia. Britain, it seemed, even if she could not provide direct help there, might provide the "peace-keeping" forces a little further west. At the end of 1964 the prime minister and minister of defense visited Washington. Wilson and President Johnson struck up an immediate rapport. The Americans impressed upon their British visitors that they regarded the British East of Suez role as being of great importance and that its continuation would be a factor in their giving Britain further economic assistance. Wilson and his colleagues also realized that a continued emphasis on Britain's role East of Suez was required to persuade Australia and New Zealand to make an enhanced contribution to the defense of Malaysia and Singapore.[54]

In addition to increased hopes for American and Commonwealth assistance the government also expected that East of Suez forces might be less expensive than forces designed to take on the Soviets in Europe. It was in this context that the government anxiously begin to scrutinize the equipment programs planned for the armed forces. Limiting the defense budget's growth soon seemed to be more urgent than ever. The new government's first Budget helped cause a serious run on the pound, and emergency action had to be taken to shore it up. Thus beleaguered financially, the government turned to a defense review. On the weekend of 21–22 November 1964, in preparation for the prime minister's American trip, a major conference was held at Chequers, the prime minister's country retreat, to sketch "the outlines" of the government's defense policy. Cabinet members were invited to Chequers, but not the "single service" junior ministers. The senior naval representatives were the first sea lord and his planning staff. At this conference Wilson announced that there was to be a "sharp cut" in the £2.4 billion budget at 1964 prices planned by the Douglas-Home administration for 1969–70. The three major military aircraft programs were under particular scrutiny. With "overstretch" confirmed by the early presentations at this meeting, Wilson committed the defense establishment to a major investigation into both commitments and forces: "Everything had to be questioned and justified where it could be justified and costed."[55] At this stage it was equipment rather than roles that would come in for the greatest attention. If commitments were indeed to be pruned, it would in all likelihood be the European commitments that went, rather than those East of Suez. Nevertheless, with the RAF even more anxious than ever to justify the American aircraft that they were now being promised if their British machines were cancelled, and with the Treasury and defense secretary increasingly viewing the carrier program as an especially wasteful project, the outlook for the Admiralty Board was beginning to look stormy. Within two weeks of the Defence Review beginning, Christopher Mayhew, the articulate minister of defense (navy) was beginning to feel that the Royal Navy would provide the "fall guys" for this particular drama.[56]

According to his own account, Mayhew asked the Naval Staff to justify the various items in their expenditure plans or "long-term costings." It became clear that either the government had to "drastically reduce the navy's commitments or drastically increase its resources."[57] The latter looked less than likely. On 28 January Chancellor of the Exchequer James Callaghan spelled out to the cabinet his plans for limiting public expenditure growth over the next five years. By 1970 he hoped to be able to lop some £500 million off the general expenditure total, £350 million of which would come from defense. By 1969–70 the defense budget would be held at £2,000 million at 1964 prices, the current expenditure total. He hoped to maintain the limit until 1975. George Brown, ebullient head of the newly created Department of Economic Affairs, emphasized the need for rapid economies. A Labour Government, he reportedly argued, had a duty to give the people the standard of living they expected in voting in the new government. Expenditure on housing and hospitals would also improve industrial relations.[58]

The National Plan published by Brown's department in September 1965 spelled out the reasoning behind the government's policy of limiting the growth of defense expenditure. "The defence effort," it argued, "pre-empts a large part of the productive potential of some of the most important and technologically advanced industrial resources and is a large user of skilled and unskilled manpower." The plan went on to argue that defense was taking up about 7 percent of national output and 5 percent of the labor force. It was consuming more resources than Britain's total investment in industrial plant and machinery, more than Britain was spending on consumer goods, and half as much again as education expenditure. Between a third and two-fifths of British research and development was defense related, and one-fifth of Britain's scientists and technologists were working on defense projects. The previous government, the document stated, had planned to keep defense at about this level as a share of national resources "in a period when a rapid increase is required in production for exports, for import saving and for the modernisation of industrial capacity and when manpower is short."[59] The balance of payments was also a problem. The £262 million of 1964–65 defense expenditure that was "direct overseas expenditure . . . is more than we can afford."[60]

By the time of the appearance of the plan, the Healey Defence Review had been in progress for almost a year. As mentioned above, it had first focused on equipment projects, and the expensive aircraft programs had come in for particular attention. In January 1965 Field Marshal Sir Gerald Templer, chairman of the committee set up to adjudicate between the navy and the RAF on air policy in 1950, was commissioned once more to act as a referee between the services as chairman of a new committee of three senior officers "to determine the most effective and economical organisation for the control of air power in support of national defence policy."[61] The terms of reference were wide, and the implication was that it might come up with radical proposals. The naval representative was the recently retired first sea lord, Admiral of the Fleet Sir Caspar John. In February the announcement was made of the final coup de grace to the P1154 project and its partial replacement by more American Phantoms, 140 aircraft being added to bring the total British Phantom order to 200. V/STOL capability would be provided by a developed version of the existing P1127 subsonic fighter/ground attack aircraft. The HS681 STOL jet transport, an aircraft of extraordinarily advanced design for the 1960s, was also cancelled to be replaced by more prosaic, but much more practical, American Hercules transports.[62]

Much was made at this time of the Phantom's capability for operations from both land and carrier bases. As the 1965 White Paper, an interim report on the Defence Review, which appeared in March put it, "dual capability would increase the flexibility of the force, perhaps making possible a reduction in its size."[63] With rationalization of air power clearly on the agenda, a terrible specter of an air force composed of the new Nimrod jet maritime reconnaissance aircraft and carrier-based Phantoms on the one hand and a fleet of transport aircraft and short-ranged ground-support fighters on the other must have begun to haunt the Air Staff. The latter types had already been joined institutionally in Air Support Command. An Army Air Corps had also been created relatively recently, much against the Air Ministry's will. Might it not be argued at some future date that the army might take over Air Support Command, especially if its combat aircraft were vertical takeoff types, like the Army Corps's helicopters? Might the Fleet Air Arm not then make a bid for the dedicated maritime aircraft? The dread prospect of partition was clearly forming; all the work of Trenchard in the 1920s to prevent such an outcome might well go for nought.

Only a long-range strike capability provided the cement for this increasingly split air force edifice. Moreover, the Royal Air Force clearly resented the strategic bombing role passing formally to the navy. When Mayhew went to see the chief of the Air Staff trying to create a united service front against the Ministry's center, he was told that the Royal Navy had Polaris and, therefore, could not expect a further share in British air power. When the review began, it was planned that the TSR2 would be the RAF's only bomber once the V bombers were phased out. It was most worrying to the RAF when this controversial aircraft was cancelled at a meeting of the Cabinet on 1 April. The price of the program was assessed at £750 million and rising. A proposed order for American F-111 aircraft of similar capability would, it was hoped, save some £300 million, but it was far from clear that the F-111s were indeed to be ordered. An investigation by what was the Cabinet Oversea Policy and Defence Committee (OPD) into an F-111 purchase and an announced option on the aircraft was all the Air Ministry had as comfort. The justification for the F-111 as a long-range theater strike capability now became the core of the RAF case. Since the Phantoms were also mentioned as TSR2 replacements, all two hundred that were to be ordered thus became necessary in the eyes of the RAF to provide the land-based RAF-operated fighter/bomber force. Although not keen on the navy's Buccaneers, the Air Staff also cast covetous eyes on them if nothing better was available. The new Mark 2 model with Rolls Royce Spey engines was a great improvement on the original version, which was both underpowered and relatively short-ranged. The "island plan" was duly revivified as a case for maintaining a British East of Suez air force in the most effective manner possible with a wholly RAF force of Phantoms, Buccaneers, and, if obtained, F-111s. The RAF planners could see clearly that this land-based force *or* the carrier force, but not *both*, could be fitted into the £2,000 million ceiling. If the carrier went and the "island plan" was endorsed, the RAF would be secure as an institution, even without the F-111.[64]

Shortly after the cancellation of TSR2, Healey set up a working party specifically to look into the question of substituting land-based for carrier-based aircraft. It was chaired by the "plain spoken, blunt, at times irascible" deputy chief of Naval Staff, Admiral Sir Frank Hopkins. Hopkins, a distinguished naval aviator and a "tremendously tough" carrier supporter, was the Navy's head of aviation and, as such, the leading naval spokesman in the controversy.[65] His committee totaled about fourteen members, with six naval officers, two civil servants, a senior RAF

Vice Admiral Sir Frank Hopkins leaving the *Ark Royal* on giving up the post of flag officer aircraft carriers. As deputy chief of Naval Staff, he led the Admiralty side in the great carrier controversy of 1965–66. (Imperial War Museum)

officer, and the balance of four to five scientists.[66] The RAF representative was the formidable assistant chief of Air Staff (Policy and Plans), Air Vice Marshal Peter Fletcher, "trained as a barrister and possessed of a quick legal turn of mind."[67] The working party supervised a study in which scenarios such as British military assistance to Malaysia were created and the relative effectiveness of land- and sea-based air power in the given context evaluated. The results were equivocal; land-based aircraft could indeed carry out some of the required tasks, but not as comprehensively as a carrier-based air force. Carrier aircraft were necessities for certain functions.[68]

Nothing had been settled, although Healey was clearly becoming committed to the F-111. He was impressed as much by the style of the RAF case as by its substance. Perhaps more importantly, his acute political instincts told him that only the RAF plan, for all its shortcomings, gave him an East of Suez policy that could be reconciled with the financial guidelines and which had some, albeit sectarian, military support. Indeed, the argument went on for the rest of the year, notably in the ad hoc groups that the defense secretary set up to deal with such problems. Joint RAF-Navy committees considered further scenarios, such as operations to rescue British civilians in Nigeria, Guatemalan invasions of British Honduras, even Argentine operations against the Falklands. The conflict was also thrashed out in the Chiefs of Staff Committee, sometimes with the prime minister present. The Naval Staff did their best and felt, to their own satisfaction at least, that they usually won the arguments on the basis of the parameters given. The Ministry's chief scientist, Sir Solly Zuckerman, gave his full support to the pro-carrier case. The carrier's supporters stressed its capability to be moved to a trouble spot to make a political point, its independence of political strings, and its relative cheapness in foreign exchange compared to land bases. The navy side questioned the costings that formed the basis of the RAF's submissions, in particular the question of the inclusion of base costs. Hopkins had served with the U.S. Navy in the Pacific during World War II. He had close relations with senior American officers, who fed him with more realistic assessments of the F-111's performance than those being used by the RAF. Hopkins and his assistants became increasingly frustrated as the political contexts of the scenarios seemed to be constantly altered by Healey's Central Staff in order to suit the limitations of land-based air power. They were particularly incensed when, in order to improve the F-111's combat radius, Australia was "moved" 600 miles in the required direction![69]

The Air Staff, used to fighting hard for survival, was significantly better fitted by its experience to cope with the new bureaucratic environment. The chief of the Air Staff, Air Chief Marshal Sir Charles Elworthy, shared Fletcher's legal education, and the pair made a formidable debating team. They argued a convincing case that even if land-based air could not do everything the carriers could, it could do enough to maintain British East of Suez commitments at acceptable cost. Much was made of the notionally superior performance of the proposed F-111 force in terms of range and payload and superior "cost per strike." The Air Force argued that twenty-five F-111s based at Singapore, a third of the total of seventy-five, would be able to equal the land-based strike capability of the single carrier the navy would be able to have on station (the navy said this underestimated the carrier's mobility). Similarly the RAF maintained that land-based Phantoms, with in-flight refueling, would be able to cover naval amphibious task forces and convoys up to a thousand miles from their bases. Land-based ex-naval Buccaneers would provide the required antishipping strike capability over a similar range.

Much was made of the carrier's supposed vulnerability, although the navy countered by quoting Vietnam experience and the ballistic-missile threat on the vulnerability of fixed shore bases. The air force also commented unfavorably on the carrier's apparent "slowness" compared to the land-based aircraft's (especially the F-111's) ability to fly at superior speed to its destination, whether it be on deployment or on a combat mission. HMS *Hermes* was especially singled out as a target for RAF studies. The little 24,000-ton ship could only carry seven Buccaneers in addition to a dozen fighters. This, it was held, was the equivalent of only three F-111s in striking power and, moreover, the F-111's would be able to travel to the required area in two days rather than two to three weeks.

The real point, however, was finance. The total cost of a carrier force was put at £1.4 billion over the next decade. This was a comprehensive figure, including the ships' running and refitting costs and aircraft, as well as the extra escorts and auxiliaries that would be required specifically for strike carriers. Infrastructure costs, e.g., dockyards, were excluded. A minimum F-111 force of fifty machines (twelve would be deployed East of Suez) costed out at some £280 million, this figure being arrived at by adding the unit costs (£2.5 million per aircraft) to the running costs over the ten-year period. Again, but much more significantly, infrastructure costs, that is airfields, do not seem to have been taken into account. On these rather special criteria the air force was able to argue that land-based air power East of Suez would cost only 40 percent the price of an East of Suez carrier force.

One weakness of the Naval Staff's case was that it seemed to accept that the RAF money had to be spent in any case, as the F-111s and land-based Phantoms were required not only for use in nuclear war in Europe but also as a vital adjunct to carriers East of Suez. In one scenario in which a carrier-based task force sailed against opposition from Australia to Singapore, operating for three months in a hostile air environment, the Naval Staff accepted that land-based air cover would be essential. Carriers could not keep up operations for ninety days against constant attacks. They could only operate for just over two weeks before having to retire for rest and replenishment. The RAF could make it appear from this that the carrier was just an *adjunct* to rather than an *alternative* to a land-based air force.

This was not the only flaw in the Royal Navy's position. Unlike the RAF, which soon reduced its ambition from seventy-five to fifty F-111s, they felt unable to lower their sights to a smaller carrier. It was a fleet carrier or nothing. Smaller, helicopter equipped, command cruisers were being planned, but as additions for the carrier fleet and as replacements for the existing three cruisers, *not* as potential centerpieces of task forces. The Naval Staff did not regard any ship smaller than their 50,000 tonner as being cost-effective. There were also elements in the service less than wholeheartedly committed to the Admiralty Board's consensus position. The supporters of the surface fleet felt that it might be able to stand on its own without the carrier. Indeed, there was a feeling that the demise of the carrier might give the surface fleet an *enhanced* role as a strike weapon. The submariners shared the surface sailors' feelings. Carriers would mean fewer destroyers, frigates, and submarines; they might mean the end of a "balanced" fleet. Both the vice chief of Naval Staff and second sea lord seem to have had their doubts, the latter being quoted at the time as saying that he did not know where the manpower for the new carriers was going to come from. Opinion within the Naval Staff was that the manpower problems were solvable, and the Admiralty Board remained officially united. Nevertheless, such differences were potentially damaging, particularly given the unity of opinion and purpose on the RAF's side.

The Royal Air Force was out to kill the carrier with little regard for the effect on interservice relations. The first sea lord, Sir Richard Luce, took the opposite view. A reticent and gentle man, he was unwilling to match such a narrow single-service view with a direct naval counterattack. As a submariner, Luce lacked the instinctive personal commitment to naval aviation that might have fired more positive leadership. Hopkins and others found the first sea lord's insistence on a statesmanlike approach deeply frustrating at times, especially when they were not allowed to expose the RAF on such pieces of "sharp practice" as the movement of continents. Perhaps conscious of Mountbatten's alienation of the RAF over the previous decade, the Admiralty Board went out of its way to conciliate the junior service. In August 1965, after one of the periodic ministerial meetings on the Review, Mayhew wrote to Healey emphasizing the need for both land- *and* carrier-based air power to keep a sufficient margin of capability for deterrence and security East of Suez. This remained Board policy despite a reconsideration of options a few months later. In the autumn the navy did consider that it might "declare war on the other two Services" by proposing cuts in the army, cancelling the F-111s, and producing a £2 billion defense policy that included the carrier force. Another option was to obtain cheap American carriers, the *Essex*-class ships in reserve in the U.S.A. Thanks to his American connection, Hopkins was able to obtain the offer of the first of three of these ships, which he urged his colleagues to accept. An ex-captain of the *Ark Royal*, the deputy chief considered these carriers superior to his old command, and certainly much sounder in material terms. He expected to be able to operate them for twenty years. The initial price was low (indeed, the first ship may even have been offered as a gift) but Hopkins's colleagues jibbed at the cost and effort required to modify the vessels to British standards. Inspection of one Essex-class vessel also revealed possible maintenance problems. Moreover, the maximum life expectancy that could be expected for a buy of up to three *Essexes* was eventually assessed as no more than about fifteen years, taking the carrier force only into the early 1980s. This was deemed to be inadequate.

Frustrated in this ploy, Hopkins felt forced to support the full-scale assault on the air force, but this policy was once more rejected by the Admiralty Board. Destroying the RAF's East of Suez posture would, Mayhew later argued, produce a capability "inadequate for the 'East of Suez' role. It . . . would be too thinly spread, would involve far-reaching dependence on the Americans for vital operational support, e.g., for long-range strike reconnaissance and its reaction time in an emergency would be comparatively slow. After considerable heart searching, we decided that, in the interests of the Service as a whole, we should not put it forwards. We knew that we alone had the expertise necessary for making a plausible cause against the RAF's strike reconnaissance requirement. But the RAF had already suffered drastic cuts. Why should our skills be exploited to secure economies in a sister Service which we believed to be unjustifiable? In this instance, we felt, the role of the Treasury officials could only honestly by played by officials of the Treasury. In addition, to be frank, we judged that in a straight fight between the new carrier and the F-111As, the odds were against us."[70]

So the Admiralty Board told the government that a carrier force was an essential part of Britain's East of Suez posture, but that its maintenance would require a budgetary ceiling higher than £2 billion. If the government still insisted on cancelling CVA 01, the Naval Staff suggested that the *Ark Royal* be refitted to squeeze the maximum life out of the existing carrier force, allowing three ships to go on to the mid-1970s. The second sea lord's department was none too keen on this option, as it prevented immediate manpower savings. Difficulties were also foreseen in naval airmen continuing to come forward once the cancellation of the new carrier was announced. At this point at least internal naval doubts were communicated to Healey's staff, but the defense minister was persuaded that the *Ark Royal* option was a viable one.

Mayhew tried to press the Admiralty Board's ideas at the highest Cabinet level, but could not do so given his status in the new Ministry of Defence structure. He was denied access even to meetings of the Oversea Policy and Defence Committee. Luce needed his minister's support when disagreeing with the formidable secretary of state in such high level, strongly politicized forums. On 8 November Mayhew wrote to Healey requesting an appearance to put the Admiralty's case at the meetings that were to take place at Chequers that weekend. This was refused, and only two or three months later was Mayhew, threatening resignation, allowed before the Oversea Policy and Defence Committee to set out his own personal position. Healey was out of the country at the time, and Wilson recognized that the political sensitivity of the situation was such that strict constitutional propriety need not be observed. Mayhew argued that the whole East of Suez presence should be greatly reduced, in which case reductions in the defense budget to £1.8 billion could be possible, or that both carriers and F-111s be procured by a defense budget increased over the government's initial ceiling. He got support from pro-European ministers such as Roy Jenkins and George Thompson, but Foreign Secretary Michael Stewart reiterated the official Foreign Office line that withdrawal from East of Suez was impractical. The withdrawal option was very much Mayhew's own. It had never been presented to the Admiralty Board, but had been created unofficially by the minister's own staff.

Mayhew's arguments were to no avail, however. Wilson and Healey seem to have been impressed both by the nature of the RAF's case and the manner of its presentation. The stress on McNamara-type cost-effectiveness studies clothed the land-based air case with an aura that fitted well with the "scientific planning" rhetoric of the administration. It is probable that Healey was pro-F111 from the start, but the prime minister may have been more open to argument. Eventually, however, Wilson saw the political utility of his defense minister's position. Both alternative options—the Admiralty's consensus position on a higher defense budget and Mayhew's personal line on major withdrawals East of Suez—were politically unacceptable. Faced by the imminent and stark prospect of CVA 01's cancellation, the Naval Staff did at last produce a plan for a navy that contained carriers and which, by cutting back on other forces, could be integrated with Mr. Healey's ceiling, but by then it was too late. The minister stated that the die was cast.

It seems a pity that the latter option was not considered before, but the main reason for the navy's losing the battle seems to have been less the content of its case than the force and skill of its presentation. Given the "political" nature of the problem facing them (F-111 as a solution to the conundrum of how to remain East of Suez on a limited budget), only a strong political campaign fought with no holds barred, both inside and outside the decision-making process, stood any chance of success. Luce was unwilling to stoop to such tactics, and Mayhew's influence was limited by his lowly status in the new institutional context. The forthcoming general election also meant that he had to tread carefully. Neither was he willing to engage in outside lobbying, and there was an insufficient attempt to construct a wide constituency of support as Mountbatten had done seven years before. Winning the intellectual argument that carriers were essential for a continued British presence East of Suez was not enough. This was a game for players, not gentlemen. It was a great pity for the Royal Navy that Mountbatten finally stepped down from the post of chief of Defence Staff in 1965. His successor, Field Marshal Sir Richard Hull, was at best only a neutral in the dispute. Indeed, the defense minister's reluctance to allow yet another extension to Mountbatten's repeatedly extended term of office may have had not a little to do with the desire to get such a powerful (and potentially unscrupulous) carrier supporter out of the way.

On Monday 14 February 1966 the Cabinet considered the Defence Review in a long meeting that went on all day. Mr. Healey made much of the fact that all the services considered an F-111 purchase essential. Some ministers attacked the policy of remaining East of Suez and buying F-111s to do so. This battle rather diverted attention away from the carrier question itself when the matter was raised after lunch. Mr. Healey used some of the RAF's visual aids to make his point. If the minister of transport's diary is to be believed, the anti-carrier argument received a new twist that afternoon: "One new carrier was just not enough to make the

CVA 01—the projected fleet carrier that was the subject of the great carrier controversy of 1965–66. Note the novel flight deck layout. (Imperial War Museum)

carrier fleet capable of doing the full job. We had before us maps showing the
range of coverage by air from a series of small islands. There was not a voice raised
in support of the carrier."[71] Barred from making a last ditch stand perhaps based
on the Naval Staff's latest proposals and making a Cabinet compromise like that
which had saved the carrier program at the end of 1954, both Luce and Mayhew
resigned.

The decision to cancel the project came just as tenders were to be invited from
shipbuilders to build the projected new aircraft carrier. Code-named CVA 01, her
design had started early in 1962 and was now well advanced. Plans were already
boxed to go to the chosen shipbuilders. At 53,000 tons the ship was to have been
bigger than any previously completed British carrier, in the same class as the
American *Midway*s or the cancelled British *Gibraltar*s of 1945. Nevertheless, this
was small by modern carrier standards. The Admiralty had insisted that size was
a crucial constraint from the start. A ship of the American *Forrestal* type, at 60–
80,000 tons or even more, would never have received Treasury approval. Not only
would the ship herself have been costly, but considerable investment would have
been necessary in new dockyards to support her. Various options were looked at
for smaller ships, and a 40,000-ton design had considerable support. Nevertheless,
it was clear that such a ship would sacrifice 50 percent of its capability for a 10
percent reduction of cost, and the design came out at about the *Eagle*'s full-load
displacement, the maximum that had any chance of financial approval. A novel
parallel deck design was drawn up to make the best use of the available space and
many "ingenious ideas were adopted" to get the maximum equipment and the

operation of aircraft in the OR346 class on to a restricted displacement.[72] Only two catapults, however, were possible against the four of a large American carrier, and both deck park and armor protection (even for the magazines) were sacrificed to save displacement. As the design progressed, CVA 01 seemed ever more "costly and unsatisfactory," especially given the usual shortages of design staff.[73] CVA 01's chief designer, L.J. Rydill, went so far as to say that "cancellation was the happiest day of my life."[74]

Not many people within MOD (Navy) felt like this, however, when the news broke that the Royal Navy was going to lose its postwar centerpiece. The bombshell was contained in the extended two-volume Defence White Paper published on 22 February 1966. This argued along the lines of a formula that had been put forward late the previous year, that the gap between resources and commitments could be dealt with by foregoing major military operations that would not enjoy direct American support. The "Defence Review" clearly set out what the "general limitations" on the role of Britain's "major military capability outside Europe" would be. "First, Britain will not undertake major operations of war except in co-operation with allies. Secondly, we will not accept an obligation to provide another country with military assistance unless it is prepared to provide us with the facilities we need to make such assistance effective in time. Finally there will be no attempt to maintain defence facilities in an independent country against its wishes."[75]

This, it was argued, allowed the carrier to be eventually withdrawn. In one of its most famous passages, the paper argued that "only one type of operation exists for which carriers and carrier borne aircraft would be indispensable; that is the landing or withdrawal of troops against sophisticated opposition outside the range of land-based air cover."[76] The roles presently carried out by carriers that would be necessary in future would be fulfilled by land-based strike reconnaissance, air defense and airborne early warning aircraft, by ASW helicopters carried in the surface fleet, and by surface-to-surface missiles mounted in ships. While the fleet was reshaped, the carriers would continue to run "as far as possible into the 1970s."[77] The *Ark Royal* option was taken, and an extensive refit for the ship was announced, together with a reduced naval Phantom buy. The Buccaneer Mk 2 strike aircraft, which had just entered service, would also continue to be procured for the navy. (Ironically enough, the first Mk 2 squadron went to sea in the much maligned *Hermes*!) As for the RAF, fifty F-111A land-based strike aircraft would be obtained which, supplemented by V bombers kept for the theater strike role, would be used for "bridging the gap" until a proposed Anglo-French variable-geometry strike aircraft appeared in the late 1970s. (The latter aircraft, incidentally, never appeared and was replaced by the Anglo-German-Italian "multi-role combat aircraft.")

The 1966 Defence Review caused shock waves to reverberate through the entire Royal Navy, but the service could, in fact, salvage much from the ashes. Despite one announced withdrawal, from the guerrilla-ridden Aden base in 1967, the East of Suez scenario was still apparently alive and well as a rationale for the deployment of the balanced fleet. Just before the publication of the Defence Review, Mr. Healey personally assured the Americans, Australians, and New Zealanders that there would be no reductions of forces while "Confrontation" lasted. When it ended, "the remaining forces, though smaller, would be better equipped" and perhaps based in Australia rather than Singapore, although the potential hosts were

Plans to equip the Royal Navy with modern dock landing ships finally came to fruition in the "East of Suez" years with the construction of the *Fearless* (seen here) and the *Intrepid*. Ironically, shortly after completion the role for which they had been designed was abandoned, but new work was soon found for them on NATO's northern flank. Both played prominent parts in the Falklands War.

none too happy at the latter idea. In any case Mr. Healey gave Singapore's prime minister, Lee Kuan Yew, the impression that Britain intended to remain in Singapore until 1979–80.[78]

To sustain this remaining commitment, many large and expensive vessels would remain in, or be added to, the Royal Navy's inventory: nuclear-powered attack submarines, a command cruiser with helicopter capability, commando carriers, and amphibious assault ships. To help screen these heavy units, a second-generation guided-missile destroyer, the Type 82, was still under development. The *Tiger*-class cruiser conversions were still to take place, now in an ASW rather than amphibious helicopter role. Nevertheless, the commitment to "thrusting power ashore" remained considerable. The new dock landing ships were just appearing. The *Fearless* was already in service, having been completed at the end of 1965. The *Intrepid* was approaching completion, and five more LSLs were also under construction. A new amphibious command structure, with a Commodore Amphibious Warfare and standing staff ready to take control of any amphibious operation that might come along, had been in being since 1964, when, in addition, the Royal Marines central organization had been integrated with the Naval Staff.[79]

Just, therefore, as the Royal Navy was becoming more amphibiously minded and capable than ever, the East of Suez role, for which the navy had been the key, was coming close to abandonment. The thoroughgoing 1966 Defence Review, intended by Wilson and Healey, as the latter assured the Australian prime minister, to be a blueprint for the next thirty years, would soon be seen as yet another futile short-term attempt to make inadequate capability cover over-ambitious commitments.[80] Only a few months after its publication, the Cabinet would be discussing eventual withdrawal from East of Suez. If the Royal Navy wanted a new case with which to argue for its continued existence into the 1980s, it would not just have to reconcile itself to a reshaped fleet. It would also have to think quickly of somewhere else for its ships to be used.

CHAPTER · EIGHT

RECALLING THE LEGIONS

The decision to abandon CVA 01 was perhaps the most traumatic shock to the Royal Navy of the entire postwar period. The fleet carrier had been central to the Royal Navy's plans and self-image for the last quarter century. The Admiralty Board decided that 1966 was the right time for a fundamental in-house review of British naval policy. There was a major change of personnel on the Naval Staff from its head, the first sea lord, downwards. Sir David Luce's replacement was Admiral Sir Varyl Begg, lately CinC Portsmouth, and previously commander in chief Far East from 1960 to 1965. Begg was essentially a surface sailor with a classic background in the gunnery branch and was thus well placed to tackle the task of reorientating the service away from complete dependence on carriers. Begg's approach was a pragmatic and realistic one, verging at times on the overcautious. His public statements loyally expressed the view that although the decision to abandon the large carrier had occurred fifteen to twenty years sooner than expected, it was eventually going to happen anyway as an inevitable result of weapons developments. He felt strongly that the circumstances of his appointment prevented any counterattack at all on the carrier question.[1]

As the main institutional framework for the in-house review, Begg set up a "Future Fleet Working Party" in April 1966 to produce an overall plan for the future navy. Its chairman was the assistant chief of Naval Staff (ACNS) since February, Rear Admiral J.H. Adams, a torpedo and ASW specialist and the first nonsubmariner to command a submarine squadron in recent times. He had also been captain superintendent of the Admiralty Underwater Weapons Establishment, but his last appointment had been command of the commando carrier *Albion*. Adams, a most able and articulate officer, was given the title ACNS(Policy) in July. This allowed him to concentrate on the long-term view, and directly subordinate to him were the Naval Plans and Administrative Planning Divisions along with the Naval Historical Branch to provide perspective. A new post of ACNS(Operations) was created with supervision of all the other previous responsibilities of the ACNS. The first ACNS(O) was Polish-born Rear Admiral J.C. Bartosik.[2]

Admiral of the Fleet Sir Varyl Begg. He had the difficult and thankless task of rebuilding the Royal Navy's morale after the loss of the fleet carriers. His period of office was not without controversy. (Imperial War Museum)

The task of the ACNS(P)'s Working Party, which was given a blank sheet of paper and six months to do its work, was a fundamental reassessment of the role and structure of the navy using the policy-planning techniques of McNamara's Pentagon. A set of assumptions on the desirable future navy were immediately tested against the expected constraints of men and money. The Working Party rightly emphasized the rising costs of both ships and personnel and the total commitment of the government to its defense expenditure ceiling of £2,000 million (at best). The financial threat to sterling was the government's prime security concern. Having established this fundamental fact, Adams's study went on to consider the national strategy that the future Royal Navy should reflect. The Foreign Office was asked for its help but could produce no statement of the future shape of British interests. The Working Party had, therefore, to make its own assessment and concluded that although a future fleet would have to have the maximum flexibility to operate anywhere, the balance of British interest was swinging steadily towards Europe. Imperial and post-imperial policing would thus become less important as a primary naval role. The fleet had to be as capable of operating in the high-threat NATO environment as outside of it. Moreover, Western strategy was moving in a direction that placed a new emphasis on conventional operations as the initial response even in areas where rapid nuclear escalation had been previously assumed. With these points in mind a paper on the "Naval Contribution" to national strategy was prepared (and shown to Mr. Healey) and this provided the basis for a study of "Naval Commitments and Tasks."[3]

Other factors were considered also: dependence on, and compatability with, allies, the state of naval technology, and the extent to which land-based RAF aircraft could provide the capabilities that were lost with the carriers. When taken together with the Naval Commitments and Tasks paper, these all came together in a central "Concept of Operations" study, which covered all aspects of naval warfare. After further consideration of constraints and factors such as the need for high operational availability, a Final Fleet Paper was drawn up. This recommended the continued construction of sophisticated surface escort vessels, although it advocated rather more austere antiair warfare "destroyers" than the cruiser-like vessels of the previous few years. Shipborne helicopters were to be utilized even more than before for such duties as surface search and attack. The Working Party's Sub-Surface Subcommittee favored a continued concentration on nuclear-powered submarines. All this was relatively unexceptional, but when it came to the question of big ships and the extent of the future fleet's "integral" air capability, the Working Party began to tread on very controversial ground indeed.

Given the need for flexibility and the possibility of operating far from the shore, Adams and his Working Party saw no alternative to a big command ship with helicopters and V/STOL aircraft to carry out three duties that could not be reliably provided by other means: airborne early warning (AEW), "probe" (investigation of distant contacts), and ASW search and strike. Adams would have been satisfied with a ship of relatively simple construction, although some of his colleagues disagreed. Whatever their exact shape, however, Begg, the first sea lord, when first briefed on the Working Party's tentative findings, made clear his hostility to any attempt to resurrect carrier-like ships. Adams and his colleagues all felt that their Working Party should have been given this vital constraint at the beginning of their study and that it was too late to turn back. Moreover, Adams had reason to believe that if the Air Staff members could be assured that the V/STOL aircraft would be RAF-operated, they would not create undue difficulties. The Working Party, therefore, persevered with the idea and included a relatively large helicopter/V/STOL ship in the final report. This led to an explosion from the implacable first sea lord. The entire Naval Staff, which had been working "flat out" on the hundred or more papers required by the Working Party, was dramatically assembled to be told that the fruits of their labors were to be shelved and not to be presented to the Admiralty Board. Adams was also told that he was not to be recommended for further appointment. He left the service at the conclusion of his duty as ACNS(P), a departure that was generally considered to have been a considerable loss to the service.

Yet the Working Party had actually achieved a great deal. It had served as both pressure and context to help the Naval Staff sort out its ideas on the nature of a fleet that would no longer be based around the traditional aircraft carrier. Officers who had played a central part in its proceedings gained promotions and went on to important posts on the Naval Staff and Admiralty Board. Admiral Sir Antony Griffin, then a rear admiral and assistant chief of Naval Staff (Warfare), became controller of the navy in 1969–71 with full charge of material policy. Admiral Sir

Ian Easton, then a captain and director of the Naval Tactical and Weapons Division, became ACNS(P) himself in 1969. Admiral Sir John Treacher, as a captain director of Air Warfare in 1966, occupied the key post of vice chief of Naval Staff from 1973 to 1975. Admiral Sir David Williams, director of plans in 1966, became second sea lord. All these officers were able to maintain a personal continuity of policy as to the shape of the navy that would be constructed in the succeeding two decades. The report did indeed provide the plan for the future; Adams and his assistants had not worked in vain.[4]

The deliberations of the Future Fleet Working Party had revealed that even if all possible capability were squeezed out of the budget, it was doubtful whether the affordable fleet could properly maintain its existing commitments. The inescapable implication was that these commitments would have to be cut. The Wilson administration was beginning to agree. The government's hope, of course, had been that the 1966 Defence Review would be a definitive act. It hoped to make no more major changes in defense policy, at least for the lifetime of the new Parliament that was elected in March 1966, shortly after the Review's publication. At that time Labour secured a handsome working majority that was a substantial vote of confidence from the electorate in its performance so far. It was soon clear, however, that the British public's opinion of the government was not shared by foreign bankers. Britain's gold and dollar reserves began to fall ominously. One reason for this was a serious strike by Britain's merchant seamen, which, by stopping exports, had a direct effect on Britain's balance of payments. The strike also increased foreign doubts about the government's ability to control domestic inflation by policies of wage restraint. The government's confidence in its own management of the economy lasted until July when the selling of sterling became particularly heavy. A "re-appraisal" of policy duly began.[5]

On 12 July Chancellor of the Exchequer James Callaghan circulated a paper calling for 500-million-pound cuts in public expenditure. Callaghan was also determined that this should include a specific extra 100-million-pound cut in overseas expenditure. At a Cabinet meeting to discuss this proposal on the 14th, it was clear that most, if not all, of these savings would come from further defense cuts. Government expenditure overseas had greatly increased since the 1950s. In 1955 it had totaled some £128 million; in 1965 payments amounted to £460 million. Moreover, a higher proportion of this expenditure was military—less than half in 1955, almost three-fifths in 1965. Although these figures seemed relatively insignificant compared to a total value of imports and exports of ten billion pounds, many observers were coming to see them as particularly damaging. This was especially so as changing world trade patterns diminished the importance of the sterling area. Until 1959 the area as a whole had usually avoided net currency losses since adverse British trade figures had been offset by a favorable overseas sterling area balance. In the sixties, however, the overseas sterling area began to follow British balance of payments trends. This was because trade between members of the sterling area was becoming less important, trade between sterling area members and other countries more so. Money spent in the sterling area, therefore, would not now necessarily come back to Britain. Defense expenditures in Malaya, for example, were now as potentially adverse in balance of payments terms as expenditures in Germany—perhaps even more so, as the Germans continued to make special provisions to offset the balance of payments costs of the British Army of the Rhine. It was easy to jump to the conclusion, therefore, that expenditure on Britain's overseas military commitments, previously cushioned somewhat by most being within the sterling area, had now apparently become a serious problem, especially when these expenditures came to four times the total "current account" balance of payments deficit. It has since been argued that the government had probably overestimated the leverage they had over the balance of payments by cutting expenditures on forces overseas. There can be little doubt, however, that the conviction that reductions in overseas force deployments would have a substantial part to play in the solution of the sterling problem had become an article of faith by the second half of 1966, particularly to a Cabinet seeking to limit the deflationary impact of their policies on the domestic economy.[6]

With little apparent difference now between the adverse effects of spending money in Germany or East of Suez, the question of where cuts were to fall became a matter of political decision. At the 14 July Cabinet meeting the prime minister had spoken of half the savings being made East of Suez and half in Germany. There was no doubt where the Parliamentary Labour Party wanted them. In May 1966, at a P.L.P. meeting, a motion calling for withdrawal from Singapore, Malaysia, and the Persian Gulf was defeated on a technicality, and both Foreign Secretary Michael Stewart and Denis Healey made conciliatory noises about an eventual withdrawal that led to anxious Australian requests for reassurances on Britain's intentions. The impending end of Confrontation with Indonesia at this time added weight to these fears, and in June, with the deputy prime ministers of Australia and New Zealand and the Australian defense minister exerting personal pressure in London, Wilson was forced to defend his own personal commitment to East of Suez before both Parliament and a skeptical audience of Labour M.P.s.

Defence Minister Denis Healey enjoying a "tot" of rum in the chief petty officers' mess on board the guided-missile destroyer *Hampshire* in the 1960s. (Imperial War Museum)

His stand was comfortably approved by the P.L.P., thanks to packing the meeting with ministers and Labour peers, but it seems that several Cabinet members, including Callaghan and Healey, were beginning to have their doubts. The preliminary consideration of a new move to join the European Economic Community (EEC) also advised against too great a reduction in the British Army of the Rhine, although the initial emphasis was on the BAOR, especially from the chancellor. For the time being ministers still stressed in public Britain's commitment to a continued presence East of Suez.[7]

At the Cabinet meeting on 19–20 July 1966 that had approved the 500-million-pound cuts, including overseas cuts of up to £100 million, it was still far from clear where the overseas reductions were going to fall. The end of Confrontation (it was formally terminated on 11 August) would clearly play a part in allowing savings in the Far East. Mr. Healey expected that these savings, together with financial contributions ("off-set costs") from Hong Kong and Libya, would total some £46 million. Fifty million more might be gained from a new "off-set" agreement with West Germany. The prime minister's 20 July Parliamentary Statement on the economic package made it clear that the government's heavy domestic programs covering industrial investment, schools, hospitals, and housing were safe. Cuts in defense, it seemed, would not only contribute significantly to the total retrenchment exercise, they would go a long way to meeting the specific overseas figure. Soon, a new total defense expenditure ceiling had been developed to replace the old one: £1.85 billion instead of £2 billion. It was also expected that up to 80 percent of the overseas savings could come from the defense budget. This cut was almost equivalent to the total foreign exchange costs of either the German or the Far East deployments.[8]

What was, in effect, a major new defense review began. More studies were carried out, attention being focused on "those areas of the defence programme which had been identified in the first review as possible candidates for economies but which, in the event, had emerged unscathed."[9] In October, after a resolution to withdraw from commitments East of Suez was passed by the P.L.P. with a large majority, Healey reported progress on his new review to a select band of his Cabinet colleagues. Significantly, the ministers were at Chequers to discuss moves towards EEC membership. Healey said that he thought it possible to get below even the £1,850 million limit. He proposed that between £250 million and £400 million should be removed from the defense budget. Costs in Germany would be cut by a third and expenditure East of Suez would be halved—the Middle East commitment possibly disappearing completely. According to some accounts, an "approximate terminal date for withdrawal" from the Far East was considered, but Defence Secretary Healey (as reported by his cabinet colleague, Richard Crossman) cited the pressure from allies as a reason for maintaining some East of Suez commitments for the time being. Crossman reports that he argued that the bullet of complete withdrawal should be bitten then and there, but that his colleagues supported the compromise Healey line.[10]

In December the Ministry of Defence/Foreign Office position came up before the Oversea Policy and Defence Committee of the Cabinet. British forces in the Far East were to be cut by one-half and forces in the Middle East and Europe by one-third. A study was to be made of total withdrawal from the Middle East, and reluctantly it was decided to do a similar piece of work on the effect of total withdrawal from Malaysia. American and Commonwealth pressure still seemed to be an important factor in reinforcing a type of imperial nostalgia on the part of Wilson and Healey. Both the prime minister and the minister of defense supported the idea of the continued relevance of dispersed "penny packages" of ships and men which, they argued, could be extremely effective in exerting a residual level of power and influence.[11]

In February 1967 the regular Defence White Paper gave some impression of how this second phase of the Healey review was going. It had been carefully worded to imply the possibility of further cuts while not unduly alarming Britain's allies. It announced defense estimates of £1,927 million at 1964 prices and also made the idea of a "continuing review" official. The success of British forces in defending Malaysia from Indonesia was emphasized, but, significantly, it was stated that: "Our aim is that Britain should not again have to undertake operations on this scale outside Europe." Nevertheless, "in the meantime," until local forces were in a position to maintain security themselves, British forces would remain. The document confirmed that British forces were to be withdrawn from Aden in 1968, but that forces in the Persian Gulf might be slightly increased to compensate. The withdrawal in the Mediterranean was to continue, while the Navy's South Atlantic Station was to be abolished.[12]

As far as the fleet was concerned, the greatest stress was still being put on amphibious forces, the two commando carriers and the two assault ships, both of the latter now being in commission. New twin-engined Wessex 5 helicopters had greatly enhanced the capabilities of the Fleet Air Arm's amphibious squadrons. Discreetly placed as second in priority came the strike carriers, which were still "a component of the highest importance," at least until new air-capable ships planned for the 1970s were ready. Next came the submarine force with two SSNs just commissioned, the *Valiant* and *Warspite,* three similar boats ordered, and a boat of a new design planned. The last of the *Oberon*-class conventional submarines was about to come into service. As for cruisers, only two conversions of the three *Tiger*-class ships into potential ASW helicopter carriers were mentioned as being in progress, and another implied cut was the mention of only one new Type 82 guided-missile destroyer as being on order, for service in 1971. Four ships had been originally projected. The Type 82 had been conceived as an enlarged *Leander* frigate (hence its "general-purpose frigate" number) with the new Sea Dart surface-to-air missile, the Australian Ikara ASW system, and an extensive electronics suite including Anglo-Dutch radar and a sophisticated ADAWS-2 combat data system. The ships were intended to act as leaders for carrier escort groups and would, it was hoped, be more cost effective than the large, light-cruiser-size "County"-class destroyers—although the Type 82 design had already grown to comparable dimensions.[13]

As for the "Counties" themselves, two modified ships were coming into service to join the four existing vessels and two more were building. The modified "Counties" were equipped with fully computerized combat information systems (ADAWS—Action Data Automation Weapons System). They carried the Sea Slug 2 missile with a limited surface-to-surface capability and it was intended to fit the new missile in the first four vessels in due course (although in the event this never happened). The *Leander*s were in full production, and the ten later Type 12s of the *Rothesay* class had begun conversion to near *Leander* standard with Wasp helicopter, im-

An early concept for the Type 82 destroyer. The design is still visibly based on the *Leander*-class frigate. Note the Anglo-Dutch "Broomstick" radar also planned for CVA 01.

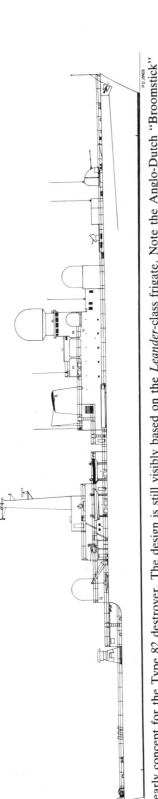

Dimensions: 507' o.a.; 490' w.l. × 55' beam
Displacement: 6,750 tons full load
Missiles: One twin Sea Dart GWS 30 surface-to-air missile system
One single Ikara GWS 40 antisubmarine missile system
Armament: One single 4.5" Mark 8 DP gun
Two single 40/70 Bofors AA guns
Four saluting guns
One Limbo triple-barrel ASW mortar
Aircraft: Facilities for a Wasp helicopter, but no hangar
Decoys: Two Corvus 3" chaff launchers
One Type 182 torpedo decoy

Electronics: ADAWS Combat Data System
One Anglo-Dutch 3D radar
One Type 1006 navigation radar
Two Type 909 Sea Dart fire-control radars
Two Ikara missile trackers
FH 5 DF system
One Type 184 medium-frequency search sonar
One Type 170 attack sonar
One Type 162M bottom-classification sonar
One Type 185 underwater telephone

The Royal Navy pioneered the use of light helicopters from surface escorts as ASW weapons delivery systems in order to capitalize upon long-range sonars (and allow the possible use of nuclear depth bombs). The Westland Wasp was the first type used, from 1963 onwards; this is HMS *Rothesay*'s example.

proved radar, and Sea Cat missiles. Conversion of the old "Ton"-class mine-sweepers into sonar-fitted mine hunters was also well under way. The fleet was still undiminished, with the same number of major combat vessels in active service as at the beginning of the decade. The whole RN "General-Purpose Combat Forces" bill came to £291 million, only an 8 percent reduction in real terms on mid-sixties figures. Something would have to be done to find a new rationale for this important investment should East of Suez by finally abandoned, as it might well be.[14]

For the time being the Royal Navy's forward planners could find but cold comfort in the possibility of a drastic rethink of NATO strategy for the North Atlantic and Europe. Although there did seem to be some extra emphasis on the reinforcement of Europe rather than on the maintenance of in-place forces, a long conventional war still seemed specifically ruled out in official British statements. Indeed, cuts in logistic tail to bring stocks into line with the expected period of conflict were called for. Although "NATO must be ready at sea, as well as on land, to demonstrate its will and its ability to respond appropriately to any act of aggression," it was "no longer realistic for the Alliance to attempt to provide maritime forces for conducting a prolonged war at sea after a strategic nuclear exchange." Broken-backed war was not about to stage a return. NATO's naval forces, like its land and air forces, were in the business of "deterrence."[15]

These ideas had much to do with Healey's campaign in NATO to resist American moves to substitute a strategy of deterrence through conventional "denial" for the existing strategy of deterrence through nuclear "punishment." This pro-nuclear policy had not had an entirely clear run through the cabinet, although Healey succeeded in getting his way for the time being.[16] Yet all was not lost for the navy. Healey's Defence Ministry was far from averse to *some* increased emphasis on an enhanced role for conventional forces in Europe and the Atlantic. There might, therefore, yet be a role for quite a large navy in the Eastern Atlantic. If the Royal Navy was to be a "trip wire," it might well be a substantial one designed to give as wide a range of options as Britain felt she could afford. Two years before, even in the heyday of East of Suez, Mayhew had set this out clearly. The Alliance, he argued, needed conventional forces at sea that could "respond to local and limited aggressive actions which, if unchecked, could gradually undermine our position. These forces must be strong enough to identify such aggression and resist it so as to face the aggressor with a choice between escalation, if he really means it, and withdrawal. Rather than naval forces for broken-backed war, therefore, NATO needs a shield force at sea to help prevent a nuclear showdown."[17] These were the ideas endorsed by the Future Fleet Working Party. Thus was a new re-orientated naval role being born that would take the service through the new traumas of East of Suez withdrawal.

The Working Party charged with coordinating the new Defence Review reported at the end of March 1967. It proposed a timetable for a phased withdrawal from East of Suez by 1975 but leaving behind a minimum military presence based largely in Australia. The precise nature of the latter deployment would be decided by a further review. These proposals were presented to the cabinet on 11 April. Some ministers feared for the alarm a withdrawal announcement would cause in Australia, but the majority wanted more drastic cuts than those recommended. Mrs. Castle, minister of transport, argued that greater savings might be obtained by a more rapid withdrawal and that, given the political costs of making the "withdrawal" in the first place, she feared that the post-withdrawal "minimum" presence, with its buildup of forces in Australia, might prove to be an expensive luxury. Crossman, lord president of the Council and leader of the House of Commons, argued for a decision that in the forthcoming negotiations with allies nothing should be done to prejudice the option of a more extensive withdrawal if required.

Crossman's views reflected those of the Parliamentary Labour Party, which had demonstrated its continued restiveness over government defense policy, when the White Paper had been approved by a much-reduced majority. (Wilson had been forced to reassert his authority in a firm speech to his back benchers.) This reflected a general left-wing tendency to play down the residual commitments of Britain's imperial past, but some of the emerging Cabinet opponents of a continued East of Suez presence, such as the Home Secretary Roy Jenkins, were on the right of the party. These critics felt that American failures in Vietnam seemed to demonstrate the limited utility of armed force in maintaining Western interests in South East Asia. Even more important, the conviction was increasing that British interests lay primarily in Europe; the government was steeling itself for a fresh application to join the EEC the next month. An enhanced commitment to European defense was the natural corollary of these moves.

The result of all this was that in April 1967 George Brown, the foreign secretary, went to Washington to a meeting of the South East Asia Treaty Organization with the news that half of Britain's forces in the area would be withdrawn by 1971 and all would be gone by 1975. The Australians and the Americans exerted great pressure that a terminal date not be announced, at least as long as the Vietnam War continued. The chiefs of staff, the defense and foreign office secretariats, and the Commonwealth prime ministers were all exerting considerable pressure on the Cabinet in the same direction. Nevertheless, the government remained committed to its phased withdrawal and residual presence plans. These proposals were a typical Wilsonian compromise; they allowed some satisfaction to be given to both sides in the argument. When Mr. Healey went out to Singapore and Malaysia to discuss the post-Confrontation withdrawal of forces and base facilities over the next year, he was able to assure the local governments that complete abandonment of deployments in the area would certainly not take place "in the next two or three years."[18]

It was at this point that an external event intervened to nudge the argument further towards complete withdrawal. This was the Arab-Israeli War of June 1967, which had an enormous effect both in terms of its direct economic impact on the British economy and because it demonstrated how little real political leverage was apparently gained by the expensive and controversial East of Suez presence. When Nasser ordered the U.N. Emergency Force out of Sinai on 19 May and closed the Straits of Tiran four days later, British intervention to break the blockade was considered. On the morning of 23 May, George Brown, Denis Healey, and the prime minister met to discuss a declaration by the maritime powers that they intended to reassert the right of innocent passage in the international waterway. At first the three seem to have agreed that military action might be necessary, but after meeting with the chiefs of staff, the defense minister soon changed his mind. As he told an emergency Cabinet meeting in the afternoon, the forces that would be required were not well deployed to take any action.[19]

British naval forces in the Indian Ocean would have to bear the brunt of any such action, with perhaps token American support. The only British carrier available was the *Hermes,* the weakest member of Britain's carrier fleet and despite a recent ten-million-pound refit to operate Mk2 variants of both the Buccaneer and Sea Vixen, only dubiously capable of taking on the apparently powerful Egyptian Air Force. Such a valuable ship could not be risked too close to potential enemy air bases, and she would stand off leaving the main work to the smaller available ships. With the *Hermes* were two "Tribal"-class frigates, the *Nubian* and *Ashanti,* and on the way around the Cape were the guided-missile destroyer *Kent,* the *Leander*-class frigate *Arethusa,* and the Type 41 frigate *Lynx.* It was a very open question whether the entire force could oppose Egyptian air defenses adequately with their missiles and guns, and there was the prospect of a humiliating withdrawal.[20]

The United States had its powerful Sixth Fleet in the Mediterranean, and the British had some forces there also. The fleet carrier, HMS *Victorious,* had just passed through the Suez Canal westbound on her way home to refit, and she was held at Malta. Emergency measures were being taken to give her a surface escort. The new frigate *Phoebe* was sent posthaste from a visit to Aberdeen in Scotland. HMS *Rhyl,* an older Type 12, was also held in the Mediterranean on her way home from the Far East, and a "Tribal," HMS *Eskimo,* on her way to Aden. The despatch to the Mediterranean of two Second Rate Utility frigates, the *Malcolm* and *Grafton*— ships almost totally unsuitable for carrier group work—was perhaps an index of how close to its bottom the barrel was being scraped. The potential British force was at best a useful addition to an American task force, but it was highly unlikely that President Nasser would allow such a fleet through the Suez Canal. The only option then would be preemptive direct action against Egyptian airfields in support of the Indian Ocean Squadron, something that raised unfortunate memories of eleven years before.

Another factor limiting Britain's own options was that her amphibious forces were tied up elsewhere. The *Bulwark* was operational in the Far East, while her sister, *Albion,* with 41 commando and an artillery battery, was apparently standing off West Africa. Civil war was breaking out in Nigeria, and the federal government there was apparently proposing British military intervention to create a neutral zone between the warring parties. British nationals might also require defense and evacuation, and the commando ship was thus required on station off West Africa. The *Albion* had loaded in great haste and eventually spent three months at sea before returning to Britain in early June.[21]

The 23 May Cabinet meeting refused to authorize any Anglo-American statement of intent to break the blockade, despite the strong advocacy of Wilson and Brown. Two days later the Cabinet agreed that purely Anglo-American action was out of the question, but there was still the possibility of a declaration of the maritime powers against the blockade. On 30 May the preparation of contingency plans for British intervention as part of an American-led "joint Maritime force" was discussed in Cabinet. Healey now strongly opposed such action on both political and military grounds. He feared that American support might be withdrawn at the last minute leaving Britain in the lurch. If she was not careful, Britain would find herself still bearing the brunt of such action with inadequate forces and very little support from elsewhere. With only one or two exceptions the Cabinet urged caution on the prime minister. It was willing to commit itself to attempts to get a declaration of the maritime powers and to contingency planning for a truly international force, but it confirmed that Britain was not going to take part if it was just going to be an Anglo-American effort. Such action would unite the Third World against an apparently overt attempt to reassert Western hegemony.[22]

As soon as the war started with Israel's attack on her neighbors, it was clear that Britain's aim was to limit the damage the war might do both to her relations with the Arab States and to her oil supplies. Ironically, given the British decision not to intervene, a bewildered President Nasser of Egypt thought that the aircraft sweeping in from over the sea had indeed come from Western carriers. The *Victorious* was at Malta at the time and the *Hermes* at Aden, both out of range, but this did not stop Arab trading reprisals, including withholding supplies of oil. Given the contemporary state of the oil market, these sanctions could not be sustained for long, but the fact that they occurred at all and had been imposed by rulers—some of whom Britain was spending scarce foreign exchange defending—had a significant impact in Cabinet. It seemed to many, including even Prime Minister Wilson, "one of the last to be converted," that the presence East of Suez was becoming "vain and costly." At the very meeting on 30 May that had confirmed Britain's unwillingness to intervene in the Middle East, the Cabinet had confirmed withdrawal from East of Suez by the mid-1970s. Wilson, however, still wished to keep a naval force in the area after withdrawal, with supporting army and air forces based in the United Kingdom. This was to reassure both the United States and Singapore. The foreign secretary still favored an Australian base, but Healey was by now against this idea. The eventual residual commitment was left studiously vague. Discussion went on, and on 6 July the Cabinet met to approve the wording of the Supplementary White Paper that would announce their withdrawal intentions. There was some debate over the rate of withdrawal, Healey and Crossman clashing over the rate of withdrawal from Singapore. The defense minister insisted that the planned 1975 time scale was the most rapid rate of withdrawal possible. The lord president argued (presciently) that the rate would soon have to increase and that a decision now would make political virtue of this necessity. The argument went in Healey's favor, but there seems to have been a consensus that Britain should withdraw from the Middle East as soon as she could shed her treaty obligations.[23]

The Government's Supplementary Statement on Defence Policy was published on 18 July. Numbers of service and support personnel in Singapore and Malaysia, including the ships' companies of warships deployed in the area, were to come down from 80,000 to 40,000 over the next seven years. By the early seventies the British presence would be largely restricted to Gurkha infantry supported by air and naval forces and with the potential for amphibious reinforcement. Present treaty obligations under SEATO and the Anglo-Malaysian Defence Agreement would be revised. Plans for beyond 1970–71 were kept vague, but it was announced that the "middle 70s" would see a complete withdrawal from British bases in Singapore and Malaysia. Nevertheless, even then there would be a capability reserved for use in the area if required. The nature and size of this "special capability" was also kept shady, but it might include "some naval and amphibious forces" kept in the Far East. The possibility of facilities in Australia was still mentioned. It seemed as if the Royal Navy might remain East of Suez after all, even if in substantially reduced strength. Despite its greater commitment to NATO and European defense, the government still could not bring itself to accept the inevitable and cut its losses East of Suez. The events of the next few months were to make the July announcement seem at best half-hearted and at worst indecisive.[24]

The July Statement made clear that the Royal Navy's future was still secure. It would "continue to play a leading part in the maritime shield forces of NATO" while being "able to perform, as far ahead as can be foreseen, a valuable peace-keeping function outside Europe by the unobtrusive and flexible exercise of maritime power."[25] Some interesting new hardware developments were announced, reflecting the thinking of the "Future Fleet Working Party." The carrier decision was, of course, confirmed, and a more detailed schedule of withdrawal from service was spelled out: The *Victorious* in 1969, the *Hermes* in 1970, with the *Eagle* and *Ark Royal* going on until the mid-1970s. The "main striking power" of the future Navy would be provided by the SSN force. The surface fleet would continue to be important, however, with a new class of "small frigate" to succeed the *Leander*. The new ship would have a new helicopter to replace the existing Wasp, a new surface-to-air missile to replace Sea Cat, and would also carry the new medium-range gun as designed for the Type 82. The fate of the Type 82 destroyer program, apparently criticized by Adams's Working Party, was now sealed; it was confirmed that only one hull would be built.

The announcement went on in an interesting way to say that the Type 82 would be developed in two forms. One successor would be a smaller Sea Dart-equipped "destroyer" that would carry a small ASW weapons-delivery helicopter. The other new ship was an acceptable variant of the unacceptable small carrier, a relatively large command cruiser to replace the *Tiger* class. Intended as flagships, these vessels would carry the Sea Dart surface-to-air missile and large Sea King ASW helicopters. Thus were announced the three types of surface combatants that would dominate the construction program of the 70s; the Type 21 frigate, the Type 42 destroyer, and, most significantly of all, at least in MOD(N)'s eyes, the large "cruiser," which would increasingly turn into a carrier replacement. The immediate air emphasis was on helicopters, however, with both the large and sophisticated Sea King for ASW duties and the new small helicopter that would make up for the lack of carrier support by combining reconnaissance and anti-surface missile capabilities with the existing ASW weapons delivery role. A Westland design was chosen, the WG-13, and arrangements were made in 1967 for its production as the "Lynx" under Anglo-French arrangements.[26]

Although the future navy, like the future army and air force, would be bigger than it would otherwise have needed to be to cover purely NATO contingencies, substantial savings had been obtained. It had seemed that the old 1966 program would, in the event, have cost marginally over the £2,000 million ceiling. With the 1967 cuts, the 1970–71 budget would only total £1.9 billion, by the mid-70s £1.8 billion. Total balance of payments savings would, it was hoped, come to £92 million by the mid-1970s and final withdrawal. In the debate on the proposals Wilson went firm on a date by which withdrawal would take place, come what may: 1977.[27]

The compromise of July 1967 was favorably received both internally within the Labour Party and externally among Britain's allies. Once again its definitive nature was stressed, although a little more dubiously than the previous year's review, given the ends still left deliberately untied. Once again, however, economic pressures all too soon swept the Wilson Government along. Within a few months there seemed little alternative to the complete withdrawal the prime minister and several of his colleagues had wished to stave off for as long as possible. For, even as the government announced its tentative withdrawal plans, a new run on the pound was beginning.

The economic measures of 1966, of which the new Defence Review had been a part, succeeded for a time. Nevertheless, the application to join the EEC and the difficulties with the balance of payments that this implied, coupled with bad trade figures and the uncertainty caused by the Six Day War, caused confidence in sterling to weaken. The closure of the Suez Canal and dock strikes in Liverpool and London in September further interfered with Britain's trade figures. Britain's continued poor balance of payments performance was all too clear by September, and the resources were draining away as the Bank of England sold gold and foreign exchange to prop up sterling's fixed parity. It looked as if Britain's adverse balance might total £500 million, even worse than the disastrous figures for 1964. Just as the Wilson Government had been dragged "kicking and screaming" into a withdrawal decision from East of Suez, so now the even more unpalatable pill of currency devaluation had to be swallowed. Further doses of deflation for its own sake were totally unacceptable to the government's supporters. The final straw was when, on 13 November, it was made clear that the International Monetary Fund would only provide support for sterling on the basis of an unacceptable level of control over internal British economic policy. The decision to devalue was taken just before midnight at a meeting between Wilson, Chancellor Callaghan, the

Cabinet secretary, and Sir William Armstrong, permanent secretary to the Treasury.[28]

The Treasury had a deflationary package of economic measures available for consideration by ministers, and these were considered at a ministerial committee, including the defense secretary, on the afternoon of 14 November. The Cabinet approved the whole package on the 16th, to take effect on the evening of the 18th. On the 20th, Chancellor of the Exchequer Callaghan announced a set of economic measures that included a further cut of £100 million in defense in the next financial year.[29] The immediate casualty was the carrier *Victorious*. She had gone into refit in June to prepare for her final commission and two months later began to prepare for recommissioning in November. The old ship's steering had always caused problems, and she had been forced back into dry dock to try to cure them. While in the dock the carrier suffered quite a serious fire in which a sailor was killed. This added to the case that, given manpower shortages and the need to make immediate savings, the carrier should not be recommissioned. On 23 November, three days after Callaghan's speech, the carrier's captain was so informed and on 13 March the ship, now stripped, was decommissioned to be sold for scrap a few months later.[30]

At first, this and other changes were announced simply as slight revisions of the basic July 1967 plan.[31] By December, however, Wilson and Roy Jenkins, the new chancellor, were sketching out a package of cuts that forced a third and final major Labour Defence Review to begin on an intense time schedule. As the prime minister later put it: "It was clear that major reductions would be required in defence and overseas expenditure and in the planned growth of social expenditure."[32] Resources had to be reallocated to investment, exports, and the replacement of imports by home-produced products. Consumption had to be reduced. The decisions were difficult ones politically. Restoring health prescription charges was a similar issue to that on which Prime Minister Wilson himself had resigned as trade minister in 1951. Postponing the raising of the school-leaving age was delaying a policy with a long pedigree in Labour policy statements. The cuts in public expenditure were also most unpalatable. Politically, it would have been impossible for the Wilson administration to have done such things without making futher cuts in defense, even if the defense cuts, with their further inroads into overseas expenditure, had not been seen as desirable in themselves. As Wilson put it: "The task of getting it [the package] through Cabinet without sensational resignations was the most formidable task I had attempted over three years of government. My greatest asset was the firmness and determination of the Chancellor in the presentation of a balanced package."[33]

Healey, and the whole foreign and defense policy establishment, were deeply unhappy at the proposed cuts. The minister himself was closely associated with some projects that were now on the chopping block, notably the order for the F-111 long-range strike aircraft. Commitments only recently negotiated would have to be revised once more, if not completely abandoned. One thing that Healey, backed strongly by the chiefs of staff, made clear was that he could not countenance any further pretence of maintaining East of Suez commitments with forces cut beyond the planned level. If the cuts were made, they would mean the end of Britain's East of Suez commitment. All the Defence Ministry could offer a shocked Foreign and Commonwealth Office was a newly designated "General Capability" that Britain's Euro-centric armed forces would have to help her extra-European friends in certain circumstances.[34]

The Defence Ministry and the Foreign and Commonwealth Offices were united in opposing the proposed cuts in Cabinet. If they could not stave off withdrawal completely, they hoped to delay it as long as possible; they suggested 31 March 1972. On 4 January Jenkins presented the Cabinet with "the toughest document on defence cuts" yet presented to the Labour Cabinet. It argued that: "Our standing in the world depends on the soundness of our economy and not on a worldwide military presence," and that drastic changes should be made in defense policy. In order to convert a £300 million balance-of-payments deficit into a £500 million surplus and to increase fixed investment of £200 million, the chancellor proposed equal cuts in civil and defense expenditure. He insisted on a 1970–71 date for withdrawal from East of Suez, i.e., before the next election. A long discussion began with cabinet evenly divided. Mrs. Castle, a supporter of withdrawal, considered that Wilson's "casting vote" was decisive. He insisted that Britain should announce her withdrawal from all her commitments East of Suez, both in the Gulf and the Far East, by the end of the financial year 1970–71. The Anglo-Malaysian Defence Agreement was to be renegotiated. There was to be no advance definition of the circumstances in which Britain's general capability was to be used. Foreign Secretary George Brown and Commonwealth Secretary George Thompson insisted that they should report back on the reaction of Britain's allies, and Healey even succeeded in getting a stay of execution on the F-111, reducing his request to thirty for European tasks and beginning a hurried investigation into savings elsewhere in defense to pay for the aircraft. The foreign secretary reported adverse American reactions to the Cabinet on 12 July; the U.S.A. was particularly anxious to retain a British presence in the Gulf. Geronwy Roberts, minister of state at the Foreign Office, announced that the Middle Eastern allies wished for an extension of a year and no announced withdrawal date. It was decided to delay a final confirmation of the East of Suez timetable, but the coup de grace was given to the F-111 on a majority of twelve to eight. The cancellation of Polaris was also considered, but the consensus was that it was a good bargain at only £20 million a year.[35]

The following day a further Cabinet meeting heard some of the horrified reactions of Britain's Far Eastern allies. George Thompson had been sounding out Commonwealth opinion while Lee Kuan Yew, Singapore's prime minister, had flown to London to press on Wilson the case against a British withdrawal until 1973. With the supporters of delay—Brown, Thompson, Michael Stewart ("first secretary of state"), and James Callaghan (home secretary)—fighting "a rearguard action with great ferocity," and other members of the Cabinet wavering in their 1971 withdrawal decision, Wilson suggested a compromise that the withdrawal from Singapore be deferred from March to December 1971. Lee Kuan Yew could take comfort that the date was now *after* the next general election. On 16 January, "Black Tuesday" as it was christened at the Ministry of Defence, Wilson made the proposals public and announced further savings of £260 million on defense by 1972–73. Apart from Hong Kong, all forces would be gone from East of Suez by the end of 1971. The particular blows for the Royal Navy were that the carriers would now be gone by 1971–72 rather than 1974–75, and the rate of nuclear submarine construction would be slowed down. With the announcement of the F-111 cancellation, both of the main protagonists of the 1964–66 carrier debate seemed to have lost. The RAF, however, had the consolation of retaining a powerful long-range striking force provided by the remaining V bombers and the Phantoms and Buccaneers acquired from the Royal Navy.[36]

In view of the way in which the Royal Navy had been making its "case" for over a decade, the East of Suez withdrawal posed an enormous challenge. Could an equivocal, and somewhat ill-defined, Atlantic role sustain the large and capable fleet that Britain still looked like keeping? Happily for the Admiralty Board, developments in NATO's strategy now came to the rescue. Mr. Healey himself seems to have played a significant role in the compromise NATO ministerial decision of December 1967 to endorse, at last, the doctrine of "flexible response." The key to this development was the condition that it should not be used as a vehicle for higher force goals. Alliance strategy should be based, it was asserted, on those forces the member states were willing to contribute. Nevertheless, the new stress on conventional forces was very significant, perhaps fundamental, and this was made clear in the 1968 Defence White Paper that appeared a month after "Black Tuesday." The main role of the Royal Navy was now clearly the maintenance of peace in Europe. The change from the nuclear emphasis of the 1967 statements was noteworthy. Britain and the other NATO members were to make force adjustments ". . . with the object of extending the conventional phase of hostilities should war break out; this would give more time in which any decision to use nuclear weapons would be taken."[37]

The new importance given to tools of crisis management was made clear by the creation of Standing Naval Force Atlantic, composed of escorts from five or six navies. The RN provided the first force commander, and indeed Britain could claim credit for having originated the concept when Admiral Sir Charles Madden as NATO CinC Eastern Atlantic had begun "Matchmaker" joint deployments of Alliance vessels in 1965. The joint squadron was intended to give SACLANT his own Alliance-wide naval force that could demonstrate resolve in a crisis, but the force also gave useful experience in the joint operation of the ships of the different NATO navies.[38]

The kind of scenarios in which this new NATO-oriented Royal Navy might play a part were shown in two significant exercises during the summer of 1968. The first was Polar Express in June and July, in which for the first time a British commando carrier, HMS *Bulwark,* was used on NATO's northern flank in the defense of Norway. The Norwegians had displayed considerable concern during the spring about the effects of the British Government's defense reviews, notably in the lack of British carrier air support in the early stages of any conflict before the main American component of the Striking Fleet arrived. Now Britain had an alternative kind of naval support to offer. A Supplementary Statement on Defence, published simultaneously with the Polar Express exercise in July 1968, made it clear that Britain's amphibious forces, notably the two commando carriers and the two assault ships, now had a primarily NATO role on both the northern and southern flanks. The *Bulwark* demonstrated what that role might be—and some of the snags of deploying too rapidly from east to west of Suez. The Wessex 5 helicopters of 848 Squadron were to be used to land the 650 men of the *Bulwark*'s embarked Royal Marine Commando. Unfortunately, the helicopters' sand filters, still fitted for Middle East service since there had not been time to remove them, made operations in the snows of northern Norway impossible. The *Bulwark* had to use her landing craft to get the troops ashore. Nevertheless, the helicopters were able to get op-erational eventually, both in a transport and in a light missile strike role against targets both on land and at sea. The "flanks" of NATO might not sustain all the increased amphibious capability of the 1960s—43 Commando was disbanded once more in November 1968—but they might well provide scenarios for most of it to remain.[39]

In September 1968 a full-scale NATO Atlantic exercise, Silver Tower, was held in which HMS *Eagle* provided Carrier Group 2 in the NATO Striking Fleet. During this exercise the Americans made only too clear their reservations about the forth-coming loss of the British carriers; there was, however, much else for other RN vessels to do in the other aspects of an exercise that included convoy protection and mine countermeasures. This was the largest maritime exercise yet staged by NATO and demonstrated the increased emphasis on conventional naval warfare as part of the Alliance's deterrent posture in the Atlantic.[40]

It was not only in northern waters that there was a significant reemphasis. The Mediterranean Fleet also began to reassert a little of its former importance. This historic major fleet had suffered perhaps most severely of all from the East of Suez priority of the early 1960s. Although British ships continued to visit Malta on work-up or on passage, by the mid-1960s the permanent strength of the Mediterranean Fleet was reduced to a single small escort squadron and a coastal minesweeper squadron. The escort squadron deployed up to four destroyers and frigates, but in 1966 the Beira Patrol (see below) and other commitments reduced the total, first to two ships and then for a period to none. The minesweeper squadron also tem-porarily lost two of its six "Tons." Effectively, Malta, with its dockyard still in British commercial hands, was a forward operating base with cadre facilities that might be expanded in the event of a major outbreak of limited war in the Eastern Mediterranean. There was now little excuse for the British fleet commander to exercise the NATO role of CinC Allied Forces Mediterranean, and in May 1967 it was announced that his post was to be abolished. On 5 June Admiral Sir John Hamilton, the last of a long line of British commanders-in-chief Mediterranean Fleet, hauled down his flag, and the few ships that Britain could spare for the Mediterranean became an outpost of the newly renamed Western Fleet. The senior British naval officer in the Mediterranean became a two-star appointment as flag officer Malta and NATO commander of the South East Mediterranean area, sub-ordinate to the American admiral at Naples, Commander-in-Chief Allied Forces South. The American instincts of fifteen to twenty years before had finally been proved correct.[41]

Even if the British had not intervened in the 1967 Arab-Israeli War, that conflict had provided the first major use of the Soviet Fleet as a diplomatic instrument, supporting Egypt both during and after hostilities. The increased presence at sea of Soviet vessels was beginning to be noticed by observers in the West, and in response to this, and to the perceived need to make some reply to the invasion of Czechoslovakia in 1968, it was decided to return major British surface units to the Mediterranean, on an occasional basis at least. First the assault ship *Fearless* was deployed there, followed by the commando carrier *Bulwark*, and then finally the strike carrier *Eagle*. The depletion of the existing permanent station forces con-tinued, however, and the minesweeper squadron was placed in reserve in 1969. When the major units were unavailable, the British presence was reduced to a single escort. Nevertheless, when a show of force was required, the Western Fleet could put on quite a brave show in the Mediterranean area. When Spanish pressure on Gibraltar looked as if it might become significant in September 1969, the forces at the rock comprised the *Eagle*, the helicopter cruiser *Blake*, two "County"-class guided-missile destroyers, and a number of other frigates and smaller conventional destroyers. The White Paper of that year announced that Britain was to deploy a "County"-class ship in the Mediterranean from 1970 and to contribute to the "On Call Allied Force in the Mediterranean," which had been agreed upon by NATO's Defence Planning Committee the previous January. It was even suggested that the Mediterranean would become the primary deployment area for Britain's amphibious forces on withdrawal from East of Suez.[42]

As the Royal Navy began the redeployment and reorientation of its forces into the new NATO context, both in the Atlantic and on both flanks, there was still unfinished business to be done East of Suez and elsewhere. The main trouble spot was Aden and its hinterland, the South Arabian Federation. Aden had become the center of British power in the area with the unified "Arabian Peninsula" command set up there in 1959 and redesignated Middle East Command in 1961. The Royal Navy's Gulf headquarters was moved from Bahrein to HMS *Sheba* at Aden in 1963, causing considerable problems in the building and furnishing of a new accommodation for Flag Officer Middle East in an old coastal artillery emplacement at Steamer Point overlooking the harbor. By then Arab Nationalist agitation was becoming a problem for the British and the local British-backed rulers as a result of the revolution the previous year in Yemen. In December 1963 following the assassination of the assistant British commissioner, major operations against dissident tribesmen in the Radfan Mountains were undertaken. Four Wessex helicopters from HMS *Centaur* helped carry troops in the opening move of this offensive, Operation Nutcracker, in January 1964. The RN helicopters were back on similar duties by May, proving better adapted to the sandy conditions than the RAF's Belvederes. On their first day back in action six Wessexes flew no less than ninety sorties. By June 26th they had flown 409 missions carrying 2,096 passengers and almost 200,000 pounds of freight.[43]

In 1964 it was announced that Aden and the Federation would receive independence by 1968, although British forces would remain. A campaign of urban violence began almost immediately in Aden itself, with Royal Navy helicopters giving occasional assistance to the army's surprise "cordon and search" counterinsurgency operations. In April 1965 ten Wessex helicopters from the *Albion* lifted a company of the Royal Anglian Regiment from their camp and dropped them in their target area within three minutes. In October 1965 the dissident Aden government was dissolved, an act backed up by the fleet carrier *Eagle*, accompanied by the Type 12 frigate *Lowestoft* and two Royal Fleet Auxiliaries, all diverted from the Mediterranean exercises. The 1966 Defence Review announced Britain's revised intention to withdraw from the base and from her support for the friendly rulers of the hinterland, but security had to be maintained in the meantime. Naval helicopters from shore bases and HMS *Albion* continued to be used to give British and South Arabian Federation forces mobility. Minesweeper patrols in the Gulf area searched for arms destined for Aden, while one of the new assault ships, HMS *Fearless*, was used to bring in reinforcements and to land in October 1966 a battalion of the Irish Guards in the Eastern Aden Protectorate by helicopter to neutralize a rebel village. When HMS *Hermes* arrived to relieve the *Victorious* East of Suez in May 1967, her ASW Wessexes were sent ashore to assist in "dissident hunting missions."

The presence of the two carriers allowed a major show of air power in support of the pro-Western forces. Over 50 Buccaneers, Sea Vixens, and RAF Hunters flew in impressive formation over Aden, but such gestures could not balance the previous year's announcement of the forthcoming British withdrawal. By the autumn of 1967 it was clear that, for once, the British had not succeeded in installing a pro-Western regime, and there was no longer any question of giving even temporary support to a friendly government, as had been clearly stated would be done as late as July. In June 1967 a date for withdrawal had finally been set, November 20th, but on November 2nd it was changed to the end of the month. The main aim was to get British forces out of the area by then at a minimum cost in life and without foreign intervention. Not only were all stores, equipment, and ammunition to be lifted by sea, but the naval support would keep the last troops in Aden operational, almost all replenishment coming from supply ships off shore. Only thus, the RAF staff historian commented was it "possible to achieve the flexibility required in this unprecedented situation." In order to extract British forces from Aden, all the large amphibious ships were deployed, the commando carriers *Albion* and *Bulwark* and the assault ships *Fearless* and *Intrepid*. The last-named ship was on her first commission and with her latest communications suite was made floating HQ. HMS *Eagle*'s Buccaneers and Sea Vixens provided air cover as the RAF presence declined and finally disappeared in November. Ship-based Wessex helicopters (RN and RAF) provided both mobility and close support for the withdrawing troops. Task Force 318, commanded by Rear Admiral Edward Ashmore, also contained the destroyer *London,* the frigates *Minerva* and *Phoebe,* and the submarine *Auriga*. It was supported by no less than eight Royal Fleet Auxiliaries.

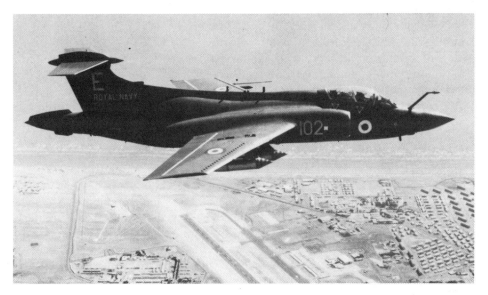

Armed with rocket packs, a Buccaneer S2 strike aircraft from HMS *Eagle*'s 800 Squadron covers the Aden withdrawal in 1967. (Imperial War Museum)

The impressive amphibious task force that gathered to evacuate Aden at the end of 1967. Left to right are the *Intrepid*, *Fearless*, and *Albion*. (Imperial War Museum)

Admiral Sir Michael Le Fanu, the last British CinC Middle East, suggested that a fleet review be held with this impressive array of ships. This was duly carried out, British High Commissioner Sir Humphrey Trevelyan taking the salute from the minesweeper *Appleton,* which later covered the final withdrawal from the inner harbor.

The last British troops ashore were 45 and 42 Commandos, Royal Marines. The former had been fighting in the Aden area since 1960, but the latter had only been deployed there since October 1967, having been landed from the *Albion* to cover the final weeks of British presence. On November 14th the final withdrawal date had been brought forward to November 29th, and on the 28th, as 45 Commando was flown out to HMS *Bulwark,* a brief ceremony marked the official end of Britain's joint Middle East Command. As Trevelyan, Le Fanu, and other senior officers flew out from the airfield, 42 Commando, supported by armed helicopters, stood guard. Finally, in the afternoon the Royal Marines were flown to the *Albion* and command of British forces devolved for the last few hours on Ashmore. British warships remained in territorial waters until midnight. There was not a little sad irony in the first deployment of Britain's complete maritime intervention forces being on the occasion of a withdrawal, moreover a withdrawal that was a rare failure of her policy of inserting pro-Western regimes in former colonies.[44]

Although Britain could cut her losses in Aden, it was harder for her to disentangle herself from Rhodesia, whose white minority refused to accept the principle of majority rule and declared independence illegally and unilaterally in November 1965. Although Rhodesia was far from the sea, a fact that made British military intervention potentially difficult, the Royal Navy played a remarkably large part in the developing crisis. First the carrier *Eagle* was called down to patrol off the Tanzanian coast to give air cover to Zambia with her Sea Vixen fighters in case of possible Rhodesian action. This duty was taken over after some weeks by RAF aircraft, but the *Eagle* remained in the area to police the oil sanctions called for, at Britain's request, by the U.N. Security Council. She spent seventy-one days at sea off the port of Beira in Mozambique, using her aircraft to keep watch on shipping movements, before being replaced by the *Ark Royal.* In addition to the carriers, destroyers and frigates were also employed, the smaller ships maintaining the blockade after the big ships' withdrawal. On her forty-two-day cruise in March and April 1966 the frigate HMS *Plymouth* attempted to stop the Greek tanker *Ioanna V,* loaded with oil for Rhodesia. At this point sanctions did not have the force of law, and the *Plymouth* had to let the ship, which refused to stop, enter Beira (although her cargo was not unloaded). Once the U.N. sanctions became mandatory, however, less than a week later, more positive action could be taken, and the Type 12 frigate HMS *Berwick* had more success with the tanker *Manuella,* which did turn away after a boarding party had been put on board.

The Beira Patrol, as it became known, was kept up year in year out, for almost a decade until, in June 1975, it became unnecessary when Mozambiquan independence cut off any chance of supplies to Rhodesia by the Beira route. The "blockade" was a frustrating task. The powers of the ships imposing it were limited, as shown drastically when the French tanker *Artois,* in any case not bound for Beira, ignored shots across her bows from the *Leander*-class frigate *Minerva.* The duty was usually dull. The "Tribal"-class frigate *Zulu* spent 124 days in 1967 sailing up and down her patrol line at twelve knots with only four boardings to enliven proceedings. The ships' companies felt it to be a somewhat futile exercise as oil was reaching Rhodesia via South Africa, if not through Mozambique. Nevertheless, the patrol did have a vital political function in demonstrating to the African States Britain's dissatisfaction with the continued fact of illegal independence. As such, the thousands of tons of fuel oil burnt and the millions of pounds spent on this activity were not entirely wasted.[45]

The Royal Navy also played another role in the developing Rhodesian situation, as a private forum for discussions between Prime Minister Wilson and Ian Smith, the head of the illegal regime. At the end of 1966 a meeting was arranged on board the cruiser *Tiger,* off Gibraltar. The cruiser was swiftly and quietly brought up from Casablanca, where she had been on a flag-showing visit. Following Rhodesian rejection of the compromise proposals thrashed out at this meeting, further face-to-face negotiations were eventually agreed upon in October 1968. The destroyer *Kent* was moved alongside the assault ship *Fearless,* this time in Gibraltar dockyard itself. Smith was given the admiral's cabin in the *Kent* as a douceur to his pride, somewhat wounded by his previous accommodation in *Tiger!* Despite these measures and conference facilities that impressed everyone, including Prime Minister Wilson, the talks were as abortive as those aboard the *Tiger.*[46]

Britain was trying to extricate herself with honor from Central Africa, but there were other colonial commitments that were going to continue apparently indefinitely. One was Hong Kong, where Mao Tse Tung's Cultural Revolution created a climate of border incidents, industrial disputes, and urban violence in which naval force was needed to maintain stability and British rule. In May 1967 the hard-worked commando carrier *Bulwark* was sent to the colony from Singapore to make a show of Britain's willingness to use force, if necessary, to maintain security. The *Bulwark* used her Wessex helicopters in a commando landing exercise in the "New Territories" on the mainland. Another carrier, this time the strike carrier *Hermes,* was in action in August using her Wessex ASW helicopters to land police and army detachments on the roofs of two skyscrapers being used as the centers of anti-government activity. Despite this activity, 1967 saw the abolition of the Hong Kong-based 8th Mine Countermeasures Squadron. HMS *Woolaston, Wilkieston,* and *Fiskerton* left the colony at the beginning of October, the decision having been taken to maintain the Hong Kong Squadron with Singapore-based ships of the 6th MCM Squadron. As well as the minesweepers, larger units of the Far East Fleet, such as commando carriers and assault ships, regularly visited the colony to maintain confidence in the British presence. In 1969 with the forthcoming run-down of Singapore, the 1967 decision was effectively reversed, and the five ships of the 6th MCM Squadron were moved up to be based in Hong Kong. It was intended to maintain a small policing squadron in the colony, and the only effect of the East of Suez withdrawal was the replacement of the squadron's sophisticated minehunters by HMS *Beachampton, Monkton, Wasperton, Wolverton,* and *Yarnton,* specially converted into "coastal patrol craft" for service at Hong Kong.[47]

Another area where a continued British presence was required was the Falkland Islands, where Argentine pressure showed signs of increasing once more. In 1966 an incident occurred in which an Argentine nationalist group staged a landing in a civil aircraft on the Port Stanley racecourse. The one remaining frigate forming the Royal Navy's South Atlantic Squadron at Simonstown, HMS *Puma,* was sent to the islands as a "temporary reinforcement."[48] This incident may well have settled doubts about the need for a more permanent naval presence in the area. For some ten years that had been HMS *Protector,* a large netlayer completed in 1936 and converted into an "ice patrol vessel." She was in need of replacement, and the original intention had been to build a new 7,000-ton icebreaker, HMS *Terra Nova.* An impressive-sounding ship with a full surveying and helicopter capability, she was a casualty of the defense reviews, and instead, in 1967 a Danish supply vessel, the *Anita Dean,* was purchased to maintain the British naval presence in the Falkland Islands and their Dependencies. As HMS *Endurance* she commissioned in 1968 and sailed on her first deployment. A small garrison of Royal Marines was placed on the island, and one of the Royal Navy's hovercraft was also based there.[49]

It may be convenient here to review briefly the Royal Navy's flirtation with the hovercraft. The financial stringencies of the 1960s did not provide the best atmosphere for investment in this new maritime technology. In 1961 an interservice hovercraft unit had been set up at the Naval Air Station at Lee on Solent to test the feasibility of the machines for a range of naval tasks ranging from rescue to ASW and amphibious warfare. A number of SRN 5 hovercraft were obtained for this unit, and these were operationally deployed to the Far East in 1965, two being used on the rivers of Borneo during Confrontation with Indonesia. Another SRN 5 was used, with limited success, in the coastal fishery protection role in home waters in 1966. Despite the problems with sea keeping, the Royal Navy now decided to purchase two hovercraft of its own, a small SRN 6 and a larger BH 7. The former craft was the one sent to the Falklands where she operated with some success, greatly increasing the mobility of the Royal Marine detachment.[50]

The 1960s also saw flurries of activity in the Caribbean as the Royal Navy continued to play its traditional role of colonial policeman throughout the decade. Although Britain was granting full independence to her larger possessions, she still remained responsible for the defense of a number of colonies and self-governing dependent islands. The political instabilities of these islands occasionally required a show of force, sometimes more. In 1956 the Royal Navy had abolished its separate America and West Indies Station, the admiral commanding having transferred to Norfolk, Virginia, as deputy supreme commander Atlantic. A commodore, however, remained as senior naval officer West Indies, from 1962 commander British Forces, Caribbean Area. That year riots and a general strike in what was still British Guiana caused the deployment of his frigates *Troubridge* and *Wizard* (both Type 15s) to land parties to help control the situation. The naval presence was soon reinforced by the three similar frigates of the Dartmouth Training Squadron (which had replaced the old training squadron of big ships), the *Vigilant*, *Urchin*, and *Roebuck*. The ships' landing parties helped contain the situation until the army arrived. The *Whirlwind* was back doing similar duty in 1964. As time went by, Cuban refugees and armed exiles caused serious problems, both of a security and humanitarian nature. In 1966 the regular station allocation of two frigates had again to be supplemented, this time by a ship taken from the South Atlantic Station. One typical deployment was composed of the new "Tribal" HMS *Tartar*, the old Type 15 HMS *Ursa*, and the Type 41 HMS *Lynx* on loan from Simonstown. Patrols were maintained off the Bahamas to stop the Cuban exiles from using the smaller, outlying islands as bases. These operations were sustained into 1968 when HMS *Eskimo*'s Royal Marines captured a small band of intruders.[51]

Internal problems in other British territories also provoked a naval response. In 1966 the Type 15 frigate *Zest* had to restore order during a strike in the Bahamas, while constitutional difficulties in St. Vincent required the sending of the destroyer *Defender* in December of that year. The trouble in St. Vincent continued into 1967 and the *Zest* was deployed from Bahamas patrol to stand off the island for a time. Riots in Bermuda in 1968 saw the arrival within a day and a half of the frigate *Leopard*, which, together with an air lift of troops, quickly reasserted British authority. Perhaps the most notable of Caribbean police activities came in March of 1969 when the island of Anguilla tried to secede from its federation with St. Kitts and Nevis. Perhaps with the Rhodesian situation in mind the government used air and sea lift in a rapid invasion to restore legal authority as quickly and decisively as possible. The frigates *Minerva* and *Rothesay* landed Royal Marines and paratroops, respectively, to take control of the air strip so that further troops— and some London policemen—could be flown in. Naval helicopters dropped leaflets to appeal to the population not to resist. There was much contemporary comment about overreaction and even Prime Minister Wilson subsequently christened the Anguilla operation as "the joke of the year" carried out in "a musical comedy atmosphere." "Mock gunboat diplomacy" it may have been, but it did succeed in preparing the way for a legal settlement more acceptable to the inhabitants. It also demonstrated that despite Rhodesia, Britain was still willing to use force if necessary to restore the law.[52]

More troublesome domestically was the future of Britain's relationship with South Africa. Here, at the Simonstown base, as late as 1967 a British vice admiral commanded what should have been a two-frigate "squadron." Both ships were rarely on station, however; in 1966 one was deployed away to the Caribbean and the other to the Falklands. Despite talk in naval circles of the continued importance of the "Cape Route," the South Atlantic Station had clearly lost its operational meaning. When this was coupled with a British arms embargo on South Africa and a considerable amount of political pressure from the ruling Labour Party for a loosening of residual ties with that country, the stage was set for withdrawal. In January 1967 the Simonstown Agreement on naval cooperation, signed a decade before, was "renegotiated," and three months later the British CinC hauled down his flag and sailed away in one of his frigates, which had returned to Simonstown from duties elsewhere. The South Africans were now placed in complete charge of naval operations around their own coast, but the Royal Navy could not quite cut the knot completely. A senior British naval officer remained on the embassy staff in Pretoria to maintain liaison.[53]

Ironically, facilities in South Africa became significant once again only a few months after the departure of the last British CinC. The closure of the Suez Canal in June 1967 meant that ships deploying East of Suez needed support facilities on the Cape Route. The Simonstown Agreement still implied a British commitment to supply naval equipment to South Africa as a quid pro quo for continued access. The Labour Government had honored the arms contracts it had inherited from its predecessor, including orders for Buccaneer maritime strike aircraft, but had refused to allow further orders, forcing the South Africans to look elsewhere, e.g., for submarines. In late 1967, conscious of her increased importance to the Royal Navy and the new significance of the Cape Route in general, South Africa renewed its pressure for Britain to sell £100 million worth of naval equipment (notably ammunition and helicopters) to help sustain and modernize its small British-built fleet. Given the parlous state of the British economy, any exports, anywhere, seemed a good idea to some Cabinet members. As in the simultaneous debate on East of Suez, the government was split. Major arguments occurred both in the Oversea Policy and Defence Committee and the full Cabinet. With the government's backbenchers in uproar, it was eventually decided not to sell any more equipment, but the affair contributed to a considerable crisis in the relationship between Defence Minister Healey and the prime minister. Healey was in favor of going through with the South African deal, and Wilson suspected this was due to pressure from the U.S.A., to which the defense minister seemed unduly vulnerable.[54] Given the problems faced by the Cabinet, such tensions were understandable, but perhaps they should not be exaggerated. A few years later Wilson was writing of Healey in very complimentary terms as the "anchorman" of Cabinet discussion whose "own grip on defence spending was such that when he responded to the Chancellor's requests he operated as an enthusiast in demanding similar sacrifices by other ministers whose control over their departments was . . . less effective."[55]

With Healey protecting it from cuts in absolute capability, the Royal Navy was duly set on course for a historic naval withdrawal to the North Atlantic and Mediterranean, at least for all but the most residual of colonial commitments. The Ministry of Defence was still reluctant to commit itself to the idea of an *all-out* war at sea as part of the NATO Alliance's new strategy. Nor was it keen on maintaining a capability to fight against a prolonged "guerre de course." Although the Americans were speaking in such terms, it was impossible for Britain to face the financial consequences of such scenarios. Nevertheless, it was clear that the emphasis of British naval strategy had decisively shifted as a result of the NATO decisions. As the under secretary of state for the navy, Mr. Maurice Foley, put it in Parliament in March:

> The concept of "shield forces" at sea is parallel to that on land, in an era of strategic nuclear deterrence and since maritime aggression is far from difficult to identify and the apparent risks are less, NATO must be constantly on the alert, with strong conventional naval forces to identify aggression when it occurs, and to prevent it from developing into a more serious conflict.[56]

This point was made again and developed in a well-informed article on the Royal Navy that appeared a few months later:

> NATO's navies could certainly by conventional means cope with a limited attack against maritime trade. Against all out trade warfare they could, like the divisions in Western Germany, win time before such a war went nuclear (and, not so incidentally, the use of a tactical nuclear weapon in mid ocean against opposing naval forces could have less dreadful consequences than the use of such a weapon in Central Europe). Because, indeed, of the nuclear deterrent, naval strategists (hopefully) consider all out trade warfare—another battle of the Atlantic—not at all probable.[57]

In his statement before the House of Commons Mr. Foley had stressed the enhancement in NATO naval capabilities that would come about because of East of Suez withdrawal, and the requirement for such improvements:

> . . . our withdrawal from overseas will enable us to increase the number of ships at immediate readiness for NATO's shield forces, and so enable us to continue to play a leading part among the European navies in the NATO maritime alliance . . . the growth of Soviet maritime strength . . . has underlined the importance of the shield forces especially in relation to the flanks of Europe, Scandinavia and the Mediterranean, where the increase in the Soviet naval presence has been most evident.[58]

Although the move from East of Suez had primarily economic motives, the improvements in Soviet naval capability (not so much in quantity of submarines and ships but in their quality and level of deployment) made a move westwards well advised. There was thus a strategic as well as a financial imperative for Britain to withdraw her fleet from colonial and post-colonial policing around the world. There were distinct echoes of fifty to sixty years before when Sir John Fisher had brought back the fleet to face threats closer to home.[59]

Yet Britain was loath to give up her world-power role completely. It was made clear in the 1970 Defence White Paper that British forces would continue to train in the Far East and that later that year a major exercise, Bersatu Padu, would be held to demonstrate the "General Capability" to intervene that Britain would retain after withdrawal. The exercise began in April, and the Royal Navy and Royal Marines played the major role, providing 9,000 of the 14,000 British service personnel involved. The *Bulwark* was deployed for the exercise, with 42 Commando, but a British strike carrier was deliberately withheld to test the feasibility of supporting operations without a carrier. There were, however, some problems with the air support provided by the land-based RAF Phantoms, and A-4G Skyhawks from the Australian carrier *Melbourne* proved more useful. The naval and marine personnel relished the opportunity to prove the point about the continued utility of naval air power.[60]

While the exercise was still in progress, Mr. Wilson decided to hold a general election. The popularity of the government had improved, and Wilson had high hopes of success. The hard and difficult decisions of 1967–68 seemed to have been worthwhile. Both the balance of payments and Britain's external indebtedness were greatly improved. The retrenchment measures of 1968, which had included the 1971 withdrawal announcement, had reduced the rise of public expenditure from 4½ percent per year to 3 percent. Further tax rises were used to limit consumption and imports. Exports and the GDP had risen between 1967 and 1970 by 27 percent and 7.7 percent respectively, consumption by 5.4 percent and imports by 17 percent. By the summer of 1970 Britain was probably in a stronger, or at least less weak, economic position than she had been in for some time.[61]

Defense economies had, of course, played their part in curbing public expenditure, with only some 5½ percent of GNP being spent on defense in 1970–71 as against the 7 percent in the early 1960s. Indeed, the government hoped to go still further and reduce expenditure after withdrawal to just under 5 percent. Already by 1 April 1970 the numbers in, and working for, the services in Malaysia and Singapore had halved compared to the years of Confrontation.[62] The continuation of this run-down, however, became a little doubtful when Mr. Heath's Conservative Party won something of a surprise victory in the June election.

The Conservative Party as the opposition had been committed to doing something to reverse the decisions both to withdraw from East of Suez and to phase the Royal Navy's carriers out of service in 1971. It soon became clear, however, that any reversals of policy would be limited. In October 1970 the new government published the results of its "critical examination" of the "armed forces and the defence programmes it inherited."[63] With a prime minister much more committed to Europe than his predecessor and with an equal determination to cut expenditure, in the short term at least, there was no room for a major reversal of policy. What the services in general, and the Royal Navy in particular, got were some minor revisions of policy but no real change of direction.

The Heath Government, with Lord Carrington as its minister of defense, proposed to cut defense expenditure from 1971–72 to 1974–75 by some £264 million, about 3 percent. The proposal was to remain East of Suez with a very small contribution to new "Five Power Defence Arrangements" for the defense of Malaysia and Singapore, to which Britain would contribute forces that would include five escorts and a possible submarine. These units would be based at Singapore where a new Maritime Joint Operations Centre was established. The cost would be £5–10 million a year. As for the carriers, the *Ark Royal,* which had been working up in the summer after her extensive £30 million refit, was to be kept "until the late 1970s" by which time the new cruisers would be becoming available.[64] In the last eighteen months of the Labour Government, there had been much discussion about providing these cruisers with Harrier V/STOL fighters, but all that had actually been promised were studies. Carrington's ministry was no more forthcoming than Healey's. All the Supplementary White Paper promised was a Harrier buy "if further study shows that their provision would be effective and give value for money."[65] In order to release resources to sustain the carrier, the conversion of the third cruiser, HMS *Lion,* to a helicopter ship was cancelled. The *Ark Royal* was fully fitted to carry the new Phantoms, but the *Eagle* required some modifications, albeit limited ones, to operate the new fighters. The government felt it could not afford the £5–10 million required for this work. More importantly, the manpower tied up in the ship, and her air group, was needed elsewhere, as were *Eagle*'s Buccaneer bombers. There were no Phantoms to spare, given RAF requirements. So, the *Eagle*'s planned demise in 1972 was to go ahead on schedule. Training of naval pilots for fixed-wing aircraft, stopped in 1966, was not to be restarted, and the *Ark Royal*'s Phantom and Buccaneer squadrons (which would be deleted from projected RAF strength) would be increasingly manned by RAF aircrew.

While certainly securing value for money out of the carrier's extensive refit, the *Ark Royal* decision meant that the Royal Navy would at times still lack air support when the ship was under repair. (The *Hermes* had ended her last commission as a fixed-wing carrier in June 1970 and was awaiting conversion to a commando carrier.) The new government, therefore, put extra life into the planning for a surface-to-surface missile system, and it was announced that the French Exocet MM 38, which was already quite advanced, would be purchased for destroyers and frigates. Work was also progressing on a submarine-based anti-ship missile system, a project that had suffered some delay in the late 1960s.

Those who had expected a U-turn in policy were disappointed. In effect, the move westwards of the Royal Navy was to go ahead as planned. Even attempts to maintain some residual presence in the Persian Gulf soon collapsed. There were deployed the seven mine countermeasures vessels of the 9th MCM Squadron and a frigate (usually of the "Tribal" class) from the Far East Fleet. By the end of 1971, the MCM Squadron had been disbanded and the ships withdrawn, the last Commander Naval Forces Gulf, Commodore Sir Peter Anson, hauling down his flag at HMS *Jufair*, the shore establishment at Bahrein, on 4 November. HMS *Intrepid,* accompanied by the frigates *Minerva* and *Falmouth,* was in attendance. October 31, 1971, was the last day of the validity of the Anglo-Malaysian Defence Agreement. That day, the ships of Britain's last "Far East Fleet" sailed past its last commander, taking the salute in the RFA *Stromness.* Led by HMS *Glamorgan* (wearing the flag of the flag officer, second in command) were the frigates *Scylla, Argonaut, Gurkha, Arethusa,* and *Danae,* together with the repair ship *Triumph.* Aircraft fom the *Albion* and the *Eagle* also took part, as did six RFAs. After this final nostalgic display, Rear Admiral J.A.R. Troup, the last Commander Far East Fleet, hauled down his flag. He was replaced by Rear Admiral D.C. Wells, RAN, the first commander of the joint-service ANZUK (Australia, New Zealand, United Kingdom) force set up by the new Defence Arrangements that came into force on 1 November. The ANZUK forces included a small joint squadron composed of British escorts and ships of the other two Commonwealth navies. The first squadron was made up of HMS *Gurkha* and HMS *Jaguar,* HMAS *Swan,* and HMNZS *Otago.* Although the naval detachment was commanded by a British commodore, there were echoes here of the long-forgotten Harwood Committee's proposals that Commonwealth forces in Singapore should be given over to an Australian flag officer's command.[66]

The events of October 31 were the prelude to the official creation of a single Royal Navy fleet command. On May 1 Admiral Sir William O'Brien, the Western Fleet commander, had taken over ultimate responsibility for Rear Admiral Troup's forces. On 1 November O'Brien's successor, Admiral Sir Edward Ashmore, was officially designated Commander in Chief, Fleet (with the rather unfortunate acronym CINCFLEET). Virtually all of Ashmore's fleet was now West of Suez, except for up to six frigates and (sometimes) a conventional submarine in the new ANZUK force, on Beira patrol or as guardship at Hong Kong.[67]

Below Ashmore were a number of subordinate commanders, notably five flag officers, one each for the newly formed First and Second "Flotillas," one for carriers and amphibious ships, one for submarines, and one for sea training. The flotillas were formed of the squadrons of frigates and destroyers based at Portsmouth and Chatham (FOF1) and Devonport (FOF2). The First Flotilla was the old command Flag Officer Flotillas, Western Fleet and the Second the previous Flag Officer, Second in Command Far East Fleet. The use of the word flotilla for such large commands was a little incongruous, but the term squadron still had NATO's imprimatur for the smaller organization that had traditionally been a "flotilla" in the Royal Navy. The aim of the new large flotilla organization was to "provide a clear and positive chain of command for operational and support purposes and provide the maximum possible association of each flotilla with its flag officer with benefits of fighting efficiency and training that this will make possible."[68] In other words, there were now three flag officers who could command three powerful tactical surface forces as required, FOF1 and FOF2 and FOCAS, the latter being designated Commander of Carrier Group 2 of the NATO Strike Fleet. Additional subordinate commands were the Hydrographer of the Navy, in charge of the Survey Fleet; Captain Mine Countermeasures; and the commanders of the residual overseas organizations in the Caribbean, South Africa, and Hong Kong. In order "to divert the highest possible share of manpower and money" into this operational fleet, a high-level committee was set up in early 1968 to examine the Royal Navy's support infrastructure ashore. As a first step to rationalization, the separate Portsmouth, Plymouth, and Chatham commands were unified in 1969 under a single admiral, CinC Naval Home Command or CINCNAVHOME, who also had responsibility for all shore training.[69]

By the early 1970s the Naval Staff had seen significant changes also. As if to mark the East of Suez withdrawal decision, it had been completely restructured in 1968. The post of DCNS was abolished and the Staff grouped into three sections, each under an ACNS. ACNS(P) continued to control Plans and NHB. He soon lost Administrative Planning to the Chief of Fleet Support (the pre-1964 fourth sea lord), but picked up the Polaris Performance Analysis Group (PPAG). ACNS(O) retained Naval Operations and Trade and took over a renamed Directorate of Air Warfare and a new combined Directorate of Naval Warfare made up of the four previous warfare, tactics, and weapons policy divisions. In 1971 the Directorate of Fleet Management Studies was added to ACNS(O)'s responsibilities. The third assistant chief of Naval Staff, ACNS(Operational Requirements) replaced ACNS(W) in 1968 with control of new Directorates of Naval Operational Requirements and Operational Analysis. This reflected the new, more professional and sophisticated approach to these subjects following the lessons of the carrier controversy and the Future Fleet Working Party. In 1972 DNOA became the Directorate of Naval Operational Studies with a "sideways" connection with PPAG. This was no doubt a prelude to planning the upgrading of Polaris. Certainly the Naval Staff was trying hard to improve the institutional framework of its planning and policy process to make it more responsive to the more complex needs of the new era.[70]

The fleet for which the revised staff structure provided the directing "brain" entered the 1970s a surprisingly impressive force despite the previous decade's rhetoric of "cuts." Some fifty-one major surface combatants were in service in European waters compared to thirty-four in 1965, an increase in surface ship strength of a third. Submarine strength in home waters was about the same, although more boats were nuclear, reflecting that about a third as much again was being spent on attack submarines as had been spent in the mid-1960s. The number of European-based mine countermeasures vessels had more than doubled from eighteen to forty-three, while instead of the entire amphibious squadron being East of Suez it was now all within the NATO area. There had been no reduction of expenditure on these forces. The total reduction in active strength was a mere five or six units, and could be accounted for by the withdrawal from service of almost all the Far East conventional submarine squadron. It was true that only one carrier remained (and money spent on these ships had been halved), but there was now almost double the number of large guided-missile destroyers, and both cruisers were fitted with ASW helicopters. Spending on major surface combatants was, in fact, 10 percent up. It was certainly arguable that, despite reductions in expenditure on the "general-purpose" navy of over a quarter since 1966, in terms of overall capability the Royal Navy was more or less in the same state in the early 1970s as it had been when the Wilson administration had taken office. What was different was that now it was no longer a post-colonial police force. Almost half the savings in the naval budget had come from closing overseas bases. A greatly reinforced fleet was deployed in home waters to face a first-class superpower opponent. The legions were home; the problem would now be to sustain them.[71]

CHAPTER · NINE

THE EASTLANT NAVY

Although it did not seem so at the time, the 1970s might be described as a kind of "Indian Summer" for the postwar Royal Navy. The decade ended with a third more money being spent on the general-purpose navy than at its beginning. The maintenance for much of the time of one aircraft carrier in commission symbolized at least the semblance of a great power naval capability and the whole East of Suez navy slotted remarkably well into its new primary Atlantic or "Eastlant" role. Not that the Royal Navy had entirely shed the capability to operate farther afield. For a time at least, British forces remained in the Mediterranean, and naval squadrons even persistently appeared in their old Far Eastern stamping grounds. Moreover, it seemed increasingly clear that the death of the Royal Navy's fixed-wing carrier capability had been somewhat exaggerated. New carrier-like ships began to appear in the shipyards, and a whole new generation of warships began to enter service, which promised that a substantial naval capability would be maintained into the 1980s and beyond. Nevertheless, signs of strain continued to show. Commitments outside the Atlantic, never as entirely forgotten as policy statements implied, became even more difficult to fulfil as the Royal Navy's roles in home waters developed a new emphasis. In the mid-1970s concentration on the Atlantic and the Channel roles became more complete, but question marks appeared even over the Eastlant forces as the manpower problem, which had been festering ever since the move to wholly volunteer services, reached near-crisis proportions. By the end of the decade, it was clear that it would be hard to avoid yet another root and branch review of Britain's defense policy in general and of her naval policy in particular.

The shape of the fleet in the early 1970s was still very much that of the East of Suez force, with the list headed by HMS *Ark Royal*, now having emerged from her last major refit. Except for her aircraft arrangements this had not been as extensive as the *Eagle*'s, having been curtailed when a 1972 disposal date was proposed. Now the *Eagle* was cannibalized for stores and spare parts to keep the other carrier going. The *Ark Royal*'s normal air group was composed of twelve Phantom FG1s of the Royal Navy's only such squadron, 892, fifteen Buccaneer

S2s of 809 Squadron, seven Sea King HAS 1 ASW helicopters of 824 Squadron, and four Gannet AEW 3 early-warning aircraft from 849 Squadron.[1] Equipped with Wessex transport helicopters were the two operational commando carriers, the *Bulwark* and *Albion*, the latter facing a doubtful future since she was next in line for a refit, and the newer *Hermes* was in dockyard hands being converted for a similar role. The *Albion* was duly paid off for scrap when the *Hermes* reentered service in her new configuration in 1973.[2]

The submarine service came next in the listings, having by now been labeled officially as the Royal Navy's main striking force. Over twenty boats were in operational service in 1972, or preparing for it.[3] Of these, some six were nuclear. The first class of SSNs was now complete, even though a shortage of design staff caused by the Polaris program had dictated retaining the basic *Valiant* type in production for longer than intended. At last, however, a new class was about to enter service. Flag Officer Submarines pushed for an improved design in the late 1960s, and Vickers was brought into the design process to expedite its development even before the first order for a new boat had been placed. The aim in the design of the new SSN-OX was to make all possible improvements without extensive research and development being necessary. Considerable changes were made in the layout of the new boats in order to simplify their design and to improve overall capability. The first member of the new class, HMS *Swiftsure*, the seventh British SSN, was laid down on 6 June 1969. The last navy minister of the Labour Government, the able and intelligent Dr. David Owen, was a keen convert to the SSN, being very impressed by operational analysis of its capabilities and potential. He used his not inconsiderable influence to put as many in the building program as possible. The aim was a total force of some twenty units.[4]

Despite official enthusiasm for the nuclear submarine program, devaluation forced a cut in the SSN building rate. This had the effect of taking nuclear submarine building away from Cammell Laird. The Merseyside yard completed its last SSN, HMS *Conqueror*, in November 1971. Vickers Armstrong of Barrow now had a monopoly on SSN construction, and although Vickers's record was better than that of its competitor, the new SSNs still did not appear with quite the speed intended. It had been hoped to get the *Swiftsure* into commission before the end of 1972; she actually appeared in April 1973. Nevertheless, during the 1970s a steady stream of *S*-class boats would appear; the *Sovereign* in July 1974, the *Superb* in November 1976, the *Sceptre* in February 1978, the *Spartan* in August 1979, and the *Splendid* in January 1980. The time of building per boat varied from just over three years to just over four. The balance of the submarine fleet was made up of the *Porpoise* and *Oberon* classes with one or two old rebuilt *A*s just surviving into the 1970s.[5]

The assault ships *Fearless* and *Intrepid* were both in commission in 1972, although it had been decided to use one as a training ship for midshipmen from the Royal Naval College, Dartmouth, to replace the squadron of three frigates (latterly Type 12s) previously used. The two cruisers *Blake* and *Tiger*, converted to carry helicopters, were also still in service, their interim Wessex 3 helicopters being replaced by Sea Kings in 1973. The "County" program of eight large guided-missile destroyers was completed in 1973, and six or seven were normally in commission. All these ships were now fitted with the ADAWS-1 computer action information system and were considered to be "high value" general-purpose combatants that might well be the heaviest ships in some future surface task group. With the possible

HMS *Bristol* emerged in 1973 substantially changed from her original plans. She proved useful for trials with new systems, such as the Sea Dart being fired here.

absence of immediate air support, some enhancement of the "Counties" antiship capability seemed prudent, and in 1972 it was announced that the newer four would be the first ships to receive the Exocet missile. HMS *Norfolk* was the first to be converted, and she fired her first trials missile in 1974. HMS *Bristol*, the one and only Type 82, was finally completed in 1973 and was employed as a trial ship for the new Sea Dart SAM and Ikara ASW missile systems. This was despite a very serious fire that gutted her steam-machinery spaces not long after commissioning. The decision to give the rather large 6,700-ton ship both full steam and Olympus gas-turbine propulsion was vindicated when the ship continued in commission on the latter engines only.[6]

The conventional gun- and torpedo-armed destroyer was almost dead by 1972 with only two ships remaining, HMS *Cavalier* in full commission and HMS *Caprice* being used as a training ship. The *Cavalier* was decommissioned that year and was eventually preserved as a museum piece; the *Caprice* continued in her training role until the end of the decade. The larger *Daring*s and the rest of the modernized *C*s had suffered slightly accelerated ends as either scrap or foreign sales in order to allow more modern frigates to come into service within the continued budgetary and manpower ceilings. The last *Daring* in service in 1970 was HMS *Diamond*, and she remained as a stationary harbor training ship before being broken up in 1981. The "Battle"- and "Weapon"-class radar pickets were also scrapped, but one rather odd survivor was HMS *Matapan*, a "Battle" that had spent almost all her life in reserve. She was given a major rebuild to convert her into a trials ship to test new sonars, notably the sophisticated 2016 planned for the "Leander" replacement frigates. The work took two years, but the ship only spent a few years in commission in her new role.[7]

The main surface escort by the 1970s was the frigate, with over sixty vessels in full commission or on trials and training duties. The Type 15 conversions of the early 1950s were by now disappearing, with only two, the *Undaunted* and the unarmed training ship *Rapid*, in the 1973–74 Strength of Fleet figures.[8] Also beginning to go to the breakers were the Type 14 "Second Rate" ASW ships, although the much rebuilt example, HMS *Exmouth*, was running as the Royal Navy's first all-gas-turbine ship to test the concept. The "First Rate" designs of the 1950s still provided the bulk of the active frigate force together with the "Second Rate" "Tribals." The 1973–74 Strength of Fleet figures listed as active ten Type 12 ASW ships (with two more on trials and training duties), four Type 61s, three Type 41s, four "Tribals" and some nineteen *Leander*s (and one more on trials work). The last of the *Leander* line, the twenty-sixth such ship built for the Royal Navy, HMS *Ariadne*, was now in service.[9] The last ten units had been built to a two-feet-wider design and had other improvements that in some ways made them a separate class. The main armament remained a Wasp helicopter for ASW weapons delivery, although the latter also carried some antisurface capability in the shape of the AS 12 missile. This had been acquired after the sinking of the Israeli destroyer *Eilat* by Soviet-made missiles fired from Egyptian motor attack craft. Without carrier cover, surface combatants needed long-range protection from such vessels.[10]

By 1972 the earliest *Leander*s were being rebuilt to carry both the Australian Ikara ASW torpedo-carrying missile and an advanced combat data computer system, ADAWS-5. The first conversion, the *Leander* herself, entered service at the end of the year. The Ikara system had looked as though it would die with the Type 82 destroyers but was kept going by its supporters. It had advantages over the

One of the Ikara ASW conversions of the *Leander* class, HMS *Euryalus*. With Ikara ASW missiles, weapons-delivery helicopter, Mark 10 mortar and variable-depth sonar, these are powerful, if very specialized, vessels.

helicopter in terms of reaction time and availability, but it lacked some of the helicopter's flexibility (such as personnel transport and antisurface capability). Hence the controversial decision was taken to remove the 4.5-inch guns from the Ikara frigates and fit the new missile forward; the helicopter was still carried aft. The nonavailability of the Lynx necessitated the retention of the Wasp helicopter. The Mark 10 mortar was also kept as the close-range ASW weapon. With modern data links allowing the missile to be fired on the sonar information provided by other vessels, the Ikara *Leanders* were extremely capable ASW platforms, albeit highly specialized ones. Three other ships were already in hand for conversion in 1972, and the eighth ship was converted by 1978. By then the original intention to create a dozen Ikara *Leanders* had been replaced by a policy of rebuilding the last eight "narrow" ships to a more flexible general-purpose format with Exocet missiles forward, a Lynx ASW helicopter, and ASW torpedoes. These ships also retained the long-range air-warning radars of the original design and were equipped with a more austere CAAIS computer fit.[11]

A new frigate appeared from a novel source in 1973. She had been built for the Nkrumah regime in Ghana, but the end of that government in 1966 had led to the cancellation of the order. The ship had lain incomplete in the Clyde for some years before being purchased by the Royal Navy. Although intended as a training ship, HMS *Mermaid*, as she was named, was used on operational duties despite her limited capabilities—two old 4-inch guns, four Bofors guns, and a Mk 10 mortar directed by some relatively unsophisticated sensors and electronics. Her diesel propulsion made her somewhat slow, and she was only suitable for such duties as Hong Kong guardship where her small crew made her an economical naval presence. She was sold off to Malaysia in 1977 after a very short career in the Royal navy.[12]

The year 1973 also marked the appearance of the initial example of the new generation of ships planned in the previous decade: HMS *Amazon*, first of the Type 21 frigates. The Future Fleet Working Party of 1966 seems to have recommended a single *Leander* replacement in the general-purpose/ASW frigate category. An outline Naval Staff Requirement was then raised calling for a relatively small vessel of 2,600 tons with a crew of two hundred. Given both the short supply and the increased cost of personnel, manpower saving was deemed to be especially important. The Sea Wolf point-defense missile system was to be carried to deal with both air and missile threats. In the antisubmarine role the primary armament would be a weapons-delivery helicopter, and either a gun or surface-to-surface missiles would be carried for antiship use. This frigate was announced in the 1967 Supplementary Statement on defense.[13]

The talk in mid-1967 was still of retaining the East of Suez policy until the mid-1970s and of a specialized naval and military capability for use in the area even after withdrawal. What seemed to be needed was a ship to serve perhaps more as a colonial gunboat than for "big war" functions, and there ensued an exercise in "writing down" the recommended frigate design in order to produce a ship that would give the maximum number of hulls for the least cost. Moreover, it was hoped that Australia, in whose bases and forces much hope was put by the supporters of a continued East of Suez presence, would cooperate to produce a joint "patrol sloop." The new controller, Rear Admiral Horace Law, and the Naval Staff seem to have had little faith in the ability of their Ships Department to produce a cheap enough design, especially since Britain's two main private warship builders, Vosper Thornycroft and Yarrow, were both claiming to be able to do much better. They pointed respectively to the 1,200-ton Vosper Mk 5 frigates building for Iran and the 1,600-ton Yarrow frigate under construction for Malaysia. Both yards claimed that they could produce a ship such as the Naval Staff required for just over 60% the cost of a *Leander*-class frigate. With the Ships Department in its usual under-manned postwar state and unable, given its other priorities, to produce a design, the opportunity was taken to declare an open competition, and in February 1968, a joint tender was accepted from Vosper and Yarrow for the design of the new vessel.[14]

The role of the ship had now changed with the withdrawal from East of Suez. The new "patrol frigate," as it had now become, would have to serve primarily in Eastlant waters. The proposed ship was not a real *Leander* replacement for Atlantic ASW duties, but still seemed a good way of getting a new class of light, cheap frigates to replace the eight old diesel ships of Types 41 and 61 at least. Admiral Law pressed on with the concept, and a revised staff requirement was soon drawn up. The ship would have to be capable of defending a convoy or task force against attack by submarines or surface ships. A self-defense capability would be provided against aircraft, missiles, and fast patrol boats (the last-named being a topical threat in 1967 with the recent sinking of the Israeli destroyer *Eilat*). With "general capability," as defined by the then minister of defense, in mind the ship would be capable of long deployments in all weathers. Even more importantly she had to be economical in crew and simple to maintain. Interestingly, a good appearance was also specified. Board approval for the requirement was obtained in July 1968, and the design was completed two months later. The first ship was ordered in March 1969 and was completed by Vosper Thornycroft, as HMS *Amazon*, in 1974.[15]

It soon became clear that the ships would not be quite as cheap as originally expected. The first ship cost over four times the intended price. Also, it proved less than easy to build all the required capabilities into the hull. Despite attempts to shut them out of the design process, the naval constructors insisted on their own standards in many areas of the design. The Australians soon found the ship too expensive for the capabilities it possessed and pulled out of the program. Despite the promise of the design, when it came to execution the high hopes of the Naval Staff in their new ship proved not to be well founded. It had been hoped to fit Sea Wolf to the ship, but it was not only the long-drawn-out development program of that missile that delayed matters. There was an insufficient margin of top weight for the system, despite an unprecedentedly high use of aluminum, in the ship's construction. The more advanced versions of the old Sea Cat system were to remain the ships' standard AA weapons for the rest of their lives. The more austere CAAIS computer system was fitted as the ships' nerve center.[16]

The new frigates came into service between 1974 and 1978, and later units were among the first ships to carry the new Lynx helicopter with its antisurface radar and ASW weapons delivery capabilities. It was found that some additions could be made within the limited margin of stability of the class. From 1977, Exocet missiles were fitted in addition to the automatic 4.5-inch gun, and ASW torpedo tubes were also added. Fast, and with good maneuverability, the Type 21s, as they were designated, were certainly rakish in appearance. They soon became popular commands and postings, although a serious fire in the lead ship in 1977, followed

Always popular by virtue of their looks were the Type 21 frigates of the 1970s. This is one of the later examples, HMS *Active*, completed with Exocet missiles.

by two losses in the Falklands War, began to cast some doubts on their ability to absorb damage. Prolonged service in heavy seas in the 1980s caused serious cracking of the hull, which had to be rectified by adding strengthening plates amidships.[17]

A project with an even higher priority than the Type 21s was the development of a new air-defense ship to replace the *Bristol*'s abortive sisters. The design for this ship accounted for much of the prior commitment of the Ships Department's draftsmen. The new Sea Dart surface-to-air missile system, first deployed in the *Bristol*, had been intended for smaller ships in the first place, and a version of the system was designed to fit into the aft section of the existing *Leander* design. In 1965 Vickers produced a private-venture 3,250-ton Type 3009 design for a combined diesel/gas turbine frigate armed with Sea Dart, the new Mk 8 gun, a Mk 10 mortar, and a weapons delivery helicopter. With the feasibility of a small Sea Dart ship clearly shown, work began in 1966 on such a vessel. Initial studies produced a ship in the £19–20 million range, almost twice the required cost limit of £11 million. In May 1967 the Admiralty Board considered the problem and authorized the naval constructors to produce a ship to meet the lower ceiling. A design, mounting Sea Dart forward, was prepared, priced at £11.25 million at predevaluation prices.

The required roles were area defense against air attack, ASW, naval gunfire support, and surveillance in the Cold War. To meet this price constraint, the ship was in essence an improved *Leander* with all-gas-turbine propulsion. There was little or no room left for modernization in the design, and everything was done to cut costs. With a full ADAWS-4 computerized-action information and fire-control system specified for the ships, even the most marginal cost-cutting methods had to be adopted, and the controller insisted on a somewhat arbitrary cut in length from over 450 feet overall to just over 400. The beam was also narrowed somewhat.

This was proved to be a less than wise decision, as it had significant adverse effects on the seaworthiness of the class for only limited savings, and after ten units had been built to this design, the last ships of the class were constructed to the original, slightly enlarged concept of their chief designer, M.K. Purvis.[18]

Although numbered in a "frigate" series like the Type 82s, the Type 42s, as they were known, were classified as "destroyers" to reflect their air-defense role. The first ship, HMS *Sheffield,* was laid down on 15 January 1970, but the second RN ship did not follow until March 1972. Another Type 42 was begun at the end of that year, two at the beginning of 1973, one in 1974, two in 1976, no less than three in 1978, one in 1979, and two in 1980.[19] More may well have been intended. The type had been an early export success, with Argentina extending to the 42 an earlier stated interest in the 3009. One was built at Vickers alongside the *Sheffield* and a second in Argentina. The Type 42s turned out as compact and relatively cost-effective warships. One contemporary assessment described the type as ". . . a compact and workmanlike addition to the Royal Navy and one admirably suited for its European role," but they remained cramped, awkward, and difficult to operate.[20] The major weakness of the design, a lack of short-range air-defense capability against small aircraft, was not considered of great importance at the time, given the nature of the threat in Eastlant waters and the expected performance of the Sea Dart missile.

Another ship planned to carry Sea Dart was the most spectacular and controversial of the new surface combatants recommended by the Future Fleet Working Party—the new helicopter-carrying command cruiser. A new cruiser had in fact already been under development for some time when the decision to cancel the CVA 01 was made in 1966. This original plan was for a helicopter-carrying, guided-missile-armed escort cruiser of about 6,000 tons with a capacity for nine Wessex ASW helicopters. Such a ship would free the CVA for purely attack functions. The end of CVA 01 meant that this smaller ship would now provide the task force with its command and control facilities and with ASW cover from a complement of the planned large Sea King helicopters. The ship would also have antiaircraft capabilities with missiles and antisurface capabilities with both helicopters and missiles. It seems that the designers now began to explore two options: a 12,500-ton cruiser of more or less conventional layout with an upper hangar for six Sea Kings (a larger version of the Italian *Vittorio Veneto* in concept), and a more radical 17,500-ton carrier-like "through deck" ship with a larger hangar for nine helicopters from the top of which the aircraft would fly. The latter design represented a more effective use of space and had the greatest development potential both for new helicopters and possible V/STOL aircraft.[21]

In early 1967 a Sketch Staff Requirement was issued that gave the studies greater weight, and in the middle of the year, despite the economic situation, the government gave approval to begin planning for the new ship. The first sea lord, Sir Varyl Begg, whose antipathy to the small carrier proposal had led to official rejection of the Future Fleet Working Party Report, leaned towards the more conventional cruiser design. He was supported in this by his vice chief of Naval Staff, Vice Admiral Sir Peter Hill-Norton, a fellow gunnery officer. In 1968, however, a change of personnel at the top swung the situation in favor of the other design. Owen, the new junior minister responsible for the Royal Navy, was inclined to go for the "through deck" design, an opinion strongly influenced by the new first sea lord,

The Admiralty Board in 1970, shortly before the change of government. The strong and dynamic team led by David Owen as under secretary of state for the Navy, and Admiral Sir Michael Le Fanu as first sea lord did much to set the Royal Navy on course for the following decade. (Imperial War Museum)

Sir Michael Le Fanu, who took up office in August. The option of a "through deck" was allowed back into the planning process and Naval Staff Target 7079 allowed both designs to be considered. Two detailed studies were carried out. The conventional layout became Study 21 and the "through deck" ship, 22. The argument of improved helicopter capacity was used to justify the latter layout. Study 22 was soon enlarged into Study 23 with a larger displacement of 18,750 tons. Operational analysis advised a capacity of at least ten helicopters to allow four in the air at all times. With Hill-Norton's departure and his replacement by Sir Edward Ashmore, the balance tilted decisively in favor of the through deck design, and in 1970 a full Naval Staff Requirement was duly drawn up for a Through Deck Command Cruiser (TDCC). Le Fanu and Owen were united in the view that it would still be imprudent to call the ship a carrier. The ship would be costly, but if necessary, "County"-class vessels were to be taken out of service prematurely to release resources.[22]

The Wilson Government had left open the question of whether V/STOL aircraft would fly from the new ships. This was an issue of considerable political sensitivity and in 1969 Owen spoke carefully in the House of Commons on the possibilities of RAF Harriers with uprated engines operating from both commando carriers and the new cruisers.[23] Le Fanu, who kept a Harrier model on his desk, also insisted that it mattered little whether pilots flying Harriers from the new ships wore light blue or dark blue uniforms.[24] The following year Owen again hedged on the question of V/STOL. A through deck, he argued, was required in any case "to allow the most effective operations of the cruiser's complement of large anti-submarine helicopters, one of its primary functions." Nevertheless, the ship's layout would give the new cruiser much greater flexibility "and it would offer significant advantages if the V/STOL option were to be taken up at any time in the future."[25] Owen and Healey, his chief, were anxious to keep the prospect of a carrier-type ship in existence. With an election due soon a public row with the Navy would be damaging.

The Harrier and its experimental predecessor were no strangers to the ships of the Royal Navy. As early as February 1963 the first P1127 prototype had landed on board HMS *Ark Royal*, and in 1966 one of the Kestrel development aircraft carried out trials on the commando carrier *Bulwark*. The RAF did not forget the potential of operations at sea when it produced the Air Staff Requirement for a service version of this aircraft, the definitive Harrier, in the aftermath of the P1154's cancellation. The machine came into service with the RAF in April 1969, and tests with fully vertical operations from the cruiser *Blake*, and in short-take-off form from the carrier *Eagle*, led to official approval for RAF Harriers to operate at sea. In 1971 No. 1 Squadron RAF performed further trials from HMS *Ark Royal* to test the concept of operating from carriers. It was clear that the Wilson Government's idea of using RAF V/STOL aircraft on carriers was not dead yet.[26]

Progress, however, was somewhat halfhearted, an important reason being that the RAF Board of MOD viewed the whole "through-deck cruiser" idea with the deepest suspicion. Relations between the Royal Navy and the Royal Air Force were uneasy at the time, despite a 1970 compromise reportedly agreed upon between the then first sea lord, Admiral Hill-Norton, and the chief of Air Staff that left tactical control of RAF Strike Command aircraft to the Air Force in return for promises always to meet naval demands for air support at sea. Rumors of continued disagreements over this matter (including its being connected with the premature resignation of CinC Western Fleet Admiral O'Brien) were fueled by reports that exercises specifically held to test RAF land-based air support of RN forces, notably "High Wood" in November/December 1971, resulted in a less than adequate performance.[27] In such circumstances Royal Navy support for its own Harriers was bound to increase, and it was just as natural for the service that had just effectively asserted monopoly rights over *all* British military aircraft to oppose them. The Royal Air Force had no money for extra Harriers in its long-term costings. Moreover, it felt that any appearance of the Royal Navy being able to defend itself in the waters around the United Kingdom would be used by the government to undermine a substantial part of the requirement for a specialized air-defense variant of the proposed multi-role combat aircraft (MRCA). The air staff seriously doubted the ability of a few subsonic Harrier-type aircraft with limited avionics and ship-based control facilities to cope with the threat of supersonic Soviet bombers. The air force was caught in something of a dilemma. Support for RAF Harriers in small carriers might assure RAF control of any maritime Harriers that were procured, but at the cost of giving support to what the air force regarded as a flawed and dangerous TDCC concept. Continued foot-dragging held the risk of giving the Royal Navy the opportunity to make the case for a naval Harrier as part of the Fleet Air Arm. In the event, the latter happened. About the time of the June 1970 election, with the new Pegasus 103 engine giving the enhanced performance the earlier Harriers had lacked, the Naval Staff initiated studies of a fully navalized "Maritime Support" version, obtaining sanction the following year for a Naval Staff Requirement to be drawn up. The Naval Staff Target document was issued in August 1972, and three months later, in November, Hawker Siddeley, the manufacturers, were contracted to do a study of the design of a specialized "Sea Harrier" for fighter, reconnaissance, and strike duties with the Royal Navy. The machine was to be capable of operating off both the TDCC-type ship and from the assault ships. To cut costs to the minimum, the basic Harrier airframe was to be unaltered. The work was effectively done in six months, and by 1973 the stage was set for a government decision to authorize the aircraft.[28]

Now, however, economic problems intervened. The Heath administration's management of the economy proved no more successful than any of its predecessors', given the structural problems with which the government had to grapple. In 1971–72 Chancellor of the Exchequer Anthony Barber, worried by increasing unemployment, attempted to reflate the economy by encouraging consumption. There was also a reversal of the previous desire to cut public expenditure, and the defense budget benefited with the announcement in the 1972 White Paper of an acceleration in the construction program. Some six major surface ships, four Type 21s and two Type 42s, were ordered as well as smaller vessels and auxiliaries. In real terms defense expenditure increased by perhaps as much as 8 percent in 1971 and 1972 on a calendar year basis. But it was something of a false dawn for the Royal Navy and the other armed forces. The year 1973 was to prove a disastrous one economically with a fall in defense expenditure in real terms.[29]

The first danger signs appeared in 1972. More problems in the docks, coupled with a high inflation rate, saw considerable withdrawals of capital from the country. The balance of payments went into sharp decline, and Britain's forthcoming entry into the EEC, timed for the beginning of 1973, promised to make the situation worse, if only temporarily. In June 1972 the pound was allowed to "float" in value, which it did in a downward direction. Given a rate of domestic inflation that was becoming a serious problem, exports were not helped much, and the balance of payments situation worsened as imports became ever more expensive. A reversal of economic course was required, and in May 1973, the chancellor of the exchequer announced cuts in public expenditure of £100 million in 1973 and £500 million in 1974. This came just at the time that a decision was required on whether to procure the Sea Harriers for the Royal Navy or not. With the chiefs of staff in any case reportedly still deadlocked on the project, delaying the Sea Harrier decision seemed an easy way both to save money and avoid controversy. Indeed, the Royal Navy was lucky that the new "cruiser" was approved before the end of the "Barber Boom" in shipbuilding. The order was in fact placed on 17 April 1973 with Vickers as the prime contractor. The yard had been chosen two years before and had already done considerable work on the design.[30]

By now the TDCC had acquired a new designation—CAH, or "helicopter carrying heavy cruiser" in the American system the MOD(N) now used. Unfortunately, the Royal Navy's grasp of the meanings of these abbreviations has never been entirely firm, and soon the accepted meaning seems to have been "cruiser (even sometimes "carrier") assault helicopter," a strange title as, at this stage, the ship had no assault role (though it acquired a secondary one in 1976). The ship had become a gas-turbine-powered 19,000-ton monster, bigger than a pre-World War I battleship, and with a greater displacement than a 1945 light fleet carrier. Between fourteen and seventeen aircraft could be carried in the hangar alone, above which there now stretched a flight deck slightly angled to avoid the Sea Dart

SAM launcher at the bows. Exocet missiles were to be carried to starboard of this system. The complement was to be between eight hundred and nine hundred, less than a third of the *Ark Royal*'s.[31]

Despite official silence on the matter, it was obvious that the new ship was intended for V/STOL, and tentative forecasts of the ship's operational complement, five Harriers plus nine Sea Kings, were openly publicized. Yet no order for the V/STOL fighters came. In October 1973 the Arab-Israeli War and the oil crisis connected with it rocked the world economy. The oil price rise seriously exacerbated Britain's balance of payments problems. Moreover, the National Union of Mine-workers used the opportunity of an energy crisis to press a wage claim against the government's policies of wage restraint. Soon Britain was in the throes of a serious power crisis, with a State of Emergency being declared by the Heath Government in November. Along with draconian power-saving measures, notably a three-day working week, massive public expenditure cuts of £1.2 billion were announced to maintain confidence in the pound. This happened just at the time that a favorable announcement on the Sea Harrier was confidently expected, the chiefs of staff now apparently supporting the concept as a "necessary addition to naval strength." Nevertheless, the project was shelved yet again. Only the cruiser herself, named *Invincible*, was certain by 1974, and she was very slowly taking shape in the three working days per week allowed at Barrow.[32]

The crisis led to a General Election in February 1974, which saw a major swing against the government that had brought the country to such a parlous situation, dramatized by the worst monthly trade figures ever. The Conservatives narrowly got the largest single block of votes, but in Parliamentary seats Wilson's Labour Party had a wafer-thin margin. Almost 20 percent of the vote went to the Liberals, but Heath was unable to pull together a coalition. On 4 March Harold Wilson became prime minister once more, with Roy Mason as his minister of defense. (Mason was a strongly pro-defense Labour politician despite being sponsored by the ever more radical National Union of Mineworkers. He had at one point stood outside collieries giving out pamphlets in favor of Polaris!) In October the government attempted to secure an overall majority, which it succeeded in doing, but only just.[33]

In opposition, Labour had committed itself to "savings on defence expenditure of several hundred million pounds per annum over a period while maintaining a modern and effective defence system," and within two weeks of taking office announced a major defense review.[34] The motives for the review were as much political as economic, as the increasing strength of the Left in the Labour Party made some genuflection in the direction of defense cuts necessary. This was especially so as the government was by no means averse to the idea of reducing public expenditure in other spheres to lower consumption and stimulate exports. Wilson could not afford a left wing revolt, even after the October election. Moreover, despite the government's initial intentions, its public expenditure plans rose steadily, fueled by increases in pay and subsidies to cushion the poor against inflation's effects. There was, therefore, some force in the argument that rises in defense expenditure should be curtailed. The old argument that resources needed to be freed for industrial investment and exports was still as valid as ever, as Mr. Healey, now chancellor of the exchequer, stressed in his Budget speech in November 1974. The government's financial deficit was also mounting to disturbing proportions (it was estimated at over 10 percent of GNP for 1975–76), which threatened to undermine international confidence in the currency.[35]

In these circumstances it was surprising that the Mason Review did so little. The planned defense program, the government announced at the end of 1974, would come down from 5.8 percent to 4.5 percent of GNP, but this would take until the next decade. The 1975 Defence White Paper spelled out substantial savings of £300 million from a program of £4,000 million in 1975–76, rising to about £500 million per year from a planned £4,300 million annual figure in 1978–79 and £750 million per year from £4,450 million by 1983–84. These annual savings, the government proudly proclaimed, would in all add up to some £4.7 billion at 1974 prices. Yet these were all savings on *future* programs. Indeed, defense expenditure was still set to *rise* in real terms over the period 1975–77, after which it would remain fairly constant. Moreover, although this meant an inevitable fall in real terms in expenditure on naval forces, the Royal Navy in one respect gained significantly from the 1974–75 Defence Review in that its share of the increased defense budget was planned to increase from 25 percent to 28 percent.[36]

Several factors conspired to produce these rather strange results. First, the political position of the government advised against too radical a real, as opposed to declaratory, defense policy, just as it necessitated playing up what "cuts" there were. The Cabinet contained a substantial number of ministers, like Foreign Minister James Callaghan, who were only too aware of Britain's defense responsibilities, particularly to NATO. Amongst the senior ministers only Chancellor Denis Healey, reflecting Treasury opinion, Employment Secretary Michael Foot, and Social Services Secretary Barbara Castle really pursued the idea that Britain's defense expenditure ought to be seriously cut to bring it down to that of her allies and trading partners—although Mr. Healey's long-standing pro-defense commitment sometimes caused him to waver in his attack. Moreover, the defense secretary, Mason, fought a skillful Cabinet battle, stressing the importance of jobs in the defense industries at a time when unemployment was becoming a serious problem and good relations with the trade unions were central to the administration's economic strategy. With shipbuilding needing every order it could get, the Royal Navy's building program and dockyard infrastructure were job-creating schemes of considerable general appeal to Mr. Wilson's Cabinet. A final factor was pressure from Britain's NATO partners, who were disturbed at some of the proposed cuts in capabilities within the Alliance area and wished to see them mitigated.[37]

That final factor decided where the axe would fall. In effect the 1974–75 Review carried the logic of 1968 to its conclusion. Britain was finally to liquidate almost all of her military commitments outside NATO. There had already been a quiet removal of forces in previous years, and by 1974 the ANZUK naval force contained but one British frigate. This was now to be withdrawn. Discussions were also held with the government of Hong Kong over the size and functions of the British force. The previous British government had decided to assign Hong Kong a permanent British frigate guardship to supplement the 6th Patrol Craft Squadron (as the MCM Squadron became in 1973). In 1972 the old Type 61 frigate HMS *Chichester* was specially converted into what was effectively a large gunboat for the task. But she had only a short time on station. As a result of the Defence Review, she was withdrawn in 1976, although the patrol craft were to remain, subsidized by the Hong Kong government. The Far East RN submarine, based once again in Australia, was also to be withdrawn. The post of senior officer West Indies was to be abolished, and the permanent deployment there of two frigates was also to be ended. The politically troublesome Simonstown Naval Agreement, the last vestige of the old South Atlantic Station, was also to go, but after some debate, it was decided that HMS *Endurance* was to remain in the Falklands.[38]

Some naval reductions were necessary within the NATO area, the emphasis being on reductions on the flanks rather than in the basic Eastlant area. The main casualty was Britain's historic naval presence in the Mediterranean. It was announced that after 1976 no surface combatants or MCM vessels were to be offered to NATO for use in this area, although British ships were to continue to visit the Mediterranean and carry out exercises. Britain was to abandon all her base rights in Malta by 1979. Affecting the northern flank also were the announced reductions in the amphibious force, with 41 Commando being disbanded upon withdrawal from Malta, HMS *Bulwark* being paid off early in 1976, her Wessex V squadron being disbanded, and HMS *Hermes* being re-equipped and redeclared to NATO as an ASW carrier.[39]

The last-named ship had already been used as a combined commando/ASW carrier in NATO's Exercise "Swift Move" in late 1973, carrying an ad hoc air group of sixteen Sea King ASW aircraft from three squadrons—her resident unit 814 Squadron, 819 Squadron, normally based at Prestwick, and 824 Squadron brought in from the *Ark Royal* (then under refit). Only four of 845 Squadron's Wessex 5 transports were retained in a weapons-delivery role, against the fourteen or more that would be borne if the ship was operating as a commando carrier. There had also been talks, abortive as it turned out, of an RAF Harrier deployment in 1974. Effectively the *Hermes*, with her more than adequate HQ facilities, had become an "interim CAH" and a fully combatant carrier once more. The ship was used for barrier patrols and to screen a U.S. carrier, pointing to the continued main "Striking Fleet" support role that maintenance of an ASW carrier would provide.[40]

To return to the amphibious reductions, it was also decided to keep only one of the *Fearless/Intrepid* pair running at any one time. Plans for a new commando helicopter and two new amphibious ships were officially abandoned, and plans for "alternate means of movement in the long term," namely the acquisition in an emergency of ferry-type merchantmen, were "in hand."[41] It was something of a blow to the Royal Marines, but much was salvaged, notably 3rd Commando Brigade with its helicopter and heavy support, a third of which (plus the aircraft) would continue to be fully arctic trained for use in Norway. By now it was clear that the Northern Flank role was one that the marines could argue well and that still meant something to the government and within the Ministry of Defence. With opposed landings becoming ever more doubtful, given the scale of the potential opposition, the Royal Marines were willing to settle, at least for the time being, for a primarily civilian shipping "pre-inforcement" role rather than an apparently rather old-fashioned "re-inforcement" one.

The 1975 White Paper made clear that certain measures, such as the acceleration of the planned conversion of the *Hermes* to the ASW role, had been done in reaction to the pleas of the NATO allies to "reconsider" the reductions perceived to be most damaging. Another compensatory announcement was the earmarking of the *Engadine*, the RFA-manned helicopter support ship, to NATO's Channel command in an ASW war role. The British also promised to continue to take part in the Naval On-Call Force Mediterranean. The government stressed that it expected the Allies to offer inducements in the form of support. Allied interdependence was also an argument for the plans to cut conventionally powered submarines. This was put over as a useful form of defense specialization, leaving conventional submarines to such navies as the Dutch, while Britain concentrated on the more prestigious nuclear boats.[42]

The Naval Staff placed highest priority on the maintenance of the cruiser program and reluctantly accepted cuts elsewhere. The accelerated withdrawal of some of the *Porpoise*-class submarines was to mean a 25 percent reduction in conventional submarine strength. The 1975 White Paper also announced that the total number of major surface combatants and MCM vessels was to come down by a seventh (14 percent). Older ships were to go sooner than intended and new construction programs were cut, some nine ships being deleted from planned building programs. Specific casualties were two Type 42 destroyers slated for ordering in 1975–76.[43] Again, however, one should be a little careful about taking these cuts at face value. Most of the reductions were in old "Ton"-class minesweepers withdrawn from the Mediterranean. In fact, close scrutiny of succeeding White Papers reveals that throughout the life of the Labour Government the total number of active major surface combatants in any one year stayed almost exactly the same, with a 5 percent fluctuation about a mean of around fifty-eight ships. Even more surprisingly, the operational submarine fleet was only a boat or two down from the Heath Government's figures. Mr. Mason's sleight of hand, and that of his successor, Mr. Mulley, was remarkable one way or the other, either in circumventing the expenditure cuts, or in padding the strength of fleet figures in the White Papers. Given the fact that the ships were there to be counted, there was more of the former than the latter.[44]

It was questionable indeed whether the "cuts" in new construction were very real either. Shipyard problems, especially shortages of skilled labor with the beginnings of the North Sea oil boom and the requirement for construction gangs for oil rigs, meant that what ships there were under construction were often subject to serious delays. There were shortfalls in electricians, coppersmiths, and steelworkers. Vickers's yard at Barrow was very seriously affected, with serious delays to the CAH and the Type 42 destroyers under construction there. The *Sheffield* took over five years from launch to completion, while HMS *Cardiff*, with workmen removed from her to sustain *Invincible*'s building, took no less than seven years, having to be towed in 1976 from Vickers where she had already spent three years, to Swan Hunter's yard on the Tyne for completion. With subcontractors delivering equipment late, it was highly questionable whether the British shipbuilding industry in the late 1970s could have built more ships than it did. The program was still quite a substantial one, with, for example, five Type 42s on the stocks and two more about to be ordered.[45]

These problems were made much worse by a tendency for the Naval Staff to change the specification of new ships several times while they were under construction. Relationships between the Ministry of Defence and the shipyards deteriorated, and litigation sometimes resulted, as in the case of HMS *Amazon*, first of the Type 21s, completed two years late at 109 percent over the expected cost. The *Sheffield*, first of the 42s, was almost as bad, two years late and 97 percent above original estimate. At the beginning of 1976 it was estimated that the five Type 42s and seven Type 21s in the yards were running eight to thirty-six months behind schedule! Delays meant increased costs—only half the increase in the cost of ships could be put down to inflation in the prices of raw materials and increases in pay scales.[46]

Rising material and personnel prices exacerbated the basic problem of the increasing sophistication, and hence increased unit cost, of warships. One example of this was the new mine countermeasures vessel. MCM work was now done more with sonar than with sweeps, and seventeen "Tons" had been converted to mine hunters with Type 193 sonars and more precise maneuvering capabilities. Work had been going on since the late 1960s on a "Ton" replacement, as part of which a new minehunter, HMS *Wilton*, was built to the old layout with cannibalized engines to test a new nonmagnetic construction medium, glass-reinforced plastic. The *Wilton* was a success, but much work was still needed to produce a design that was even cleaner magnetically and acoustically. The resulting ship, HMS *Brecon*, was built in the late 1970s, but at about £24 million was an exceptionally expensive ship for her size. Even though following vessels would be over a third cheaper, there could be no question of a new *Brecon* for every one of the forty or so "Tons" operational or on training duties. A dozen *Brecon*s were programmed, and this seems to have been left unchanged by the Mason Review.[47]

Another program that demonstrated even more clearly the problems of increased costs was the definitive Type 12 *Leander* replacement, the Type 22 frigate, the first of which had been ordered as one of the last actions of the Heath Government at the end of February 1974. This ship had had something of a troubled birth, having originated in 1968 as the Ships Department's 3,000-ton answer to the problem of a proper Eastlant frigate at the time of the Type 21 controversy. It soon became tangled up in Alliance politics as the possibility of a cooperative venture with the Dutch was explored. The latter, however, were not interested in the proposed Sea Wolf point-defense missile system, while the British did not like the idea of being constrained in length by Dutch docks or letting down their regular suppliers to buy Dutch materials. By July 1970 a purely British Naval Staff Requirement for the new ship had been drawn up, and the concept of collaboration was completely abandoned at the end of the year. With the cooperation of Yarrow, the designated shipbuilders, the new ship took shape to an enlarged design. Relations with the shipbuilders seem to have been somewhat uneasy because of Yarrow's doubts about the solidity of the program, given the financial background of the early 70s, and there were reportedly contractual difficulties, which, along with the defense cuts of 1973, delayed the ordering of the prototype.[48]

The 22 had by then grown into a 3,500–4,000-ton ship with a capacity for *two* Lynx helicopters, since doubling the helicopter capacity meant an increased probability of one aircraft being available, but in the event, no Type 22 frigate would have a permanent flight of two helicopters until the mid-1980s; the first ships went to sea with but one Lynx. The main sensor was to be the new and powerful 2016 sonar with a reputed range of up to sixty miles under certain conditions. The ship would carry four Exocet missiles and two 40-mm guns, while point-defense from aircraft and missiles was to come from two six-round Sea Wolf missile launchers and their associated radars. On test, in the trials ship HMS *Penelope*, Sea Wolf was proving to be an exceptionally capable missile with a capacity to engage even

The most expensive and sophisticated frigates built for the postwar Navy are the Type 22s. HMS *Brilliant* seen here distinguished herself in the Falklands War. She is one of the earlier vessels of the class; later ships are increased in length.

4.5-inch shells. The fully automatic system GWS 25 required no less than five FM 1600B computers, and there was another computer to control the sonar and a sixth to provide the CAAIS system that coordinated the whole weapons suite with the ship's sensors. The hardware-intensive computer solution was matched by the propulsion system where an all-gas-turbine system, like that for the Types 42 and 21, was controlled remotely from the ship's control room. All this complexity had saved manpower, which was limited to a maximum complement of about 225 against a *Leander*'s figure of over 250, but it significantly increased the ship's price. The first Type 22 frigate, HMS *Broadsword,* which Yarrow completed in 1979, cost almost *twice* the price of a contemporary Type 42! Despite this, however, the program was to go forward, and the 1975 Review announced that a further ship would be ordered that year from Yarrow. It is not clear how many of the nine "cancelled" ships of the 1975 Review were 42s and how many 22s, but at least fourteen 22s seem to have survived to be in the program in the late 1970s.[49]

The main role of these large and extremely sophisticated new frigates would be to act as "inner layer" escorts to carriers or cruisers in ASW task forces. Their procurement was, therefore, to a considerable extent predicated on the continuation of the cruiser program, and this assurance was specifically given in the March 1975 White Paper.[50] Indeed, two months later, with an eye to potential exports (Iran was showing considerable interest), it was finally announced that twenty-four Sea Harriers were to be ordered to fly from the new ship. This meant three thousand jobs with Hawker Siddeley (airframes), Rolls Royce (engines), and Ferranti (avionics), plus a thousand more if the Iranians took the bait (which they did not). What a Labour Government had taken away and a Conservative Government had not felt able to give back, a new Labour Government committed in theory to saving "thousands of millions of pounds" on defense now returned. The Naval Staff could congratulate itself on the success of almost a decade's hard advocacy and subtle bureaucratic in-fighting. The Royal Navy was back in the jet-fighter business. Indeed, at the time of the Harrier announcement, it was also stated by Mr. Mason that two more expected ASW cruisers would be ordered. It seemed almost a formality, therefore, when the orders were actually placed in May 1976 and December 1978, respectively, both with Swan Hunter on Tyneside, an area of considerable unemployment. Each cruiser meant jobs for four thousand men with several hundred more working for subcontractors.[51]

The success story seems even more remarkable when the events after the 1975 White Paper are reviewed. For the economic crisis that provided the background for the defense review became steadily more serious. In fact, the Defence White Paper emerged when still further cuts in public expenditure were in the air. On 27 February a major argument occurred in the Cabinet with Roy Mason fighting "like a tiger" to defend his future budget as set out in the draft White Paper. Mrs. Castle, worried about forthcoming cuts in social services, led the attack. The chancellor now defended Mason's plans, but the prime minister decided that the figures mentioned in the Defence Review were to remain "provisional." Exactly how provisional was, however, still a matter of some doubt. The following week the Cabinet in its final approval of the White Paper merely agreed that defense was as subject to review as any government program. Mrs. Castle threatened resignation if reductions in social services preceded further reductions in defense. Impatiently she referred in her diary to Mr. Healey as a "broken reed" on the defense cuts question.[52] Nevertheless, the chancellor and his assistants were making it increasingly clear that there was no choice but for further public expenditure reductions to deflate the overheating economy. These cuts would have to include defense.[53]

The package, a billion pounds in extent, was unveiled to the Cabinet on 25 March 1975. Negotiations continued over the next three weeks between Joel Barnett, as chief secretary to the Treasury, and the spending ministers. Mason, fresh from his "Review" and armed with the chiefs of staffs' words that they would not be responsible for carrying out present policies if the Treasury's full demands were met, resisted as strongly as ever. He would only concede half the £200 million the chancellor demanded. The decision went to the full Cabinet where, despite the pressure of both the Treasury ministers and the Social Services secretary, the defense cuts for financial year 1976–77 were only increased to £110 million. The cut was not significantly greater than in other areas much closer to the government's supporters' hearts, like food subsidies, the nationalized industries, education, and health. The usual principle of "equal misery" was being followed, and the 1976–77 defense budget was larger in real terms than that of 1971–72.[54]

Inflation remained a very serious problem in 1975 with prices rising higher than ever. High public expenditure was held by the government and Treasury to be a contributing factor to this. Unemployment was also steadily rising and by early 1976 stood at over a million. The government was determined that capital should be released to take up this manpower slack. This also meant reductions in the resources planned to be taken up by the public sector, including the armed services. In December there seems to have been a confrontation between the chancellor and the service chiefs in the Oversea Policy and Defence Committee, which made the chancellor "very angry" and more determined to get defense expenditure reduced by a further £400–450 million. On 16 December the public expenditure plans were discussed in Cabinet, with Mason showing his usual "ferocious fluency"

in defense of his funds. All he would concede was £100 million. The prime minister ·
tried to compromise and suggested Mason produce a paper on the implications of
a £275 million cut, but before this could be, Wilson allowed Mason to backtrack
still further by making the extra £175 million conditional on Britain's ability to
maintain her treaty obligations.[55]

The Expenditure White Paper published in February 1976 spelled out both the
rationale for the cuts and their consequences for defense. The government's purpose
was to "ensure that the increase in national output in the next three or four years
is not appropriated for use in the public sector, but instead is available to put the
balance of payments right, to provide for increased productive investment and to
allow a modest increase in private consumption." The defense budget was being
pegged at £4.54 billion (at 1975 prices). This meant a further reduction of only
£193 million for defense as the Health and Social Services secretary had feared.
Mason had indeed "got away with it." The government argued that it could achieve
its defense cuts, and those of April 1975, by "reductions in support, not the front
line." It went on to say that the reductions in expenditure would not "impinge on
the essential elements of our contribution to NATO."[56] The two ways of obtaining
the savings specifically mentioned were greater subsidies from Hong Kong and the
reduction of civilian manpower. The defense cuts were much smaller than those
proposed for housing or capital expenditure in the nationalized industries, and this
balance was stoutly opposed by the left wing of the Labour Party, which voted it
down in Parliament but would not pursue the opposition to the level of throwing
out the government.[57]

Reductions in government expenditure did not stave off steadily mounting pressure on the pound. Wilson, perhaps sensing the deluge to come, announced in
March 1976 that he was to be replaced by that old friend of the Royal Navy, Jim
Callaghan, a wartime acting lieutenant and later junior navy minister of the Attlee
years. Callaghan continued to take a great interest in the navy; he requested and
received constant updates of the position of the fleet. Alas, these ships and submarines were little defense from the financial threat. The month after the new
prime minister took office, sterling hit a new low of $1.70. By July the chancellor
was back in Cabinet asking for another billion pounds in expenditure cuts. When
Barnett began his negotiations once more, Mason dug in his heels again but found
no support, even from Callaghan, normally a strong supporter of defense expenditure. The prime minister, who personally intervened, made it clear that there
was no alternative but to defer some defense programs. Mason recognized that he
would have to shed still more expenditure and was forced eventually to settle for
losing a hundred million pounds, 10 percent of the total cuts. Even given this
sacrifice, the other ministers fought a steady rearguard action in several days of
Cabinet debate.[58]

Despite everything the government did to placate financial interests at home
and abroad, the sterling crisis deepened still further, and in September 1976 the
chancellor was forced to return dramatically from Heathrow airport as he was
about to set out on a journey to an international financial conference. By October
the pound was at an all-time low of $1.50. An International Monetary Fund credit
with strings attached seemed the only alternative. As a preliminary, yet another
round of expenditure reductions was set out with defense losing another thirty
million pounds, 60 percent of what the Treasury had rather optimistically asked.

Fred Mulley, the new defense minister, proved to be a little less successful than his predecessor in defending his budget, although he was to show remarkable skill in squeezing the maximum capability out of it. The IMF demanded still greater cuts, and some dramatic Cabinet meetings ensued in early December. Defense gave up a hundred million pounds for 1977–78 and 230 million for 1978–79, but the arguments over reductions elsewhere in the government's plans were more bloodstained as the total "package" was constructed.[59]

Given such weak economic foundations and the enormous political difficulties in making cuts in social services, it is hard to criticize the Wilson and Callaghan governments for cutting too much in defense or naval terms. Indeed, it is surprising that they did not go further. Real expenditure on the "general-purpose" Navy fell by less than 7 percent from 1975 to 1977. The government continued to stress its aim of maintaining front-line capabilities, but the reductions in tail rather than in teeth could only go so far in improving "efficiency" before operational capability began to suffer. The easy cuts to make in support and ammunition stockpiles did have an effect on the readiness of the fleet. The simple truth of the matter was that Britain, as usual, was trying to squeeze a little too much defense out of an inadequate budget.

This was especially true as far as the Royal Navy was concerned, as extra calls began to be made on the finite resources of the naval budget. From the earliest times the Royal Navy had been Britain's offshore policeman. Nevertheless, the

One of the "Ley"-class mine-location vessels, the *Bromley*, after four years in reserve, was commissioned in January 1959 as HMS *Watchful* for inshore fishery protection duties. She served in this role until 1966 when she was taken out of service to be scrapped.

service had always tended to regard such duties as not the most central of its concerns. Yet the developing technologies of seabed exploitation were fast increasing the importance of the offshore estate and the need to keep it in good order. One of the few bright spots on the British economic horizon was the prospect of opening up the great fields of oil and gas in the North Sea. This increasing utility of the sea as an area in itself to be exploited rather than as just a transport medium was reinforcing the tendency to "enclose" the oceans. These claims were also directed towards the control of more traditional economic activities such as fishing.

Fishery protection had been very much a minor naval duty for most of the postwar period. On its reconstitution the immediate postwar Fishery Protection Squadron had amounted to the frigate *Stork* and three ocean minesweepers in the North Sea, two corvettes, a minesweeper, and two motor launches on the south and west coast, and another corvette in the Scottish area. The *Algerine*-class ocean minesweepers provided the backbone of the squadron in the 1950s with six of these ships on duty, but towards the end of the decade they were replaced by four of the small "Second Rate" Type 14 frigates and four "Ton"-class coastal minesweepers. The two motor launches of the Channel Division were replaced by inshore minesweepers.[60]

The smaller craft were to maintain sovereignty over Britain's three-mile limit, but the role of the Type 14s was more "offensive," protecting British trawlers off Norway and Iceland from molestation by foreigners exercising their perceived fishing "rights." The main problem had been with Iceland, who imposed a twelve-mile fishing limit around her coast on 1 September 1958. Two days later a British trawler was arrested. The Fishery Protection Squadron had already received temporary reinforcement to deal with such problems, and the Type 12 "First Rate" frigate *Eastbourne* came to the rescue, removing the Icelanders' boarding party and putting them ashore in a whaler. As a gesture, the boat was given to the Icelanders. Some four British ships, plus an auxiliary, were soon on station.

As confrontation between trawlers and Icelandic Coast Guard vessels mounted, the British maintained naval protection, even big *Daring*-class destroyers being deployed on the duty. These powerful warships did not overawe the trawler-type patrol vessels of the Icelandic Coast Guard, which tried to use their little 47–57-mm guns to stop foreign trawlers, especially when these were within the old four-mile fishing limit. In 1959 the *Thor* fired a dozen shots in an attempt to capture one British boat, and one round near-missed the destroyer HMS *Contest*. The latter replied with four rounds of practice shot, successfully driving off the gunboat. There had been the odd collision also, as when the destroyer *Chaplet* rammed the Coast Guard vessel *Odinn* in May 1958. The latter was soon replaced by a new 1,000-ton patrol vessel of the same name. Their life having been made too difficult by the activities of the Icelanders, the British reluctantly accepted the new limit in 1961. By that time four *Darings*, thirteen other destroyers, and nineteen frigates had been on duty in Icelandic waters. The regular Type 14s suffered especially severely from the weather and had to be given extra strengthening.[61]

By the time this "First Cod War" came to an end in 1961, British trawlers were also having trouble around the Faroe Islands. One one occasion when a Danish frigate, an ex-British "River"-class ship, the *Neils Ebbeson*, moved to make an arrest, the trawler *Red Crusader* tried to make an escape. The Danish warship pursued, firing as she did so, and the Aberdeen trawler was holed. The Type 15 frigate *Troubridge* and the minesweeper *Wotton* of the FPS came to give assistance and escorted the trawler to Aberdeen, its home port. At that time the Faroe Islands did not officially claim a twelve-mile exclusive fishing zone, but when they did so in 1964, British warships were deployed to assert British rights while negotiations were held.[62]

In September 1964 Britain herself extended her exclusive fishing zone to twelve miles around her shore but, with an eye on Icelandic and Faroese waters, gave vessels that traditionally fished around Britain special permission to continue their activities. The British twelve-mile zone put a greater strain on the frigates and minesweepers of the FPS, which on occasions in succeeding years were themselves firing across bows to arrest boats. Sometimes more unconventional projectiles were used, as on one famous occasion when an especially successful minesweeper used a well-placed potato as its "minimum force" to stop a particularly troublesome poacher. Fishery protection duties also provided the last operational role for the fast attack craft in the Royal Navy. Two gas-turbine-powered 89-ton *Brave*-class fast patrol boats, built too late to serve in the defunct coastal forces organization, were used on fishery protection duties from 1962 to 1970. Their high speed proved useful and the fast 165-ton boat, *Tenacity*, built by Vosper Thornycroft as a private venture, was hired in 1971 and then purchased to retain the capability for the rest of the decade.[63]

With twelve miles the accepted fishing limit, the Icelanders took the lead in 1972 in pushing the boundary out further, to fifty miles. This included the richest fishing grounds for the cod, haddock, and flatfish that were the quarry of the British boats, and the British strongly opposed the Icelandic move. The Icelanders had strengthened their Coast Guard with another new, purpose-built, 1,000-ton vessel, the *Aegir*, and this ship opened "hostilities" with an ingenious and effective net cutter that cut the nets of a British trawler on 5 September. The British at first shied away from using warships, but instead hired large and powerful tugs that could come off best in ramming encounters with the Icelandic ships. This stratagem was unsuccessful, and in mid-May 1973, the trawler owners insisted that larger warships be sent in or they would withdraw. By that time there were two frigates just outside the limit, HMS *Cleopatra* and HMS *Plymouth*, and they were already flying their Wasps over the disputed zone. On the 19th the two ships moved in with a third frigate, the *Lincoln* (a Type 61), staying just outside to await relief by the helicopter-equipped *Leander*-class ship HMS *Juno*. Although there were a number of serious incidents before the end of May, the first collision, between the *Aegir* and the *Scylla*, did not occur until 7 June. In July HMS *Leopard* told the *Aegir* that if she opened fire with her 57-mm gun, the frigate would reply with her 4.5-inch weapons, although the British ships were strictly ordered not to use their overwhelming firepower offensively. The only device that *could* be used offensively was one that could cut the Icelanders' cutting gear. The Heath administration's reluctance to send in warships in the first place reflected a desire not to push the crisis too far. The government had to balance its fishing interests against the much more important strategic interest of keeping Iceland in NATO. British trawlers who engaged in counter harassment of Icelandic trawlers were told to desist, but collisions between Icelandic Coast Guard vessels and British frigates steadily mounted; the *Lincoln* and *Aegir* on 17 July, the *Arethusa* and *Odinn* three days later, the *Andromeda* and *Odinn* on 10 August, the *Apollo* and *Aegir* on the 29th, and the

Jaguar and *Thor* (a veteran that had served throughout the 1958–61 confrontation) on the night of 9/10 September. The Icelanders claimed that the British had adopted a deliberate policy of ramming and threatened to cut off diplomatic relations after the last incident, and two more collisions, the *Lincoln* and *Aegir* on the 22nd and the *Whitby* (an older Type 12) and *Thor* on the 27th, dramatized the seriousness of the situation.[64]

Eventually the British Cabinet decided that the situation was getting out of hand and that the Icelanders really meant to cut off diplomatic relations, an act that would have serious repercussions on NATO. The British forces and the tugs were duly withdrawn on 3 October. A compromise was reached in London the following month in which limited British fishing rights were conceded for two years. This second "Cod War" came at a time when the British were becoming rather more conscious of the need for their own strong maritime police force. The ability of the Icelandic "gunboats" to take punishment and apply minimum force effectively seemed to contrast markedly with the performance, creditable though it was, of the large, sophisticated warships "fighting with their arms pinioned," and with insufficiently sturdy hulls to stand the rigors of a conflict for which they had not been primarily designed.

At about this time, in fact, the Ministry of Defence seems to have commissioned a Working Party to look at the whole question of policing in the "Offshore Tapestry," the complex weave of resource interests that Britain herself would, given the trend of international opinion, soon be defending as assiduously as the Icelanders were defending theirs. The first sign of a new emphasis on offshore protection was the ordering of what promised to be a large class of coastal patrol vessels based on the RAF's *Seal*-type air-sea rescue boat. For longer range duties a series of studies was carried out that led to the drawing up of design parameters that seemed to be met by the type of 778-ton vessel already in use by the Scottish Office to police northern waters. One of these vessels, the *Jura*, was borrowed from the Scots by the Royal Navy in 1975, and an order was given to Hall Russell of Aberdeen for five slightly larger copies to be named after islands off the British coast. In the meantime an old naval tug, the *Reward,* was commissioned as a warship to complement the *Jura* on offshore patrol duties.[65]

The tough and seaworthy little "Islands," built in Aberdeen, would not have been out of place in the Icelandic Coast Guard, which in 1975–76 fought out its last, and perhaps most bitter, battle with the Royal Navy. For the Icelanders once more led the way in the extension of fishing zones, having declared a 200-mile limit in mid-1975 to take effect in October, except for the British who would have the right to fish until their existing agreement ran out in November. As soon as it did, the Icelanders began to take action against British trawlers, and back came the frigates to protect the British boats from harassment, net cutting, and arrest.

HMS *Leopard* was the first to reach the scene on 25 November. Before this third Cod War ended in June 1976, some twenty-two frigates had seen service in it—nine *Leander*s, six Type 12s, two Type 14s (one, HMS *Exmouth,* the modified all-gas-turbine trials ship), two "Tribals," a Type 41, a Type 61, and HMS *Mermaid.* These, along with some nine tugs, were required to counter the actions of six Icelandic Coast Guard vessels supplemented by two leased trawlers. There were at least forty-nine collisions recorded during the conflict, with the *Diomede, Gurkha,* and *Salisbury* recording no less than six bumps each. The *Gurkha* was not a great success due to the "Tribals' " lack of maneuverability, and no further vessels of this type were sent; on the other hand the old Type 14 frigates, although in their declining years, proved much more capable of mixing it with the gunboats. All but six of the frigates engaged had at least one collision. The vulnerability of the frigates was once more shown. Damage and the desire not to overtax the crews with duty that was both frustrating and demanding made the maintenance of seven ships on patrol (the standard strength) a great strain on the fleet's programmers. Other deployments had to be abandoned. Two frigates, HMS *Lincoln* and HMS *Jaguar,* veterans of earlier conflicts, were in fact taken out of the operational reserve at Chatham, now but a tiny "Standby Squadron." These ships were fitted with wooden protecting buffers on the bows, but they never had a chance to show their capabilities as "rams" since the Cod War was brought to a conclusion before they were placed in full commission. They were, however, temporarily left in service to cover the enforced absence of the worst-dented ships.[66]

This time Iceland did indeed break off diplomatic relations, and she also began to make noises about leaving NATO. This, coupled with the heavy costs of the operation and Britain's interest in a 200-mile zone for herself, led to another compromise in which a limited number of British boats would be allowed to fish in Icelandic waters until December 1976.[67] Britain enacted her own 200-mile limit on 10 December, only ten days after all British trawlers had left Icelandic waters, the British zone being absorbed into a more general EEC fishing zone at the beginning of 1977. The *Jura* and the "Ton"-class mine countermeasures vessels of the Fishery Protection Squadron were ready to police the area when it came into being, but sadly, the *Reward* had been sunk in a collision in the Firth of Forth in August. The first two new *Seal*-type craft, the *Kingfisher* and *Cygnet,* soon proved to be bad sea boats, thus precluding their use on extended patrols. They did, however, come in useful for Northern Ireland security work, a commitment necessitated by the "Troubles" that had begun in 1969. (Two small converted tenders, commissioned as the *Alert* and the *Vigilant,* were also used in Northern Iceland waters.) The next two "Birds," as they were known by the Royal Navy, the *Sandpiper* and *Peterel,* were sent to the Royal Naval Reserve as training ships and eventually finished up at the Royal Naval College, Dartmouth, as "Attached Training Vessels." No more were built.[68]

Somewhat more successful sea boats (although not as good as hoped for) were the "Islands," the first of which, HMS *Jersey,* entered service at the beginning of 1977. Before her four sisters were all in commission a further two were ordered. They were much criticized for their lack of helicopter capabilities and even more for their low maximum speed of sixteen knots, but they provided just the "presence" required among the fishing vessels and oil rigs of the 270,000 square miles of water for which the British now had responsibility. To get away even from a ship like the *Jersey,* a fast fisherman would have to cut his nets, an expensive sanction the Icelanders had found was very effective in itself. Nevertheless, it was recognized that the "Islands" were something of a "quick fix," and in the late 1970s Naval Staff Target 7040 was drawn up for a more capable and flexible vessel with helicopter facilities that would displace almost 1,500 tons. Hall Russell of Aberdeen, the builders of the "Islands," took the risk of laying down a ship to this new specification before getting an order, which, much to the yard's relief, arrived belatedly in 1980, along with another for a second ship. Both OPV 2s were in service by 1982. New technologies were also explored for the offshore policing role. After tests with a commercial vessel, a fishery protection hydrofoil designed for the Japanese was ordered "off the shelf" from Boeing at a cost of just over £6 million. She was commissioned in 1980 as HMS *Speedy*.[69]

These improvements in capability reflected to some extent the significant subsidy the Defence Budget was now receiving from other government departments for services rendered in the offshore area. The 1978 Defence White Paper demonstrated this for the first time. Some £5.27 million, just over a third of the total "offshore tasks" budget, was recoverable from the Department of Energy and the Departments of Agriculture and Fisheries for both England and Scotland. This covered the running costs of those vessels (and RAF Nimrod aircraft) engaged in joint fishery protection and offshore oil and gas installation protection duties. The Royal Navy received just over £2 million of this for the "Offshore Division" of its Fishery Protection Squadron. The remaining "Coastal Division" vessels, plus old Sea Devon transport aircraft used for surveillance, plus HQ facilities, cost only £3.16 million of "naval" money. A small extra contribution to the running costs of both ships and the Sea Devons was, however, obtained from the Department of Trade for the extra costs incurred by the navy in its role of policing the Dover Straits traffic separation scheme.[70]

A third of the total "Offshore Tasks" budget was taken up by hydrographic surveys reflecting the new emphasis on this long-standing Royal Navy commitment caused by the movement to enclose the seas. The Hydrographic Service had spent the immediate postwar years surveying the new wrecks that were strewn around the shipping routes off the coast of Britain. The service had available four prewar converted minesweepers and a slightly larger 1,140-ton vessel, HMS *Challenger*. For inshore work there were half a dozen motor launches. In the late 1940s four incomplete "Bay"-class frigates were converted into *Cook*-class survey ships to allow four ships to be used for overseas duties with four, plus the motor launches, kept at home. The overseas craft at this time were opening up the rivers of British Borneo for trade.[71]

The early 1950s saw the construction and delivery of a new, much larger, purpose-built survey ship, HMS *Vidal*, one of the first RN vessels to be equipped with a helicopter. The latter was used for air survey photography and transfer of shore observers and stores. The ship also carried three small survey launches. By the time she entered service in 1954, the Admiralty charts were being modernized to take account of radar and radio aids, and there was a new emphasis on underwater surveying for submarine purposes and ASW. The *Vidal* was only a limited success; she suffered considerable teething troubles with her power plant, which was of naval configuration, being a test bed for the diesels of the Type 41 and 61 frigates. Critics also argued that this installation made her too manpower intensive for her surveying task.[72]

By 1957 there were only six operational survey ships, the *Vidal*, the four *Cook*s, and the *Shackleton* (the only other surviving prewar ship, the *Scott*, was in refit). They operated all around the world from Britain's coasts to the Mediterranean, the West Indies, off Africa, in the Middle East, off Malaya, around Hong Kong, and even in the Southwest Pacific, where Admiralty charts needed updating. Six motor launches surveyed the South and East Coasts. These latter small craft were

Mainstays of the survey fleet in the immediate postwar years were four converted "Loch"/"Bay"-class frigates. Here is HMS *Cook*, completed in 1950 and put in reserve fourteen years later after service all over the world.

replaced from 1958 with the construction of three purpose-built inshore survey craft, the *Echo, Egeria,* and *Enterprise.* These ships appeared briefly with 40-mm guns on the forecastle, a mark of their wartime role of inshore minehunter. Complete replacement of the other survey MLs had to wait until the early 1960s, when two "Ham"-class inshore minesweepers were converted to a similar configuration to the *E*s.[73]

There was an intention to replace the two remaining prewar ships with another new-construction vessel that would have a secondary warship role, but the manpower squeeze of the early 1960s enforced a change of plan. In order to reduce the ship's complement, a commercial layout was adopted, based on that of an existing civilian research ship. The resulting ship, HMS *Hecla,* was laid down in 1964, and orders for two sisters were placed at the same time as the withdrawal of the converted frigates began. The latter had been far and wide in their work, the early sixties having seen them in the Pacific, the Indian Ocean, and the South Atlantic. With the two extra *Hecla*s earmarked for continued overseas work, two "Ton"-class coastal minesweepers were converted to survey vessels to cover the ex-frigates' home duties. This was an interim measure while six purpose-built, rather larger 800-ton coastal survey craft, were constructed, an order that was cut to four ships in the defense review process in 1967, two for home use and two for overseas.[74]

The shape of the hydrographic flotilla lasted into the 1970s—four oceangoing vessels (the *Vidal* being replaced by a new modified *Hecla*-class ship, HMS *Herald*), four coastals, and five inshore vessels. Their work acquired new relevance since not only had the seabed developed a new economic value, but the ever-deepening draft of tankers made accurate charts of the Channel essential. In 1974 the increasing demands for accurate knowledge of the oceans led the minister of state for defense to set up a Hydrographic Study Group. The report of this group the following year recommended a major increase in investment with four more coastal craft and three more inshore ships. The program was priced at some £34 million over the seven years to 1981. Nothing was done to implement this plan, although there were at least no cuts in the survey fleet. One of the inshore vessels was kept going with a civilian crew, while an inshore minesweeper temporarily replaced one of the specialized vessels, HMS *Egeria,* when the latter was damaged by fire.[75]

Not only survey ships continued to show the White Ensign around the world. Despite its primary Atlantic role the Royal Navy was loath to give up the capacity to operate worldwide. British imperial nostalgia could be legitimized by the requirement to demonstrate the "general capability" to operate outside the NATO area, a capacity that reflected the residual interests and commitments the United Kingdom retained around the globe. The Royal Navy itself, unhappy with a future that limited it to cold, grey, northern seas, and with centuries of experience in colonial and post-colonial peacekeeping duties in more congenial warmer climes, encouraged as much as possible an emphasis on these worldwide commitments. The concept of the "Group Deployment" was born, in which relatively powerful balanced squadrons of warships were sent on wide-ranging cruises, visiting areas of interest and exercising with friendly navies.

These became regular events in the 1970s. To support the Heath Government's policy of a token presence East of Suez, the helicopter cruiser *Tiger,* the nuclear submarine *Dreadnought,* and accompanying escorts went to the Far East in 1973. The following year a smaller squadron, led by the destroyer *Fife,* deployed into the Indian Ocean.[76] Despite the election of a new government, with its rhetoric of a complete abandonment of Britain's wider military roles, September saw the most ambitious group deployment yet. Under the command of the then Flag Officer First Flotilla, Vice Admiral Henry Leach, flying his flag in HMS *Blake,* Task Group 317.2 sailed all the way around the world. With the *Blake* were five frigates, the *Leander, Diomede, Achilles, Falmouth,* and *Lowestoft,* and the SSN *Warspite.* As the official press release had it:

> An important purpose of the deployment has been to visit those countries with which the United Kingdom is friendly and has strong trade connections. Every opportunity has been taken to exercise with ships and aircraft of foreign navies in order to further already well established friendly relations and demonstrate the effectiveness and potential of the ships that the Royal Navy possesses.[77]

The group joined with the carrier *Ark Royal* and the destroyer *Hampshire* in Brazilian waters for exercises with the Brazilian Navy before coming home.

The month after Leach arrived home the pattern of large/small-scale deployments was maintained when HMS *Glamorgan* set out with five frigates on another round-the-world voyage.[78] For the rest of the 1970s, as the deployments continued, a cruiser was available to act as flagship, and it was felt that the new cruisers/carriers would provide even more capable centerpieces for the 1980s.[79] The Naval Staff welcomed this diversion from being "mesmerised by the Eastlant area." In 1978 Admiral Sir Terence Lewin, the first sea lord, explained the situation thus: "The real value of Group Deployments lies much more in the opportunities they give for maintaining world wide expertise among our officers and men than the chance to exercise with non-NATO navies."[80] Clearly, despite appearances, the Eastlant Navy had a wider relevance.

A more permanent naval presence was also maintained in the West Indies, especially after Guatemala began to threaten the dependent territory of Belize more seriously from November 1975. A frigate serving in what the contemporary White Paper called the West Indies "Station" was sent to provide a reassuring presence and a Royal Marine reinforcement for the garrison. The frigate reappeared whenever tension increased in subsequent years, as in 1977, and by 1979 it had become a formal deployment as "Belize guardship . . . at short notice to be on station in Belizean territorial waters." The deployment continued into the 1980s despite Belizean independence. The operational assault ship was also regularly deployed into the Caribbean at intervals in her combined training and operational role.[81]

The mid-1970s saw the Royal Navy carry out two significant operations in the Mediterranean area. One was helping clear the Suez Canal. With the Egyptian regime of President Sadat disentangling itself from its Soviet connections, a process fully encouraged by Western governments, Britain offered a small mine counter-measures flotilla to contribute to the clearing of the Suez Canal after the Yom Kippur War. Three coastal minehunters, the latest glass-reinforced plastic vessel, *Wilton,* and the older vessels *Maxton* and *Bossington,* together with their mother ship *Abdiel,* spent seven months in mid-1974 on mine clearance, and the *Abdiel* returned in 1975 with the *Sheraton* and the *Hubberston* to complete the work. During the first phase of the clearance, in July 1974, another kind of "clearing up" operation took place when the commando carrier *Hermes,* the destroyer *Devon-*

Since 1970 the large Westland Sea King helicopter has formed a vital part of the Royal Navy's antisubmarine warfare capabilities. This is an HAS 5 in service since 1980 with Sea Searcher radar, dipping sonar, and advanced sonobuoy capability. The operation of such large helicopters provides the primary rationale of the Royal Navy's ASW aircraft carriers.

shire, and the frigates *Andromeda, Brighton,* and *Rhyl* (supported by four Royal Fleet Auxiliaries) evacuated 1,500 civilians of various nationalities from Kyrenia in northern Cyprus following the Turkish invasion of that island. The *Hermes,* carrying sixteen Wessex 5 transport helicopters of 845 Squadron and the four Sea King ASW helicopters of 814 Squadron had landed 41 Commando to help safeguard the security of the British sovereign base areas, but there seems to have been little question of more offensive intervention, despite Britain's status as guarantor of the independence and integrity of the island. Reinforcements, including the carrier *Ark Royal,* were not too far away but were not deployed, leaving the available British ships vulnerable to Turkish air power. When the Turks accidentally bombed and sank their own destroyer, the *Kocatepe,* her survivors were picked up by the *Andromeda,* the RFA *Gold Rover,* and the Sea Kings of 814 Squadron. One of the latter landed on the *Andromeda,* the first time such a large helicopter had done so on an RN frigate.[82]

Britain's unwillingness to act more positively to safeguard the independence of Cyprus was a sad reflection on the limits of her real power in the Mediterranean, and in 1975 the Defence Review announced the decision to recognize realities and withdraw from Malta. The island, independent since 1964, elected the neutralist government of Mr. Dom Mintoff in 1971, which took over the dockyard and tried to renegotiate the existing defense agreement with Britain. The negotiations were not easy, and British soldiers and service families were withdrawn with the assistance of the cruiser *Blake* and commando carrier *Bulwark.* Eventually a deal was arrived at in March 1972 whereby the United Kingdom would continue to use the base until March 1979 in return for various payments, including an annual fee of £14 million. The base was henceforth to be used for British ships alone. Malta ceased to be a NATO base, and the South East Mediterranean Command's recent departure to Naples was confirmed. British ships continued to visit Malta on work-up or in transit, and the attempt was made to maintain as permanent a presence as possible with available resources. In 1977 some fifty-seven separate British warship visits took place, and the *Ark Royal* visited the island for the last time in November 1978, a month before her withdrawal from service. In 1979 the final closing of the naval base began, and in March, three RFAs and the guided-missile destroyer *London* arrived to evacuate personnel and material, including the last of the Commando. With due ceremony the British flag was lowered over the base, and on 1 April HMS *London* sailed away, carrying Rear Admiral Oswald Cecil, the last of a long line of British naval commanders at Malta. Henceforth, although British warships would still appear periodically in the Mediterranean, the "guard-ship" at Gibraltar would be at the farthest east British base.[83]

Despite the continued withdrawal from permanent commitments "East of Gibraltar," the government's defense program was still too ambitious to be fitted comfortably into its budget. A factor that did much, albeit temporarily, to square the financial circle was the government's policy of wage restraint adopted with increasing success in 1977–78. The administration, reluctant to push the trade unions too far by statute, tried to show the private sector a good example by limiting salary increases in the public sector. This significantly helped the defense budget to meet the costs of its overloaded program. In 1977, as for many years before, more defense money was going on wages, 40 percent, than on equipment,

37 percent. By 1979 the relationship was reversed, with equipment going up to 40 percent and pay coming down to 37 percent.[84]

Yet, as had been the case with cuts in support activities, a price had to be paid, and it was heavy. Indeed, by 1979 the armed forces in general, and the Royal Navy in particular, were in the throes of a manpower crisis. To put this into perspective we must return for the last time to the mid-1960s, when we looked at this chronic problem in detail. The effect of the defense reviews of that period on naval manpower had been somewhat negative, both in recruiting and retention. In 1966–67 significant shortages were apparent in officer recruiting. Perhaps even more ominously, only a quarter of ratings (rather than a third in 1964) were re-enlisting when they had completed their initial nine years of service. The numbers of men on twelve-year engagements re-enlisting showed a similar fall. The cuts of 1967–68 mitigated the situation to some extent as the manpower requirement was reduced. Vote A, the authorized strength of the service (including Royal Marines), came down from its 1960s peak of 98,600 in 1965 to 95,100 in 1968. There was a second slump to just over 90,000 in 1969. It had been announced in 1968 that some 16,000 naval officers and men were to go by 1973–74, but the relatively poor recruiting/retention situation meant that only a small number of compulsory redundancies were necessary. Nevertheless, the manpower future after cuts looked a little bleak, and in a signal to the fleet in early 1968, Sir Varyl Begg had felt forced to stress the opportunities for foreign travel that the future Eastlant navy would still offer. Contrary to some previous ideas, foreign deployment (within limits) was now felt to be an incentive for men to stay in the service.[85]

Begg had become very concerned about service morale and "felt that the Navy now needed an injection of self-confidence, requiring talents different from his own."[86] Le Fanu, his chosen successor, was very much the man to do this. His last job had been CinC Middle East, where he had kept up morale during the difficult Aden withdrawal. Le Fanu cultivated the media to project a positive public image for the navy and he also did much to encourage a similar effect for the "management" within the service. Considerable changes took place in the administration of the Royal Navy. A new system of "continuous" ship commissions was introduced, in which ships remained in commission between long refits, men being drafted on board for not longer than thirty months: half that period might be deployment abroad. Le Fanu even felt confident enough to abolish the 150-year-old rum ration that had now become an anachronism. The service now required active brains to operate complex equipment and not an anesthetic to mitigate the boredom and monotony of life in "pre-electronic" warships. There was, however, considerable reluctance in some quarters to abolish the "tot," given the already dubious state of morale, and Owen, the navy minister, insisted that the service retain for general welfare purposes the sum of money that would otherwise have gone on rum. He also insisted that ratings be given a beer ration and noncommissioned officers be given drinking privileges like their commissioned superiors. The last "tots" were issued at the end of July 1970. By this time Le Fanu had contracted leukemia and, to the dismay of the service, had to give up the promised post of chief of Defence Staff. At the beginning of the month in which the rum ration was to end a new first sea lord took office, Sir Peter Hill-Norton, who early in 1971 was elevated to his predecessor's designated post of CDS. The professional leadership of the navy was left to Sir Michael Pollock.[87]

The election of a Conservative Government in 1969 with its protestations of a high priority for defense helped consolidate a manning situation that had already been showing signs of improvement in the last years of the Wilson Government. The first statement of the Heath Government on defense manpower pointed to the problem that the low level of recruitment in the 1960s had left. Male other-rank recruits for all three services had fallen "disastrously" from 40,000 in 1966–67 to 28,000 in 1968–69, and even the improved figures for 1969–70 were still 25 percent below requirements. Officer shortages were still a problem, the Royal Navy being picked out for specific mention. The paper committed the government "to make life in the Services sufficiently attractive to compete successfully in all respects with civilian employment; and to enhance the status of military service in the national life."[88]

Things looked good in the early 1970s. Naval officer recruitment was up for both short career and full career commissions. Recruitment and re-engagement of other ranks also increased significantly. Pay was improved with the concept of a "military salary," which put single and married men on the same rates, and an improvement was made in the rules for payment of separation allowances. Ship commissions were also extended in length to bring stability into the lives of naval personnel. The last Heath Defence White Paper of 1973 stated almost proudly that naval officer recruitment was now within 91 percent of target for full career officers and that over half the naval ratings were prolonging their period of service. Given the continued cuts in Vote A from 86,000 in 1970 to 81,200 in 1973, this was a more or less satisfactory situation, although there were still shortages in some specializations. It was significant perhaps that the Defence Review of 1974–75, which planned to reduce the Royal Navy by another 6 percent between 1974 and 1979, necessitated only a thousand compulsory redundancies from manpower reductions of five times that size.[89]

In its Defence Review of 1974–75, the Wilson Government did little to help the manpower situation, as the potential recruit was more likely to listen to news reports of "defense cuts" rather than notice the government's continued real commitment to a powerful first-line fleet. Officer recruitment went down, although rating recruitment remained satisfactory for a time; then that declined also. By 1979 the rather complacent comments of previous White Papers had been replaced by an admission of the seriousness of the manpower situation. It was not just that too few people had been coming in to meet requirements. The recruiting targets themselves, it seems, had not been high enough; therefore, they had been increased for 1978–79 "to relieve overstretch and improve operational capability; and to make good losses by premature voluntary release."[90] Nevertheless, the increased number of people recruited, unsurprising given the high national level of unemployment and the perception that things were not going to improve, was insufficient to meet the increased targets. Moreover, it could do little, at least in the short term, to help the hemorrhage of skilled technical manpower.

The holding down of public sector pay was steadily biting as skilled personnel recognized the opportunities that still existed "outside" and left the service. The 1979 White Paper frankly and drily summed up the problem:

> The total number of men and women leaving the Services, for all reasons during 1978, continue to include an unusually high outflow among the more experienced

and highly skilled categories following request for voluntary release. If current rates of outflow from this source continue, the consequences in the loss of trained officers and men will be serious for the armed forces and the Government attaches great importance to correcting this trend.

The paper admitted that dissatisfaction with pay was one of the main reasons for the outflow; but it also cited other contributory factors, notably the deteriorating conditions of service, including the turbulence and increased separation that had been "unavoidable consequences" of the 1974–75 Defence Review.[91]

The real problem was the failure of the government to match its defense program with adequate resources. Trying to do too much with too little always put a strain on the people caught up in the attempt, for despite the Callaghan administration's attempts to check the growth of the defense budget, the strength of the fleet was higher than that it had been for some time. The official figures show that the prime minister, who as a junior minister had fought to retain old frigates in reserve almost thirty years before, had not forgotten his old instincts. The 1978–79 White Paper listed no less than sixty-one major surface ships in service or preparing for it, the highest figure since 1962–63. This figure included no less than three carriers, the *Ark Royal* in her last year of service, and the *Hermes* and *Bulwark* resuscitated as ASW carriers, while the *Invincible* was close to her belated completion. The new "cruisers" were increasingly obvious replacements for the three carriers, not the existing cruisers, and this was symbolized by the decision to name the third "through deck" CAH, ordered in 1978, *Ark Royal.* A new type of SSN, a third-generation boat named *Trafalgar,* was under construction and more were planned. Six Type 42 destroyers were listed and the *Broadsword,* the first of the Type 22s, was among the forty-two frigates. Six "Counties" and HMS *Bristol* remained in full commission.[92]

This level of strength was impossible to sustain if for no other reason than there would soon not be enough men to man it. It looked as if by 1980–81 the number of major surface ships would be no more than fifty, as particularly manpower-intensive vessels like the *Blake* and *Tiger,* and the older "County"-class destroyers, were slated for withdrawal. It was not that extra money was not provided. In 1977, at the NATO meeting of defense ministers, Defence Secretary Mulley committed the Callaghan Government to a steady 3 percent rise in real terms in defense expenditure. The 1978–79 naval budget showed a significant rise back to mid-seventies levels and a new high for the entire decade. Yet even with these increases it was not possible to pay for new equipment and for skilled sailors to operate it. The accelerated pay rise promised by the Conservatives, who swept into office in the spring of 1979, only promised to make the equipment program difficult to sustain. As informed outside observers were pointing out, the fundamental problem was that the defense program was overloaded.[93] It needed cutting to match what the country was willing to afford. This would soon dawn on the strong-minded new prime minister, Margaret Thatcher. When it did, the Royal Navy began to realize that perhaps the 1970s had not been such a bad decade after all.

CHAPTER · TEN

WHICH WAY FORWARD?

The paradoxes of British defense policy were clearly illustrated by the events of 1979. One of the last acts of the Labour Government, originally elected on a pledge to cut defense expenditure by hundreds of millions of pounds, was to order in March and April the last three Type 42 destroyers (all to the new "stretched" design) and two new Type 22 frigates, the first stretched Batch 2 ships. These vessels would together cost over £500 million. Two months later in June the Thatcher Government, committed to raising Britain's defense expenditure, announced the decommissioning of the cruiser *Blake* and five frigates. There have been questions of electoral interest in the shipbuilding orders so close to polling day. Given the manpower crisis, there was certainly little option but to decommission the ships. Yet both acts illustrate clearly the fact that the relation of government party to naval policy was by no means as clear as some commentators would have one believe.[1]

Indeed the new government's commitments to raise service pay, necessary as it was to staunch the outflow of personnel and which gave some substance to the administration's pro-defense rhetoric, created as many problems as it solved. The Callaghan administration had followed an "equipment-heavy" naval policy. Paying the going rate for the personnel meant either savings on equipment or increases in budgetary allocations. The published naval budgets for the early 1980s were indeed the highest since the new methods of accounting had begun in 1966, but the government did not wish to go any further.

The Thatcher Government's commitment to severe cuts in public expenditure meant that, although defense rapidly climbed in the relative standings of individual items of government expenditure, the real increases were no more substantial than those planned by the Callaghan Government. Indeed, advantage was taken of not having spent all the 1979–80 budget to claim an increase of 3.5 percent in real terms in defense expenditure for 1980–81. In reality the government was planning to spend £180 million *less* than the Callaghan administration had planned for 1980–81, not enough to sustain the armed forces' equipment budget, given rising costs of some 5 percent.[2]

Some administrative savings were possible, but there were pressures for more fundamental changes. A Defence Programme Working Party was set up by the

Ministry's permanent secretary, Sir Frank Cooper, to suggest an approach to re-shaping the defense program in a more affordable direction that would be more rational than equal cuts spread between the three services. The Working Party, composed of a senior civil servant, a general, and an air vice marshal, recommended cutting naval programs in order to sustain the continental commitment. At a week-end meeting, the Royal Naval College, Greenwich, was once more the scene of interservice strife as, led by Admiral of the Fleet Sir Terence Lewin, Chief of the Defence Staff, the navy claimed "that their entire shipbuilding program would be ruined by the cuts." The RAF, as keen in debate as they had been fifteen years before, answered with figures "slipped to them by friendly civil servants" showing that the navy would still have a substantial building program even with the proposed cutbacks.[3]

The navy could not avoid rescrutinizing their programs and cutting some of their more ambitious features. This was done with some reluctance. At the time of the 1974–75 Defence Review, an in-house study of "The Navy in 1985" seems to have generally concluded that the emphasis in naval procurement ought to remain on high-quality vessels even at the expense of smaller numbers. Ideas for cheaper, less-capable ships were generally not followed up, despite work by the Forward Design Group of DG Ships. Several "future light frigate" concepts were explored in the 1970s, some of considerable austerity. By 1978 a Type 24 design had emerged as a "simple ship which could act as a towed sonar ship for the RN" and be suitable for export. Again, little official interest was shown, but by 1980, encouraged by the new Navy Minister Keith Speed, there was, at last, a growing recognition of the need for more austere warships. A new range of ships was investigated, a developed version of the cheaper frigate, a more austere mine countermeasures vessel, and even the use of mercantile hulls as V/STOL-helicopter carriers.[4] Plans for new, highly impressive air-defense destroyers were cancelled. The Naval Staff had produced the Type 43, a 6,000-ton ship planned to mount both Sea Dart area-defense missile launchers and Sea Wolf point-defense systems fore and aft, a 4.5-inch gun on the forecastle, Exocet missiles over the stern, and a large helicopter in a hangar amidships (with flight deck above between the funnels). Not only would this ship have cost too much—at least £200 million per unit (probably much more)—but its manpower requirements, at almost 350 men, were too great also.[5] First the design was reduced in scope to a more austere Type 44; then it was cancelled completely. The best the navy could hope for in air defense was a modernization program for the existing Type 42s with an upgraded Sea Dart system.

Yet the savings promised by the cuts in new destroyers were far in the future. More immediate problems were soon pressing the government. The foundation of the new administration's financial management was the annual "cash limit," which departments were not allowed to exceed. Overspending in one year had to be offset by cuts in the next. Reluctantly the government was forced to increase the defense cash limit during 1980–81, but even this was not enough to cover expected costs. The effects of both the government's deflationary policies and the world recession were to lower civil demand for British industry. Contractors, therefore, concentrated on their defense contracts and presented the bills significantly faster than expected. Dramatic measures proved necessary to limit the budgetary impact of this. To save £100 million, an emergency "moratorium" was placed on spare parts and equipment purchases from August to November 1980, with a period of "strin-

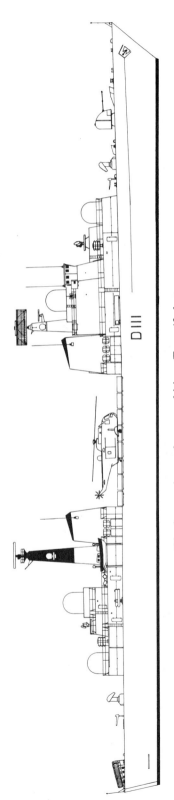

D III

The impressive and over-ambitious Type 43 destroyer

Missiles:	Two twin Sea Dart surface-to-air missile systems
	Four sextuple Sea Wolf short-range anit-missile missile systems
	Four MM 38 Exocet surfact-to-surface missiles
Armament:	One single 4.5" Mark 8 DP gun
	Two single 20-mm Oerlikons
	Two STWS triple torpedo tubes
Decoys:	Two Sea Gnat chaff launchers
	One Type 182 torpedo decoy

Electronics:	ADAWS Combat Data System
	One Type 1022 air-search radar
	One Type 1006 navigation radar
	Four Type 909 Sea Dart fire-control radars
	Two Type 910 Sea Wolf fire-control radars
	SCOT Satellite Communications System
	Type 184 search sonar
	Type 162M bottom classification sonar
	Type 185 underwater telephone

gent economy" for the rest of the financial year. Fuel expenditure was restricted, and ships' programs were curtailed. These measures, which had a hint of desperation about them, caused considerable confusion. They were, moreover, perhaps unnecessary, as the Defence Budget, swelled by a Supplementary Estimate, was in the end underspent by a figure almost the same as that it was calculated saved by the moratorium![6]

To make matters worse for the Defence Ministry, its future financial allocations were now attacked as part of the government's general response to the disappointing results of its financial strategy. In fact, the proposed budget for 1981–82 was reduced to a level no higher than 1980–81. (The uncontrolled increase of 5 percent one year and nothing the next was held to constitute around 3 percent for two years!)[7] Both the prime minister and her defense secretary, Francis Pym, were becoming frustrated: the latter with the constraints on his budget, given the government's supposed intentions vis-à-vis defense, the former with Pym's apparently lackadaisical approach to financial management. At least one navy departmental civil servant, himself frustrated that government pro-defense rhetoric was not matched in practice, leaked documents to the press showing Treasury pressure on Pym and chiefs of staff concern at proposed cuts in programs. In January 1981 in a Cabinet reshuffle, Pym was "kicked upstairs" to the job of leader of the House of Commons and was replaced by the gaunt figure of Mr. John Nott, an ambitious merchant banker who had previously been a junior Treasury minister at the center of the government's cash limits policies. The implications were clear; as Speed later put it: "There was considerable speculation in the Press that John Nott had been put into defence to do a hatchet man's job that Francis Pym was not prepared to countenance. A few months after his appointment I was told . . . that this was certainly so."[8]

Nott inherited a set of force-level reductions made necessary by the government's cuts in the forthcoming 1981–82 Budget. HMS *Bulwark* was to be decommissioned six months earlier than expected, the abolition of 41 Marine Commando (which had been given a brief new lease on life in 1977) was confirmed, and ship orders were deferred, notably the Type 22 frigates and the twelve projected trawler-type minesweepers that had been announced in the Callaghan administration's last Defence White Paper. These ships were intended for use as "Extra Deep Armed Team Sweep" vessels to cater to the deep-water mine threat. Two ships had been chartered in 1978 to test the concept, but the four purpose-built vessels planned for 1980 did not appear. It was clear that they would not appear in 1981 either.[9]

But these cuts were simply pecking at the surface. John Nott had something much more substantial in mind. His merchant banker's instincts led him to take notice of the ideas of those critics who argued that there was a serious mismatch between planned force levels and future defense budgets. As the resulting supplementary Defence White Paper put it: "Our current force structure is . . . too large for us to meet the need within any resource allocation which our people can reasonably be asked to afford."[10] Nott decided to take the bull by the horns. The unusually direct wording of the White Paper made clear the extent of his and the government's aim:

> We cannot go on as we are. The Government has, therefore, taken a fresh and
> radical look at the defence programme. We have done this in terms of real

defence output—the roles our forces undertake and how they should in future
be carried out—and not in terms of organisation. It is increasingly essential
that we tackle the business of defence in this way, and manage it in terms of
total capability rather than Service shares.[11]

There were strong echoes of Duncan Sandys, almost a quarter of a century
before, in the way Mr. Nott imposed his will on the Ministry of Defence. The
twelve-week exercise was carried out at a break-neck pace, with "sheaves of reports" being commissioned by the secretary of state. Nott asked the three services
for their ideas on their changing roles and functions so that he could assign rational
priorities between them. He found some difficulty, he later said, in getting satisfactory answers from the navy. As he put it on television in early 1986 " . . . and
I tried and tried and tried to get rational analytical and coherent answers from the
Royal Navy but normally failed to do so." He turned, therefore, to his central staff
"to get properly argued pieces about the Royal Navy's attitude to how they saw
things in the Eastern Atlantic." To Nott it seemed that the navy itself was arguing
more on grounds of sentiment than anything else, "The navy is the navy is the
navy and you are a fool if you do not understand what it is for." This was not
enough for a minister who felt that he was seeking to "analyse these questions"
and who had not got "enough money to do everything."[12]

Yet another meeting was arranged at Greenwich at which the Defence Ministry's
civil servants stressed the need for spending cuts if defense expenditure was not
to take a politically unacceptable share of gross domestic product in the late 1980s.
A paper by the chief scientific adviser, Sir Ronald Mason (upon whom Nott was
increasingly relying as a source of "independent" advice), argued that the Royal
Navy was spending too much on ships and too little on weapons. Nott was apparently convinced and ordered his private office to draw up new spending targets;
reportedly these targets were to leave the "RAF better off, the Army about the
same and the Navy considerably worse off." Not surprisingly, Speed and the Admiralty Board counterattacked. After a meeting that lasted late into the evening,
a paper was produced that spelled out the implications of this policy. Much of the
fleet, the Board argued, would have to be scrapped. Some in the Ministry were
unimpressed by a paper that seemed to them "extremely thinly argued and clearly
designed to cause the maximum political embarrassment." Nevertheless, with the
Admiralty Board threatening resignation en masse, and the chiefs of staff deadlocked, a committee was set up under Bernard Day, assistant under secretary
(Operational Requirements) to examine the minister's proposals. Understandably,
the committee's meeting with naval representatives was somewhat acrimonious.
One official described it as " . . . the most emotional, illogical and abusive meeting
I have ever sat through in my entire civil service career." The Royal Navy team,
led by its own assistant under secretary of state, Michael Power (son of Admiral
of the Fleet Sir Arthur Power), insisted that Nott's proposed cuts could not be
limited to support. The front-line fleet would inevitably suffer severely, and Power
reportedly asserted that such a reduced fleet was not "the sort of Navy I would
send any son of mine to sea in."[13]

The identification of Power with "his" service demonstrates the extent to which
the 1964 "unification," always limited, had been undermined. The civil servants
serving the separate services had become once more, through their common work
on the service long-term costings, most powerful spokesmen—despite their osten-

sible responsibility to the "Centre." But with a minister as single-minded as Nott, even this support was not enough. Eventually Speed felt constrained to make a speech on 15 May that called for the maintenance of existing naval strength. Two days later he was asked to resign and, when he refused, was personally dismissed by Prime Minister Thatcher. The following day he left the Ministry of Defence amidst remarkable scenes of support from naval officers, including First Sea Lord Sir Henry Leach. Speed was the last junior minister of the navy. It was eventually decided to abolish the separate service appointments with two tri-service junior ministerial appointments instead. Speed's departure, which came just before a debate in the House of Commons, led to considerable back-bench Conservative criticisms and may have had some effect on the proposals themselves that were announced on 24 June in a supplementary White Paper called "The Way Forward." Its number, Command 8288, was to become infamous in British naval circles.

What had worried all three service chiefs (who had used their little-used right of access to the prime minister) was Mr. Nott's general assault on the defense budget to bring it into line with political realities. After various alternatives had been considered, it was decided that the 3 percent increase was to be interpreted in its most restrictive possible form, 21 percent over seven years from the 1978–79 baseline. This was a reduced budget compared to that published in the White Paper two months before. What still concerned the admirals, however, was the way the cuts were distributed. The secretary of state remained firmly against an "equal misery" set of cuts all around. Budgetary shares were to be decided by an analysis (as far as the time available allowed) of what Britain's defense priorities ought to be and how best they could be fulfilled. First, however, the priorities had to be set, and both the government and the chiefs of staff seem to have been in agreement that the top priority had to be the maintenance of the strategic nuclear deterrent.[14]

The question of Britain's strategic nuclear future had become a live issue by 1981 because of the Thatcher Government's commitment, announced in 1980, to provide for a Polaris replacement system. Even before Polaris came into service the question of a follow-on system to maintain its credibility against ABM defenses had been considered. Back in 1967, the highly secret small Cabinet committee that Wilson used to consider nuclear questions had rejected the option of acquiring the Poseidon missile with multiple independently targeted re-entry vehicles (MIRVs). Poseidon had been offered informally by the Americans, but questions of both political and financial prudence prevented its adoption. The Heath government was offered Poseidon by U.S. Secretary of Defense Melvin Laird in 1970 but delayed taking a decision. Moving to MIRV would make cancellation by a future Labour government much more likely. The Royal Navy also opposed Poseidon as it would take scarce funds away from conventional forces. Finally, in 1972, when Mr. Heath was in Washington, the Americans let him know that they would prefer *not* to be asked to sell Britain Poseidon due to Strategic Arms Limitation Talks (SALT) considerations. Instead of a new missile an idea first discussed in great secrecy in 1967 was continued, that of upgrading the Polaris missiles. The Wilson Government had been on the point of moving to a formal feasibility study of such a project when it fell, and the Heath Government actually took the decision. This led to a project definition study in 1972 that called for a five-year program estimated to cost some £175 million. The Heath Government pondered the matter through

1973, but in January 1974 decided to proceed with the program. The domestic crisis conditions in which the decision was taken meant that little money was allocated to the project for the time being. It was up to the winner of the election to decide whether to go further or not.[15]

The Wilson administration decided not to reverse the decision but to continue it in great secrecy, a secrecy directed as much at their own back-benchers as anyone else. The decision was taken in April 1974 by a small committee composed of the prime minister, Home Secretary Roy Jenkins, Foreign Minister James Callaghan, Chancellor Denis Healey, and Defence Secretary Roy Mason.[16] Some £46.5 million was allocated to continue the work for another year while the project was examined as part of the Mason Defence Review. It was in this context that the issue reached the full Cabinet in November 1974. The prime minister assured his colleagues that "there would be no Poseidonisation and no MIRV." The force was cheap and gave a unique entree to U.S. thinking. Wilson stressed the diplomatic advantages of maintaining and modernizing the force. He quoted a "unanimous" decision of the Oversea Policy and Defence Committee in favor of retention and modernization. Opposition was half-hearted, only Mrs. Castle (on her own evidence) being "more emphatic," in her statements. The conclusion was that the Cabinet approved maintaining and modernizing the force "with a few expressing dissent." The cost of modernization was quoted to the Cabinet as £24 million per year. Despite this approval it does not appear that the "definitive Cabinet decision" was taken (apparently in committee) until September 1975.[17]

The "stop-go" and highly secret nature of the program did nothing to reduce its cost. By 1976 this had more than doubled in real terms, and in cash terms was about £600 million. By 1980, with the Thatcher Government announcing the extent of the project officially, the cost had been over £530 million at 1972 prices, or a billion pounds at contemporary values. "Chevaline," which went into service in the summer of 1982, is reported to consist of a maneuvering spacecraft (post-boost vehicle) on each missile loaded with two or three warheads and a large number of balloon decoys. The warheads (themselves inside balloons to make them indistinguishable from the decoys) are directed at the same target area but on a number of widely differing trajectories. In order further to enhance penetration all of one submarine's missiles are fired at the same target area, the payloads being timed to appear simultaneously to present the largest number of threats on enemy radar. The warhead balloons and decoy balloons were specifically designed to exhaust the exo-atmospheric "Galosh" antiballistic missile (ABM) system defending the Soviet capital.[18]

Yet neither Chevaline nor any other improvements to Polaris could keep the submarines running beyond the 1990s, or assure the maintenance of a viable missile system into the next century. A decision was relatively urgent. Mr. Callaghan was in favor of maintaining a British nuclear force but recognized the grave political difficulties of going against the government's declared policy of not procuring a successor to Polaris. At the beginning of 1978 officials asked for approval to be given to studies of just such a successor system. A highly secret committee of four, the prime minister, Chancellor Healey, Foreign Secretary David Owen, and Defence Minister Fred Mulley, was set up to consider the matter. Two working parties were convened to give the committee advice, one under Sir Michael Duff of the Foreign Office on the wider implications of Polaris replacement and one under Sir

Ronald Mason of the Defence Ministry on the technical options. The two carried on their work in great secrecy, and the studies were "without ministerial commitment." "Recommendations" were not required, only the consideration of "options." The various studies sponsored by the working groups were brought together in the Duff-Mason Report for submission to the group of four. The report recommended retention of a British strategic nuclear force if it could be afforded financially. As for technical options, the report recommended an expanded force given further expected improvements in Soviet defenses. A new submarine-launched ballistic missile (SLBM) seemed the strongest contender, although Owen was an enthusiast for cruise missiles fired from submarines. At the Guadeloupe Summit at the beginning of 1979 Callaghan and President Carter discussed options on new American systems, including the Trident C-4.[19]

The election now intervened. Mr. Callaghan was careful to word Labour's manifesto in order to allow possible Polaris replacement, but the election of Mrs. Thatcher, with a firm commitment to the deterrent, removed previous inhibitions completely. In mid-1979 Defence Minister Pym renewed contacts with the Carter administration on the question of Britain's deterrent. At the year's end Mrs. Thatcher and President Carter personally reaffirmed their commitment to continuing discussions and their agreement on "the importance of maintaining a credible British strategic deterrent force." The material from the Duff-Mason Report was re-presented to the committee Mrs. Thatcher set up to consider the matter. Coded "MISC7," the committee was composed of Prime Minister Thatcher, Foreign Secretary Lord Carrington, Chancellor of the Exchequer Sir Geoffrey Howe, Home Secretary William Whitelaw, and Defence Secretary Pym. The decision went in favor of the American Trident C-4 SLBM to be fitted in a new generation of submarines. On the day the Trident decision was to be announced in Parliament, 15 July 1980, the full Cabinet rubber-stamped it, despite the reservations of some ministers who were worried about costs. Pym duly announced the decision to Parliament.[20]

The Trident decision helped stimulate a considerable debate about the place of nuclear weapons in Britain's defense posture and the cuts in spending on conventional forces that such a program might bring. The Royal Navy at this stage was generally supportive of the decision, as it was by no means clear who would pay these expenses. The Trident sales agreement was a favorable one and the official Ministry of Defence line was that effectively there would be no special target for savings to subsidize the program. The events of early 1981 changed some, but by no means all, minds in MOD(N) about the costs of Trident and also made it clear that there would indeed be a price to be paid in other areas of defense.[21]

There seems little doubt that Mr. Nott insisted that changes be made in the budgetary mechanism for costing the strategic deterrent. According to Keith Speed, who was one of those whose views underwent alteration, "The Navy was saddled with virtually the entire bill for the Trident submarine and missile programme." He contrasted this with the situation in "the early 1960s, when the Polaris missiles and submarines were being acquired," when "the cost was designed to fall on the defence budget as a whole rather than be at the expense of one Service."[22] With a tidy chunk thus taken out of the "sea systems" long-term costings, themselves already reduced by £600 million or so per annum (at 1982 prices) by the time Trident would be paid for, the supporters of the more conventional aspects of the naval program had to revise their opinions.[23] Although some, notably the senior submariners and others intimately connected with the program, found it difficult to change their minds on Trident, others, some very senior, began to speak of the "cuckoo in the nest" of the naval program.[24] The fact that many in the Royal Navy had never really taken the SSBN role to their hearts became increasingly obvious. Nevertheless, Mr. Nott's logic was impeccable. SSBNs were warships, and impressive and expensive ones at that. They were, in fact, the most important warships Britain possessed, given the government's defense priorities. It was only right that they should not only come from the naval part of the costings but, indeed, that they should have first call upon them.

If the stress on the SSBNs was not enough, the next Nott defense priority stressed more naval forces of a type that had not been at the center of the service's priorities for three decades. This second priority was "Defence of the Home Base," something that the secretary of state felt particularly strongly had been neglected in the past. The expensive hardware for this role was an expanded and re-equipped RAF fighter force, but the Royal Navy's mine countermeasures role was confirmed too. Indeed, there was even a stress on the *use* of mining to defend shipping and ports. These relatively unspectacular forces would thus be the next in line for the reduced naval budget, but money spent on mines meant less for warships. Some officers of the Naval Staff might be gratified that they were at last to get their converted trawlers and new cheaper minehunters, as well as a continued, even expanded, buy of "Hunts," but this seemed a little less welcome if the price paid was fewer major surface combatants.

It was indeed the future of the surface fleet that soon became the critical issue of the Nott Review as it was fought out in the Defence Ministry in February, March, and April of 1981. First the priority of the Eastlant role itself had to be settled. There was no question of doing away with it completely, but its priority vis-à-vis the commitment of land and air forces to the continent of Europe had to be settled if a useful framework for the allocation of funds was to be defined. There was apparently some reluctance by the chiefs of staff to make a decision on this point, but Nott insisted and got the advice, strongly supported by the Foreign Office, that the logic of the previous three decades and more still held good. Nott's defense review clearly stated that forward defense of the German Federal Republic was "the forward defence of Britain itself."[25]

So the primary role for the largest part of the Royal Navy became officially priority number four of Britain's whole defense effort. If that was not bad enough for an Admiralty Board that had become ever more angry, disillusioned, and frustrated, the defense secretary insisted that there should be some changes in how that priority should be fulfilled.[26] The Naval Staff was perhaps a little unfortunate in that circumstances had conspired to weaken the case for surface escorts. As early as 1974 an informed observer had written that he (and presumably his naval informant) regarded the convoy as "played out." By the 1980s, doctrinal thought was moving even further away from the ideas confirmed by past experience. Nothing demonstrated this better than the "Ocean Safari" NATO exercise of 1981. The exercise demonstrated that direct defense of shipping carrying troops and supplies across the Atlantic had been apparently abandoned in favor of an experiment with a new concept of "defended lanes" in which warships, including the new carrier *Invincible*, were to be used to "sanitize" areas through which shipping moved. The

Naval Staff's own thinking had, rightly or wrongly, clearly moved to a priority of "containment" operations to keep Soviet forces beyond the Greenland-Iceland-U.K. gap and "defense in depth" by offensive use of ASW groups. In any case, operations in support of the NATO strike fleet still seemed to be the first call on the Royal Navy's forces.[27]

In these circumstances it was only too easy for Mr. Nott's advisers, notably Sir Ronald Mason, the chief scientific adviser, to stress the importance of land-based maritime air power and submarines, both nuclear and conventionally powered, as the truly vital assets in any conventional deterrent force for the Eastern Atlantic. The Defence Operational Analysis Establishment (DOAE) at West Byfleet produced computer studies that Sir Ronald used to produce a scenario that Mr. Nott found convincing enough. Unescorted merchant ships would be rushed along an idiosyncratically named "shipping band" defended by prowling RAF Nimrods. "Barrier operations," Mason argued, would also help to keep enemy submarines at bay, using aircraft and mines in the gaps themselves and submarines beyond them to the north. Sir Ronald conceded that there might still be a role for the frigate as a vehicle for the new "towed array" long-range sonars for area defense of the "shipping band" or for barrier patrols, but with no convoys any requirement for true escort forces began to wither away. Perhaps correctly, Sir Ronald posed serious questions about the utility of the carrier-centered task force for "area" ASW. The Naval Staff officers, with their own doubts and uncertainties about the shape of maritime warfare in the 1980s, seem to have found it difficult to counter such objections. Indeed, they felt that they were never given a proper opportunity to do so. Certainly it was clear that Mr. Nott felt that the defense of shipping in convoy was the least important facet of modern naval warfare. Impressed by the latest intelligence of the long-range Soviet missiles such as the SS-N-19, he felt that the convoy scenario was, in his scientific adviser's words, "very fragile." In such a context, arguing a case for the ASW carrier (CVS) group, excellent though Mason admitted it was for "the defence of a small area against high level threats," was extremely difficult.[28]

With no strategic rationale for the surface fleet, Mr. Nott had to come up with more "economic" criteria to determine its size. In announcing his proposals Mr. Nott made the rather remarkable observation that no strategic rationale lay behind the cuts he was forced to make in the naval surface ship programs! Instead there had been a much more arbitrary decision based on the planned cuts in dockyard support.[29] As late as August 1980, after a major study, the government had announced its decision to retain all four of the home dockyards, Devonport, Portsmouth, Rosyth, and Chatham.[30] Now this decision was reversed. Two were to be closed, Chatham and Portsmouth, although the latter would remain as a naval base. This would make substantial savings and, given major reductions in the refit and maintenance program, would still allow the maintenance of some fifty frigates declared to NATO. Eight of these would be in operational reserve, the "Standby Squadron." It might have been much worse. Reportedly, a frigate force of under thirty ships had been considered at one point in the review.[31]

Nevertheless, fifty ships was a reduction of nine vessels compared to the existing NATO force declaration, including *Leander*-class vessels, whose modernization program was to be ended. Indeed, mid-life modernization as a concept was to be officially abandoned, a program of such refits for the Type 42s being specifically ruled out. Extensive improvements planned for the Sea Dart missile system were cancelled. Question marks were also placed over the continuance of the Type 22 ASW frigate program. Instead of modernized *Leander*s and new 22s, a new Type 23 frigate, "simpler and cheaper than the Type 22" was announced for future procurement. The ending of mid-life modernizations would, it was argued, significantly increase (by some 12 percent) the availability of the reduced fleet.[32]

The Royal Navy's big ships came in for especially great reductions. It was announced in Command 8288 that although the three remaining Royal Marine Commandos would be retained, both LPDs, *Fearless* and *Intrepid*, were to be phased out, the latter in 1982 and the former in 1984. Not even the hard-fought-for command cruisers, now officially "ASW carriers," were safe. Mr. Nott had been rather dismissive about them during the May debate. "I do not believe," he said, "that we would order them if we were making the decision today."[33] A force of two of these ships only was to be maintained. The *Hermes* was to disappear as soon as the *Illustrious* was commissioned, and it soon became clear that the *Invincible* would be sold on completion of the *Ark Royal*. (Australia was soon announced as a potential buyer.) The main role for these ships would be "out of area" operations for which Mr. Nott considered them "ideal."[34]

There was a significantly enhanced emphasis on such operations "beyond the NATO area" in Command 8288. "Britain's own needs, outlooks and interests," Nott argued, "give her a special role and special duty in efforts of this kind." In these efforts "the Royal Navy has a particularly valuable role."[35] He alluded to the "Armilla Patrol" of two warships that had been maintained since the outbreak of the Gulf war the previous year. The intention of this patrol was to safeguard free passage for merchant shipping in the Gulf of Oman. The first two vessels were the Type 22 destroyer *Coventry* and the Type 21 frigate *Alacrity*. They had been detached from one of the regular "out of area" group deployments, Task Group 318, which had sailed from Britain to the Far East in 1980 to be the first ever RN visitors to the People's Republic of China.[36]

Mr. Nott specifically re-emphasized such activities—with the full support of the Naval Staff. In some of the few passages of 8288 that the Staff would have unequivocally welcomed, Mr. Nott announced that: "We intend to resume from 1982 onwards the practice of sending a substantial naval task group on long detachment for visits and exercises in the South Atlantic, Caribbean, Indian Ocean and further east. We intend to make particular use of the new carriers, with Sea Harriers and helicopters, in 'out of area' deployment. We will co-ordinate all these deployments and exercises as fruitfully as possible with the United States and other allies, as well as other countries with whom we have close defence relations."[37]

So the Atlantic was to be left primarily, and perhaps increasingly, to the Royal Navy's submarines. The force of SSNs was to be expanded, Nott announced, to seventeen boats, five more than the existing force of twelve. The first of the new 4,500-ton *T* class of quieter SSNs, HMS *Trafalgar*, was about to be launched, and more were on order or planned. Much was made of this increase in strength, although Mr. Speed made it clear that it was not as large as the previous program of the Naval Staff, which had aimed at a force of twenty vessels. In the debate on the Nott proposals, serious doubts were cast on the SSN building program, given the construction of the four Trident boats in the single available yard at Barrow, and also the capability to keep up-to-date with refits, given the closure of the major

SSN refit facility at Chatham. The effects of limited refit capacity were soon demonstrated by the fate of HMS *Dreadnought*, the first British SSN, which suffered
quite serious machinery damage in 1980 (reportedly cracks in the cooling system)
necessitating reactor shutdown. At the time of 8288 she was about to enter Chatham
for a refit intended to keep her running until about 1988. The problems of changing
over to Devonport as the major refit facility and Devonport's relative inexperience
in the work made taking up the facilities for such a limited amount of future service
inadvisable and, after some debate, the decision was taken to withdraw the boat
from service, the first Royal Navy SSN to suffer the fate. By the end of 1984 total
T-class SSN orders had reached six, which allowed for the *Dreadnought*'s eventual
replacement within the target force of seventeen boats to be attained in the early
1990s.[38]

Mr. Nott also confirmed that the conventional submarine, or SSK, was not dead
in the Royal Navy. The 1970s had been a struggle between those who wished to
concentrate on the SSN and those who argued the case for the SSK for both the
training role and shallow-water surveillance operations. The 1974–75 Working
Party seems to have come out in favor of at least considering a new program of
conventional boats, and a decision was made to prepare an outline requirement
for a new conventional submarine. This was approved, and five preliminary options
were looked at in a range of sizes from 500 to 2,500 tons. These five options were
soon reduced to four proposed boats of 2,510 tons (A), 2,000 tons (B), 1,210 tons
(C), and 710 tons (D). The Naval Staff found that the two smaller boats, although
half the price of the larger, were too limited in capability even for surveillance and
training. The two larger boats, on the other hand, promised to be expensive. In
1977, therefore, the larger designs were scaled down and redesigned to take existing
sensors and tactical data handling systems. This produced an 1,850-ton "Option
E" design that was 10 percent cheaper than "Option B" and was chosen as the
basis for an Outline Staff Target. The latter was approved with a few modifications
that increased displacement to 1,960 tons submerged. Before a full Naval Staff
Target was issued, the boat's weapons, sensor, and action-information equipment
were reassessed and improved. The cost went up once more by 15 percent. This
became the Naval Staff Target, but when this came up for endorsement by the
Ministry of Defence's Operational Requirements Committee, the latter doubted
its export potential and recommended further modifications to increase chances of
foreign sales. In the end the Naval Staff reluctantly combined their 2,250-ton
submarine with the Vickers "VSEL 2500" export design to produce the 2,400-ton
Type 2400, around which the definitive Naval Staff Requirement, approved early
in 1980, was written. Fuel capacity was increased as was space in general for
improved upkeep and reliability and greater development potential. As the program
appealed to Mr. Nott's pro-area ASW, pro-submarine, pro-"cheaper" platform
tendencies, it survived 8288. The Admiralty Board gave their approval in August
1981, but it took more than two years, until November 1983, for an order finally
to be placed for the first of the class, HMS *Upholder*. Completion date was set for
1987–88.[39]

The conventional submarine program fitted in with another of Mr. Nott's "hob-
byhorses" in 8288, the need to spend money on "weapons" rather than "platforms."
This accounted for his assault on the "expensive" surface ship program, although
a closer look at the problem would have revealed that over 60 percent of the cost

of a Type 22 frigate was taken up by weapons systems and their related sensors and fire control. It might be argued, however, that the continuing sad saga of British underwater weapons development did indeed reflect an over-concentration on expensive "platforms" rather than the weapons they carried. In 1981 the primary British submarine-launched anti-surface ship weapon was still the fifty-four-year-old Mk 8 torpedo! There had been talk of a submarine-launched anti-ship missile system for many years, and in 1980 HMS *Churchill* actually carried out trials with the American Harpoon system. The year after the Nott review Sub-Harpoon finally entered service, HMS *Courageous* being the first SSN fitted. This program had been seriously delayed by the financial stringencies of the late 1970s and early 1980s, negotiations for the sale having been completed in 1977.[40]

The late arrival of the Sub-Harpoon was especially important given the problems faced in giving anti-surface capability to the Mk 24 "Tigerfish" wire-guided homing torpedo. Despite fifteen years of development work, the limited number of Mk 24s procured in 1974 was only suitable for ASW, and even then it took another five years for them to achieve fleet weapons acceptance. The MOD1 "Tigerfish" with anti-surface as well as anti-submarine capabilities had been under development since 1972, but it was taken into service in 1980 without having passed its fleet weapon acceptance trials. Unreliability was a serious problem, and in 1982 an official Ministry of Defence investigation (the fourth in the Mk 24 program in thirteen years!) concluded that no project management had satisfactorily coordinated all the different organizations concerned with the torpedo's development. Hence, interface problems between various sub-systems had been severe. A Consolidation Programme (CP), begun as a result, tried to provide improved project management as well as better technology, and on contract acceptance trials in 1985 the MOD2 prototype achieved 80 percent reliability. A "dismayed" House of Commons Public Accounts Committee looking at the torpedo question that year hoped that the Mk 24 CP program might be curtailed as a result of the development of its "Spearfish" replacement. By 1986, however, it looked as if all 600 Mk 24s would be converted to MOD2 standard as "Spearfish" would not be available for service until the end of the decade.

"Spearfish" had been under development by Marconi since 1981, a Naval Staff Requirement for an advanced heavy torpedo having been issued the previous year. An American weapon, the improved Mk 48, had been considered, but Marconi eventually won the competition, not least because the "Spearfish" program could be combined with the same manufacturer's "Stingray" advanced lightweight torpedo project. Lightweight torpedoes, previously only helicopter-delivered, were now even more important in the Royal Navy as surface ships were being fitted with STWS (Ship-Launched Torpedo Weapon System) tubes as their primary close-in ASW armament. U.S. Mk 44 and Mk 46 weapons were still the standard British lightweight torpedoes in 1981, but "Stingray" production was just beginning after just over a decade's development. It entered service the following year for helicopter delivery; a larger-caliber STWS-2 was under development to allow it to be fired from surface ships.[41]

Weapons improvements were, however, less obvious than reductions in the fleet. Plans were soon being announced for the withdrawal from service in 1983 of HMS *Hermes*, which had just been put back in commission after a £40 million refit and installation of "Ski jump" for the more efficient operation of Sea Harriers. The remaining six, active, large guided-missile "destroyers" were now to be decommissioned in the mid-1980s. In the near term the *London* was to be sold to Pakistan and the *Norfolk* to Chile; the *Antrim* and *Glamorgan* would decommission in 1984; the *Fife* and *Bristol* would follow soon afterwards. The Type 12 frigates would be down to two active units by 1985 with the decommissioning of the *Berwick*, *Brighton*, *Falmouth*, and *Rhyl* in 1982, the unarmed trial ship *Londonderry* (recently converted at a cost of £23 million) in 1983, and the *Lowestoft*, *Rothesay*, and *Torquay* in 1984. The *Leanders* would also be reduced with the premature ending of their modernization program. Only five "Broad-Beam" or "Batch 3" ships, the *Andromeda*, *Charybdis*, *Hermione*, *Jupiter*, and *Scylla* were to be given the £70–80 million conversion into "mini Type 22s" with 2016 sonar, Sea Wolf point-defense missiles, Exocet surface-to-surface missiles, and a Lynx helicopter. The remaining four "Broad-Beam" ships were bound either for sale (HMS *Bacchante* to New Zealand) or the Standby Squadron. HMS *Juno*, earmarked for conversion to "Batch 2" Exocet configuration, was to be reconfigured as a training ship to replace HMS *Torquay*. Even the Ikara units were to be reduced, the *Dido* by sale to New Zealand, and the *Naiad*, *Euryalus*, and *Aurora* to the Standby Squadron, which in the second half of the 1980s would be entirely composed of *Leanders*.[42]

A significant improvement being added to some of the surviving *Leanders* was towed-array sonar, a technical development whose performance had much to do with the operational background to the 8288 decisions. Towed arrays seem to have first entered service with the Royal Navy in Polaris submarines for self-defense purposes. This 2023 array, based on an American design, was later joined by the 2024 designed to give SSNs a long-range search capability. A towed array consists of a string of passive sonar receivers that is towed behind the listening unit, on which the received signals are analyzed by modern data-processing techniques. Results from trials on a surface ship version in the *Lowestoft* exceeded expectations, and plans were well advanced for fitting the 2031 surface ship arrays; four Exocet *Leanders* were earmarked as "Group 2A" for modifications that necessitated top weight reductions, including the loss of long-range radars. The ships thus converted were the *Cleopatra*, *Sirius*, *Phoebe*, and *Argonaut*.[43]

Abandoning further work such as this and the more expensive "Batch 3" conversions would play a major part in achieving Mr. Nott's planned savings. In all, the Royal Navy's long-term financial expectations for the next nine years had been slashed by "several billion pounds . . . more than twice the cuts applied to the Army and over seven times those applied to the Royal Air Force." However, even before the events of spring 1982, which shattered the high hopes of Mr. Nott's Review, significant alterations had taken place that promised greater than expected naval expenditure. Following a personal visit to the *Fearless* by the secretary of state, and a second look at the projected costings, it was decided to keep the two assault ships "to maintain our capability to conduct operations on NATO's northern flank . . ." and "also out of area." It is also possible that there were deeper reasons for the retention of these ships. Reportedly, the Americans asked for their retention in return for favorable terms in a second Trident deal announced in 1982.[44]

This reflected a considerable escalation of the program, an escalation that was serious in its implications. The original 1980 plan was to build new versions of the *Resolution* class, but in July 1981 it was decided to utilize the new PWR2 propulsion system for the new SSBNs. Given the long service life expected for the new boats, this seemed advisable, and the same logic dictated a new 2054 sonar suite as well. It was also decided to give the SSBNs the enlarged missile tubes of the American *Ohio*-class submarines in order to allow the option of modernization with the later Trident D-5 missile. There would, however, be only sixteen tubes instead of twenty-four. The longer core life of the PWR2 meant such enhanced availability that plans for a fifth boat that had been considered could be finally abandoned, but the cost of the program had increased by £475 million to £5.6 billion. Britain's Trident submarines were to displace almost 16,000 tons, making them twice the size of previous British SSBNs and three times the size of an SSN. It was later reported that the old battleship/carrier names had been suggested for these "boats," as befitted their status: *Vanguard, Vengeance, Venerable,* and *Victorious.*[45]

The decisions on the submarines had all been taken by the autumn of 1981. The situation was then further complicated by President Reagan's announcement that Trident D-5 would enter service earlier than planned, by December 1989, before Britain's new SSBNs would be in service. The British government did not want to be caught out again with the "logistical, operational and financial penalties" of deploying a system soon to be replaced in the American inventory.[46] There thus seemed little alternative to adopting the more expensive D-5. It was hoped that cost-cutting measures could restrain too much price escalation. A reduction to twelve tubes was considered, but the savings were considered too marginal to warrant the reduction in capability that would result. Significant savings were, however, achieved by deciding to forego a separated British stockpile of missiles and to share the American assembly and refurbishment facility at King's Bay, Georgia. This was even more important as the project was already suffering from serious cost escalations due to the decline of the pound against the dollar. In fact, the decision to go for D-5 only added another £390 million to the existing price tag: missiles were after all only 17 percent of the total cost of the program. The drop of the pound from 2.36 dollars to 1.78 dollars between September 1980 and March 1982 and general inflation were the major culprits for the increased estimated Trident cost in 1982 of £7.5 billion, an increase of 50 percent over the original 1980 estimate.[47]

Until Trident entered service, the Polaris force would continue. The improved Chevaline warhead system, despite some problems in testing, entered operational service in 1982 after successful firings at the American range at Cape Canaveral earlier in the year. A £300 million program to re-motor the Polaris missiles was also announced "to ensure their operational reliability."[48]

The extra costs implied by the enhancement of the SSBN forces promised naval budgetary difficulties in the future. In the shorter term, older problems of over-loading began to re-assert themselves as Chancellor of the Exchequer Sir Geoffrey Howe maintained with increasing rigor the "cash limits" policy. There seemed little money to spare to reverse apparently minor cuts made in 1981, notably the decision, taken over strong Foreign Office opposition, to withdraw HMS *Endurance*, the permanent Falklands naval presence. At the beginning of 1982 the F.O. stepped up its campaign to reverse the decision so that the correct signals could be given to Argentina of British intentions not to withdraw precipitately from the Falkland Islands. The Foreign Office ministers, Lord Carrington and Richard Luce, had an ally in Captain N.J. Barker of the *Endurance* who repeatedly sent back to London disturbing messages of increasing Argentine hostility. These, however, tended to

The ice patrol ship *Endurance*, Britain's Falkland Island presence since her purchase in 1967. Her withdrawal was often discussed, but when finally announced, helped lead to the war that ensured her continued deployment. (Imperial War Museum)

be dismissed as merely efforts to maintain the ship on station. Given his budgetary difficulties, Mr. Nott had to refuse a personal approach from Carrington in January. A counterproposal that the Foreign Office rather than the Ministry of Defence should pay for the *Endurance* was refused in turn by the Foreign Office. Acceding to such a proposal would set an unfortunate precedent; as far as the F.O. was concerned the entire navy existed, if necessary, to act as an executor of British foreign policy.[49]

The stage was being set for the most remarkable and unexpected naval event of the postwar era, the Falkland Islands War of 1982. In this conflict the Royal Navy would suffer its worst warship losses of the post-1945 period and score its greatest success in projecting power over many thousands of miles to the other side of the world. Contrary to the policy pronouncement of sixteen years before, Britain would indeed have to carry out an opposed landing without the support of allies. At the end of February 1982 such an outcome still seemed a little outrageous, even given the violent Argentine reaction to apparently successful talks between British and Argentine ministers in New York. The Foreign Office, anxious at this outcome, stepped up the pressure to keep the *Endurance* on station. It was considered that Argentina might well increase pressure on the Falklands and might even take some kind of limited military action before the end of the year. Prodded by Downing Street, it was decided to review the defense contingency plan, which led to contacts with the Ministry of Defence. The Foreign Office also decided to prepare a paper for an early meeting of the Defence Committee of the Cabinet that would include yet another request for the *Endurance*. At this point it seems that ministers were told by officials of the events of five years before when the Callaghan Government had been faced with a similar and apparently more serious situation.[50]

The mid-1970s had seen a significant rise in tension over the Falklands. At the beginning of 1976 ambassadors were withdrawn. The occasion was the beginning of a major British survey of the economic potential of the islands. In February 1976 the civilian research ship *Shackleton* was shot at by an Argentine destroyer. The *Shackleton* incident then won a temporary reprieve for the ice patrol ship *Endurance*, which had been a proposed casualty of the Mason Review. At Prime Minister Callaghan's request a frigate was sent as a temporary replacement. Callaghan also asked the chiefs of staff to produce a paper on military options. This report pointed out the difficulty and expense of defending the islands by maintaining a garrison of superior strength. If the Falklands fell, however, there would be no alternative to an amphibious landing, complete with the support of a carrier task force. Such a counter-invasion would be a "major operation" at "very long range."[51]

Negotiations during the rest of the year served to defuse the situation, but in December 1976 HMS *Endurance*'s helicopters discovered an Argentine force on Southern Thule, in the South Sandwich Islands. The government protested about this, but played the situation down lest it force a move to a "Fortress Falklands" policy, which it wished to avoid if at all possible. Nevertheless, a junior Foreign Office minister, Mr. Ted Rowlands, visited Argentina in February 1977 when it was feared that the Argentines might increase their military pressure. Rowlands knew that there was a Group Deployment composed of HMS *Tiger*, the SSN *Churchill*, and five escorts in the area that might be diverted if necessary. In the event, the British did not have to employ this threat.

In the autumn, as Argentine impatience with the British began to manifest itself once more, Foreign Secretary David Owen got wind of increased Argentine activity in the area of the Falklands and asked for a report. This revealed that the Argentines had arrested Bulgarian trawlers and even fired on a Soviet boat. The Argentine ships had orders to sink foreign vessels if necessary. It seemed as if Southern Thule (having been abandoned for the Antarctic winter), was to be reoccupied by the Argentines, contrary to arrangements made with Rowlands. The situation seemed bad, and a full Joint Intelligence Committee report was set in motion, along with an exploration of military options. Owen, a keen SSN enthusiast since his days as navy minister, suggested one be sent, but the MOD preferred a surface-action group of frigates, which would have better communications with home. The visibility of such a force, however, might well do more harm than good in provoking the Argentines, and Owen opposed the sending of any surface force other than the *Endurance*, whose withdrawal was cancelled.

The final policy was thrashed out in three meetings of the Oversea Policy and Defence Committee in November 1977. The JIC report suggested that some aggressive Argentine move might well take place in connection with the next round of negotiations in December. Both Prime Minister Callaghan and Owen felt that a precautionary naval presence was necessary, therefore, and an SSN ought to be sent to cruise covertly about the islands to be unveiled should anything untoward occur. The SSN, however, would not be able to communicate very well with London, so a surface ship command link was required. This could be provided by two frigates, which did not have to be provocatively close to the islands. As the chiefs of staff put it in their submission " . . . it was preferable not to deploy the two frigates in the immediate vicinity. It would be adequate to have them a thousand miles out in the Atlantic. There would be no problem to them being at sea for a month, and they could use the time for the purpose of exercises. The fleet submarine could, on the other hand, be deployed close to the islands on a covert basis. . . . This small task force would, therefore, be able to respond flexibly to limited attacks of aggression. . . ."[52] Rules of engagement were worked out, as always, at the highest level. If necessary, a maritime identification zone fifty miles around the islands would be set up inside of which any Argentine warship would be asked to explain its actions. In certain circumstances the submarine would be authorized to open fire. The actual members of this task group seem to have been the SSN HMS *Dreadnought* and two Exocet-equipped frigates, the brand new Type 21 *Alacrity* and the just-refitted *Leander*, *Phoebe*. The frigates were indeed deployed a thousand miles to the north, well "over the horizon."

These precautionary measures were kept very quiet. The purpose of the force was an option should things go wrong, rather than a diplomatic bargaining chip. It is still unclear whether the Argentinians go wind of it. In any case the ships were withdrawn in late December, following the relatively successful outcome of the talks. Despite some jitters in early 1978, a new force was not reconstituted, but continued plans to withdraw the *Endurance* were successfully resisted by Callaghan and Owen. She was kept on station on a year-to-year basis until a less naval-orientated successor government allowed the Ministry of Defence to have its way with the ship. As to the general question of naval reinforcement, the consensus in March 1982 among ministers and officials was that although contingency plans ought to be explored, no action should be taken. Mrs. Thatcher asked Mr. Nott on the 8th how quickly Royal Navy ships could be deployed to the islands if they should be required. The Ministry of Defence replied on the 12th with a list of ships deployed at that time in the Caribbean and West Atlantic areas and the news that a frigate with RFA support would take almost three weeks to get to the islands. Submarines seem not to have been suggested, perhaps due to MOD(N)'s desire not to give any further encouragement to Mr. Nott's enthusiasm for them.[53]

In reality the Argentines, now led by a new and more aggressive military junta determined to use an external success to cover problems at home, were drawing up contingency plans of their own for invasion if negotiations failed. The first plan was to use a scrap-metal dealer called Davidoff, who had a legitimate contract to dismantle a disused whaling station on South Georgia, as a cover to land a small band of special forces, Group Alfa, on the island. In the event, in mid-March, the Argentine Junta decided not to put Operation Alfa into effect, but the landing of Davidoff's civilians by an Argentine naval auxiliary did take place on the 19th. This was immediately reported, first to the Falklands and then to London, along with news of the party's rather provocative activities, including raising the Argentine flag. Prodded by Falklands Governor Rex Hunt, London decided on March 20th to send the *Endurance* and her Marines to evict the troublesome foreigners. Three days later, however, much to the disgust of everyone on board, she was ordered to hold back and remain off Grytviken. Despite this attempt at non-provocation, the Argentines, informed of the intention to remove their nationals, decided to put their contingency plans into operation. Another auxiliary, the *Bahía Paraíso*, sailed with Group Alfa for South Georgia, and the troops were ashore before midnight on the night of the 24th/25th. The following day the British found out that the Argentine Navy was sending warships to the South Georgia area to threaten the *Endurance*. Nevertheless, Lord Carrington counseled caution at a Cabinet meeting that day, which Mr. Nott missed because of a NATO Nuclear Planning Group meeting in the United States. It was decided that it would be a good idea if the Ministry of Defence reconsidered its plans on withdrawing the *Endurance*. Yet no decision was taken to send further reinforcements.[54] As one study of the campaign has put it: "This must be considered a serious error of judgement."[55]

Too overt a naval presence, however, could have been seen as provocation. Indeed, the *Endurance*'s activities *were* seen as such. By 26 March the Junta was apprehensive that a diplomatic disaster would result if the Davidoff party and Group Alfa were captured and the British reinforced the island. This, coupled with the obvious domestic dissatisfaction with the Junta's internal policies (which was about to take the form of demonstrations in Buenos Aires), would endanger the regime. The time had come, it seemed, to capture the Falklands and the dependencies. D-day was fixed at 1 April, and the amphibious task group for the main islands was ready to go, having been exercising for the previous week in the Gulfo San Roman. Two corvettes had already been detached from maneuvers to reinforce the South Georgia detachment and protect the Alfa force from the *Endurance*. The whole operation was code-named "Blue," which now encompassed Operation "Alfa" in South Georgia and Operation "Rosario," the taking of the main islands.[56]

On the 26th, after a transatlantic telephone call with Mr. Nott, the junior defense minister, Mr. J. Wiggin, informed the Foreign Office that the *Endurance* was to remain on station, at least for the time being. He stressed, however, that no final decision on her future or funding had been made. Indeed, he went so far as to say that "the Ministry of Defence could not justify paying for her retention."[57] The subject of this continuing squabble was at the end of her regular deployment and was coming to the end of her supplies. It was necessary, therefore, to send a replenishment vessel to resupply her. The RFA *Fort Austin* at Gibraltar was duly prepared to sail on the 29th. The Ministry also resubmitted its document on defense options with the addition of a proposal to send a nuclear submarine. Not until Monday 29 March did Prime Minister Thatcher and Lord Carrington agree, on their way to an EEC meeting in Brussels, that a submarine should, in fact, be sent. The closest available SSN was the modern boat HMS *Spartan*, at that time supporting the First Flotilla of destroyers and frigates commanded by Rear Admiral J.F. ("Sandy") Woodward, exercising in the annual "Spring Train" series off Gibraltar. With live torpedoes quietly transferred from an alongside SSK, she was on her way within forty-eight hours, with an estimated passage time to the Falklands of ten days. Two more boats at the Scottish base at Faslane, the *Splendid*, the newest in the fleet, and the *Conqueror*, were available, but they could not be sent immediately. They eventually departed for the South Atlantic on 1 April and 4 April, respectively.[58]

The first sea lord, Sir Henry Leach, and the Naval Staff were, however, convinced that submarines would not be enough. As one account has put it: "There now grew in the minds of Leach and his Staff a most remarkable prospect, that of a full British battle fleet putting to sea in earnest against a not inconsiderable foe. To most senior officers such a concept was not merely fantastic in the context of the 1980s, it would also become impossible in a few years when the carrier and amphibious assault groups had been phased out. This was precisely the unforeseen contingency Leach had always argued that the Navy had to be equipped to meet, and there were certainly overwhelming strategic arguments for sending a large task force which Leach began to assemble that very day. He would be the first to admit that there were overwhelming political ones as well."[59] Late that night CINC-FLEET, Admiral Sir John Fieldhouse, on board the destroyer HMS *Glamorgan* observing "Spring Train," was informed of the possibility of sending a full "balanced" task force. The next day Fieldhouse summoned Woodward to his flagship. The admirals shared a common submarine background, but now they discussed policy if a surface task force was required. Woodward then returned to his flagship, HMS *Antrim*; Fieldhouse went back to London.[60]

By 31 March London recognized that "Operation Blue" was about to begin, and the *Endurance* was ordered back to Port Stanley. In the evening, somewhat fortuitously, Sir Henry Leach was the senior service representative at a meeting in the prime minister's room in the House of Commons. The chief of Defence Staff, Admiral of the Fleet Sir Terence Lewin, was away on a visit to New Zealand, and his deputy, the chief of the Air Staff, had not been invited. Leach rushed to the House on his own initiative after a day visiting the surface weapons establishment at Portsmouth to express to Nott his dissent from a pessimistic Ministry of Defence briefing the secretary of state had just received. Contrary to his ministry's view, the first sea lord told Prime Minister Thatcher that a full task force could be available for sailing to retrieve the situation within a few days. "He also hazarded the political view that, if an Argentine invasion did occur, the Navy not only could but should respond."[61] Leach's enthusiasm appealed to the prime minister more than the Ministry of Defence's caution, and it was agreed that forces should be put on the alert. It has been argued that if it had not been for the first sea lord, "it is unlikely that the fleet would have sailed so soon, and as a result more cautious counsels might have gained wider currency."[62]

April 1 did not see the Argentine invasion; it was delayed by twenty-four hours because of bad weather. That day, however, did see meetings of the Cabinet, its Oversea Policy and Defence Committee (OD) and the chiefs of staff. The committee decided not even to attempt to send reinforcements to the tiny island garrison, but at the chiefs of staff meeting Leach brushed aside the reservations of his two colleagues to the idea of a relief task force. Defence Secretary Nott was also becoming convinced of the practicality and political desirability of sending a naval task force. Despite the fact that there had been no studies of the likely level of opposition, the decision in principle was duly taken to send such a fleet. Leach returned to the Ministry in the early hours of 2 April to give orders to Woodward to "form his ships into a task group and prepare to go south." Despite the fact that no specific decision on the timing of its despatch had yet been made, the first sea lord made the confident directive: "The task force is to be made ready and sailed."[63]

On 2 April, the day of the Falklands invasion, orders were issued to Admiral Woodward to gather together his most suitable vessels and sail for the south. Some of the "Spring Train" ships were deemed unsuitable: the Ikara *Leanders Aurora*, *Dido*, and *Euryalus* with their specialized ASW armament, the unmodernized *Leander Ariadne* and the potentially valuable Sea Wolf-equipped Type 22 HMS

Battleaxe, which was in need of repairs at home. The Type 21 *Active* was also sent home. Some eight vessels were chosen to make up the initial force: the "County"-class guided-missile destroyers *Antrim* and *Glamorgan*; the Type 42 destroyers *Sheffield*, *Coventry*, and *Glasgow*; the Type 22 frigate *Brilliant*; the Type 21 *Arrow*; and the old Type 12 HMS *Plymouth*, which had already departed for a long deployment in the West Indies, but which was hastily ordered to return. Two more "Spring Train" frigates, the Type 22 *Broadsword* and the Type 12 *Yarmouth*, were initially ordered to continue with plans to sail to the Indian Ocean, but within a few days both had been ordered to turn back to join the Falklands-bound forces. On 4 April Woodward transferred his flag to the *Glamorgan*, and the *Antrim* and *Plymouth* were detached to press on to South Georgia. By 11 April Woodward's six remaining ships had reached Ascension Island.[64]

The core of the task force had still to arrive from Britain. On the 2nd, orders were issued to bring to immediate readiness the two carriers *Hermes* and *Invincible*, the assault ship *Fearless*, the two available frigates *Alacrity* and *Antelope*, four landing ships logistic, and 3rd Commando Brigade, Royal Marines. After prodigies of organization and improvisation, these ships and men were soon at sea, the two carriers leaving Portsmouth on 5 April to the cheers of assembled crowds. The *Hermes* had been loaded with twelve Harriers, her own 800 Squadron's aircraft, augmented by reinforcements from 899 Squadron, the Sea Harrier training unit. She also carried nine Sea King ASW helicopters of 826 Squadron and nine Sea King transports of 846 Squadron. The *Invincible* carried eight Sea Harriers (three more than usual) and eleven Sea Kings of 820 Squadron.

On 4 April Fieldhouse suggested the establishment of a maritime exclusion zone around the islands in order to blockade the invaders. On the 7th a two-hundred-

The centerpiece of the Falklands Task Force, the "carrier battle group" of *Hermes* and *Invincible*. The Royal Fleet Auxiliary *Tidepool* had been sold to Chile but was retained for the duration of hostilities.

mile-radius zone was announced to take effect from 12 April when the nuclear submarines were due to arrive on station to enforce it. The Cabinet was also anxious to get surface units as far south as possible in case negotiations enforced a "freeze" on military movements. Captain J.F. Coward of HMS *Brilliant* was put in charge of the three Type 42s and HMS *Arrow* to advance to a position in the South Atlantic equidistant from Port Stanley, Buenos Aires, and South Georgia. Woodward, in the *Glamorgan*, doubled back north on 14 April to meet the carriers and their three accompanying frigates, *Broadsword*, *Alacrity*, and *Yarmouth*. The following day he transferred his flag to the *Hermes*, which had the best communications suite. The same day the *Invincible* finally completed a week-long repair to her main gearbox that had necessitated the ship running on half power since 17 April. With two now fully operational carriers under his immediate command, Woodward became commander of the task groups in the South Atlantic. By now all the surface ships had been designated Task Force 317, and the submarines Task Force 324. Fieldhouse at Northwood as CINCFLEET retained overall command of both these task forces.

The first phase of the British counterattack was the taking of South Georgia, where the Argentinian Force Alfa, with naval support, had captured the British settlement of Grytviken on 7 April, against considerable resistance from the Royal Marines landed there by the *Endurance*. The *Antrim* and *Plymouth* had been sent on ahead of the rest of the task force, in company with the fleet tanker *Tidespring*, in which was embarked "M" Company 42 Commando, which had been flown to Ascension with the intention of being sent ahead to recapture the island. The *Antrim*'s commander, Captain B.G. Young, was task group commander. In addition to the *Plymouth*'s Wasp, the force had three medium helicopters, two Wessex 5 transports in the *Tidespring*, and a Wessex 3 ASW machine in the *Antrim*. On 14 April the task group met the *Endurance* (with her two Wasps), and the whole group closed South Georgia to execute "Operation Paraquat." The recapture started badly when both Wessex 5s were lost on the 22nd extracting special forces, who had overestimated their powers of endurance, from Fortuna Glacier. The *Brilliant*, with her Lynx helicopters, was ordered to join the *Antrim* group as soon as possible to replace the losses. Her ASW capabilities were also invaluable as it was soon clear that there was an Argentine submarine in the area. She was the *Santa Fe*, an old ex-American boat that was transporting personnel to the island. The submarine HMS *Conqueror* had been directed to the South Georgia area to support the landings, but it was the *Antrim*'s Wessex 3 that found the surfaced submarine, on radar, close to the captured base at Grytviken on the morning of 25 April. The Wessex attacked with Mk 11 depth charges, which damaged the *Santa Fe* aft. Fearful of homing torpedoes, the submarine did not dive but continued to dash for Grytviken. A Lynx from the *Brilliant* duly dropped a MK 46 torpedo which was, as expected, ineffective against a surfaced target. More useful were the Wasps from the *Endurance* and *Plymouth*, which scored a number of hits with AS12 wire-guided missiles. A ballast tank was ruptured by a near miss and holes made in the submarine's "sail" by the missiles made diving even more noisy and dangerous. As the *Santa Fe* came alongside at Grytviken, a final AS12 shattered its periscope, snort, and radio antennae. The boat was abandoned, which did little for the morale of the defenders. Landings then took place by helicopter, as a Wasp from the *Endurance* directed the 4.5-inch guns of the *Antrim* and *Plymouth* in a 235-round bombardment that completed the destruction of the Argentines' will to resist. As the first wave of the assault closed the settlement, the Argentines at Grytviken surrendered, followed by the rest of Force Alfa at Leith the following day, 26 April.

On 18 April Woodward had set sail for the south with what was now known, perhaps a little inappropriately, as the "Carrier Battle Group." Yet this was the role that the two ASW carriers would have to fulfil. It was especially ironic that the *Hermes*, for over a decade a real strike carrier, should now be sailing into her first action having been reconfigured for a new and inappropriate role. Nevertheless, her much larger aircraft capacity still gave her a greatly enhanced capability compared to the command cruiser *Invincible*, a carrier in name only. If worst came to worst, these two ships would have to cover an opposed landing, the kind of operation Mr. Healey had specifically ruled out when he scrapped CVA 01 sixteen years before. The feeling in London was growing that some military action was inevitable, but there were also hopes that the mere presence of the task force, plus a gradually escalating pressure on the islands, might well persuade the Argentines to see reason and come to an acceptable settlement before an actual landing. The carriers and escorts made rendezvous with the ships sent on ahead on the 24th, and on the following day passed latitude 35° south. The *Brilliant* also soon rejoined the battle group to provide a Sea Wolf-equipped close escort, or "goalkeeper," for each carrier, an odd role for these primarily ASW ships and one that led to much dangerous close maneuvering. The Staff decision not to insist on point-defense systems to the carriers themselves, one dictated by shortage of funds more than anything else, now seemed to have been a weak one. The dedicated air-defense ships, the three 42s, were placed twenty miles "up threat" from the carriers to provide more distant missile cover with their Sea Darts and radar early warning with their 966 sets. The ASW carriers, intended for Atlantic operations under friendly air cover, had not been provided with their own early-warning aircraft.

The arrival of the "Carrier Battle Group" allowed the government, from 1100 GMT on 30 April, to extend the maritime exclusion zone into a total exclusion zone, or TEZ. By now a "War Cabinet" was in session. Officially it was called the Committee on the South Atlantic and was coded OD(SA) to represent its status as a sub-committee of the Oversea Policy and Defence Committee of the Cabinet. OD(SA) was composed of the prime minister, foreign secretary, defense secretary, home secretary, Conservative Party chairman, attorney general, and chief of Defence Staff. On 30 April it authorized military action against the Falklands. The following day, 1 May at 0130 Greenwich time, the Battle Group entered this area and prepared for combat. The carriers were to follow up a Vulcan long-range air strike on the Falkland Islands' main air strip at Port Stanley. The Sea Harriers were also to attack a smaller strip at Goose Green. Woodward's action was "to provide a demonstration of force to convince doubters on both sides that he was in earnest; it would also . . . force the Argentinians to commit and reveal their capabilities and weaknesses."[65] Nine aircraft were sent against Port Stanley and three against Goose Green. The *Invincible*, with her modern aircraft-direction equipment, acted as air defense, fighter cover, and antiair warfare coordination ship (as she did throughout the campaign). The attacks were completed without loss, and the BBC's correspondent in the *Hermes* was able to make the famous statement that he had counted the same number of aircraft coming back as had left. Three Argentine Pucara light strike aircraft were destroyed on the ground by cluster bombs at Goose Green.

Later that day Woodward sent in a surface bombardment group composed of the *Glamorgan*, *Alacrity*, and *Arrow* to continue the pressure. Ships' helicopters provided platforms for the forward observers. Sea Harriers chased away an Argentine Navy light strike flight of Turbo-Mentor aircraft. Already the Argentine Air Force had sent over their first probe with Mirage III fighters, but the latter were not willing to engage the Sea Harriers at low altitude, where the slower, but much more maneuverable, British aircraft had a clear advantage. The Argentines also knew that Britain had much better heat-seeking missiles. Another indecisive meeting of Sea Harriers and Mirages occurred in the afternoon, but to little effect. By this time another group of warships was operating close to the island, an ASW hunting group of the *Brilliant*, *Plymouth*, and Sea King helicopters, looking for the modern German-built submarine *San Luis*, thought to be in the area.

At last, thinking the British were carrying out a landing to retake the Falklands, the Argentines put in a full air strike with Canberras, Daggers (Israeli-built versions of the Mirage), and Skyhawks with Mirage and Dagger fighter cover. Daggers attacked the bombardment group, near-missing the *Glamorgan* and *Alacrity*, and hitting the *Arrow*, but only with cannon fire. The three British ships found that their 965 air-warning and 992 target-indication radars could not deal adequately with the ground-clutter problem. The *Glamorgan* fired a Seacat missile that missed the fast-crossing target. The Sea Harriers, however, directed by fighter controllers in the *Brilliant*, *Coventry*, and *Glamorgan*, had a good afternoon shooting down a Mirage, a Dagger, and a Canberra, and damaging another Mirage so that it was forced to put down at Port Stanley—where it was shot down by Argentine AA fire. This first air engagement had a decisive effect. The Argentines decided that because of its advantages of armament and low-altitude maneuverability the Sea Harrier could not be engaged in air combat: all further Argentine air strikes were intended to avoid the British combat air patrols.

The war was now on, and Argentina prepared for revenge with its carrier and surface fleet. On 27 April the Argentine Navy had deployed Task Force 79 to resist any attack on either the islands or Argentina herself. It was initially in two parts, Task Group 79.3 in the south (the old 6-inch cruiser *General Belgrano* and two Exocet missile-fitted ex-U.S. destroyers), and in the north Task Groups 79.1 and 79.2, the carrier *Veinticinco de Mayo* (ex-HMS *Venerable* of 1945), and Argentina's two Type 42 destroyers. On 1 May, after the British raids, Task Group 79.4 was constituted as the central prong of Argentina's trident with three remaining French-built Exocet-fitted frigates. At 1855 (GMT) on the evening of 1 May, the northern and central groups were given freedom of action to attack the invasion force, which the Argentines believed to be disembarking troops near Port Stanley. When it became clear that this was not the case, the Argentine command seems to have tried to recall their groups, but the latter pressed on, further encouraged by reconnaissance reports of a probable British carrier. The old problem of operating modern aircraft from the little British light fleet carriers, which the British themselves had faced in the 1940s and 1950s, now ruined Argentine intentions. Before dawn on 2 May, in a calm that was both unusual for the area and most fortunate for the British, it was soon clear that the old carrier was not going to have enough wind over the deck to catapult bombed-up Skyhawks with a full load of fuel. The British might have been caught in as vulnerable a state as the Japanese were at Midway, but the Argentine plan was aborted shortly after 0400 GMT. Also abortive was an attempted strike by two land-based Exocet-fitted Super Étendards that missed their in-flight refueling point, and an attempted attack by the *San Luis* that launched at some British escorts a homing torpedo whose guidance wire broke. In no sense were the Argentines holding their fire.[66]

On the evening of 30 April, with the decision to mount the air attacks next day and in accordance with the British announcement of a week before that any threat to the task force perceived as such by the British would receive a violent response, HMS *Splendid*, which was guarding the northern sector was given authority to sink the carrier if she found her. Although the *Splendid* did make long-range towed-array sonar contact with the escorting destroyers, she never found the *Veinticinco de Mayo* herself, perhaps to the relief of the foreign secretary, Francis Pym, and the attorney general, Sir Michael Havers, who were worried about the legal propriety of the move. Not so lucky, however, was the *Belgrano* group, which had not been instructed to play a part in the attack but had been ordered instead to continue on patrol in the south, guarding against possible intervention from around Cape Horn. On the afternoon of the 30th the *Conqueror* had detected a replenishment tanker on her 2024 towed-array. The *Conqueror* refined her bearing by periodically slowing and taking fixes and closed the *Belgrano* group, being ordered at midnight to attack if the enemy penetrated the Total Exclusion Zone. At 1300 GMT the *Conqueror* sighted an old cruiser and signaled this back to London an hour later. For about twenty-four hours the *Conqueror*'s captain, Commander C.L. Wreford Brown, trailed the group as it patrolled its "beat" outside the exclusion zone, first going southeast, then due east, and finally at 0800 GMT on the 2nd, turning westward. At 1400 GMT, when she raised her mast for routine signals, the *Conqueror* received a garbled message from London. This was, in fact, a change in the rules of engagement to allow attacks on Argentine ships outside the exclusion zone, first sent to British submarines at 1230. Wreford Brown, a thoughtful, introspective officer, was suffering severe communication problems due to damage to his masts caused by heavy seas. He had no desire to start a war without authorization and held his fire, signaling back to London the *Belgrano*'s recent change of course. Ironically enough, while this was going on, the *Belgrano* was ordered to continue westward to get to shallow water to protect her from SSNs. The rules of engagement change was confirmed to the *Conqueror* at 1700 GMT (1400 local time). Wreford Brown replied at 1730 that he understood the rules of engagement change and that he intended to attack. The nuclear submarine went to action stations at 1800. It took almost another hour for him to maneuver from several miles astern to within 1,400 yards of the *Belgrano* and her escorts. The *Conqueror* then fired a spread of three Mark 8 torpedoes. Wreford Brown chose Mark 8s primarily because their large warheads stood a better chance of penetrating the cruiser's armor and bulges. The torpedoes scored hits on the cruiser, which quickly rolled over and sank. The third torpedo hit the destroyer *Hipolito Bouchard*, but did not explode. The ship, however, received some damage and began to withdraw. The third ship, the *Piedra Buena*, dropped depth charges that seem to have inhibited the *Conqueror*'s activities for a time.[67]

It has now been revealed that Woodward himself had taken the initiative in unleashing the *Conqueror*. An admiral noted for intellectual subtlety and depth, and fully cognizant of the potential effectiveness of surface action groups against carriers, he had a high regard for the potential danger posed by the *Belgrano* group. The Argentines had proved quite competent when trained by the British at Portland. As a submariner he also recognized the possibility of the *Conqueror* losing contact as the Argentines advanced northwards over the shallows of the Burdwood Bank. So, in the early hours of 2 May (0710 GMT) he had sent a signal via Northwood to the *Conqueror* to attack the *Belgrano*. The *Conqueror* never received that message, which was immediately countermanded by Flag Officer Submarines Admiral Sir Peter Herbert. This explains a signal sent to the *Conqueror* at 0915 GMT that the *Belgrano* was not to be attacked until the rules of engagement were changed. Given this specific caution it is hardly surprising that Wreford Brown showed some circumspection when the genuine rules of engagement change was made. CINCFLEET, Admiral Fieldhouse, reportedly sent an angry signal to the task force commander, but Woodward had made his point. When Lewin, the chief of Defence Staff, visited Northwood later that morning, he was made aware of Woodward's obvious concern. Together the admirals seem to have decided that they should support the man on the spot. Moreover, they calculated that the loss of the *Belgrano* might so demoralize the Argentine surface navy that it would effectively abandon the war. Lewin and Fieldhouse went to Chequers, where members of the "War Cabinet" were due to meet in the afternoon and thus were available for an impromptu session before lunch without their other professional advisers. In Lewin's words: "We had this little meeting which lasted about twenty minutes, explained the situation and got agreement that they could now attack any Argentine warship that they intercepted outside territorial waters. This was telephoned through to Northwood and transmitted about 1300." (British Summer Time, 1200 GMT). The *Conqueror*'s later message about the change of course was not forwarded to the War Cabinet, who had no doubt been given a clear exposition of Woodward's perception of danger. It is even possible that it was told of the latter's action in trying to unleash the submarine himself. In any case, in the circumstances, it was difficult for Prime Minister Thatcher and her associates to overrule such a strong military consensus. Political circumstances did not seem to them to justify it. It is possible that the whole *Belgrano* affair, which culminated in the unsuccessful prosecution of the Ministry of Defence civil servant Clive Ponting in 1984–85, had as its root the government's unwillingness to show the successful way it had been manipulated into a significant escalation by its naval subordinates. Certainly the full hopes of the British naval command proved justified. The *Veinticinco de Mayo* and the Argentine surface navy stayed within their territorial waters for the remainder of the war.[68]

On the night of 2/3 May a clash occurred between the task force's helicopters and an Argentine patrol vessel, the *Alfarez Sobral*, on a mission to rescue a shotdown air crew. The boat fired at a Sea King, which called in Lynx helicopters from the *Glasgow* and *Coventry*. The Lynxes were equipped with the new Sea Skua radar-homing missiles, which scored at least one hit. The *Sobral* had its bridge blown away with the loss of her captain and seven members of the crew. The British thought they had sunk one vessel and damaged another, but the one Argentine vessel involved got back home a week later.

If Woodward had known it, the Argentine submarine threat had been neutralized, at least for the time being. Harried for twenty-four hours by helicopters that dropped depth charges and at least one torpedo, the *San Luis* had retreated, but there was still a potent enemy air threat. Quite how potent was demonstrated on 4 May when the Étendards scored a significant success. That morning the battle group was steaming to the southeast, about 100 miles off Port Stanley. The three Type 42 destroyers were disposed in an arc about twenty miles ahead of the carriers. The familiar radar emissions of the Type 42s were picked up by an Argentine Navy Neptune reconnaissance aircraft, and two Exocet-fitted Super Étendards were scrambled from Rio Grande airfield to attack the British task force. Being fully aware of the techniques for dealing with British long-range radar of their own, the Étendards kept below the searching lobes, popping up to 120 feet to acquire targets and fire missiles. HMS *Glasgow* obtained all too brief contacts both of the Étendard radars on her passive electronic warfare (ESM) receiver, and of the aircraft themselves on her own search radar. As these fleeting contacts were assessed in the *Invincible* and as the *Glasgow* fired chaff rockets, one of the Exocets locked on to HMS *Sheffield*, the closest target. With tragic ill-luck the *Sheffield* had chosen this moment to indulge in routine satellite communications, which had the effect of degrading her ESM capabilities. She was hit on the starboard side, the missile

The Royal Navy's first loss of the Falklands War: HMS *Sheffield* burns after being struck by an Exocet missile. In the first days of hostilities both sides were more vulnerable than they later became. (Imperial War Museum)

entering on an angled trajectory and piercing deep inside the unsuspecting destroyer.

A large fire broke out in the ship, fueled by the rocket's own unburnt propellant and the ship's wiring, hydraulic fluid, and galley fat. Reportedly, there were problems with the ship's firefighting equipment, an index both of the inevitable inexperience and shortcomings one finds at the beginning of a war, and perhaps the lack of unspectacular backup equipment that results from an overloaded defense program where the less spectacular tends to be neglected. The missile cut the ship's water main on impact. At 1751 (GMT) Captain Salt ordered abandon ship despite the efforts of his crew and those of HMS *Arrow* and HMS *Yarmouth* that came alongside. The *Yarmouth*, which had been narrowly missed by the second missile, had been firing its mortars at suspected submarine contacts as the destroyer burned. The threat of submarine attack and magazine explosion were primary factors in the decision to take off the *Sheffield*'s crew. Later, attempts were made by HMS *Yarmouth* to tow the burnt-out hulk to meet a tug which would tow her home, but in heavy seas the ship capsized and sank on 10 May. The 4th of May also saw another British reverse, the first Sea Harrier loss, when an aircraft attacking Goose Green was shot down by AA fire.

The losses of 4 May had a significant effect on Woodward's thinking. They demonstrated that a too-aggressive use of the battle group was dangerous, given its technical weaknesses. The admiral pondered "how he and his fleet could solve the conundrum of the air threat without being destroyed by it."[69] If one of his precious carriers were hit and put out of action, then every military option available to the British government would have disappeared. Both ships and aircraft had to be husbanded. So the battle group kept its distance, and the Sea Harriers restricted themselves to relatively ineffective high-level bombing. A discouraged Woodward held back his surface units until the night of 8 May when HMS *Brilliant* was sent to see what enemy forces she could draw out north of Falkland Sound, and HMS *Alacrity* bombarded the Port Stanley area. On 9 May a novel surface action unit was created to maintain the offensive, the 42/22 "Combo," a combination of the two escort types that between them could deploy a Sea Dart long-range SAM launcher, Sea Wolf point-defense missiles, a 4.5-inch gun, a 966 long-range air-search radar, and 997/998 doppler radars that could deal with ground clutter. The two ships could act on each other's sensor information using electronic data links. Given the capabilities at hand, the principle was a sensible one although it created a number of practical problems.

The Combos could both bombard and engage aircraft, and the first one, composed of the *Coventry* and *Broadsword*, duly appeared off Port Stanley. The *Coventry* fired a Sea Dart at a Hercules flying in supplies and at a Puma helicopter. The former turned away, but the latter was destroyed, Sea Dart's first ever kill. The *Coventry* also claimed two Skyhawks, but it seems these were lost in an operational accident caused by poor visibility. The *Coventry* was also involved in the other major action of the day, directing a Harrier to bomb and strafe the Argentine surveillance ship *Narwhal*.

Other ships kept up the bombardments at night, and on the 10th the *Alacrity*, operating in the Sound between the islands primarily to test the area for mines, blew up the supply ship *Islos de los Estados* with accurate 4.5-inch fire. The *Alacrity* and a companion were then attacked by the *San Luis* north of San Carlos, but again the torpedo wire broke. Two days later another Combo, the *Glasgow* and *Brilliant*, was bombarding Port Stanley airfield. The aim was to draw out the Argentine Air Force, and eight Skyhawks duly attacked. At first, as planned, the Sea Wolf missiles worked magnificently. The *Brilliant* shot down two aircraft, and a third crashed trying to evade a missile while being damaged by pieces from the second casualty. When the next wave came in, however, the fire-control computer was confused, partly by the *Glasgow*'s 4.5-inch fire and partly by its preference for individual missiles rather than groups of aircraft: the system refused to work. With Sea Dart also unusable in the conditions, the ships only had a few light guns to protect them. The Skyhawks narrowly missed the *Brilliant*, but one bomb passed straight through the *Glasgow*, damaging her so badly that she was out of action for the remainder of the war and had to be sent home. Given their narrow escape, the ship's company cannot have been too unhappy at their withdrawal. The Sea Wolf software, optimized for anti-missile work, was adjusted as rapidly as possible to improve its capability against relatively large targets such as aircraft.

The loss of the services of another long-range SAM ship helped demonstrate that the strategy of maritime pressure and blockade was not working under the pressure of the Argentine aerial counterattacks. The lack of airborne early warning made the option of moving the battle group west of the islands too risky. Some measures were, however, taken to improve the situation. On the evening of 17 April HMS *Invincible* steamed to the west of the Falklands to launch a Sea King helicopter of 846 Squadron carrying Special Air Service (SAS) men equipped with electronic receiving and transmitting equipment that would allow them to provide covert early warning of Argentine raids. The group of eight men were landed in Argentina and provided a vital service to the ships until the fall of Port Stanley, when they were taken off by submarine. The helicopter, prevented by bad weather from returning to the *Invincible*, had to land in Chile were it was burnt by its crew.[70]

There seemed little alternative to an amphibious landing, despite the lack of complete air superiority. With a last, remarkably generous, British negotiating proposal rejected by an Argentine government that seemed, in any case, beyond reason (and which still might have felt it had a reasonable chance of success), on 18 May the chiefs of staff presented an invasion plan to the full Cabinet. On the 19th, with rejection confirmed, Woodward was authorized to proceed with the invasion, "Operation Sutton" as it was code-named. The whole operation was by now known as "Operation Corporate."

By the 18th the Amphibious Task Group, commanded by Commodore M.C. Clapp (Commodore Amphibious Warfare), had joined Woodward's battle group. The assembly of this force, carrying 3rd Commando Brigade reinforced by two parachute battalions, had been an extraordinary achievement given the short time available. By 9 April, the week after the decision to make open preparations to prepare a task force, the 3rd Commando Brigade, reinforced by the 3rd Parachute Regiment, a SAM battery, and two armored reconnaissance troops, were embarked in HMS *Fearless*, the four LSLs *Sir Galahad*, *Sir Geraint*, *Sir Lancelot*, and *Sir Percivale*, the Royal Fleet Auxiliaries *Stromness*, *Fort Austin*, and *Resource*, and two converted merchantmen, the huge 45,000-ton cruise liner *Canberra* and the 5,500-ton P & O ferry *Elk*. They were soon joined at Ascension Island by the second LPD *Intrepid* (rapidly mobilized from reserve with an ad hoc crew), another

LSL *Sir Tristram*, the 13,000-ton Ro-Ro ferry *Norland*, and the 4,200-ton *Europic Ferry* with another battalion and a field artillery battery. The ships had been sailed rapidly to achieve maximum political effect: tactical loading had been ignored. This necessitated much activity at Ascension, reloading and transferring equipment between ships, as well as exercises by the troops ashore. The five slow LSLs eventually sailed on 30 April, followed by the *Canberra* and *Elk* on 6 May and the rest on the 8th. With the amphibious ships were the destroyer *Antrim*, which had transferred her South Georgia prisoners to the *Antelope* for transport back to Ascension, the frigates *Argonaut* (an Exocet *Leander*), *Ardent* (a Type 21), and the large container ship *Atlantic Conveyor*, converted into an aircraft transport/ auxiliary carrier. She had sailed from Britain on 25 April with four Chinook and six Wessex transport helicopters and a replacement Lynx. At Ascension she acquired more aircraft, eight Sea Harriers of the newly formed 809 Squadron and six RAF Harrier GR3s of No. 1 Squadron. A Sea Harrier was kept on deck to provide VTOL fighter cover as the ship sailed south.

The Amphibious Task Group came together on 17 May, and two days later massive "cross-decking" of men and equipment took place. This was more extensive than Clapp and the landing force commander, Brigadier Julian Thompson, had planned. London, conscious of the vulnerability of three units (40 and 42 Commandos and 3rd Parachute Battalion) in one ship, the *Canberra*, ordered the dispersal of the troops into other vessels. This duly took place by landing craft and helicopter. A Sea King containing Special Air Service personnel crashed, killing twenty-two of its passengers and crew. A happier event for the task force on the 19th was its reinforcement by the four remaining GR3 Harriers of No. 1 Squadron,

HMS *Hermes* launches a Sea Harrier during the Falklands War. The stacking of bombs on deck seems to show little regard for the Argentine air and missile threat. (Imperial War Museum)

which had flown down with the aid of in-flight refueling. There were now twenty-five Sea Harriers available for combat air patrols (fourteen in the *Hermes* and eleven in the *Invincible*) and ten GR3s for ground attack (all in the *Hermes*). These were somewhat exiguous resources with which to cover a landing within range of a significant, if not especially sophisticated, enemy air force. Given the quarrels of the past, it was also interesting to see FAA and RAF Harrier squadrons operating side by side.

On 20 May (D minus 1) the ships closed up into antiaircraft formation for the run in to the chosen landing place, the sheltered bay of San Carlos Water on the northwest side of East Falkland, where it was felt that the hills would help protect the force from Exocet missiles. Already on the night of 14/15 May a special forces raid on the nearby airstrip of Pebble Island, which had been supported by HMS *Glamorgan*'s guns, had destroyed ten Pucara and Turbo-Mentor light attack aircraft and a Prefectura Naval Skyvan transport. The weather on the 20th was just what the British needed—rough, rainy, and misty. Thus protected, with the *Antrim*, *Brilliant*, *Broadsword*, *Yarmouth*, *Plymouth*, *Ardent*, and *Argonaut* providing cover with their missiles and guns and the *Invincible* close by in support, the Amphibious Task Group closed in. The latter consisted of HMS *Fearless* and HMS *Intrepid*, the RFAs *Sir Galahad*, *Sir Lancelot*, *Sir Tristram*, *Sir Percivale*, *Stromness*, and *Fort Austin*, and the *Canberra*, *Norland*, and *Europic Ferry*. That evening the *Antrim* sped away to carry out an operation to neutralize Argentine positions on Fanning Head, both by landing a patrol by helicopter and by bombardment. The frigate *Ardent* also departed to bombard Darwin and the Goose Green airfield to the south of San Carlos, in support of an SAS troop that was acting both as a diversion and to pin down Argentine reserves.

The first amphibious ships anchored at the entrance to San Carlos Water rather later than planned at about midnight local time (0400 GMT). Further delays were caused by a defect in the *Fearless*'s ballast pump, and the difficulties of the 2nd Parachute Battalion in the *Norland* (untrained in the art of night embarkation into landing craft) in getting into the *Intrepid*'s landing craft standing alongside. Eventually, 40 Commando, a combat engineer vehicle, and four light tanks from the *Fearless* were embarked in four LCUs and four smaller LCVPs, and the 2nd Parachute Battalion safely made it in their four LCUs. HMS *Plymouth*, the first ship into Falkland Sound, gave close support. Led by a Royal Marine major with intimate knowledge of the Falklands coastline, the landing craft sped at rather more than the planned six knots into San Carlos. The paratroopers waded ashore on "Blue Beach Two," south of San Carlos Settlement, on time at about 0830 GMT. A few minutes later 40 Commando went ashore at "Blue Beach One" to the north of it. The landing craft then returned to pick up 45 Commando and 3rd Parachute Battalion from the *Stromness* and *Intrepid*. The former were landed at "Red Beach" at Ajax Bay opposite San Carlos Settlement, the latter (at around 1130 GMT) at "Green Beach" on the north bank of the Port San Carlos inlet. It was here that the only Argentine opposition was encountered, but the small Argentine half company was easily driven away.

As dawn broke the Amphibious Force moved into San Carlos Water, both to gain the protection of the hills and to land guns and other equipment, including vital Rapier air-defense missiles. All the warships, except the *Plymouth*, remained outside San Carlos Water itself in a protective line of guns and missiles. The first of the expected counterattacks came in the form of a Macchi 339 light attack aircraft of the Argentine Navy, which inflicted rocket and cannon damage on HMS *Argonaut*. Then a group of Daggers flew in from the mainland and attacked the warships, which replied with missiles and guns. A Sea Wolf missile from HMS *Broadsword* accounted for one of the aircraft, but the Daggers succeeded in damaging HMS *Antrim*, the main antiair coordinating ship stationed inside Falkland Sound. She was raked by cannon fire and hit by two bombs. One bounced off the forecastle to explode harmlessly in the water. The other penetrated deep inside the ship, narrowly missing two highly explosive Sea Slug missiles, but causing considerable damage by its impact. The height at which the 1,000-lb. bomb had been released, however, prevented it going off, a good omen for the future. The *Antrim* had to move inside San Carlos Water to get the bomb defused, but this enabled her to provide the ships inside, especially the great white bulk of the *Canberra*, with direct protection. The *Broadsword* also suffered damage from cannon fire.

The next attack came from Goose Green-based Pucara counterinsurgency aircraft tasked with shooting down British helicopters. One of the first pair of Pucaras was prevented from taking off by the start of the *Ardent*'s delayed dawn bombardment: the other was shot down by an SAS man with Stinger missiles. A second pair of Pucaras, searching for the artillery observers controlling the attacks on their airfield, were attacked by Sea Harriers, which shot one down. Argentine Skyhawks now found the *Ardent*, but their attack was unsuccessful. Sea Harriers from the *Hermes* were vectored in and found another group of Skyhawks, which they engaged with Sidewinder missiles, shooting down two.

These early attacks were just a foretaste of what was to come during the afternoon. The Argentines got better as they gained experience, but so did the British. HMS *Antrim* remained remarkably active in her fighter control role, despite her damage, but she was supplemented by HMS *Brilliant* using an ad hoc combination on a Sea Wolf doppler radar and computer system and an executive officer with much experience of aircraft direction. This compensated for the fact that the *Brilliant*'s Sea Wolf missiles were unable to cope with the clutter problem in San Carlos Water, where the frigate had moved to join the damaged *Antrim* and to give more support to the amphibious ships. Guided by the control ships, Sea Harriers successfully dealt with one of the afternoon's first wave of Daggers, but Skyhawks attacking from the south smothered the *Argonaut*'s defenses, putting two 1,000-lb. bombs into her. Neither exploded (a particularly fortunate occurrence, as one ended up in the ship's Sea Cat magazine!), but the ship lay immobile in the water.

The survivors of the Dagger formation took on the *Ardent*, which had moved up to be the southernmost member of the "gun line." Unluckily, she was now suffering from a malfunction with her Sea Cat system. The lack of defense meant that the Argentine aircraft could now attack from a proper height, and this time one bomb went off, inflicting severe damage on the stern of the ship and putting all her major weapons out of action: the Sea Cat launcher was blown completely off the ship. The ship was then attacked by Air Force Skyhawks and, with only 20-mm and machine guns to protect her, suffered more hits from exploding bombs in the stern area. Next came Navy A-4Q Skyhawks with special 500-lb. "Snakeye" bombs, configured for low-level release, which scored even more hits, although all three aircraft were shot down by the *Hermes*'s Sea Harriers, one Argentine aircraft also being helped on its way by *Ardent's* light AA gunfire. It was small revenge for the *Ardent*, which had to be abandoned. She eventually sank after a total of seven hits by bombs that exploded and two that did not. At the same time as the *Ardent* was suffering her death blows, HMS *Brilliant* was strafed by Daggers. The 30-mm shells caused temporarily catastrophic damage to the Sea Wolf's computer input channels, but the damage was quickly repaired.

In the entire day the British Sea Harriers shot down four Daggers, five Skyhawks, and a Pucara. Antiaircraft fire accounted for a Pucara and the *Broadsword's* Dagger, but the relative "ineffectiveness" of the AA armament of the ships was more apparent than real. Their fire had played a decisive role in their protection of the amphibious ships. It forced the Argentine aircraft to fly so low that most of the bombs they were using failed to arm. Moreover, it made it impossible for the aircraft that had actually penetrated the Sound to make effective attacks at all, despite the obvious vulnerability of ships such as the *Canberra*. With the *Plymouth, Antrim, Brilliant,* and the transport ships themselves putting up a considerable barrage of gunfire inside the Sound, and the ships outside drawing fire, the surface ships carried out their role with considerable success and were a decisive complement to the Sea Harriers, especially as the Argentines insisted on going for the warships rather than the more valuable amphibious vessels. It must also be remembered that the surface ships provided the Sea Harriers with vital forward radar control and direction facilities without which the fighters would have been much less effective. Nevertheless, it was considered prudent during the morning to disembark 42 Commando, being kept in reserve, from the *Canberra*. That night, and in some haste, the liner was withdrawn on orders from London. Plans to use her as a floating forward dressing station had to be abandoned. The *Norland* was ordered out also. The balance of the threat meant that it was better to have them at sea facing a limited submarine threat rather than as continued "sitting ducks" for aircraft in San Carlos Water. Nevertheless, many vital stores went with the two ships.

The next day, the 22nd of May, was relatively quiet. In the evening the *Brilliant* and *Yarmouth* were ordered to find and capture the Falkland Islanders' supply vessel *Monsunen*, being used by the Argentines on transport duties along the south of the Falklands between Falkland Sound and Port Stanley. An attempt to board with Special Boat Service personnel by means of the *Brilliant's* Lynx helicopter failed due to heavy fire, but the merchantman was driven ashore and was of no further use to the Argentines.

The Argentine air offensive began again in earnest on the 23rd. The Skyhawks, which unlike the Daggers had a little fuel in reserve for tactical maneuvering, were finding it a little easier to avoid Sea Harrier patrols. The task force had been reinforced on 21 and 22 April by the arrival of the Type 42 destroyer *Exeter* and two Type 21s, the *Ambuscade* and *Antelope*. The *Antelope* was sent almost immediately in to the islands on 23 April to replace the previous day's losses. Her Lynx used her Sea Skua missiles to set on fire the Argentine supply vessel *Rio Carcarana* at Port King on the western side of Falkland Sound. The ship had defied both Sea Harriers and the *Argonaut's* Lynx, but the *Antelope's* helicopter succeeded in finally sinking her. It was to be the frigate's only offensive action of the war. Even as her helicopter was returning from the successful mission, four Argentine Air Force A-4B Skyhawks attacked the *Antelope*. One flew so low that it struck

The most successful ship with the Sea Dart missile in the Falklands War was HMS *Exeter* with four Argentine aircraft to her credit. The *Exeter* was the first Type 42 to be fitted with the 1022 radar instead of the 966 modification of the 1950s-vintage 965.

the ship's aftermast. Two bombs hit that at first failed to explode. Unluckily, attempts to defuse them that evening failed and the ship blew up. Despite this important reverse, the synergistic Sea Harrier and AA systems proved effective in dealing with most of the attacks, the land-based Rapier missiles now adding to the Argentine's discomfort. Only two Argentine aircraft seem actually to have been lost, a Skyhawk attacking the *Antelope* that was shot down by multiple hits from the frigate's 20-mm Oerlikon gun, a Sea Wolf missile from the *Broadsword*, and a Rapier missile from the shore, and a Dagger shot down by a Sea Harrier; more importantly, the remaining ships in the Sound survived.

The following day saw the same story, with repeated air attacks in "Bomb Alley" that failed to inflict any catastrophic damage, although two LSLs, the *Sir Galahad* and *Sir Lancelot*, were hit by bombs that failed to explode. The ships were neutralized while the weapons were defused. A Skyhawk was brought down over San Carlos Water by the multiple effects of missiles and guns, while the Sea Harriers' Sidewinders dealt with three Daggers. Woodward had placed a "42/22 Combo," composed of the *Coventry* and *Broadsword*, to the northwest of the landing area off Pebble Island to improve radar fighter control and act as a "missile trap," and it was control from this unit that dealt with all three of the shot-down Daggers. The next day, 25 May, Argentina's national day, the Argentine Air Force claimed its revenge. An increased intensity of attack was expected, and Woodward moved the carriers closer to the islands to give the Sea Harriers more time on station. The *Coventry/Broadsword* "Combo" had mixed fortunes, but the balance of its luck was bad. During the morning, due to the Sea Darts' magazine doors being jammed by dried salt, the *Coventry* was unable to get missiles on to her launcher quickly enough to engage a high-flying reconnaissance aircraft. This was probably a C130 on a target acquisition mission for a dawn Skyhawk strike specifically directed on the troublesome pair of ships. The *Coventry* had better luck with one of the Skyhawks, however, which was shot down by a long-range Sea Dart shot, causing the mission to be aborted.

The *Coventry*'s good shooting continued when she struck a Skyhawk that had attacked the San Carlos anchorage, but which had been unable to release its bombs. With even more reason to dispose of the threat posed by the two ships the Argentines mounted another raid specifically targeted on the *Coventry* and *Broadsword*, now reported to be fifteen miles off Pebble Island. The day's earlier successes, inflated by a false Sea Wolf claim of a small, slow aircraft over the islands, had given the two ships too great a degree of confidence in their weapons. The "Combo" decided to trust its missiles rather than the fighters under its control when it was attacked. The first pair of Skyhawks seemed to be headed for the *Coventry*, which put up a barrage of gunfire that may have forced the aircraft to go for the *Broadsword* instead. The Type 22 had Sea Wolf locked on, but at the last moment the system's computer was again confused by one apparent "target" turning into two and refused to continue the engagement. One bomb hit, bouncing off the sea into the ship's side, coming out on the flight deck and falling into the sea beyond, carrying with it the nose of the frigate's Lynx helicopter. The next pair attacked the *Coventry*, which had again called off its Sea Harrier due to Sea Dart having locked on to the Argentines. Unfortunately, due to background clutter and evasive action by the Argentine pilots, the missile missed. The problems of operating a point-defense system on one ship and an area-defense one on another now became evident. Both ships were maneuvering violently, and the *Coventry* found herself masking the arcs of fire of the *Broadsword*. Three of the Skyhawks' 1,000-lb. bombs hit and exploded; the *Coventry* heeled over and sank an hour after being hit.

If this were not enough, the main battle group now came under another attack from two Exocet-fitted Super Étendards flying from Rio Grande in Tierra del Fuego. Escorts were by now using their Lynx helicopters on anti-missile barrier patrols listening for tell-tale radar echoes. The *Invincible* also carried a Lynx equipped with anti-missile electronic countermeasures. The whole carrier group was at a much greater state of combat efficiency than it had been at the time of the *Sheffield* fiasco. HMS *Ambuscade* spotted the Exocet attack and fired chaff, which decoyed away one of the missiles from striking her. The warships' chaff rockets proved to be adequate anti-Exocet protection, but this only had the effect of leading the missiles to the less well-equipped supply ships deployed deliberately "up-threat" of the vital carriers. The unlucky ship was the *Atlantic Conveyor*, about to move into the islands to unload her helicopters and other much-needed supplies, including equipment for a Harrier landing strip. Possibly both missiles hit her, causing uncontrollable fires. She had to be abandoned, a serious and significant loss, but not as serious as would have been one of the carriers. It was, however, at least arguable that one of the frigates would have been a less unacceptable casualty. The 25th of May was perhaps the Argentines' best day of the war, with a destroyer and a vital supply ship sunk in exchange for three Skyhawks shot down. As well as the *Coventry*'s kills, the third Skyhawk was downed by hits from guns, and, possibly, a

Rapier missile over the San Carlos anchorage. After the sinking of the *Atlantic Conveyor*, it was decided to equip the *Hermes* as well as the *Invincible* with an electronic surveillance and decoy Lynx helicopter.

Nevertheless, despite their efforts, the Argentine Air Force and Naval Air Force could not deny the British the use of the sea to such an extent that their operations on land were affected. The Harriers of No. 1 Squadron continued to give useful air support to the advance of 3rd Commando Brigade; Sea Harriers, surface ships, and Rapier SAMs kept the air threat at bay over the islands and over the task force. The *Fearless* and *Intrepid* brought down a Skyhawk with 40-mm fire on 27 May, and two days later a shore-based Rapier claimed another Dagger. The Argentine forces in West Falkland were also contained as much as possible, partly by a series of night bombardments begun by HMS *Plymouth* on 26 May with an attack on Fox Bay. Her sister Type 12, the *Yarmouth*, carried out a similar attack in the early hours of the following day. Their old Mark 6 gun mountings proved more reliable than the newer automatic Mark 8 mountings in the Type 21s. The *Arrow*, tasked with supporting the famous advance of the 2nd Parachute Regiment on Goose Green on 28 May, was forced to cease fire for a time due to faults. She made up for it by staying on station almost an hour longer than ordered. The same day, in minor revenge for the bombing of the *Coventry* a C-130 target acquisition aircraft was shot down by two Sea Harriers vectored on to the target by the frigate *Minerva*. No more such missions were flown by the Argentines, although C-130 transports, avoiding Sea Harriers, combat air patrols, and Sea Dart missiles, were able to fly in and out of Port Stanley until its recapture by the British.

On 30 May the Argentines mounted a last determined air attack on the British ships with two navy Super Étendards carrying the last available air-launched Exocet and air force Skyhawks carrying 500-lb. bombs. The Skyhawks were to follow the Exocet in to finish off the ship the missile hit; it was hoped that the ship would be a British carrier. Unfortunately for the Argentines, the attack was concentrated on the Type 21 frigate *Avenger*. The latter was closing the islands to engage in "Operation Brewers Arms"—the landing of a small Special Boat Service patrol to keep the area on West Falkland opposite San Carlos clear of any Argentine forces who might be directing the air attacks. She was passing HMS *Exeter* in the battle group screen. The Type 42 detected the attack first, but there was considerable confusion that led to the *Avenger* missing the warning and then mistaking the direction of the attack. Skillful handling retrieved the situation and kept the frigate in a cloud of chaff, which decoyed the Exocet away to splash harmlessly in the sea. A Sea Dart from the *Exeter* blew up a Skyhawk (for a time the *Avenger* was convinced that the flash of this explosion was one of her 4.5-inch shells destroying the Exocet!), but the other three A-4Cs closed the *Avenger*, which then engaged them with gunfire. Two dropped their bombs harmlessly into the sea, one was shot down, crashing into the sea alongside the British frigate. The two surviving Argentine pilots allowed wishful thinking to get the better of them. They were convinced that they had attacked the *Invincible*! The lucky *Avenger* continued with her mission, closing the islands that night. She carried out various bombardments and used the *Ambuscade*'s Lynx (her own having broken down) to insert the patrol near Mount Brisbane.

The *Avenger* was part of a further welcome reinforcement that Woodward had received to supplement his depleted screen. On the 26th of May, HMS *Bristol* had

Extensive modernization was planned for the "broad-beamed" *Leander*s in the 1980s to bring them close to the standard of a Type 22. The program was curtailed by the Nott defense review to five ships. This is the first, HMS *Andromeda*, which served in the Falklands War. Note the considerable alterations, Sea Wolf missile launcher forward, Exocet missiles, extended flight deck, and loss of funnel cap to save top-weight. Less obvious is the addition of a 2016 sonar.

arrived as leader of a group of escorts, the Type 42 destroyer, HMS *Cardiff* (diverted from the Armilla patrol), the first of the rebuilt Sea Wolf-equipped Batch 3 *Leander*s HMS *Andromeda*, the Batch 2 Exocet *Leander*s HMS *Minerva* and HMS *Penelope*, and the Type 21s HMS *Active* and HMS *Avenger*. On the way south both the *Bristol* and the *Cardiff* had fired Sea Dart missiles at an Argentine Boeing 707 being used to monitor British reinforcements south of Ascension. These two ships, together with HMS *Exeter* meant that Woodward now had effectively re-placed all his lost area-defense guided-missile ships. The *Andromeda* also gave him the flexibility to use pairs of Type 22s more offensively without denuding his carriers of their point-defense antiaircraft and anti-missile "goalkeeper" Sea Wolf escorts. Extra submarines were also sent south, the SSNs *Courageous* and *Valiant*, and the quiet conventional boat *Onyx*, specially suitable for special forces operations. The nuclear submarines maintained the blockade of the Argentine Navy and also used their radar to give early warning of air raids. The 6,000-ton North Sea oil support ship, *Stena Seaspread*, had arrived at South Georgia on 15 May to maintain and repair the task force vessels that were suffering wear and tear as well as battle damage. (The old repair ship *Triumph* would have been useful in this role, but she had been finally scrapped in 1981!) A few days later an area east of the Falklands was designated the Tug, Repair, and Logistic Area (TRALA), in which the work of maintaining and supplying the task force could take place. The extent of the work undertaken at sea was impressive; the *Stena Seaspread*'s divers could even replace a frigate's broken screw propeller blade. The *Stena Seaspread* was but one of forty-eight ships "taken up from trade" (STUFT), mobilized with amazing speed to supplement twenty-four Royal Fleet Auxiliary and Royal Maritime Auxiliary Service vessels to form the whole Falklands Task Force deployed before hostilities ended. It was a remarkable demonstration of "British Sea Power" in a traditional sense.

On 27 May more ground reinforcements had arrived at South Georgia, the three battalions of 5 Infantry Brigade in the impressive bulk of Britain's largest liner, the *Queen Elizabeth II*. Covered by HMS *Antrim* and *Endurance*, she transferred her troops to the *Canberra* and *Norland* and left for home on the 29th, carrying the survivors of the sunken ships. Used for the transfer were five converted Hull trawlers that had been mobilized to act as the 11th Minesweeping Flotilla for the task force, and the patrol vessels *Leeds Castle* and *Dumbarton Castle*, which were being used as despatch vessels between the South Atlantic and Ascension. Troops of 5 Brigade were soon at San Carlos, where they reinforced the thrust on Stanley, already begun by the marines and paratroops. On 30 May Major General Jeremy Moore, Royal Marines, took over command of what was now a division-sized command on shore.

The logistics of the ground forces in the difficult Falklands terrain depended on helicopters. The loss of the three Chinooks and six Wessexes in the *Atlantic Conveyor* had, therefore, been a serious blow. The Wessexes belonged to one of the three new operational helicopter squadrons re-formed by the Royal Navy in April and May 1982. 825 Squadron was commissioned with ten ASW Sea Kings (mainly from the training squadron 706 at Culdrose) with their sonar removed for transport duties. The aircraft came south with the *Queen Elizabeth II* and in the *Atlantic Causeway*, a sister of the ill-fated *Atlantic Conveyor*. In addition to the surviving Wessex 5 squadron, 845, some of whose aircraft were taken south in RFAs and the *Intrepid* at the outset of the hostilities (and some of whose machines were based at Ascension), two more Wessex squadrons were re-formed. 847 Squadron was set up with aircraft from miscellaneous second-line sources on 5 May and moved south in the *Atlantic Causeway*, and the helicopter support RFA *Engadine*. It helped make up for the Wessexes lost by 848 Squadron, commissioned from the second-line 707 Squadron on 19 April at Yeovilton, which had lost half its strength in the *Atlantic Conveyor*. 848 Squadron's remaining six Wessex 5s deployed in three RFAs survived, but were heavily used for replenishments at sea rather than duties ashore. (825 and 847 Squadrons disbanded in September 1982 and 848 Squadron at the end of November.)

The army reinforcements included two Guards battalions who were fresh from their sentry boxes at Buckingham Palace entertaining the London tourists. These soldiers found marching across the island difficult, and given the shortage of helicopters, it was decided to send them by sea. On the night of 5 June the *Intrepid* lived up to her name and used her landing craft to carry the Scots Guards to Bluff Cove, south of Stanley. An attempt to repeat the operation with the Welsh Guards failed, and it was now decided that the LPDs were too valuable to risk on such duties, being almost regarded as "capital ships." LSLs were already being used successfully to bring in supplies to Teal Inlet, north of Stanley, and the *Sir Tristram* had already been sent to Bluff Cove with ammunition. Now her sister, the *Sir Galahad*, her previous bomb safely defused, was loaded with two companies of Welsh Guards and supporting troops.

The stage was set for disaster. Communication failures and lack of experience by local commanders in the basic principles of amphibious operations meant that the *Sir Galahad* remained fully loaded off the settlement at Fitzroy for five hours in broad daylight. The air threat seemed much less. Sea Dart-equipped Type 42 destroyers now covered the islands with disturbing efficiency. On 6 June a tragic breakdown in communications led to a British Army Air Corps Gazelle being shot down by HMS *Cardiff*. At the other extreme of altitude the Argentines now found that their high-flying Learjets being used for reconnaissance were not safe, the *Exeter* adding to her kills on 7 June with a copybook Sea Dart engagement of one. The Fitzroy situation, however, caused the Argentine Air Force to seize its chance. A combined assault of fourteen Daggers and Skyhawks was arranged, ten of which reached the islands. The Daggers were diverted from their primary target by HMS *Plymouth*, which spotted them as she sailed from San Carlos Water. Set upon by five aircraft, the old frigate put up a barrage of 20-mm shells, Sea Cat missiles, and small-arms fire. The main 4.5-inch guns could not be brought to bear. Once again the aircraft were forced to attack from too low. The *Plymouth* was hit by four bombs, but all failed to explode. The main damage came from a Mark 10 mortar round that was knocked by one of the Argentine bombs and did explode, causing a fire that proved troublesome but not dangerous. The five Skyhawks almost missed the LSLs, but on turning spotted the targets. With little opposition they bombed the two ships from the correct height. Both ships caught fire, and a major rescue operation had to be mounted. The affair cost the British almost a hundred casualties. The Argentines renewed the pressure later in the day, but ground fire and Rapier missiles kept one wave at bay, and three of the Skyhawks of a second attack were disposed of by Sea Harriers from the *Hermes*, albeit after the Argentines had sunk a landing craft from the *Fearless*. These three Skyhawks were almost the last kills of the war, the *Exeter* claiming the very last one when she again demonstrated the high-altitude capabilities of Sea Dart, this time against a Canberra bomber on 13 June, the day before the Argentine surrender.

The final attacks of the two-phase land battle for the heights around Stanley on the night of 11/12 June went in under cover of the guns of Woodward's warships. The ships of the force had been carrying out bombardments throughout the war, keeping the Argentines around Stanley off balance. The 4.5-inch guns were the major weapons, but HMS *Glamorgan* even fired off some of her spectacular, if dubiously effective, Sea Slug missiles in the surface-to-surface role. On the night of the 11th the *Glamorgan* was with the *Yarmouth* and *Avenger* to the south of Stanley. After several hundred rounds had been fired (despite mechanical problems with *Avenger*'s gun), the three ships moved out to the east. The *Glamorgan* "cut the corner" into an area covered by Exocet missiles that had been unloaded from Argentine surface ships and flown to the Falklands to defend Stanley. A missile was fired that was quickly spotted. The large destroyer turned away, but the Exocet caught her a glancing blow near the hangar, where it caused the ship's helicopter, full of fuel and ammunition, to explode.

The *Glamorgan* was soon under repair alongside the *Stena Seaspread*. She was one more damaged member of an increasingly worn-out force. Admiral Woodward later made it clear that he was becoming worried about the condition of his command as wear and tear took its toll, and the operational margins became even narrower. By the end of July "only one-eighth of the [air defense] systems were available to us. If the opposition had found us then we'd have been in a very poor way."[71] For him and his ships and aircraft, the surrender came none too soon. It only remained for the *Endurance, Yarmouth,* and tanker *Olwen,* and the tug *Salvageman* to be sent down to Southern Thule, where the Argentines surrendered without resistance. It was fitting that the *Endurance,* her position now secure, should be in at the end of a conflict of which in some ways she had been at least partly the cause.

The Falklands campaign was an extraordinary and timely demonstration of British sea power. The first sea lord could not have wished for a better "show." Two full brigades had been transported 8,000 miles and sustained in combat; the islands had been recaptured; the enemy's surface fleet had been blockaded after the loss of one of its largest warships; his air forces had been held at bay and heavy losses inflicted upon them. Sea Harriers had shot down eighteen aircraft with their formidable AIM-9L missiles, three with cannon fire, and a large C-130 Hercules with both. They also forced down a Puma helicopter, making a grand total of twenty-three air-to-air kills. Sea Harriers also destroyed five aircraft on the ground, and RAF Harriers, flying from the carriers, another four. Between them, therefore, the *Hermes* and *Invincible* accounted for thirty-two enemy aircraft. Sea Dart missiles shot down six Argentine aircraft (and one British), Sea Wolf missiles four (with a contribution to a fifth). Naval gunfire claimed two aircraft and contributed to another four kills. In all, the Royal Navy had played a direct part in the destruction of some forty-seven enemy aircraft, although it had, of course, played a decisive role in the destruction of all 100 Argentine aircraft. British losses had not been too high: two destroyers and two frigates sunk; six Sea Harriers and four RAF Harriers, twenty-one naval helicopters and three RAF helicopters lost. Eighty-four RN personnel had been killed, a remarkably small death toll compared with World War II experience, and a tribute to modern survival suits and the effectiveness of the helicopter as an instrument of rescue.

For the next six months the lessons of the campaign were dissected within the Ministry of Defence, and at the end of 1982 a Supplementary Defence White Paper appeared entitled "The Falklands Campaign: The Lessons." This paper argued that the campaign had vindicated the principle of the "balanced fleet," the "ability of British amphibious forces to react swiftly and effectively to emergencies in and away from the NATO area" and the "crucial" role of nuclear-powered attack submarines in modern naval warfare. Accusations that RN surface ships were especially vulnerable due specifically to overuse of aluminum in construction were denied, although the paper went on to say that "important lessons have been learnt about the rapid spread of smoke and fire in ships, and about the use of materials which can prove hazardous in fires." Extra means to improve the fire resistance and damage-control capabilities of ships were promised.[72]

The problem of air defense was addressed at some length. It was argued that Task Force 317 had had to operate in conditions for which it had not been designed, far from land-based fighter or early-warning cover and far from American carriers. The paper fairly vindicated both Sea Dart and Sea Wolf and promised improvements to both. The vital importance of airborne early warning was stressed, especially against missile-equipped aircraft. Sea Kings were being converted with radars for use in this role, and two were already deployed in HMS *Illustrious* when she sailed after her accelerated commissioning to relieve the *Invincible* off the

Second of the through-deck cruisers was HMS *Illustrious*, commissioned in 1982, seen here with her Sea Kings and Sea Harriers on deck. Also visible is the Vulcan Phalanx close-range AA armament rapidly fitted as the ship was rushed to completion during the Falklands War.

Falklands in the late summer. (By staying on station so long *Invincible* was able to record on her way home 155 days of continuous carrier operations, breaking the record held by the USS *Dwight D. Eisenhower*.)

The *Illustrious* was also carrying Vulcan Phalanx point-defense guns to enhance her air-defense capabilities. These weapons, like the formidable AIM-9L missiles of the Sea Harriers, were expressions of the extraordinary help given to Britain by the U.S. Defense Department. Critics asked why such measures in point-defense and AEW had not been taken before. The technology had been available for some time. Those who had felt for a long period that British ships were lacking in close-range AA armament and had believed the argument that such systems were too difficult to fit were a little perplexed to see ships' boats suddenly disappear to be replaced by 20-mm guns, both old and new, and twin 30-mm mountings. It seemed to some that lack of war experience, coupled with an overoptimistic performance assessment of missiles and a fixation with the Soviet air threat of large, high-flying aircraft and large transonic or supersonic missiles coming in at high angles of attack had misled the Naval Staff in their determination of weapon fits.[73]

The new White Paper, particularly the final part entitled "The Future," seemed to say that the basic architecture of British defense set out in Command 8288 was to remain with little change. The four "pillars" of policy were reaffirmed with a "major maritime capability in the Eastern Atlantic and Channel" still listed fourth.[74] The paper, however, significantly increased the emphasis on the "out of area" role, claiming that measures were already at hand to consolidate and improve these capabilities. Both the financial flexibility obtained by the Nott process, with some margin of spare cash being available for redeployment, and Mr. Nott's success in gaining extra money from the government's contingency fund over and above the 3 percent increase in real terms to fund Falklands costs and replacement, meant that "we can now finance significant force enhancements over the next few years." The paper listed those already made: more Sidewinder air-to-air missiles; the accelerated introduction of the Sea Skua; the Sub-Harpoon antiship missiles for SSNs; new software for Sea Wolf to ensure its capability against aircraft targets; Vulcan Phalanx for the *Illustrious*; and general improvements in the fleet's electronic-warfare capabilities. What the Royal Navy welcomed most, however, was the confirmation that the *Invincible* was to be retained. Three carriers would allow two to be kept running at all times, but the need for economy was not entirely forgotten. It later became clear that it had not been felt necessary to increase the numbers of aircraft. Two carrier air groups of Sea Harriers and Sea Kings were deemed sufficient, even for three ships.[75]

The Falklands White Paper announced more ship orders, with the potentially doomed Type 22 program getting a new lease on life. Eight had been ordered before the war, and it seemed the program might stop at that. Four more ships were now added to the class to replace the Falklands losses, and these, plus two more units already planned, brought the total number of Type 22s back to fourteen, closer to "pre-8288" levels. The four final ships of the class were to be a modified Batch 3 design with a 4.5-inch gun on the forecastle, improved missiles (eventually announced as Harpoon), point-defense gun armament to complement Sea Wolf, and provision for towed-array sonar and a large ASW helicopter. The first of these cruiser-like ships was given a cruiser-like "County" name, HMS *Cornwall*; together with her sister HMS *Cumbria* (later changed to *Cumberland*) she was ordered in December 1982. The remaining pair, the *Campbeltown* and *Chatham*, were not ordered until January 1985. To make the point of the rationale for the extra Type 22 orders, the last two of the previous batch of six "stretched" Exocet-armed ships were named, on being laid down, HMS *Sheffield* and *Coventry*. These "Batch 2" vessels and their immediate predecessors, HMS *Brave* and HMS *London*, were also to be fitted with the enlarged flight deck and a large helicopter to prosecute towed-array contacts. The first "Batch 2" Type 22, HMS *Boxer*, on commissioning in January 1984 while not quite to this standard, introduced the advanced CACS-1 combat data system as well as an improved 2031 towed array, a new bow position for the 2016 sonar, and a water displacement fuel system to give significantly increased range.[76]

Older ships were to win reprieve as a result of the conflict. Late 1981 had seen the Standby Squadron larger than it had been for some time—some ten frigates. Half of these ships had been mobilized during the war to help maintain NATO and other commitments. All had been officially "for disposal," the two Type 12s *Berwick* and *Falmouth* appearing as such in the 1982 Defence White Paper, and the three "Tribals," *Zulu, Gurkha,* and *Tartar,* in that for 1981(!).[77] The need to maintain a slightly larger escort fleet meant that a first line of fifty-five escorts was to be maintained into 1984.[78] This involved keeping eight of the ships scheduled for decommissioning under earlier statements; the destroyer *Glamorgan* (which was, nevertheless, not to be refitted), the unmodernized Batch 3 "gun *Leanders*"; the *Achilles, Apollo,* and *Ariadne*; the "Ikara *Leanders*," the *Aurora, Euryalus,* and *Naiad*; and one of the Type 12s (originally planned to be the *Rhyl* but eventually the *Berwick*). The other old escorts given a new lease on life in 1982 were finally withdrawn from service in 1983–85. The number of *active* frigates, after rising to a peak of forty-two in 1983–85 (equivalent to the late 1970s figures), fell slightly to forty in 1984–85 and slumped to thirty-four in 1985–86, the lowest figure for twenty-three years.[79]

A "lesson" of the Falkland War that went unmentioned in the White Paper was the embarrassment that had been caused by the task force's tactical nuclear capabilities. During the 1960s the Royal Navy had received a new generation of British-built tactical nuclear weapons, WE177 kiloton-range hydrogen bombs for use by carrier-based aircraft, and nuclear depth charges for use by ASW helicopters. The numbers of the latter were not large, perhaps only some two dozen or so deployed in certain antisubmarine frigates as well as larger ships. The Royal Navy was always very sensitive about these weapons, although their presence was revealed in the 1980 Defence White Paper. According to a usually well-informed source, around 75 percent of Britain's nuclear depth charges were sent south with Task Force 317. The War Cabinet was informed and an RFA rapidly sent to retrieve them before the ships entered the combat zone. The led to a decision to keep the stockpile ashore in peacetime, although the navy will never confirm or deny whether ships are carrying nuclear weapons or not. This has led to embarrassment, such as when HMS *Invincible* was refused dry-docking facilities in Australia during the 1983–84 "Orient Express" deployment. Nevertheless, the Royal Navy has been loath to give up a tactical nuclear role; indeed, the 1985 White Paper carefully and defiantly announced a new nuclear capability: "Free fall nuclear bombs can . . . be delivered by Sea Harriers of the squadrons in service with the Royal Navy's *Invincible* class of aircraft carriers."[80]

As for amphibious forces, the 1982 supplementary White Paper announced that a replacement for the *Sir Galahad* would be built and that it was hoped that the damaged *Sir Tristram* (in use as an accommodation ship at Port Stanley) would eventually be repaired. In the meantime two temporary replacements were chartered and renamed the *Sir Lamorak* and *Sir Caradoc*. Indeed, the whole concept of "Ships Taken Up from Trade" (STUFT), about which the Royal Navy was somewhat skeptical before the conflict, had been triumphantly vindicated. Especially impressive were the air-capable conversions, the *Atlantic Conveyor* and *Atlantic Causeway*. Largest of all was the 28,000-ton *Astronomer*, which took thirteen helicopters south in June and then operated in a helicopter support role using American "Arapaho" equipment. In April 1983 this ship was chartered on a more permanent basis to become the Royal Fleet Auxiliary *Reliant*. A year later another ship, the *Contender Bezant*, chartered late in the Falklands War as a helicopter carrier, was purchased outright from her owners to whom she had been returned. Officially a replacement for the RFA *Engadine*, the impressive new 22,000-ton *Argus* would be an auxiliary carrier in all but name.[81]

Other ships purchased for naval use were three oil-rig supply vessels that were armed with 40-mm guns and commissioned as the *Guardian, Protector,* and *Sentinel* for Falklands patrol duties. A longer-established colonial flotilla also got replace-ments in the mid-1980s. Seventy-five percent paid for by the Hong Kong Govern-ment was a new flotilla of five 700-ton patrol vessels of the "Bird"-class. Armed with the Italian OTO-Melara 76-mm gun, the first ships set sail for the Far East in 1984 to replace the old "Ton"-class converted minesweepers.[82]

The increased priority for homeland defense also renewed interest in small craft, despite the Naval Staff's immediate response to the financial squeeze of scrapping the little squadron of unarmed fast training boats, the hovercraft unit, and the hydrofoil *Speedy*. The year 1983 saw the first of a series of small motor patrol craft enter service with the dual role of training reservists in peace, and acting in a port-defense role in war. Five were initially obtained, windfalls from a cancelled Middle East order, but the were to be followed by no less than fourteen more of a different design for delivery in 1985–86. Also intended to be manned by reservists were the 850-ton EDATS minesweepers named after rivers. By 1982–83 half as much again was being spent on MCM forces as in 1979–80. In all, the Royal Navy planned to spend a billion pounds on its MCM fleet over the fifteen years from 1984. This, it was hoped, would produce a modern fleet of fifteen "Hunts" (an expanded pro-gram), twelve "Rivers," and twenty new "single role minehunters." There were

Name ship of the class of five vessels built in 1983–84 for patrol work in Hong Kong is HMS *Peacock*. Three-quarters of the building and maintenance costs of these vessels have been met by the Hong Kong government.

contingency plans to double this fleet in a crisis using trawlers and suitable RN vessels. Mr. Nott's new priorities had clearly had some effect.[83]

Yet another sign that the Naval Staff was getting more small ship orientated was the announcement made by Admiral Sir Lindsay Bryson, the controller, at the 1983 Royal Navy Equipment Exhibition that an OPV-based corvette was being considered for general "presence" duties with the emphasis on "out-of-area" operations. The following year submissions were asked for from various companies to produce a suitable concept for the OPV3, and two or three ideas were to receive development funds in 1985. It had been hoped to order the first of about six ships in 1986 at a cost of £25–30 million each, but the whole idea rested on MOD(Navy)'s ability to fit the vessels into its groaning budget. In the end, the idea was quietly dropped, after consideration had been given to hiring a prototype built and financed by private industry.[84]

Another ship looking for a place in the budget was a new type of dock landing ship to replace the *Fearless* and *Intrepid* in the 1990s. A major internal debate began in 1984 over the future of these ships. The departing commandant general Royal Marines made the point forcibly that specialist amphibious shipping was still required to act as the core of any amphibious force, be it in the NATO area or elsewhere. His point was confirmed by the exercise "Bold Gannet" in September of that year, in which severe practical difficulties were encountered landing troops from "Ro-Ro" and container ships. The problem was that of cost: it would not be easy to pay for new landing ships and all the other types required by the Naval Staff. Following a chiefs of staff study, a new priority for the Northern Flank was announced in the 1985 Defence White Paper. This flank was now clearly part of the "European Mainland," the third pillar of Mr. Nott's priorities. Yet even this could not expedite the ordering of new amphibious shipping. The 1985 White Paper made clear that the Ministry of Defence was still far from making a decision: "We are considering a range of options for providing a future amphibious capability once the existing specialized ships come to the end of their planned life." In early 1986 it was reported that these studies, which were considering the conversion of container ships into commando carriers and the modernization of the *Fearless* and *Intrepid* with new engines and equipment, were pointing towards an affordable amphibious forces replacement program. In July 1986 it was reported that £450 million had been set aside in the Ministry's long-term costings to cover the project. The Royal Navy hoped that this would cover two container-ship-based aviation support ships, and two vessels capable of docking landing craft. Harland and Wolff were working on the former concept and Swan Hunter on the latter. Completely new dock landing ships were being considered, as well as a service life extension for the existing LPDs. A firm decision to keep the amphibious assault role was announced at the end of 1986, but nothing specific on procurement policy.[85]

By 1986 the amphibious forces case was being argued once more firmly in a NATO context, but this had probably been less clear a year or two before. In 1982 Admiral Sir John Fieldhouse became first sea lord and chief of Naval Staff after leading the Fleet Command to its Falklands victory. Fieldhouse made numerous public statements that emphasized operations outside the NATO area as a major reason why Britain possessed a balanced fleet. Indeed, at times, he even went so far as to say that Britain's worldwide role had "increased many fold." This high-level view, which seemed to fly in the face of the considerable reduction in Britain's overseas commitments described earlier in this book, found more moderate articulations elsewhere. As the vice chief of Naval Staff, Vice Admiral Sir Peter Stanford, put it in an important conference in London in the autumn of 1983, "Did not the Falklands Campaign teach you something about the need to react to the contingent circumstances of an uncertain and violent world, outside the institutionalised Euro-Atlantic situation, in areas where conflict is endemic?" It was clear from the thrust of his remarks that he regarded the probability of such contingencies as a powerful argument in favor of a balanced fleet to deal with the unforeseen.[86]

The Royal Navy, which had always had cultural and emotional problems in coming to terms with the loss of the empire for which it had provided the primary defense, was suffering from the warm afterglow of her last imperial war. It was perhaps only natural that the Falklands War had resurrected folk memories of empire that could be dressed up in fashionable new terminology. In 1983, the year that saw the "Falklands Factor" sweep Mrs. Thatcher triumphantly back into office, the chiefs of staff had examined "Britain's likely role outside the NATO area." The following year's Defence White Paper, unlike its predecessors, duly gave a major heading to "Beyond the NATO Area." The paper quoted recent events in the Middle East, both the Iran-Iraq war and the crisis in Lebanon. The Royal Navy had played a significant part in both areas. The "Armilla Patrol" had continued, with New Zealand help, throughout the Falklands War, to give Britain the opportunity to take part in any Western action to keep open the vital Straits of Hormuz. As the Gulf War escalated in early 1984, a small MCM squadron of four ships, the *Gavinton, Kirkliston, Brinton,* and *Bossington* was sent to the Mediterranean in May with a "STUFT" mother ship, the *Oil Inspector*, to help deal with a possible mining threat. These vessels were used in the second half of 1984 to deal with mysterious mines that appeared in the Red Sea. Off Lebanon British ships, HMS *Fearless* and later RFA *Reliant*, had stood offshore as the British considered withdrawal of their peacekeeping forces, and eventually the *Reliant*'s helicopters helped in the evacuation. The 1984 Paper also drew attention to the purchase of the oil rig support ship *Stena Inspector* (mobilized during the Falklands War to replace the *Stena Seaspread*) as RFA *Diligence*, "to provide afloat support for naval vessels operating a great distance from their bases," and to give "a considerable enhancement to the 'out of area' capability of the destroyer/frigate force and of conventional submarines."[87]

Perhaps the Naval Staff were making the most of the national political mood. As long as the Falklands remained fresh in the public memory, the maximum amount of value had to be squeezed from it. If "out-of-area" commitments had been increased by the need to protect "Fortress Falklands," then a good argument was provided for a larger Royal Navy. Moreover, it did not fly in the face of the established priorities to use money made available by the war to reverse some of the 1981 cuts. Contrary to appearances, John Nott did not pursue an anti-navy vendetta. He had never disagreed that surface naval forces were appropriate for "out-of-area" contingencies. If money was available for these, well and good. Mrs. Thatcher, with her strong personal commitment to the Falklands, could hardly avoid paying a higher price in defense spending than previously planned. For Falklands commitments demanded the constant presence of a significant British squadron. A typical South Atlantic patrol in 1983 was made up of five ships, the Type 42 destroyers *Cardiff* and *Exeter*, the "Exocet *Leander*" HMS *Penelope*, the unmodified *Leander* HMS *Achilles*, and the Type 21 HMS *Active*, with an RFA tanker and RFA storeship in support. Both the *Reliant* and *Diligence* were primarily intended to support this deployment, which was both a burden in its significant drain on what should have been primary NATO commitments and an asset in terms of Naval Staff arguments for more ships.[88]

For a time the Royal Navy's strategy seemed to be working. The excellent relationship between the first sea lord and the prime minister was exploited to obtain government approval of the Staff target.of a destroyer/frigate force of fifty ships. The naval planners of the 1980s viewed this magic figure as an irreducible minimum, just as their predecessors of the 1920s and 1930s had argued for seventy cruisers. The 1984 White Paper announced that instead of an eight-ship Standby Squadron, all fifty members of the late-1980s escort fleet would be active. The dilemma that had faced the Royal Navy since 1945 of the balance between active units and the reserve seemed as if it had finally been settled in favor of the former. The Admiralty Board had claimed that there might well be insufficient time to bring the eight standby vessels forward from reserve, an interesting use of the "short-war" argument in the Royal Navy's favor![89]

The navy was also helped by the arrival at the Ministry of Defence in 1983 of a new secretary of state, Michael Heseltine. Heseltine had a reputation to rival Nott's as a cost cutter, but his approach was fundamentally different from his predecessor's. The new defense minister, troubled by mild dyslexia and more interested in diagrams than documents, was not especially concerned with a detailed matching of defense priorities and force levels. Larger-scale solutions, notably radical new management practices best described in charts, would stave off the Ministry's financial problems. Indeed, for his first few months in office Heseltine had little time to spare for any substantial considerations of defense policy. Mrs. Thatcher had chosen him to lead the propaganda campaign against the Campaign for Nuclear Disarmament in the run up to the General Election in June. This preoccupation did not make it any easier to defend the defense budget from further cuts. Somewhat humiliatingly, Heseltine was forced to accept a £230 million cut in his cash limit the very week the 1983 Defence White Paper was published with higher figures. In August, as the new government began seriously to review its public expenditure plans, there were reports of a major struggle over whether the 3 percent growth in real terms in the defense budget, already seriously eaten into by extra Falklands costs (despite transfers from the central contingency fund), would continue beyond 1986, the year the commitment to NATO ran out. Heseltine fought back strongly, but could not stand up to the formidable new chancellor, Nigel Lawson, supported by the new foreign minister and ex-chancellor, Sir Geoffrey Howe. In a battle that lasted over the winter, the planned cash provision for defense edged steadily downwards. The 1984 Defence White Paper held out hopes for some real growth in expenditure into 1986–87, but its 1985 successor made it clear that 1985–86 would be the last year of a 3 percent increase in real terms in the defense budget. Even the effectiveness of that increase (in cash terms to over £18 billion) was hostage to the dubious fortunes of the government's counterinflation policy. From 1986–87, when the costs of defending the Falklands were taken into account, the planned increases in defense expenditure were barely ahead of expected inflation rates. The defense cake was certainly not going to be getting any bigger—indeed, it might well be getting smaller in real terms. Competition for slices of it would, therefore, be the more intense.[90]

If defense costs continued to expand ahead of general inflation rates, the problem would indeed be acute. Some analysts—those who had pointed out the overloading of the 1970s and who had been listened to by Mr. Nott—argued that the defense program as planned would cost much more than the allocated sums, perhaps some £4.6 billion more by 1988–89. Mr. Nott, now Sir John and out of government, agreed. The official Ministry of Defence line, supported in its turn by an alternative set of outside analysts, was that prudent marginal adjustments would solve the problems of successfully managing the defense program. When introducing the defense segment of the revised public expenditure proposals in February 1984, Mr. Stanley, a junior defense minister, argued that there would be no reduction in program and commitments. Three solutions were offered: more cost-effective equipment, reduced manning levels, and overall improved management.[91]

The navy's greater use of merchant-manned Royal Fleet Auxiliaries fitted in well with the Heseltine approach. So also did the acceptance that the Type 22's successor frigate would have to be significantly cheaper. Yet the difficulties of cost-cutting without undue losses in capability were vividly demonstrated when the new Type 23 frigate design was unveiled in 1984. The original Outline Staff Target of spring 1981 had specified a £70 million ship, little more than a tug for a towed-array sonar, and a platform for a large ASW helicopter to prosecute contacts. The ship would just refuel and rearm the aircraft, not maintain it. Endurance would be limited and maintenance requirements reduced. In 1981–82 the design was debated by the Naval Staff and the "central" Defence Staff as it progressed through the Naval Staff Target phase. The second Spey gas turbine was first removed and then replaced. A hangar was added and then an extra Sea Wolf tracking radar. The ship's length was steadily increased; the requirement to land the Sea King as well as the projected EH101 helicopter increasing it still further.

The Falklands experience of 1982 seemed to dictate further alterations to reduce flammability and smoke hazards, and to improve damage control. A gun was added to the design, and a renewed desire to add some "stretch" potential to the ship increased its length to the maximum that could be accommodated in the frigate complex at Devonport (123 metres). The changes were so extensive that the design was resubmitted to the Ministry of Defence's Operational Requirements and Defence Equipment Policy Committee. The Admiralty Board gave their approval to the detailed design in mid-1983. The resulting Type 23 had become a £110 million ship, an expensive and highly capable vessel with the latest "Computer Assisted Command System." A new variant was to be developed to coordinate the frigate's impressive new radars and electronic suites, a comprehensive sonar fit with a hull-mounted set as well as towed array, the latest Dutch point-defense gun systems, Sea Wolf and Harpoon missiles, the latest helicopter, and a 4.5-inch gun. If this level of capability was required, then there was little alternative to a high cost level, but the Naval Staff could take some pride in the significant savings in both money and manpower that the ship would still achieve. Despite its increased price, a "23" would cost almost 25 percent less than a basically equivalent Type 22. One way of saving manpower was to emphasize the role of the RFA supply ship as a helicopter maintenance vessel as well as a source of fuel and provisions, and this

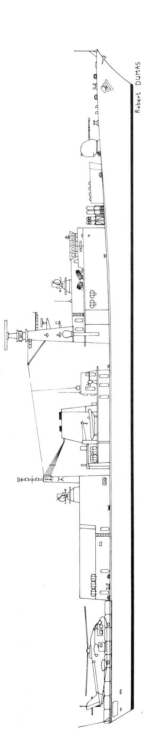

Robert DUMAS

The "Duke"-class Type 23 frigate

Dimensions: 133.0 × 16.1(15.0 w.l.) × 4.3
Displacement: 3,700 tons full load
Missiles: Eight Harpoon surface-to-surface missiles
                One Sea Wolf GWS.26 vertical-launch group
Armament: One 4.5" Mark 8 DP gun
                One 30-mm Goalkeeper gatling AA
                Two 30-mm Rarden AA
                Four 324 torpedo tubes
                One EH.101 ASW helicopter
Electronics: One 1007 radar
                One 996 Mod. 1 radar
                Two 911 Sea Wolf fire-control radar
                One 2050 sonar
                One 2031(2) towed linear passive array sonar
                One UA-F1 passive array
                One Decca Cygnus jammer
                Four Shield chaff launchers

was the essence of the new "one-stop" oiler replenishment vessel (AOR) design announced in the summer of 1984. The enhanced importance of this ship was demonstrated by its much greater self-defense capability than previous RFAs. The first £130 million AOR RFA *Fort Victoria* was eventually ordered in 1986, after acrimonious debate between rival shipyards. A second ship was to follow "as soon as possible."[92]

The new Type 23 was an important ship, destined for production in various forms in the 1990s, to replace all existing escorts from the *Leander* to the Type 42. The class name eventually decided upon was "Duke," which allowed the reuse of geographical names with advantages of local connections. In the meantime, although the ultra costly (but, perhaps, cost-effective) mid-life modernizations were still officially abandoned, a significant set of improvements was begun on the Type 21s and 42s. The former were in need of drastic hull strengthening to hold them together after the South Atlantic swells had demonstrated quite serious weaknesses in their design. Exocet missiles were fitted to those ships still not so equipped, and improvements in sensor fits were also promised. The Type 42s began to receive new radars and still further planned improvements were announced. Enhanced point-defense, including Sea Wolf capability for some vessels, was perhaps in prospect.[93]

Another apparent partial reversal of policy was the announcement in 1984 that a new survey vessel was to be built, HMS *Roebuck*. The 1981 Defence Review had seen the apparent abandonment of new hydrographic vessels and the beginnings of moves to place as much of this duty as possible on to the budgets of other government departments. In 1983 a merchant ship was obtained for operation with a joint Board of Trade/Royal Navy survey party. The *Roebuck*, however, an 800-ton vessel in the same category as the existing *Beagle* class, would be an entirely RN vessel. It was hoped, nonetheless, that when she came into service her duties would be paid for by other government departments. The year 1984 also saw the enhancement of the RN's capabilities in another aspect of marine exploration with the final acceptance into service of the Seabed Operations Vessel, HMS *Challenger*. Delayed almost two years by problems with her builders (during which time the oil rig support vessel *Seaforth Clansman* had been chartered to fill the gap) the *Challenger* had cost some £100 million by the time she was accepted into service.[94]

With ships costing so much, manpower savings were more crucial than ever. Yet this could not go too far. Throughout the postwar period the major constraint on the Royal Navy's shape and size has been more a shortage of personnel than a lack of money or ships. The laying up in April 1984 of the manpower-intensive *Hermes* as a static training ship over eighteen months before the *Ark Royal*'s entry into service (delayed by the Falklands War) in November 1985 and the later sale of the *Hermes* to India in 1986 dramatized the situation, as did the new stress on the merchant seamen of the RFA to man increasingly "combatant" vessels. To maximize combat strength, cuts in "tail" were stressed. The 1984 White Paper, which announced that a higher proportion of the defense budget was going on equipment than even in the Callaghan years, showed that the personnel strength of the Royal Navy was slightly reduced from 59,300 in 1979 to 58,600 in 1984. It was now approaching the crisis manning levels of late 1979/early 1980, and the present and intended fleet could only be maintained by a determined effort to get people to sea. The Admiralty Board had promised the minister that it could get the two thousand men required to man its eight extra frigates without any increase in the above-planned totals. The White Paper spelled out how this was being done and how far it was hoped the process would go:

> The Royal Navy is drawing on skills and experience within the fleet to reduce the shore training load; this and a vigorous drive to secure economy in all forms of shore support will reduce the numbers of men employed ashore by 25 per cent between 1981 and 1988. Three shore establishments will have to be closed by the end of 1985 and others will close later. The search for greater efficiency will continue in the longer term; in the five years after 1988 a further fall of 15 per cent in shore based numbers is expected . . . . By the early 1990s total naval manpower numbers are planned to be some 11,000 lower than in 1981 before the Defence Review which led to Command 8288.[95]

Finally, Mr. Heseltine promised more efficient management in the ministry itself. New management techniques were to be used but, most important of all, the central organization of British defense was to be reformed to a greater extent than at any time since 1964. The general principles were revealed in the 1984 White Paper, the details in a supplementary document three months later. Already since 1981 there had been moves to a greater centralization: the abolition of the service ministers, and, more important, Sir Terence Lewin's strengthening of the position of the chief of Defence Staff. No longer did this officer have to reflect the consensus of the three service chiefs and only give his own views in the case of a fundamental difference of opinion. He could now give his own "defense" advice, as he had done to the "War Cabinet" during the Falklands conflict. The Ministry of Defence Central Staff was also "reorganised so that it could look at resource allocations across the board rather than theatre by theatre or service by service."[96]

In 1984, the logic of the Lewin/Nott reforms was to be carried a stage further. Heseltine pulled no punches in his 1984 Defence White Paper. He argued that the Thorneycroft/Mountbatten reforms had not solved the problem of creating a truly unified British defense policy. "The Ministry of Defence," the paper said, "had survived as a federal structure, based on three largely autonomous Service Departments . . . this organisation is less economical than it should be . . . lines of accountability and responsibility for decision making are blurred . . . it is clear that the organisation must be changed to cut overheads, improve accountability and encourage delegation and the more efficient use of resources."[97]

To improve the situation, a combined Defence Staff was to be set up incorporating much of the Naval Staff that was, under the minister's original proposals, to be abolished. The first sea lord and the admiralty board were to be left with problems of personnel, training, logistics, and supply—the servicing of strategic, operational, and tactical policies decided on by the Central Staff. To aid still further a stronger central determination of priorities for expenditure and allocation of resources, an Office of Management and Budget was to be set up under a senior permanent civil servant. This organization replaced the senior single-service civilian officials, the service deputy secretaries, who had previously played a key role in the debate on resource allocation. It was yet another vital step away from a "single-service" representation in the higher echelons of policy making, especially when combined with the move to the OMB of the civil divisions concerned with long-term costings and issues of service "size and shape." This meant the end once more of the core of "pro-navy" civil servants and much greater "central" control of new shipbuilding and naval equipment programs.

In July 1984, just before the publication of the White Paper setting out these proposals, Sir John Fieldhouse and his two colleagues went to see Mrs. Thatcher to express their reservations over some of these changes, especially the abolition of the separate staffs for each service. They failed to obtain any substantial alteration of policy, but the chiefs did get a very significant concession: small staffs for each individual service were after all to be retained. Effectively, this allowed the three chiefs of staff "enough personnel to be able to formulate single service views on strategy, and thus provide the secretary of state with some opportunity to receive alternative views on defence policy." The new, much smaller "Naval Staff" consists of four sections under a single ACNS: the Directorate of Naval Warfare; the Directorate of Naval Operations and Training; a new Directorate of Naval Staff Duties; and a civilian Secretariat (Naval Staff) fully under the first sea lord's and ACNS's authority in the spirit of the new "integrated" staff (see diagram). DNSD contains officers whose task, albeit on a reduced scale, is to carry out similar planning and other duties as those once carried out by the "abolished" staff divisions.[98]

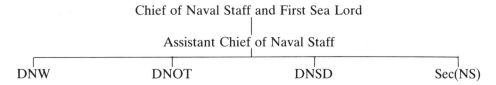

Chief of Naval Staff and First Sea Lord

Assistant Chief of Naval Staff

| DNW | DNOT | DNSD | Sec(NS) |

How the naval interest would do in this new bureaucratic context remained to be seen. There were signs of attempts to improve the capacity of the service and its officers to argue a "naval case." Yet, 1966 aside, it could hardly be said that the predecessors of the new model naval staff had done that badly. Despite the enormous economic problems of the postwar period, Britain still deployed the world's third most powerful navy, with almost every naval system available — ballistic missiles and nuclear-powered attack submarines (the latter the only significant quantity not in superpower hands), conventional submarines, aircraft carriers, SAM destroyers, ASW frigates, minehunters and sweepers, patrol craft, and amphibious warfare vessels. Despite a slight drop after 1985, British naval spending was still higher in real terms than it had ever been in any previous peacetime decade. Major surface ships were consuming half as much money again as they had in the mid-1960s, attack submarines over twice as much. When the total displacement of the active British fleet was considered, it showed little decline over the carrier-centered so-called "big ship" navy of twenty years before. (See Appendix 2.)

Whether this story of relative success would survive the financial crunch of the mid- and late 1980s depended on the extent of that crunch and the forensic skills of the naval officers within the new staff structure. Optimists saw in the new structure a refreshing move away from the politics of "equal misery" compromises and service special pleading that had worked against the navy in the past. Others remembered the Royal Navy's slightly equivocal record in the "fighting of its corner" in unfamiliar environments. The complete dependence on the new Office of Management and Budget for financial advice seemed a particular weakness as it meant the "centre" would have a "monopoly of information" about what was affordable.[99]

The key to it all, however, was the state of the British economy, a much more fragile and battered structure in comparison to its predecessors than the Royal Navy of the 1980s in comparison to its forebears. There were too many uncertainties to make definite predictions. Trident was still a hostage to the pound's exchange rate against the dollar. As the latter plummeted down in January 1985 to near parity, things looked serious, but the recovery of sterling, coupled with the reductions in development cost, limited the damage. At a notional $1.28 to the pound (significantly less than the actual exchange rate), the 1986 Defence White Paper put the cost of the Trident program at £9.87 billion at current prices. Whatever the cost, the system was so central to Prime Minister Thatcher's views on defense policy that it would stand or fall with her, and while she remained in office, the program ground inexorably on. HMS *Vanguard* was ordered on 30 April 1986, Vickers insisting on substantial financial safeguards against cancellation. But if Trident did remain, then it was questionable that conventional forces in general, and the general-purpose navy in particular, could be maintained undiminished for what were, after all, in the prime minister's eyes at least, lower priority tasks in British defense policy. Of course, these tasks might not *remain* low on a *future* government's priority list, perhaps that of a government committed, like the Labour Opposition, to a nonnuclear defense policy, a concept that implied a "longer war."[100]

Choices could not be avoided. By the mid-80s there were signs in the press that the old symptoms of overstretch and overload in defense policy were beginning to show once more. Renewed reports appeared concerning the Ministry of Defence's problems of fitting its programs in being into the planned budget. Despite official denials, it looked as though Mr. Heseltine had not pushed back the specter of hard choices as far as he would have liked. The 1985 Defence White Paper commented confidently on the Ministry's ability to "plan flexibly to match the forward programme to the available cash and to make appropriate provision for contingencies." "The defence programme," it asserted, "should not be seen as a rigid plan stretching ten years ahead, establishing commitments in detail to exact equipment numbers with specified in service dates."[101] The House of Commons Defence Committee was unimpressed. It feared that the "cumulative effect of managing the defence budget in the manner endorsed in the White Paper may result in a defence review by stealth." By this it meant a series of defense decisions based on "short term financial considerations" rather than a long-term plan. The committee foresaw the future as a period of "considerable difficulties leading to cancellations, slowing down of acquisitions and the running on of equipment beyond its economic life-span."[102]

The Royal Navy's frigate program was a case in point. As a well-informed journalist pointed out in March 1985 " . . . unless the Government dramatically improves its rate of ordering new escorts the Navy faces the prospect of operating an increasingly aged fleet of destroyers and frigates with rising maintenance costs and diminishing effectiveness."[103] This required an ordering rate of some three ships a year, but the rate since 1979 had been only nine ships in six years, and four of these were Falklands replacements paid for from special funds. The nine ships included the last two Type 22s, finally ordered in January 1985, and HMS *Norfolk*, the first Type 23 that had been ordered from Yarrow at the end of October 1984. The 1985 Defence White Paper promised only to "negotiate an order for the second vessel at Swan Hunter as soon as this can sensibly be done." Tenders were to be invited for two more Type 23s. These announcements had the marks of decisions taken under pressure and, in any case, as the House of Commons Defence Committee tartly commented: "The announcement of a decision to invite tenders does not constitute an order: on the basis of the number of ships building and the age profile of the present destroyer/frigate fleet faster progress will have to be made if the Government's stated policy of ordering three ships each year is to be achieved."[104]

By 1986 little had been done to remedy the situation; indeed, to delay ordering the new frigates into another financial year, the shipbuilders were asked to re-tender for the three outstanding Type 23s. This successfully delayed matters until July 1986, when Yarrow was finally given orders for HMS *Argyll* and HMS *Lancaster*, and Swan Hunter received its delayed order for HMS *Marlborough*. There were rumors that the Ministry of Defence was seeking to make up for lost time by expediting further Type 23 orders, but the program's long-term future looked somewhat bleaker than originally intended. The Royal Navy still hoped for more improved Type 23s after the eight ships of the first batch, but it was also showing a greater than usual interest in the latest plans for a common NATO frigate for its future air defense requirements in the 1990s. Such international projects were much harder to cancel. At the other end of the scale, older ships were being decommissioned, some earlier than expected. Falklands veterans HMS *Yarmouth* and HMS *Glamorgan* went for scrap in 1986, while the Ikara *Leander*s HMS *Leander* and HMS *Galatea* were being put into a reconstituted "Standby Squadron" along with five old "Ton"-class MCM vessels. The *Glamorgan* was the Royal Navy's last Sea Slug ship, her sister HMS *Fife* having lost her launcher on conversion for Dartmouth Training Ship duties. The virtual disarming of HMS *Juno* for navigational and engineering training meant that only the addition of the yet-to-be-completed HMS *London* brought the navy's total of effectively combatant destroyers and frigates to the magic fifty. Indeed, in the House of Commons at the beginning of July the government stated that its commitment was now only to maintain an escort fleet of "about fifty" ships. On the submarine front things seemed a little brighter. The year 1986 saw the ordering of a seventh "T"-class nuclear submarine, HMS *Triumph*, three more "U"-class conventional boats, the *Unicorn, Unseen,* and *Ursula,* and the continuation of the modernization of nine of the *Oberon*s with a new 2051 bow sonar, 2046 towed array, and improved fire-control equipment. (The *Opossum* had been the first boat so treated, in 1984.)[105]

The continued erosion of the surface fleet increased the load on the ships remaining, causing the kind of problems that the Labour Government of two decades before had called "over-stretch." Reportedly, the Royal Navy was committed in 1985 to tasks that required some ten more escorts than it actually possessed. "Time devoted to evaluating equipment, to local exercise and routine maintenance" was being cut to less-than-desirable levels. The amount of time a frigate spent at sea had gone up from about seventeen weeks to twenty-six, 10 percent more time at sea than during World War II, and 300 percent more time than the ships of the interwar navy spent away from harbor. There was understandable concern that such "levels of activity may lead to a decline in the fighting efficiency of ships and their crews."[106]

As job satisfaction diminished in 1985–86, trained manpower was beginning to leave the navy. Shortages of seagoing officers meant that some older ships were "operational" with only half their normal complement of warfare and watchkeeping officers. This shortage was reported to be a major factor in the premature demise of the *Leander* and *Galatea*. To help solve the problem in the longer term the manpower target for the early 1990s was increased from Mr. Nott's 56,000 to 63,000, and recruiting was stepped up; the navy was trying to recruit 800 hundred officers per year in 1986, compared to some 530 per annum in the early 1980s. This put an obvious strain on the training system, precisely the area that was being cut to maintain the front line. Senior officers voiced open concern in 1985 at the inadequate training being given to both seamen and junior officers. As the professional demands on naval personnel were increasing, so training periods were being cut. Minor accidents led to fears being expressed on the safety of ships at sea. Such reductions in efficiency were all the more pernicious for their lack of proper quantification.[107]

In 1986 new professional and political masters were seen grappling with these naval problems. At the end of 1985 Sir John Fieldhouse was promoted to admiral of the fleet and chief of Defence Staff, another vote of governmental confidence in him, as under the old system it would have been the Royal Air Force's turn to provide the CDS. He was replaced by Admiral Sir William Staveley. On 9 January, in sensational circumstances, Michael Heseltine walked out of a Cabinet meeting and resigned over his disagreement with Mrs. Thatcher on the future of the bankrupt Westland helicopter company. Heseltine, typically, saw European cooperation as a large-scale "macro-solution" to Western defense problems and attempted to arrange for a European consortium to take over: Thatcher preferred an American-backed bid and, as usual, got her way. The new minister of defense was Mr. George Younger, the ex-secretary of state for Scotland. Younger, who almost twenty years before had opposed the disbanding of his old regiment, the Argyll and Sutherland Highlanders, had no intention of departing from his predecessor's line of avoiding difficult decisions as long as possible. The 1986 Defence White Paper made this clear: " . . . suggestions have been made that Britain can no longer sustain all its defence roles and that as a consequence a fundamental review of defence policies is necessary . . . there is no strategic case for drastic change to any of these roles, nor is there any necessity for such an approach, given the massively increased resources that the Government has committed, and continues to commit to defence."[108]

The problem was that the same White Paper made it only too clear that those resources were going to decline in real terms over the next few years. The 1986–87 defense budget of £18.5 billion and its two proposed successors were increased in cash terms compared to their predecessors, but these increases still meant a 6 percent cut in real terms. The White Paper bravely continued to rehearse the continued benefits of the Heseltine efficiency program, but it did admit that some "difficult decisions were in prospect balancing the maintenance of front line strength against procurement of new equipment." Naval Staff briefing documents accidentally revealed to the press in the summer clearly revealed serious problems of matching resources to requirements at all levels: ships, submarines, manpower, research and development. Even Trident was behind schedule and £219 million over budget. Both an effective defense of his ministry's plans and a less restrictive government policy on public spending (with a possible 1987 election in the offing) allowed Mr. Younger to increase his 1986–87 budget by £75 million and diminish the overall cut by 1989–90 to minimal levels (0.25%) when new spending plans were announced at the end of 1986. Nevertheless, there was clearly insufficient cash to fund every desired program, and the expenditure figures for the two years 1987–88 and 1988–89 showed still further marginal cuts.[109]

In these circumstances there seemed little alternative to yet more slow but steady nibbling away at the surface fleet. This needed a strong rationale to protect it from further cuts. The continued emphasis on "out of area" was still tempting, both in terms of appeal to a government committed to supporting the United States in dealing with a "global" Soviet threat and in terms of the appeal of balmy tropical waters to present and future officers and men. British carrier groups continued to cruise across the globe, exercising with a wide variety of friendly navies. In 1983–84 HMS *Invincible* led the "Orient Express" deployment to the Far East and Australia. In 1986 HMS *Illustrious* was due to lead a "westabout" round-the-world cruise, "Global 86," but she suffered a serious fire that prevented her joining HMS *Beaver*, HMS *Manchester*, HMS *Amazon*, and their three supporting RFAs for over four months. As the fire occurred off Britain, she was saved the embarrassment that the *Invincible* faced in trying to get into dry dock in Australia, and being refused because of her possible possession of nuclear weapons. Yet such voyages, major exercises like "Swift Sword," planned for late 1986 (which would see a British carrier and amphibious task force back in the Gulf of Oman), and the more mundane commitments of a pair of ships on Armilla patrol, a reduced Falklands commitment, plus a retained Caribbean guardship, meant that full attention could not be given to NATO activities. Moreover, the positive political pay-offs of such "out of area" activities were sometimes hard to identify. When yet another evacuation operation took place at Aden in January 1986, it was significant that HMS *Newcastle* and HMS *Jupiter* were far from welcome, and even the noncombatant RFA *Brambleleaf* was denied access, due to her warlike appearance. The more colorful Royal Yacht *Britannia* fortuitously was available to provide more acceptably packaged naval skills. It was far from clear that Britain's warships gave her such obvious political leverage "out of area" that they were worth foregoing other, more obviously relevant, forces closer to home. It was doubtful in the extreme that "out of area" would offer the solace for the nineties that "East of Suez" had done for the sixties. Times had changed: colonies had been given up, and the awful lesson of "Black Tuesday" 1968 ought not to have been so easily forgotten. Extra-European commitments, even perhaps the Falklands, were essentially expendable. Although the United States might well demand at least a gesture of European naval support outside the NATO area, and the Royal Navy might well supply it, such requirements would not sustain a large general-purpose navy of major surface warships against the calls of competing defense commitments. "Out of area" capability was an additional reason for having a navy, not a fundamental one.[110]

Developments in American naval strategy were reemphasizing once more the Royal Navy's Atlantic role. As the U.S. Navy began more clearly to articulate its newly defined "Maritime Strategy" in 1985–86, the Royal Navy found itself in demand as a supplier of submarines and ASW battle group escorts for forward operations in the Atlantic in general and the Norwegian Sea in particular. In the context of an "Ocean Safari" NATO naval exercise in 1985 at which great emphasis was placed on a carrier offensive deep into Arctic waters, it was announced that Britain's Anti-Submarine Group Two was now "Anti-Submarine Warfare Striking Force Atlantic" with a crucial role up to 400 miles ahead of the American carriers of the main NATO Striking Fleet. It was a moot point whether a British ASW Striking Force would have the air defenses to enable it to take on the full might of the Soviet Northern Fleet's powerful land-based air arm. Those aware of the lessons of history might also wince at the new emphasis on "offensive fleet" operations. Nevertheless, such announcements demonstrated once more the vital contribution of British naval forces as perceived by the United States. The arguments set forth in the early 1950s about influence and control over the world's largest navy still had more than a little force.[111]

The older established arguments for the Royal Navy were looking somewhat threadbare by 1986. Britain might still be an island, but she was no longer the maritime nation that she had been. Her merchant fleet, which had remained the world's largest until the 1960s, was in serious, and possibly terminal, decline, as was her shipbuilding industry. The number of "seafarers" in the British merchant fleet had almost halved from 61,000 in 1981 to 35,000 in 1985.[112] This caused serious worries in maritime circles about Britain's ability to provide military shipping, given some future requirement to project power. The more far-reaching implication was that Britain would cease to regard herself as a "sea power" of any kind, with potentially disastrous results for the Royal Navy. The pattern of British trade was now overwhelmingly Eurocentric, making it economically as well as strategically vital to put European security at the top of the United Kingdom's defense priorities, after the protection of the home islands themselves.[113] All these circumstances made it doubly unwise for supporters of the Royal Navy to take their stand on traditional "world-wide" sea power rhetoric. The "sea blindness" of which Sir John Fieldhouse had consistently grumbled was grounded in a fundamental reality.[114] The maritime activities at sea that still mattered to the United Kingdom were essentially local—trade with Europe, the exploitation of Britain's continental shelf and fisheries. This was not necessarily a good maritime foundation for the maintenance of the kind of navy with which most in the Royal Navy were happiest, an "open-ocean" force of some considerable reach and with every capability from light aircraft carriers to nuclear-powered submarines. Yet, after all, overwhelming strategic reasons for the maintenance of such a fleet remained. Maintaining European security through the North Atlantic alliance demanded a capacity to cross the Atlantic against opposition. This in turn demanded substantial sophisticated surface forces as well as submarines. The essence of the NATO bargain was that the U.S.A. would not underwrite the security of Europe without substantial European help. The Royal Navy provided precisely that help in any future Atlantic battle. Moreover, the security of the Northern Flank of NATO was a vital British national security interest, especially as viewed from the northern parts of the British Isles. Although there might be some doubts about the full implications of the American Maritime Strategy, there was a real need to project British military power there to maintain forward defense.

There was an excellent naval case in all this that Admiral Staveley's naval staff were beginning to recognize; one firmly bound up with NATO and Europe. This also meant, however, that in any future defense review, whether self-consciously styled such or not, the scope for cutting Britain's land and air forces on the continent was essentially limited. There was only one candidate for pruning, the government's main "naval" priority, Trident. A remarkable consensus seemed to have grown up outside the government that even if Britain was to remain a nuclear power, Trident D-5 was somehow overambitious. Certainly with first call on Royal Navy funds it was a serious "cuckoo" in the naval nest. The new HMS *Vanguard* would be an even more serious drain on the rest of the navy than her predecessor had been. She was also, perhaps, a less potent status symbol. For a year or two cancellation might be possible, but it was an open question whether by the time a new government came to office, perhaps as late as 1988, the option would remain. If the *Vanguard* and her sisters did enter service, the Royal Navy would still be at the center of Britain's defenses, but it would be a navy of a new kind, one directed at the heart of a continental empire and a monument to the end of old-fashioned sea power as generations of British seamen had known it.

APPENDICES

APPENDIX · ONE

RN UNITS LISTED AS "ACTIVE"

	Major Surface Combatants	Major Combat Units	Battle-ships	Carriers	Cruisers*	Destroyers	Frigates	Sub-marines
1948–49	81	107	2	4	16	34	25	26
1949–50	80	110	2	5	15	33	25	30
1950–51	80	112	—	5	14	34	27	32
1951–52	81	113	—	4	13	28	36	32
1952–53	84	123	—	5	12	31	36	39
1953–54	79	116	1	5	11	31	31	37
1954–55	75	112	1	4	10	27	33	37
1955–56	73	116	1	4	9	29	30	43
1956–57	70	112	—	4	9	29	28	42
1957–58	65	104	—	4	8	27	26	39
1958–59	64	102	—	4	6	24	30	38
1959–60	64	96	—	3	6	23	32	32
1960–61	63	94	—	4	5	20	34	31
1961–62	62	92	—	4	5	20	33	30
1962–63	61	91	—	4	6	20	32	30
1963–64	59	94	—	4	7	12	36	35
1964–65	60	97	—	4	6	13	37	37
1965–66	61	96	—	4	6	10	41	35
1966–67	58	93	—	4	7	9	38	35
1967–68	58	94	—	3	6	14	35	36
1968–69	60	92	—	2	6	11	44	32
1969–70	56	84	—	2	7	2	45	28
1970–71	57	84	—	2	6	1	48	27
1971–72	54	79	—	2	8	1	43	25
1972–73	55	78	—	1	8	1	45	23
1973–74	59	86	—	1	10	—	48	27
1975–76	60	84	—	1	11	1	47	24
1976–77	57	80	—	2	8	2	45	23
1977–78	55	79	—	2	8	3	42	24
1978–79	61	84	—	3	9	6	43	24

	Major Surface Combatants	Major Combat Units	Battle-ships	Carriers	Cruisers*	Destroyers	Frigates	Sub-marines
1979–80	57	80	—	2	7	6	42	23
1980–81	50	74	—	2	4	7	37	24
1981–82	52	74	—	2	5	9	36	22
1982–83	55	78	—	3	3	11	38	23
1983–84	58	80	—	3	4	9	42	22
1984–85	58	81	—	2	4	12	40	23
1985–86	51	76	—	3	2	12	34	25
1986–87	49	76	—	3	3	10	33	27

Source: Contemporary *Statements on the Naval Estimates*, later *Defence Estimates*, except for 1965–66 when, in the absence of figures from the White Paper, they were produced in *House of Commons Debates* 2 March 1965, Columns 218–22. There was no Defence White Paper in 1974–75, hence the gap above.

*"Cruisers" include large "destroyers" of the "County" and *Bristol* classes.

APPENDIX · TWO

"STANDARD" DISPLACEMENT
OF ACTIVE UNITS

	Major Surface Combatants	Major Combat Units	Average M.S.C.	Average Sub.	Average M.C.U.
1948–49	365,000	393,000	4,500	1,100	3,680
1949–50	383,000	415,000	4,790	1,060	3,770
1950–51	334,000	367,000	4,180	1,030	3,280
1951–52	284,000	315,000	3,510	970	3,790
1952–53	332,000	370,000	3,960	960	3,010
1953–54	363,000	399,000	4,590	970	3,440
1954–55	331,000	367,000	4,420	970	3,270
1955–56	355,000	397,000	4,860	990	3,430
1956–57	308,000	350,000	4,390	1,010	3,120
1957–58	298,000	337,000	4,580	1,020	3,240
1958–59	279,000	318,000	4,350	1,030	3,120
1959–60	242,000	281,000	3,780	1,210	2,920
1960–61	270,000	307,000	4,290	1,190	3,270
1961–62	278,000	315,000	4,490	1,240	3,430
1962–63	247,000	288,000	4,050	1,360	3,160
1963–64	274,000	323,000	4,640	1,410	3,440
1964–65	286,000	339,000	4,760	1,430	3,490
1965–66	294,000	344,000	5,070	1,441	3,590
1966–67	289,000	347,000	4,980	1,660	3,730
1967–68	245,000	308,000	4,230	1,740	3,280
1968–69	222,000	290,000	3,710	2,120	3,160
1969–70	214,000	284,000	3,820	2,520	3,390
1970–71	233,000	296,000	4,090	2,350	3,530
1971–72	234,000	298,000	4,340	2,540	3,770
1972–73	199,000	260,000	3,620	2,650	3,340
1973–74	210,000	286,000	3,560	2,810	3,330
1975–76	225,000	293,000	3,750	2,820	3,490
1976–77	227,000	297,000	3,980	3,040	3,710
1977–78	231,000	300,000	4,190	2,870	3,790
1978–79	274,000	351,000	4,500	3,210	4,130

	Major Surface Combatants	Major Combat Units	Average M.S.C.	Average Sub.	Average M.C.U.
1979–80	215,000	291,000	3,780	3,280	3,630
1980–81	163,000	245,000	3,270	3,410	3,310
1981–82	193,000	269,000	3,710	3,450	3,630
1982–83	211,000	290,000	3,840	3,430	3,720
1983–84	220,000	297,000	3,800	3,500	3,710
1984–85	202,000	284,000	3,480	3,540	3,500
1985–86	199,000	272,000	3,900	2,950	3,580
1986–87	209,000	306,000	4,270	3,620	4,040

Source: As Appendix I, worked out with displacements from *Jane's Fighting Ships*; Pink Lists were used to help elucidate the "Strength of Fleet" figures in early "Statements" on the Naval Estimates.

APPENDIX · THREE

UNITS LISTED AS ENGAGED
IN TRIALS AND TRAINING

	Major Surface Combatants	Major Combat Units	Battle-ships	Carriers	Cruisers*	Destroyers	Frigates	Sub-marines
1948–49	45	53	2	5	2	18	18	8
1949–50	46	50	2	3	2	20	19	4
1950–51	39	39	1	3	2	18	15	—
1951–52	40	40	1	4	2	18	13	—
1952–53	40	40	1	5	2	13	19	—
1953–54	42	42	—	4	2	19	17	—
1954–55	31	31	—	6	1	3	21	—
1955–56	30	30	—	4	1	3	22	—
1956–57	31	31	—	3	1	3	24	—
1957–58	28	28	—	2	1	2	23	—
1958–59	24	24	—	—	1	2	21	—
1959–60	16	20	—	—	—	2	14	4
1960–61	20	23	—	—	—	3	17	3
1961–62	19	21	—	—	—	2	17	2
1962–63	19	21	—	—	—	1	18	2
1963–64	17	18	—	—	—	1	16	1
1964–65	17	19	—	—	—	1	16	2
1965–66	16	17	—	—	—	—	16	1
1966–67	18	19	—	—	—	—	18	1
1967–68	16	17	—	—	—	—	16	1
1968–69	11	12	—	—	—	—	11	1
1969–70	9	10	—	—	—	—	9	1
1970–71	10	10	—	—	—	1	9	—
1971–72	9	9	—	—	—	1	8	—
1972–73	10	10	—	—	—	2	8	—
1973–74	6	6	—	—	—	1	5	—
1975–76	4	4	—	—	—	1	3	—
1976–77	4	4	—	—	—	1	3	—
1977–78	3	3	—	—	—	1	2	—
1978–79	1	1	—	—	—	—	1	—

	Major Surface Combatants	Major Combat Units	Battle-ships	Carriers	Cruisers*	Destroyers	Frigates	Sub-marines
1979–80	2	2	—	—	—	—	2	—
1980–81	1	1	—	—	—	—	1	—
1981–82	1	1	—	—	—	—	1	—
1982–83	1	1	—	—	—	—	1	—
1983–84	1	1	—	—	—	—	1	—
1984–85	1	1	—	1	—	—	—	—
1985–86	1	1	—	—	—	—	1	—

Source: As Appendix 1.

*"Cruisers" include large destroyers of the "County" and *Bristol* classes.

APPENDIX · FOUR

UNITS LISTED AS IN RESERVE
OR UNDER REFIT

	Major Surface Combatants	Major Combat Units	Battle-ships	Carriers	Cruisers*	Destroyers	Frigates	Sub-marines
1948–49	220	251	1	5	13	65	136	31
1949–50	212	243	1	5	12	65	129	31
1950–51	203	237	4	5	10	61	123	34
1951–52	200	224	4	7	11	65	113	24
1952–53	197	211	5	4	12	66	110	14
1953–54	199	215	4	2	13	67	113	16
1954–55	206	226	4	2	15	70	115	20
1955–56	198	212	4	7	14	58	115	14
1956–57	178	191	5	7	12	44	110	13
1957–58	167	184	5	6	11	36	109	17
1958–59	98	113	1	5	8	30	54	15
1959–60	99	114	1	5	8	30	55	15
1960–61	87	102	—	4	5	29	49	15
1961–62	71	91	—	4	3	25	39	20
1962–63	60	75	—	3	4	22	31	15
1963–64	61	76	—	1	4	24	32	15
1964–65	51	59	—	1	4	22	24	8
1965–66	39	48	—	1	3	18	17	9
1966–67	28	38	—	1	4	11	12	10
1967–68	27	38	—	2	3	2	20	11
1968–69	25	36	—	2	3	5	15	11
1969–70	28	40	—	1	4	9	14	12
1970–71	20	28	—	1	5	5	9	8
1971–72	19	30	—	—	4	1	14	11
1972–73	15	27	—	—	3	—	12	12
1973–74	13	20	—	—	1	—	12	7
1975–76	10	18	—	—	—	—	10	8
1976–77	15	24	—	1	2	—	12	9
1977–78	16	23	—	1	2	—	13	7
1978–79	13	20	—	—	1	—	12	7

	Major Surface Combatants	Major Combat Units	Battle-ships	Carriers	Cruisers*	Destroyers	Frigates	Sub-marines
1979–80	15	23	—	—	3	—	12	8
1980–81	20	28	—	1	3	—	16	8
1981–82	10	20	—	—	1	—	9	10
1982–83	6	15	—	—	1	—	5	9
1983–84	4	13	—	—	—	—	4	9
1984–85	3	12	—	—	—	—	3	9
1985–86	8	16	—	1	1	—	6	8
1986–87	7	14	—	—	—	2	5	7

Source: As Appendix 1.

*"Cruisers" includes large "destroyers" of the "County" and *Bristol* classes.

APPENDIX · FIVE

ACTIVE UK ROYAL NAVY PERSONNEL
IN THOUSANDS
(Including Royal Marines)
(as at 1st April Each Year)

	REGULARS		National Servicemen	Total
	Men	Women		
1949	120.1	7.3	17.1	144.5
1950	123.0	6.0	11.0	140.0
1951	125.6	5.4	7.2	138.2
1952	135.5	5.1	4.6	145.2
1953	133.7	5.2	6.7	145.6
1954	121.0	5.0	7.8	133.8
1955	114.2	4.7	9.5	128.4
1956	106.6	3.9	11.6	122.1
1957	102.7	3.7	9.6	116.0
1958	97.8	3.5	5.3	106.6
1959	95.8	3.6	2.2	101.6
1960	93.7	3.5	0.6	97.8
1961	91.9	3.3	0.1	95.3
1962	91.0	3.3		94.3
1963	92.3	3.5		95.8
1964	94.1	3.5		97.6
1965	95.0	3.6		98.6
1966	94.1	3.7		97.8
1967	93.2	3.8		97.0
1968	91.3	3.8		95.1
1969	86.7	3.5		90.2
1970	82.7	3.3		86.0
1971	79.2	3.3		82.5
1972	78.9	3.5		82.4
1973	77.6	3.6		81.2
1974	74.7	3.6		78.3
1975	72.5	3.7		76.2
1976	72.2	3.9		76.1

	REGULARS		National Servicemen	Total
	Men	*Women*		*Total*
1977	72.2	4.0		76.2
1978	71.3	4.0		75.3
1979	68.6	3.8		72.4
1980	68.1	3.8		71.9
1981	70.2	4.1		74.3
1982	69.0	4.0		73.0
1983	67.9	3.9		71.8
1984	67.4	3.9		71.3
1985	66.7	3.7		70.4
1986*	64.8	3.4		68.2

Source: Contemporary "Statements" on Defence Estimates.
*Estimate.

APPENDIX · SIX

NAVAL ESTIMATES 1946–47—1964–65
(Including Supplementary Estimates)*

	Current £ (million)	1970 £ (million)	(Index (1964–65 = 100)
1946–47	275	679	105
1947–48	197	444	68
1948–49	169	364	56
1949–50	189	395	61
1950–51	203	412	63
1951–52	279	524	81
1952–53	332	581	89
1953–54	330	578	90
1954–55	353	607	93
1955–56	341	565	87
1956–57	349	545	84
1957–58	351	538	83
1958–59	389	583	90
1959–60	371	556	86
1960–61	398	584	90
1961–62	413	593	91
1962–63	464	638	98
1963–64	440	591	91
1964–65	496	650	100

*Source: Statements on the Naval Estimates for each year (Defence Estimates for 1964–65). Figures are net, subtracting U.S. aid and other receipts.

APPENDIX · SEVEN

EXPENDITURE ON "NAVY GENERAL-PURPOSE COMBAT FORCES" 1965–87

	Current £ (million)	1970 £ (million)	Index (1965–66 = 100)
1965–66	294	377	100
1966–67	309	376	100
1967–68	291	346	92
1968–69	301	339	90
1969–70	280	298	79
1970–71	295	295	78
1971–72	301	276	73
1972–73	330	280	74
1973–74	419	330	88
1974–75	n/a	n/a	n/a
1975–76	632	371	98
1976–77	726	346	92
1977–78	843	344	91
1978–79	1,017	378	100
1979–80	1,131	384	102
1980–81	1,461	420	111
1981–82	1,663	422	112
1982–83	1,861	422	112
1983–84	2,149	465	123
1984–85	2,493	512	136
1985–86	2,505	490	130
1986–87	2,625	487	129

Source: Relevant "Statement" on the year's defense estimates.

N.B.: These figures do *not* include such items as reserves and auxiliary formations, some research and development, training, war stocks, and other common services. Also the figures from 1984–85 are not fully comparable with "those earlier years" due to "the functional attribution of Royal Navy expenditure and manpower having recently been reviewed and improved."

APPENDIX · EIGHT

EXPENDITURE ON DIFFERENT TYPES
OF NAVAL FORCES 1966−87
(Units—millions of 1970 pounds)

	Total	Amphibious Forces	Aircraft Carriers	Sub-marines	Major* Surface Ships	Mine Counter-measures	Other Ships	Aircraft	Overseas bases
1966−67	376	18	22	32	101	9	50	85	60
1967−68	346	15	21	38	99	8	43	92	30
1968−69	339	16	18	44	91	7	44	93	26
1969−70	298	16	19	49	94	6	40	48	27
1970−71	295	17	13	44	108	6	39	44	24
1971−72	276	18	9	41	112	6	38	33	18
1972−73	280	18	6	43	123	7	37	33	13
1973−74	330	16	8	51	150	10	54	26	16
1975−76	371	17	5	68	180	11	50	23	18
1976−77	346	14	7	53	155	14	52	32	17
1977−78	344	12	6	53	156	17	47	38	13
1978−79	378	10	10	58	184	19	47	38	10
1979−80	384	12	8	67	172	17	54	37	13
1980−81	420	13	7	73	183	22	59	45	14
1981−82	422	13	7	86	175	23	53	44	15
1982−83	422	12	16	105	144	34	46	45	14
1983−84	465	13	30	101	156	34	62	52	11
1984−85	512	18	21	72	156	31	115	70	13
1985−86	490	18	17	85	160	31	98	73	8
1986−87	487	16	15	84	157	29	91	60	9

*"Cruisers," "destroyers," and "frigates."

N.B.: Due to "rounding" up and down and the extra "fleet headquarters" heading introduced in 1975−76, the individual figures may not add up to the total in the left-hand column. In 1984−85 some £43 million at 1970 prices was put under a further new heading "Naval bases and operational support." In 1986−87 this figure was £32 million. These base and support costs have been redistributed on a proportional basis in the above table.

APPENDIX · NINE

FIRST SEA LORDS, 1945–87
BRIEF BIOGRAPHICAL PROFILES

1943–1946—Sir Andrew Cunningham (Viscount Cunningham of Hyndhope).

One of the greatest leaders of men in the history of the Royal Navy, Andrew Cunningham was born in 1883 and entered the training ship HMS *Britannia* as a cadet in 1897. As a midshipman he saw action in the Naval Brigade in the Boer War. His first command came in 1908 in the shape of Torpedo Boat Number 14. Cunningham developed a great liking for destroyers and took command of HMS *Scorpion* in 1911, serving in her until 1918. He won the first of three Distinguished Service Orders in the Dardanelles campaign. A second DSO followed service in the Dover Patrol in the latter part of the war (including the raid on Zeebrugge in 1918), and a third DSO was awarded for service in the Baltic in 1919. Promoted captain in 1920, Cunningham commanded destroyer flotillas and a destroyer base and then became flag captain on the American and West Indies Station in 1926. He later commanded the new battleship *Rodney*. Receiving his flag in 1932, Cunningham became first rear admiral (destroyers) in the Mediterranean and then commander Battle Cruiser Squadron and second in command Mediterranean Fleet. The immediate prewar period saw Cunningham at the center of power as deputy chief of Naval Staff, deputizing for the terminally ill Sir Roger Backhouse. The change around in commands caused by Backhouse's death saw Cunningham promoted acting admiral and CinC Mediterranean, the Royal Navy's premier sea command. From 1939 to 1942 Cunningham led that fleet through victory and adversity, becoming the Royal Navy's most famous and heroic combat commander of the war. Moved briefly, at a sensitive time, to be head of the British Admiralty Delegation in Washington in 1942, Cunningham returned to become Allied naval commander for the "Torch" landings under General Eisenhower and from January 1943, CinC Mediterranean as an Admiral of the Fleet. Created Baron in 1945 and Viscount in 1946, Cunningham died in 1963.

1946–1948—Sir John Cunningham

No relation to his more famous predecessor, John Cunningham was born in 1885 and entered the Royal Navy as a *Britannia* cadet in 1900. He soon demonstrated considerable intellectual and professional caliber, scoring five firsts in his sub lieutenants' examinations. Specializing in navigation, an unusual background for a future first sea lord, he served both at sea and in the Navigational School as an instructor. After being sunk in the pre-dreadnought *Russell* in the Mediterranean, Cunningham served in battle cruisers, culminating in an appointment in 1920 as navigation officer in the brand new HMS *Hood,* largest capital ship of her time. After service as executive officer of the Navigational School, 1921–23, he was appointed "Master of the Fleet" before spending three years as a captain on the directing staff of the Senior Officers' War Course. Cunningham went to sea in command of the cruiser/minelayer *Adventure* in 1929, but returned to the Admiralty for duty in Plans Division, before becoming its director. In 1933 he was appointed to command the battleship *Resolution* and served as flag captain to the CinC Mediterranean during the Abyssinian crisis. Cunningham got his flag in 1936 and served on the Naval Staff, first as ACNS, then ACNS(Air), and finally as fifth sea lord, helping organize the naval takeover of the Fleet Air Arm. In 1939 he was given command of the First Cruiser Squadron, first in the Mediterranean and then off Norway in 1940, from where his flagship evacuated the Norwegian royal family and government. After service in the unsuccessful Dakar landings in 1940, Cunningham was created fourth sea lord in 1941 and as such organized the wartime fleet's logistics. In 1943 he was appointed CinC Levant, which involved him in the disastrous Dodecanese operations. This did not stop him succeeding his namesake as Allied naval CinC Mediterranean. Admiral of the Fleet Sir John Cunningham died in 1962.

1948–1951—Bruce, Lord Fraser of North Cape

Bruce Fraser, perhaps the greatest of all postwar first sea lords in all-around ability, was born in 1888 and entered HMS *Britannia* in 1902, the last first sea lord to be trained under the old training scheme. After early service, largely in battleships, Fraser specialized in gunnery and passed top of his class, soon becoming one of the leading officers in the field. For the first half of World War I he served in Mediterranean and Middle Eastern waters in the old cruiser *Minerva.* Missing the Battle of Jutland due to service at the Gunnery School, HMS *Excellent,* Fraser was appointed gunnery officer and then executive officer of the battleship *Resolution* from 1916 to 1919. This was followed by command of an ill-fated anti-Bolshevik expedition to Baku which led to his imprisonment in a Soviet jail in 1920. Returning home, Fraser was reappointed to the *Excellent* as commander (G) and then to the Ordnance Directorate in the Admiralty where he helped design a new, fully effective fire-control system. He became fleet gunnery officer in the Mediterranean before being promoted captain and appointed senior officer, Tactical Course at Portsmouth. Fraser then served as head of the Tactical Section, later Division, Naval Staff before commanding the cruiser *Effingham,* flagship of the East Indies Station, from 1929 to 1932. After a short period commanding the new cruiser *Leander,* Fraser became Director of Naval Ordnance in 1933. Appointed as captain of the carrier *Glorious* in 1936, Fraser received his flag eighteen months later. He became chief of staff to the CinC Mediterranean Fleet for a year before being appointed third sea lord and controller in 1939. After supervising the equipment of the Royal Navy at one of the crucial periods in its history, Fraser moved to the Home Fleet, first as vice admiral Second Battle Squadron, then as commander-in-chief. Flying his flag in the battleship HMS *Duke of York,* Fraser masterminded the Royal Navy's last major gunnery action against an enemy battleship, the *Scharnhorst,* on 26 December 1943. Promoted full admiral in 1944, Fraser was moved to the Eastern Fleet and then in December became first CinC of the newly formed Pacific Fleet, which he led against the Japanese under American overall command in 1945. Raised to the peerage, he became CinC Portsmouth in 1946 before being appointed first sea lord in 1948. Lord Fraser died in 1981.

1951–1955—Sir Rhoderick McGrigor

Born in 1893, Rhoderick McGrigor entered the Royal Navy through the new Selborne Scheme and the Royal Navy Colleges Osborne and Dartmouth. After service at the Dardanelles in destroyers and in the battleship *Malaya* at Jutland, he became a torpedo specialist. Service followed in the East Indies, at the Admiralty, and in Spanish waters during the Civil War before McGrigor went to the China Station as chief of staff. McGrigor's command of the battle cruiser *Renown* as part of Force "H" in 1940–41 was short due to early promotion to the flag list and the post of ACNS(Weapons). There then followed active duty in the Mediterranean as force commander in the landings at Pantelleria and Sicily, and then liaison work with the Italian Navy. Returning to northern waters and the First Cruiser Squadron, McGrigor carried out operations in Norwegian and Arctic waters in 1944–45 before going to the Admiralty as VCNS in the early days of peace. In 1948, as a full admiral, McGrigor became CinC Home Fleet at the time of its immobilization and supervised its reconstitution into an operational force. He was CinC Plymouth in 1950–51. Sir Rhoderick McGrigor died suddenly after surgery in Aberdeen in December 1959.

1955–1959—Louis, Earl Mountbatten

Certainly the most famous and remarkable of postwar first sea lords and perhaps the most extraordinary naval officer of the twentieth century, Louis Francis Albert Victor Nicholas Battenberg was born in 1900, son of Prince Louis of Battenberg, first sea lord at the outbreak of the First World War (which caused the family to change its name in 1917). A great-grandson of Queen Victoria, Battenberg entered the Royal Naval College, Osborne, in 1913. After Dartmouth he went to sea as a midshipman in Admiral Beatty's flagship, HMS *Lion,* in 1916. Moving to the fleet flagship, *Queen Elizabeth,* in 1917, Mountbatten served in a submarine and in patrol craft before accompanying his cousin, the Prince of Wales, in the battle cruiser *Renown* on his tours to Australia, India, and the Far East in 1920–21. Specializing in signals, Mountbatten had several appointments as communications officer, culminating in the post of fleet wireless officer Mediterranean Fleet 1931–33. After commanding two destroyers and service in the Naval Air Division, Mountbatten began the war as captain in command of the Fifth Destroyer Flotilla in HMS *Kelly.* After being mentioned in despatches twice, and eventually sunk in the Mediterranean, he was placed briefly in command of HMS *Illustrious* before being promoted in the acting rank of vice admiral, adviser on and then chief of Combined Operations (with a seat on the Chiefs of Staff Committee). In 1943 he became an acting admiral and supreme allied commander South East Asia until 1946, when he became a viscount. He was appointed Viceroy of India to oversee independence and went on to be India's first governor general. Created both baron and earl in

1947, Mountbatten returned to his normal naval duty and status as a rear admiral and commander of the First Cruiser Squadron in the Mediterranean the following year. After duty as fourth sea lord from 1950 to 1952, Earl Mountbatten of Burma became CinC Mediterranean, taking over the NATO post of CINCAFMED in 1953. In 1959 Mountbatten became chief of Defence Staff, a post he held until 1965. He was assassinated by an IRA bomb in 1979.

1959–1960—Sir Charles Lambe

Charles Edward Lambe was born in 1900 and entered Osborne in 1914. After service in the battleship *Emperor of India* from 1917 to 1919, he became a torpedo specialist. After serving in the Mediterranean and passing Staff College, Lambe served in the cruiser *Hawkins* in the East Indies and then on the staff of Rear Admiral A.B. Cunningham in command of Mediterranean destroyers. After being executive officer of the Torpedo School, HMS *Vernon,* in 1935, Lambe was appointed equerry to King Edward VIII and then King George VI. Promoted captain in 1937, he commanded the cruiser *Dunedin* and then in 1940 became assistant director Plans on the Naval Staff. He rose in the Plans Division to become director and had a crucial role in wartime strategic decision making. In 1944 Lambe, a private pilot, took command of the carrier *Illustrious.* After distinguished service in the Indian Ocean and Pacific he returned to the Admiralty as ACNS (Air). By now one of the navy's leading aviation experts, Lambe went on to be flag officer Flying Training in 1947, commander Third Aircraft Squadron in 1949, and flag officer (Air) Home in 1951. After a period as CinC Far Eastern Station and promotion to full admiral, he became second sea lord and chief of Naval Personnel in 1955, helping to supervise the "Way Ahead" cuts. From 1957–59 Lambe was CinC Mediterranean. Due to illness, Lambe's period as first sea lord was brief, and he died a few months after retirement in 1960.

May 1960–August 1963—Sir Caspar John

Son of the noted artist Augustus John, Caspar John was born in 1903 and entered the Royal Navy as a cadet in 1916. After service in the battleship *Iron Duke,* he began his connection with naval aviation as a sub lieutenant in the new carrier *Hermes.* Specializing as a pilot in 1926, something of a professional risk in the era of dual control of naval aviation, John advanced in both naval and RAF rank to be commander RN and wing commander RAF by 1936. After service in the Air Division of the Naval Staff, John became executive officer of the heavy cruiser *York,* being mentioned in despatches. A captain in 1941, he became director general of Naval Aircraft Development and Production and then assistant attaché (Air) Washington and head British Naval Air Service in the U.S.A. This was at a time when U.S. aircraft and training facilities were vital to the growth of the wartime Fleet Air Arm. Appointed to command the escort carrier *Pretoria Castle* in 1944, John moved to the new light fleet carrier *Ocean* in 1945. After command of the Royal Naval Air Station, Lossiemouth, he returned to Whitehall as deputy chief Air Equipment and director of Naval Air Organisation and Training. Getting his flag in 1951 John commanded the Third Aircraft Carrier Squadron and Heavy Squadron Home Fleet until 1952, was chief Naval Air Equipment 1952–53, and deputy controller Aircraft 1953–54. As a vice admiral he was flag officer (Air) Home 1955–57 and, as a full admiral, VCNS from 1957–1960. The only fully fledged naval airman to be first sea lord, he became an Admiral of the Fleet in 1962. Sir Caspar John died after a long retirement in 1984.

1963–1966—Sir David Luce

Born in 1906, John David Luce passed through the naval colleges and eventually entered the submarine service, commanding three boats in the period 1936–41. Ending the war as a captain, Luce commanded the Royal Naval Air Station Ford from 1946 to 1948. He then moved to the Admiralty as deputy director Plans and in 1951 went to sea in command of the cruisers *Liverpool* (until 1952) and *Newcastle* (until 1953). After a period as director of the Staff College, Luce was appointed naval secretary to the first lord of the Admiralty, a post in which he received his flag. In 1956 he became flag officer (Flotillas) Home Fleet and as a vice admiral moved on in 1958 to be flag officer Scotland. CinC Far East Station from 1960, Admiral Sir David Luce was appointed first CinC British Forces Far East in 1962. He died in 1971.

1966–1968—Sir Varyl Begg

Born in 1908 Varyl Cargill Begg was the first first sea lord to enter the navy through the Special Entry at eighteen. After service on the China Station, in the West Indies and Mediterranean, Begg specialized as a gunnery officer in 1933. He later served as gunnery officer of the cruiser *Glasgow* (1939–40) and battleship *Warspite* (1940–43), winning the Distinguished Service Order at the Battle of Matapan. Promoted captain in 1947 he commanded the Gunnery School at Chatham and then the Eighth Destroyer Flotilla in the Far East where service in the Korean War brought him a bar to his DSO and a mention in despatches. After commanding HMS *Excellent,* the Gunnery School, in 1952–55 he moved to the training carrier *Triumph* in 1955–56. Achieving his flag in 1957, Begg served as chief of staff to CinC Plymouth until 1958 and then was commander Fifth Cruiser Squadron and second in command Far East Station 1958–60. A vice admiral from 1960 and a full admiral from 1962, Begg was VCNS from 1961 to 1963 and CinC Far East from 1963 to 1965, the period of Confrontation with Indonesia. His last appointment before replacing Sir David Luce was CinC Portsmouth and NATO Commander in Chief Channel. Admiral of the Fleet Sir Varyl Begg lives in Hampshire.

1968–1970—Sir Michael Le Fanu.

Born in 1913 Michael Le Fanu (of French Huguenot descent) entered the Royal Naval College Dartmouth in 1926. After service largely in destroyers he became a gunnery specialist in 1938. The following year Le Fanu became gunnery officer of the light cruiser *Aurora,* where he greatly distinguished himself both in the Norwegian campaign (mention in despatches) and the Mediterranean (Distinguished Service Cross). In 1942 he joined the staff of CinC Home Fleet and in 1944 became gunnery officer of the battleship *Howe,* which served in the Indian Ocean and Pacific. Le Fanu was appointed liaison officer with the Americans, a post he held with great success, helping arrange the events on board the USS *Missouri* in Tokyo Bay. The Unites States Government presented him with the Legion of Merit. Promoted early to commander, Le Fanu became experimental commander at HMS *Excellent* and then executive officer of the cruiser *Superb*. His first appointment as captain was naval assistant to the third sea lord, whose "hardware" aspects were more familiar than those of his next post, in charge of the Third Anti-Submarine Training Squadron. Special duty under the chief scientist investigating nuclear matters was followed by a year's course at the Imperial Defence College. Le Fanu was then appointed to command the boys' training establishment, HMS *Ganges,* before going to sea once more in command of the fleet carrier *Eagle.* Le Fanu was the first Director General Weapons from 1958 to 1960 and then became flag officer second in command Far East Station. From 1961 to 1965 he was third sea lord and controller, being promoted vice admiral in 1961 and full admiral in 1965. The joint service CinC Middle East post followed, whose main preoccupation was the Aden evacuation. Following his highly successful period as first sea lord, Admiral of the Fleet Sir Michael Le Fanu was due to become chief of Defence Staff, but he was prevented from doing so by illness that caused his death in 1970.

1970–1971—Sir Peter Hill-Norton

Born in 1915 Peter John Hill-Norton entered the Royal Naval College Dartmouth in 1928. After serving as a midshipman in a cruiser and two battleships he went on to serve as a lieutenant in the battleship *Ramillies* and the cruiser *Sussex* before doing the long gunnery course at Whale Island in 1939. After periods in the AA cruiser *Cairo* and heavy cruiser *Cumberland,* Hill-Norton ended the war as gunnery officer of the battleship *Howe* in the Pacific. After a similar appointment in the cruiser *Nigeria,* he was promoted commander and served in the Naval Ordnance Division at the Admiralty. Hill-Norton then went to sea as executive officer of the new fleet carrier *Eagle,* a post which led to promotion to captain in 1952. After a period as naval attaché to Argentina, Uruguay, and Paraguay, Hill-Norton commanded the large destroyer *Decoy* and carrier *Ark Royal,* with a period on the Naval Staff in between. Gaining his flag in 1962, Hill-Norton served as ACNS and then flag officer second in command Far East Fleet. A vice admiral by 1965 he became deputy chief of Defence Staff (Personnel and Logistics) and then second sea lord and chief of Naval Personnel. After a period as VCNS and promoted full admiral, Sir Peter Hill-Norton became CinC Far East in 1969. His period as first sea lord was short as he was promoted in Le Fanu's place to be chief of Defence Staff, a post he held until 1973. Chairman of the Military Committee of NATO from 1974 to 1977 Admiral of the Fleet Sir Peter Hill-Norton became Baron Hill-Norton of South Nutfield in 1979.

1971–1974—Sir Michael Pollock

Born in 1916 Michael Patrick Pollock entered the Royal Naval College Dartmouth in 1930. Specializing in gunnery, in 1941 he served during the war in the battleship *Warspite,* the cruisers *Arethusa* and *Norfolk,* and the destroyer *Vanessa.* Promoted captain in 1955 he served in the Plans Division of the Naval Staff and as director of Surface Weapons, and he also commanded the Portsmouth Squadron in the destroyer *Vigo* in 1958–59. His final command was the carrier *Ark Royal,* which led to a flag and the post of ACNS. Flag officer second in command Home Fleet from 1966–67, Pollock became flag officer Submarines and NATO commander Submarines EASTLANT in 1967. The year 1970 saw promotion to admiral and appointment as controller of the navy in charge of naval material. Admiral of the Fleet Sir Michael Pollock lives in active retirement in Wales.

1974–1977—Sir Edward Ashmore

Born in 1919 to a naval family, Edward Beckworth Ashmore entered Dartmouth in September 1933. He served as a midshipman in the cruiser *Birmingham* on the China Station and then in the fleet destroyer *Jupiter* and the escort destroyer *Middleton*, in which he won the Distinguished Service Cross in 1942 on Malta convoy duty. Specializing in signals and communications, in 1943 he served on the staff of CinC Home Fleet and then as flag lieutenant and communications officer with the Fourth Cruiser Squadron in the Pacific, being mentioned in despatches in the Okinawa campaign. After qualifying as a Russian interpreter, he served as assistant attaché in Moscow and was promoted to commander while squadron communications officer of the Third Aircraft Carrier Squadron in 1950. After serving in the radio equipment department in the Admiralty, Ashmore commanded the frigate *Alert* on the Far East Station and then was executive officer of HMS *Mercury*, the Communications School. Promoted captain in 1955 he was assistant chief of staff(Communications) on the staff of NATO's CINCNORTH and then commanded the Sixth Frigate Squadron in HMS *Blackpool*. From 1960 to 1962 Ashmore was director Plans on the Naval Staff and then (as a commodore) held the same post on the central Defence Staff. In 1963–64 he received another commodore's appointment as senior naval officer West Indies and commander British Forces Caribbean Area. Ashmore was promoted rear admiral at the beginning of 1965 and served for two years as assistant chief of Defence Staff(Signals). In 1967 he returned to operational duty as flag officer second in command Far East Fleet. The following year Ashmore was promoted vice admiral and in 1969 he became VCNS. As a full admiral he became CinC Western Fleet in September 1971, being created the first CINCFLEET in November of that year. Due to the ill health of Marshal of the Royal Air Force Sir Andrew Humphrey, Admiral of the Fleet Sir Edward Ashmore held the post of chief of Defence Staff from February to August 1977. He is now a director, Racal Electronics Ltd.

1977–1979—Sir Terence Lewin

Terence Thornton Lewin was born in 1920 and joined the Royal Navy in 1939. He served during World War II in the battleship *Valiant* at home and in the Mediterranean, and in the destroyer *Ashanti* on convoy duty in the Mediterranean and Arctic, during the "Torch" landings and in the Channel on anti-shipping raids off the French coast. He obtained a Distinguished Service Order and was mentioned in despatches three times. His first command was the destroyer HMS *Corunna* in 1955–56 and he was executive officer of the royal yacht *Britannia* in 1957–58. Promoted captain, he commanded the Dartmouth Training Squadron in the frigates *Urchin* and *Tenby*, and by 1964–65 was on the Naval Staff as director of the Naval Tactical and Weapons Policy Division. Lewin then went back to sea in command of HMS *Hermes* and then, gaining his flag, became ACNS(P) in 1968–69 and flag officer second in command Far East Fleet in 1969–70. The early 1970s saw Lewin successively VCNS, CINCFLEET, and CINCNAVHOME before he became first sea lord. In 1979 Admiral of the Fleet Sir Terence Lewin became chief of Defence Staff, a post from which he retired in 1982 to be created Baron Lewin of Greenwich and, in 1983, a Knight of the Garter.

1979–1982—Sir Henry Leach

Son of Captain J.C. Leach of HMS *Prince of Wales* who lost his life when the ship was sunk, Henry Conyers Leach was born in 1923 and entered the Royal Naval College Dartmouth in 1937. From 1941 to 1946 he served in the cruiser *Mauritius* in the South Atlantic and Indian Ocean, in the battleship *Duke of York* (during the *Scharnhorst* sinking), and in destroyers in the Mediterranean. A gunnery specialist, from 1947 he served in several appointments including that of gunnery officer in the modernized cruiser *Newcastle* in the Far East 1953–55. He also passed the Staff Course in 1952. After staff appointments from 1955 to 1959, Leach's first command was the destroyer *Dunkirk*. After completing the Joint Services' Staff Course he then became chief staff officer (Plans and Operations) with the Far East Fleet, moving in 1965 to the frigate *Galatea* as captain(D) 27th Escort Squadron and Mediterranean. After being director Plans on the Naval Staff, he took command of the commando ship *Albion* in 1970. Leach was back at the Admiralty as ACNS(P) in 1971 and became flag officer First Flotilla in 1974–75. A senior central staff appointment followed as vice chief of Defence Staff, followed by that of CINC-FLEET in 1977–79, the Royal Navy's main operational command. Admiral of the Fleet Sir Henry Leach now lives in active retirement in Hampshire, being chairman of St. Dunstan's, the organization for the blind.

1982–1985—Sir John Fieldhouse

Sir John Fieldhouse was born in 1928, son of Sir Harold Fieldhouse, a distinguished local government officer. After being a cadet at the Royal Naval Colleges at Dartmouth and Eaton Hall, John Fieldhouse became a midshipman in the East Indies Fleet in 1945–46 before entering the submarine service in 1948. Fieldhouse commanded the conventional submarines *Acheron*, *Tiptoe*, and *Walrus* and (in 1964–66) the nuclear submarine *Dreadnought* (he is a member of the Institute of Nuclear Engineers). The Joint Services Staff Course was the prelude to an appointment as executive officer of the carrier *Hermes*. In 1967 he was promoted captain and commanded the Polaris Squadron from 1968 to 1970. After being appointed to a surface command, the frigate *Diomede*, in 1971 Fieldhouse commanded the NATO Standing Naval Force Atlantic as a commodore. From 1973–74 he was director of Naval Warfare, followed by gaining his flag and a period as flag officer Second Flotilla in 1974–76. After commanding the submarine service as flag officer Submarines in 1976–78 and being in charge of material matters as controller in 1978–81, Admiral Sir John Fieldhouse became CINCFLEET in 1981. As such, he had operational responsibility for the conduct of the Falklands War. He became Chief of Defence Staff at the end of 1985.

1985–____—Sir William Staveley

William Doveton Minet Staveley, the grandson of Admiral Sir Doveton Sturdee, victor of the Battle of the Falkland Islands in 1914, entered the Royal Naval College as a cadet in 1942. His first ship as a midshipman was the cruiser *Ajax* in the Mediterranean in 1946 and, after service as a junior officer on the South Atlantic station in the cruisers *Nigeria* and *Bermuda*, Staveley served as flag lieutenant to Admiral Sir George Creasey, CinC Home Fleet in his successive flagships HMS *Indomitable* and HMS *Vanguard* in the period 1952–54. After serving on the staff at Dartmouth, Staveley went to the Royal Yacht and then became first lieutenant of the destroyer *Cavalier*. After attending Staff College at Greenwich, he served on the staff of CinC Nore and flag officer Medway before being promoted to commander and being appointed as senior officer with the 104th (later the 6th) Minesweeping Squadron, Far East Fleet. Service on the staff of flag officer Sea Training was followed by command of the *Tribal*-class frigate *Zulu*. Promoted captain in 1967, Staveley became assistant director, Naval Plans, followed by two years in command of the assault ship *Intrepid,* and a year as captain of the commando carrier *Albion*. After a course in 1973 at the Royal College of Defence Studies, he was director Naval Plans from 1974 to 1976. As a flag officer, Staveley had a succession of key appointments, flag officer Second Flotilla, flag officer Carriers and Amphibious Ships, chief of staff to CINCFLEET, and vice chief of Naval Staff. Sir William Staveley succeeded Sir John Fieldhouse, first in the Fleet Command in 1982, and then as first sea lord in 1985.

Sources: Relevant Volumes of *Dictionary of National Biography, Who's Who,* and *Navy Lists*; also biographical notes held by Naval Historical Branch.

APPENDIX · TEN

FIRST LORDS OF THE ADMIRALTY AND NAVY MINISTERS, 1945–1981

In 1945–46 the first lord was a senior minister and member of the Cabinet. After the creation of the Ministry of Defence, the post became one of medium grade, usually associated with a seat in the House of Lords rather than the more politically important House of Commons. The first lord still had access to the Cabinet, however, on request, a right that was lost in 1964 with the creation of a unified Ministry of Defence. Separate service representation was, however, kept at the mid-grade "Minister of State" level within the Defence Ministry until 1967 when it was reduced to junior "Parliamentary Under Secretary" status. In 1981 even that level of separate political representation in the government was abolished as still tending to lead to too great a level of ministerial identification with sectional service interests. Since that date there has been no "Navy Minister" as such.

FIRST LORDS OF THE ADMIRALTY

1945–1946—A.V. Alexander

Albert Victor Alexander was born in 1885 in Weston Super Mare, the son of a blacksmith who died in his son's first year. His mother moved to Bristol, and to help support her Albert Victor left school at thirteen to become a boy clerk with the Bristol School Board. By 1919 he was chief of the Higher Education Department of Somerset County Council. His involvement with the Local Government Officers Union led him into the Co-operative movement. After service in the Artists Rifles in World War I he left the army with the rank of captain and joined the Parliamentary Committee of the Co-operative Congress, which led to his election as Labour and Co-operative candidate for Hillsborough, Sheffield, in 1922. In 1924 he was parliamentary secretary to the Board of Trade in the first Labour Government, and when labour regained office in 1929 he became first lord of the Admiralty. The crisis of 1931 saw Alexander lose both his portfolio and his parliamentary seat, but he regained the latter in 1935 becoming Opposition spokesman for naval affairs. In May 1940 he became first lord in Churchill's coalition government and continued in this post, except for the brief interlude of the Churchill caretaker administration, in Attlee's Labour Government. Alexander left the Admiralty in October 1946 to become minister without portfolio in preparation for becoming the first minister of defence under the postwar system at the beginning of 1947. Created Lord Alexander of Hillsborough in 1950, he became chancellor of the Duchy of Lancaster. A prominent member of the Labour Opposition in the House of Lords after 1951, he led the Party there from 1955 to 1964. He died in 1965.

1946–1951—George, Viscount Hall

A Welsh miner for thirteen years from the age of twelve, George Henry Hall was born in Penhiwceiber Glamorgan in 1881. He came into Labour politics via the South Wales Miners Federation and was elected M.P. for Aberdare in 1922, a seat he held until 1946. Civil Lord of the Admiralty in the 1929–31 Labour Government, Hall became parliamentary under secretary of state at the Colonial Office in the early years of Churchill's wartime coalition. He moved back to the Admiralty briefly as financial secretary in 1942–43 and then moved on to the Foreign Office as parliamentary under secretary for the rest of the war. In Attlee's Government he became secretary of state for the Colonies, but moved both to the House of Lords as Viscount Hall of Cynon Valley, and to the Admiralty, in 1946. He died in 1965.

1951—Francis, Lord Pakenham

A great contrast in background to his working-class predecessors, the last Labour first lord was a member of a long-standing noble family. Educated at Eton and Oxford he worked for a time in the Conservative Party Economic Research Department and then as a lecturer in politics at Oxford. By 1938 he was a Labour parliamentary candidate, and after brief service in the territorial army became personal assistant to Sir William Beveridge, author of the British welfare state proposals. After a brief period as a government whip in the House of Lords, he began his ministerial career in Attlee's Government as parliamentary under secretary of state War Office 1946–47, chancellor of the Duchy of Lancaster 1947–48, and minister of Civil Aviation 1948–51. Succeeding his brother as Sixth Earl of Longford in 1961, he served as leader of the House of Lords, colonial secretary, and lord privy seal in Harold Wilson's Government 1964–68. He is also well known as a historian, author, and social reformer.

1951–56—James P.L. Thomas, Viscount Cilcennin

James Purden Lewes Thomas was born in 1903 of Welsh-Irish descent. The grandson of a naval officer, he was educated at Rugby and Oxford, and after unsuccessfully standing as Conservative candidate for Llanelly in 1929, became Member of Parliament for Hereford in the 1931 general election. After a brief period as Stanley Baldwin's assistant private secretary, he became parliamentary private secretary to the dominions secretary from 1932–35 and colonial secretary in 1935–36. He was PPS at the Foreign Office in 1937–38 and returned to government in 1940 in Churchill's Coalition in the same position at the War Office. After a period at the Treasury from 1940–43, Thomas was financial secretary at the Admiralty until the end of the war. Following the defeat of the party at the general election, Thomas became vice chairman of the Conservative Party helping create the conditions for the election victory in 1951 that led to his appointment as first lord. Created First Viscount Cilcennin in 1955, he became lord lieutenant of Herefordshire in 1957 and died in 1960.

1956–57—Quentin, Viscount Hailsham

A senior member of today's Conservative Government, Quentin McGarel Hogg was born in 1907. Educated at Eton and Oxford he distinguished himself academically and became a lawyer before being elected as Conservative M.P. for Oxford in 1938. After service in the army (Rifle Brigade) in World War II, Hogg's first experience of government was as parliamentary under secretary for Air in 1945. He succeeded his father as Viscount Hailsham in 1950. After his relatively brief period as first lord, Lord Hailsham continued in increasingly senior government appointments and was leader of the House of Lords 1960–63. A prominent member of the Conservative party by then he disclaimed his peerage in 1963 to contest, unsuccessfully, the party leadership. He was created Baron Hailsham of St. Marylebone (his seat as an MP 1963–70) in 1970 to become lord chancellor of Britain, a post he relinquished on the Heath administration's defeat in 1974, but which he took up again in Mrs. Thatcher's administration in 1979.

1957–1959—George, Earl of Selkirk

George Nigel Douglas-Hamilton, Tenth Earl of Selkirk, was born in 1906 and succeeded his father to the title in 1940. Educated at Eton and Oxford he became a Scottish lawyer and was prominent in both Scottish local government and administration and the Royal Auxiliary Air Force in the 1930s. He saw distinguished service in the RAAF during World War II. A government whip in the House of Lords 1951–53, Selkirk entered Churchill's Government as paymaster general in 1953, becoming chancellor of the Duchy of Lancaster in 1955. Following his departure as first sea lord he became U.K. commissioner in Singapore and delegate to the South East Asia Treaty Organization until 1963. After involvement with various organizations in the 1960s and 1970s, the Earl of Selkirk lives today in retirement in Dorset and London.

1959–1963—Peter, Baron Carrington

Born in 1919 Peter Alexander Rupert Carrington succeeded to the title as Sixth Baron Carrington in 1938. Educated at Eton and the Royal Military Academy Sandhurst, Lord Carrington saw service with the Grenadier Guards in World War II. His first ministerial post in 1951 was as parliamentary secretary with the minister of agriculture, moving in the same position to Defence in 1954. He was high commissioner (i.e., ambassador to a Commonwealth country) to Australia in 1956–59. Following his time as first lord, Lord Carrington became leader of the House of Lords, and then led the Conservative Opposition in that House from 1964–70. Secretary of State for Defence for most of the Heath administration, Lord Carrington was briefly energy secretary before returning to the Opposition front bench in the Upper House. Foreign secretary in the Thatcher administration, Lord Carrington had to resign over the Falklands affair, but was appointed secretary general of NATO in 1984, a post he presently holds.

1963–1964—George, Earl Jellicoe

George Patrick John Rushworth Jellicoe, born in 1918, is the son of the British Commander-in-Chief at the Battle of Jutland and first sea lord 1916–17, whom he succeeded as second earl in 1935. Educated at Winchester and Cambridge he had distinguished service in the Coldstream Guards and Special Air Service during the

Second World War and entered the diplomatic service in 1947 serving as first secretary in the embassies to the United States of America, Belgium, and Iraq. In the last-named post he was deputy secretary, Baghdad Pact. Earl Jellicoe entered the Macmillan Government in 1961 as a parliamentary secretary in the Ministry of Housing and Local Government, being promoted to minister of state Home Office in 1962.

MINISTERS OF DEFENCE (ROYAL NAVY)

1964—George, Earl Jellicoe

Earl Jellicoe, the last first lord, continued in office under his new title until the defeat of the Douglas-Home Government at the 1964 election. He was deputy leader of the Opposition in the House of Lords from 1967–70 and then became lord privy seal, civil service minister and leader of the House of Lords in the Heath administration. Earl Jellicoe lives in Wiltshire and London and is chairman of the Medical Research Council.

1964–1966—C.P. Mayhew

Christopher Paget Mayhew was born in 1915, educated at Haileybury and Oxford and served in the army during World War II, being mentioned in despatches. He became a Labour MP for South Norfolk in 1945, losing his seat in 1950 but gaining a new seat, Woolwich East in 1951, which he held until 1974. A parliamentary secretary at the Foreign Office for most of the Attlee administration, Mayhew did much writing and broadcasting in the years of Opposition before being appointed navy minister in 1964. Resigning over the carrier decision, he returned to the back benches and writing, notably about his interest in the Arab side of the Palestine Question, and the European movement. He left the Labour Party in 1974 to become a Liberal, but lost his seat at the second election of that year. Chief Liberal party spokesman on defense in 1980, Christopher Mayhew became Baron Mayhew of Wimbledon in 1981.

1966–1967—J.P.W. Mallalieu

Born in 1908, the son of a member of Parliament, Joseph Perceval William Mallalieu was educated in both Britain and America (University of Chicago) before entering journalism in the 1930s. After service in the Royal Navy from 1942–45 (which he made the basis of two books), he became in 1945 Labour MP for Huddersfield, later Huddersfield (East), holding the seat until 1979. After service as a parliamentary private secretary in the Air and Food Ministries in the Attlee administration, Mallalieu was appointed under secretary of defence (Royal Navy) in the Wilson administration in 1964. Promoted to full ministerial status on Christopher Mayhew's resignation, Mallalieu moved to the Board of Trade after the abolition of his post and then was minister of technology in 1968–69. Knighted in 1979 Sir William Mallalieu died in early 1980.

UNDER SECRETARIES OF STATE FOR DEFENCE (ROYAL NAVY) 1967–1981

1967–1968—M.A. Foley

Maurice Anthony Foley was born in Middlesborough in 1925. An electrical fitter, youth organizer, and social worker, he became a trade unionist and was elected

Labour MP for West Bromwich in 1963. Appointed under secretary of state in the Department of Economic Affairs in Harold Wilson's administration, he moved to the Home Office in 1966. On leaving his Royal Navy post he spent the rest of the Wilson administration as PUS in the Foreign Office. Since 1973, when he resigned his seat, Mr. Foley has been deputy director general of the Development Directorate at the Commission of the European Economic Community in Brussels.

1968–1970—Dr. D.A. Owen

David Anthony Owen was born in Devon in 1938 and was educated at Bradfield and Cambridge. Following in his father's footsteps, he trained in medicine and practiced until 1966 when he was elected Labour party member for the Plymouth Sutton parliamentary seat, which he has held ever since (as "Plymouth Devonport," with re-drawn boundaries, since 1974). A brief appointment as parliamentary private secretary in the Defence Ministry led to Owen's appointment as PUS for the Royal Navy in 1968, the youngest navy minister ever. In opposition, Dr. Owen became Defence front-bench spokesman, although disagreements over EEC policy led to his resignation. In the second Wilson administration Dr. Owen first served at the Ministry of Health, first as PUS, then as minister of state. He then moved to the Foreign Office in 1976 as minister of state to Anthony Crossland. On the latter's death, Mr. Callaghan appointed Dr. Owen to be foreign secretary. After the 1979 defeat, Dr. Owen aligned himself with the other leading members on the right of the labour party who split away to form the Social Democratic party in 1981. He became party leader in 1983 and is presently one of the leading Opposition politicians in the United Kingdom.

1970–1972—P.M. Kirk

Peter Michael Kirk was born in 1928 and was educated at Marlborough, Oxford, and Zurich. After some time as a journalist, he was elected in 1955 to the Conservative seat at Gravesend, becoming a member of the U.K. delegation to the Council of Europe before serving briefly as PUS for the army from 1963 to 1964. Losing his seat in 1964 he became MP for Saffron Walden in 1965 and continued to show a great interest in European affairs, culminating in his becoming leader of the Conservative Delegation to the European Parliament in 1973. He was knighted in 1976. Sir Peter Kirk died in 1977.

1972–1974—P.A.F. Buck

Born in 1928 Philip Antony Fyson Buck was educated at Ely and Cambridge and became a barrister in 1954. Elected Conservative MP for Colchester in 1961 he was parliamentary private secretary to the attorney general in 1963–64. In opposition, Antony Buck was secretary of his party's Home Affairs Committee, but became vice chairman, and then chairman, of the Defence Committee before his appointment as junior minister for the navy. Now a prominent back bencher he chairs his party's Defence committee once more. Knighted in 1983 Sir Antony now sits for the new seat of Colchester North.

1974–1976—F.A. Judd

Born in 1935 Frank Ashcroft Judd was educated at the London School of Economics. After unsuccessfully contesting Sutton and Cheam for Labour in 1959, Mr.

Judd was secretary general of International Voluntary Service before winning the Portsmouth West seat for Labour in 1966. (In 1974 his seat changed to Portsmouth North). He was parliamentary private secretary to the Ministry of Housing in the first Wilson administration. After two years as PPS to Mr. Wilson as Opposition leader, Judd moved to be a Defence Opposition spokesman, a prelude to his period as navy minister in Mr. Wilson's second government. He moved to the Ministry of Overseas Development post as PUS, then as minister of state before replacing David Owen at the Foreign Office as minister of state in 1977. Losing his seat at the general election, Frank Judd returned to his overseas development interests and has been director Voluntary Service Overseas since 1980.

1976–1979—A.E.P. Duffy

Albert Edward Patrick Duffy was born in 1920 and took a doctorate at the London School of Economics after service in World War II with the Royal Navy. A university lecturer from 1950, he was Labour MP for Colne Valley from 1963 to 1966 and reentered Parliament for Sheffield Attercliffe in 1970. He became parliamentary private secretary to the Ministry of Defence in 1974, moving to be PUS for the navy when Mr. Callaghan took over as prime minister. In opposition, Mr. Patrick Duffy has been a leading Labour spokesman on defense issues.

1979–1981—H.K. Speed

Born in 1934 Herbert Keith Speed entered the Royal Navy as a cadet, was educated at Dartmouth and served as an officer from 1947 to 1956. After a period as a marketing manager in the electronics industry, Keith Speed worked for the Conservative Research Department from 1965 to 1968 before becoming MP for Meriden in 1968, and Ashford in 1974. An assistant government whip and junior minister at the Treasury and Department of Environment in the Heath administration, Speed became an Opposition spokesman on local government and home affairs. He did, however, maintain an active membership in the Royal Naval Reserve, which he ceased on his appointment as PUS for the navy. An opponent of the Nott Defence Review, Mr. Speed was dismissed by Mrs. Thatcher, and since then he has maintained the position of back bench critic of government policy, especially on defense issues.

Sources: *Dictionary of National Biography* and *Who's Who*.

NOTES

Chapter One

1. For the basis of this thesis and its fuller exposition, see P. Kennedy, *The Rise and Fall of British Naval Mastery* (London: A. Lane, 1976; 2nd ed., London: Macmillan, 1983), especially chapters 6–8.

2. Ibid., chapter 10. Also see G. Peden, *British Rearmament and the Treasury* (Edinburgh: Scottish Academic Press, 1979). For detailed naval policy, see S. Roskill, *Naval Policy Between the Wars*, 2 vols. (London University Press, 1968, 1976).

3. S. Roskill, *The War at Sea*, 4 vols. (London: His Majesty's Stationary Office, 1954–56). The best one-volume account is also by Roskill, *The Navy at War 1939–45* (London: Collins, 1960), published in the U.S.A. under the title *White Ensign* (Annapolis, Md.: U.S. Naval Institute, 1960).

4. Wartime strengths taken from lists compiled from relevant "Pink Lists" by Naval Historical Branch made available to the author. For losses, see *Ships of the Royal Navy: Statement of Losses During the Second World War* and *Amendments No. 1* (His Majesty's Stationery Office, 1947 and 1949). Also *Brassey's Naval Annual* 1946, pp. 55 and 151, and appendices to Roskill, *War at Sea*, vol. 3, part 2.

5. For the effects of World War II on the foundations of British sea power, see Kennedy, *Rise and Fall*, chapters 11 and 12.

6. "The Atomic Bomb—Its Influence on Naval Warfare and Naval Policy," Public Record Office (PRO), Admiralty and Secretariat Papers, ADM1/17259.

7. Much of the following is drawn from *The Naval Warfare Manual* BR1806(48), copy held in Naval Library, Ministry of Defence, Empress State Building, London.

8. For Attlee himself, see K. Harris, *Attlee* (London: Weidenfeld & Nicolson, 1982). For his use of committees, see P. Hennessy and A. Arends, *Mr. Attlee's Engine Room: Cabinet Committee Structure and the Labour Government 1945–51* (Glasgow: University of Strathclyde, 1983).

9. For the development of the Admiralty as an organization, see N.A.M. Rodger, *The Admiralty* (Lavenham: T. Dalton, 1979).

10. BR1806(48). For quotations, see pp. 24–25.

11. For the evolution of the Staff see notes kindly placed at the author's disposal by the Naval Library, Empress State Building, London.

12. BR1806(48), p. 25.

13. "Composition of the Post War Navy." Paper B435 of 12 September 1945 in PRO, Board of Admiralty Minutes and Memoranda, 1945, ADM167/124. For earlier work see papers in PRO, First Sea Lord's Records, ADM205/53.

14. "The Post War Navy and the Policy Governing its Composition." Paper B424 of 17 July 1945 in ADM167/124.

15. PRO, Cabinet Defence Committee (Operations), DO(45) 6th Meeting, 14 September 1945, CAB69/7. For Dalton's perspective on the problems of this period, see his autobiography, *High Tide and After* (London: Muller, 1962), and B. Pimlott, *Hugh Dalton* (London: Jonathan Cape, 1985).

16. "Size and Deployment of the Armed Forces on 30 June 1946," PRO, Chiefs of Staff Committee memorandum, COS(45)565 in CAB80/97.

17. DO(45) 11th Meeting, 29 September 1945, CAB69/7. It might be said that this meeting established the basic principle of British defense policy making for the whole postwar period.

18. The main source for the discussion of cancellations is "Cancellations of Orders for Ships," ADM1/19096. For details of 1943 carriers, see Memorandum B425 in ADM167/124 and Ships Cover 698. For description of ships mentioned, also see *Conway's All the World's Fighting Ships* (hereafter *Conway's*) 1922–46; R. Chesneau, *Aircraft Carriers of the World 1914 to the Present* (London: Arms & Armour Press, 1984), and A. Raven and J. Roberts, *British Cruisers of World War II* (London: Arms & Armour Press, 1980). The difference between a *Majestic* and *Colossus* is best explained in Ships Cover 666C (folio 56) (National Maritime Museum).

19. WP(44)764, copy in ADM205/53.

20. Quoted in "Battleship Committee," ADM1/17251.

21. ADM205/53.

22. B403 in ADM167/124.

23. For the fullest account of the discussions, see "Battleship Committee," ADM1/18659.

24. ADM1/19096.

25. Ibid. Also see Board Minute 4046, 7 November 1945, ADM167/124.

26. DO(45) 13th Meeting, 7 November 1945, CAB69/7.

27. ADM1/19096 and Board Minute 4052, 7 December 1945, ADM167/124.

28. ADM1/19096.

29. Board Minute 4046 and Appendix, 7 November 1945, ADM167/124. Also CP(45)291 in CAB69/7.

30. DO(45)22 "Sale and Scrapping of Warships," CAB69/7.

31. Naval Air Personnel Committee Reports, ADM116/5528.

32. "Report on the Internal Organisation of Naval Aviation" presented to the first lord 26 February 1945 (the "Evershed Report"), B404 in ADM167/124. The order AFO 5631/46 can be found in ADM1/24535. It was approved by the first lord on 27 August 1946.

33. "State of the Fleet Arm," ADM116/5534.

34. "Disposal of American Aircraft," ADM1/15576.

35. ADM116/5534. Also see O. Thetford, *British Naval Aircraft since 1912* (London, 1978), D. Hobbs, *Aircraft of the Royal Navy Since 1945* (Liskeard: Maritime Press, 1983), and A. Vicary, *Naval Wings* (Cambridge: P. Stephens, 1984).

36. "Future of the Aircraft Industry," ADM1/17395.

37. PRO, Admiralty and Secretariat Cases, ADM116/5534.

38. Thetford, *British Naval Aircraft*, p. 402.

39. ADM1/19009.

40. Based on "New Types of Aircraft," 30 December 1945 in ADM205/64. For general carrier details, see Chesneau, *Aircraft Carriers*.

41. Ships Covers 587C and 666C, fol. 56, and Chesneau, ibid.

42. "Admiralty Production for the Period 1 October–31 December 1946," DO(45)28 in CAB69/7.

43. ADM116/5534. R. Sturtivant, *The Squadrons of the Fleet Air Arm* (Tonbridge: Air Britain, 1984), pp. 165, 205, 214, and 474. For air-dropped weapons, see DNC General Correspondence, vol. 72, fol. 48 (National Maritime Museum).

44. For Australian negotiations, see J. Goldrick, "Carriers for the Commonwealth," paper presented to the 1985 Naval History Symposium at the U.S. Naval Academy, Annapolis. For documents on deal, see ADM205/69. For French negotiations see PRO, Cabinet Memorandum CP(46)95, CAB129/7 and for Dutch PRO, Cabinet Defence Committee DO(46)3 CAB131/12. See also Chesneau, *Aircraft Carriers*, pp. 58, 126, 187–88.

45. "Estimated Strength and Distribution of the Royal Navy During the Year to 30 June 1946 by Quarters and Numbers of Men and Women Under Training at These Dates," DO(45)39, CAB69/7.

46. "The Manpower Situation—January 1945," B399 in ADM167/124.

47. See Carew, *The Lower Deck of the Royal Navy 1900–39* (Manchester University Press, 1981). Also comments in Memorandum B426 of 28 August 1945, "Personnel Problems in Relation to the Aftermath of the War" in ADM167/124.

48. See letters from Admiral Dalrymple Hamilton to first lord 7 November 1945, Alexander Papers AVAR 5/10/67, Archive Centre, Churchill College, Cambridge.

49. D. Wettern, *The Decline of British Sea Power* (London: Jane's, 1982), p. 2.

50. "Provisional Personnel Requirements for the Post War Armed Forces," ADM116/5658; PRO, Cabinet Memorandum CP(45)161 in CAB129/2; PRO, Cabinet Defence Committee paper DO(46)7 in CAB131/2.

51. PRO, Cabinet Defence Committee, DO(46) 1st Meeting, CAB131/1.

52. DO(46) 3rd Meeting, CAB131/1.

53. "Memorandum on the Size of the Armed Forces—Report by the Chiefs of Staff," DO(46)20 in CAB131/2.

54. Ibid.

55. DO(46) 5th Meeting, CAB131/1.

56. Memo. B446, Board Minutes and Memoranda, ADM167/127. DNC General Correspondence vol. 72, fols. 1, 13, 48, and 62 and vol. 73, fol. 68. For fate of *Majestics*, see *Conway's 1947–1982*, part 1, p. 124.

57. Memoranda B 471 and B 476 and Board Minutes 4104 and 4112, ADM167/127 for modernization decisions. DNC General Correspondence, ibid. and vol. 72, fol. 64.

58. DNC General Correspondence, vol. 72, fols. 23, 48, and 62, vol. 73, fols. 22, 51, and 68, vol. 76 part 2, fol. 141.

59. Memorandum B483 and Board Minute 4119, ADM167/127. See also document 7/6 in ADM205/64.

60. The quotation is from Admiral Sir Manley Power who had worked with both. For it and the Roskill assessment, see S. Roskill, *Churchill and the Admirals* (London: Collins, 1979) p. 217.

61. DO(46)52 in CAB131/2.

62. DO(46)66; ibid.

63. Minutes included in DO(46)97, CAB131/3.

64. Ibid.

65. Government White Paper, The Central Organisation for Defence, (Cd. 6923).

66. Montgomery of Alamein, *Memoirs* (London: Collins, 1958), p. 483.

67. F.A. Johnson, *Defence by Ministry* (London: Duckworth, 1980), p. 22.

68. See correspondence in A.V. Alexander papers.

69. See obituary in the *Times*, 9 November 1965.

70. "Compulsory Service Arrangements Subsequent to 1948," B488 in ADM167/127.

71. Ibid. and Board Minute 4122, ADM167/127.

72. DO(46) 27th Meeting, CAB131/1. See also papers DO(46)117 and DO(46)119, CAB131/3.

73. DO(46) 28th Meeting (17 October), CAB131/1.

74. DO(47)4 and DO(47)9, CAB131/1.

75. DO(47)9, ibid.

76. DO(47) 2nd Meeting, CAB131/5.

77. Paper CP(47)221 of 30 July 1947, CAB129/20. See also Pimlott, *Hugh Dalton*, pp. 480–81, and Dalton, *High Tide*, pp. 193–94.

78. DO(47)63, 2 August 1947, CAB131/4.

79. "Main Effects on the Navy of a Reduction of National Service from Eighteen Months to One Year," Memorandum for chiefs of staff by the first sea lord, COS(47)77 in PRO, Chiefs of Staff Memorandum DEFE5/4. Also references in "Future Defence Policy, Naval Peacetime Requirements," Memorandum B520 in ADM167/129.

80. DO(47)4, CAB131/4.

81. COS(47)5 in DEFE5/3 and Minutes of COS Meeting 13 January 1947 in PRO, Chiefs of Staff Minutes DEFE4/1.

82. COS(47)33 in DEFE5/3.

83. This document, JP(46)164, was not released when hitherto closed pieces of the PRO file Joint Planning Committee CAB84/84 were released in April 1983, but the shape and nature of the study can be deduced from the documents at the next two references.

84. COS(47)72 and COS(47)78 in DEFE5/4.

85. COS(47) 54th Meeting DEFE4/3.

86. COS(47)79 DEFE5/4. For a more extended discussion, see the author's "The Post War 'Ten Year Rule'—Myth and Reality" in the *Journal of the Royal United Services Institute*, December 1984.

87. The document itself is still closed. Its terms of reference COS(47)84 are available in PRO, Chiefs of Staff Committee Minutes DEFE4/3 and 4/4. Its main features are, however, reflected in an open document COS(47)227 in DEFE5/6.

88. COS(47)114, DEFE5/4.

89. COS(47)142, DEFE5/4.

90. Memorandum B520 in ADM167/129.

91. See Minute by Permanent Under Secretary in reference 93.

92. Board Minute 4171, ADM167/129.

93. COS(47)178, DEFE5/5.

94. Memorandum B526 of 8 August 1947 in ADM167/129. Also COS(47)184, DEFE5/5.

95. Board Minute 4182, ADM167/129 and DO(47)68, CAB131/4.

96. DO(47) 20th Meeting, CAB131/5.

97. DO(47)74, CAB131/4.

98. "Pink List" for December 1947, Naval Library, Ministry of Defence.

99. "Disposal of Certain of H.M. Ships," DO(47)96, CAB131/4.

100. DO(47) 27th Meeting, CAB131/4.

Chapter Two

1. PRO, Cabinet Defence Committee DO(48)1, CAB131/6.

2. DO(48), ibid.

3. DO(48) 2nd Meeting, CAB131/5.

4. Joint Intelligence Committee document JIC(47)76(0) discussed at the 14th Meeting of the COS in 1948, PRO, Chiefs of Staff Committee Minutes DEFE4/10. This document is still classified, but its content can be inferred from later discussions.

5. Title of a paper by Foreign Secretary E. Bevin of 3 March 1948, PRO, Cabinet Memorandum CP(48)72, CAB129/25.

6. CM(48) 19th Conclusions 5 March 1948, PRO, Cabinet Minutes CAB128/12; COS(48) 35th Meeting 9 March 1948, PRO, Chiefs of Staff Committee Minutes DEFE4/11.

7. COS(48)77(0), PRO, Chiefs of Staff Committee Memoranda DEFE5/10.

8. "State of the Home Fleet—1 March 1948" in First Sea Lord's Records ADM205/69. Also contemporary "Pink Lists."

9. DO(48)46, CAB131/6; DO(48) 13th Meeting 27 July 1948, PRO, Cabinet Defence Committee CAB131/5.

10. DO(48)49, CAB131/6; DO(48) 14th Meeting 30 July 1948, CAB131/5.

11. DO(48)55, CAB131/6 and discussion in Defence Committee 23 August 1948, CAB131/5; Cabinet decision in CM(48) 57th Conclusions, CAB128/13.

12. Contemporary "Pink List."

13. The Production Programme is Memo B539 in PRO, Board of Admiralty Minutes and Memoranda ADM167/131; for carrier modernization plans see Memo B533 and Board Minute 4195 in ADM167/129 and Memo B539 in ADM167/132. For specially useful material on carrier plans, see Ships Covers 587C (fleet carriers) and 740 and 791 (light fleet carriers).

14. Ships Cover 760, "Fleet Aircraft Direction Escort."

15. See Memos B539 and B556 in ADM167/131. Also J. Simpson, *Understanding Weapon*

Acquisition Processes: A Study of Naval Anti-Submarine Aircraft Procurement in Britain 1945–55, vol. 2. (PhD Dissertation presented to University of Southampton, 1976.)

16. Simpson, ibid.; COS(48) 99th Meeting.

17. Memo B556, ADM167/131. Also see J.M. Milne, *Flashing Blades over the Sea* (Liskeard: Maritime Books, 1980), pp. 5–25.

18. For biography see R. Humble, *Fraser of North Cape* (London: Routledge & Kegan Paul, 1983).

19. Memo B577 "Naval Estimates 1949/50," ADM167/133; DO(48) 23rd Meeting, CAB131/5; DO(48)83, CAB131/6.

20. "Manning Difficulties," Memo B595, ADM157/133.

21. Memo B567, ADM167/131.

22. DO(49)43, CAB131/7.

23. For the Committee's beginnings, see COS(48) 166th and 168th Meetings, DEFE5/18. For its report, see DO(49)47 in CAB131/7 or COS(49)113 in DEFE5/13. For Harwood, see *Who's Who* for the period. For Lambe, see memoir by O. Warner, *Admiral of the Fleet* (London: Sidgwick & Jackson, 1969). The Committee's own file is at PRO Ministry of Defence Register Files, General Series, DEFE7/592.

24. COS(49) 48th Meeting in DEFE4/20 and Board Memo B588 ADM167/133; Minute 4283, ADM167/132.

25. Ibid. and COS(49)68th and 77th Meetings in DEFE4/22. Subsequent COS discussions on the report are conveniently gathered together in DEFE7/592.

26. COS(49)214, DEFE5/14.

27. Minutes of SM/M(49)18 in DEFE7/592.

28. DO(49)51, CAB131/7; GEN296/1 First meeting, CAB130/53, DEFE7/609. For a short chronology of the Harwood Process and the defense planning process to January 1950, see DEFE7/593.

29. "Shape and Size of Future Navy and Armed Forces," ADM205/83.

30. "Revised Restricted Fleet," Memo for the Board B590 of 23 May 1949, ADM167/133; Board Minute 4285, ADM167/132.

31. COS(49)236, DEFE5/15 and DEFE7/609. See also ADM205/84.

32. The Parker Committee file is at PRO, Ministry of Defence, Major Committees: Minutes and Papers DEFE10/65. Its working documents are in DEFE7/609–613.

33. CAB128/16, 48th, 50th, 53rd, 54th, and 55th Conclusions.

34. CP(49)205 in CAB129/37. Approved at CAB(49) 61st Conclusion, CAB128/16.

35. See DO(49) 19th, 20th, 21st, and 22nd Meetings, CAB131/8.

36. See DEFE6/7 for the evolution of the plans in 1948. See also Annexe to JP(50)9 in PRO, Joint Planning Committee DEFE6/12 for useful summary of the early planning processes.

37. Plan "Sandown," JP(48)106, DEFE6/7.

38. Plan "Doublequick," JP(48)132, DEFE6/7.

39. Correspondence between Power and Fraser in First Sea Lord's Records ADM205/69 and ADM205/72.

40. JP(48)132, DEFE6/7.

41. JP(49)135, DEFE6/11.

42. JP(49)147, ibid.

43. Memos B610, B611, B612, and B613, ADM167/133 and Board Minutes 4319 and 4320, ADM167/132. Also see memos B646 and B650 and Board Minute 4371, ADM167/135.

44. ADM205/74.

45. Battleships paper in ADM205/69; Fraser quotation in ADM205/72.

46. ADM205/74.

47. ADM205/69.

48. Ibid.

49. Thetford, Vicary, Hobbs, and Sturtivant, op. cit.

50. "New Construction Programme, 1950/51" B645 in ADM167/135.

51. B655 and Board Minute 4393 in ADM167/135.

52. B656 and Board Minute 4394 in ADM167/135 for *Victorious*.

53. "Pink Lists" for carrier complements. Ships Covers 740 and 741 for *Majestic* modifications.

54. B626 "Cruiser Programme" and Board Minute 4345, ADM167/135. See also Ships Cover "Cruisers General" 790 and ADM116/5632. Also M. Critchley, *British Warships Since 1945*, Part 1 (Liskeard: Maritime Books, 1981), pp. 60–65.

55. Ships Cover 790 "Cruisers General" fol. 5. See also meetings of the Ship Design Policy Committee in ADM116/5632. DNC General Correspondence vol. 73, fol. 80 for heavy cruiser conversion proposal.

56. SDPC(49) 1st Meeting, 27 January 1949 in ADM116/5632. For more on these cruiser designs, see the ships described in *Conway's 1947–82*, part 1, p. 150 and in A. Preston, "The RNs 1960 Cruiser Designs," *Warship*, July 1982.

57. Copies of the Edwards' paper can be found in ADM205/83 and ADM205/84. See also DNC General Correspondence, vol. 78, fol. 117 (especially for abilities relative Soviet cruisers), ADM116/5632 and entry in *Conway's 1947–82*, part 1, p. 152.

58. Memos B569, ADM167/131 and B589, ADM167/133 and B629 and B682, ADM167/135. For sonar, see Hackmann, *Seek and Strike* (London: Her Majesty's Stationery Office, 1986), pp. 346–48.

59. Memo B582, ADM167/133 and Board Minute 4278, ADM167/132; Hackmann, op. cit.

60. Memo B583, ADM167/133 and Minute 4279, ADM167/132.

61. Board Minute 4290, ADM167/132; Memo B623 and Minutes 4335, ADM167/135.

62. Memo B634, ADM167/135. For the final quotation, see Board Minute 4488, ADM167/136.

63. Board Minute 4361, ADM167/135.

64. Memos B652 and B653, Board Minutes 4390 and 4361.

65. Memos B551 and B552, ADM167/131; Memos B658 and B659 and Minutes 4396 and 4397, ADM167/135. For details of these and other frigates, see L. Marriott, *Royal Navy Frigates 1945–1983* (Shepperton: Ian Allan, 1983).

66. Memo B641 and Minute 4366, ADM167/135. See also ADM205/74.

67. A list is included in the report of the Maritime Air Defence Committee at PRO, Chiefs of Staffs: Committees and Sub Committees, DEFE8/23. This source provides a wealth of information on the expected shape of a new Battle of the Atlantic.

68. See for example, Plan "Galloper" JP(49)134, 1 March 1950 in DEFE6/11.

69. See Ships Cover 719 "Oyster—Counter Measures." See also J. Worth, *British Warships Since 1945, Part 4, Minesweepers* (Liskeard: Maritime Books, 1984).

70. Memos B605, B606, B607, and B617, ADM167/133; Board Minutes 4313, 4314, 4315, and 4325, ADM167/132; Hackmann, *Seek and Strike*, pp. 344 and 439.

71. Harris, *Attlee*, pp. 442–47.

72. COS(50)101, DEFE5/20; DEFE8/23; Thetford, *British Naval Aircraft*; Simpson, op. cit., vol. 2, especially chap. 6.

73. Exchange of correspondence in File 6 ADM205/74.

74. Letter to Sir Richard Fairey of 21 April 1950 quoted in Simpson, op. cit., p. 305.

75. COS(50) 74th Meeting, DEFE4/31.

76. File 6, ADM205/74.

77. COS(50)139 of 1 May 1950. The actual paper is still withheld from the PRO, but much can be gleaned from the discussions on it and the Continental Commitment questions at chiefs of staff meetings recorded in DEFE4/29. The quotation is from COS(50) 46th Meeting. See also COS(50)93 of 16 March in DEFE5/20.

78. DEFE8/23.

79. Ibid.

80. See for example, JP(49)149 in DEFE6/11. See also Grove, "The Post War Ten Year Rule—Myth and Reality," *R.U.S.I. Journal*, December 1984.

81. DO(50) 15th Meeting, CAB131/8. The minister's paper is DO(50)56, CAB131/9. See also the chiefs of staff paper "Ability of the Armed Forces to Meet an Emergency," DO(50)58, ibid.

82. CM(50) 50th Conclusion, CAB128/18.

83. Memo B685, ADM167/135.

84. See RAP/P(51) in DEFE7/671, "Progress of Rearmament Programme."

85. For Cabinet decision on pay increases and National Service, see CM(50) 53rd Conclusions, CAB128/18, 12 August 1950.

86. CM(50) 52nd, 54th, and 55th Conclusions, CAB128/18. See also CP(50)181 of 31 July 1950 in CAB129/44. For the Admiralty's hopes of U.S. aid, see B654, ADM167/135.

87. Memo B671 "Shape and Size of Fleet, Fraser Plan," Board Minute 4407, ADM167/135; also as COS(50)323 in DEFE5/23. The whole rearmament plan is DO(50)81 in CAB131/9. For the origins of the seaward defense boat, see File 3, ADM205/74.

88. CM(50) 87th Conclusions, CAB128/18.

89. The Admiralty's proposals and the Parker Committee's comments therein can be found in DEFE10/65.

90. DO(51) 1st Meeting, CAB131/10.

91. CP(51)20, CAB129/44. CM(50) 7th and 8th Conclusions, CAB128/19.

92. Harris, *Attlee,* pp. 468–80, and M. Foot, *Aneurin Bevan, vol. 2* (London: Davis Poynter, 1973) for two contrasting views of this crisis.

93. JP(50)73 in DEFE6/13; JP(50)59 at the same reference contains a useful summary of the beginnings of NATO planning as seen from London; see also DO(51)105 in CAB131/11.

94. Board Minute 4481, ADM167/136.

95. See the papers at DEFE7/671 for the problems faced by the rearmament program. All contemporary Ships Covers contain clear signs of strain also. Especially see Cover 694 "*Hermes* Class."

96. Plans Division paper of 2/51. Ships Cover 694/1.

97. Folio 24 "DNC Annual Progress Report—Light Fleet Carriers," Ships Cover 694.

98. Ships Cover 771 and file 13 in ADM205/74.

99. See note 101. Also Sturtivant, *Squadrons of Fleet Air Arm*, and contemporary "Pink Lists."

100. Simpson, op. cit., vol. 3; Thetford, *British Naval Aircraft*; Vicary, *Naval Wings* (Cambridge: Patrick Stephens, 1984); P. Birtles, *De Havilland Vampire, Venom and Sea Vixen* (Weybridge: Ian Allan, 1986), p. 94; and B. Fiddler, *Sea Vixen* (Yeovilton, Friends of the Fleet Air Arm Museum, 1985), pp. 3–4. The navalized Swift is mentioned in Folio 38, Ships Cover 694.

101. Ships Cover 805.

102. Ships Cover 798.

103. Ships Cover 810. For a drawing, see *Conway's 1947–84,* vol. 1, p. 159.

104. References in DEFE7/671, also see *Conway's 1947–84.*

105. Annexe 1 to JP(49) in DEFE6/11.

Chapter Three

1. PRO, Ministry of Defence: Register Files: General Series, DEFE7/671. Also DO(51)94 and 97, Cabinet Defence Committee CAB131/11.

2. "Urgent Economic Problems," DEFE7/676.

3. PDP/M(51)2. Minutes in DEFE7/676.

4. Paper PDP/P(51)2, ibid.

5. PDP/M(51)4, ibid.

6. CC3(52)3, PRO, Cabinet Minutes CAB128/24.

7. For the chancellor's paper, see C(52)10, PRO, Cabinet Memoranda CAB129/48. For minutes of meetings, see CC(52)7 and 25, CAB128/24.

8. COS(51)701 quoted in D(53)3, PRO, Cabinet Defence Committee CAB 131/13.

9. The 1951 paper COS(51)701 is quoted heavily in DP(52)17, PRO, Joint Planning Committee, DEFE6/20. See minutes of COS meetings for February–April in DEFE4/52 and 53.

10. Dictionary of National Biography.

11. For Sir Ian Jacob, see references in F.A. Johnson, *Defence by Ministry*, and *Who's Who*, which also see for Brundrett. The former was kind enough to grant the author an interview. The latter's papers are in the Archive Centre, Churchill College, Cambridge.

12. Relevant meetings are recorded in PRO, Chiefs of Staff Committee Minutes, DEFE4/54.

13. As such it is still withheld from the Public Record Office (it should be D(52)26 in Cabinet Defence Committee, CAB131(12)); the following is based on quotations in related documents, notably GEN411/19 in Cabinet Committee's CAB130/77, various papers in DEFE7/677, D(52)41 in CAB131/12, and D(53)14 in CAB131/13.

14. COS(52) 29th Meeting, DEFE4/52.

15. "British Overseas Obligations," C(52)202 in CAB129/53.

16. The proceedings of this committee are in CAB130/77. The "Metal Using Industries" report is GEN411/2.

17. See GEN411/19 in CAB130/77. The Defence Committee meeting was DO(52) 8th Meeting, CAB131/12.

18. GEN411/20, CAB130/77.

19. GEN411/7th Meeting, ibid.

20. CC72(52), CAB128/24.

21. DEFE7/677, Papers 2, 9, and 13.

22. D(52)45, CAB131/12.

23. D(52)46, ibid.

24. C(52)316 and C(52)310 in DEFE7/677 and CAB129/56.

25. DO(52) 11th Meeting, CAB131/12.

26. C(52)393 and 394, CAB129/56.

27. CC94(52), CAB128/25.

28. COS(53)94, DEFE5/44.

29. This can be followed in DEFE4/59 and 61.

30. ADM205/89 and COS(53) 76th Meeting, DEFE4/76.

31. Ibid., DEFE4/76.

32. See dispute with Chief of the Air Staff COS(53) 80th Meeting, DEFE4/76.

33. Paper 15, ADM205/89.

34. See Appendix i to minutes of COS(53) 80th Meeting DEFE4/76; also papers in ADM205/89.

35. Paper 16, ADM205/89.

36. Papers in ADM205/89; for Churchill's illness, see Lord Moran, *Winston Churchill: The Struggle for Survival 1940–65* (London: Constable, 1966).

37. MISC/P(53)54, Paper 11, ADM205/90.

38. For Thomas quotation, see his papers of 6 October in ADM1/25103. For details of *Vanguard,* see Ships Cover 612D; Paper 11 ADM 205/90 for *Vanguard's* costs.

39. ADM1/25103.

40. D(53)47, CAB131/13.

41. ADM205/91.

42. Ibid.

43. COS(53) 131st Meeting and other remarks in DEFE4/66.

44. Papers in ADM205/89.

45. For McGrigor's thoughts, see Paper of 30 October 53 in ADM205/91. For change in aircraft policy see ADM1/25076.

46. For N113, see COS(52)392 in DEFE5/40. For strike aircraft plans, see Ships Cover 818. For NA39's beginnings, see M. Allward, *Buccaneer,* pp. 6–17.

47. On *Implacable's* delay, see Minutes of PDP/M(51)2, DEFE7/676. For new carrier, Ships Cover 818.

48. PRO, Chiefs of Staff Committees and Sub Committees DEFE8/39 and 40 for the somewhat dilatory proceedings of this committee. No report seems to have been produced by the end of 1953.

49. COS(52)75, DEFE5/44.

50. For fleet carrier abandonment, see Ships Cover 818; for aircraft plans, see ADM1/25076, and for new small carriers, ADM1/25149.

51. ADM1/25076. See also ADM205/94 and ADM205/102.

52. "The Role of the Aircraft Carriers," ADM1/24695.

53. Ibid.

54. Corrected Minutes of Meeting RDP/M(53)8, ibid. This is one of the few available sets of minutes of a ministerial meeting on the Radical Review.

55. Ibid.

56. Draft DP(M)(53)14 in ADM1/24695.

57. JP(50)43. DEFE6/12.

58. See DO(51)25 for a summary of the story, CAB131/11. For Cabinet discussion, see CM51 16th and 27th Conclusions CAB128/19. For *Times* quotation, see *Brassey's Annual 1951,* pp. 12–13. See also Shinwell's comments at DO(51) 4th Meeting, CAB131/10.

59. VCNS put forward the argument quoted at DO(51) 5th Meeting, CAB131/10.

60. *Brassey's Annual 1952,* pp. 12–13. See also DO(51)25, CAB131/11 for origins of Channel proposals.

61. See DO(51)62 in CAB131/11 and JP(52)10 and JP(52)59 in DEFE6/20 for statements of British position. Minutes of meeting between Admiral Fechteler and the British COS are at COS(52)60th Meeting in DEFE4/53. For final solution, see *Brassey's Annual, 1953,* p. 12. See also Ziegler, *Mountbatten* (London: Collins, 1985), pp. 515–21.

62. For IBERLANT question, see Section 8F of ADM205/102.

63. See commentary on the Ministry of Defence's Paper DP(M)(53)13 by Director of Plans, Paper 6 in ADM205/92.

64. Reference to DP(M)53 6th Meeting. Section G of ADM205/94.

65. RDP/P53(30) in ADM205/93.

66. Both ADM205/93 and ADM205/94 contain defenses of the N113 and the DH110. See the latter for aircraft order question and the former for the Admiralty–Ministry of Defence controversy.

67. Paper 21, ADM205/93. For savings, see Admiralty paper of 19 January 1953, ADM205/93.

68. ADM205/94.

69. Section E of ADM205/94 and Paper 15, ADM205/95.

70. For the attack on Coastal Command, see ADM205/92, 94, and 95.

71. A report of this appears in ADM205/93 as "Enclosure to First Sea Lord's No. 2829 of 22 December 1953."

72. Paper 1, ADM205/96.

73. See papers at 8A, "Long Term Plan for the Navy" in ADM205/102.

74. All quotations from "The Navy of the Future" and covering notes, 8A, ADM205/102.

75. Papers in ADM205/96. For GEN 464, see P. Hennessy, *Cabinet* (Oxford: Basil Blackwell, 1986), pp. 136–37.

76. ADM205/96 and 97. The "Report of the Committee on Defence Policy" is C(54)250 in CAB129/69.

77. "United Kingdom Defence Policy," D(54)43, CAB131/4, paras. 1–13. For the H Bomb decision, see CC(54)47 and 48, CAB128/27.

78. Ibid, paras. 14–24.

79. Paper 1, ADM205/96.

80. CC(54)54th Conclusions, CAB128/27.

81. Biographical information from relevant volumes of *Who's Who.* Nigel Birch is now Lord Rhyl. For rebuttal of Birch, see Section 8C of ADM205/102. For biography of Lord Swinton, see J.A. Cross, *Lord Swinton* (Oxford University Press, 1982).

82. "Defence Policy," C(54)329, para. 8, CAB129/71.

83. C(54)329, ibid., paras. 9–11.

84. Ibid., paras. 12–13.

85. Ibid., paras. 14–16.

86. Ibid., para. 17.

87. For briefing and Newell note, see ADM205/99.

88. C(54)332, "Defence Policy: The Fleet Air Arm," CAB129/71, para. 1. For description of Thomas, see Ziegler, *Mountbatten,* p. 526.

89. Ibid., paras. 2–8.

90. "Defence Policy: Minesweepers," C(54)332, CAB129/71.

91. CC(54) 73rd Conclusions, CAB128/27.

92. Ibid.

93. ADM205/99.

94. Statement on Defence, 1955 (Cmnd. 9391), especially see para. 21. For correspondence mentioning American arrays and "New Look Atlantic" plan, see Sections 8C and 8F of ADM205/102.

95. The Navy Estimates 1955–56, Explanatory Statement (Cmnd. 9396).

96. For the development of mirror landing aid, see P. Beaver, *The British Aircraft Carrier* (Cambridge: P. Stephens, 1984). For details of *Eagle* and *Ark Royal*, see respectively D. Brown, *Carrier Air Group, HMS Eagle* (Windsor: Hylton Lacy, 1972) and M. Apps, *The Four Ark Royals* (London: Kimber, 1971).

97. *Conway's 1945–1982,* Part 1, p. 143 and Ships Covers 694 and 694/1. For debate on modernization, Section 8b in ADM205/102.

98. For the transfer of light fleets to training duties, see ADM1/25074. This file also contains useful information on light fleet modification plans. For fleet carrier fates, see Critchley, *British Warships*, part 1.

99. For squadron details see Sturtivant, *Squadrons*. For aircraft, Hobbs, *Aircraft of the Royal Navy*, and Thetford, *British Naval Aircraft*. For Firefly 7 and Gannet problems, see Simpson, op. cit. For torpedoes, see A. Preston, "From Fancy to Stingray," *Warship*, vol. 5, no. 18. pp. 192–99.

100. Ships Cover 612D.

101. The above cruiser discussion is based on Ships Covers 790, 817, and 839; also see ADM1/25074 and ADM205/90, 91, and 102.

102. ADM1/18620.

103. DO(49)62, CAB131/7, which contains a long DRPC "Review of Guided Weapons Research and Development Policy" (to August 1949). DO(50)96, CAB131/9 covers the acceleration of the program. For the early vicissitudes of the program, see a document in ADM205/69. Missile details are also contained in the "Guided Weapon Ship," Ships Cover 789. For "Terrier," see Memorandum B672 and Board Minute 4410, ADM167/135, and Board Minute 4489, ADM167/136.

104. Ships Cover 789; see also discussion in ADM205/102.

105. Folio 214, ADM116/5632 for end of cruiser/destroyer; ADM1/23473 for failure of the new gun; also Cmnd. 9396 para. 12; *Conway's 1947–82*, part 1, p. 152. For the new fleet escort, see D.K. Brown, *A Century of Naval Construction* (London: Conway, 1983), p. 215; for the building program of the class, see ADM205/96.

106. For the Type 15s and 16s see L. Marriott, *Royal Navy Frigates*, pp. 33–43; J. Lambert, "HMS *Rapid*, a Type 15 Fleet Destroyer Conversion" in *Warship*, vol. 2, no. 6, pp. 120–26, and "HMS *Terpsichore*, A Type 16 Fast Anti-Submarine Frigate of 1953," *Warship*, vol. 2, no. 7, pp. 179–85. For Type 18s, see Ships Cover 810; Type 62s Ships Cover 798. For *C* class, see Ships Cover 805 and Cmnd. 9396, para. 13.

107. For 1953 program, see ADM205/96. For Type 61 plans, see ADM205/89. For programmes executed, see Marriott, op. cit., and Critchley, *British Warships*, part 5. For Indian frigate orders, see *Conway's 1947–82*, part 3, p. 339.

108. ADM205/96; Ships Cover 798; Brown, op. cit., pp. 14–19; Marriott, ibid; and Critchley, ibid.

109. The OMS Ships Cover is 815. For other MCM vessel details, see Worth, *British Warships Since 1945*. For sonar, see Hackmann, *Seek and Strike*, pp. 344 and 489.

110. Cmnd. 9396, para. 28.

111. Ibid., paras. 30–33 and 51–58. ADM1/25074 makes clear the connection between the decommissionings and *Ark Royal's* commissioning. For restoration of term "Fleet Air Arm" and the reasoning behind it, ADM1/24535. For General Service Commissions, see A.C. Hampshire, *The Royal Navy Since 1945* (London: Kimber, 1975), p. 106.

Chapter Four

1. Board Memorandum B424, "The Post War Navy and the Policy Governing its Composition," 17 July 1945. ADM167/124.

2. Contemporary "Pink Lists" Naval Library M.O.D. Also Statement of the First Lord of the Admiralty Explanatory of the Naval Estimates 1949–50, Cmnd. 7632.

3. PRO, Admiralty and Secretariat Papers, ADM1/18683.

4. The following account is based on the Admiralty files on the Yangtse Incident: PRO, Admiralty and Secretariat Cases ADM116/5695, 5696, 5698, 5707, and 5740. See also L. Earl, *Yangtse Incident* (London: Harrap, 1950) and C.E. Lucas Phillips, *Escape of the Amethyst* (London: Heinemann, 1957).

5. For this final correspondence, see Pack 12 in ADM205/72.

6. ADM116/5713 and 5753 conveniently contain the material on the above. See also Pack 12 in ADM205/72.

7. DO(49) 21st Meeting, PRO, Cabinet Defence Committee, CAB131/8.

8. COS(50) 27th, 32nd, 33rd, and 35th Meetings PRO, Chiefs of Staff Committee Minutes DEFE4/29.

9. JP(50)19 is an enclosure to COS(50)35th Meeting, ibid.

10. Wettern, *Decline of British Sea Power,* pp. 48–49.

11. ADM116/5862.

12. Wettern, op. cit., pp. 69 and 83.

13. The account of the Korean War, unless otherwise stated, is based on the Admiralty records of the war. There are to be found in files ADM116/5777–8, 5794–9, 5856–8, and ADM1/23260 and 23537–23999 (not inclusive). Also useful for British operations is M.W. Cagle and F.A. Manson, *The Sea War in Korea* (Annapolis: U.S. Naval Institute, 1957).

14. DO(50) 11th Meeting, CAB131/8.

15. DO(50) 15th Meeting, ibid.

16. COS(50) 24th Meeting, DEFE4/60.

17. A. Short, *The Communist Insurrection in Malaya* (London: Muller, 1975), pp. 371–72; Lucas Phillips, *Escape of Amethyst*, p. 47; Thetford, *British Naval Aircraft*, p. 169, and Wettern, *Decline*, p. 106.

18. COS(52)313, 321, and 442 in PRO, Chiefs of Staff Committee Memoranda DEFE5/40. COS(52) 84th and 87th Meetings DEFE4/54.

19. Sir David Lee, *Eastward: A History of the Royal Air Force in the Far East 1945–72* (London: Her Majesty's Stationery Office, 1984), p. 154; also see Milne, *Flashing Blades*, pp. 20–23.

20. Statement of the First Lord of the Admiralty Explanatory of the Naval Estimates, 1948–49, Cmnd. 7337.

21. Ibid., and Wettern, *Decline*, p. 85.

22. For Cabinet discussion, see CP(51)212 in CAB129/46 and C(51) 51st Conclusions, CAB128/19. See also Wettern, op. cit., pp. 56–57, and Sir David Lee, *Flight from the Middle East* (London: HMSO, 1980), pp. 55–56.

23. The sources for the following account are ADM116/5541, 5543, and 5544; and E. Leggett, *The Corfu Incident* (London: Seeley, 1974).

24. The sources for the following are "War Diaries and Reports of Proceedings of the Mediterranean Fleet," ADM116/5638, and "Illegal Jewish Immigration into Palestine," ADM116/5648.

25. See J. Cable, *Gunboat Diplomacy 1919–79* (2nd ed., London: Macmillan, 1981) for the analytical framework for these comments. For the visit to Saudi Arabia, see ADM116/5638.

26. ADM116/5638. For Power's hostile view of Israelis, see correspondence in ADM205/72.

27. ADM116/5638.

28. Ibid. It is interesting to note that the Foreign Office letter of appreciation for the visit was signed by "J.E. Cable," then a relatively junior F.O. official.

29. ADM205/72.

30. A.D. Nicholl, "The Work of the Navy in the Suez Canal," *Brassey's Annual, 1952.* For evolution of "Rodeo," see PRO, Chiefs of Staff Committee Memoranda and Joint Planning Committee files, DEFE5 and 6, also ADM1/23919.

31. CC8(52), CAB128/24 and Nicholl, op. cit.

32. COS(52) 47th Meeting, DEFE4/53. ADM1/23562.

33. CC72(52), CAB128/25.

34. CC91(52), CAB128/25.

35. ADM1/25058.

36. COS(53)199, DEFE5/45.

37. J.D. Ladd, *The Royal Marines* (London:Jane's, 1980); ADM1/25058.

38. *Brassey's Annual* 1952, p. 114; 1953, pp. 158–59; 1954, pp. 289–92; 1955, pp. 332–33. See also "The Navy Estimates 1955–56 Explanatory Statement" (Cmnd. 9396), para. 93.

39. *Brassey's Annual* 1948, pp. 12 and 21–22.

40. Account based on the Exercise Report at ADM116/5780. For 815 Squadron, see R. Sturtivant, *The Squadrons of the Fleet Air Arm*.

41. *Brassey's Annual* 1952, pp. 107–8; Sturtivant, op. cit., for 1st CAG.

42. *Brassey's Annual* 1951, pp. 34–35; 1952, p. 110.

43. *Brassey's Annual* 1952, pp. 110–11, 113.

44. *Brassey's Annual* 1953, pp. 159–61; Ships Cover 612D for *Vanguard*'s armament problems.

45. For two contrasting accounts for Exercise Mariner, see *Naval Review* vol. 41, pp. 365–73, and *Brassey's Annual*, pp. 285–88. For carrier complements, contemporary "Pink List."

46. Wettern, *Decline*, pp. 10, 16; *Brassey's Annual* 1948, p. 12. Statement of the First Lord of the Admiralty Explanatory of the Naval Estimates, 1948–49 (Cmnd. 7337), p. 12.

47. The *Times*, 2 January 1983; Wettern, op. cit., p. 66; COS(52) 44th Meeting DEFE 4/52; JP(52)25 (terms of Reference), DEFE6/20.

48. The Royal Marines' Report of Proceedings is at ADM1/24866; *Snipe*'s at ADM1/24867.

49. *Bigbury Bay*'s Report of Proceedings is at ADM1/24905. The Dundee Island affair is from COS(53), 142nd Meeting.

50. Wettern, op. cit., p. 84; Statement of the First Lord of the Admiralty Explanatory of the Naval Estimates 1954–55 (Cmnd. 9079); COS(53) 108th, 110th, 112th Meetings, DEFE4/65.

51. Speech given on receiving the Freedom of the City of Edinburgh. *Brassey's Annual* 1954, pp. 29–34.

52. For a remarkably informative account of this first test see *Naval Review*, vol. 41, 1953, pp. 277–83.

Chapter Five

1. Sir Anthony Eden, *Full Circle*, pp. 370–71; Ziegler, *Mountbatten*, p. 525; "The Navy and the Hydrogen Bomb War," PRO First Sea Lord's Records ADM 205/102.

2. J. Terraine, *The Life and Times of Lord Mountbatten* (London: Hutchinson, 1968), pp. 174–75; Ziegler, op. cit., p. 530; J.D. Brown, "Mountbatten as a First Sea Lord," *Journal of the Royal United Services Institute for Defence Studies*, June 1986, p. 64; Hampshire, *The Royal Navy Since 1945*, pp. 137–38; W.J. Crowe, *The Policy Roots of the Royal Navy 1946–63* (Dissertation presented to Princeton University, 1965), p. 152.

3. Statement by the First Lord of the Admiralty Explanatory of the Navy Estimates 1956–57 (Cmnd. 9697), paras. 23–27.

4. Statement on Defence 1956 (Cmnd. 9691), paras. 15, 20–26.

5. Ibid. Annexe II and Cmnd. 9697, Abstract of Navy Estimates.

6. Hampshire, op. cit., pp. 137–39. For Indian orders, see *Conway's 1947–82*, part 2, p. 339.

7. Eden, op. cit., p. 371.

8. Ibid. This is obviously a quotation from an official document.

9. Ibid., pp. 372–74, 424. Ziegler, *Mountbatten*, p. 528, for Mountbatten's "selling" the navy to Eden.

10. "An Appreciation of Our Capabilities and a Review of Our Requirements in Combined Operations," 28 February 1947, COS(47)43 in PRO, Chiefs of Staff Committee Memoranda DEFE5/3; JP(47)71 and discussion thereon at COS(47) 70th Meeting PRO, Chiefs of Staff Committee Minutes DEFE4/4.

11. COS(47) 48th Meeting, DEFE4/5; B. Fergusson, *The Watery Maze* (London: Collins, 1961), especially pp. 384–88.

12. COS(47)43 resubmitted in a revised form as COS(47)129, DEFE5/4.

13. Ibid. and COS(47) 70th Meeting, DEFE4/4.

14. COS(47)157, DEFE5/5.

15. Ibid.

16. Ibid. and B616 in PRO, Board of Admiralty Minutes and Memoranda ADM167/129; DNC General Correspondence, vol. 74, fol. 48, for technical details.

17. COS(47)204, DEFE5/6.

18. B589 and B590 in ADM167/133. For Harwood, see notes 23–28 in chapter 2. For decision to suspend amphibians, see DNC General Correspondence, vol. 78, fols. 36 and 134.

19. COS(50)295, DEFE5/23.

20. JP(52)1, DEFE6/20 discussed at COS(52 45th Meeting, DEFE4/53. Also see COS(52) 67th Meeting DEFE4/54. The abortive LSD's Ships's Cover is 838; it also contains material of the contemporary landing craft plans.

21. For the vehicle position, see COS(52)291, DEFE5/40 and COS(52) 69th Meeting, DEFE4/54. For Thomas's complaints, see COS(53) 21st Meeting, DEFE4/60.

22. COS(53) 124th Meeting. Ladd, *Royal Marines*, pp. 266, 297–98, 375.

23. Fergusson, *Watery Maze*, p. 386; Statement by the First Lord of the Admiralty Explanatory of the Naval Estimates 1956–57 (Cmnd. 9697), para. 30; Ladd, op. cit., pp. 291, 298; D.J. Sutton, ed., *The Story of the Royal Army Service Corps and Royal Corps of Transport* (London: Leo Cooper with Secker & Warburg, 1984), pp. 488–90.

24. D.M.J. Clarke, *Suez Touchdown* (London: P. Davies, 1966), pp. 8–9.

25. Unless otherwise stated, the account of the Suez Operation is drawn from H. Thomas, *The Suez Affair* (London: Penguin, 1970); A. Beaufre, *The Suez Expedition 1956* (London: Faber, 1969); R. Fullick and G. Powell, *Suez: The Double War* (London: H. Hamilton, 1979); K. Love, *Suez: The Twice Fought War* (London: Longmans, 1969); Clarke, op. cit.; Ladd, op. cit.; Ziegler, *Mountbatten*, chap. 41; N. Polmar, *Aircraft Carriers* (London: Macdonald, 1969), pp. 575–81; K. Burns and M. Critchley, *HMS Bulwark 1948–1984* (Liskeard: Maritime Books, 1986); "Operations in Egypt—November to December 1956," Supplement to the *London Gazette* of Tuesday 10 September 1957 (General Keightley's official despatch), published 12 September 1957; and R. Rhodes James, *Anthony Eden* (London: Weidenfeld & Nicolson, 1986), see p. 460 for Cabinet document quoted.

26. Wettern, *Decline*, pp. 128–29; D. Brown, *Carrier Air Groups HMS Eagle*, p. 22.

27. K. Macksey, *The Tanks* (London: Arms & Armour Press, 1979), pp. 123–38 gives an interesting account of this fiasco and the operational activities of British armor at Suez.

28. Ziegler, op. cit., p. 547.

29. The following account of the Sandys Exercise is based on L.W. Martin, "The Market for Strategic Ideas in Britain," *American Political Science Review*, vol. 56, no. 1, March 1962; P. Darby, *British Defence Policy East of Suez* (Oxford University Press, 1973); P. Ziegler, *Mountbatten*, chap. 42; H. Macmillan, *Riding the Storm* (London: Macmillan, 1971); F.A. Johnson, *Defence by Ministry*, chap. 4; C.J. Bartlett, *The Long Retreat* (London: Macmillan, 1972), chap. 5; Crowe, *The Policy Roots*, chap. 5; Darby, op. cit., pp. 107–22.

30. Crowe, *The Policy Roots*, p. 184.

31. Ibid., p. 185.

32. W.P. Snyder, *The Politics of British Defence Policy 1945–62* (Columbus and London: Benn, 1964), p. 164.

33. Martin, op. cit., p. 28.

34. Ziegler, op. cit., p. 549.

35. Quoted in Crowe, op. cit., p. 242.

36. For Mountbatten as a bureaucratic politician, see Ziegler, op. cit., p. 328. The quotation and reference to 50 percent cuts is at p. 551. For Lambe, see O. Warner, *Admiral of the Fleet*, especially p. 176 for his relationship with the first sea lord.

37. Ziegler, op. cit., p. 552.

38. Defence: Outline of Future Policy (Cmnd. 124), paras. 1–7.

39. Ibid., paras. 8–16.

40. Ibid., para. 24.

41. Ibid., paras. 37–39.

42. The Navy Estimates 1957–58, First Sea Lord's Explanatory Statement (Cmnd. 151).

43. Ibid.; D.K. Brown, *A Century of Naval Construction*, pp. 214–18.

44. Plans in Ships Covers, ADM1/25074 and DEFE/671 compared with performance in contemporary *Jane's Fighting Ships, Conway's 1947–1982*, part 1, and M. Critchley, *British Warships Since 1945*, part 1.

45. Cmnd. 151, para. 23; J.D. Brown, "Mountbatten as a First Sea Lord," p. 66.

46. Cmnd. 151, para. 27; Brown, ibid., p. 66; Contemporary *Jane's* and *Conway's 1947–82,* part 1; Wettern, *Decline*, p. 143.

47. Cmnd. 151, paras. 39 and 65–73.

48. Ibid., paras. 15–17; Simpson, op. cit. vol. 3; Crowe, *The Policy Roots*, pp. 205–6; Allward, *Buccaneer*, pp. 12–13.

49. Crowe, op. cit., p. 205; Milne, *Flashing Blades*, pp. 24–25, 34–35; D. Hobbs, *Aircraft of Royal Navy*, pp. 98–99.

50. Ziegler, *Mountbatten*, p. 551.

51. Darby, *British Defence Policy*, pp. 114–15.

52. Ziegler, op. cit., p. 552.

53. Crowe, op cit., pp. 191–92; Martin, "Market for Strategic Ideas," pp. 31–33; Snyder, Politics of British Defence Policy, pp. 168–69; Ziegler, op. cit., pp. 551–52.

54. Crowe, op. cit., pp. 197–99; Ziegler, op. cit., p. 553.

55. Ibid., pp. 199–202; Ziegler, ibid.

56. Ibid., p. 202; Ladd, *Royal Marines*, p. 375; Hampshire, *Royal Navy Since 1945*, p. 172.

57. Wettern, *Decline*, p. 155; Explanatory Statement on the Naval Estimates 1959–60 (Cmnd. 674), paras. 26–29; Burns and Critchley, *HMS Bulwark*, pp. 26–27.

58. Crowe, op. cit., pp. 204–5; J. Simpson, *The Independent Nuclear State* (London: Macmillan, 1983), p. 153; Ziegler, op. cit., p. 553 and footnote 26; Allward, op. cit., chap. 2 for NA39/Buccaneer development.

59. Letter quoted in Ziegler, ibid., p. 554.

60. Report on Defence (Cmnd. 363), para. 44.

61. Navy Estimates 1958–59, First Lord's Statement (Cmnd. 371), paras. 14–17.

62. Ibid., paras. 42–57.

63. Cmnd. 371 and 674, Abstracts of the Navy Estimates. Also "Progress of the Five Year Defence Plan" (Cmnd. 662).

64. Quoted in Crowe, *Policy Roots*, p. 209. For Lambe's being chosen as first sea lord, see Ziegler, *Mountbatten*, pp. 564–65.

65. First sea lord's newsletter quoted in Ziegler, op. cit., p. 554. For the Coastal Command question, ibid., p. 589.

66. See note 11, chap. 1.

67. J.D. Brown, "Mountbatten as First Sea Lord," p. 65; the change occurred in Defence Council Instruction 651/68.

68. Hampshire, *The Royal Navy Since 1945*, pp. 107–11.

Chapter Six

1. For place of submarine service in the postwar navy, see *The Naval War Manual 1948* BR1806, Naval Historical Library. For subsequent changes of title, see Navy Lists.

2. "A Balanced Post War Fleet," ADM205/53.

3. For ASW priority, see Admiralty letter M/TASW 289/47 of 8 January 1951 in PRO Admiralty and Secretariat Papers, ADM1/25252. The other quotations are from papers in ADM205/83.

4. "Pink Lists" for submarine strength. Also "Composition of the Post War Navy," Memo B435, PRO, Board of Admiralty Minutes and Memoranda, ADM167/124 and "British Post War Submarine Potential," ADM1/19301.

5. Contemporary "Pink Lists"; "Future Defence Policy Naval Peacetime Requirements," Memo B250, ADM167/129; "Shape and Size of the Armed Forces," DO(48)3, CAB131/6; "Revised Restricted Fleet," Memo B590, ADM167/133.

6. "Pink Lists" and "British Submarine War Plan," ADM1/24783.

7. General submarine characteristics from *Conway's All the World's Fighting Ships 1947–82,* part 1, pp. 137–38; Contemporary *Jane's Fighting Ships*; M. Critchley *British Warships*

Since 1945, part 2; N. Friedman, *Submarine Design and Development* (London: Conway, 1986), p. 58 for *S* class conversions; Board Minute 4046, ADM167/124; Board Minute 4109 and Memo B474, ADM167/127 for building plans.

8. Ship's Cover 778 "*T* Class Conversions," DNC General Correspondence, vol. 73, fol. 113, and vol. 74, fol. 68.

9. Ibid.; Board Memos B589 and B590, ADM167/133.

10. SDPC(49)20 in ADM116/5632; Ship's Cover 728/A "Experimental Submarines"; Board Memo B604, ADM167/133; Board Minute 4312, ADM167/132. See also DNC General Correspondence, vol. 73, fol. 113.

11. Board Memo B620, ADM167/135; *Conway's 1947–82*, part 1, p. 168.

12. ADM 1/25252. For sonar details, see W. Hackmann, *Seek and Strike*, pp. 289, 430, and 435.

13. ADM1/25252.

14. Ibid.

15. Ship's Cover 787, "*T* Class Conversions"; *Conway's*, p. 168; Critchley, *British Warships*, pp. 34–35.

16. Ship's Cover 787; *Conway's*, p. 169. For picture of *Tradewind*, see *Jane's Fighting Ships* 1950–51, p. 47.

17. For BQR-3 references, see ADM1/25252. For sonar details Hackman, op. cit., pp. 352–53 and 437. For photographic evidence, see *Jane*'s and Critchley op. cit.

18. Hackmann, ibid., the quotation is from p. 343. See also N. Friedman, *Submarine Design*, p. 152.

19. Hackmann, ibid., pp. 314–15, and ADM1/25252.

20. Hackmann, ibid., p. 343; A. Preston, "From Fancy to Stingray," *Warship*, vol. 5, pp. 193–99.

21. Preston, ibid., p. 195.

22. Board Memorandum B665 and Minute 4398, ADM167/135; *Conway's*, p. 170; Hackmann, op. cit., pp. 352–53, 439–40; Friedman, op. cit., pp. 61–62.

23. *Conway's* and Hackmann, ibid.

24. *Conway's*, pp. 137–38; Critchley, op. cit.; Contemporary "Pink Lists."

25. Critchley, op. cit., pp. 66–67; *Conway's*, p. 168. For nuclear role, see ADM205/102 8A "Long Term Plan for the Navy."

26. Conway's, p. 771; Friedman, op. cit., pp. 61–63.

27. Crowe, *Policy Roots*, pp. 253–54.

28. Ibid., pp. 255–56. For quotations, see Plans Division Paper ADM205/102, Section 8A.

29. See Crowe, op. cit., p. 256; Simpson, *The Independent Nuclear State*, pp. 116–23. For Mountbatten's role and quotations, see Ziegler, *Mountbatten*, p. 558. For U.S. fears of attack, see Section 8C of ADM205/102.

30. Ziegler, ibid.; D.K. Brown, *Century of Naval Construction*, pp. 233–34.

31. Simpson, op. cit., p. 122; also Ziegler, ibid.

32. Brown, op. cit., p. 232; Crowe, op. cit., pp. 258–59.

33. Ziegler, op. cit., p. 558 (for quotation); Crowe, op. cit., pp. 260–62; Simpson, op. cit., pp. 122–23.

34. D.K. Brown, op. cit., p. 234; Crowe, *Policy Roots*, p. 263.

35. D.K. Brown, op. cit., pp. 232–35; *Conway's*, pp. 132 and 170–71; Friedman, *Submarine Design*, pp. 83–85.

36. Ziegler, *Mountbatten*, p. 359; D.K. Brown, op. cit. p. 235.

37. Brown, ibid., p. 238, *Conway's*, p. 171.

38. See "Long Term Plans for the Navy" in ADM205/102. Also Crowe, *Policy Roots*, pp. 274–76; G.M. Dillon, *Dependence and Deterrence* (Aldershot: Gower, 1983).

39. Quoted in Sir Ian McGeoch, "The British Polaris Project" in *Perspectives upon British Defence Policy 1945–70*, papers on a conference held at the University of Southampton, April 1974, pp. 127–28.

40. Ziegler, op. cit., pp. 560–61.

41. Crowe, op. cit., pp. 268–69; for the Avro 730 and Blue Steel, see D. Wood, *Project Cancelled* (London: Macdonald and Jane's, 1975), chap. 8.

42. For the evolution of the independent nuclear doctrine, see A.J. Pierre, *Nuclear*

Politics (Oxford University Press, 1972), and A.J.R. Groom from "The British Deterrent" in J. Baylis, ed., *British Defence Policy in a Changing World* (London: Croom Helm, 1977). For British bomb development see J. Simpson, *The Independent Nuclear State* (London: Macmillan, 1983); for Mountbatten and the October 1958 COS Meeting, see Ziegler, *Mountbatten*, p. 561.

43. Crowe, op. cit., pp. 270–82.

44. H. Macmillan, *Pointing the Way* (London: Macmillan, 1973), pp. 251–52.

45. Crowe, *Policy Roots*, pp. 280–81; McGeoch, op. cit., pp. 132–33.

46. Macmillan, op. cit., pp. 253–55; J. Baylis, *Anglo-American Defence Relations 1939–54* (London: Macmillan, 1973), pp. 98–101.

47. Quoted Ziegler, op. cit., p. 594.

48. Ibid. and Watkinson in the House of Commons, quoted Crowe, op. cit., p. 283.

49. J. Simpson, "The Polaris Executive: A Case Study of a Unified Hierarchy," *Public Administration*, vol. 48, p. 383.

50. Brown, *Century of Naval Construction*, p. 239.

51. Crowe, *Policy Roots*, p. 284.

52. Ibid., pp 284–85.

53. Ibid., pp. 286–87.

54. H. Macmillan, *At the End of the Day* (London: Macmillan, 1973), pp. 343 and 355; Baylis, *Anglo-American Defence Relations,* pp. 102–3.

55. Macmillan, ibid., pp. 356–57.

56. Ibid., pp. 357–60. I.J. Galantin, Jr., "The Resolution of Polaris," U.S. Naval Institute *Proceedings*, April 1985, p. 81.

57. Macmillan, op. cit., p. 363.

58. Simpson, "The Polaris Executive," pp. 383–84.

59. Brown, op. cit., p. 239; Simpson, ibid., pp. 384–87; Dillon, *Dependence and Deterrence*, chap. 3.

60. Crowe, op. cit., p. 288.

61. McGeoch, "British Polaris Project," p. 139.

62. Galantin, op. cit., pp. 83–84; Dillon, op. cit., pp. 33–35; Macmillan, *At the End of the Day*, p. 363.

63. Galantin, op. cit., p. 84 for quotation; Dillon, op. cit., pp. 35–40; Simpson, "The Polaris Executive," pp. 387–89; the Agreement is reprinted in Baylis, *Anglo American Defence Relations*, pp. 126–36.

64. Ziegler, *Mountbatten*, p. 595.

65. Simpson, "The Polaris Executive," pp. 385–86; D.K. Brown, *Century of Naval Construction*, p. 240.

66. Dillon, op. cit., p. 35. See also Brown, ibid.

67. Daniel quoted in Brown, ibid., p. 239.

68. Dillon, op. cit., chap. 5, gives a full description of the shipbuilding problems and building dates. See Pierre, *Nuclear Politics*, chap. 10, for a discussion of the Wilson Government's attitude towards Polaris.

69. Announced in Parliament and quoted in Wettern, *Decline*, p. 320; and McGeoch, "British Polaris Project," p. 143.

70. Wettern, ibid., p. 293.

71. Statement on the Defence Estimates 1965 (Cmnd. 2592), Annexe D, and Statement on the Defence Estimates 1975 (Cmnd. 5796).

72. See *Conway's 1947–82*, part 1, p. 171, for building dates.

73. For an indication of contemporary submarine deployment, see map of fleet dispositions in *The Naval Review*, vol. 49 (1961), opposite p. 124. The formation of the new squadron is noted in the Statement on the Navy Estimates 1960–61 (Cmnd. 949) para. 9.

Chapter Seven

1. For the best study of the whole "East of Suez" question, see P. Darby, *British Defence Policy*.

2. Darby, ibid., pp. 143–45.

3. Darby, ibid., p. 147; D. Hawkes, *The Defence of Malaysia and Singapore* (London: R.U.S.I., 1972), chap. 2.

4. Darby, ibid., p. 154.

5. Sir David Lee, *Flight from the Middle East*, p. 167; N. Brown, *Strategic Mobility* (London: Chatto & Windus, 1963), pp. 91–93.

6. Darby, op. cit., pp. 197–98; Lee, op. cit., p. 171.

7. The account of Kuwait is based on N. Brown, op. cit., pp. 88–96; Darby, op. cit., pp. 244–49; Wettern, *Decline*, pp. 194–95; Ladd, *Royal Marines*, pp. 303–5; Lee, op. cit., chap. 9; Burns and Critchley, *HMS Bulwark*, pp. 38–39; C.N. Barclay, "Britain's Strategic Reserve and Sea-Borne Task Forces in Action," *Brassey's Annual 1962; Naval Review*, vol. 49, pp. 398–400, and vol. 50, pp. 39–42. For British political background, see H. Macmillan, *Pointing the Way*, pp. 382–87.

8. Darby, ibid., 218.

9. Ibid.

10. Statement on Defence 1962: The Next Five Years (Cmnd. 1639), para. 3.

11. Ibid., para. 9.

12. Ibid., paras. 26 and 24.

13. Explanatory Statement on the Navy Estimates 1962–63, Cmnd. 1629. For the *Leander* see L. Marriott, *Royal Navy Frigates 1945–83* (Shepperton: Ian Allan, 1983); C.J. Meyer, *Leander Class* (Weybridge: Ian Allan, 1986); N. Brown, op. cit., pp. 206–7; M.K. Purvis, "Post War RN Frigate and Guided Missile Destroyer Design, 1944–69," *Naval Architect*, October 1974. For Type 19, see D.K. Brown, *Century of Naval Construction*, p. 230. See Ladd, *Royal Marines*, for Commando improvements.

14. See for example the reference in contemporary "World in Action" TV program, "£60 a second," the transcript of which is in D. Crow, *World in Action 63* (Manchester and London: Arrow Books, 1966), pp. 54–71. (The program was so critical the Independent Television Authority forbade its showing!)

15. W.J. Crowe, *Policy Roots*, p. 232.

16. *Conway's 1947–82*, part 1, p. 174.

17. Cmnd. 1629, para. 2 (next came a brief account of Kuwait).

18. Ibid., pp. 14–15.

19. Ibid., paras. 6, 33, and 68–72.

20. *Conway's 1947–82*, part 1, pp. 80–81 and 133–34, and part 2, p. 395.

21. For interesting 20,000-ton carrier designs of 1954, see ADM1/25149; in November of that year it was stated that the "smallest worthwhile carrier" was now considered to be 30,000 tons. See also Ships Cover 789. For late 1950s policy, see Crowe, op. cit., p. 218.

22. Ibid., p. 219; Ziegler, op. cit., pp. 586–88.

23. Ziegler, *Mountbatten*, p. 580.

24. Ibid., p. 219–21; Wood, *Project Cancelled* (London: Macdonald & Jane's, 1975), pp. 190–97.

25. Ibid., pp. 221–22, 224; Darby, *British Defence Policy*, pp. 261–66 for a full account of the "island plan."

26. Cmnd. 1629, para. 5.

27. Crowe, op. cit., p. 222; Darby, op. cit., pp. 266–67.

28. Cmnd. 1639, para. 33.

29. Wood, op. cit., pp. 214–18.

30. Darby, op. cit., p. 267.

31. Crowe, op. cit., pp. 225–26.

32. Ibid., pp. 227–28.

33. Ibid., pp. 228–29.

34. Ibid., pp. 229–31; Wood, op. cit., pp. 218–24; interview with Sir Frank Hopkins, August, 1985.

35. Ziegler, *Mountbatten*, pp. 608–9.

36. Ziegler, ibid., pp. 584–85.

37. F.A. Johnson, *Defence by Ministry*, pp. 102–8; Ziegler, ibid., pp. 609–12.

38. Johnson, ibid., pp. 109–16; Ziegler, ibid., pp. 614–19.

39. Johnson, ibid., pp. 118–19; M. Howard, *The Central Organisation of Defence* (London: R.U.S.I., 1970), pp. 18–19; Ziegler, pp. 619–20.

40. Johnson, ibid., p. 120; Howard, ibid., pp. 16–19; *Naval Review* vol. 52, p. 321.

41. Ziegler, op. cit., pp. 582–84; pp. 620–22.

42. *Naval Review*, vol. 50, pp. 453–54.

43. Ladd, *Royal Marines*, p. 307; J.L. Moulton, "A Brush-Fire Operation—Brunei, December 1962," *Brassey's Annual 1963*, chap. 10; Wettern, *Decline*, p. 208; H. James and D. Shiel Small, *The Undeclared War* (London: Leo Cooper, 1971), part 1; Sir David Lee, *Eastward*, chap. 16.

44. Wettern, op. cit., pp. 229–30; Ladd, op. cit., pp. 313–14; N. Polmar, *Aircraft Carriers*, pp. 640–43.

45. Sir Frank Cooper, "Economic Constraints on Britain's Defence Planning" in G. Till, ed., *The Future of British Sea Power* (London: Macmillan, 1986), chap. 6a.

46. Darby, *British Defence Policy*, pp. 249–50.

47. Cmnd. 1629, p. 17.

48. Wettern, op. cit., pp. 203–4.

49. Statement on Defence 1984, Cmnd. 2270, paras. 62 and 66 and Annexe A.

50. C. Mayhew, *Britain's Role Tomorrow* (London: Hutchinson, 1967), p. 137.

51. Statement on the Defence Estimates 1966, part 1, the *Defence Review*, Cmnd. 2901, paras. 7 and 8.

52. The account of "Confrontation" is based on J.A.C. Mackie, *Kronfrontasi: The Indonesia-Malaya Dispute 1963–66* (Oxford University Press, 1974); James and Shiel Small, op. cit., part 2; Darby, op. cit.; Wettern, op cit.; Ladd, op. cit.; Sir David Lee, *Eastward*, chap. 17; Burns and Critchley, *HMS Bulwark 1948–1984*, pp. 47–52.

53. Quoted in Darby, op. cit., p. 284.

54. Ibid., p. 285; Chin Kin Wah, *The Defence of Malaysia and Singapore* (Cambridge University Press, 1983), p. 127; Barbara Castle, *The Castle Diaries 1964–70* (London: Weidenfeld & Nicolson, 1980), p. xiv for the Wilson-Johnson relationship.

55. H. Wilson, *The Labour Government 1964–70* (London: M. Joseph, 1971), p. 42; also see Darby, op. cit., pp. 286–87.

56. Mayhew, op. cit., p. 132. Also interview with Lord Mayhew, July 1985.

57. Ibid.

58. Castle, op. cit., p. 5.

59. The National Plan (Cmnd. 2764), p. 182, para. 3.

60. Ibid., para. 2.

61. Statement on the Defence Estimates 1965 (Cmnd. 2592), para. 190.

62. Wood, *Project Cancelled*, pp. 224 and 231; Wettern, *Decline*, p. 249.

63. Cmnd. 2592, para. 29.

64. For the best account of TSR2, see G. Williams, F. Gregory and J. Simpson, *Crisis in Procurement: A Case Study of the TSR2* (London: R.U.S.I., 1969). For Mayhew and the Chief of the Air Staff, interview with Lord Mayhew. For Cabinet discussion, see R. Crossman, *The Diaries of a Cabinet Minister, Volume 1* (London: Hamish Hamilton, 1975), pp. 190–91, and Wilson, op. cit., pp. 89–90. Wilson gives the date wrongly as March 31st, perhaps sensitive to the day's implications! For the trade-off between the carrier and aircraft plans, see W.S. Johnson, "Defence Budgetary Constraints and the Fate of the Carrier in the Royal Navy," *Naval War College Review*, June 1973, pp. 16–18. See also Darby, *British Defence Policy*, pp. 299–300.

65. Johnson, *Defence by Ministry*, p. 21; Mayhew, interview.

66. Darby, op. cit., p. 300.

67. Johnson, op. cit., p. 21.

68. Mayhew, *Britain's Role Tomorrow*, pp. 139–40.

69. This paragraph and the rest of the carrier controversy account is based on the previously cited accounts of Mayhew, Johnson, and Darby; also the interviews with Lord Mayhew and Sir Frank Hopkins.

70. Mayhew, op. cit., p. 142.

71. Castle, op. cit., p. 107.

72. *Conway's 1947–82*, part 1, p. 239.

73. D.K. Brown, op. cit., p. 239.

74. Ibid., p. 240.

75. Statement on the Defence Estimates 1966, part 1, The Defence Review (Cmnd. 2901), chap. 2, para. 19.

76. Ibid., chap. 3, para. 4.

77. Ibid., para. 7.

78. Chin, op. cit., pp. 128–30.

79. Ladd, op. cit., pp. 315 and 327.

80. Chin, op. cit., p. 28 for promises to Australians as reported by Prime Minister Harold Holt.

Chapter Eight

1. Wettern, *Decline*, p. 276. Also, Naval Historical Branch archives.

2. Ibid. Also, interview with Rear Admiral Adams, July 1985.

3. Ibid.; the magazine *Navy* published useful material on the Working Party in their December 1966 issue, p. 414, and the January 1967 issue, p. 23.

4. Adams interview.

5. For a good account of the economic problems of this period, see M. Stewart, *The Jekyll and Hyde Years: Politics and Economic Policy Since 1964* (London: Dent, 1977); chaps. 3 and 4 cover this paragraph.

6. Crossman, *Diaries*, pp. 567–68; Castle, *Castle Diaries*, pp. 142–45; for alternative views of the effects of defense expenditure on the sterling problem, see S. Strange, *Sterling and British Policy* (Oxford University Press for the Royal Institute for International Affairs, 1971), and D. Greenwood, *The Economics of the East of Suez Decision*, (Aberdeen, Studies in Defence Economics No. 2, 1973); for the balance of payments problem, see R.N. Cooper, "The Balance of Payments" in R.E. Caves, ed., *Britain's Economic Prospects* (Washington, D.C.: Brookings Inst., 1968); for two enlightening articles on the changing shape of British trade and its effect on the sterling problem, see C.R. Conan, "Sterling: the Problems of Diagnoses" and "Sterling: the Problem of Policy" in *Westminster Bank Review*, August and November, 1967.

7. Chin, *Defence of Malaysia*, pp. 130–32; Crossman, op. cit., pp. 539–41; Castle, op. cit., p. 143; P. Gordon Walker, *The Cabinet* (Heinemann Educational, 1972), pp. 140–41; Greenwood, op. cit., p. 10.

8. Crossman, op. cit., pp. 577–78; Castle, op. cit., p. 150; Wilson, *Labour Government*, Greenwood, op. cit., p. 10.

9. Greenwood, ibid.

10. Chin, op. cit., p. 134; Wilson, op. cit., p. 297; Crossman, *Diaries*, vol. 2, pp. 81–88.

11. Crossman, ibid., pp. 155–56.

12. Castle, *Castle Diaries*, p. 215; Statement on the Defence Estimates 1967 (Cmnd. 3203), quotations from para. 26.

13. Ibid., paras. 15–24; Purvis, "Post War RN Frigate," p. 194; *Conway's 1947–82*, part 1, p. 155.

14. Cmnd. 3203, paras. 25–30; Purvis, op. cit., p. 193; *Conway's 1947–82*, p. 154; Marriott, *Royal Navy Frigates*, p. 56.

15. Cmnd. 3203, paras. 14–15.

16. Crossman, op. cit., vol. 2, pp. 215–16.

17. House of Commons Debates, 11 March 1965, columns 656–57.

18. For the above account, see Chin, op. cit., p. 59; Castle, op. cit., pp. 240–41; Crossman, op. cit., vol. 2, p. 308; Gordon Walker, *The Cabinet*, pp. 142–43; Wilson, *Labour Government*, pp. 376–78.

19. Castle, op. cit., pp. 257–58; Crossman, op. cit., vol. 2, p. 356; see also the "imaginary" Cabinet meeting in Gordon Walker, op. cit.; in this the Defence Secretary is quoted as saying ". . . since we cannot bring effective force to bear we should not try to."

20. For the *Hermes*'s refit and activities, T. Dyson, *HMS Hermes 1959–84* (Liskeard: Maritime Books, 1984), pp. 49–50.

21. For naval movements see Wettern, *Decline*, pp. 291–92 and *Navy*, July 1967, p. 244.

22. Castle, op. cit., pp. 259–60; Crossman, op. cit., vol. 2, pp. 356–58.

23. Gordon Walker, op. cit., pp. 143–44; Castle, op. cit., pp. 259–60 and 273–74; Crossman, op. cit., vol. 2, p. 435.

24. Supplementary Statement on Defence Policy, 1967 (Cmnd. 3357).

25. Ibid., chap. 4, para. 2.

26. Milne, *Flashing Blades*, pp. 65–66.

27. Cmnd. 3357, chap. 5, paras. 1–3.

28. For background to devaluation, see Stewart, *Jekyll and Hyde Years*, pp. 81–83; also, Wilson, op. cit., especially pp. 447–56.

29. Wilson, ibid., pp. 454–61; Crossman, *Diaries*, pp. 575–77.

30. M. Apps, *Send Her Victorious* (London: Kimber, 1976), pp. 238–45.

31. Darby, *British Defence Policy*, p. 322.

32. Wilson, op. cit., p. 479.

33. Ibid.

34. Ibid., p. 483; Darby, op. cit., pp. 323–24.

35. For quotations, see Castle, *Castle Diaries*, pp. 348–50; for discussion, also see Crossman, op. cit., vol. 2, pp. 634–35, 646–48.

36. Castle, ibid., pp. 356–57 (quotation); Crossman, ibid., pp. 650–53; Darby, op. cit., p. 325.

37. Statement on the Defence Estimates (Cmnd. 3540), chap. 1, para. 8.

38. Wettern, op. cit., p. 301.

39. Ibid., pp. 308–9; D. Wettern, "On NATO's Northern Flank," *Navy*, July 1968; Supplementary Statement on Defence Policy 1968 (Cmnd. 3701), para. 22; Ladd, *Royal Marines*, p. 375; Burns and Critchley, *HMS Bulwark*, p. 61.

40. Wettern, op. cit., p. 312.

41. Ibid., p. 279; Hampshire, *Royal Navy Since 1945*, pp. 247–48; P. Elliott, *The Cross and the Ensign* (Cambridge: Patrick Stephens, 1980), p. 186.

42. Wettern, op. cit., pp. 336–38; Statement on the Defence Estimates 1969 (Cmnd. 3927); D. Wettern, "On NATO's Northern Flank," *Navy*, July 1968, pp. 248–49.

43. For the account of Aden, see Wettern, *Decline*, pp. 256, 284, 295–96; Ladd, *Royal Marines*, pp. 316–25; Lee, *Flight from the Middle East*, chaps. 11–13; J. Paget, *Last Post: Aden 1964–67* (London: Faber and Faber, 1969).

44. The quotation is from Paget, ibid., p. 246; Dyson, *HMS Hermes*, pp. 49 and 58 for the fly past. For final withdrawal, see *Navy*, January 1968, p. 30; Burns and Critchley, op. cit., p. 60; and *Navy News*, February 1968, p. 10.

45. For Beira Patrol, see Wettern, ibid., pp. 262–63, 284–85, 319.

46. Wilson, *Labour Government*, pp. 307–21, 567–70.

47. Wettern, op. cit., pp. 291, 296, 325; Cmnd. 3540, chap. 2, para. 13; Cmnd. 3927, chap. 2, para. 13.

48. Wettern, op. cit., p. 279; Cmnd. 3203, chap. 2, para. 49.

49. *Navy*, May 1964, p. 157, and April, 1967, p. 118; Wettern, op. cit., p. 295; *Naval Review*, vol. 52; *Navy News*, February 1968, p. 14; J. Worth, *British Warships*, pp. 2, 81, 105, 116, 118–19.

50. Wettern, op. cit., p. 198, 241, 254, 278, 293.

51. *Naval Review*, vol. 50, p. 331; Hampshire, op. cit., pp. 140, 230.

52. Wilson, op. cit., pp. 625–26; Wettern, op. cit., pp. 279 and 329.

53. Hampshire, op. cit., p. 247.

54. Crossman, *Diaries*, vol. 2, pp. 597, 635; Wilson, op. cit., pp. 470–76.

55. Wilson, op. cit., p. 480.

56. House of Commons Debates 11 March 1968, column 1008. This was in the context of a most interesting debate in which the Opposition's defense spokesman, Enoch Powell, mounted a most perceptive and penetrating exposé of the recent strategic changes.

57. *The Economist*, 15 June 1968.

58. House of Commons Debates, 11 March 1968, col. 1009.

59. For the earlier "recall of the legions," see P. Kennedy, *Rise and Fall*, chap. 8.

60. J. Marriott, "Exercise Bersatu Padu—Long Range Reinforcement on Trial," *International Defense Review*, September, 1970, pp. 286–90.

61. M. Stewart, *Jekyll and Hyde Years*, chap. 4.

62. Statement on the Defence Estimates, 1970 (Cmnd. 4290).

63. Supplementary Statement on Defence Policy 1970 (Cmnd. 4521), para. 1.

64. Ibid., para. 12. For the political background for ANZUK, see Chin, *Defence of Malaysia*, chap. 9.

65. Cmnd. 4521, para. 15.

66. "Singapore Without the Royal Navy," *Navy*, October 1971. For Gulf policy, see Lee, *Flight from the Middle East*, pp. 279–80. See also *Navy News*, May 1971, pp. 20–21, November 1971, pp. 20–21, and December 1971, pp. 18 and 31.

67. L. Phillips, "HMS Warrior, the Flagship in Upper Suburbia," *Navy International*, January 1972; Statement on the Defence Estimates 1972 (Cmnd. 4891).

68. L. Phillips, op. cit., p. 5.

69. Hampshire, *Royal Navy Since 1945*, pp. 248–49; *Navy News*, April 1968, p. 1, and May 1969, p. 10.

70. Naval Historical Branch notes.

71. See table in *Navy International*, February 1972, p. 3.

Chapter Nine

1. M. Apps, *The Four Ark Royals*, pp. 221–39.

2. *Conway's 1947–82*, part 1, pp. 143, 146.

3. Cmnd. 4891, Annexe C.

4. D.K. Brown, *Century of Naval Construction*, p. 254.

5. For submarine commissioning dates, see *Conway's 1947–82*, part 1, pp. 171–73.

6. *Conway's 1947–82*, part 1, pp. 154–55.

7. Ibid., pp. 152–54; Wettern, *Decline*, p. 304.

8. Statement on the Defence Estimates 1973, Cmnd. 5231, Annexe D.

9. Ibid.

10. Marriott, *Royal Navy Frigates*, pp. 75–80; C.J. Meyer, *Leander Class*; Wettern, *Decline*, pp. 296–97, 334.

11. Marriott, op. cit., pp. 79–82. Meyer, op. cit.

12. Marriott, op. cit., pp. 94–96.

13. Cmnd. 3357, chap. 2, para. 4.

14. Marriott, op. cit., p. 97; "The Type 21 *Amazon* Class Frigate," *Navy International*, December 1971.

15. Ibid.

16. *Conway's 1947–82*, part 1, p. 166.

17. Ibid.

18. D.K. Brown, op. cit., p. 246; D. Wood and R.B. Pengelley, "Britain's Type 42 Destroyer," *International Defense Review*, no. 6, December 1971, pp. 571–76. L. Marriott, *Type 42* (Shepperton: Ian Allan, 1985), gives an interesting and useful, if slightly "rose-tinted" description of the class.

19. *Conway's 1947–82*, part 1, p. 156.

20. A. Preston, "The Sheffield Class—Origin, Evolution and Characteristics," *Navy International*, March 1975, p. 12.

21. For development of the "TDCC" concept, see D.K. Brown, *Century of Naval Construction*, pp. 254–57, 333; D. Wood, "The Through Deck Cruiser Concept," *International Defense Review*, vol. 6, no. 6, 1973, and R.B. Pengelley, "The Royal Navy's *Invincible* Class Cruisers," *International Defense Review*, no. 8, 1979.

22. R. Baker, *Dry Ginger* (London: W.H. Allen, 1977), pp. 224–25.

23. House of Commons Debates, 10 March 1969, cols. 993–94.

24. Baker, op. cit., p. 225.

25. House of Commons Debates, 9 March 1970, col. 921.

26. F.K. Mason, *Harrier* (Cambridge: Patrick Stephens, 1981), pp. 122–24; B. Gunston, "Sea Harrier, History and Prospect," *Navy International*, February 1976.

27. Wood, "The Through Deck Cruiser Concept" for RAF opposition to the TDCC; Wettern, *Decline*, p. 375 for the O'Brien rumor; also see Wettern, "High Wood, An Exercise to Test RAF Cover for the RN," *Navy International,* January 1972.

28. Mason, op. cit., pp. 129–31; Gunston, op. cit., and *Harrier* (Shepperton: Ian Allan, 1984), p. 86.

29. M. Stewart, *Jeckyll and Hyde Years*, chap. 5, pp. 138–50 for economic background; Cmnd. 4891, chap. 1, para. 10; D. Greenwood, "Defence and National Priorities Since 1945" in J. Baylis, ed., *British Defence Policy in a Changing World*, p. 191.

30. Stewart, ibid., pp. 150–73; Wood, op. cit., p. 749, *Navy International*, May 1973, pp. 3, 7.

31. Wood, op. cit., p. 747; Pengelley, op. cit., p. 1335.

32. Stewart, op. cit., pp. 173–87; Gunston, "Sea Harrier, History and Prospect," p. 17; *Navy International*, January 1974, p. 11.

33. A. Sked and C. Cook, *Post War Britain, a Political History* (London: Harvester P., 1979), pp. 327–30, 338–340.

34. Statement on the Defence Estimates 1975, Cmnd. 5976, para. 1.

35. Stewart, op. cit., pp. 202–3.

36. Cmnd. 5976. For an exposition of the "positive" side of the 1974 Review, see D. Greenwood, "Sights Lowered: The United Kingdom's Defence Effort 1975–84," *RAF Quarterly*, autumn 1975.

37. For Mason's frank comments on the Review, see "Setting British Defence Priorities," *Survival*, September/October 1975, a transcript of a lecture to the International Institute for Strategic Studies. For some impression of the dynamics of Cabinet decisions, see Joel Barnett, *Inside the Treasury* (London: Deutsch, 1982), and B. Castle, *The Castle Diaries 1974–76*, pp. 206 and 227.

38. Cmnd. 5976, especially paras. 33–44.

39. Ibid., especially paras. 26–32.

40. For "Swift Move," see D. Wettern, "The Royal Navy Tries the CVS Concept," *Navy International*, November 1973.

41. Cmnd. 5976, para. 27a.

42. Ibid., para. 45.

43. Ibid., para. 46.

44. See appendix.

45. For delays, see *Daily Telegraph*, 4 December 1975 and *Conway's 1947–83*, part 1, for completion dates.

46. *Daily Telegraph*, 23 January 1976.

47. D.K. Brown, *Century of Naval Construction*, pp. 260–61; *Conway's 1947–83*, part 1, p. 181; R.B. Pengelley, "The Royal Navy's New Mine Countermeasures Vessel," *International Defense Review*, no. 1, 1979.

48. R.B. Pengelley, "The Royal Navy's Type 22 Frigate," *International Defense Review*, no. 1, 1980.

49. Ibid.; for description of Sea Wolf and its trials, see "Sea Wolf/GW25, The Royal Navy's Anti-Missile Missile System," *International Defense Review*, no. 5, 1976.

50. Cmnd. 5976, para. 10a.

51. Gunston, "Sea Harrier," *Navy International*, February 1976, pp. 17–18; Wood, The Royal Navy's Invincible Class Carriers, *International Defense Review*, no. 8, 1979, p. 1340.

52. Castle, op. cit., 1974–76, pp. 324 and 333.

53. Barnett, *Inside the Treasury*, pp. 62–66.

54. Ibid., pp. 64–66; Castle, op. cit., 1974–76, pp. 351–54 and p. 360; Greenwood in Baylis, ed., *British Defence Policy*, p. 191.

55. Castle, *Castle Diaries 1974–76*, pp. 581, 596–97, 601.

56. Public Expenditure to 1979–80 (Cmnd. 6393), part 1, para. 17, and part 2.1, para. 3. Also *Castle Diaries 1974–76*, pp. 602 and 625.

57. Barnett, op. cit., p. 87.

58. Ibid., pp. 89–96.

59. Ibid., pp. 97–111.

60. Wettern, op. cit., pp. 5 and 149; contemporary "Pink Lists" for late 1940s.

61. Wettern, op. cit., pp. 157–58, 168–69; contemporary *Jane's* for details of Icelandic ships; J. R. Hill, "The Rules of Engagement," *Navy International*, April 1975.

62. Hill, ibid.; Wettern, op. cit., pp. 193–234.

63. Hill, ibid.; *Conway's 1947–83*, vol. 1, pp. 177–78.

64. For an Icelandic view of these events, see J. Jønsson, *Friends in Conflict: The Anglo Icelandic Cod Wars and the Law of the Sea* (London: Hamden, 1982), pp. 109–53. See also *Keesings Contemporary Archives*, 1973, 26028 and 26237.

65. I. McGeoch, "Inshore–Offshore," *Navy International*, March 1977; contemporary *Jane's*, and *Combat Fleets of the World*.

66. Jønsson, op. cit., pp. 155–83; D. Wettern, "Cod War," *Navy International*, July 1976.

67. Jønsson, ibid.

68. *Navy International*, February 1977, pp. 6–7; contemporary *Jane's* and *Combat Fleets of the World*.

69. *Conway's 1947–82*, part 1, pp. 175–76; contemporary *Jane's*.

70. Statement on the Defence Estimates, 1978 (Cmnd. 7099), table 5.

71. Contemporary *Jane's*; Wettern, op. cit., pp. 13, 25.

72. See "The Hydrographer and the Navy," *Naval Review*, vol. 46, p. 208; Wettern, ibid., p. 111, for duties at this time.

73. "The Report of the Hydrographer of the Navy for 1957," *Naval Review*, vol. 46, pp. 419–28. See contemporary *Jane's* for ship development.

74. Contemporary *Jane's*.

75. Ibid.; J.E. Moore, "Surveying in the Balance," *Navy International*, October 1975. Also comment in *Navy International*, December 1975, p. 26.

76. Cmnd. 5976, chap. 3, para. 57.

77. News release 58/75 of 10 June 1975 (in IISS Newspaper Files).

78. Cmnd. 6432, chap. 2, para. 45.

79. D. Wettern, "Task Group East of Suez," *Navy International*, June 1978.

80. Admiral Sir Terence Lewin, "A Very Good Run for Your Money," *Navy International*, August 1978, p. 9.

81. Quotations from Cmnd. 6432, chap. 2, para. 58, and Cmnd. 7474, para. 242.

82. For Suez clearing operations, D. Wettern, "Clearing the Canal," *Navy International*, October 1974; "Operation Rheostat—Suez Canal 1974," *Ships Monthly*, November 1974; *Navy News*, July 1975, p. 11; for Cyprus, see Dyson, *HMS Hermes*, pp. 86–87, *Navy News*, August and September, 1974, and J. Cable, *Gunboat Diplomacy*, pp. 26–27.

83. P. Elliott, *The Cross and the Ensign*, pp. 186–200.

84. Statement on the Defence Estimates 1977 (Cmnd. 6735), para. 301, and Statement on the Defence Estimates 1979 (Cmnd. 7474), para. 301.

85. Figures from relevant Statements on Defence Estimates. Also see Wettern, *The Decline of British Sea Power*, p. 304.

86. Baker, *Dry Ginger*, p. 217.

87. Baker, op. cit., chap. 18 for Le Fanu's time as first sea lord. Hampshire, *The Royal Navy*, p. 106.

88. Cmnd. 4521, paras. 33 and 36.

89. Contemporary Statements on Defence Estimates.

90. Statement on the Defence Estimates, 1979 (Cmnd. 7474), para. 401.

91. Ibid., para. 403.

92. Cmnd. 7099, Annexe D, Table 1.

93. Especially David Greenwood. See for example the paper written by him and J. Drake, "The United Kingdom's Defence Programme and Budget," Aberdeen Studies in Defence Economics No. 17 (Aberdeen, 1980).

Chapter Ten

1. *Navy International*, June 1979, p. 53; Defence in the 1980s: Statement on the Defence Estimates 1980, vol. 1 (Cmnd. 7826-I), para. 332; K. Speed, *Sea Change* (Bath: Ashgrove, 1982), pp. 78–79.

2. D. Greenwood, "NATO's Three Per Cent Solution," *Survival*, November/December 1981, pp. 245–46; Command 7826-II, table 2.2.

3. D. Leigh, "A Ministry All at Sea," *The Observer*, 3 March 1985.

4. D.K. Brown, *Century of Naval Construction*, pp. 268–69; the Type 24 was exhibited at the RN Equipment Exhibition at Greenwich in 1979. See *International Defense Review* 9/1979, pp. 1560–61; Speed, op. cit., pp. 89–90.

5. Brown, ibid., p. 268; Speed, op. cit., p. 90.

6. Statement on the Defence Estimates 1981, vol. 1 (Cmnd. 8212), paras. 807–9; Leigh, op. cit.

7. Greenwood, op. cit., p. 255.

8. Speed, op. cit., p. 99. Also see Leigh, op. cit.

9. Ibid.

10. The United Kingdom Defence Programme: The Way Forward (Cmnd. 8288), para. 4.

11. Ibid, para. 6.

12. Remarks in the program "MOD," BBC2, 9 April 1986.

13. See Leigh, op. cit. for an interesting account of these proceedings.

14. See Speed's account in *Sea Change*, chap. 7. For the identification of the service staffs and their civil servants, see M. Hobkirk, "The Heseltine Re-organisation of Defence: Kill or Cure?" *Journal of the R.U.S.I.*, March 1985, p. 47.

15. D. Greenwood, *Reshaping Britain's Defences* (Aberdeen Studies in Defence Economics, No. 19, 1981), pp. 17, 21; Speed, op. cit., pp. 101–2.

16. P. Hennessy, *The Cabinet*, pp. 148–50; P. Malone, *The British Deterrent* (London: Croom Helm, 1984), pp. 67–68; Dillon, *Dependence and Deterrence*, pp. 108–11, 116–18; Simpson, *The Independent Nuclear State*, pp. 171–75. See also *Financial Times*, 6 February 1973 and *Le Monde*, 7/8 February 1973.

17. For 1974 decision, BBC TV program, "Panorama," 21 July 1980, and Hennessy, ibid., pp. 150–51; Castle, *The Castle Diaries 1974–76*, pp. 227–28 for Cabinet discussions. See Simpson, op. cit., p. 176, for final quotation.

18. Dillon, op. cit., p. 114; *Jane's Defence Review*, vol. 2, no. 23, pp. 1068–69. For Moscow targeting and the fullest description of Chevaline, J. Barry, "*Our Bomb: The Secret Story*," Channel 4 television, April 1986.

19. Barry, ibid.; Hennessy, op. cit., p. 154.

20. House of Commons: Fourth Report from the Defence Committee, Strategic Nuclear Weapons Policy, pp. 228 and xxxviii; Barry, ibid.; Hennessy, ibid., pp. 154–56.

21. Speed, *Sea Change*, pp. 162–64.

22. Speed, ibid., p. 102.

23. Ibid.

24. For the first sea lord's attitude, see Sir Henry Leach, "Britain's Maritime Forces: The Future," lecture to the Royal United Services Institute, 9 June 1982, printed in the Institute's *Journal*, September 1982, p. 13.

25. Command 8288, para. 16.

26. Speed, op. cit., p. 103.

27. J. Winton, *Convoy* (London: M. Joseph, 1983), p. 349; D. Wettern, "Defended Lanes v Convoys," *Navy International*, December 1981; for the earlier sign of an anti-convoy "offensive task force" decline, see H. Stanhope, "Royal Navy Planners to Look to Fresh Horizons," the *Times*, September 1974; quoted also in J. Cable, *Britain's Naval Future* (London: Macmillan, 1983), p. 129.

28. See R. Mason, "Problems of Fleet Balance" in G. Till, ed., *The Future of British Sea Power* (London: Macmillan, 1984).

29. Greenwood, *Reshaping Britain's Defences*, pp. 41–42.

30. Speed, *Sea Change*, pp. 92–93.

31. Command 8288, para. 29.

32. Ibid., para. 29; also see House of Commons Debates 8 July 1981, columns 280–81 for a defense of the new modernization policy. For a well-informed reference to the reduced frigate options, see Admiral Sir James Eberle, "Britain's Naval Programme," *Naval Forces*, no. 6, 1984, p. 39.

33. House of Commons Debates, 19 May 1981, col. 165.

34. Ibid.

35. Command 8288, paras. 32 and 34.

36. Command 8212-I, paras. 412–13; *Navy International*, December 1980, p. 771.

37. Command 8288, para. 34.

38. Ibid., para. 26; Speed, op. cit., p. 113; for reports of *Dreadnought*'s damage and refit plans, see *Navy International*, December 1980, p. 773, and October, 1981, p. 602. See Statement on the Defence Estimates 1984 (Command 9227-i), para. 434, and *Jane's Defence Review*, 29 September 1984, for *T*-class program.

39. "New Diesel Submarine for Royal Navy," in *Navy International*, July 1983; "The Vickers Type 2400 Diesel Electric Submarine" in *International Defense Review* 8/1983; A. Preston, "Progress on the Type 2400," *Jane's Defence Review*, 14 April 1984; the most authoritative account is P. Wrobel, "Design of the Type 2400 Patrol Class Submarine," a paper presented to the Royal Institute of Naval Architects in April 1984 and published in the *Naval Architect*, January 1985.

40. J.R. Hill, *The Royal Navy Today and Tomorrow* (Shepperton: Ian Allan, 1981), p. 36 and *Navy News*, March, 1980, pp. 1 and 19.

41. E.R. Hooton, "The British Torpedo: on Track at Last?" *Military Technology*, vol. 9, no. 7, and House of Commons Twenty-Eighth Report from the Committee of Public Accounts, Session 1984–85, "The Torpedo Programme," HC391.

42. See contemporary *Jane's* and answers to parliamentary questions in House of Commons debates for the evolving disposal plans. Also *Ships Monthly*, January 1982 and June 1982.

43. *Combat Fleets of the World* 1984–85 (Annapolis: Naval Institute Press, 1984), pp. 256, 271–78.

44. Statement on the Defence Estimates 1982 (Command 8259-I), para. 237.

45. E.R. Hooton, "The United Kingdom's Trident Programme," *Military Technology*, vol. 10, no. 1, 1986; *Jane's Defence Review*, 25 February 1984, p. 268.

46. Command 8529-I, para. 114.

47. Hooton, op. cit., pp. 21–22.

48. Command 8529-I, para. 125.

49. The Falkland Islands Review: Report of a Committee of Privy Councillors (Command 8787), paras. 114–18.

50. Ibid., paras. 146–48; M. Hastings and S. Jenkins, *The Battle for the Falklands* (London: M. Joseph, 1983), pp. 53–54.

51. See the *Times* for 15 January 1983 for an account by the then Foreign Office junior minister Ted Rowlands. This has been supplemented and corrected with the help of interviews with Dr. David Owen.

52. Quoted by Rowlands, ibid.

53. Command 8787, paras. 152–53.

54. Ibid., paras. 161–94. R. Perkins, *Operation Paraquat* (Chippenham: Picton, 1986), pp. 48–52.

55. Hastings and Jenkins, op. cit., p. 59.

56. Ibid., pp. 59–60.

57. Command 8787, para. 204.

58. Ibid., paras. 205 and 213; Hastings and Jenkins, op. cit., p. 61.

59. Hastings and Jenkins, ibid., p. 62.

60. Ibid., pp. 62–63.

61. Ibid., p. 67.

62. Ibid., p. 68.

63. Ibid., p. 71; also Command 8787, paras. 239–51.

64. The account of the Falklands War, unless otherwise stated, is based on the following sources: "Despatch by Admiral Sir John Fieldhouse GCB, GBE, Commander of the Task Force Operations in the South Atlantic April to June 1982," Supplement to the *London Gazette*, 13 December 1982; A.R. Burden, M.I. Draper, D.A. Rough, C.R. Smith, and D.L. Witton, *Falklands—The Air War* (Twickenham: British Aviation Research Group, 1986), a monumental reference work whose extremely well-researched and detailed infor-

mation has usually been preferred to that in other sources; M. Middlebrook, *Operation Corporate* (London: Viking, 1985); House of Commons, Third Report from the Foreign Affairs Committee Session 1984–85, "Events Surrounding the Weekend of 12 May 1982"; Hastings and Jenkins, *Battle for the Falklands*; J. Ethell and A. Price, *Air War South Atlantic*; R. Perkins, *Operation Paraquat*; The Falklands Campaign: The Lessons (Command 8758); R. Scheina, "The Malvinas Campaign," U.S. Naval Institute *Proceedings*, May 1983, and "Where Were Those Argentine Subs?" ibid. March 1984; J.R. Briasco and S.M. Huertas, *Falklands: Witness of Battles* (Valencia: Federico Domenech, 1985); G. Underwood, ed., *Our Falklands War* (Liskeard: Maritime Press, 1983); Cdr. M.R. Morgan, RN, *Antrim's War* (privately published, 1983); Lt. Cdr. J.L. Muxworthy, RN, *Canberra, The Great White Whale Goes to War* (privately published, 1982); D. Rice and A. Gavshon, *The Sinking of the Belgrano* (London: Secker and Warburg, 1984); H. Tinker, *A Message from the Falklands* (London: Penguin, 1982); H. McManners, *Falklands Commando* (London: Kimber, 1984); J. Thompson, *No Picnic* (London: Secker and Warburg, 1985); M. Arthur, ed., *Above All, Courage* (London: Sidgwick and Jackson, 1985); R. Villar, *Merchant Ships at War, The Falklands Experience* (London: Conway Maritime Press, 1984); J. Godden, ed., *Harrier, Ski Jump to Victory* (London: Brassey's, 1983); P. Way, ed., *The Falklands War* (London: Marshall Cavendish, 1982). See also 1982–83 issues of *Globe and Laurel*; special unclassified Falklands issue of *Flight Deck*, the FAA house journal; Vice Admiral Sir Ted Horlick, "Naval Engineering Achievements in the Liberation of the Falklands," *Proceedings of the Institution of Mechanical Engineers*, vol. 1980, no. 11; also E. Briffa and G. Williams, *In the Wake of HMS Sheffield*, BBC2, broadcast twice in 1986.

65. Ethell and Price, *Air War South Atlantic*.

66. Ethell and Price, ibid.; Scheina, USNIP articles; extracts from O.R. Cardoso, *La Trama Secreta*, quoted as Appendix 11 in House of Commons Foreign Affairs Committee Report; *The New Statesman*, 24 August 1984; Rice and Gavshon, op. cit., p. 77.

67. Rice and Gavshon, ibid.; House of Commons Foreign Affairs Committee Report; A. Gavshon, "*The First Strike Philosophy that Sank the Belgrano*," *The Guardian*, 28 January 1985; the *Times*, 15 February 1985; the *New Statesman*, 31 August 1984; C. Ponting, *The Right to Know: The Inside Story of the Belgrano Affair* (London: Sphere, 1985), pp. 85–99; for signals to and from the *Conqueror*, see House of Commons Foreign Affairs Committee Report, pp. 183–84.

68. For important new information on Woodward and *Conqueror*, see the *Guardian*, 11 June 1985. For Lewin quote, see Gavshon in the *Guardian*, 28 January 1985.

69. Hastings and Jenkins, *Battle for the Falklands*, p. 156.

70. For an account of this sensitive operation, see "Operation Eavesdrop," *The Daily Express*, 14 March 1983.

71. Rear Admiral J. Woodward, "Command at Sea" in M. Arthur, ed., *Above All, Courage* (London: Sidgwick and Jackson, 1985), p. 327.

72. Command 8758, paras. 210, 211, and 220.

73. Ibid., paras. 225–32.

74. Ibid., para. 302.

75. Ibid., para. 306 (for quotation); for aircraft question, see *Daily Telegraph*, 24 May 1985.

76. *Combat Fleets 1986/87* (Annapolis: Naval Institute Press, 1986); *Warship World*, vol. 1, no. 1, 1984.

77. *Ships Monthly*, August 1981; Command 8212-I, Annexe C, and Command 8529-I, Annexe C.

78. Command 8758, para. 331.

79. *Ships Monthly*, February 1983; see also strength of the fleet figures in Statements on the Defence Estimates 1983, 1984, and 1985.

80. Command 9430-I, para. 408; for earlier reference, see Command 7826-I, para. 221; for details of stockpile and Falklands, see D. Campbell, "Too Few Bombs to Go Round," *New Statesman*, 29 November 1985.

81. "RFA *Reliant* and the Arapaho concept" and "First Report—RFA *Argus*," *Warship World*, vol. 1, no. 7, summer 1986.

82. *Jane's* and *Combat Fleets*.

83. Speed, *Sea Change*, pp. 111–12; *Jane's Defence Weekly*, 24 November 1984, pp. 946–47.

84. *International Defense Review* 11/83, p. 1609, and 11/85 p. 1810; *Jane's Defence Weekly*, 20 October 1984, p. 681, and 22 June 1985, p. 1195.

85. *Jane's Defence Review*, 6 October 1984, p. 563, and 19 July 1986, p. 43; Command 9430-I, paras. 204 and 430; *Daily Telegraph*, 9 January 1986.

86. For Fieldhouse interview, see "Interview with the British First Sea Lord," *Navy International*, July 1985. For Stanford, see "The Current Position of the Royal Navy" in G. Till, ed., *The Future of British Sea Power* (London: Macmillan, 1984).

87. For the chiefs of staff study, see the *Times*, 16 August 1983; Statement on the Defence Estimates 1984, Command 9227-I, p. 29, and para. 403.

88. E.J. Grove, "After the Falklands," U.S. Naval Institute *Proceedings*, March 1986; *Navy News*, February 1983, p. 9.

89. Command 9227-I, para. 436.

90. M. Linklater and D. Leigh, *Not With Honour* (London: Sphere, 1986), chap. 2; *The Observer*, 28 August 1983; D. Greenwood, "Managing the Defence Programme and Budget," *Three Banks Review*, June 1984; Command 9227-I, para. 203; Command 9430-I, paras. 501–3; Third Report from the House of Commons Defence Committee, Session 1984–85, "Defence Commitments and Resources and the Defence Estimates, 1985–86."

91. For the two alternative views, see, on the one hand, D. Greenwood, ibid., and "Economic Constraints and Political Options" in J. Baylis, ed., *Alternative Approaches to British Defence Policy*; and on the other J. Small, A. Thompson, and G. Kennedy, *Is There a Defence Spending Crisis?* Defence Finance Report No. 1 (Edinburgh: Heriot Watt University, 1984); for Stanley reference, see the *Times*, 28 February 1984.

92. The Type 23 frigate was described in *Navy International*, June 1984, and *Military Technology*, vol. 9, issue 9, 1985; for the most authoritative source on Type 23 development and a useful guide to contemporary procurement in general, see Vice Admiral Sir Lindsay Bryson, "The Procurement of a Warship," a lecture to the Royal Institution of Naval Architects, June 1984, in *The Naval Architect*, January 1985. For the AOR, see *Jane's Defence Weekly*, 3 May 1986, p. 785, and the *Times*, 4 April 1986.

93. *Ships Monthly*, September and November 1984.

94. Ibid., September 1984. For HMS *Challenger*, see *Jane's Defence Weekly*, 17 November 1984, and *Warship World*, vol. 1, no. 1.

95. Command 9227-I, paras. 220–21.

96. M. Hobkirk, "The Heseltine Re-organisation of Defence"; see also Command 8529-I, paras. 507–9.

97. Command 9227-I, para. 211.

98. Hobkirk, op. cit., pp. 46–47; The Central Organisation for Defence (Command 9315); the *Times*, 9 and 19 July 1984.

99. Hobkirk, op. cit., p. 49.

100. For Trident cost, Statement on the Defence Estimates 1986 (Command 9763-I), para. 406. For *Vanguard* order, *Navy International*, June 1986, p. 382, and *Jane's Defence Review*, 10 May 1986, p. 823.

101. Statement on the Defence Estimates 1985, Command 9430-I, para. 503.

102. House of Commons, Third Report from the Defence Committee, Session 1984–85, "Defence Commitments and Resources and the Defence Estimates 1985–86."

103. Rodney Cowton, "The Royal Navy's Uncertain Future—I", the *Times*, 23 March 1985.

104. See note 103; also Command 9430-I, para. 435; the *Times*, 27 December 1984; the *Daily Telegraph*, 3 May 1984, described the three frigate tenders as "a considerable surprise within the Ministry of Defence."

105. D. Wettern in the *Daily Telegraph*, 27 January and 15 February 1986, and in *Navy International*, "Maritime Defence: Still Dwindling Assets," July 1986. Also other reports in the *Daily Telegraph* by P. Pryke, 2 July 1986 and P. Webster, 10 July 1986; *Navy News*, August 1986, p. 1; *Warship World*, summer 1986, p. 19.

106. R. Cowton, "The Royal Navy's Uncertain Future—II," the *Times*, 26 March 1985; see also D. Wettern, the *Daily Telegraph*, 1 February 1986.

107. D. Wettern in the *Daily Telegraph*, 9 April and 3 May 1985, and 2 January and 1 February 1986.

108. Command 9763-I, para. 118. For the Westland affair, see Linklater and Leigh, *Not With Honour* (London: Sphere, 1986). For the lost documents, see *The Mail on Sunday*, 14 September 1986 and the *Sunday Times*, 21 September 1986. For Younger's defense of his budget, see *Jane's Defence Review*, 8 November 1986, p. 1075, and 15 November 1986, p. 1145.

109. Ibid., para. 503.

110. For the burden of "out of area" on NATO commitments, see Cowton, The *Times*, 23 March 1985. For deployments, see *Navy News* for the relevant dates; for well-argued alternative views to the author's on "out of area," see J. Cable, *Britain's Naval Future* (London: Macmillan, 1983), and J. R. Hill, *British Sea Power in the 1980s* (Shepperton: Ian Allan, 1985), and *Maritime Strategy for Medium Powers* (London: Croom Helm, 1986).

111. The *Daily Telegraph* and the *Times*, 30 and 31 August 1985; for the U.S. Navy's "Maritime Strategy," see the brochure published with U.S. Naval Institute *Proceedings* in January 1986; see also Grove, "After the Falklands" for the Royal Navy's long-term problems in continuing to play a part in strike fleet strategy.

112. Wettern, "Maritime Defence," *Navy International,* July 1986, p. 441.

113. A.D. Couper, "The Shipping Industry," in G. Till, ed., *The Future of British Sea Power* (London: Macmillan, 1984).

114. See, for example, the *Sunday Times*, 1 September 1985.

BIBLIOGRAPHY

Primary Sources

The main sources for the first four chapters were the Admiralty (ADM), Cabinet (CAB), and Defence (DEFE) records held at the Public Record Office at Kew in London. The main classes of records consulted were:

ADM1	Admiralty & Secretariat Papers
ADM 116	Admiralty & Secretariat Cases
ADM 167	Board of Admiralty Minutes and Memoranda
ADM 205	First Sea Lord's Records
CAB 69	Cabinet Defence Committee (Operations) (to 12/46)
CAB 79	Chiefs of Staff Committee Minutes (to 12/46)
CAB 80	Chiefs of Staff Committee Memoranda (to 12/46)
CAB 84	Joint Planning Committee (to 12/46)
CAB 128	Cabinet Minutes
CAB 129	Cabinet Memoranda
CAB 130	Cabinet Committees
CAB 131	Cabinet Defence Committee
DEFE 4	Chiefs of Staff Committee Minutes (from 1/47)
DEFE 5	Chiefs of Staff Committee Memoranda (from 1/47)
DEFE 6	Joint Planning Committee (from 1/47)
DEFE 7	Register Files: General Series
DEFE 8	Chiefs of Staff: Committees and Sub Committees
DEFE 10	Major Committees: Minutes and Papers

Also of great use were the records of the Director of Naval Construction kept at the National Maritime Museum, Greenwich. These are largely composed of "Ships Covers," both for individual classes of ships and certain categories of vessel, e.g. "Cruisers (General)." The DNC General Correspondence files held at the National Maritime Museum with the Covers also proved of considerable value.

The Naval Historical Branch Library of the Ministry of Defence at Empress State Building in London were most helpful in providing access to now unclassified "Pink Lists," the contemporary records of the disposition of the fleet, biographical material on naval officers, and notes on the evolution of the Naval Staff, including the first postwar issue of "The Naval War Manual."

Certain records at Churchill College, Cambridge, were also consulted, notably the papers of Lord Alexander of Hillsborough and those of Sir Frederick Brundrett.

In addition to the above documents, official publications were also of great importance. Notable among these were:

The Annual "Statement" on the Naval Estimates (to 1963)
The Annual "Statement" on the Defence Estimates and Supplementary Statements on Defence issued in certain years
Parliamentary Debates (Hansard)
Reports of the House of Commons Select Committees on Defence and Foreign Affairs

Other official publications are cited (with command numbers where relevant) in footnotes.

Unpublished Dissertations

No work on the postwar Royal Navy can ignore Admiral W.J. Crowe's doctoral dissertation "*The Policy Roots of the Royal Navy 1945–63*" presented to Princeton University in 1965. Also of great value was Dr. John Simpson's monumental three volume "*Understanding Weapon Acquisition Processes: A Study of Naval Anti-Submarine Aircraft Procurement in Britain 1945–55*" presented to the University of Southampton in 1976.

Secondary Sources

Memoirs and Diaries
No naval memoirs by leading participants in postwar policy-making process have been published. The following memoirs and diaries, however, were of value.

Castle, B. *The Castle Diaries 1974–76*. London: Weidenfeld and Nicolson, 1980.
———. *The Castle Diaries 1964–70*. London: Weidenfeld and Nicolson, 1984.
Crossman, R. *The Diaries of a Cabinet Minister*. 3 vols. London: Hamish Hamilton 1975–77.
Dalton, H. *High Tide and After*. London: Muller, 1962.
Eden, R.A. *Full Circle*. London: Cassell, 1960.
Macmillan, H. (Lord Stockton). *Riding the Storm*. London: Macmillan 1971.
———. *Pointing the Way*. London: Macmillan 1973.
———. *At the End of the Day*. London: Macmillan 1973.
Montgomery, B.L. *Memoirs*. London: Collins, 1958.
Moran, Lord. *Winston Churchill: The Struggle for Survival*. London: Constable, 1966.
Shinwell, E. *Lead with the Left*. London: Cassell, 1981.
Wilson, H. *The Labour Government 1964–70*. London: M. Joseph, 1971.

Biographies

The following biographies contained useful material.

Baker, R. *Dry Ginger*. London: W.H. Allen, 1977.
Bullock, A. *The Life and Times of Ernest Bevin, vol. 3, Foreign Secretary*. London: Heinemann, 1983.
Cross, J.A. *Lord Swinton*. Oxford University Press, 1982.
Foot, M. *Aneurin Bevan Vol 2*. London: Davis Poynter, 1973.
Harris, K. *Attlee*. London: 1982.
Humble, R. *Fraser of North Cape*. London: Routledge and Keegan Paul, 1983.
Nicolson, N. *Alex: The Life and Times of Field Marshal Lord Alexander of Tunis*. London: Weidenfeld & Nicolson, 1973.
Pimlott, B. *Hugh Dalton*. London, 1985.
Rhodes, James R. *Anthony Eden*. London: Weidenfeld & Nicolson, 1986.
Terraine, J. *The Life and Times of Lord Mountbatten*. London: Hutchinson, 1968.
Williams, P. *High Gaitskell, Political Biography*. London: Cape, 1979.
Ziegler, P. *Mountbatten*. London: Collins, 1985.

Books and Monographs

Allward, M. *Buccaneer*. Shepperton: Ian Allan, 1981.

Apps, M. *The Four Ark Royals*. London: Kimber, 1971.

———. *Send Her Victorious*. London: Kimber, 1976.

Arthur, M. *Above All Courage: The Falklands Front Line: First Hand Accounts*. London: Sidgwick & Jackson, 1985.

Barnett, J. *Inside the Treasury*. London: Deutsch, 1982.

Bartlett, C.J. *The Long Retreat*. London: Macmillan, 1972.

Baylis, J. *British Defence Policy in a Changing World*. London: Croom Helm, 1977.

———. *Alternative Approaches to British Defence Policy*. London: Macmillan, 1983.

———. *Anglo-American Defence Relations 1939–84*. 2nd ed. London: Macmillan, 1984.

Beaufre, A. *The Suez Expedition 1956*. London: Faber, 1969.

Beaver, P. *The Modern Royal Navy*. Cambridge: P. Stephens, 1982.

———. *The British Aircraft Carrier*. Cambridge: P. Stephens, 1984.

———. *Fleet Command: British Armed Forces Today, 2*. Shepperton: Ian Allan, 1984.

———. *Invincible Class*, Shepperton: Ian Allan, 1984.

Birtles, P. *DeHavilland Vampire, Venom and Sea Vixen*. Weybridge: Ian Allan, 1986.

Briasco, J.R., & S.M. Huertas. *Falklands, Witness of Battles*. Valencia: Federico Domenech, 1985.

Brown, D. *Carrier Air Group, HMS Eagle*. Cambridge, 1972.

Brown, D.K. *A Century of Naval Construction*. London, 1983.

Brown, N. *Strategic Mobility*. London: Chatto & Windus, 1963.

Burns, K., and M. Critchley. *HMS Bulwark 1948–1984*. Liskeard: Maritime Books, 1986.

Cable, J. *Gunboat Diplomacy*. London: Macmillan, 1981.

———. *Britain's Naval Future*. 2nd ed., London: Macmillan, 1983.

Cagle, M.W., & F.A. Manson. *The Sea War in Korea*. Annapolis, U.S. Naval Institute, 1957.

Carew. *The Lower Deck of the Royal Navy 1900–39*. Manchester, 1981.

Caves, R.E. *Britain's Economic Prospects*. Washington, D.C.: Brookings Inst. 1968.

Chesneau, R. *Aircraft Carriers of the World, 1914 to the Present*. Annapolis, Md.: Naval Institute Press, 1984.

Chin, Kin Wah. *The Defence of Malaysia and Singapore: The Transformation of a Security System*. Cambridge University Press, 1983.

Clark, D.M.J. *Suez Touchdown*. London: P. Davies, 1964.

Critchley, M. *British Warships Since 1945*. Part 1, *Battleships, Carriers, Monitors and Cruisers*. Part 2, *Submarines, Depot and Repair Ships*. Part 3, *Destroyers*. Part 5, *Frigates*. Liskeard: Maritime Books, 1981–84.

Darby, P. *British Defence Policy East of Suez*. Oxford University Press, 1973.

Dillon, G.M. *Dependence and Deterrence*. Aldershot: Gower, 1983.

Dow, J.C.R. *The Management of the British Economy*. Oxford University Press, 1964.

Dyson, T. *HMS Hermes: A Pictorial History*. Liskeard: Maritime Books, 1984.

Earl, L. *Yangtse Incident*, London: Harrap, 1980.

Elliot, P. *The Cross and the Ensign*. Cambridge; Patrick Stephens, 1980.

Ethell, J., & A. Price. *Air War South Atlantic*. London: Sidgwick & Jackson, 1983.

Fergusson, B. *The Watery Maze*. London: Collins, 1961.

Fiddler, B. *Sea Vixen*. Yeovilton, 1985.

Foot, M. *Aneurin Bevan, Vol. 2*. London: Davis-Poynter, 1973.

Friedman, N. *Modern Warship Design and Development*, Greenwich: Conway, 1979.

———. *Carrier Air Power*. Greenwich: Conway, 1981.

———. *U. S. Naval Weapons*. London: Conway, 1983.

———. *Submarine Design and Development*. London: Conway, 1984.

Fullick, R., & G. Powell. *Suez: The Double War*. London: H. Hamilton, 1979.

Godden, J. *Harrier: Ski Jump to Victory*. London: Brasseys, 1983.

Gordon Walker, P. *The Cabinet*. London: Heinemann Educ., 1972.

Greenwood, D. *The Economics of the East of Suez Decision*. Aberdeen Studies in Defence Economics. No. 2, 1973.

Greenwood, D., and J. Drake. *The United Kingdom's Defence Programme and Budget*. Aberdeen Studies in Defence Economics. No. 17, 1980.

Greenwood, D. *Reshaping Britain's Defences*. Aberdeen Studies in Defence Economics. No. 19, 1981.

Gunston. *Harrier*. Shepperton: Ian Allan, 1984.

Hackmann. *Seek and Strike: Sonar, Anti-submarine Warfare and the Royal Navy 1914–54*. London: H.M. Stationery Office, 1984.

Hampshire, A.C. *The Royal Navy Since 1945*. London: Kimber, 1975.

Hastings, M., & S. Jenkins. *The Battle for the Falklands*. London: Michael Joseph, 1983.

Hawkes, D. *The Defence of Malaysia and Singapore*. London R.U.S.I., 1972.

Hennessy, P. *Cabinet*. Oxford: Basil Blackwell, 1986.

Hennessy, P. & Arends. *Mr Attlee's Engine Room*. Glasgow: University of Strathclyde, 1983.

Hill, J.R. *The Royal Navy Today and Tomorrow*. Shepperton: Ian Allan, 1981.

———. *British Sea Power in the 1980s*. Shepperton: Ian Allan, 1985.

Hobbs, D. *Aircraft of the Royal Navy Since 1945*. Liskeard: Maritime Press, 1983.

Howard, M. *The Central Organisation of Defence*. London, R.U.S.I., 1970.

Hubbard, K., & S. Simmons. *Operation Grapple: Testing Britain's First H-Bomb*. Weybridge: Ian Allan, 1985.

James, H., & D. Shiel Small. *The Undeclared War*. London: Leo Cooper, 1971.

Johnson, F.A. *Defence by Ministry*. London: Duckworth, 1980.

Jønsson, J. *Friends in Conflict: the Anglo-Icelandic Cod Wars and the Law of the Sea*. London: Hamden, 1982.

Kennedy, P. *The Rise and Fall of British Naval Mastery*. London: A. Lane, 1976.

Ladd, J.D. *The Royal Marines*. London: Jane's, 1980.

Lee, Sir David. *Flight from the Middle East*. London: Her Majesty's Stationery Office, 1980.

———. *Eastward: A History of the Royal Air Force in the Far East*. London: Her Majesty's Stationery Office, 1984.

Leggett, E. *The Corfu Incident*. London: Seeley, 1974.

Linklater, M., and D. Leigh. *Not With Honour*. London: Sphere, 1986.

Longstaff, R. *The Fleet Air Arm*. London: Hale, 1981.

Love, K. *Suez, The Twice Fought War*. London: Longmans, 1969.

Mackie, J.A.C. *Kronfrontas: the Indonesia-Malaya Dispute 1963–66*. Oxford University Press, 1974.

Macksey, K. *The Tanks*. London: Arms and Armour Press, 1979.

Malone, P. *The British Deterrent*. London: Croom Helm, 1984.

Marriott, L. *Royal Navy Frigates 1945–1983*. Shepperton: Ian Allan, 1983.

———. *Type 42*. Shepperton: Ian Allan, 1985.

Mason, F.K. *Harrier*. Cambridge: Patrick Stephens, 1981.

Mayhew, C.P. *Britain's Role Tomorrow*. London: Hutchison, 1967.

Meyer, C.J. *Leander Class*. Shepperton: Ian Allan, 1984.

Milne, J.M. *Flashing Blades over the Sea*. Liskeard: Maritime Books, 1980.

McManners, H. *Falklands Commando*. London: Kimber, 1984.

Muxworthy, J.L. *Canberra, the Great White Whale Goes to War*. (Privately published, 1982.)

Morgan, M.R. *Antrim's War*. (Privately published, 1983.)

Paget, J. *Last Post Aden 1964–67*. London: Faber and Faber, 1969.

Perkins, R. *Operation Paraquat*. Chippenham: Picton, 1986.

Phillips, C.E.L. *Escape of the Amethyst*. London: Heinemann, 1957.

Pierre, A.J. *Nuclear Politics*. Oxford University Press, 1972.

Polmar, N. *Aircraft Carriers*. London: Macdonald, 1969.

Ponting, C. *The Right to Know: The Inside Story of the Belgrano Affair*. London: Sphere, 1985.

Popham, H. *Into Wind*. London: H. Hamilton, 1969.

Raven, A. & J. Roberts. *British Cruisers of World War II*. London: Arms & Armour Press, 1980.

Rice, D., & A. Gavshon. *The Sinking of the Belgrano*. London: Secker and Warburg, 1984.

Rodger, N.A.M. *The Admiralty*. Lavenham: T. Dalton, 1979.

Roskill, S. *The War at Sea*. London: HMSO 1954–56.

————. *The Navy at War 1939–45*. London: Collins, 1960.

————. *Churchill and the Admirals*. London: Collins, 1979.

Short, A. *The Communist Insurrection in Malaya*. London: Muller, 1975.

Simpson, J. *The Independent Nuclear State*. London: Macmillan, 1983.

Small, J. *Is There a Defence Spending Crisis*? Edinburgh Defence Finance Report No. 1984.

Sked, A., and C. Cook. *Post War Britain: A Political History*. London: Harvester Press, 1979.

Snyder, W.P. *The Politics of British Defence Policy 1945–62*. Columbus, London: Benn, 1964.

Speed, K. *Sea Change*. Bath: Ashgrove, 1982.

Stewart, M. *The Jekyll and Hyde Years: Politics and Economic Policy since 1964*. London: Dent, 1977.

Strange, S. *Sterling and British Policy*. Oxford University Press for the Royal Institute of International Affairs, 1971.

Sturtivant, R. *The Squadrons of the Fleet Air Arm*. Tonbridge: Air Britain, 1984.

Sutton, D.J., ed. *The Story of the Royal Army Service Corps and Royal Corps of Transport*. London: Lee Cooper with Secker & Warburg, 1984.

Terraine, J. *The Life and Times of Lord Mountbatten*. London: Hutchinson, 1968.

Thetford, O. *British Naval Aircraft Since 1912*. London: Putnam, 1978.

Thomas, H. *The Suez Affair*. London: Penguin, 1970.

Thompson, J. *No Picnic: 3 Commando Brigade in the South Atlantic*. London: Secker and Warburg, 1985.

Till, G. *Air Power and the Royal Navy*. London: Jane's, 1979.

————. *The Future of British Sea Power*. London: Macmillan, 1984.

Tinker, D. *A Message from the Falklands*. London: Penguin, 1982.

Underwood G. *Our Falklands War*. Liskeard: Maritime, 1963.

Vicary, A. *Naval Wings*. Cambridge: Patrick Stephens, 1984.

Villar, R. *Merchant Ships at War: The Falklands Experience*. London: Conway Maritime Press, 1984.

Walker, P. Gordon. *The Cabinet*. London: Heinemann Educational, 1972.

Warner, O. *Admiral of the Fleet*. London: Sidgwick & Jackson, 1969.

Wettern, D. *The Decline of British Sea Power*. London: Jane's, 1982.

Williams, E.L. *Crisis in Procurement: A Case Study of TSR-2*. London: R.U.S.I., 1969.

Wood, D. *Project Cancelled*. London: Macdonald & Jane's, 1975.

Worth, J. *British Warships Since 1945, Pt. 4: Minesweepers*. Liskeard: Maritime, 1984.

Reference Works

Brassey's Annual (later *Defence Yearbook*)
Combat Fleets of the World
Conways All the World's Fighting Ships, vols. 3, 1922–45, and 4, 1947–82 (Parts I and II).
Dictionary of National Biography
Jane's Fighting Ships
Keesing's Contemporary Archives
Who's Who

Journal Articles

The following journals have been of value both for specific material and as background: article references can be found in footnotes.

International Defense Review
Jane's Defence Review and *Jane's Defence Weekly*
Journal of the Royal United Services Institute for Defence Studies
Naval Achitect
Naval Forces
Naval Review

Naval War College Review
Navy, from *1972 Navy International*
Ships Monthly
Survival
The United States Naval Institute *Proceedings*

The following specific articles from other journals should also be mentioned:

Conan, C.R. "Stirling—The Problems of Diagnosis." *Westminster Bank Review*, August
    1967.
Conan, C.R. "Stirling: The Problem of Policy." *Westminster Bank Review*, November 1967.
Greenwood, D. "Sights Lowered: The United Kingdom's Defence Effort 1975–84." *RAF
    Quarterly*, Autumn 1975.
Greenwood, D. "Managing the Defence Programme and Budget." *Three Banks Review*,
    June 1984.
Martin, L.W. "The Market for Strategic Ideas in Britain." *America Political Science Review*,
    vol. 56, no. 1, March 1962.
McGeoch, I. "The British Polaris Project." *Perspectives Upon British Defence Policy* 1945–
    70, conference at University of Southampton, April 1974.
Simpson, J. "The Polaris Executive: A Case Study of a Unified Hierarchy." *Public Admin-
    istration,* vol. 48.

Newspapers

The *Times*, the *Guardian*, the *Daily Telegraph, Navy News*.
   (The press files at the International Institute for Strategic Studies and at the Council for
Arms Control were of great value in finding relevant articles.)

INDEX

Note: All ships not otherwise designated are Royal Navy vessels (HMS).